Le Roy Fitch

Le Roy Fitch

The Civil War Career of a Union River Gunboat Commander

MYRON J. SMITH, JR.

McFarland & Company, Inc., Publishers
Jefferson, North Carolina, and London

The present work is a reprint of the illustrated case bound edition of Le Roy Fitch: The Civil War Career of a Union River Gunboat Commander, *first published in 2007 by McFarland.*

LIBRARY OF CONGRESS CATALOGUING-IN-PUBLICATION DATA

Smith, Myron J.
Le Roy Fitch : the Civil War career of a Union river
gunboat commander / Myron J. Smith, Jr.
p.   cm.
Includes bibliographical references and index.

ISBN 978-0-7864-7737-1
softcover : acid free paper ∞

1. Fitch, Le Roy, 1835–1875.
2. United States. Navy—Officers—Biography.
3. Ship captains—United States—Biography.
4. Gunboats—United States—History—19th century.
5. Naval convoys—United States—History—19th century.
6. United States—History—Civil War, 1861–1865—Riverine operations.
7. Tennessee—History—Civil War, 1861–1865—Riverine operations.
8. Ohio River—History, Naval—19th century.
9. Tennessee River—History, Naval—19th century.
10. Cumberland River (Ky. and Tenn.)—History, Naval—19th century.
I. Title.

E467.1.F58S65   2014   359.3092—dc22   [B]   2007012857

BRITISH LIBRARY CATALOGUING DATA ARE AVAILABLE

© 2007 Myron J. Smith, Jr. All rights reserved

No part of this book may be reproduced or transmitted in any form or by any means, electronic or mechanical, including photocopying or recording, or by any information storage and retrieval system, without permission in writing from the publisher.

Cover images: Commander Le Roy Fitch, 1870; pen and ink drawing of the U.S.S. *General Price* by Samuel Ward Stanton (both images from the Naval Historical Center)

Manufactured in the United States of America

McFarland & Company, Inc., Publishers
Box 611, Jefferson, North Carolina 28640
www.mcfarlandpub.com

For Dennie

Contents

Preface	1
List of Abbreviations	9
ONE: A Close-Knit Family and Unheralded Youth, 1835–1856	11
TWO: From Sea to Brown Water, 1856–March 1862	23
THREE: New Madrid to Memphis, March–June 1862	42
FOUR: Brothers and Guerrillas, June–September 1862	57
FIVE: Tinclads, Logistics and Rivers	72
SIX: Guerrillas and the Nashville Lifeline, August–December 1862	90
SEVEN: Fighting Irregulars and Guarding Convoys, January–June 1863	112
EIGHT: Morgan, May–July 1863	167
NINE: Chattanooga, August–December 1863	208
TEN: Building a Fleet, Fort Pillow, and a Second Summer on the Ohio, January–September 1864	239
ELEVEN: Johnsonville, September–November 1864	267
TWELVE: Nashville, December 1864–January 1865	291
THIRTEEN: From Brown Water to Blue and Home, January 1865–April 14, 1875	335
Notes	359
Bibliography	391
Index	407

Preface

THE ERUPTION OF THE WAR BETWEEN THE STATES, better known as the Civil War, occasioned the largest conflict ever seen on the North American continent. Most of the Southern states, for several reasons, elected to secede from the United States of America and go it their own way in a confederacy. There were a few border states which would also be contested. In general, however, with the Allegheny Mountains as the dividing line, the fighting was divided into two main theaters: East and West. There was of course the nautical component of the coastlines where a Union blockade was, with varying degrees of success, maintained and the open oceans where Confederate commerce raiders sailed. Additionally, there were the rivers, the great early to mid-19th century communications arteries.

Despite one or two incursions, the southern bank of the Ohio River was soon seen as the northern boundary of Rebel aspiration and disposition, despite various cries emanating from politicians and firebrands to carry the war further. The Southern states had to defend their collective territory from Yankee invasion. For the North, any plan to counter Confederate resistance necessitated military conquest of the rebellious regions. For such a strategy to be successful in the West, complete control of the navigable reaches of the Mississippi, Cumberland, and Tennessee rivers had to be seized by armed force. Although other Western rivers, such as the Kanawha, Green, White, Yazoo, Red, and Arkansas would also be battlegrounds, it was these big three tributaries which were crucial. Railroads had entered the transportation mix by the 1860s along with the animal-powered wagons of the eons, but for sheer bulk logistical support of invading armies, river shipment of men and goods with steamboats remained key. This fact was as well known in St. Louis, Louisville, Cincinnati and Washington, D.C., as it was in Richmond.

As a part of its overall strategy for independence, the Confederate government, with aid from the states, established a number of citadels and fortified positions. In the East, nearly every coastal city from New Orleans to Richmond had fortifications, many strengthened from pre-war citadels. Along the Western rivers, key river towns were protected, starting with Columbus, Kentucky, and Paducah, Kentucky. Forts Henry and Donelson were established to guard Nashville, Tennessee, while Island No. 10 and Fort Pillow shielded

Memphis. Further down, of course, Vicksburg, Mississippi, was the most significant of all Rebel river bastions.

To accomplish its Western aims, the Lincoln government had to physically push south, often along the rivers. In addition to capturing territory, it had to maintain commerce where it existed and open it where it did not. This was a much easier goal to conceptualize—as was early done in a grand strategy known as the Anaconda Plan—than to accomplish. On top of all the difficulties associated with military combat, the Yankees also faced the twin problems of logistical support and counterinsurgency operations. Getting enough men and materiel to the appropriate spots and countering attacks from members of non-regular indigenous populations both turned out to be significant challenges, occasionally as formidable as winning battles.

The War Department, with help from the U.S. Navy, quickly built an improvised gunboat fleet unit, designated in its first year while under army control as the Western Flotilla. The first three boats were converted steamers known from their protection as timberclads. Following right behind them was the backbone of the organization, eight purpose-built ironclad vessels designed by Samuel Pook and constructed by St. Louis salvager James B. Eads. Supplemented with several auxiliary craft, manned by naval personnel, and operated from a ramshackle base at Cairo, Illinois, these warships joined the military in amphibious operations on the Mississippi, Tennessee, and Cumberland. From Belmont, Missouri, to Forts Henry and Donelson and the capture of Nashville and from Island No. 10 past Memphis to the vicinity of Vicksburg, the Western Flotilla's heavy units smashed at Confederate objectives from the water while U.S. Army soldiers attacked from the land.

During the late spring of 1862, the Western Confederacy found that large portions of its territory, including much of Kentucky, Missouri, the Arkansas shoreline along the "Big Muddy," and middle and western Tennessee, were in Northern hands, some parts more solidly than others. The Federal goal of reaching down the Mississippi toward Helena and Vicksburg was pushed from Cairo and St. Louis while, simultaneously, Nashville became the hub of a great Yankee supply chain. The importance of Tennessee's capital city, the first seat of Rebel state government reclaimed by the Union, was enhanced by the trade links run into it. The railroad and, most importantly, the Ohio and Cumberland steamboat routes from Cincinnati and Louisville made functional the Union supply chain from factory to field. While the principal adversarial armies maneuvered south of Nashville and above Vicksburg, the growing Union logistical flow down the rivers and over miles of unguarded track to Nashville became a tempting target for Confederate raiders and irregular forces.

The importance of opening "The Father of Waters" and the heavier draft of the ironclads forced the War Department to operate its most powerful flotilla units on the deeper Mississippi River. This was true even after the Navy Department took over the organization in October 1862, renaming it the Mississippi Squadron. Army support and the protection of civil and military steamers on the Ohio, Cumberland, and Tennessee was left to the smaller timberclads, which could not themselves proceed far on those streams at certain times of year. Although the skippers of the oak-backed gunboats had considerable latitude in their action, the missions chosen and operations undertaken were administered centrally from Cairo, the flagboat of the flotilla commander, or the tent or command post of the local army theater commander.

As the size and momentum of the Western campaign took the ironclads farther from Cairo and the demand for supplies and troops was consequently boosted, there were not enough gunboats available to go where they were needed. Atop these physical and governance issues, Federal forces in the West increasingly faced full-scale insurgency. Grayclad cavalry and irregular soldiers struck back at the invaders with increasing skill and ferocity, concentrating on what the Allies before D-Day would call the "Transportation Plan." Wherever possible, they would attempt to sink any steamer or derail any train headed south of Louisville. Additionally, as Mark Grimsley has noted, guerrillas and partisans enforced secessionist political order on those rural parts of the countryside not controlled by the Confederate government and not fully controlled by the Union. Butternut riders also terrorized African Americans and Southern Unionists alike.

Opposing this dynamic of Southern resistance necessitated innovative tools and leadership. Regular Union troops into the summer and fall of 1862 waffled back and forth in their counterinsurgency policies (before eventually toughening in the period after a disastrous joint Army-Navy expedition up the White River in June). It was sometimes hard for the bluecoats and bluejackets to determine whether Southerners engaged in irregular combat were official soldiers or guerrillas. Additionally, determination of just how much covert local support was enjoyed by either was difficult. Naval and military officers saw the requirement for more suitable tactics and craft with which to guard their lifelines and battle the Rebel irregulars. From this need on the nautical side emerged the light draught and thin-metal protected gunboat known to history as the tinclad. Additionally, strong local leadership was authorized by the Western river navy to lead the battle against all who would interfere with waterborne Northern logistics and amphibious objectives.

The professional U.S. Navy officers chosen to command in the Western riverine force were drawn from billets throughout the sea service. There were not very many of these people and thus they were supplemented by a large number of volunteer officers, many with practical local steamboat experience. At the top of the command during its War Department tenure was a flag officer (equivalent to a major general) and, when it was turned over to the Navy, an actual or acting rear admiral. The fighting seamen Foote, Davis, Porter, and Lee held these posts. Below them came a number of captains, commanders, lieutenant commanders, and lieutenants. Administrative expertise such as that shown by Captain Alexander M. Pennock was vital, but even more reliance, perhaps much more so than in the East, was placed upon the individual initiative of those in lower ranks. Whether in command of individual warboats or, later, entire subunits, known as districts, these men were invaluable to the successful achievement of Union goals.

"Many of the younger officers, too junior to have important sea commands during the course of the war, performed outstanding jobs in individual commands," wrote naval historian Bern Anderson in 1962. "Henry Walke and Leroy Fitch, on the Western rivers ... to name a few, fall within this category."[1] Literary coverage of the entire naval war pales in comparison to that fought on land and when one considers the nautical phase, that percentage assigned to the rivers of the West is quite small. There are no campaign histories devoted exclusively to the naval war on the upper rivers, the Ohio, Cumberland, and Tennessee.

Below the rank of rear admiral, there are no biographies of river commanders save one, Seth Ledyard Phelps, the ironclad captain whose papers were recently edited into print by Jay Slagle.[2] Several, such as Henry Walke, famous as the first commander of the gunboat *Carondelet*, have left memoirs. Those who commanded light draughts or even entire districts are, individually and as a group, without remembrance, even in periodical profiles.[3]

At least one man in this latter group seemed to be everywhere there was action after

September 1862. By war's end, he was the senior junior officer in the Mississippi Squadron in terms of time served and the most experienced fighter in the western fleet. He fought three of the South's most feared cavalry leaders—Morgan, Wheeler, and Forrest—contended with all manner of irregulars along the river banks, provided succor to Federal sympathizers, participated in amphibious operations with the U.S. Army, oversaw the Union supply chain on three rivers, built a fleet of gunboats on the lower Tennessee, and commanded part of the time from within a monitor during the last decisive battle in the West. A lieutenant commander from Logansport, the Hoosier is mentioned in almost every Western chronicle with a river reference, but until now his life history has not been published. His name was Le Roy Fitch and he was 26 years old when the war began.

While waiting for the U.S. Army to come up to strength for an advance on Vicksburg in 1862, Flag Officer Charles H. Davis upgraded his ships and his organization, with some attention to counter-guerrilla operations. He added new light draft tinclads to guard the upper rivers and found a man he knew well to lead them. According to Prof. Richard West, an advance division of gunboats was established "under Commander Le Roy Fitch to patrol the Ohio, Tennessee, and Cumberland Rivers." It matched another unit Rear Admiral Porter would set up under Captain Henry Walke to watch "the Mississippi between Helena and Vicksburg."[4] Although Captain Pennock was officially named to oversee the "mosquito flotilla" as Fitch's unit was initially known, the Indiana sailor was its executive and was, in fact, the man in charge of mounting all operations, patrols, and convoy escorts.

Le Roy Fitch was the younger half brother of Graham Newell Fitch, a prominent Logansport physician and politician who served in Washington, D.C., as both a congressman and a senator. It was Graham Newell, 25 years older than his partial sibling, who found young Le Roy a berth at Annapolis, from which he graduated in 1856. Upon his graduation, Fitch quickly advanced to the rank of master and, in the process, met and served under Commander Charles H. Davis in the pursuit of Nicaraguan filibuster William Walker. When war came, the Hoosier initially served off Pensacola before taking a training billet at the New York Navy Yard. There he had a chance to familiarize volunteer officers and recruits with the use of his favorite weapon, the 12- or 24-pounder. Dalhgren howitzer.

In March 1862, Lieutenant Fitch was assigned to the Western Flotilla, then under the command of Flag Officer Andrew Hull Foote. His first duty was as skipper of the fleet auxiliary and ordnance boat *Judge Torrence*. Aboard the *Torrence*, he participated in the campaigns to reduce Island No. 10 and to capture Fort Pillow and Memphis. During these three offensives, he was undoubtedly able to visit frequently with his brother, Graham Newell, who was colonel of the accompanying 42nd Indiana Volunteer Infantry, and his nephew, Quartermaster Henry S. Fitch. Toward the end of May, the injured Foote was succeeded in squadron command by Flag Officer Davis, the same Davis who was the young Fitch's first captain. Already acquainted with Colonel Fitch from his time as a U.S. senator, Davis did not initially let on that he knew that the colonel's half brother, Le Roy, was in his command. It was not until the youngster demonstrated outstanding leadership in the salvage of a Confederate boat sunk in the Battle of Memphis that Davis knew that the colonel's brother was the right man for a more important assignment.

From the time of his selection that summer to what was, for all practical purposes, an independent command through the end of the war, Le Roy Fitch was indomitable. He gained a reputation for his prosecution of counterinsurgency warfare and as an innovator of protective measures for the massive number of contract steamboats which churned the

Ohio, Cumberland, and Tennessee rivers supplying the advancing Union armies. Though not a flamboyant man, Fitch could write a self-flattering dispatch, several of which were later reprinted in Northern newspapers. Well regarded by Rear Admiral Davis from his time as a midshipman, he was not initially a favorite of Rear Admiral Porter, under whom he served longest. Porter, however, had the good sense to recognize the straight-forward bulldog officer as a competent leader. Despite constant battles with high ranking army officers who did not understand the nature of the rivers or basic organizational requirements of waterborne escort, Fitch received his superior's continued support. In the process, the Hoosier became the finest innovator and practitioner of the art of convoy in the entire Civil War Union Navy. After Fitch's death, Porter would have nothing but praise for the Indiana sailor. Fitch, if anything, may remind the student of convoys or the reader of World War II Battle of the Atlantic literature of the highly-regarded British escort commander Vice Admiral Sir Max Horton.

In his efforts to safeguard Northern shipping, Le Roy Fitch found himself not only an innovator in convoy and patrol work, but an active participant in Federal amphibious operations and a fireman who was often called upon to steam toward points under Confederate attack, real or imagined. After battling the Confederate horsemen of Wheeler and Forrest at Dover, Tennessee, in February 1863, he fought back against Rebel gunners attempting to sink his Nashville-bound convoys from high points along the Cumberland River. At one point, he reluctantly found it necessary, in accordance with stiffening Union anti-guerrilla policy, to burn the entire town of Palmyra as an object lesson. The Indiana sailor joined with Alfred Ellet's revolutionary Mississippi Marine Brigade and other military forces to assist the sendoff of Colonel Abel D. Streight's "mule raid" into Northern Alabama. In July 1863, he gained his greatest fame when he organized all available vessels to contain the great Indiana-Ohio incursion of Brigadier General John Hunt Morgan. His careful calculations and a deeper-than-usual Ohio River allowed him to prevent the colorful raiders from escaping back to the South.

After his brilliant exploit against the Confederate horsemen, Morgan's nemesis returned his attention to the Cumberland convoys in the fall of 1863. The great contest for the city of Chattanooga brought the opportunity for detached duty. After first consulting on the project, Fitch directed the construction and outfitting of a fleet of gunboats by army engineers at Bridgeport, Alabama, for use on the Upper Tennessee River. In March 1864, it was Fitch who was called upon to steam to Fort Pillow after it was sacked by Forrest's raiders in what many regarded as an atrocity. When Major General Sherman pushed off from Atlanta and the coast, it was the Logansport seaman who, under the overall direction of Acting Rear Admiral Samuel P. Lee, provided local naval support at the time of the Nashville campaign. Called upon at the last minute in November to prevent an unfolding disaster, Fitch was unable to actually forestall the now-savvy gunners of Nathan Bedford Forrest from scaring the defenders of Johnsonville, Tennessee, into destroying their big supply base.

In December, Fitch was determined not to fail the huge army of Major General George Thomas during its defense of the state's capital city from General John Bell Hood's approaching Rebel army. In a number of valiant engagements, the Hoosier officer, from within the monitor *Neosho* and backed up by the famous ironclad *Carondelet* and tinclads, battled Rebel gunners on the left of Hood's line as they blockaded the Cumberland west of Nashville in Bell's Bend. The Confederates lost at Nashville and the war rapidly wound down in the West in early 1865, coming to an end after Appomattox. Fitch, while on shore duty in late

April, had the great satisfaction of knowing that his flagboat, the U.S.S. *Moose*, was engaged in that theater's last naval fight with guerrillas. When the Civil War ended, the Indiana sailor had served in his theater longer than any other junior officer and, in less than three years, had engaged in more combat and support operations and escorted more convoys than any other naval officer in the West. He was still just 29 years old.

Le Roy Fitch was like a Civil War shooting star. He came on the scene from obscurity, provided great public service to his nation, and then, in the decade left to him, faded. The years from 1865 to 1875 were a period of decline for both the U.S. Navy and for the Logansport seaman. Following a year instructing at the Naval Academy, he, like other officers, waited at home for one of the declining number of available postings. From 1867 to 1868, he commanded the gunboat *Marblehead* in the Atlantic and Caribbean. Thereafter, he remained in Logansport until the summer of 1870, when he became the executive officer of the Pensacola Navy Yard, gaining with it a promotion to the rank of commander. Following his Florida deployment in February 1872, Fitch was given an assignment at the Navy Department in Washington, D.C., which occupied the remainder of the year.

On the personal side, Fitch was married, with a loving wife and daughter about whom little is known. It was later reported that Le Roy withdrew to Logansport at the beginning of 1873 due to illness. He lived in obscure retirement in his community for two years, apparently indulging his passions for painting and sport shooting. A lingering illness forced him to bed in January 1875 and caused his death in April.

Except in the pages of those Civil War naval histories touching upon the Western waters, the memory of Le Roy Fitch faded quickly. Even the author of his April 1875 obituary in the Logansport *Daily Star* was moved to comment that citizens of his hometown knew little "of the brilliant career and eminent services of this young officer whose record is thus suddenly terminated." Although only in his late 20s, Fitch "was often placed in positions that would have taxed the knowledge, discretion, and energy of men a score of years his senior, but in all he acquitted himself well.

"Responsibilities of duty called from his all the latent and deep worth of his abilities and his shipmates and companions in the service all bear record to his ability, promptness, and discretion in the performance of his duties" recalled his hometown newspaper. "His life was short. Its best years passed in the limits of our war, were filled with deeds of usefulness that do honor to his memory and to his family."[5]

Admiral David Dixon Porter, who knew Fitch both during the war and after at the U.S. Naval Academy, became a great admirer of the Indiana officer. A decade after the commander's death, Porter wrote:

> Although his command was not a large one, this young officer was often mentioned [in dispatches] for gallant and efficient service, and he ever displayed sound judgment, no matter in what position he was placed. His officers and men, inspired by his spirit, were conspicuous for their bravery.
>
> The gallant Fitch never shrunk from the performance of any duty however hazardous. He was always under fire whenever opportunity offered, not owing to chance circumstances, to which sluggards often attribute a man's reputation for heroism, but to a determined will. This gallant officer gained little promotion for his war services, and his highest recognition was a complimentary letter from the Secretary of the Navy on the occasion when he brought about the capture of General John Morgan, the celebrated Confederate partisan leader.

Years later, the historian of the Cumberland River, Douglas Byrd, opined:

This officer carried out these instructions and all subsequent tasks assigned to him with zeal and ability. He is another of the lesser known officers who deserve far greater credit than history has so far accorded for the part he played in the victory of the North. He was the officer who did more than anyone else to keep the Cumberland open.[6]

Any attempt to understand the life of a person requires at least some familiarity with the subject's family background. This task is often immensely simplified through the work of family genealogists and caches of papers, letters, or diaries authored by the biography's subject. Good sources sometimes become easier to obtain when the subject comes from a noted lineage and his papers are in private hands or public repositories. In the case of the Fitch brothers, we have a large Indiana family with three siblings of at least a modicum of contemporary fame. Unhappily, none left behind a paper trail and none have had their lives previously described save in short entries in various histories or directories. About all that is left to work with in the way of papers is the public record and a few newspaper columns.

Since first writing about Le Roy Fitch in a 1971 *Indiana Historical Bulletin* article, I have been squirreling away information on the commander for use in a biography about him which I hoped to write one day—unless someone beat me to it. In those 30 years, I have, as the bibliography shows, reviewed a mound of material, very little of which focused on the sailor's personal life. Throughout the lengthy literary due diligence process, I was actually most surprised to find just how few non-governmental primary sources were available not only on the seaman, but on his brothers, especially Senator Graham Newell.

Despite the work of a dedicated family genealogist, John T. Fitch, this lack of sources and previous detailed exposure, both personal and professional, has meant that Le Roy, his 25-year-senior half brother, Graham Newell Fitch, and Graham Newell's son Henry S. are almost totally forgotten today, even in their hometown. In 1960, Will Ball, then president of the Cass County Historical Society in Indiana and one of the last in the Logansport community to write about the Fitches, declared "this writer has seldom, if ever, come across a family as badly 'scrambled' as the Fitch brothers."[7] It was not my purpose to write a triparte biography of the Fitch brothers, but, in the process of constructing a narrative on one, the intertwined activities of the other two have come at least partially to light and, as appropriate, are included. It is hoped this may be useful.

The stories of other junior officers in the Union's inland navy deserve to be told. These include regulars like Henry Walke, James W. Shirk, William Gwin, James A. Greer, Frank Ramsey, Elias K. Owen, George M. Bach, Byron Wilson, Thomas O. Selfridge, Jr., and George Brown. If data can be found, a number of volunteer officers would also be good subjects and, indeed, profiling any of these acting volunteer lieutenants could be used as a springboard for a useful review of the entire Civil War Federal volunteer navy officer program: Henry A. Glassford, Charles G. Perkins, George J. Groves, Edward M. King, William R. Hoel, and Jason Goudy. Rear Admiral Davis needs a new biography and no one in the annals of the Mississippi Squadron deserves a profile more than Fleet Captain Alexander M. Pennock. The field is ripe for the picking by Ph.D. candidates or others interested in harvesting from one of the few untapped Civil War fields yet remaining. I hope to dip again one day.

A number of people and libraries helpfully provided insight and information during the years this work has been in gestation. Chief among these are John T. Fitch, Cambridge, Massachusetts; John T. Brock, reference librarian, Logansport–Cass County Public Library, Indiana; Mary C. Stuart, former co-curator, Cass County Historical Society, Indiana; Paul

Kroeger, Logansport, Indiana; Robert W. "Bob" Henderson, Jr., former chairman, Battle of Nashville Preservation Society; Dr. Thomas F. Beckner, Greeneville, Tennessee; and Donal Sexton, Greeneville, Tennessee.

Others who assisted were David Kitchell, Logansport *Pharos-Tribune,* Indiana; Jennifer A. Bryan, current head and Alice S. Creighton, former head, Special Collections and Archives, U.S. Naval Academy; Michael Cart, former director of the Logansport–Cass County Public Library; Stephen E. Towne, Indiana State Archives; Graham Denby Morey, Indianapolis; Hobart Leslie, Logansport; Rebecca A. Livingston, Archives I Reference Branch, Textual Reference Division, National Archives, Washington, D.C.; Eric L. Mundell, head of Reference Services, Indiana Historical Society Library; Maj. Robert R. Mackey, Washington, D.C.; and Chuck Sherrill, Reference Department, Tennessee State Library and Archives.

Myron J. Smith, Jr.
Greeneville, Tennessee
Spring 2007

List of Abbreviations

Army

Rank	Abbreviation	Rank	Abbreviation
General	Gen.	Major	Maj.
Lieutenant General	Lt. Gen.	Captain	Capt.
Major General	Maj. Gen.	Lieutenant	Lt.
Brigadier General	Brig. Gen.	Sergeant	Sgt.
Colonel	Col.	Corporal	Cpl.
Lieutenant Colonel	Lt. Col.	Private	Pvt.

Navy

Rank	Abbreviation	Rank	Abbreviation
Acting Rear Admiral	Acting Rear Adm.	Lieutenant Commander	Lt. Cmdr.
Rear Admiral	Rear Adm.	Acing Volunteer Lieutenant	none
Flag Officer	none	Lieutenant	Lt.
Commodore	Cdr.	Acing Volunteer Master	none
Captain	Capt.	Master	none
Commander	Cmdr.	Acting Volunteer Ensign	none
Acting Volunteer Lieutenant Commander	none	Ensign	Ensign

CHAPTER ONE

A Close-Knit Family and Unheralded Youth, 1835–1856

ANY ATTEMPT TO UNDERSTAND THE LIFE of a person requires at least some familiarity with the subject's family background.[1] Before we can pass on to the Civil War exploits of Le Roy Fitch, it is necessary to undertake such immediate family spadework as is required in order to give the reader a sense of the man's background and allow informed supposition concerning his career development.

Although Hoosier Cmdr. Fitch died in 1875, his story actually began 89 years earlier, on April 11, 1784, with the birth of his father, Frederick Fitch, in Washington County, New York, which is in the northeastern section of the state. Its eastern boundary is the New York–Vermont border, part of which is along Lake Champlain. Interestingly, in 1784, the name of that political entity, Charlotte County, was changed to honor the first U.S. president.[2]

The future naval officer's father was a physician and surgeon in New York state who practiced medicine learned in the traditional apprentice fashion. This gave him much hands-on knowledge, but probably led him, like other men so trained, to the use of some outmoded procedures and to prescribe some medicines questionable by today's standards.[3]

Sometime prior to 1808, Frederick Fitch moved west to the small farming village of Bellona, in the eastern part of New York's Genesee County, which is located between Rochester and Buffalo. Bellona would be renamed Le Roy in 1813, and the city would become famous as the town where Jell-O was invented and first marketed.[4]

Life could not have been bad and must have been busy for a healer in this or any small U.S. community of that day. On December 4, 1808, Dr. Fitch married Mary "Polly" Capen, who had been born four months before him, on January 20, 1784. Almost exactly a year later, on December 6, 1809, the couple's first son, Graham Newell Fitch, was born. It would later be recorded that he was the first white child born in Le Roy. A daughter, Mary Ann, would follow on November 10, 1811.[5]

Caught up in the American invasion of Canada during the War of 1812, Dr. Fitch was named a corporal in the cavalry troop of a Capt. Peters and served with his unit as it moved toward Ontario. British and Indian forces under Gen. Sir Isaac Brock defeated these Americans under Gen. Stephen Van Rensselaer at the Battle of Queenstown Heights, near Niagara Falls, on October 13. Fitch was wounded quite seriously, losing a leg, and was returned to Le Roy, where he was discharged on October 16. Despite his handicap, which he chose not to perceive as such, Dr. Fitch was able to continue his practice of medicine and, on August 13, 1815, he and Polly had another daughter, Henrietta Bradley. A second son, Egbert Bensen Fitch, would be born on an undocumented date and die in Tazewell County, Illinois, sometime around 1844.[6]

Meanwhile, Graham Newell Fitch became the apple of his war-veteran father's eye. "Inheriting from his ancestors a well-developed physical system and a vigorous intellect," according to historian Thomas B. Helm, "he was allowed all of the educational privileges the locality and vicinity afforded." While these were not top rate, they were, nevertheless, "sufficient to lay the foundation of a career of usefulness." During the 1820s, he traveled into the next county south to study at Middlebury (later Wyoming) Academy in Wyoming, New York. This was followed by schooling at Geneva College. At an early age, Graham Newell elected to follow in Dr. Fitch's footsteps and become a physician. To do so, he would pursue what historian Thomas Neville Bonner called a grafting "of newly organized lecture courses in practical science onto a program of apprenticeship or hospital training undertaken at the student's own initiative."

Young Fitch served a period of apprenticeship with his father in Le Roy and also studied locally with Dr. Asa Freeman. His medical study was undertaken at the College of Physicians and Surgeons of the Western District of New York at Fairfield. There the course of study may not have differed much from that described by a Connecticut contemporary who later recalled that:

> the typical medical practitioner had attended one set of lectures for five or six months, perhaps less, and then the following year, he heard these same lectures again. He might have worked with a practicing doctor, a remnant of the old medical tradition, but he might have had no apprenticeship at all.

A later historian of early medical education was more blunt: "The student often finished his formal education without having been alone with, much less touched a patient." Dr. Fitch had the good fortune to receive both clinical experience and some of the best formal training then available to students outside of New York or Philadelphia.

Just after completing his medical training in 1832, Graham Newell married Harriet Valerie Satterlee. The new Mrs. Fitch, born in Le Roy in September 1809, was the daughter of Luther and Hannah (Swenzey) Satterlee, who had moved to Brookhaven, Suffolk County, New York. Tragically, the family suffered a devastating loss when Polly Fitch died in Le Roy on December 28, 1833. The Fitches were still in mourning when Harriet gave birth to a son, Henry Satterlee, in Le Roy on March 5, 1834.[7]

The first four or five decades of the 19th century in the U.S. were marked by beginning of the Industrial Revolution and continued westward movement, one fueled by the chance for many citizens and immigrants alike to begin life anew, to obtain and own land, or to strike it rich. The generations that settled the western portions of New York and Ohio and moved to Kentucky and Tennessee now joined or gave way to those who pressed on into Indiana and Illinois. The small prairies and tough sod of those midwestern locations

One. A Close-Knit Family and Unheralded Youth (1835–1856)

challenged the pioneers, but repaid them. The ground, in the words of Samuel Eliot Morison, a famous historian noted for his maritime writing, "taxed their strength but repaid it with bountiful crops of grain; where shoulder-high prairie grass afforded rich pasturage for cattle and groves of buckeye, oak, walnut, and hickory furnished wood and timber."[8] Dr. Frederick Fitch, who had moved west himself as a young man, and his son, the newly-minted physician, Graham Newell Fitch, both decided to move the family farther west and seek a fresh beginning.

The location chosen for the Fitch family transfer was Logansport, at the junction of the Wabash and Eel Rivers, in Indiana. A large Native American village, Kenapakomoko, had existed until recently at this site just six miles north of town on the Eel River. Named for a Shawnee chief, the community, settled in 1827, is located 69 miles northeast of Indianapolis and 43 miles northeast of Lafayette; it is the county seat of Cass County, organized in 1829. Frederick, Graham Newell, Harriett, and the Fitch children duly arrived in the farming village in July 1834. On December 29, Dr. Frederick married Rachel Thomas. In 1835, probably following the birth of Graham Newell and Harriet's daughter Martha on February 22, the patriarch of the Fitch clan and his new wife, with daughter Mary Ann, moved on to another farming community, Pekin, Illinois, county seat of Tazewell County, which is located on the banks of the Illinois River 10 miles south of Peoria. It was here that Le Roy Fitch was born on October 1. Possibly named for his father's former New York hometown, the future naval hero was the first offspring of Dr. Frederick and Rachel Fitch. Although various histories have shown his name variously as LeRoy or Leroy, the correct representation is Le Roy. Ironically, steamboat traffic, with which he would be intimately concerned during the Civil War, was becoming increasingly important to the local Pekin economy the year he was born.[9]

While Dr. Frederick and his family were in Illinois, Dr. Graham Newell Fitch established a

Graham Newell Fitch (1809–1892) was 25 years older than his half brother Le Roy and outlived him by 17 years. A physician and Logansport Democratic politician, Graham Newell was the boy's mentor, guardian, and later, most likely his first teacher on matters of counterinsurgency. Graham Newell served from 1836 to 1839 as a Hoosier state legislator, from 1849 to 1853 as a U.S. congressman (during which time he secured Le Roy's appointment to the new U.S. Naval Academy), and from 1857 to 1861 as a U.S. senator. Upon the outbreak of the Civil War, he raised the 46th Indiana Volunteer Infantry and led it into battle at Fort Pillow, Memphis, and at St. Charles on the White River, spring-summer 1862. Injured, he retired to private medical practice. Although active, he never sought another political office and, unlike most retired officers, did not employ in civil life his earned military title (courtesy John T. Fitch).

Built in 1834 this Federal-style structure was one of the first large homes constructed in Logansport. English-made bricks for the structure and Italian fireplaces were delivered via the Wabash and Erie Canal. Owned by Graham Newell Fitch and home to Le Roy for much of his life prior to his departure to the U.S. naval Academy, the house also later became famous for a willow tree supposedly from St. Helena, Napoleon's place of exile. The home originally faced 7th Street and overlooked the town's business district; prior to the Civil War, it was a stop on the Underground Railroad for fugitive slaves seeking freedom in Michigan. The home remained a private residence until 1952 (courtesy Paul Kroeger).

very successful practice back in Logansport and was becoming widely known as a successful GP and surgeon. Life in 1830s Indiana was hard and could be dangerous. Disease and epidemics of cholera and other sickness were constant. Like his father, Graham Newell took care of whatever ailments afflicted people, whether they came to see him or he made house calls, visiting them on horseback. Broken bones, "fever 'n ague," and even amputations were commonplace. If the latter were necessary, they occurred without anesthesia—the patients were held or tied down often on kitchen tables, given huge doses of whiskey, cut with unwashed blades, and bandaged with strips from whatever garments were handy. The travelling physician met many Cass Countians professionally during his first two years in the community and also encountered others when he served as captain of the Logansport Dragoons (in which organization brother Egbert Benson was a private), a unit of the Indiana militia.[10]

The Indiana militia of the 1830s, the state's primary defense against Indians some years before, was in a period of decline. Work clothes replaced uniforms for soldiers, and women often accompanied their men to the required April and September musters (now often supplemented with July 4 gatherings which were more party than drill). Instead of guns, some men carried canes, hoe handles, sticks, or cornstalks. Officers, no doubt including Graham Newell, were "still attired in some sort of uniform," but they usually "spent more time electioneering than drilling." Still, there was a period in September-October 1836 when, for awhile, it appeared that some sort of combat might occur. The story of the only actual Hoosier militia activity of the 1830s is told by a military expert:

> The "Peru Blues" were called up on September 25, 1836 on the report of Col. G.W. Ewing that the Potawatomi Indians had allegedly risen against the government. Another company [Logansport Dragoons] joined the Blues near Logansport, where the real reason for the call-up was discovered. Col. Ewing had appropriated all the money to have been paid as annuity to the Potawatomi, claiming that the Indians owed the full amount of their annuity to his firm. The captains of the militia sided with Col. Pepper, the paymaster, against Ewing, and forced him to return the money to Pepper. The Indians were given their annuity, and the militia returned home on October 1.[11]

In 1836, undoubtedly because of his local medical practice and perhaps as a result of his leadership in the fall's call to arms, Graham Newell Fitch was chosen to represent Cass County in the Indiana State Legislature at Indianapolis. Of his service, it was later reported that "as a legislator in the State councils, he proved himself equal to the responsibility intrusted [sic] to him." Meanwhile, Dr. Frederick returned to Indiana from Pekin to help out with his firstborn's growing Logansport medical practice.[12]

For the Fitch family, as for Logansport itself, the years 1837–1839 were times of success and satisfaction, with only one real clan setback. On March 1, 1837, Mary Ann Fitch married Stephen Bradley; the couple would have one child. The same year, the Wabash and Erie Canal, which originated in Toledo, Ohio, reached the Indiana town. The second of two daughters, Emma, was born to Graham Newell and Harriet Fitch on January 15, 1838. A month later, on February 17, Logansport was incorporated as a city. The joy which was widely shared at the beginning of the year, however, turned to grief in the fall. Mary Ann Fitch died on October 24. She was buried in the community's Mt. Hope Cemetery, the first of many Fitches to be interred in that location. Graham Newell was returned to the state Legislature in 1839. Egbert Fitch moved to Pekin, Illinois, in October 1839 where his son, Frederick, was born the following year; in 1850, young Frederick and his mother, since remarried, returned to Logansport.[13]

Upon his return to Logansport from Indianapolis in 1840, Dr. Graham Newell Fitch purchased a magnificent property and stately brick home at 711 East Market Street in the city. Many of the English-made bricks used to finish the house were brought to Logansport by the Wabash and Erie Canal; the fireplaces were imported from Italy. The homestead included several outbuildings and a beautiful sunken garden. The residence was near the doctor's office on Third Street, around the corner from the 200 block of Market Street. The little frame building stood as late as 1958. From this office, undoubtedly shared first with his father and certainly with his later partner, Dr. Asa Coleman, Fitch's name and fame became "household worlds ... throughout the upper Wabash Valley." In addition to the home in town, Fitch, in 1859, also acquired a 375-acre farm about three miles west of town along the Wabash and Erie Canal. This abode, with its stately home and barn, together with spacious acreage was called Ravine Farm. A series of waterfalls running through the property, later called by some the most beautiful place in the county, became known as Fitch's Glen. There was a large turn basin less than two blocks from the back door. It was no coincidence, wrote a county historian, that both Fitch houses were within sight of the progressive canal. "It was the best mode of travel in Cass County during the 1840's."[14]

Little is known about the early years of Dr. Frederick and Rachel Fitch's firstborn son, Le Roy. It may be—indeed, has been—suggested that water and vegetation may have played some part in his formative period. The latter supposition, which came about because of his alleged trans-ocean transport of a tree sprout, is known to be a legend. On the side of reality, however, we know that the Wabash and Erie Canal, which reached the city in 1837, crossed the Eel River in 1840 over an aqueduct, which followed the route of the city's present day Fifth Street. The city prospered as warehouses sprang up to store and disperse the region's grain and other goods. Small transport craft of all kinds traversed the canal as it progressed over its open segments, starting on Lake Erie and traveling over the Maumee River to Fort Wayne and hence down the Wabash, via Terra Haute on toward the Ohio River at Evansville. These could be easily seen from older brother Graham Newell's house. The canal was undoubtedly a recreational and visual magnet for many local citizens, grownup and youngsters alike. Daily horse-drawn packet boats which came into town by beginning of the 1840s took the place of steamboats, the other novel river transport of the age. Hardly any of those engine-powered vessels came to Logansport because they could not ascend that far. The ignominy of the *Republican*, which had to be towed into town by oxen all the way from Lafayette in 1834, demonstrated the physical impossibility of larger craft reaching the seat of Cass County. Thus the canal would flourish in Logansport until the first railroad came in 1855, four years after Le Roy's departure for the U.S. Naval Academy.[15]

Vegetation did not play an actual part in the young life of Le Roy Fitch, though later there was the tree legend. It concerned a certain weeping willow tree sprout from an unusual place supposedly planted in the northeast corner of the formal garden of Dr. Graham Newell Fitch's home on Market Street during 1840. The story first came to notice when published in Dr. Jehu Powell's 1913 county history and even today it appears in the Web pages of the Cass County Historical Society. It is reprinted here in part with acknowledgement to that site.

> Le Roy Fitch, half-brother of Dr. G. N. Fitch, was in the United States Navy for many years. In 1840 he was an officer aboard the United States war ship that was appointed to escort the remains of Napoleon Bonaparte from the Island of St. Helena back to Paris for permanent sepulture. When at St. Helena he secured a sprout of a willow tree that stood at the head of Napoleon's grave on that island and brought it home with him and planted it on the Fitch lot, corner of Seventh and Market Streets, where it grew into a large tree.

It is a fact that the body of Napoleon I, who died on the tiny South Atlantic island on May 5, 1821, was returned to France in December 1840 and laid to rest in a great public ceremony. The existence of the Logansport willow tree is also not in dispute. It stood in front of the Fitch house, near a sundial, on the lot line and, by 1913, reached a diameter of nearly two feet. When George Seybold, founder of the Seybold Dry Goods Company, purchased the garden plot early in the 20th century, he found that an iron fence had been put up around the property with a curve in the fence around the tree designed to preserve it. There was no U.S. Navy escort for the French frigate *La Belle-Poule* when she transferred Napoleon's corpse; neither Fitch nor anyone else from the U.S. military witnessed the seaborne mission. Even if such a duty was performed by the American navy, Le Roy Fitch would not have been present because he was only five years old at the time. Thus the question arose of who brought the tree sprout to the doctor's front yard and did it come from St. Helena, where it supposedly shaded the grave of the French emperor.[16]

Historian William Ball of Logansport, who also repeated the Le Roy Fitch tree story in one of his "This Changing World" pieces for the local newspaper, later reviewed his sources and re-examined the tale. A former neighbor of Dr. Graham Newell Fitch had, he revealed, informed him that Cmdr. Fitch, indeed, transported the sprout. This was the same Le Roy Fitch, he noted, who married the daughter of Maj. Benjamin H. Smith, a prominent city resident. It was an interest in finding details of that couple's relationship, needed as a footnote in a report on the city's first hospital which he was then writing, which caused Ball to dig deeper. Eventually, after considerable stack time in the Logansport Public Library, Ball discovered the navy man's date of death—and the truth of the story.

By the 1850s, Mrs. Harriet Fitch, wife of then Senator Fitch, who had earlier served in Congress, was well known in the Washington, D.C., area. During her time in the nation's capital with her husband, she took an interest in the preservation of the home of President Washington at Mount Vernon. She became a participant in the Mount Vernon restoration movement and a member of the Mount Vernon Ladies Association, which purchased and undertook the residence's renovation. From 1859 to 1880, she served as Indiana vice-regent for the group. Another "anonymous neighbor" of the Fitches informed Will Ball that it was Harriet Fitch who brought the sprout to Logansport and planted it, "rather than her half brother-in-law." This twig probably appeared in Indiana about 1860 and, rather than from St. Helena, it may have come from Mt. Vernon.[17]

Le Roy's unheralded childhood continued to unfold in Logansport during the 1840s. Given his family's position, we can surmise that he was properly raised (his father and older half-brother were both Episcopalians) and that his education did not suffer. Like all young Midwestern men, he learned how to ride horses and to shoot. We know from a review of columns in the local press that he had a talent for painting in oil and watercolors, as well as drawing in pencil, though none of his art seems to have survived. Artistic ability was a trademark of several 19th Century U.S. naval officers, the most noteworthy being Adm. Henry Walke, whom Le Roy would doubtless meet while serving in the Mississippi Squadron in 1862–1863.[18]

The older members of the Logansport Fitch clan were not inactive during the early years of the 1840s. Le Roy's father, Dr. Frederick, was, so far as we know, still practicing medicine. He and Rachel gave birth to a second son, Leander, on July 17, 1841, but despite the best efforts of his father and half-brother, the infant died on August 4. Another boy, Henry Alvord, was born to the senior Fitch, aged 60, and his wife on July 7, 1844. With his youngest half brother enjoying good health, Graham Newell accepted a position with Rush Medical College in Chicago. From the fall of 1844 to 1847, he would serve as chairman of that school's department of theory and practice. He was not in Logansport when Rachel Thomas Fitch died on October 2, 1846, nor when his father and half-brothers moved into the large house on East Market Street.[19]

Following the spring term of 1847, Graham Newell returned to Logansport from Illinois. While practicing medicine, he also found himself a candidate for Congress, winning election to the House of Representatives in the August election. Historian Helms suggests that "not naturally a politician, Dr. Fitch, from force of circumstance was drawn, perhaps not unwillingly, into the arena of politics, where his commanding talent and energy marked him as the people's choice." Fitch would represent Indiana's Ninth Congressional District until 1852. While his oldest son was away in Washington, Dr. Frederick Fitch died on March 18, 1850, and was buried on the East Market Street property. Graham Newell became guardian for Le Roy and Henry Alvord, then aged 14 and 6 respectively. When the Military Land Bounty Act of September 28, 1850, was passed, the congressman attempted to obtain for his young charges those shares to which their father was entitled. Graham Newell would conscientiously file numerous claims on their behalf over the next several years.[20]

On January 7, 1851, as the direct result of his half-brother's action, Le Roy Fitch was appointed to the U.S. Naval Academy from the Ninth District of Indiana. He was 14 years and 10 months old and had passed a relatively simple entrance examination. Arranging for his much younger sibling to attend this six-year-old institution was perhaps the greatest gift Graham Newell could offer, one greater than he might have imagined. The young Logansport resident was lucky in his brother's timing. The system whereby prominent families, senior naval officers, or others with political connections could get their sons into the school via the navy secretary or president was about to end. On August 31, 1852, the U.S. Congress would take over the power to set qualifications and would thereby transform Annapolis "from a finishing school for the elite to a national institution." Young Fitch might still have warranted appointment, but the process for him could have been much more demanding.

Traveling from Indiana, perhaps for the first time, the acting midshipman on probation arrived at Annapolis, Maryland, and entered the school there on the Severn River with 37 other freshmen at the beginning of its academic year on October 1, 1851. He, like the other newcomers, was resplendent in his freshly-acquired uniform, mandatory for the first time with this class.[21]

"School" is the wrong term to employ in connection with the pedagogical operation then centered on ancient Fort Severn, but only by a few months. Navy secretary George Bancroft originally moved the new naval school from Philadelphia to Annapolis in 1845. Initially, a five year course of study was offered, with the middle three spent in apprenticeship at sea. The training facility Fitch entered experienced a significant reform in 1850, being turned from a two year residential course of study into a full-fledged naval academy. The renamed institution adopted a curriculum stretched to seven years with the first two and last two spent in residence at the Maryland facility. The four years of consecutive residential study was phased in starting with Fitch's class and practice cruises were substituted for the three consecutive years at sea. All of this was part of a search for professionalism that veered away from the American individualist precedent of the Jacksonian era.

Until the introduction of the Naval Reserve Officers Training Program in 1925, the college on the Severn would be the only source of new regularly-commissioned U.S. Navy officers. Administered from Washington, D.C., as a sub-unit of the Bureau of Ordnance and Hydrography, it was governed by a distant oversight board and a local academic board, made up of a superintendent, a commandant of midshipmen, and professors in the academy's six schools: naval tactics and practical seamanship, gunnery and infantry tactics, mathematics, science (the school of natural and experimental philosophy), ethics and English, and modern languages. The superintendent was Cmdr. Cornelius K. Stribling, a veteran, like Dr. Frederick Fitch, of the War of 1812, while the commandant of midshipmen was Lt. Thomas T. Craven.[22]

The course of academic study under the academy's 1851 reforms was now vastly enhanced and improved over that available in the late 1840s. Ten plebes in 1851 chose the newly-available accelerated four-year path, which would be phased in during the decade. This approach permitted midshipmen to skip ahead, or accelerate, to higher classes by taking exams early. Under this transitional program, plebe (freshman)-class midshipmen could, after successfully passing their tests, advance in their second years to become third classmen or youngsters, while those in their junior and senior years would be known as second classmen and first classmen, respectively.

Six students would graduate in the college's first accelerated graduation on June 10, 1854; Le Roy Fitch was not one of these, having elected to complete the still-possible longer regiment. Professor James R. Soley in his 1876 sketch of the USNA reviewed the transitional period, noting that "the old and new systems worked side by side, compelling a provisional arrangement of studies."

Whether or not he was able to see any family members during his plebe year—Graham Newell was still in Congress until after Christmas—the Logansport teenager would have been able to report home that he was one of 23 plebes successfully promoted on June 16 into the academy's second class.[23]

The school year 1852-1853 was important to the professional education of Le Roy Fitch. In the first semester, the college received over 200 muskets to be used in infantry training together with a number of model sailboats to be employed as visual aids in teaching fleet tactics and ship maneuvers. In November, Lt. John A. Dahlgren arrived from the Bureau of Ordnance to superintend installation of a roofed-over naval battery of 32-lb. cannon. These guns, which replaced older U.S. Army fieldpieces, allowed Fitch and his classmates their first chance to work real cannons of the type they could expect to oversee in years ahead.

Upon the completion of exams at the end of June, the Hoosier joined others from his class on their first required summer training cruise aboard the academy's dedicated warship. Under the able leadership of Lt. Craven, 35 third- and first-class midshipmen traveled from Annapolis to the New York Navy Yard in July to join the complement of the 16-gun sloop-of-war U.S.S. *Preble*. Craven had taken the *Preble* on the academy's first summer training cruise 12 months earlier and its success led to a seaborne educational practice which has continued to this day. Once aboard, the lads were divided into port (left) and starboard (right) watches, were assigned lockers and mess seats, and were named to one of four gun crews, an ammunition-passing powder division, or a masters (quartermasters, lookouts, helmsmen) division.

Once the *Preble* put to sea, all aboard were subjected to the whims of ocean and weather and trained continuously on every type of sailor duty. For a young man from Indiana who had grown up alongside the banks of a canal perhaps reading of warships in the pages of James Fenimore Cooper and for whom a keelboat was probably a grand sight, this first opportunity on blue water must have been exhilarating. In 1851, the *Preble* sailed the U.S.

East Coast. Fitch and his classmates in 1852 were able to visit points further away, including the Azores port of Fayal; Madeira, Santa Cruz and Palma in the Canaries; and St. Thomas in the Caribbean before returning to Chesapeake Bay in September.[24]

During his second class year, Acting Midshipman Fitch's education in small arms and artillery intensified. Superintendent Louis M. Goldsborough, who succeeded Superintendent Stribling in 1853, brought in a battery of six Prairie Howitzers with caissons and, for the first time, the young naval cadet was able to spend time training on the light cannon type with which he would be forever identified. It was about this time that something of the 18 year old's living conditions at the naval school was revealed.

During 1851–1853, several midshipman dormitories were completed on the grounds of the naval academy. These held a total of 98 two-person rooms, each 15 feet square. These quarters were outfitted with a pair of iron beds, one table, two chairs, and several other hygiene-connected items. Despite the fact that African American attendants, who were mostly likely slaves, did much of the work (including bringing in water and brushing clothes and shoes), many students objected to a rule which required that they clean their rooms and make up their beds. Some went so far as to petition the superintendent in November 1853 requesting "that we may have servants to make up our beds and sweep out our rooms." Others objected that "during the past month, we have been compelled from time to time not only to light our lamps, bring up our wood and make our fires, but also to black our boots and in some cases to bring our water from the pump." The superintendent did not reply.[25]

His appointment secured by his half brother, Congressman Graham Newell Fitch, 16-year-old Le Roy Fitch entered the U.S. Naval Academy at Annapolis, Maryland with 37 others on October 1, 1851. Graduating No. 10 in his class on June 20, 1856, the new junior officer was 21 years old and would know no other life than that of a seaman for the next 17 years. This is one of only two photographs of Fitch known to exist; the other was taken in 1870 just five years before his death (Captain Robert F. Bradford Collection, Naval Historical Center).

In his excellent study of the antebellum naval academy, Charles Todorich discusses a point about midshipmen in the early 1850s which, when reviewed together with Fitch's USNA discipline record, displays the free-spirited nature of the future naval hero better than most available contemporary sources. There were present on the Severn in those years a number of midshipmen (known as Oldsters) still following the seven year curriculum, which valued practical application over theoretical study. Many of these young gentlemen thought the academy's new order, with its attention to codes of strict discipline, scholarship, and other "theoretical truck," was derogatory. These Oldsters went out of their way to bend or break academy rules as it suited them. For its part, the leadership of the academy, from Cmdr. Stribling on down, could do little more than offer demerits for infractions. The poor behavior by some of the older students had an adverse influence on a number of the newer men and sometimes led to cases among them of "idleness or fractiousness."

There is no doubt that the institutional "regs" were tough; indeed, most could not even be considered at a civilian college in 2007. Still in the context of the times, much of the unruliness by the newer midshipmen was in the nature of antics or pranks, with no physical harm done or disrespect intended. There was, however, one plague of serious portent—drunkenness—and another of disgust—tobacco—which attracted many midshipmen. The misuse of alcohol, which remains a problem in American higher education, was a moral difficulty that continued at the academy throughout the decade. Tobacco use, too, was seen as an evil and it was also, with little luck, discouraged. George Dewey, famed admiral of the Spanish-American War and a third classman the year Fitch graduated, chewed tobacco and later wrote that the weed "was the habit of the acting midshipmen in keeping with the universal male habit of the time."

There is no direct evidence that Le Roy Fitch drank too much or was disrespectful, plotted against academy authority, or was otherwise idle. There is verification, from his demerit record, that he did at least occasionally smoke and did not always follow all rules to the letter. A review of his conduct record in 1854-1855 shows a total of 41 demerits on the year including these incidents: receiving unauthorized visitors, 3; talking at recitation, 1; a dirty room, 1; absent from French recitation, 2; absent from section formation or exercise, 2; not in uniform in the city, 1; smoking, 1; neglect of duty as officer of the day for not finding absentees, 1. There were 34 demerits in 1855-1856 for these and other incidents: violating an order to change his room (linen?) weekly, 1; clothes "adrift" in room, 1; room out of order, 1; receiving unauthorized visitors, 2; absent from class or roll-call, 3; neglect of duty by not preserving order at exercise, 2.[26]

During his academy years, young Fitch took, in addition to his practical courses in gunnery, tactics, and seamanship, a variety of additional academic courses designed to stand him in good stead in his future profession. Among these were mathematics, astronomy, navigation, and surveying as taught by the noted Professor William Chauvenet. Other disciplines covered included mechanics and physics, ethics, international law, geography, history, grammar, composition and rhetoric, French and Spanish, and drawing. Given what we know of his interest in art, it is possible that this subject, along with surveying, gave him the opportunity to show initiative and personal flair and may have been among his favorite pastimes.

The curriculum Fitch studied was very conservative rather than progressive. Rote memory was valued far more than creative analysis or original thinking. No less a giant of American naval philosophy than Alfred Thayer Mahan, a plebe the year Fitch graduated, was known to believe that his college was not a hotbed of intellectualism. Admiral Dewey, writing years later, opined that the academy in his day was simply "one endless grind of acquiring knowledge" and that the "relentless examinations permit of no subterfuge of mental ability." Still, like others who made it through to the end, he was proud to note that when men graduated they "were well grounded.... The things that we knew we knew well."

The Hoosier doctor's son also participated fully in the cultural and social life pre-war Annapolis had to offer and was witness to important visitors. Like all cadets or aspiring U.S. naval officers, the teenager was instructed not only in the values and tasks of his occupation, but in the more refined components of a social and intellectual life far more formal and often more rigorous than today's.

On holidays and other occasions, lectures and parties were held and soirees were common in the city of Annapolis and at the academy. In preparation for these and other life encounters, the midshipmen learned how to act correctly in all social circumstances; manners were taught, as was dancing. This attention to sophistication was probably not lost on the town's young ladies, who were permitted to attend the academy's social functions. Chaplain George Jones' Lyceum was the academy center for historical exhibits of all manner while noted personages, including U.S. presidents Fillmore and Pierce, visited during Fitch's college years.

In 1852, Millard Fillmore came to the state capital to observe the departure of Commodore Matthew C. Perry's squadron for Japan. Later in that year, the Dutch frigate *Prince of Orange* arrived on a goodwill visit that permitted American midshipmen to mix with those from The Netherlands. A fiery speech was given at the governor's mansion in January 1856 by Louis Kossuth, whom all of the midshipmen were invited to hear and meet. Even more impressive than the program of the Hungarian revolutionary was the visit of President Franklin Pierce in April 1856. The purpose of his presence was to personally inspect the new U.S.S. *Merrimac*, which was commissioned on February 20, before returning overland to the White House. Under the command of Capt. Garrett J. Pendergast, the giant steam frigate had dropped anchor off Annapolis on an important stop on its inaugural cruise. Midshipmen, officers, and townspeople alike toured aboard the ship during its stay, while the secretary of the navy and members of the Congress also came from Washington to see the vessel. The day Pierce arrived, he was treated to a 21-gun salute, as well as a review of the ship's batteries and capabilities. The 14th chief executive concluded his stay with attendance at a grand naval ball attended by a multitude.[27]

Cmdr. Joseph F. Green was named commandant of midshipmen in May 1855 and it was he who led First Classman Fitch and that year's complement of 35 officer trainees up to New York in July to join the *Preble*'s summer cruise. Storms seemed to follow the sloop between every port on her voyage along the eastern seaboard from Eastport, Portland, Provincetown, to Boston. Still, the sloshing wet life of shipboard was assuaged perhaps a little during the Portland stop. There a Mrs. Little gave the midshipmen a ball, complete with good food and local young ladies. This break reportedly amused and improved several of the aspiring leaders, giving them a taste of "polite life" to compare with the "rough and tumble experience of a seaman." Throughout the sunny months at sea, the first classmen each took turns standing as either navigator or officer of the deck.[28]

When the *Preble* returned to Chesapeake Bay in September 1855, Acting Midshipman Fitch had completed much of his theoretical training in seamanship and gunnery and had received a chance to leaven it with practical experience. This education would only be expanded while on active sea duty over most of the next six years. Even though the future brown-water warrior would make his greatest military contribution in command of steam-powered vessels, about which neither he, nor any of his classmates, had any Annapolis training, it can be argued that the opportunities presented to him at the naval academy had been seized and would contribute greatly in turning a grassland physician family's son from an unknown boy into an enterprising officer of great organizational and leadership ability.

Le Roy Fitch graduated Number 10 in his class on June 20, 1856, receiving his diploma from Capt. Goldsborough in a simple ceremony in the 300-seat academy chapel. The next day he received leave to return to Logansport. The Hoosier was warranted 1856 academy graduate 10 on June 30. He was 21 years, eight months old.[29]

CHAPTER TWO

From Sea to Brown Water, 1856–March 1862

LE ROY FITCH, WHO OBTAINED HIS MAJORITY the previous October, returned home to Logansport for a summer of leave on June 21, 1856, the day after his graduation from the U.S. Naval Academy. His warrant, denoting his class rank at no. 10 and dated June 30, would be received in Indiana. It is uncertain from the record whether he had returned home since his departure for Annapolis in 1851 or if he had seen any of his Indiana family since his half-brother, Dr. Graham Newell Fitch, completed his term of congressional service in March 1853.

When Graham Newell, who did not stand for reelection the previous fall, and his wife, Harriet, returned to Logansport in the spring of 1853, they were able to resume their active Cass County medical, social, and political life. The patient load was no less than it ever was and the physician continued to address the varied health concerns of the area's growing population. Everywhere he went, the militia veteran, "a man perhaps a little above medium height, erect and straight as an arrow" always dressed formally: "high silk hat, well brushed; knee-length black Prince Albert coat; nicely blacked boots, the high tops of which were hidden by his striped trousers; brocaded vest, and gold-headed cane, without which no gentleman ever went on the street." Mrs. Fitch, too, had a significant influence on various women's groups around the town and was aided at home by the work of a servant, Jason Major. Dr. Fitch "attained an unusual degree of success in his profession" and his wife, as was the case with many doctors' wives, became an important exponent of community progress.

Although there is no evidence that Midshipman Fitch shared the political ambition which gripped his older half brother, he was undoubtedly familiar with the public discord then building in the nation. He could not have been but aware that the Cass County Democratic Party and indeed allies throughout the Wabash region looked to Graham Newell for civic leadership. A statewide election in 1855 placed the new Republican Party in control of the lower house of the Indiana legislature. To avoid the possibility of a Republican U.S. senatorial choice coming from a full session in a time years before the 17th Amendment to the Constitution permitted direct election, the Democratic controlled state senate simply refused to permit the whole deliberative body to meet in joint session. Le Roy would be long at sea before the standoff was concluded. Following the 1856 election, in which the Democrats regained control of both chambers of the Indiana statehouse, they "heedless of Republic attempts to bolt and cause no quorum unless given the Senator of whom they had been 'robbed' in 1855, pressed through the election of Jesse Bright and Graham Fitch, the so called 'bogus' Senators." Graham Newell, himself, would later admit that his election may not have been legal. These political developments were in the future; in the meantime, there were other family members to catch up with or on and local advances to experience.[1]

Le Roy's half sisters, Martha and Emma, were still at home. The former would marry Charles H. Denby, Sr., a Union Officer in the Civil War and a diplomat. Emma would become the wife of Graham Newell's partner, Dr. Asa Coleman.

Henry Alvord, the navy man's younger natural brother, was now 12 years old and was attending school while living with his half uncle and Harriet V. His older half brother Henry Sattelee, 22, studied at Georgetown University while Graham Newell served in Congress, as well as under Horace P. Biddle, presiding judge of the Eighth Judicial District and future Indiana Supreme Court jurist. Henry completed his studies at St. Mary's College in Chicago, taking his law degree from Albany Law School in 1855. He was just beginning to practice law in the "Windy City." In 1858, President James Buchanan would appoint him U.S. attorney for the circuit and district courts of Northern Illinois, but he would not take his seat before an ugly U.S. Senate fight over the move between Graham Newell and Stephen A. Douglas of Illinois. Henry would hold his post until 1861.[2]

The Wabash and Erie Canal, alongside of which Le Roy may have played years earlier, continued to flourish as its course ran near the home of the seaman's older half-brother on Market Street. The 468-mile waterway, longest of its kind in the United States, connected Toledo on Lake Erie with Evansville on the Ohio River. Just as it did before he went away to college, it continued to permit farmers to bring produce from all over Indiana's north central region into the city and to the county's small towns, like Lewisburg and Georgetown. It was then shipped on to Toledo and Cleveland, Ohio, and as far as Buffalo and Albany, New York.

Since at least the 1840s, packet boats for people and freight ran up and down the canal, while stagecoaches provided transport north and south of Logansport. Unhappily, by the time Midshipman Fitch came home for this visit, the canal he had known when he was younger was in a terrible state of disrepute. "The daily line of canal packets now running on the Wabash and Erie Canal, from Fort Wayne to Terre Haute, is at this time," one reporter wrote the previous September, "one of the most consummate swindles ever palmed-off upon the traveling public.... We advise everyone, who seeks anything like comfort in their travels, to avoid the canal packets."

At about the same time the canal was being criticized the previous year, a new form of transportation arrived in town—the railroad. Just as it would for generations of Cass Countians to follow, it undoubtedly caught the young officer's attention. The iron system, operated by the Newcastle and Richmond Rail Road, was still in its infancy when Le Roy Fitch first saw it. Indeed, the premier locomotive arrived only the previous July and it was, irony of ironies, floated down the Wabash and Erie Canal from Toledo. From Logansport, the engine was "hauled across the Wabash River to the south side, at the time known as Taberville, to a turntable." Still, it was a beginning and in time Logansport would become a rail hub, hosting nine lines spreading out from the city in different directions.[3]

Before leaving Logansport and a seldom-interrupted 23 years afloat, Le Roy may have become acquainted with one other local person whom we must profile. Mary "Mollie" Smith was one of two daughters of Lt. Col. Benjamin H. and Mary "Polly" Smith, who resided in a large two-story frame house on the southeast corner of Court and Third Streets. Mary Smith's parents were described by Cass County historian Will Ball in a 1960 newspaper column. "Smith himself," wrote Ball, "was a large man, an 'introvert' as the eggheads say, given to sober thought. Polly, on the other hand, was a lively, charming, vivacious woman quite small, always exerting herself to make her guests feel at ease." Polly Smith's father, Elihu Smith, founded the first newspaper north of the Ohio River, in Vincennes, in 1804. The other daughter, Susan, known as "Tune," later married Jesse Taber, son of 1828 Logansport pioneer Cyrus Taber. It was Mary who would, at some point and why not this one, catch the sailor's eye. The two would marry four years hence. In late October 1856, orders arrived requiring the Hoosier midshipman to report to the New York Navy Yard in Brooklyn.[4]

Having arrived at the country's second biggest naval facility by early November, Le Roy Fitch reported aboard the U.S.S. *Wabash*, which had steamed up from Washington, D.C., on October 23. The 4,650 ton screw frigate, a sister to the steamer *Merrimac* which the midshipman had visited at Annapolis in April, was commissioned at Philadelphia on August 18 under the command of Capt. Frederick K. Engle. The warship, named for the home region of the Indiana Fitch clan, was actually 1.6 feet longer than the *Merrimac* and 5.2 feet wider, but her depth of hold was actually a foot less. Designed by John Lenthall for a complement of 642 officers and men, the ship's 40 smoothbore cannon made her a powerful symbol of American might for the Home Squadron, the Navy's principal fleet. Fitch was sent aboard the *Wabash* to take passage south, together with his new commanding officer, to another ship, the U.S.S. *St. Mary's*.

Aboard the flagship, Fitch made the acquaintance of the Home Fleet commander, Cdr. Hiram Paulding, and, more importantly, his own new captain, Cmdr. Henry H. Davis. The Navy's greatest hydrographer and a scientist of note, Davis, 49, had, since the 1840s, published numerous scholarly articles on tides and helped found the *American Ephemeris and Nautical Almanac* during his just completed tour at Harvard University. Just as the *St. Mary's* would be Fitch's first ship, the sloop of war would be Davis' first command. He hoped to use the vessel to sail in search of new guano (bird excrement) islands. Before the invention of artificial fertilizers, seabird dung was the world's best source of nitrogen; it was heavily harvested by 19th-century European and North American traders and sold to farmers to replenish exhausted soils. First up on Davis' list was Jarvis Island, a tiny speck about a mile square located 22 nautical miles south of the equator and 200 miles southwest of Easter Island.[5]

Built in 1843-1844 at the Washington Navy Yard and commissioned in the fall of 1844, the flush-decked sloop of war *St. Mary's* weighed 958 tons and had a complement of 195. The sailing ship was 149.3 feet long, with a beam of 37.4 feet and a draft of 18 feet. Sailing ship historian Howard I. Chappelle has recorded that she had "a plain round stern and almost upright stem ... much deadrise and was rather sharp-ended." She was armed with 18 32-pounders and six 8-inchers. The *St. Mary's*, under Cmdr. Theodorus Baily, had operated as a unit of the Pacific Squadron but was due to be relieved. To that end, Bailey put into Panama City, Panama, in December where he and his men handed over the ship to Davis and his replacement crew, which had taken passage across the isthmus from Aspinwall (Colon) via the American Panama Railroad Company route completed the year before.[6]

Cmdr. Davis and the *St. Mary's* were delayed in their departure for Oceania by political events in Central America. Indeed, they would be called upon to address a concern more often associated in the public mind with European colonial areas, especially in Africa, than the Western Hemisphere. A dreamer and schemer, William Walker of Tennessee, lawyer, medical doctor, and journalist, had earlier taken the steps necessary to launch the first of three attempts to create a Central American military empire. This crude mercenary approach would leave a bad taste for Yankees in the mouths of regional citizens for decades to come.

On May 4, 1855, with fifty-six followers called "filibusters," Walker sailed from San Francisco for strife-torn Nicaragua, where one of the belligerent factions had invited him to come to its aid. In October, Walker and his mercenaries seized a steamer on Lake Nicaragua belonging to the Accessory Transit Company, a U.S. corporation dominated by Cornelius Vanderbilt, that transported freight and passengers across the isthmus. The Nashvillian was able to surprise and capture Granada, the capital and his opponents' stronghold, and make himself master of Nicaragua. Peace was then arranged between the factions, a puppet provisional president was put into place, and Walker, as troop CO, became *de facto* leader.

Cmdr. Charles H. Davis (1807–1877) was, besides Fitch's brother Graham Newell Fitch, one of the most important figures in the life of Le Roy Fitch, and quite probably the most inspirational to him professionally. A learned scholar, skilled diplomat, and highly regarded officer, Davis was Fitch's first captain, on the *St. Mary's*. Later, during the Civil War, the two would serve together again and Davis would create the berth that made Fitch's career (*Battles and Leaders of the Civil War*, Vol. 1).

At the dawn of 1856, two officials of the Accessory Transit Company plotted a very hostile corporate takeover. Funds were funneled to Gen. Walker and the company brought in his replacement mercenaries from America without fee. Claiming that Vanderbilt's firm had violated its charter, Walker seized its property and turned it over to the two conspirators for use of their concern, the Transit Company. As this intrigue unfolded, Nicaragua's new Walker-dominated government was formally recognized on May 2 by President Pierce, who had declared the Nicaraguan conflict a civil war. On June 3, the Democratic National Convention, to which Graham Newell Fitch was one of the delegates, expressed its sympathy with the efforts being made to "regenerate" Nicaragua. The same month internal dissention and Walker's plans to colonize the country with pro-slavery U.S. citizens from the southern states brought about the defection of figurehead chief executive Patricio Rivas. Undeterred, Walker, while chiding some of his followers for their half-hearted support, simply became Nicaragua's *de jure* president.

In the months thereafter, agents of millionaire Vanderbilt, working with Rivas and others, were able to encourage a coalition of neighboring Central American states, led by Costa Rica, to make war on Nicaragua while, internally, a revolt was fermented in attempt to break Walker's supply line by assisting rival interests. In the process, a number of American citizens, en route via Central America to the California gold fields, were killed. The British, by the instrument of their Royal Navy, were also interested in the isthmian region. Concerned over potential American ambitions, they, too, focused more closely upon the conflict. As the fighting intensified, the allies enjoyed some success, particularly in gaining control over the logistical aspect of the campaign. A highlight for Walker, however, was the November 23 defeat of the four-gun Costa Rican brig *Eleventh of April* by his lighter schooner *Granada*.

During the entire time of the Nicaraguan adventure, the U.S. Pacific and Home Squadrons kept tabs on Walker, intensifying oversight following a massacre of U.S. citizens in October 1855. In mid–January 1857, Pacific Squadron CO Commodore William Mervine ordered Cmdr. Davis to halt prepa-

Nashville-born lawyer, doctor, and adventurer William Walker (1824–1860) was determined to establish a pro-slavery military dictatorship in Central America. His 1856 activities in Nicaragua were watched by Cmdr. Davis, to whom he surrendered when his situation deteriorated in 1857. Walker tried again in 1860, but was caught and executed (James Roche, *The Story of the Filibusters*, 1891).

rations for his guano island expedition and instead sail to San Juan del Sur to witness the possible final destruction of the filibusters and to guard American lives.

The final battle of what Nicaraguans called the National War (1856-57) took place in the spring of 1857 around and in the town of Rivas, on Lake Nicaragua, near the Costa Rican border. When the *St. Mary's* arrived off San Juan del Sur on February 6, Davis found that, while Walker was, in fact, cornered in Rivas, his adversaries were unable to mount a final assault. Walker had some hope for relief as mercenary reinforcements were known to be en route from San Francisco. So far, the American filibuster was able to beat off the attacks of the Central Americans and Davis did not believe there would be a quick resolution of the conflict. Consequently, the commander hoped to sail for Jarvis Island and return before any showdown. That would not happen. Instead of departing, the sloop of war would remain into the spring as her captain sought to negotiate an end to the fighting. The diplomatic and potential military confrontation with Tennessean Walker or his opponents was not something Davis relished.

A week before the *St. Mary's* dropped anchor, the 500 replacement filibusters landed at Greytown, on the Atlantic across Lake Nicaragua from Rivas, and began an effort to fight their way through Costa Rican forces to Walker's relief. This they were unable to do despite over a month of determined attacks. On April 11, the Central American allies mounted an assault on Rivas, but were beaten off. Of the 463 mercenaries who remained alive and in command of the town at the conclusion of the battle, more than half were sick or wounded. The Americans were surely doomed to defeat, by attrition if nothing else, but still they held on.[7]

On separate occasions toward the end of April, Captain Davis sent his three lieutenants, John Maury, Thomas T. Houston, and David P. McCorkle, into Rivas to learn firsthand details of the situation in the besieged stronghold and to bring out American dependents. All three reported the filibusters' situation hopeless. Walker, it was said, was known to believe that, if worse came to worse, he could escape on the *Granada*, which was then anchored at San Juan del Sur. On April 29, Davis decided to attempt to put an end to the Nicaraguan conflict and, together with Surgeon I. Winthrop Taylor and a small party which included several seamen and possibly Midshipman Fitch, visited Walker and the leader of the Central American allies, Gen. Jose I. Mora. Before departing for the interior, Davis gave First Lieutenant Maury, temporary commander of the 20-gun sloop, strict orders concerning the *Granada*. If Walker was expelled from Rivas during the time Davis was away, the mercenary ship should be considered a pirate ship and seized before the renegade Americans could sail it away. Mora agreed to the neutral Yankee's effort to end the bloodshed and, following three meetings over the next two days, Walker, too, was convinced that his cause was lost and that quitting was the best option for personal survival. On May 1, the Nashville native surrendered himself, his followers, and his ship to the protection of the U.S. Navy captain. Walker and his staff were transported down to Panama City while most of his men were escorted on foot across the isthmus; both groups were returned to the U.S.[8]

Once the spring's Nicaraguan interlude was concluded, the *St. Mary's* was free to undertake her delayed Pacific voyage and to seek geologic and hydrographic data and, yes, guano deposits. The first stop would be Jarvis Island where, back in March, two Americans, representing the American Guano Company, had landed from the Honolulu-based schooner *Liholiho* and claimed the whole pile for their expedition's investors under terms of the U.S. Guano Act of 1856. When the *St. Mary's* arrived at the island at the end of May, Cmdr. Davis surveyed it and made a formal territorial claim in the name of the U.S. Compared to the political activity of the premier months of his first command, most of the next two years of pure scientific sailing must have been a great pleasure for the Davis, the scholar.

In 1858, Charles Davis and his officers faced a different challenge when they were stranded at Mare Island. The ship, after several years of constant service, had put into the port for a refit. This could not be completed in a timely fashion because funds to complete the service were not forthcoming. As the captain and his crew spent the next six months waiting for completion of the work and the attendant paperwork, the lure of riches in the California gold fields tempted many people from all walks of life to come from far and near to "get rich quick." Desertions among the ship's sailors, as well as shipyard mechanics, ran rampant. Still, there were compensations. Cmdr. Davis struck up what was to be a life-long friendship with the yard's chief, Cmdr. David Glasgow Farragut. The two men would meet again during the Civil War, as subordinates at Port Royal and as fleet leaders at Vicksburg.

It was the early weeks of September 1858 before the *St. Mary's* could sail south to resume cruising off Central America. Walker or some other filibuster could be expected to create additional mischief in the area and the Navy had to remain on the alert. Finally, three years after this chapter was begun, the warship's story was continued under different authorship.

The *St. Mary's* was relieved at Panama City, Panama, in January 1859 and her officers and crew returned stateside.⁹

After departing the *St. Mary's*, Commander Davis, whom Midshipman Fitch would not see again until May 1862, was granted leave for six months before returning to Harvard University to supervise the Nautical Almanac Office. Fitch, too, was given a vacation, but on April 6, 1859, he was sent to examination. This he took on April 29 and, on May 6, he was notified that he had passed; his commission as a passed midshipman was dated April 29, No. 7. The same day, May 6, he was ordered to the U.S.S. *Savannah* as Acting Master; he was able to join the ship by May 31.¹⁰

The U.S.S. *Savannah*, the second ship with that name in the U.S. Navy, was a 1,726-ton sailing frigate which was originally laid down at the New York Navy Yard in July 1820. She was one of nine ships from a class prototype design of naval architect William Doughty. For a variety of reasons, the warship remained on the building stocks until launched on May 5, 1842. She was not actually commissioned until October 15, 1843.

The cruiser, similar in design to the U.S.S. *President* of the War of 1812 except for "an ugly round stern, combined with quarter galleries," was 175 feet long with a beam of 45 feet and a depth of hold of 22.4 feet. Her battery comprised 44 cannons and her crew numbered four hundred. Her sister *Cumberland* would be sunk and another sister, the *St. Lawrence*, would be damaged by the C.S.S. *Virginia* at Hampton Roads on March 8, 1862.¹¹

The *Savannah* had been inactivated in November 1856, but was now recalled to serve as Home Squadron flagship for Cdr. Garret J. Pendergast. From New York to Florida and New Orleans, the aging frigate would sail in Mexican and Central American waters between July 1859 and November 1860. There, although not directly involved, she would help to protect American lives and monitor the situation between the parties engaged in Mexico's War of the *Reforma*. The men aboard would also hear tales of the renewed activities of an old Fitch "acquaintance," William Walker. During this cruise, the Hoosier officer was promoted twice in 1859. On July 12, he was warranted passed midshipman no. 7, dating back to April 30, while on Sept. 8, he was warranted Master, dating back to Sept. 5. The Mexican government of Benito Juarez was recognized by the U.S. on December 14.

In the spring of 1860, as the Mexican conflict raged, William Walker once more heard the trumpet call of mercenary opportunity and sprang into action, this time in Honduras. With a tiny band of followers and an invitation from a dissatisfied group on one of the Bay Islands, he attempted to prevent the transfer of that real estate from the U.K. to Honduras. During the summer, he moved over from the island and captured the city of Trujillo, while simultaneously causing the local British customs receipts to disappear. Money spoke just as loudly then as now and when the 11-gun steam sloop H.M.S. *Icarus* arrived, its captain, Cmdr. Norvell Salmon, informed Walker directly that his activities on the mainland and the island, together with the loss of the cash, were unacceptable to Her Majesty's government. Finding himself surrounded by Hondurans, Walker attempted the same ploy he had with Charles Davis of the U.S. Navy; he would surrender and hope to be taken safely out of harm's way. The British were not, however, willing to accommodate the American. When he came aboard the *Icarus*, Walker was promptly thrown into irons and then handed over to the Hondurans at Trujillo. There he was executed on September 12.

At the time of Walker's death, the War of the *Reforma* in Mexico had only a few months more to finish playing out, but the role of the U.S. Navy in keeping American civilians and interests in the nation safe intensified along with the final battles. The forces of President

Juarez made steady progress, defeating their adversaries at Silao (August 10) and Guadalajara (November 1). Although the oversight role of the Home Squadron would continue as before even through the fall of Mexico City to Juarez on January 1, 1861, Master Fitch and his colleagues aboard the *Savannah* would not be observers. Early in November, the frigate completed her assignment and her crew was rotated. On November 19, Fitch was ordered detached from the *Savannah* and allowed to return home on three months leave.[12]

On only his second visit back to Logansport since his naval academy graduation, Le Roy Fitch married Mary Smith at the city's Calvary Presbyterian Church on December 4, 1860, the Rev. Martin M. Post officiating. While it is relatively certain that much of the bride's family was present, is it not known for certain who represented the groom's family. It is a fairly safe bet that his 16-year-old brother, Henry Alvord Fitch, may have been the 25-year-old naval officer's best man, although, it may have been Frederick Fitch, his 20-year-old nephew by Uncle Egbert. Half sisters Emma and Martha would have been present, but his half brothers were out of town. Henry S. was performing his duties as U.S. attorney for northern Illinois while Graham Newell, who had not been a candidate for reappointment the previous fall, was, with his wife, Harriet, in Washington, D.C. In the little over two months that Le Roy and his bride would have to spend together in Indiana, the storm clouds of civil war, gathering for some years, spread ominously across the land. To say that the political situation was tense in the wake of the election of Illinois native Abraham Lincoln to the White House on November 6 would be a huge understatement.

The day before Le Roy's wedding, the second session of the 36th U.S. Congress assembled in the nation's capital. President James Buchanan's constitutionally required state of the union message of that date recognized that the slave states had certain grievances and deprecated the possible dissolution of the Union, but simultaneously announced that the Federal government was impotent to prevent it. In the days that followed Buchanan's speech and the opening of Congress' last pre-war session, newspapers from big cities and small would intensify their reporting of the uncertainty-filled public discourse. Many sectional leaders from the south threatened secession while significant blocks of northern citizens would either seek compromise to avert the Union's dissolution or demand that the government stand fast and impose its laws in the south.

On December 18, Sen. John J. Crittenden offered a compromise, rejected by Lincoln and his followers, that would have recognized even further the "rights" of the slaveholders. Graham Newell Fitch, an ally of the president, was strongly committed to compromise, both on political grounds and because of the perceived impact the crisis was having upon the national economy.

With land travel primitive, uncertain, and time-consuming, the people of America's central section during the first six decades of the 19th century were dependent upon water transportation on the Mississippi River and its 50 navigable tributaries. Despite differing geographic features, the great rivers of the area helped to create a regional unity from differing political interests, fostering networks of rural market exchanges between various communities in the south and larger, more urban centers of the north. This trade had a significant impact on both regional and national outlooks.

Flatboats and keelboats like those seen on the Wabash and Erie Canal, and steamboats on the "Father of Waters" and such streams as the Ohio, Cumberland, Tennessee, White, Red, Wabash, and Kanawha moved both people and goods and provided the backbone of the region's commerce. Even with the coming of the railroad, among the possibilities most feared by those at the northern end of the river system as the secession movement unfolded in 1860-1861 was the creation of a hostile, southern, indeed, foreign, power which could choke off trade. As the soon-to-be-called Confederates became increasingly aggressive and the civil war threatened, opinion and concern in the upper Midwest crystallized behind the slogan "Free Navigation of the Mississippi." Many northerners were beginning to consider the extreme measures which might be necessary to protect their vital water arteries to the south and to the world in the event compromise failed.

Senator Fitch participated in the ferocious legislative debates which surrounded the Crittenden Compromise and the several other proposals designed to find some middle ground between the crisis' extremists. Though not seen that day, the work of the peace advocates was really doomed on December 20 when South Carolina enacted an ordnance of secession.

The administration of President Buchanan demonstrated impotence and confusion as the collective national waiting for Lincoln's March 4, 1861, inaugural raced along. The U.S. Congress, despite the election of many new Republican members, failed to fill the chief executive's void by refusing to come down strongly for either compromise or enforcement. In the end, the weak congressional effort to prevent an armed split proved unsuccessful and its supporters, Fitch among them, were largely be branded appeasers. Still, in something of a footnote, Senator Fitch was the last U.S. senator to speak on the floor of the national legislature before President Lincoln took his oath of office. As was reported in the March 16 issue of *Harper's Weekly*:

> On Monday, 4th, both Houses met at 10 A.M., but no business of consequence was transacted. In the Senate, Senator Fitch, of Indiana, spoke against time to kill a gas company's charter. At noon the session terminated.

Years later, Cass County historian Thomas B. Helm recalled in his profile of the doctor that Graham Newell's "senatorial experience ... ended his active political life."[13]

On the Fitch family front, Le Roy was the only member with long-standing national employment to enjoy public favor in the new year, 1861. On January 12, he received word that he had been promoted to the rank of lieutenant; his commission would be delivered on March 1, backdated to January 12. Meanwhile, time was running out for half brother Henry S. Fitch to continue in his post as U.S. attorney for the Northern District of Illinois. Knowing his position was entirely dependent upon the unlikely spoils pleasure of the new president, Henry S. wrote to Abraham Lincoln on January 31, 1861, offering to resign his position at the end of June. Given that Le Roy was still in town awaiting orders, it is quite possible that he was able to greet Graham Newell and Harriet V. upon their return from Washington, D.C., in early March. At the beginning of April, Le Roy was ordered to the Philadelphia Navy Yard. There he would take passage south aboard the U.S.S. *Water Witch* to join the complement of the U.S.S. *Wyandotte*.[14]

The 378-ton *Water Witch* was the third incarnation of a side-wheel steamer originally commissioned with a one-of-a-kind experimental propulsion system. When that unique power plant did not work out, the vessel was twice rebuilt. On April 8 when Lt. Fitch reported aboard, the 150-foot light gunboat was completing a refit begun on November 1; he was joined aboard by Lt. Commanding August S. Baldwin, who would be the *Wyandotte*'s new commander. On April 10, the *Water Witch* put to sea headed for Key West, Florida. Two days later, troops under Gen. Pierre Beauregard began the bombardment of Fort Sumter in Charleston Harbor, South Carolina, the opening shots of the War of the Southern Rebellion or Civil War.

The *Water Witch* dropped anchor among the ships of the newly formed Gulf Blockading Squadron off Pensacola on May 2 and Lieutenants Baldwin and Fitch reported aboard the *Wyandotte*, a far larger warship. The first appearance by Lt. Fitch in the Navy's Civil War Official Record series now occurs as the result of Capt. Henry Adams' May 3 report to new Navy Secretary Welles concerning the disposition of vessels and officers of his command. We reprint the message in whole in order to show the local state of affairs as the Hoosier sailor began his initial wartime service.

> U. S. FRIGATE SABINE,
> Off *Pensacola, May 3, 1861.*
>
> Sir: I have the honor to inform you of the arrival of the *Water Witch* yesterday from Key West. Owing to the nonarrival of the New York steamer at Havana in time, she brought no later intelligence from the United States than had previously been received by the *Mohawk*. The *Water Witch* will be immediately employed in carrying out your instructions regarding the mail between this place and Key West. For the sake of expedition I may sometimes judge it best to send her direct to Havana. The steamer *Philadelphia* arrived this morning with military stores. The boats of the squadron are now engaged in landing them. The *Illinois* was discharged and sailed yesterday. The following changes have been made in the distribution of officers to the ships: Lieutenant Commanding Baldwin and Lieutenants Stillwell and Fitch have joined the *Wyandotte*; Lieutenant Williamson has returned to the *Brooklyn*; Lieutenant Murdaugh, whose resignation I lately forwarded, I have ordered to the *Supply*; Lieutenant Jones, of the *St. Louis*, to the *Supply*; Lieutenants Maxwell and Hopkins from the *Supply* to the *Sabine*. I hope to get the *Supply* off in about a week.
>
> The *Water Witch* sails today for Tortugas, carrying an Army officer who is to bring down some military stores in her. She will go to Havana and Key West for the mail and to make arrangements for its speedy conveyance in future.
>
> Very respectfully, your obedient servant,
>
> H. A. ADAMS,
> *Captain, and Senior Officer Present.*
>
> Hon. GIDEON WELLES
> *Secretary of the Navy.*[15]

It is an interesting bit of trivia that the first warship Le Roy Fitch served in during the Civil War began life as a merchantman, the Philadelphia-built *Western Port*. Most of the vessels he would serve in or captain hereafter during the great conflict would have a past or future in civilian service. Like so many of the other craft in his future, the *Western Port* was originally employed on charter. By the spring of 1861, she was a full-fledged naval vessel, having been purchased into the Navy on June 6, 1859, and christened *Wyandotte* after the Native American tribe. The 453-ton screw-steamer was 162.4 feet long, with a beam of 24.3 feet and a draft of 13.6 feet, had a complement of 90 and was armed with four 32-pounders and one 24-pound howitzer. She was sail equipped and often employed her canvas.

Most of the excitement, if such it may be termed, in *Wyandotte*'s cruise off Florida during the opening weeks of the secession had already occurred by the time Fitch joined the ship. After safeguarding Key West in early December 1860, the steamer put into Pensacola's dry dock in midmonth for minor repairs. She was refloated on January 9, 1861, and refused to surrender when Confederate forces took over the Pensacola Navy Yard three days later. Instead, she towed Cmdr. Henry Walke's supply ship *Supply*, loaded as she was with military dependents, out to sea. The *Wyandotte* transported troops from Fort Barrancas to Fort Pickens on February 10 and regularly patrolled the inner shore of Santa Rosa Island to prevent Rebel soldiers from attacking Fort Pickens by land. On April 2, the ship's captain, Lt. Commanding O. H. Berryman, died and Lt. J. R. M. Mullany became acting commander. Mullany's vessel was a participant in the daring nighttime reinforcement of Fort Pickens on April 12, the day of the firing upon Fort Sumter, S.C. On April 17, *Wyandotte* received a new acting captain, Lt. J. C. Williamson, and also took U.S. Army Engineer Corps Capt. Montgomery C. Meigs on a reconnaissance of Santa Rosa Island.

The *Wyandotte* which Baldwin and Fitch joined on May 2 was a very tired ship. Capt. Adams had reported to the Navy Department on April 18 that the ship was expected "every day to break down." Her engine was "much worn" and "for the past 100 days her fires had only been out for 24 hours."

The *Wyandotte* remained off the Florida coast for the next four months engaged in patrol and transport assignments. In May and June, she cruised several times back and forth between Pensacola and Key West; These trips were performed after May 17 as a unit in the Gulf Blockading Squadron. On August 23, she proceeded to the New York Navy Yard for major repairs. It would later be recorded that, prior to her relief, "she narrowly escaped shipwreck [and] was finally declared unseaworthy and returned North for repairs. The officers and crew were therefore discharged on their arrival."[16]

The New York Navy Yard, which had been commanded by future Western Flotilla flag officer Capt. Andrew Hull Foote from October 1858 until August 1861 but which was now led by Cdr. Hiram Paulding, was located on Brooklyn's Walabout Bay, across the East River east of Manhattan. The largest naval facility in the U.S., it was a site for major warship construction and repair as well as the primary renovation location for almost 200 of the 300 merchant or captured vessels converted into Atlantic coast blockade ships. It had a labor pool of about 1,650 in 1861, but that would later grow to almost 6,000 workers. From a personnel viewpoint, it was also a major source for new seamen taken into the Union Navy.

The *Wyandotte* anchored off the Brooklyn repair facility on September 16, 1861. Lt. Fitch was detached and required to remain in town awaiting orders. On September 28, he was posted to the old 74-gun ship-of-the-line *North Carolina*, then serving as the New York Navy Yard's receiving ship, where he would also perform ordnance duty. The *North Carolina*, which had been housing newcomers to the fleet since 1839 and was one of the old wooden battleships serving that need in U.S. ports, was equipped with one 32-pounder and four 9" smoothbores.

Le Roy Fitch worked with both the laborers and new recruits flooding into the Navy Yard in the fall of 1861. He was often called upon for advice with the ordnance being installed aboard the ferryboats and other ships being converted for blockade duty. Additionally, it fell to him to provide basic gunnery education for at least some of the volunteer officers and seamen being assembled to crew the new warship additions. The process and procedures of mass induction of manpower as practiced in the receiving ship must have been instructive as he would later be called upon to follow a similar pattern while finding men for his river gunboats.

The first step aboard a man-o'-war for new recruits was their signing of shipping articles. These were legal contracts officially witnessed by a navy officer at a recruiting rendezvous

A receiving ship at Brooklyn's New York Navy Yard at the outbreak of the Civil War, this inactive three-decker battleship was home to new recruits as well as to Lt. Fitch from September 1861 to March 1862. During his time as the *North Carolina*'s ordnance specialist, he trained new recruits in gunnery and offered his expertise to yard workers outfitting emergency warships for the Union blockade (Naval Historical Center).

(recruiting station). Once the papers were signed, the recruits were sent (by government transport or in some cases by private means for which they were reimbursed) to a receiving ship. These were, like the *North Carolina*, floating collection points where the new men would receive required medical exams (usually very basic if not downright primitive), uniforms (civilian clothes were discarded or recycled home) and eating utensils. Navy discipline and activity (such as cleaning ship) followed, together with as much rudimentary nautical training (like drilling at the big cannon) as was possible before the men were shipped out to units of the fleet.[17]

While Lt. Fitch was in New York, the rum-hating 56-year-old Flag Officer Foote, Cdr. Pauling's predecessor as yard commandant, was leading the U.S. Army's inland gunboat flotilla to victory in the Western theater. On March 3, 1862, the Hoosier lieutenant was detached from the New York Navy Yard and posted to Cairo, Illinois, where he would take command of one of the ordnance steamers recently outfitted for the Western Flotilla. Before, however, we transfer our attention to the brown water scene where Fitch would achieve recognition, we should review military developments centered on the great rivers south and west of Indiana.

When news of Fort Sumter's fall on April 13 and President Lincoln's call-up were received in St. Louis, Missouri, the well-known and wealthy engineer-riverman James B. Eads wrote to his friend Attorney General Edward Bates. Eads, later made famous by his construction of the St. Louis bridge, called for aggressive action to defeat the Rebels and suggested he had a plan that might prove helpful in wresting the lower Mississippi away from the South. In the attorney general's April 17 acknowledgment, Bates advised Eads that the riverman's presence would soon be required in the nation's capital, as "it will be necessary to have the aid of the most thorough knowledge of our Western rivers and the use of steam on them."

Eads arrived in Washington and on April 29 was taken by Bates before President Lincoln and the cabinet to explain his ideas for creating a river navy to aid in a joint U.S. Army-Navy campaign to recover the river valley. The proposed campaign would be based on a navy operating from the low-lying town of Cairo, Illinois, where the Ohio River flowed into the Mississippi and where those two streams physically separated pro–Union Illinois from the border states of Kentucky and Missouri. Eads later delivered his ideas in writing to an appreciative Navy Secretary Welles. In the confusion, excitement, and inter-service rivalries which marked the Federal buildup, Eads' plan was to be amalgamated into one sponsored, financed, and controlled by the War Department which, in peacetime, exercised jurisdiction over inland waterways.[18]

On May 1, 1861, Union Army chief Gen. Winfield Scott, a hero of the Mexican War, wrote to Lincoln describing a strategy for crushing the rebellion. At the heart of his Anaconda victory plan lay the idea of strangling the South along the Mississippi and its tributaries, using inland river highways to mount and support amphibious assaults to crush the strong points of the divided parts, eventually reopening the mighty stream to United States commerce. Scott based his strategy on a powerful U.S. Navy coastal blockade and called for a decisive "movement down the Mississippi to the ocean, with a cordon of posts at proper points ... the object being to clear out and keep open this great line of communication." Although this game plan had its critics, it was, with modifications, successfully followed. The Confederacy, for its part, devised no real countermeasures to the Union strategy and such preparations as could be made to resist the scheme would, in the end, prove useless.[19]

The first problem faced in implementing the Eads-Scott strategy was one of materiel: there were no Union gunboats on the rivers. On May 16, 1861, Cmdr. John Rodgers, USN, was ordered to report to Brig. Gen. George B. McClellan at Cincinnati "in regard to the expediency of establishing a naval armament on the Mississippi and Ohio Rivers." McClellan, earlier in the month, recommended to Scott that three gunboats be constructed to protect the occupation of Cairo, Illinois, and Secretary Welles quickly cut the orders which would send the sailor west to serve as nautical advisor to the soldiers. Although Rodgers would fall under Army orders and funding, he would be allowed to make requisitions upon the Navy Department for ordnance—and make all the recommendations the generals would hear. In addition to establishing at Cairo what would become the inland navy's administrative seat and one of its most important bases, Rodgers, with the help of two subordinates and Naval Constructor Samuel M. Pook, purchased and oversaw the conversion at Cincinnati of three river steamers: the *Lexington*, *Conestoga*, and *A. O. Tyler* (shortened to *Tyler*). Laboring in the face of a civilian-military logistical nightmare, the Navy men were able to get these three steamers outfitted, armed, and crewed, and, following a low-water delay, down to Cairo by August 12, 1861. With the timberclads (so called because of their wooden armor) in hand, the U.S. Army could begin implementing the Scott-Eads plan and the naval war on inland waters could proceed.[20]

Meanwhile, on August 7, James B. Eads, who had never built a boat, ship, or any other kind of nautical craft, found himself the winner of a War Department contract for the construction of seven ironclad gunboats to be delivered at Cairo by October 10. Designed by Pook and sometimes called Pook Turtles, or more commonly, the City Series, these vessels were designed to provide the heavy punch necessary to achieve the riverine goals of the Anaconda plan. The big sisters would be almost identical when completed. Built around a casemate pierced for 13 guns and constructed with many sub-contracted components at yards in Mound City, Illinois, and Carondelet, Missouri (a St. Louis suburb), Eads' vessels were named for prominent river cities: *Carondelet, St. Louis, Louisville, Cairo, Cincinnati, Mound City,* and *Pittsburg* (the Pennsylvania city did not employ an "h" at that time). Delays in construction, usually because of financing, caused the craft to be delayed well beyond their initial delivery dates. In addition to these purpose-built ironclads, two larger conversions would be made using existing steamers. Thus the snagboat *Submarine No. 7* was reborn as the *Benton* and the ferryboat *New Era* became the *Essex*. Various tugs, auxiliary steamers, and a number of barges converted into heavy mortar platforms were also ordered or purchased.

As the construction and conversion of the vessels for the War Department's Western Flotilla progressed, non-materiel problems for this Union effort arose. Cmdr. Rodgers ran afoul of many people, including Eads and St. Louis commander Gen. John C. Fremont, a popular hero still politically useful to the Lincoln administration. On August 9, Fremont wrote a Washington friend: "I don't like Commander Rodgers who is in charge of the gunboat operations—will you ask to have him removed." By month's end, Rodgers, whose little-appreciated yeoman service was indispensable to the Western Flotilla's creation, was ordered east. Secretary Welles' replacement made on August 26 was the 56-year old Capt. Andrew Hull Foote.[21]

Between September 1861 and January 1862, Capt. Foote literally struggled with the U.S. Army, as well as the builders and contractors, to complete his flotilla. In November he was promoted to the rank of flag officer (equivalent to a land force major general) largely to give him the inter-service clout necessary to finish his project. Samples of potential gunboat achievements were constantly provided by the timberclads as they undertook support and reconnaissance missions up and down the rivers. One of the "more serious of these affairs," as Alfred Thayer Mahan would put it years later, occurred on November 7. Disembarking from chartered steamboats, about 3,000 Union soldiers under Brig. Gen. Ulysses S. Grant assaulted Belmont, Missouri, across the Mississippi River from the Confederate fortress at Columbus, Kentucky. That town had been seized by Rebel troops on September 4, thereby ending Kentucky's hopes to remain neutral. Although repulsed, Grant's people received significant support from the gunboats, causing the future commander in chief of all Union ground forces to thereafter become one of the navy's greatest enthusiasts. Operationally on Western waters after the Battle of Belmont, "nothing of importance," as Mahan has it, "occurred in the year 1861." Work on the ironclads and mortar rafts was pushed and efforts to redress serious shortcomings in the recruitment of enlisted men and willing pilots continued. Anyone who would listen was asked to assist with the manpower crisis; even local newspapers ran tales promoting the "ease" of gunboat life over that experienced by the Army's new recruits:

> The pay of the sailor is somewhat more liberal than that of the soldier, and his duties, include no long marches or wet encampments. He gets his meals and his grog with unfailing regularity and has always, besides, a dry bed—luxaries [sic] which a soldier can seldom count on.

The seven City Series ironclads were finally accepted by the government on January 15, 1862. The recruitment knot was still untied and consequently, only four of the vessels would be ready to steam to Fort Henry, the first big test for these river warships.[22]

At the beginning of the Civil War, the economic value of Tennessee, where Le Roy Fitch would play his key role starting in the fall of 1862, and the northern parts of Alabama and Georgia, was underappreciated in many circles in the South. Although the value of sectional trade may have been understood, the politics of warfare in that time required that major attention be focused on the two perceived seats of power, Washington and Richmond; "On to Richmond" was both an all-absorbing battle cry and an approach to securing victory. Confederate military leaders from Robert E. Lee to Leonidas Polk, Gideon Pillow, and Albert Sidney Johnston all really failed "to grasp fully the importance of the munitions-producing area of Georgia, Tennessee, and Alabama" and failed, accordingly, to plan for its defense.

This rebellion's heartland area was very worthy of protection. The value of the resources available in Tennessee alone are illustrative. Utilizing saltpeter acquired from the caves of East Tennessee, the South's largest gunpowder mills manufactured their deadly powder along the Cumberland River northeast of the state capital. Nashville, the most cosmopolitan U.S. city below the Ohio River (save New Orleans) and a major railroad hub, was also Richmond's greatest war production center. Located along a big loop on the southern bank of the Cumberland River, it is, as succinctly put by Anne J. Bailey, historian of a later campaign, geographically "near the center of a bowl-like valley formed by a string of ridges." City and surrounding Davidson County concerns turned out cannon, small arms, cartridges, saddles, blankets, and all manner of other accouterments. Significantly, because 90 percent of all the copper available in the South came from the region surrounding Duckville, Tennessee, it was the major supplier of available copper percussion caps. In addition to war materiel, the state's foodstuffs were critical to the associated states' success. In this one Civil War historian has opined that "in the total production of corn, hogs, cattle, mules and horses, the lower Middle Tennessee zone was one of the richest in the *entire Confederacy*."

Failure to protect these assets would have a drastic and tragic impact upon the fortunes of the South if invasion did not come along the Mississippi corridor. Still, as it has been suggested by regional historian Byrd Douglas, this development may not have been caused by an overall Southern appreciation for Tennessee's importance. While the Confederacy "was criticized and may have seem indifferent to forwarding the men and tools of war" as might have been expected, "it should be remembered," Douglas wrote in 1961, "that the Confederacy was an infant republic" as yet unable to defend its totality. Each southern state was initially responsible for its own protection as all of the seceding states were clinging "to the traditional doctrine of 'States Rights'"—which had many faults requiring time and patience to overcome.

The Scott-Eads plan for the Union's reduction of Confederate positions in the West and an associated great move south along the Mississippi River was not a secret. Indeed, when Tennessee became the last seceded southern state on June 8, 1861, the outline of the Yankee scheme was widely accepted as strategy on both sides of the Mason-Dixon Line and a guide to the way the Western conflict would be fought. At Nashville, which is located 280 miles northeast of Memphis and 206 miles southwest of Lexington in Kentucky, Governor Isham G. Harris, following this logic, fully expected that his northern border was safe due to Kentucky's neutrality. Not having any particular reason to believe that northern generals would operate outside of the Scott plan, Harris, together with his military advisors, Maj. Gen. Leonidas Polk and Brig. Gen. Gideon J. Pillow, believed that most of the fighting involving Volunteer state patriots, more of whom would bear Confederate arms than from any other state save Virginia, would occur along the state's Mississippi River border. Indeed, Brig. Gen. Pillow went so far as to write one concerned citizen that "nothing of military importance [is] to be gained by [the Yankees] ascending [the] Tennessee River." Thus most available troops of Tennessee's provisional army, including engineers and artillery, were ordered west to help protect a chain of defenses running south from Island No. 10 (the 10th island in the Mississippi south of the Ohio) to Memphis. The noted Tennessee community, located 790 miles by the river from New Orleans and 240 from Cairo, stood on an elevated bluff on the left bank of the Mississippi River. It had to be kept out the hands of Union troops; not only was it the termination of the Memphis and Charleston Railroad, but was " a place of much business activity, being the distributing point for the produce of West Tennessee." Thus it was that only 4,000 soldiers guarded the Cumberland Pass and the vital economic areas of Middle Tennessee at the time James B. Eads was building ironclads near St. Louis.[23]

When Brig. Gen. Pillow's forces, acting on orders from Maj. Gen. Polk, took over Columbus on September 4, 1861, they violated Kentucky's "neutrality" and threw the entire northern border of Tennessee open to invasion. Brig. Gen. Grant, for his part, quickly seized the Ohio River community of Paducah, Kentucky, which sat at the mouth of the Tennessee River, and Smithland, at the mouth of the Cumberland River. As rivers in the region flow north, the two were, at those points, upstream from Tennessee. When Gen. Johnston took charge of Confederate western forces during the month he chose to concentrate his defense on what Brig. Gen. Grant later described as "a line running from the Mississippi River at Columbus to Bowling Green and Mill Springs, Kentucky." It was Governor Harris who sent engineers down the Cumberland and Tennessee to look for places to erect forts. Work, which progressed only slowly, was begun on two main defensive positions: one named Fort Donelson (after West Point graduate Daniel S. Donelson, Tennessee's attorney general) on the Cumberland River and the other, 12 miles northwest on the Tennessee River, called Fort Henry (in honor of Gustavus A. Henry, the state's senior Confederate senator). Fort Donelson was mostly abandoned until October.[24]

Union supporters and a number of Yankee generals now believed that a strike into the heart of the western Confederacy via the Tennessee and Cumberland Rivers would pay huge dividends. As famed Civil War authority Allan Nevins would write in 1960, "A mere glance at the map would seem to reveal that the Tennessee-Cumberland river system offered the North a heaven-sent opportunity to thrust a harpoon into the very bowels of the Confederacy." In early October, Lt. Phelps by Army request began a series of probing reconnaissance cruises to Forts Henry and Donelson with the U.S.S. *Conestoga*. Following one of these trips, on December 10, he confirmed persistent rumors that the Rebels were building gunboats on the Cumberland, one at Clarksville and another at Nashville. He strongly recommended immediate armed incursions on both streams.

Maj. Gen. Henry Halleck, "Old Brains" as he was known, reviewed the strategic situation in the West in the weeks following his November 1861 posting to Cairo as one of two senior Union military commanders in the West. U.S. Army organization in the region was, by presidential order, just now being reconfigured into what would prove to be two rival departments. One was Halleck's Department of the Missouri, which covered several states west of the Cumberland River. The other, under Maj. Gen. Don Carlos Buell, was the Department of the Ohio; it came with specific access to the Ohio and Cumberland Rivers. It did not take Halleck, for one, long to determine that thrusting Nevins' harpoon into the area of Middle Tennessee between the rivers could be "the turning point of the war." Still, neither he nor Maj. Gen. Buell authorized any move against the two Tennessee fortifications.[25]

In the weeks before Christmas 1861, Confederate generals Johnston and Polk began to realize the importance of the Nashville area economic contribution to the Rebel war effort and started to focus their attention upon improving the defenses of the Tennessee and Cumberland Rivers. After all, as Gen. Johnston wrote to Polk on October 31, an enemy invasion down the two rivers "may turn your right with ease and rapidity." Polk, reacting to supply concerns, was able to assure Johnston that "I am glad to say, too, that I am having an increase of power and other munitions," while in a report to President Jefferson Davis, he confided that he was taking extraordinary measures to secure the region's available foodstuffs for Confederate States succor. Work on strengthening Forts Henry and Donelson was stepped up.[26]

The *Conestoga* continued her reconnaissance patrols on the Cumberland and Tennessee as 1862 dawned. On January 6, Lt. Phelps observed: "It is now too late to move against the works on either river, except with a well-appointed and powerful naval force." That force became available on January 16 when Flag Officer Foote was able to inform Washington, "The seven gunboats built by contract were put in commission today." The theater commanders, Halleck and Buell, were unable to come to agreement upon a plan of advance. Still, once the foot soldiers' timing and objectives with regard to the forts were determined, the Navy finally had ironclad power to support whatever waterborne or combined assault mission might be chosen. Several more timberclad probing missions, as well as several military diversions, were meanwhile completed before month's end, designed to confuse the Rebel defenders.[27]

Before proceeding further, it may be best to digress and review the seasons of navigation on the Western waters. From the beginning of the steamboat period in the 1820s to its end in the 20th Century, all riverboat activities were governed first and foremost by the moisture or lack thereof in the various seasons. These seasons were different in different parts of the Mississippi River system, depending upon geographical location. It was generally recognized that river depth increased as one moved from a stream's headwaters to its mouth or from tributary to main river. Rains, snow, floods, and drought determined the river depths and thus the size of vessel which could operate in any given stream at any given time. In the words of famed steamboat historian Louis Hunter: "Each part of the river system rose and fell almost continuously according to a variety of controlling conditions, many of which were not shared by other parts at the same time." In practice, the maxim became: the smaller the river or the lower the stream, the lighter the boat draft required.

Usually beginning in the early spring, melting snow and ice plus rain swelled streams. These ran into the smaller rivers, like the Nolichuckey in Tennessee, which, in turn, ran into the intermediate tributaries like the Tennessee River, and then eventually raised the levels of the trunk rivers, Mississippi, Ohio, etc. This annual "spring rise" marked the opening of the steamboat navigation season, the duration of which was different for every river depending upon its ecology and physical characteristics, particularly shoals. The steaming period on the larger rivers depended not only on this one rise, but on various rises or freshes, which were, in turn, determined by the weather.

Generally, the hotter summer months saw a drop in the river stages, particularly in the upper half of the Mississippi Valley; water levels could fall so far as to greatly restrict navigation or prohibit it entirely. In the Ohio, Cumberland, and Tennessee Rivers, and even the White River in Arkansas, the low water period usually began sometime in June and ended about the last of September. Severe thunderstorms could result in a fresh, which might, at least briefly, allow intensification of previously restricted gunboat activities. Skilled rivermen aboard both naval and civilian steamers could tell a river's stage, rising or falling, by using a lead or even watching driftwood.

Other physical aspects of the Western rivers not appreciated by those unfamiliar with them included such concepts as crooked channels; those watery paths were not straight, but tended to weave across the different expanses, often revealing themselves by depth or color. In a September 17, 1862, report to Navy assistant secretary Gustavus V. Fox, Flag Officer Charles H. Davis sought to convey some sense of this phenomenon to the uninitiated:

> There are no fixed channels in these great rivers, as there are in the sounds, estuaries, and harbors of the Atlantic; quite otherwise; the channels are always changing, not only from year to year, but from season to season, during the period of rise and fall particularly.

Often times, little hills, plateaus, bars, or even islands appeared in the rivers. At one point, it was noted that some 98 islands could be seen in the Ohio River. Additionally, boulders, unmarked sunken boats, and thick foliage could pose dangers. Trees often grew right down to the banks, and, largely due to erosion, just as often fell in; as snags, they could hit and even sink steamboats. Rapids, particularly the Falls of the Ohio at Louisville and Muscle Shoals, on the Tennessee about 250 miles above its mouth, were the most dangerous navigational obstructions, though swift currents were always to be avoided.

The fall rise, which was more unpredictable as to its beginning or end than that in the spring, could often be counted upon to provide good steaming into December. Commonly, the main rivers in our Western theater of operations did not freeze in wintertime and, as in the upcoming Fort Henry and Fort Donelson campaigns or during the 1864 Battle of Nashville, riverine warfare activities could be continued. Conventional wharves were few; boats could and did tie up along or push into banks as required.[28]

At the end of January 1862, Maj. Gen. Halleck received intelligence that the defenders of the Tennessee river forts might be reinforced by fresh troops from Virginia. On January 29, he authorized Maj. Gen. Grant to take Fort Henry on the Tennessee River. Heavy rains slowed the arrival of the bluecoats, but the Navy had no problem with the rising water in the stream. When the federal gunboat and transport fleet arrived at Bailey's Ferry near Fort Henry, they were spied by Rebel lookouts; the defenders witnessed a most novel sight. "Steamboats," wrote Cumberland River historian Douglas, "had been used for many various purposes, but never before in an amphibious military operation to transport an entire army." On February 6, following a spirited hour and half morning exchange between Rebel gunners and those aboard the *Essex, Cincinnati, Carondelet,* and *St. Louis,* Fort Henry, nearly awash due to its low lying position, was surrendered to Flag Officer Foote. Yankee soldiers did not arrive on the scene until the afternoon, by which time the soggy citadel's main Confederate garrison had escaped to Fort Donelson.

As most of the ironclad fleet returned to Cairo, the three timberclads under Lt. Phelp's orders, undertook a two-day armed reconnaissance up the river, capturing the steamer *Eastport* being converted into a gunboat and continuing on to Florence, Alabama, where they were halted by the river's natural obstruction, the Muscle Shoals. The three warships, with their prize, returned to Cairo just in time to join Flag Officer Foote's flotilla as it moved on its next target: Fort Donelson on the left bank of the Cumberland River, 12 miles southeast of Fort Henry and north of the little town of Dover.

Fort Donelson's guns were not at water level; indeed, its formal cannons were mounted on a bluff some one hundred feet high overlooking a straight stretch in the river below. It would later be praised as "the strongest military work in the entire theater of war." On February 14–15, the ironclads *Carondelet, St. Louis, Louisville,* and *Pittsburgh*, supported to the rear by the *Conestoga* and *Tyler*, steamed within 600 yards of the Rebel batteries and engaged them in furious close-range exchanges of fire. This time the gunboats did not prevail as plunging fire took a terrible toll on the ships and their sailors, including a wound to the fleet commander which would eventually lead to his death. "Actually, the Western Flotilla at Fort Donelson was," as historian Douglas later noted, "thoroughly whipped by the land batteries." Still, the navy men contributed materially to the victory achieved when the bastion surrendered to General Grant on February 16. Indeed, the stronghold and its 15,000 defenders were captured far more quickly than Confederate leaders, who anticipated the result, had hoped. A week earlier, on February 7, Gen. Johnston had issued orders for an orderly withdrawal from Bowling Green, Clarksville, and Nashville designed to allow retrieval of as much ordnance, ammunition and materiel as possible, including machinery from the foundry in the latter city.[29]

The Confederate defense line in the West was shattered by the twin Union triumphs on Tennessee's waterways, two of "the most significant battles of the Civil War." Confederate commander Johnston was forced to advance the timetable for his evacuation; troops departed Bowling Green, Kentucky, on February 17 and over the next week soldiers marched out of Nashville while stores and equipment were sent to Chattanooga. The Union occupied Clarksville on February 19 and Tennessee's capital on February 24–25. "The loss of Nashville had a paralytic effect upon the Confederacy, politically, psychologically, and from a military standpoint."

In addition to Nashville's loss, Columbus was about to be abandoned and control of the Mississippi River was yielded as far south as Island No. 10. Gen. Pierre G. T. Beauregard, of Fort Sumter fame, then in the West, summed up the Confederate position in a March 3 memorandum cited in the official record; the main Southern forces, he reported, now occupied a line from Island No. 10 down across West Tennessee to Corinth, Mississippi, and in between those extremes lay a number of small defensive outposts at Fort Pillow, Union City, Paris, and Jackson.

Washington's control, however tenuous, was largely established over Kentucky and a portion of Middle Tennessee. By neglecting to safeguard the approaches to the heart of the Tennessee Valley, the South was forced to give up the more navigable expanses of two water routes pointed at its center together with a major manufacturing center. Nashville, a city central to this biography, would remain an occupied community until the end of the war. It was questionable but hoped by Southern leaders that the retreat further into the interior would make the Western Confederacy stronger.[30]

It is at this point that Le Roy Fitch enters the action-oriented portion of our story, arriving at Cairo sometime around the end of the first week of March 1862.

CHAPTER THREE

New Madrid to Memphis, March–June 1862

On March 3, 1862, Lt. Le Roy Fitch was detached from his duties as an ordnance officer at the New York Navy Yard in Brooklyn and ordered to join Flag Officer Andrew Hull Foote's Western Flotilla. He would arrive at Cairo, Illinois, that Army squadron's base, in about a week. Traveling West on the transport available 143 years ago, it is unlikely that time permitted a visit to the Fitch family in Logansport. Still, the mail and telegraph services probably kept the lieutenant aware of developments at home and thus we take a few paragraphs here to review them.

Without a doubt, the greatest thrill in the naval officer's life, save perhaps his marriage to Mary Smith, was when he received word that he had become a father. A healthy daughter, Marie L, had been born on January 15, probably at the home of Col. Smith. Like Mozart's offspring, history will not record much detail about the youngster, only that she would live 27 years longer than her father, dying on April 30, 1902.[1]

Older half-brother Dr. Graham Newell Fitch had returned from Congress on March 8, 1861. A Democrat who had supported President James Buchanan and the peace movements of December 1860, he was branded a traitor and appeaser in some quarters. One Cass County historian later believed those labels unfair as the physician "esteemed principles above mere partizanship [sic] and was not slow to manifest disapprobation when his party seemed disposed to pursue a course of policy in antagonism with his better judgement." Another suggested that "regardless of his attitude before the outbreak of hostilities, he lined up on the right side" when it was time.[2]

Following President Lincoln's April–May 1861 call for three-month volunteers, Indiana communities recruited and dispatched numerous infantry regiments to Union service. The Southern victory at the First Battle of Bull Run on July 21 brought home to Hoosiers, as to others across the North, that the war would not, as some had suggested, be a short affair. Rather, the bloodletting would intensify into a major internecine struggle. As became the custom, men from cities and towns, villages and rural areas from Illinois to Massachusetts and down into the border states answered the North's call by flocking to central communities, where leaders eagerly recruited them into military companies and regiments, often under officers elected or appointed by state governors. As the number of enlistments rose, state political leaders were able to determine which units would serve where and how and under what circumstances and whose command.

As Cass, White, and Carroll counties had already sent six companies of infantry to battle with regiments from other locales, Indiana governor Oliver P. Morton promised that he would accept a Logansport-based regiment if that city would quarter it at no expense to the legislature or executive branch in Indianapolis. Agreeing to meet the challenge, Dr. Graham Newell Fitch, state senator Richard Patten DeHart, Newton Scott, and Thomas Bringhurst were authorized by the governor on September 30 to raise a regiment and to rendezvous with it at Logansport. Fitch was appointed colonel, with Scott as lieutenant colonel, Bringhurst as major, and DeHart as adjutant. Dr. Asa Morton, Col. Fitch's medical partner, became the group's assistant surgeon, serving until Dec. 26, 1862. Governor Morton provided much encouragement in his message to the city leaders: "Build your barracks, hurry up your company organization, and put them in camp."

Constructed with money provided by public subscription, a barracks was set up and made habitable over the next week; recruiting was stimulated by handbills and speeches, and enlistment papers were signed by the men on Logansport's West Side, a block or so north of the later-day Franklin School. The camp, as the unit's historian recorded, "was fully organized and under discipline by October 7," the day the 46th Regiment of the Indiana Volunteer Infantry officially came into existence. Another member of the Fitch family reporting to the rendezvous was Frederick Fitch; after Fort Sumter, he had enlisted as a private in Co. K, 9th Indiana Volunteers, but he was allowed to resign from that outfit on July 29 and sign enlistment papers from his uncle, Col. Fitch, which made him a private in Co. I of the Logansport unit.[3]

After 40 days of equipping and drilling, during which time "an inferior article of Enfield rifles was received," the volunteer regiment was mustered into the service of the U.S. on December 12. The formal morning ceremony was presided over by a regular Army officer and witnessed by over 4,000 area citizens. As part of the proceedings, the officers and men all took an oath of allegiance and, on behalf of the regiment, Col. Fitch accepted a "handsome" national flag presented by the citizens of Logansport. Then, led by the Logan Band, the town's brass ensemble, the men undertook a line of march to the railroad depot, where they boarded a train for Lafayette. From there, by rail, steamboat and overland trek, the soldiers traveled to the Ohio River and hence, after several halts along the way, reached Cairo, Illinois, on February 23, 1862. The group's two brigades were now split between the second and third divisions of 39-year-old Maj. Gen. John Pope's brand new Army of the Mississippi. Col. Fitch, with the Second Brigade, which also included the 43rd Indiana Regiment, was attached to the Second Division. Both brigades now marched, via rough, swampy ground, to Commerce, Mo, and hence began their participation in the siege of New Madrid and the siege and capture of Island No. 10, Mississippi River.[4]

Gen. Pierre G.T. Beauregard, now commander of the Confederate Army of the Mississippi, was forced to revisit his regional strategy following the surrenders at Forts Henry and Donelson in mid–February and the evacuation of Columbus on March 2. His choice of a stronghold from which to defend the Mississippi River fell upon Island No. 10, about 40 miles south of Columbus, and nearby New Madrid, Missouri. Under the command of

Brig. Gen. John P. McCown, heavy batteries were placed at both locations (19 cannon were at the former and 21 at the latter) and 8,000 soldiers manned the earthworks. Island No. 10, where a large loop appeared in the stream (no doubt looking from the air like an inverted S), was seen as a natural citadel. Her newly-emplaced Rebel cannon could halt the passage of unauthorized boats downstream and could fire upon any attempting to move north around the bend. The Mississippi's current here was such that any boat disabled by the guns would be carried to the island's shore, where it could be captured. A floating battery and a light Confederate gunboat flotilla augmented the big guns. If the location had a weak point, it was logistical access. Supplies could move upriver by boat past Point Pleasant, Missouri, to the island and New Madrid or be taken 12 miles south to Tiptonville, Tennessee, and then brought up overland by wagon. If Tiptonville and its road to the river were captured, the garrison would be trapped.

Flag Officer/Rear Adm. Andrew H. Foote (1806–1863) was the second commander of the U.S. Army's Western Flotilla and the man to whom Le Roy Fitch reported for Western theater duty in March 1862. The veteran Foote, who had guided his squadron in the battles at Fort Henry and Donelson, appointed the Logansport sailor to command the ammunition steamer *Judge Torrence* during the upcoming campaigns against Island No. 10, Fort Pillow, and Memphis. Succeeded by Flag Officer/Rear Adm. Davis in late spring, Foote died a year later of wounds received at Fort Donelson (Library of Congress).

To capture Island No. 10, Union forces first needed to isolate it and this was the reason Maj. Gen. Pope's army began its siege of New Madrid on March 3. The Missouri town initially proved too strong to capture or reduce and so Yankee troops initially by-passed it. Troops marched and hauled guns around the Missouri community and placed a battery downriver at Point Pleasant, thereby cutting off water shipments to Island No. 10. Heavy siege cannon were brought up to pound New Madrid, and on March 14 its Confederate garrison evacuated across the river. There would be no reinforcement because the 16,000 men under Maj. Gen. Earl Van Dorn in Arkansas which might have been sent to help were defeated on March 7–8 by Brig. Gen. Samuel R. Curtis' 5,000 fewer Yankees in the Battle of Pea Ridge.[5]

Following its ordeal at Forts Henry and Donelson, the U.S. Western Flotilla returned to its base at Cairo for repair and replenishment. Although several individual reconnaissance and individual boat missions were undertaken, it would be some time before Flag Officer Foote believed his command ready to launch another large operation. Despite requests from the Army that the gunboats mount a demonstration "upon Island No. 10 & if possible assist Maj. Gen. Pope," the Navy leader declined, seeking "two or three days" more to repair his warships. He would use the time not only in material restoration, but to replenish supplies, victuals, and ammunition and to apportion 600 desperately-needed and recently-arrived Army of the Potomac

The waterfront of the Illinois facility shown later in the war with an unidentified tinclad moored to the bank. Cairo was the main Mississippi Valley administrative and logistical facility for the Union's inland navy throughout the war. It featured ways for hauling vessels out of the water, a receiving ship, and a large wharf boat, for ordnance, commissary stories, shops, and officers quarters. The town of Cairo was often labeled during the war as one of the most unwholesome places anyone could visit (*Miller's Photographic History of the Civil War*).

soldiers among his boats. Once distributed around the fleet, the men would be turned into freshwater sailors. These men were in addition to 350 "offscourings of the Army" received earlier who were so unsuitable that two companies of local soldiers had to be detailed to guard them. Additionally, a number of the 38 new mortar boats (actually, floating barges) under construction by James B. Eads at Carondelet, Mo., were completed. These and the fleet would be supplied during upcoming operations by specially-outfitted ordnance boats, the *Great Western* and the *Judge Torrence*, six-year-old vessels both acquired for the Army on February 10. The new commander of the latter steamer would be 27-year-old Lt.-Commanding Le Roy Fitch.[6]

When Lt. Fitch arrived at Cairo from New York at the beginning of the second week of March, he found the river town that was now funneling Yankee forces south to be a bustling, unclean, and not inexpensive community. In the words of *New York Times* correspondent Franc Bangs Wilkie, the most famous Western theater newsman, it was a "mud hole of a town." Five years after the Civil War was over, one traveler passing through en route downriver found the situation unchanged in the town which

> to-day is the vilest hole above ground, if the streets formed by introducing foreign soil can be said to be above-ground; for the open lots formed by the streets were partially filled with

water covered with green scum, and which was also the receptacle for offal, dead animals, and other offensive refuse. Turn which way you would the sight was unspeakably disgusting. The streets were knee-deep in mud, and it seemed impossible to transact business upon them when horses and wagons were required.

A levy surrounded Cairo, designed some said, more to hold the mud in than the river out. The quartermaster's offices, the makeshift naval base, some work barges and wharf boats were on Ohio Street at the river's edge. West of Ohio Street was Halliday Street, home to saloons and dance halls, while farther west was Commercial Street, reserved for proper businesses and even a theater. Daniel Pollard, master of the civilian steamer *V. F. Wilson*, recalled that "the generals seemed to think this place is special, but the soldiers all say, they had plenty of mud where they came from, and that we should just give it to the Rebs and let them wallow in it."

The most notable hostelry in the town was the five-storied Saint Charles Hotel (later the Halliday Hotel) on Ohio Street, where the young officer may have stopped, seeking news of his older half-brother or the conflict in general. Reporter Wilkie noted that the place "was always jammed to repletion by officers, contractors, speculators, Hebrew dealers, river men, Northern visitors, correspondents, and scores of other classes." More than likely most war news of interest was obtained at the army and navy headquarters building. Certainly, he was not long on the scene before he learned the proper to say the city's name (it is "pronounced 'Kerro,' not 'Kyro' or 'Kayro'"). Neither newsman or sailor would be surprised to one day to learn that from 1,756 inhabitants in 1857 the population would swell to 8,000 by 1865—it may have seemed that most of the 8,000 were already in town.[7]

The Cairo riverfront along Ohio Street was almost a mile in length; there the gunboats, transports, and freighters laid along the bank or levee, with a few anchored out on the water. It was easy to see the big ironclads of the Western Flotilla being patched up and a number of chartered steamboats moving

The 12- and 24-pounder Dahlgren boat howitzer was of great interest to Le Roy Fitch from his time at the Naval Academy. Fitch was known for his proficiency with the weapon, which could be mounted in nautical craft of all sizes or placed on a wheeled-carriage and employed as a field piece. The naval howitzer was the principal ordnance employed upon the light-draught tinclad gunboats Fitch would command from 1862 to 1865 (*Naval Ordnance Instructions, 1866*).

across the rivers providing service not only to his squadron, but to U.S. Army Quartermaster Corps as well.

Fitch was able to observe workers laboring on new gunboat construction, while noting that the finishing touches of conversion were placed not only on his *Judge Torrence*, but also on the other ammunition ship, the *Great Western*. It was, of course, with his own craft that the new skipper, something of an ordnance specialist, was most concerned.

The *Judge Torrence* was a wooden 700-ton steamboat which was originally constructed in 1857 at Cincinnati, Ohio, from which she was home ported. The vessel, acquired by the Army on February 10, was 179.1 feet in length and had a 45.6 foot beam and a nine foot draft. Steam from three boilers, passed via a pair of engines, with each with a 20" cylinder diameter and 8 foot piston stroke, powered the side-wheels. At full speed (which was seldom, if ever, attempted), the boat could reach six knots (seven mph) with the current. Some years later, it would be recorded that her armament consisted of a pair of 24-pound smoothbore howitzers.

As an ammunition ship, the *Judge Torrence* would join the *Great Western* in the dangerous task of transporting all of the powder and shot, replacement ordnance, and extra small arms required by the Western Flotilla on its upcoming missions. It would also have on hand a number of additional boat howitzers which could be mounted for land expeditions.[8]

Among the projectiles to be carried in the upcoming campaign against New Madrid and Island No. 10 were those 204-lb. shells (each loaded with seven pounds of gunpowder), each costing $15, intended for the 38 mortar boats which James B. Eads was finishing upstream near St. Louis. It would later be recorded that about 3,500 13-inch shells could be stored on the *Judge Torrence*. When at her duty station, the boat would be resupplied by other craft bringing them down about 100 per trip.

The unpowered mortar boats—essentially rectangular barges—were about 65 feet long with 25 foot beams. Their sides, pointed at the bow and stern, were each graced with an iron-plated sloped bulwark between six and seven feet high, with those to port and starboard stretched back three-quarters of the length. An iron-covered hatch for egress was cut into the stern bulwark. Each bulwark was waterproofed and corked to a height of two feet to allow the craft, which floated at deck level, to survive the tremendous recoil. A canvas covering was available to shield the crew from sun or rain.

A single iron 17,210-lb. 13-inch seacoast mortar was mounted in the center of the reinforced deck of each boat; the entire Rodman mortar bed carriage weighed 4,500 pounds. This weight, added to the boat's center reinforcement of layers of logs laid at right angles to each other, increased the overall heaviness of each craft to 13 tons. Eight small chambers held the powder and shot; the shells were loaded into the muzzle via a small derrick. The full charge of powder required to launch the giant hollow bullet from an elevation of 41 degrees to its extreme range of 3.5 miles was 23 pounds. Lesser amounts of propellant and elevation would shorten the range.

The craft were initially tested off Cairo on February 9 and the results, witnessed by St. Louis *Missouri Democrat* reporter George W. Beaman, were exciting, promising, and potentially as dangerous for the crews as for the enemy. The noise and concussion from the firing was shocking, made more so by the bulkheads. During one of the trial shots using only a 15-lb. powder charge, "the cap of the gunner was carried away from his head and he was almost taken off his feet." The major lesson taken from the successful shoot concerned the ironed sides of the craft; "if they are permitted to remain, some plan will have to be devised by which the gunners, at each discharge, may get outside of them." In practice, the crew would load the mortar, leave through an escape hatch onto the rear part of the deck, and fire by yanking a lanyard, not forgetting to put their hands over their ears and flex their knees against the concussion. The repeated blasts would, in practice, cause the middle of the boats to settle and the ends to rise, thereby causing them to fill with water. After two or three shots, only the buoyancy of the boats' solid timber centers kept them afloat until they could be bailed out.[9]

Flag Officer Foote had earlier requested that Capt. Henry E. Maynadier, who was serving with the U.S. 10th Infantry Regiment in Washington, D.C., be detailed as mortar boat ordnance officer. It was Maynadier, a native Virginian and a veteran of service in Utah and in the Yellowstone region from 1857 to 1861, who oversaw the transfer West of the 350 "offscourings of the Army" detailed by Maj. Gen. George B. McClellan to Foote at the end of February, probably from the 10th's Company B, which had just been broken up. Given the upcoming close working relationship between the ammunition handlers and the mortar men, it is probable that Fitch and Maynadier came to know each other fairly well.[10]

As the Ides of March approached, Foote continued to ready his fleet, making every preparation possible to ensure that when he took it into action, success would follow. Bitter lessons of vulnerability were learned about the ironclads in Tennessee and it was also known that, from their earlier shakedowns, they could not successfully be anchored from the stern and held against the Mississippi's current. A disabled boat would undoubtedly fall into Confederate hands. "I will be very cautious," he wrote Secretary Welles on March 12, "as I appreciate the vast responsibility of keeping our flotilla from falling into the rebels' hands, as it would turn the whole tide of affairs against us." To one commander, he would write, "our gunboats are to be used as forts ... the army must do the shore work." The potential effectiveness of the mortars on the Upper Mississippi was then unknown.

A number of these scows were constructed in the early months of 1862 and employed in the Union campaigns against Island No. 10 and Fort Pillow, and later at Vicksburg. The ammunition boat *Judge Torrence*, under the command of Lt. Le Roy Fitch, carried the shells employed by the giant 13-inch mortars (Lossing's *Pictorial Field Book of the Civil War*, Vol. 2).

On March 14, the Army of Maj. Gen. Pope occupied New Madrid. Early that morning, elements of the Western Flotilla departed Cairo to join in the campaign. The *Benton*, leading six Pook turtles, and the *Conestoga* were followed by the *Judge Torrence* and *Great Western*, plus five steamers towing 14 mortar boats, and several USQM-chartered steamers for 1,200 soldiers under Col. Napoleon Buford. The procession paused at Columbus, now a Union base, during the afternoon to take the tow on two more mortar barges, before reaching Hickman, Kentucky, at dusk.

Over the next two days, the Western Flotilla initiated the waterborne softening-up of Island No. 10's defenses. The mortar boats were placed along the Missouri shore, with gunboats to protect them, but, their position was extremely unfavorable in that they fired at extremely long range over Phillips Point. The huge shells flew high into the air and 30 seconds later exploded. Unhappily, the barge gunners could not see their targets and could not independently gauge the fall of their shot. Only when word was received from observers on other craft could corrections be made. As might be imagined and was widely recorded at the time, the noise of the bombardment was tremendous. Still, even after the expenditure of 733 shells in 48 hours, not a single Confederate casualty attributable to the shooting occurred on the island. As Capt. Maynadier later reported: "Most of the shells were fired with large charges over the bluff, with a view to reach the camps and storehouses in the hollow beyond; in this the success was very limited."[11]

The Island No. 10 operation from the river now turned into a siege. For the next 20 days, the mortar boats pounded the Rebel defenses with powder and shot supplied via the *Judge Torrence* and *Great Western*. "Heavy firing was constantly heard at Island No. 10" by Col. Fitch and the men of the 46th Indiana Volunteers downstream at Riddle's Point. Aboard the mortar boats and steamers tied to or anchored near the Missouri shore above the citadel, soldiers and sailors remained tense. False alarms of Confederate boat attacks or shore raids were constant. Between 9 P.M. and 10 P.M. on April 19, an alarm, false as it turned out, was raised concerning the pending approach of a Rebel force by land. In the only "action" report concerning the ammo boat to make it into the ORN during the entire campaign, the mortar fleet abstract log for that date recorded: " The *Judge Torrence* slipped her moorings from the shore, got underway, and stood out into the middle of the stream. Quiet was soon restored and the boat returned to her anchorage." Still, there was very little sleep aboard the Union ships, just as there was little on the island.[12]

Despite a change in Confederate command on Island No. 10, the digging of an innovative U.S. Army canal, and continued shelling by gunboats and mortars, the situation is this part of the Western theater remained largely unchanged. Despite earlier hopes, the thousands of mortar bombs and gunboat shells being dropped in and around the river fortress were not having the intended effect. Indeed, one later analysis bluntly stated that the greatest failure from a Union perspective during the campaign was "the complete ineffectiveness of long-range shelling." The mortar shells forced the defenders to move their camps out of range and dig bombproof shelters for the batteries. Captured prisoners confessed that the fireworks were a "great annoyance to the daily labors of the garrison," but otherwise caused little actual damage.

For all intents and purposes, the standoff at Island No. 10 ended on the night of April 4–5. Under cover of a thunderstorm, Cmdr. Henry Walke successfully ran the *Carondelet* past the river bastion's cannon and halted off New Madrid. In the words of Capt. Mahan, "The passage of the *Carondelet* was not only one of the most daring and dramatic events of the war; it was also the death-blow to the Confederate defense of this position." After the

Pittsburgh followed down next evening, Maj. Gen. Pope had two ironclads with which to cover the crossing of his men from the Missouri shore to Tennessee. The Confederate stronghold was cut off by lunchtime on April 7; the next evening it was surrendered to Flag Officer Foote. Three Confederate generals, 4,500 soldiers, and 109 artillery pieces were now taken off the table. "The circumstances as connected with the surrender of this position, with all its guns, ammunition, &c., are," wrote an editorialist for the *Richmond Press* on April 14, "humiliating in the extreme."[13]

Although the victory at Island No. 10 was universally hailed throughout the North, it was quickly overshadowed. While the campaign was underway, Union Maj. Gen. Henry Halleck was also attempting to concentrate aforce on the Tennessee River for a move to capture the Confederate railroad center at Corinth. Simultaneously, the Rebel armies of Albert Sidney Johnston and Pierre Beauregard were also gathering their forces together in the Mississippi center. The two Union forces to be employed to accomplish Halleck's aim were the Army of the Ohio, Maj. Gen. Don Carlos Buell, which was moving down from Nashville, and two divisions of the Army of the Tennessee (Maj. Gen. Grant), which established a depot at Pittsburgh Landing. Even as John Pope's troops were outflanking Island No. 10, Johnston, having divined Halleck's objective, launched his own surprise against the Yankees at Shiloh Church (near Pittsburgh Landing). Gen. Johnston was killed during the famous and bloody battle, which was a near-run victory for the Federals. Still, the triumph caused theater leader Halleck to reassess his approach into Mississippi and to decide, among other things, to bring Maj. Gen. Pope's Army of the Mississippi inland on April 15 to help his advance. The twin Confederate reversals at Shiloh and Island No. 10 meant, in fact, that the large scale battle for the upper Mississippi Valley was over; Fort Pillow and nearby Fort Randolph could be outflanked from the east and Memphis could not really be protected. Sensing this probable consequence in events and that his Union army was now in control of Middle Tennessee and almost all of West Tennessee, Maj. Gen. Halleck chose to leave only one small U.S. Army brigade of 1,200 men attached to the Western Flotilla for garrison duty—Col. Fitch's 46th Indiana Volunteers.[14]

When Maj. Gen. Pope and his men went upriver aboard 20 steamers on April 16, the Memphis guardian, Fort Pillow, was already under Western Flotilla bombardment. Located atop the nearly vertical Chickasaw Bluffs on the Tennessee shore three miles above Plum Point Bend (opposite Craighead's point) and near Fulton, about 60 miles south of Island No. 10, it was originally established as something of a reserve defense point. It ranked in order of importance after Columbus and Island No. 10. Following the Shiloh bloodbath, Gen. Beauregard ordered it strengthened.

Forty heavy cannon were placed in Fort Pillow's enhanced earthworks, which were now manned by 6,000 Rebel soldiers. Many of the guns were placed in water batteries which extended for a mile and half up and down the shoreline. Although the post bore a heavy load of defensive responsibility, many in the South were unconvinced that it could hold out or save Memphis. "If Fort Pillow falls, of course, Memphis goes with it," the *Richmond Examiner* reported on April 27. In the same article, it was noted, "There is little panic in Memphis, however. The people are quietly, if not almost callously, anticipating the worst."

As they had at Island No. 10, Capt. Maynadier's mortar boats, from a point above Craighead's Point near Osceola, Arkansas, lofted their projectiles into the air toward Fort Pillow. Meanwhile, Col. Graham's Hoosier soldiers stood guard duty for them on the wet and low shore each hot day, while an ironclad remained nearby in the river on a 24-hour rotation. By night, the brigade, however, returned aboard its two transports, the *Emma* and *Graham*. Despite an initial flurry of fiery give and take between the Yankee ironclads and several boats of the Confederate River Defense Force, which had come north from New Orleans, the mortar bombardment of Fort Pillow would continue for the next seven weeks. As at Island No. 10, the *Judge Torrence* and the *Great Western* provided ordnance support.

"Up to the 9th of May," the historian of the 46th Indiana later wrote, "nothing of interest occurred." Still, it was for this time frame that we have the closest we are going to get to a written acknowledgement that three male members of the Logansport Fitch clan were likely in contact in the Mississippi River war zone around this time. On page 27 of the unit chronicle, the brigade historian recorded three sentences of interest: "Col. Fitch commanded the brigade." "Henry S. Fitch, came to Osceola as brigade quartermaster." "Le Roy Fitch was in command of the *Torrence*, a magazine boat, belonging to the navy." With the ammunition boats tied up to the shore near the troopships, it is impossible for this writer to believe there would not have been family contact.[15]

This nearly-contemporary rendering clearly outlines the major rivers and towns of the Western Theater. It can safely be referred to for much of our story (Lossing's *Pictorial Field Book of the Civil War*, Vol. 2).

Flag Officer Foote was by this time suffering badly from his Fort Donelson wound, so badly that three surgeons from his fleet recommended he go home to Cleveland on leave to recover. The flag officer recognized this wisdom and petitioned the Navy Department to name his friend Capt. Charles H. Davis as his deputy while he was on leave or as his successor. When Davis arrived at Osceola on May 9, Foote was worse and quickly departed back up the river for Ohio. Davis, Le Roy Fitch's first commander back on the *St. Mary's*, became *de facto* flotilla CO and would remain so for over a month. Among those greeting Davis upon his arrival were Col. Fitch, his younger half brother, and other ship commanders. The elder Fitch brother showed Davis two editions of a Memphis newspaper critical of Confederate leaders and opined to the newly-arrived Navy man that he expected the Rebel leaders "would be stimulated to some effort of a desperate nature."

The first Civil War engagement between opposing naval squadrons occurred on May 10, 1862. In "a smart affair," eight Rebel gunboats, CSS *General Bragg*, *General Sumter*, *General Sterling Price*, *General Earl Van Dorn*, *General M. Jeff Thompson*, *General Lovell*, *General Beauregard*, and *Little Rebel*, "came up in gallant style" and attacked Davis' fleet off Plum Point Bend on the Tennessee shore, disabling the ironclads *Cincinnati* and *Mound City*. The Confederates quickly withdrew under the guns of Fort Pillow. While admitting its "dash and spirit," Union officers brushed off the fight as a skirmish, and historian Mahan would write that it was "the only service of value performed by this irregular and undisciplined force [Confederate River Defense Force]."[16]

The assault on Fort Pillow's defenses continued apace after the Plum Point episode. The Union mortars continued to throw shells at the Southern defenders. As a later writer would have it, "nothing of interest occurred at Fort Pillow for the next two weeks." That view was not altogether accurate. In mid–May, Capt. Davis invited Brig. Gen. Isaac F. Quinby, commander of the District of the Mississippi at Columbus, to come down with additional soldiers to join with Col. Fitch in an enhanced reconnaissance of Fort Pillow, which might turn into an Island No. 10-type bypass operation. To help assure the success of this expedition, Davis on May 16 ordered mortar chief Capt. Maynadier to secure four mounted boat howitzers from Lt. Fitch on the *Judge Torrence*. He was to hold these in readiness to join Col. Fitch and to provide them with a number of artillerymen from the mortar boats (number specified by Lt. Fitch) to serve as crews.

Quinby duly arrived on May 19 and he, together with Fitch, met with Davis to plan a joint operation. If the Army could set up a protective shore battery below and opposite on the Arkansas shore, he would attempt to run several gunboats past Fort Pillow. Although the soldiers tried on the night of May 22, the poor condition of the ground prevented the only course of action possible "carrying the guns and ammunition along a levee for a distance of three miles," all of which was commanded by Confederate batteries. The brigadier general and his men returned to Columbus two days later.

The overall lull at anchorage near Fort Pillow changed on May 26 when Col. Charles Ellet, Jr., and his independent Mississippi Marine Brigade showed up at the Yankee anchorage. Outfitted with several steamboats reinforced at their bows for ramming other river craft, the strange unit, the product of a March special arrangement between War Secretary Edwin Stanton and Ellet, was not welcomed by either Capt. Davis or Col. Fitch. Twice in the next several days Ellet met with Davis trying to obtain cooperation for some sort of joint operation, but twice the naval chief put him off. Finally, on June 2, Ellet penned Stanton that he would move against the Confederates with Davis' support or without.

Meanwhile, the big gun barges continued to pound away. On June 2, Davis received a curious demonstration that confirmed what he heard: "These mortar-men are said to be very careless." One of the gunners had a cylinder of loose powder on his shoulder and proceeded to light up a cigar—"his head was blown off."

As June dawned, the soldiers of the 46th Indiana sought "weak and assailable points" in the Fort Pillow defenses. Fitch hoped that he and the navy could carry the place in a joint army-navy operation. Indeed, at least two efforts were planned by Davis and Fitch to launch joint attacks on Fort Pillow on June 4 and 5, but these were spoiled either by interference from Ellet's "foolish movement," or by the Rebel decision to cut and run. In the darkness of June 4–5, as elements of the Hoosier contingent began to drop down toward Fort Pillow, scouts discovered that it was abandoned and everything moveable, save some heavy guns, were withdrawn by the retreating Rebels. Ellet later reported to Secretary Stanton that he and his men "before daylight" on June 5 were the first to plant "the stars and stripes on the fort." The 46th Indiana historian, in defense of his colleagues to whom the honor belonged, later refuted this claim simply and sternly: "Colonel Ellet is mistaken in his facts." Coordination between the Fitch-Davis team and Ellet was now icy at best and both sides complained about one another to their superiors.

During the morning of June 5, Col. Fitch and the men of the 46th Indiana, together with some detachments of sailors, secured Fort Pillow and prepared to embark on the regiment's two transports. At the same time, Col. Ellet, without a nod to the USN, took three rams 12 miles downriver to Fort Randolph, where he did, in fact, take over abandoned Fort Randolph and raise the Union flag. He then rounded to and returned upriver.

Davis assisted the wounded Foote and officially took over the Western Flotilla when Foote was invalided east. With military support from the 46th Indiana Volunteer Infantry under Col. Graham Newell Fitch, Davis secured Federal victories at Fort Pillow and Memphis in April to early June 1862. During this time, the Fitch family was represented in the theater not only by the colonel, but by Lt. Fitch and Graham Newell Fitch's son, Maj. Henry S. Fitch (Library of Congress).

After lunch, elements of Capt. Davis' fleet began to move down the river toward Memphis, leaving the *Pittsburgh* and *Mound City* behind to co-ordinate with Col. Fitch, who was assigning his Company B to hold the fortress. Some miles below, the Ellet rams and Yankee ironclads passed one another, but no hail was made; even if the desire was present, neither fleet could have communicated with the other because no system of signals had been devised for such a purpose. After arriving at Fort Pillow, Ellet sent a report to Secretary Stanton and then started his eight rams back down.

At 8 P.M., the Western Flotilla gunboats anchored at the lower end of Island No. 45, then a mile and a half above Memphis. The mortar boats, tugs, commissary boat, the *Great Western* and Lt. Fitch's *Judge Torrence* tied up for the night to the bank of Island No. 44, a bit further upstream. The embarked companies of the Indiana regiment tied up for the night at Fort Randolph. As darkness fell, the Mississippi Marine Brigade group halted anchored

In the only major fleet action of the Civil War, the union flotilla of Flag Officer Davis, operating with a fleet of U.S. Army rams, routed the Confederate River Defense Force on the waters off Memphis. All three members of the Fitch family present witnessed all or part of the action (Henry Walke, *Naval Scenes and Reminiscences of the Civil War*, 1877).

some 16 miles above Memphis. No one aboard any of the ships knew that the Confederate River Defense Force was secured at the Memphis levee.[17]

At dawn on Friday, June 6, CSS *Earl Van Dorn*, *General Beauregard*, *General M. Jeff Thompson*, *General Bragg*, *General Sumter*, *General Sterling Price*, and *Little Rebel* of Commodore Montgomery's Confederate River Defense Fleet cast off, dropped below Railroad Point, and were drawn up in a double line in front of Memphis. There they were seen through Federal spyglasses and, at 4:20 A.M., the U.S. flagship *Benton* and the Pook turtles *Louisville*, *Carondelet*, *St Louis*, and *Cairo* began to drop downstream toward the Rebel warships, which had, meanwhile, opened fire. As the two squadrons approached, Col. Ellet, who was charging to the sound of the guns, suddenly appeared with the rams *Monarch* and *Queen of the West* and attacked at full steam.

The close action which followed the appearance of the Yankee rams was dramatic, with fast-paced give-and-take fighting between the ships of Ellet and Montgomery ensuing before the heavier ironclads could come up. After smashing into the *Lovell*, the *Queen of the West* was rammed by the *Beauregard* and disabled; Colonel Ellet was mortally wounded. The *Beauregard* and *General Sterling Price* then aimed at the *Monarch*, missed, and collided, with the *General Sterling Price* the worse for the assault. The *Beauregard* was rammed by the *Monarch* and sunk by a shot from the *Benton* as Davis' boats came closer. The surviving Rebels began to flee and an hour-long running duel ensued that carried the opposing units 10 miles downstream past President's Island. In the end, only the *Van Dorn* escaped, with all the others either captured, sunk, or grounded on the river bank to avoid sinking. Cdr. Montgomery and Brig. Gen. M. Jeff Thompson, who had both promised better results, "were hurried," as the latter subsequently reported to Gen. Beauregard, in their "retirement from Memphis."[18]

Memphis, built high on bluffs like Fort Pillow, was not fortified; its only defense was the swift boats of the Confederate River Defense Fleet. During the battle, the bluffs were lined with 15,000 Tennessean and other witnesses, most of whom were dreadfully disappointed by the outcome of the fighting. The Yankee mortar boats did not participate in this fight and their commander chose to jump on one of the tugs accompanying the ironclad squadron and join in on the fringes of the fight. Although Lt. Fitch, who was equally unengaged, may have joined the Army captain, it was Capt. Maynadier who took charge of the ruined *Beauregard* and its crew. He took in hand other prisoners during the combat, both survivors in the water and those who "returned and delivered themselves up after their vessels had been deserted." The historian of the 46th Indiana reveals that Federal sailors and soldiers manning yawls picked up a hundred prisoners and confined them aboard the chartered steamer *Henry Von Puhl*. During this process, a pickup band on one of the transports "played 'Dixie' for the comfort of the shivering rebels."

The citizens of Memphis now awaited their fate as a white flag was hoisted over their town. The *Memphis Argus* reported later that day, "Many ladies were seen with tears trickling down their cheeks, humiliated at the triumph of the Federal boats." It was also noted that "the train which left on the Mississippi and Tennessee road was jammed and crammed by our citizens, many of whom remained until the last opportunity to get away." Cut off and unable to get underway, eight steamboats, valued by later survey at $40,375, were seized as prizes.

In light of the white flag, Charles River Ellet was charged by his father to go ashore, seek the city's surrender, and raise the Stars and Stripes over the city's customhouse and post office "as an emblem of the return of the community 'to the care and protection of the Constitution.'" With three soldiers, the youngster managed to get through the jeering mob and, under the personal protection of the 300 pound Mayor Park, was able to get the bunting flying in a makeshift fashion from the roof of the post office. The men were shot at, but not hit; they were, however, caught on the roof when citizens shut the trapdoor behind them. With his son at the crowd's mercy, the ram fleet CO got a message to Davis advising him that his 19-year-old had taken possession of the city, but now needed help.

Capt. Davis and Col. Fitch now undertook to arrange the city's surrender with Mayor John Park. As the local civil authorities were recognizing the inevitability of occupation by people from three different Yankee organizations (USA, USN, and MMB) and Davis, Fitch, and Park were engaged in necessary correspondence on that topic, Col. Fitch ordered his troop transports run in and tied up. Freed by soldiers from the ram *Lioness*, the Ellet party returned from the post office to the landing as the U. S. Army transport, the *Henry Von Puhl*, carrying CRDF survivors, came to off the levee. As the other boats eased in about 11 A.M., a company was sent ashore to keep back the dense and excited crowd, a stone-throwing portion of which had earlier attempted to trap the two flag-hanging members of the Ellet Brigade. By Fitch's order, other soldiers from the steamers stormed ashore and up onto the city bluff to chop down a large Confederate flag nailed to a tall pole—the last fluttering symbol of Rebel rule.

At 3 P.M. on the afternoon of June 6, Col. Fitch met with Mayor Park and the Memphis city council and worked out the terms under which U.S. authority would operate. The municipal government would be allowed to function and, together with Union soldiers, would enforce the law and maintain order. Memphis, the terminus for four railroads, was actually an important prize for the Union. Not only would it become a major Army supply base, but a naval base operated there before the war would be reopened and upgraded into a major river fleet center.[19]

With the one-sided Union triumph at Memphis coupled to that more spectacular victory won by Flag Officer Farragut at New Orleans on April 24, organized Confederate naval power on the Mississippi River was ended. Save for river fortifications, an upcoming short appearance by the armor-clad C.S.S. *Arkansas*, and the continuous pin-prick raids of guerrillas or partisans, the Western Flotilla was free to traverse the Mississippi River from its source down to Vicksburg, Mississippi, and all of the rivers of the Ohio and Tennessee valleys.[20]

CHAPTER FOUR

Brothers and Guerrillas, June–September 1862

As soldiers of the Indiana Brigade were taking possession of Memphis and Southern forces were moving south after having evacuated Corinth, Mississippi, Maj. Gen. Ulysses S. Grant, who played almost no major role in the fall of either, assessed the Union's strategic situation in the area.

> The railroad from Columbus to Corinth was at once put in good condition and held by us. We had garrisons at Donelson, Clarksville and Nashville, on the Cumberland River and held the Tennessee River from its mouth to Eastport. New Orleans and Baton Rouge had fallen into the possession of the National forces so that now the Confederates at the west were narrowed down for all communications with Richmond to the single line of road running east from Vicksburg.

Grant and other Northerners, notably Maj. Gen. William T. Sherman and Western Flotilla commodore U.S. Navy Capt. Charles H. Davis, believed that the capture of that road, together with possession of the Mississippi River from Memphis down to Baton Rouge, was a matter of war-winning significance. "It would," Grant later wrote, "be equal to the amputation of a limb in its weakening effects upon the enemy." It was argued then, and later much more frequently, that a well-led combined operation might have achieved those aims. But it was Maj. Gen. Henry Halleck who was in charge at Corinth, and he now elected to disperse his force, "the largest army ever assembled west of the Alleghenies."

Exact figures are disputed, but, in general, it is believed that the Union armies in the west totaled about 137,000 effectives (those not sick, wounded, or otherwise unfit for service) against 105,000 Confederates. On June 3, Maj. Gen. John A. McClernand and Maj. Gen. Lew Wallace of the Army of the Tennessee were sent to the Mississippi Central Railroad center at Bolivar. Maj. Gen. John Pope, who was chasing Rebel general Beauregard south of Corinth, was ordered the next day to break off his pursuit. On June 9, the divisions of Maj. Gen. Sherman and Brig. Gen. Stephen A. Hurlbut were sent to Memphis, while Maj. Gen. Don Carlos Buell was ordered to take his men to Chattanooga, repairing railroads en route. Halleck, who had broken up his overall command into a series of wings back on April 30, cancelled that formation on June 10 and their previous names, Armies of the Tennessee (Grant), Ohio (Buell), and Mississippi (Pope) respectively, were restored. Halleck wrote letters from his Corinth headquarters for the next five weeks and otherwise did little other than demand that local railroads be improved.

This inactivity left Confederate forces under Gen. Braxton Bragg, the new theater commander appointed in June, to refresh and reequip, to undertake the difficult mission of halting the advance of Union troops into the heartland, and to plan and execute a counterattack into Kentucky. What was immediately available to accomplish these goals was a combination of guerrilla attacks, cavalry raids, and relatively small Rebel army counterinitiatives, all of which had one overriding goal: sever Northern lines of communications and prevent Maj. Gen. Buell from reaching Chattanooga. Irregulars and partisans raided throughout the region attacking their favorite targets: railroads, overland wagon trains, and river supply steamers.

As he pushed toward Chattanooga, Buell was unable to repair his first railway, the Memphis & Charleston, as quickly as Confederate raiders could destroy key links. A switch to the Nashville & Chattanooga Railroad was just as fruitless. Gen. Bragg's Army of Tennessee occupied Chattanooga on July 24; his army arrived in the mountainous city on the Tennessee River by riding the rails from Tupelo, Mississippi, via Mobile. It would now be his aim to march up into Kentucky across the Cumberland plateau. During this period, Bragg was aided substantially both by his cavalry and by the great obstruction of the Tennessee River, Muscle Shoals. The shoals were, wrote historian Donald Davidson in 1948, "in effect a flank guard, as good as a mountain range, or better." This was because the Confederate leader knew that, east of the rapids, any army coming against him must move overland by road and railroad; Muscle Shoals prevented interference with him by steamer or gunboat.

Meanwhile, on July 16, Halleck departed east to become general in chief of all Union armies; fifteen days later, he telegraphed Maj. Gen. Grant, whom he had left in charge of troops in the Corinth-Memphis-Columbus area, leaving it up to him to figure out what to do next: "You must judge for yourself the best use to be made of your troops. Be careful not to scatter them too much."[1]

In the first weeks after the fall of Memphis on June 6, 1862, the sailors and soldiers reporting to Capt. Davis and Col. Graham Newell Fitch were occupied with matters in and around the Tennessee city. Ashore, the Hoosier bluecoats provided support to the civilian government. On the banks of the Mississippi, workers from the Western Flotilla attempted to salvage as many of the former Confederate warships as possible while their commander pondered what moves he could make next. Although steamboat traffic northward up the Mississippi was quickly being reestablished, the first period of occupation would not be easy for a people "more or less in sympathy" with the Confederate cause. In fact, upon his arrival, Maj. Gen. Sherman would find "the place dead; no business doing, the stores closed, churches, schools, and every thing shut up."

Without significantly more troops than the 1,200 or so of the 46th Indiana, it was useless to head downriver toward Vicksburg, the obvious next big target in the brown water war. It would be better, Davis reasoned, to continue raising and repairing the Confederate vessels sunk on June 6 and make the captured steamers serviceable for future use. Additionally, as news of the Halleck force realignment trickled in, the scholar-seaman determined to run small sweeps up the White and Arkansas Rivers until more soldiers actually reached

Four. Brothers and Guerrillas (1862)

Sunk during the Battle of Memphis, the C.S.S. *General Sterling Price* was thought to be lost. A skilled salvage effort led by Lt. Le Roy Fitch allowed the vessel to be reclaimed. So impressed was Flag Officer Davis with the achievement that he not only ordered his young acquaintance to skipper the vessel on its run north for rebuilding, but arranged that he thereafter be given an independent command (pen and ink drawing by Samuel Ward Stanton, Naval Historical Center).

Memphis and a firmer plan for their use was available. This choice would have a direct impact on the fortunes of the Fitch family warriors then in the Tennessee community.[2]

In his account of the fleet action to Navy secretary Gideon Welles written on the evening of the battle, Capt. Davis reported that, of the eight Confederate warships engaged, only the *General Van Dorn* had escaped. The seven others remained in various states of wrecked or arrested condition off the city: *General Price, General Lovell, General Beauregard* sunk in action, *General J. Thompson* captured, but blown up; and *General Bragg, General Sumter,* and *Little Rebel* all captured. It was anticipated that the surviving captured craft could be repaired, either at Memphis or Cairo. Indeed, within a day or so, Lieutenants-Commanding Henry Erben and Joshua Bishop were placed in command of the *General Bragg* and *General Sumter*, respectively, and dispatched upriver to Cairo. It was not expected that any of the other Rebel boats could be saved.

Col. Charles Ellet, Jr., the wounded commander of the Mississippi Marine Brigade, whose rams had done such fearsome damage fighting close-in amongst the Confederate warships, claimed the *Little Rebel* as a prize of war. Several memorandum, some heated, were exchanged between the marine leader and the flag officer over the next couple of days as the former pressed his case to no avail. Meanwhile, the *General Sterling Price* became the object of both a MMB and Western Flotilla salvage operation.[3]

The *General Price*, or *Sterling Price* as she was also sometimes known, was constructed in Cincinnati in 1856 and entered commercial service as the *Laurent Millaudon*. The 633 ton, wooden side-wheeler steamer was 182 feet long, with a beam of 30 feet and a depth of hold of 9.3 feet. Early in the war, she was taken into Confederate service, converted into a ram armed with four 9-inch Dahlgren smoothbores, and made a unit of the Confederate River Defense Force. In a short June 10 review entitled "Incidents of the Naval Engagement at Memphis," Col. Ellet detailed the fate of the *General Price* during the June 6 battle. At a point early in the fight, the *Monarch* side-swiped the Confederate boat, shearing off its starboard paddle wheel. The *Price*, employing its port side wheel, made it to the Arkansas shore, where it then accidentally collided with the Ellet ram *Queen of the West*. Totally disabled, she began to slowly sink. Her crew of 81 was able to surrender to marines sent aboard from the *Queen* and was rescued in an orderly manner. The *General Price* settled and "it was at first supposed could be easily raised."[4]

On June 7, Ellet, calling the *General Sterling Price* "a very valuable steamer already armed for gunboat service," sought the use of the fleet auxiliary *Champion No. 3* to assist in raising the rebel steamer.

The *Champion No. 3*, a civilian transport, towboat, and wrecking boat of unknown tonnage, was chartered by the USQM earlier in the year for use in those capacities by the Western Flotilla. The main 20-inch steam pump of the *Champion No. 3* was duly applied as salvage efforts were quickly undertaken. Ellet assured Secretary of War Edwin Stanton the next day that he was salvaging the steamer and proposed to add it to his ram fleet.

The work of reclaiming the *General Sterling Price* from the Mississippi River began on June 9 and was watched with interest by Yankee tars on vessels moored in the river and by those aboard passing tugboats and other small craft. Among those attracted to the operation was Lt. Le Roy Fitch, commander of the ammunition boat *Judge Torrence*. Fitch was curious to see the process of reviving a dead ship, and, like others, was disappointed that the enterprise initially went poorly. After being hauled up, the warship's port shaft was accidentally let go and lost in four fathoms of water. Then the *Champion No. 3*'s main pump broke down, at which point the civilian contractors decided to suspend salvage activities.

Lt. Fitch, who appears to have been innocent of salvage experience, apparently went aboard the hulk next morning and spoke about the outlook for the *General Sterling Price* with a number of the officers then on board her, who were themselves wondering if another attempt to get her up should be made. From the tone of his reports and their recipient's responses, it was Fitch who convinced the men to try again. Chief Engineer Samuel Bickerstaff, a second master named Newton, and pilot Samuel G. Sheely all agreed that they would be willing to help Fitch renew the effort; the captain, officers and men of the *Champion No. 3* promised their "cheerful and energetic cooperation" if the ordnance man could get authority. All agreed that if the smaller pump of the *Champion No. 3* could be employed, it would not be difficult to get the ram afloat. In that spirit of optimism, Fitch sought permission from flotilla chief Davis.

Although both Ellets and Davis were faced with other pressing matters, Davis agreed to the new salvage plan. For approximately three days, Fitch, Bickerstaff, Newton, and Sheely, with help from the officers and men of the *Champion No. 3*, labored in the mud and water "with the most unbounded perseverance and energy." Probably employing an armored diving suit and glass-windowed helmet, divers undoubtedly had gone under water, as was common practice in riverboat salvage, and made repairs prior to pumping. Finally, on June 15 in a letter written aboard the *Judge Torrence*, Lt.-Commanding Fitch was able to proudly report to his boss, "I have the honor to inform you that the steamer *Sterling Price* is afloat and her hull is apparently in good condition." The lost shaft was found and buoyed for later recovery.

Four. Brothers and Guerrillas (1862)

Capt. Davis was overjoyed to learn that the *General Sterling Price*, which many expected would have to be written off, was available for restoration and addition to the fleet. The commodore immediately sent over a message to the *Judge Torrence* acknowledging his pleasure in receiving the junior officer's letter. Davis readily applauded the achievement, asking that Fitch call all of those participating in the enterprise together and read them his words of public thanks. "In emergencies like these," Davis advised, "everything depends upon the superior intelligence of the directing minds and upon the faithful and untiring industry of the working hands." The captain, who had known Lt. Fitch years earlier and who was now even better acquainted with his older half brother, the colonel, added for the younger man's benefit the sentiment that he would "be happy, when the occasion offers, to show my just appreciation of the manner in which both the intelligence and industry were displayed on this occasion." That appreciation began to manifest itself next morning when Fitch was detached from the *Judge Torrence* and made prize captain of the *General Sterling Price*, his full-fledged warship command.

The *General Sterling Price* was now repaired for a trip to Cairo. Earlier, Col. Fitch and Capt. Davis, having determined the value of the eight steamers taken at the Memphis wharf the day of the battle, had reached an informal understanding for the repair of four of them: *Victoria*, *H. R. W. Hill*, *Mark R. Cheek*, and *Acacia*. The work was done under the supervision of and on the account of the 46th Indiana quartermaster, now acting quartermaster for Memphis, Capt. Henry S. Fitch, the colonel's son. Davis now saw to it that the refloated Rebel warship was also patched up by Capt. Fitch, just as soon as his uncle could get it across river to the dock.[5]

While Union troops fanned out over parts of Tennessee, Alabama, Mississippi, and Kentucky under Maj. Gen. Halleck's June dispersal orders and Confederate troops regrouped under their new leader, Gen. Braxton Bragg, major campaigning in the West slowed almost to a standstill. This is not to say that the fighting ceased. On the contrary, in the words of historian Benjamin Franklin Cooling, "the conflict became a 'war in the shadows' in which rebel horsemen garnered most of the honors." Southern units both official and unofficial, military raider, partisan, and guerrilla, struck back at the Yankee invaders, hitting Union outposts, small or isolated contingents, supply dumps, loyalist leaders and homesteads, and most especially, rail and water transport and telegraph communications.

Everywhere Southern men fought to stem in other ways that loss of ground they were unable to prevent on the battlefield. The potential for this sort of contribution to the war effort was recognized by the Confederate Congress when, on April 21, it passed a Partisan Ranger Act; in 1864, the legislation would be revoked as unworkable.

If you were a Yankee invader or sympathizer in Tennessee, Kentucky, or some other Southern state, the differences between the types of insurgents shooting at your steamer, destroying your home, burning your supplies, killing your straggling troops or foraging parties, tearing up railroad tracks, or pillaging in some other fashion probably did not matter any more to you than did the destruction of homes, theft of livestock, destruction of railroad rolling stock, or murders committed upon Southerners by Union troops or supporters. The noted British military historian, John F. C. Fuller, once wrote: "The Federal soldier was semi-regular and the Confederate semi-guerrilla." Yet, in fact, there was, as Dr. Robert M. Mackey notes, a real difference between the various kinds of attackers, if not the outcome of their assaults.

In the spring-summer of 1862 as the Rebel irregular menace became more fully appreciated by the Union army in the West, Maj. Gen. Halleck asked the German immigrant jurist Francis Lieber, then at Columbia University, to give his legal opinion on the matter. Guerrillas, a 19th century term first applied to Spanish irregulars in the Napoleonic wars, were seen by Lieber as unpaid volunteers who were not part of an army but who joined together in self-constituted bands to take up arms against (or who also faded away from) invaders. They often wore no uniform and quarter was seldom given or expected in combat or after capture. Partisans, on the other hand, were more elite military groups, special forces if you will, who wore uniforms and undertook unconventional activities, like stealthily capturing opposing generals. Lieber, whose thoughts were contained in his *Guerrilla Parties Considered with Reference to the Laws and Usages of War*, also known as the "Lieber Code," noted that raiders were regular cavalry units usually sent to attack targets of substance, like railroads, supply centers, and river shipping, rather than political or soft targets such as farmers or shopkeepers. As the war went on, "guerrilla" became an epitaph employed primarily by Northerners to mean groups, primarily of Southerners, engaged in any type of unconventional or irregular warfare from cavalry raids to bushwhacking.

So widespread did this irregular "pestilence" become for Northerners over the summer months of 1862 that it was not only the names of cavalrymen like John Hunt Morgan and Nathan Bedford Forest which caused panic in Union circles, but those of lesser remembered irregulars, like Adam Rankin Johnson of Kentucky and T. Alonzo Napier of Benton County, Tennessee, to name two of hundreds. Throughout large swaths of the mid–South, unconventional small-scale combat became more than just a part of the war; to its victims and perpetrators, it became the war itself. All of the evils we've come to know in insurgent and counterinsurgent warfare in our own time, save possibly suicide bombings, were experienced during the Civil War.[6]

As 1862 passed, the true differences between cavalry operating as special force raiders and small bands of unorganized bushwhackers were recognized in some higher Union headquarters. It also came to be understood that in many areas, such as Middle Tennessee, "civilian animosity and guerrilla marauding ... were," as historian Steven V. Ash has put it, "two sides of the same coin." Indigenous guerrilla bands, in addition to fighting within provincial, hometown boundaries, were also of major assistance to regular CSA cavalry raiders. Forrest, Morgan, and others received intelligence, food, horses and forage, and recruits from these sometimes informal, always irregular people. As Union Brig. Gen.. James S. Negley later wrote: "The wealthy secessionists ... are undoubtedly aiding and sympathizing with these guerrilla parties. Many of their sons are with them."

Though not always appreciated, the difference between regular troops and guerrillas was recognized at the time. Maj. Gen. Don Carlos Buell, whose logistics suffered as much from Rebel raiders as any Northern commander, objected to one investigating panel that the troops of Generals Forrest and Morgan were being unjustly labeled. "They are as much troops," he said, "as any in the rebel service." There was a difference between those riders "and what we understand by 'guerrillas.' I know of no reason for giving them a character which does not belong to them, for they are not 'guerrillas' in the proper sense of the term." The principal problem for Federal authorities seemed to lay with accepting the truth about just how widespread the underlying local support was for the insurgents and in developing measures to deal with both the fighters and with those actively assisting them. The challenge existed not only in Tennessee and Kentucky, but wherever Union troops inserted themselves in the South.

Four. Brothers and Guerrillas (1862)

There was at least one high level systematic and organized Rebel effort to create and harness guerrilla bands, "in the proper sense of the term," to a state's defense. This measure would be, in effect, to quote irregular warfare historian Robert Mackey, an effort "to give the Yankee army a taste of what Napoleon's army experienced in Spain." In late May, Maj. Gen. Thomas C. Hindman, a one-time U.S. congressman, was sent by Richmond to reorganize the defense of Confederate Arkansas, which was then in a state of turmoil, with most of her soldiers east of the Mississippi. When Hindman and his entourage arrived at Little Rock on May 30 (after stopping en route to liberate a quantity of arms and $1 million from Memphis banks), they found Arkansas virtually defenseless and facing an invasion by Yankee troops from Missouri.

As commander of the new Trans-Mississippi District, Hindman immediately set to work building up as much resistance as possible to halt an expected Northern influx. Martial law was declared, all supplies and munitions were taken in hand, rationing was introduced, and men were conscripted to reform a conventional army. Building a new regular military force would take time and to help buy that time, Hindman authorized the raising of independent guerrilla companies to fight behind enemy lines. His decree, General Order No. 17, later known as the "Bands of Ten" order, specifically called upon the populace (meaning primarily Caucasian males) to organize into independent 10-man companies, each under the leadership of an elected captain. "Without waiting for special instructions," the little non-uniformed outfits were ordered to undertake guerrilla activities "for the more effective annoyance of the enemy upon our rivers and in our mountains and woods." When the general order took effect on June 17, Arkansas found that it had mobilized a guerrilla army "but without providing for the command and control needed to oversee the independent companies."[7]

It would fall to Col. Fitch to be among the first Union commanders to experience the concentrated and persistent sting of Hindman's people's army during his upcoming outings into the wilds of Arkansas. The shock and revulsion felt at his opponent's tactics would not only stymie the progress of his last campaigns, but also poison his opinion of all irregular operations. It cannot come as a surprise then that, in younger half-brother Le Roy's upcoming naval operations, lessons were learned from his half brother and elsewhere. These provided motivation and some of the tactics the enterprising sailor would employ in his riverine counterinsurgency campaign against those hostile armed Southerners who dared to approach any river's edge he could reach—be they guerrillas, partisans, or raiders.

While Le Roy Fitch was occupied with the salvage of the *General Sterling Price*, Capt. Davis received a message which would, in the end, send the young lieutenant along on the path to his greatest contribution while simultaneously leading to his physician older half brother's exit from the war. Maj. Gen. Samuel R. Curtis, who had earlier won the victory at Pea Ridge, was frustrated in his effort to march his Army of the Southwest from Missouri to northeastern Arkansas. Out of supplies and forage and harassed by Rebel guerrillas, Curtis fell back behind the White River near Batesville and petitioned Maj. Gen. Halleck for help.

When the Curtis message, sent via wire from St. Louis, reached Corinth on June 8, the Western commander, who appeared to some to have been erratic of late, sprang into action. The telegraph sang again with pleas for support, this time to both Secretary of War Stanton and Capt. Davis. Due to technical problems and outages caused by irregulars, both Stanton and Davis received their messages two days later. Like Halleck, both moved. The secretary forwarded his to Navy secretary Welles asking the former Connecticut newspaperman to order Davis' support while Davis was already moving on Halleck's request, planning an expedition to open army communications on the White River.[8]

In response to the Army entreaty, Capt. Davis revised an earlier scheme he had devised to chase Confederate steamers and a few gunboats reported to be in the White and Arkansas Rivers. His plan was, instead, scaled back to ascend the White River up to Jacksonport. Knowing that the Arkansas stream was falling and short of lighter-draught gunboats, Davis sought Charles Ellet's cooperation in a joint enterprise to the White. Ellet, who was dying, responded by saying the request was made on very short notice and if it were to be granted, Davis would have to surrender command of the expedition to Ellet's associate U.S. Army Lt. George E. Currie, commander of the ram *Mingo*. Although Davis would gain use of the three available Ellet rams and one of the soldier's tugs, he could not bring himself to agree to a force "acting under divided authority." Consequently, Davis called upon his senior captain, Augustus H. Kilty of the U.S.S. *Mound City*, to put together a small task group and lead it on an expedition to the White River.[9]

Cmdr. Kilty's group included the *Mound City* as flagship, plus the Pook turtle *St. Louis*, the timberclad *Lexington*, and the tugboat *Spitfire*. Delays in assembling the force pushed back the expedition's departure date until June 13. Early that morning, the four boats got underway for the White River, 181 miles below. News then came in that the Confederates had sunk a heavy timber raft in the lower reaches of that target stream and were planning to defend it with sharpshooters and artillery.

Next day, the chartered steamer *White Cloud*, loaded with supplies for the Army of the Southwest, arrived at Memphis from St. Louis. Her captain immediately called upon Capt. Davis asking for escort. Davis, who was expecting the request, already had Lt. George Blodgett's timberclad *Conestoga* tasked to the duty. What he did not have was marines to clear away the Rebel raft.

Meeting with Col. Fitch, the navy chief provided a verbal briefing of the White River enterprise and asked for his help (which request was so important as to also be put into writing), even going so far as to remind him of Maj. Gen. John Pope's original orders that the Hoosier soldiers cooperate with his flotilla. Graham Newell Fitch quickly appreciated the gravity of the situation as Capt. Davis outlined it. If his men did not help the bluejackets, they would be unable to run supplies up to Curtis, who would be trapped and maybe lost.[10]

By evening, Col. Fitch had the men of the 46th Indiana embarked upon the steamer *New National*. At 5 A.M. on June 15, the Hooser expedition pushed off. With the *Conestoga* in the van, the steamers *Jacob Musselman*, *New National*, and *White Cloud* steamed downstream, attempting to catch up with Cmdr. Kilty's *Mound City* group, which had entered the White River earlier in the day. Having learned of the Fitch mission, the warships anchored at the Arkansas cut-off, awaiting the soldiers' arrival.

The *Conestoga* task group entered the White River at 5:25 A.M. on June 16 and joined up with the *Mound City* unit; together, the force steamed fifty miles up the river, dropping anchor at 4:30 in the afternoon at a point some 77 miles above the river's mouth. Col. Fitch and Cmdr. Kilty, acting in consultation, decided to send a reconnaissance toward St. Charles, which lay eight miles further upriver. Two groups, one on foot and one aboard the replacement tug *Spiteful*, subsequently reported a pair of Rebel batteries, zeroed in on the river and supported by an unknown number of troops, were deployed near the city.

In fact, the defenders had placed wooden obstructions and sunk three boats in the river, including Capt. Joseph Fry's gunboat C.S.S. *Maurepas*. Two gun emplacements were hastily thrown up on a high bluff back from the left bank of the river, armed with cannon unshipped from the C.S.S. *Pontchartrain*, then at Little Rock, and sent down to St. Charles by rail and water. A pair of 32-pounders were situated in a battery on the bluff and two 3-inch guns were located 400 yards below, with another four small cannon available. CSN Lt. John W. Dunningham and 50 *Pontchartrain* tars manned the cannon, supplemented by men from the *Maurepas* and 50 Confederate soldiers, all under the overall command of Capt. Fry, a pre-war USN lieutenant, and Capt. A. M. Williams of the CSA Engineers, made ready as the Union army-navy commanders determined to move upon them next morning.[11]

The Fitch-Kilty plan was relatively simple: the gunboats would attack the Rebel emplacements from the river while the Indiana soldiers came against them from behind. This is the same plan that Le Roy Fitch and Brig. Gen. Richard Johnson would employ against the Confederate batteries at Bell's Mill, near Nashville, in December 1864. The gunboats moved out at 6 A.M. on June 17, steaming to a point just below the batteries while Companies A, B, and G of the 46th Indiana went ashore "about two miles below the town and just below where a little bayou put out." It then pushed up to within 300 yards of the top of the bluff where the 32-pounders were mounted. As they waited, Signal Corps Lt. George Gray and two soldiers were sent to scout the enemy "fort."[12]

The ironclad Yankee gunboats began a close-in firefight with the shore batteries while the Hoosier troops were climbing. Cmdr. Kilty, believing his cannonade was effective, moved the *Mound City* inshore when suddenly there was a great explosion. A 68-pound Read projectile from one of the guns in the upper battery had smashed through the turtle's iron and penetrated its steam chest, filling the boat with scalding steam and driving the crew overboard into the river. The stricken vessel drifted to the right bank of the river, where Capt. Fry called upon the few survivors aboard to lower their flag. When this didn't occur, Fry reportedly ordered his men "to shoot all in the water that attempted to escape." Lt. Gray and his men, secreted upon a knoll, saw the tragedy and also witnessed that "the enemy then came out of the fort and rushed the river bank, firing at the men in the water and on the boat ... they shot and killed all they could."

Some years later when Jeanie Mort Walker published her biography of Fry, by then "the Cuban Martyr," she included a number of interviews (most anonymous) with eyewitnesses, all of whom denied the charges that Fry ordered his men to fire. "I know them [the assertions] to be false," commented U.S.S. *St. Louis* executive officer John V. Johnston, a former packet captain, "they never had any foundation whatever." Fry himself reportedly admitted "in after times when 'fighting his battles o'er again'" stationing riflemen to open fire on Yankee small boats reportedly moving to cut off his retreat.

As the encounter continued, the other Union gunboats now moved to take up the firing. Meanwhile, Lt. Gray and his party, briefly detained by but escaping from Rebel pickets, made it back to report to Col. Fitch. "Do you suppose I can take the works from the rear?" asked the Hoosier; Gray replied "yes," and so, 10 minutes after the *Mound City* disaster, Fitch ordered the gunboats to cease firing. Led by Gray and Fitch, the 46th Indiana then carried the Rebel position "in the most dashing and gallant manner, and with no loss of [bluecoat] life." Eight Southern defenders were killed in the attack and 29 were captured, including Capt. Fry. With no further fortifications upriver and only the *Pontchartrain* to offer resistance, the costly St. Charles victory in effect gave the North control of the White River.

While Lt. Fitch was salvaging the C.S.S. *General Sterling Price,* Col. Graham Newell Fitch's command participated with a naval task group in an abortive effort to relieve a force under Brig. Gen. Samuel R. Curtis believed trapped in Arkansas. Steaming up the White River, the force was engaged near St. Charles and a Confederate shot into the steam drum of the U.S.S. *Mound City* resulted in significant casualties. In reaction to Southern attacks on survivors and general hidden riverbank assaults on naval craft, Col. Fitch announced, in one of the first major statements of Union counterinsurgency policy, that local civilian populations would be held responsible for hostile activities by irregular forces operating in their regions. This philosophy, endorsed in Federal military circles, was undoubtedly passed on from brother to brother within several months (*Harper's Weekly,* 1862, via Naval Historical Center).

As the action ended, the *Mound City* was towed out of danger by the *Conestoga*. The Confederate shot into her steam drum left 125 of her 175-man crew dead or mortally wounded, one of the greatest single ship losses for the Union Navy in the entire war. The deadly effects of pressurized steam, long known to steamboatmen, were made plain to landsmen and soldiers alike. Screams from the wounded and dying broke morale and the gunboat commanders became reluctant to proceed; falling water only heightened their unease.[13]

On the evening of June 17, soldiers of the Indiana Regiment buried the dead of both sides. The butcher's bill from the ironclad was later determined to be 82 men killed by gunshot wounds or scalded to death, with 43 others drowned, or shot while struggling in the water. Only three officers (not including Commander Kilty) and 22 men escaped uninjured. Col. Fitch and others were appalled by the "inhumanity" of Confederate attacks against the *Mound City* men who had jumped overboard. In his June 19 report of the action, Fitch recorded that scarcely had the sailors abandoned their ship before:

> A party of the enemy's sharpshooters descended the bluff from batteries and, under cover of fallen timber on the river bank, commenced murdering those who were struggling in the water, and also firing upon those in our boats sent to pick them up at the same time, another party of the enemy, concealed in the timber on the opposite of the river, pursued the same barbarous course.

Fitch went on to further express his outrage and that of his men:

> So strongly marked was the contrast between this conduct on their part and that of our sailors and soldiers at Memphis, who risked their lives to save those of the enemy who had been driven into the river by steam or flames, as to excite an intense desire upon the part of the land forces to end the scene and punish punish the barbarity.

Capt. Davis, upon hearing accounts of the tragedy, wrote home that the "scene of horror was rendered more frightful by the enemy's shooting our wounded and scalded men in the water and by firing into the boats of the other vessels of the squadron which came to the assistance of the poor, helpless, drowning, and scalded victims.... This barbarous conduct on the part of the enemy," Davis concluded, "will lead to terrible retaliation. The men of the squadron are now very much excited and vow vengeance." David Dixon Porter, who would succeed Flag Officer Davis as squadron commander in October, later directly suggested that the ship's death toll was so high because Rebel sharpshooters purposely shot Union sailors struggling in the White.[14]

On June 18, Col. Fitch, in response to a request from the ironclad's acting captain, Jonathan A. Duble, sent a 46th Indiana lieutenant and 48 enlisted men to help man the *Mound City*. The ship would be left at St. Charles while the *St. Louis, Lexington, Spiteful* and the two transports pushed on upriver. After passing Adams Bluff early on June 19, the gunboats and troopships were engaged in a running series of off-and-on firefights with Rebel soldiers and guerrillas firing at them from the riverbank. The Hoosier soldiers on the *White Cloud* and *New National* were favorite targets and four Union men died in the attacks.

The squadron came abreast of Clarendon at mid-afternoon, at which point it halted. Col. Fitch went ashore to speak with persons gathered at the wharf who, although professing neutrality, were sternly warned that "firing on the boats from the banks of the river would not be permitted, and if it was connived at by the citizens, they would be held accountable and their property destroyed." The night, with the river still falling, the *St. Louis* and her consorts reached Crooked Point Cut-off, 63 miles above St. Charles. There the commanders of the *St Louis* and *Lexington*, alarmed by the fall of the river and advised about it by the knowledgeable White River pilot aboard *White Cloud*, informed an unhappy Fitch that the expedition must turn back. Although the physician argued strenuously against retreat, the advance was abandoned and next morning the boats returned to St. Charles.

Flag Officer Davis, upon receiving word of the St. Charles tragedy, dispatched Cmdr. John A. Winslow and the U.S.S. *Cincinnati* to St. Charles, where the Pook turtle arrived on June 21. There the future commander of the U.S.S. *Kearsarge* during her victory over the Rebel raider *Alabama*, met with the navy men and Col. Fitch, and determined to lay to at St. Charles awaiting orders. The next day, as the Yankee sailors and bluecoated soldiers awaited some decisions from their leadership and the *Conestoga* paddled up toward Memphis carrying after-action reports and requests for orders, Arkansas guerrillas hiding in the dense nearby foliage began sniping at them. One man each on the *Lexington* and *New National* was killed.[15]

News having come in from informants that the Rebels firing at them were from Monroe County, Col. Fitch and Cmdr. Winslow decided that a punitive expedition would be dispatched to that region. Early on the 22nd, four companies from the 46th Indiana, led by Maj. Thomas Bringhurst, were sent aboard the *Cincinnati* and *Lexington*, which then proceeded up Indian Bay. Frequently, the warships would halt and heavily armed landing parties were put ashore and notices signed by Col. Fitch were posted addressed "To the Inhabitants of Monroe County, Arkansas." In short declarative sentences, the locals were informed that guerrilla bands raised in their vicinity had fired from the woods upon the United States gunboats and transports on the river in a mode of warfare Fitch labeled as "that of savages." They were warned not to aid the guerrillas because, if they did, the Federal government would hold them responsible, revisit them, and confiscate or burn their homes. Fitch's broadside was "the first open declaration by Federal authorities that guerrilla attacks would be followed by Federal punitive measures against the civilian populace."

When the troops returned to St. Charles, they learned that the Confederate irregulars had been shooting at the ships in their absence, though no casualties resulted. Although Fitch did not order any Monroe County habitat burnings, he may have wished he had. Before the Indiana colonel could organize any more raids or poster placements, Cmdr. Winslow pulled the plug on the Hoosier's activities. The navy man was specifically warned that he "must at once leave the river" to avoid being trapped by low water and by the morning of June 25, all of the vessels were back at the mouth of the White. In a letter home two days earlier, Flag Officer Davis summed up the failed White River situation, assigning the reversal "to the low stage of the river." On June 25, he pointed out another detail not commented upon in official reports: "We are having now one of the hot terms and it is worse, I think, than Central America."[16]

Up the Mississippi at Memphis, wheels were turning to send Col. Fitch and his Hoosiers back up the White River in a second attempt to reach Maj. Gen. Curtis. Responding to a June 25 request by Maj. Gen. Halleck for another logistical effort, Maj. Gen. U. S. Grant, who arrived in the West Tennessee city two days earlier to be put in charge of the effort, agreed to dispatch additional transports. On June 26, Flag Officer Davis promised to provide escorting warships and so, by June 29, five additional steamers bearing supplies and elements of the 34th and 43rd Indiana Volunteer Infantry, all covered by the *Conestoga*, reached the mouth of the White River.[17]

While Halleck, Grant, and Davis were at work upriver, there now occurred one of those rare, but not unheard of, exchanges of personal viewpoints between opposing Civil War commanders. On June 25, Maj. Gen. Hindman, having heard of Col. Fitch's Monroe County declaration, sent a letter to the former U.S. senator-now-warrior setting out his position concerning his use of irregulars, even taking the precaution of enclosing a printed copy of his General Orders No. 17 so that Fitch might "act advisedly." In his missive, Hindman bluntly stated that he, as a Confederate department commander, personally, even if Fitch did not, recognized the local guerrillas "as Confederate troops, and I assert as indisputable the right to dispose and use those troops along the banks of the White River, or wherever else I may deem proper, even should it prove annoying to you in your operations." He closed with a warning that should Fitch's retaliatory threats be "executed against any citizens of this district," his people would retaliate, man for man, against any Federals falling into their hands.[18]

A man known for his oratory since at least the 1830s, Graham Newell Fitch, who was mightily annoyed at this juncture both with the results of his Arkansas adventure and Hindman's audacious message, replied three days later. "You will permit me to suggest that your objections to my proclamation come with ill grace from you," the colonel wrote, "when accompanied with your own order above referred to." That order, the soldier frankly stated, "is but an encouragement to rapine and murder upon the part of those in this State, if there be such, so lost to all sense of honor as to avail themselves of your permission to commit such depredations.... Your threat," he declared, "will not deter me from executing the letter of my proclamation in every case in which my judgment dictates its propriety or necessity."[19]

Escorted by the timberclads, the Yankee troopships, bearing almost 1,500 Indiana troops, began back up the White River on June 29. Intensive small-arms attacks on the boats began on June 30; the men of the *New National*, for example, could by day's end, point to 30 places where bullets had passed through their boat. This expedition, continuously plagued by Hindman's fighters, came to within about a mile of Clarendon where it ground to a halt because the water was too low and filled with dead trees. Upriver, Maj. Gen. Grant detailed the 24th Indiana down to Fitch's assistance, giving its commander orders for Col. Fitch not to take any risks.

By the morning of July 4, it was determined to start up the White again. After a brief program of patriotic tunes from the band of the 34th Indiana, the boats pulled away. That evening, Rebel troops, having avoided pickets, surprised a recreating swim party of sailors and killed Chief Engineer Joseph Huber of the *Lexington*.

Guerrillas and Southern sympathizers were simultaneously having an impact in Union-occupied Memphis. The correspondent of *Harper's Weekly* recorded on July 5 that Maj. Gen. Wallace was forced to shut down the Memphis *Argus*. "The vicinity of the city" he wrote, was infested with guerrillas, many of whom are engaged in burning cotton in the southern counties of Mississippi and other points." On the bright side, "trade in Memphis is rapidly improving. Boats going north are filled to their utmost capacity with passengers and freight."

On July 6, an overland sweep by 800 men from the four Hoosier regiments, accompanied by a pair of boat howitzers, resulted in an inconclusive skirmish near the Grand Prairie, close to the town of Aberdeen, Arkansas. A second sweep the next day engaged several Confederate parties, but was equally nonproductive. On July 8, the troops returned aboard their transports while intelligence was studied which indicated that Maj. Gen. Curtis was about 30 miles away to the north near the Cache River. Before this data could be acted upon, July 6 dispatches arrived from Maj. Gen. Grant recommending that, because he could send no more men and the rivers were still falling, Fitch return to St. Charles.

This second wilderness trek, every bit as arduous as the first, turned out to be equally fruitless, with the only benefit, if such it be counted, that the casualty list was confined to men shot by snipers. The number of Hoosiers killed by guerrilla attacks during the two incursions was at least seven. On July 15, a month after he had departed Memphis, Col. Fitch led his men out of the White River to Helena. There he and they were greeted by soldiers of Maj. Gen. Curtis' army, who had safely reached the river town by another route the day before. "A more ill-conceived and fruitless affair could not have been contrived than this combined foray into the Arkansas wilds," wrote historian Rowena Reed. By summer, as Robert Mackey points out, guerrillas infested the entire White River valley.[20]

Despite the failure of Col. Fitch's White River gambit, that exercise resulted in the germ of a counterinsurgency position for a number of influential Union generals. It would not be one of leniency; the concept of "winning hearts and minds" would not be popular in numerous Federal army or navy circles after what the Hoosiers experienced. Responses to perceived guerrilla attacks by Federal military units and warships, whether by legitimate soldiers or unregulated bands and regardless of location, would become almost standardized. Homes, farms, or towns would be burned or sometimes ransomed; prisoners would be taken and often jailed. Both Grant and Sherman certainly drew the line, offering little protection to non-uniformed and unorganized irregulars.

Grant's General Order No. 60 of July 3 echoed the "Fitch doctrine," in as much as Union commanders who suffered losses from guerrillas were authorized to seize personal property from Rebel sympathizers in the immediate vicinity. Grant, like Fitch, saw the people as responsible for policing their areas and suppressing unregulated incidents "being so pernicious to the welfare of the community where it is carried on." Historian Noel C. Fisher has indicated that Maj. Gen. Sherman strongly concurred with and applied the principle of community responsibility for guerrilla activities and believed that reprisals would help people see the wisdom of acting to halt such actions. Total war, as it was later known and of which counterinsurgency operations were a part, also had a serious impact on the civilian population and contributed to the continuing disharmony between occupier and resident. "Rural women left alone in cabins and on farms were repeatedly robbed of livestock and food items as troops looked for food to feed their armies."

Employing often harsh measures, Union soldiers afloat and ashore would now wage a continuing and intense struggle against the guerrillas, as well as uniformed raiders, and those viewed as sympathetic to them. Protecting land and water communications lines in a war of logistics was now viewed as vital. Maintaining Federal control of the rivers, rail routes, and roads became a paramount mission for the all Yankee land forces, as well as the Western Flotilla. If the guerrillas and partisans could not be beaten off, it would be impossible for the North to guarantee a dependable flow of supplies and munitions to its field armies. At this point and for some time to come in the West, there would be few real lines, enemy or friendly, save around Nashville, Memphis, and a few other communities. "Large areas," wrote the modern British observers Cornelia and Jac Weller, "were not and could not be totally controlled by either side save for short periods."

"Without an adequate naval force to challenge the Union naval activities, the Confederates could only resort to guerrillas," wrote several well-known Civil War historians just a decade ago. To win the war against them, at least from a riverine viewpoint, required new strategy and tactics, as well as equipment. Many regular as well as volunteer U.S. naval officers would participate in the shadowy and unglamorous battle with several, like Lt. Cmdr. Seth Ledyard Phelps and Acting Volunteer Lieutenant Henry A. Glassford, taking starring roles. None would, however, come to represent the human instrument of U.S. naval counterinsurgency on Western waters more completely than 27-year-old regular Navy Lt. Le Roy Fitch then guiding the *General Sterling Price* up the Mississippi toward Cairo. With strong, though distant, support from his superiors, Fitch, would soon have an opportunity to display previously untapped leadership skills and a "knack for improvisation" of the kind recently revealed in the raising of the former Rebel ram. With energy and a ferocious devotion to the Union, he would write his name on almost every major or minor anti-guerrilla, anti-partisan, and anti-raider operation undertaken anywhere near water in the Ohio and Tennessee valleys during the remainder of the war.[21]

As the wartime star of the young lieutenant rose, that of his older half brother now rapidly faded from the battlefield. It is thus appropriate to conclude this chapter with a summary of the departure of Graham Newell Fitch.

After its White River adventure, the 46th Indiana Regiment was stationed at Helena, where, according to its historian, it "went into a thorough renovation." New uniforms, horses, wagons and other equipment was provided and numerous recruits from home filled the ranks. On August 3, Col. Fitch led the regiment, as part of a larger force under Brig. Gen. Alvin P. Hovey, on a four day trek to Clarendon in pursuit of a reported Confederate force. Although no regulars were met, guerrilla sniping killed four men and wounded several others. About this time, Col. Fitch was hurt in a manner not recorded; the injury disabled him from further service, forcing him to resign and take leave.

On September 2, following the acceptance of his resignation, the 46th Indiana was drawn up for a final review by its first commander. His speech on this sad but proud occasion reminded the men of their achievements and enjoined them to do nothing "that might tarnish the good name of the regiment or the honor of Our State." He closed by asking the officers and men "to be kind to one another and remember that the discipline they were under" was for their own good. Three cheers followed the talk. Later, when the group's story was told, it was recorded of Col. Fitch: "The departure of the colonel was regretted by all the members of the regiment. His care of the men endeared him to all." Will Ball, the Logansport historian, reported simply that Fitch, "who had lined up on the right side," was in the end a war hero who "fought with distinction."

Upon his return to Logansport, Graham Newell Fitch resumed his medical practice, and continued as an informal advisor to the local Democratic Party. In 1868, he was a delegate to the Democratic National Convention in New York City, which nominated the presidential ticket of Seymour and Blair. From 1878 until 1883, he taught surgery at the Indiana Medical College in Indianapolis. He died in Logansport on November 29, 1892, and was interred in Mount Hope Cemetery.[22]

Following the final salute of the Indiana regiment on September 2, 1862, it is almost certain that ex–Col. Fitch, who never used that title in his later civilian life, returned up the Mississippi from Helena. It is quite probable that he traveled home to Logansport via Memphis and Cairo, then probably up the Ohio River, via Paducah and Shawnetown, either to the mouth of the Wabash River or more likely on to Evansville. By his own record, it is known that Le Roy Fitch was in both Cairo and Paducah between September 3 and 6 and made his headquarters at Evansville, where he was held by low water between September 12 and 29. It is inconceivable to this writer that the brothers Fitch did not meet in one of those towns and perhaps discuss the colonel's trials in the White River first hand. Such a rendezvous could explain the sailor's blunt verbalization of his relative's "doctrine," in September 11 orders to a subordinate sent on an anti-guerrilla sweep: "Should you be fired into at Caseyville, or any resistance offered, destroy the place at once. You are authorized to make arrests of such persons as you may, in your own judgement, deem proper."[23]

CHAPTER FIVE

Tinclads, Logistics and Rivers

IN THE SUMMER OF 1862, WESTERN FLOTILLA commander Flag Officer Charles H. Davis, assorted of his subordinates such as Lt.-Commanding S. Ledyard Phelps and Fleet Captain and Cairo station chief Commander Alexander M. Pennock, to say nothing of various influential Union military leaders, including such landsmen as Maj. Gen. Grant, Sherman, and Col. Fitch, as well as quartermasters like Capt. Henry Wise and Henry Fitch, well understood the necessity of winning the anti-partisan–guerrilla war and protecting vital lines of communication. To do that, however, more than superb leadership would be required on land or river. In the Mississippi and Tennessee valley areas of the South where terrain and weather often dictated campaign or skirmish outcomes large and small, new tactics and significantly more and improved equipment was required. If the Western Flotilla, in particular, was to make a significant contribution, it would need not only to creatively apply its new appreciation for local resistance tactics and possible countermeasures discussed in the last chapter, but also required more gunboats. These gunboats had to be of a light draft sufficient to go where the big ironclads available or a-building could not. For purposes of this account, those places were the Ohio, Tennessee, and Cumberland Rivers.[1]

Of the fighting units in Flag Officer Davis' U.S. Army squadron in the summer of 1862, the Pook turtles were purpose built, the *Benton* and *Essex* were rebuilt specialty craft (snagboats), and only the timberclads *Lexington*, *Tyler*, and *Conestoga* were true conversions from common river steamers—and their renovation into warships predates our story. The nine ironclads were very heavy, with drafts ranging from six foot for the *Mound City* to nine feet for the *Benton*, were extremely slow going upstream, and were needed for major operations, especially in the Vicksburg campaign. The three timberclads were spread too far and wide to adequately cover the upper part of the Mississippi River, and the other major streams, the Ohio, Tennessee, and Cumberland. Yet to fully appreciate the manner and rationale under which the Western Flotilla began its warship re-equipment requires some familiarity with the river steamers then available.

By the 1850s, Western river steamboat evolution was essentially complete; the vessel's form, retained into the early 20th Century, was that of lightly-constructed, flat-bottomed craft with multiple decks rising high above their waterlines. Mark Twain remembered a sidewheeled steamboat which appeared at his hometown of Hannibal, Missouri, as being a "handsome sight, too."

> She is long and sharp and trim and pretty; she has two tall, fancy-topped chimneys, with a gilded device of some kind swung between them; a fanciful pilot-house, all glass and "gingerbread," perched on top of the "texas" deck behind them; the paddle-boxes are gorgeous with a picture or with gilded rays above the boat's name; the boiler-deck, the hurricane-deck, and the texas deck are fenced and ornamented with clean white railings; there is a flag gallantly flying from the jack-staff.

In general, the appearance of these commercial passenger-carrying packets changed little from the antebellum days of Mark Twain to that of one visited by George Ward Nichols in 1870:

> From her keel to the roof of the upper cabin she includes forty feet. Above that is the "Texas," as it is called, which is an upper row of cabins, where the officers quarters are, and upon the top of which is imposed the pilot-house. The main cabin is plainly but well furnished, with large staterooms on either side. Below it is the main deck, where the big boilers and furnaces and engines are. Below this deck again there is a deep, spacious hold, where a thousand or fifteen hundred tons of freight may be stowed away.... Perhaps the most ornamental and most needful parts of this noble creature, as we see her from the outside, are the two big black smoke-stacks.

Official terminology for the decks in Nichols' colorful layout description was, in fact, slightly different. Borrowing from the detail provided in Adam Kane's excellent recent *The Western River Steamboat*, let us elaborate. Directly above the cargo hold was the open main deck which hosted all of the machinery, a blacksmith's shop, deck passenger berths (bunks, actually), heads, and hatches covering stairs into the hold. Most passengers were accommodated in cabins on either side of a deck-long central hallway, often called the saloon, on the boiler or upper deck. This next deck up from the main deck was equally as wide as the one below it and also contained washrooms, a bar and a saloon, a pantry, and a baggage room. The saloon hallway was also the dining and social area. The after part, closed off at night by folding doors, was set aside for ladies and children and was usually equipped with a piano. The clerk's or business office was located in the forward part of the saloon hallway. The exterior of the boiler deck was largely surrounded by a covered walkway, also called a gallery or a guard; sometimes, the bar and a barbershop were located on this area. The largely-open roof of the boiler deck was known as the Hurricane Deck. The open portion usually had skylights to illuminate the saloon on the boiler deck directly below. Forward and covering about a third of the deck were cabins for crew and overflow passengers and it was these which were known as the Texas. The pilot house was located atop the Texas and was ringed with windows for the pilots; it was either somewhat centered or built on the forward edge. On civilian boats, ladies and gentlemen in escorted groups were often allowed to visit the pilot house to enjoy the steamer's best view of the surrounding countryside.

Built from multiple sections of sheet iron, the smokestacks Nichols referenced above were actually known, per Mark Twain, as chimneys in everyday parlance. The pair came up through the superstructure from the forward end of the boilers below and were essential, as in the case of a fireplace, to the provision of an air supply that aided in the process of fuel combustion. These chimneys were tall, usually between 75 and 90 feet above water, and were often viewed as an aesthetic necessity.[2]

Imprecisely-built and easily repaired, the engines powering Western riverboats were of the lighter-weight, high-pressure variety rather than the low-pressure condensing engines employed elsewhere. Very fuel inefficient, the horizontally-oriented poppet-valve engines, with their relatively-small, but long, cylindrical iron boilers, were located on the main deck, and, indeed, occupied a large part of it. The boilers were, as former acting assistant paymaster E. J. Huling remembered, "provided with places where the sand and sediment from the water can be blown out at short intervals when the boat is running." Two or more engines and three or more boilers per vessel were common. The engine cylinder was about one foot to 20 inches in diameter with a three to five foot piston stroke. The fuel employed was wood or coal and given the manner of construction, with various rough approximations in valve, flue, and head fittings, the engines, particularly when overly-stoked to obtain speed or poorly maintained, were dangerous. The *Sultana* disaster of 1865 provides the worst example, but steamboat explosions were common. Later turned back into commercial craft, the tinclads *Kenwood* (14) and *Glide II* (43) were both destroyed by boiler explosions.[3]

The steamboat's power plant provided the energy to turn paddle wheels, which were uncomplicated and fairly easy to repair if damaged. True, the water thrown up with each turn was a waste of fuel, but that was not a significant concern when wood was easily available and did not detract from the restoration advantage. Obstructions, snags, logs, and ice caused much damage which could often be readily fixed by the boat's carpenters.

During the first half of the 19th century, most Western river craft were powered by side-wheels of fairly significant diameter and width (30 foot diameter and 12 foot width was common), which were mounted about one-third of the length forward from the boat's stern. These big wheels, located in special housings, were particularly helpful in steering the vessels and at those times, as was very common, when it was necessary to back out into a stream after making a bows-on landing. This was the same arrangement as was employed by steamers on the Hudson River and elsewhere in the east.

It has been recorded that side-wheel packet boats, which could also haul cargo on their main decks and in a shallow hold, were much longer on the Mississippi River than on the Ohio, while the latter tended to have their wheels located farther aft. This difference occurred because of the need for those plying between Cincinnati and the west to get through the locks of the Louisville and Portland Canal, built around the Falls of the Ohio at Louisville.

In contrast to the side-wheel boats, stern-wheelers endured a more difficult time in getting established in the years before the Civil War. They were seen as slower and harder to handle. However, rear propulsion did make significant technical gains and was beginning to win larger acceptance by operators. This trend would continue, particularly in the two decades after Appomattox. Pilots and captains, and during the war, the U.S. Navy, recognized that these rear-wheeled boats, generally smaller in size than the side-wheeled packets, offered some major rewards over their two-wheeled rivals.

Stern-wheelers were less prone to hit things in the water or to need to stop to avoid ramming floating objects. The rear wheel location offered a built in advantage to those needing to get boats off bars or over shoals. Most importantly, the removal of the propulsion wheels from the sides to the rear meant that builders, on about the same hull tonnage, could do away with the heavy side wheel houses and provide these types with greater beams, thereby lightening draft. The square-sterned boats each possessed at least three rudders, which were connected by rods "in a rude sort of way, but very strong." Approximately the same size cargo could be carried by stern-wheelers, but the craft could operate in drier seasons, earning more return. "To obtain lightness of draft in relation to tonnage and cargo capacity became the primary object of steamboat builders from an early date," wrote Louis C. Hunter in 1949, "and remained so throughout the steamboat era. The true western river steamboat was first and last a shallow-water boat."

Another advantage was a certain convenience in the use of the vessels as towboats. Instead of towing barges or other boats astern, connected by long lines (towlines), sternwheelers could lash their tows forward and push them. This practice allowed for greater control over the tows in crooked channels or swift currents.

When it came to the handling of the two different types when employed as tinclads, both had advantages. As Gary Matthews wrote in a message on the Civil War Navies Message Board:

Steamboats on the Western rivers, including those converted into light draught tinclads, were propelled by paddle wheels. The *Minnie Bay* is an example of the side-wheeler steamer configuration, with one housed paddle wheel on each side of her hull. The sternwheeler *R. R. Hudson* shipped a single wheel aft. Both craft were active on the Ohio River after the war (West Virginia State Archives).

In order for a stern-wheeler to come about in a narrow river, the pilot had to put the boat's bow or stern into the bank and then allow the current to swing the opposite end around, whereas a side-wheeler could simply go ahead on one wheel and back on the other. The independent side wheels could also be used to steer a boat if her rudder or steering ropes were damaged, which was a fairly common occurrence.

Rear Adm. Porter, when he came on the scene, definitely preferred side-wheelers, which did not employ tubular boilers. If given a choice, he would have his boats constructed new with extra-large boilers and large cylinders. As it was, he would have to take many sternwheelers not only because of their shallow draft, but because he could "put in more guns."

In short, the maxim expressed in Chapter 2 became ever more important by the summer of 1862, particularly as the river stages around the craft of the Western Flotilla declined:

"the smaller the river or the lower the stream, the lower the boat draft required." It was Flag Officer Davis and the Cairo base chief, commander Alexander M. Pennock, who would put this requirement into useable naval terms.[4]

Although credit for coming up with that germ of an idea which evolved into the light-draught Union gunboat type later known as the tinclad is usually assigned to Flag Officer Davis, the concept was actually the brainchild of two other men: Maj. Gen. Henry Halleck and Cmdr. Alexander M. Pennock. They were not initially looking to create a new class of warship, but rather to gain some additional strength on the Tennessee River.

While on Tennessee River patrol near Florence, Alabama, on April 21, the U.S.S. *Tyler*, under Lt.-Commanding William Gwin, captured the Confederate transport *Alfred Robb*, the last Rebel vessel afloat on that stream. The 86-ton *Robb*, which had been eluding the timberclads since the fall of Fort Henry in February, was a wooden-hulled stern-wheeler built at Pittsburgh, Pennsylvania, in 1860 and employed in commercial service until taken into Confederate service at some undetermined time in 1861. After administering the Federal oath to the boat's pilot, Joseph N. Smith, Gwin placed an 11-man prize crew on the vessel and renamed her *Lady Foote* in honor of his commander. Foote would find the latter action embarrassing and, as soon as he learned of the well-intentioned honor, have the *Robb*'s name restored.

"Old Brains" Henry Halleck (1815–1872) was Western theater commander until July 1862 when he was ordered to operate, principally as chief of staff, from Washington, D.C. In mid–May, Halleck had urged upon Flag Officer Davis the conversion of the captured Confederate steamer *Alfred Robb* into the first light draught gunboat for the Tennessee River. He shared with Fleet Captain Alexander Pennock the true parentage of the tinclad (*Battles and Leaders of the Civil War*, Vol. 1).

By order of Flag Officer Foote and at the urging of Maj. Gen. Halleck, who was deeply impressed by the sterling roles played by the *Tyler* and *Lexington* in the April 6 Battle of Shiloh, the two timberclads remained on the Tennessee River into May while the *Robb* was sent to Cairo for disposition.

As he continued his approach to Corinth, Halleck was informed by Lt. Gwin on May 17 that his warships would have to depart the Tennessee due to falling water. Though "Old Brains" was not pleased by this development and, in fact, asked that Gwin remain as long as it was deemed safe, he recognized that a boat with a draft much lighter than the six foot of the 420 ton sidewheeler *Tyler* or her compatriot, the 362-ton *Lexington*, was required. Writing to Gwin from his camp on the Corinth Road the same day, the west's top general stated his view simply: "I think the *Robb* should be fitted up to render us all the assistance possible on the [Tennessee] River." Halleck's message to Gwin was forwarded to Capt. Davis three days later.[5]

With the Western Flotilla now engaged in the campaign against Fort Pillow, Capt. Davis temporarily assumed its command on May 9 from the injured Flag Officer Foote. In the next week, the squadron would, as noted in Chapter 3, invest that bastion and fight an engagement with the Confederate River Defense Force at Plum Point Bend. During the remainder of the month, the ironclads and mortar boats continued to smash at Confederate defenses. While these activities occupied Davis and his sailors, Alexander M. Pennock, in his capacity of fleet captain and Cairo naval base commander, was daily attending to the myriad of administrative matters behind the lines, while attempting to keep an eye on Rebel activities in the areas of the Ohio, Tennessee, and Cumberland Rivers.

Cmdr. Pennock, who came to play an important oversight role in the counter-guerrilla activities of Lt. Cmdr. Fitch on those three named rivers, was, like Cmdr. Henry Walke, then serving farther down the Mississippi, a native of Virginia. Pennock, like Tennessee's David Farragut, remained loyal to the Union. After years at sea (1828–1859), he had served as a lighthouse inspector in New York State until plucked back into the mainstream by the Navy Department in September 1861. He was sent West with Flag Officer Foote to help oversee the construction of the Pook Turtles and to handle flotilla equipment; he became fleet captain that October. In January 1862, he took over command of the Cairo naval station. Pennock would hold his post through 1864, gaining during his

Fleet captain of the Army's Western Flotilla and the Navy's Mississippi Squadron from September 1861 to April 1865, Alexander Pennock (1814–1876) was one of the Civil War's most able administrators. Not only did he have charge of the Western navy's logistical operation, but, in the absence of his flag officer or admiral during the Vicksburg campaign, was also in charge of operations on the upper rivers. In the fall of 1862, the newly promoted Lt. Cmdr. Le Roy Fitch was made executive officer to Pennock in charge of the light draft fleets on the Ohio, Mississippi, and Cumberland Rivers. Pennock largely allowed Fitch autonomy in guarding those rivers, sending in occasional reports (Library of Congress).

tenure "a reputation as one of the best wartime executives of the navy." While serving at Cairo, Pennock, who brought his wife out to be with him, lived in quarters on the receiving ship, where he frequently enjoyed the company of junior officers and visitors at dinner. His friend and colleague Quartermaster George D. Wise would confide to Flag Officer Foote at the end of July 1862 that Pennock "is a good officer for equipment and repairs, and his health is suffering from continued residence in this part of the country."[6]

Among Pennock's responsibilities was supervision of the construction, outfitting, and supply of new or captured warships and the repair, outfitting, and supply of others. Thus it was that the *Alfred Robb* came into his care when she arrived at the Cairo river base from up the Tennessee. In a May 21 letter to Davis, the fleet captain advised "in accordance with the suggestion of General Halleck in his letter of May 17, I shall prepare the *Robb* so as to protect her pilothouse, etc., against rifle shots from the shore." The next day, the Western Flotilla chief, who had received Pennock's report by a swift dispatch boat, replied that the "fitting up" of the *Robb,* as she was sometimes known, was all right.

On June 3, Cmdr. Pennock again communicated with his distant chief in one of a series of detail-laden reports he would compose on what was often called "general matters." In addition to a variety of miscellaneous flotilla detail, the fleet captain explained that the renovation of the *Robb* was well underway. "She will carry four howitzers," he wrote, "and be well supplied with small arms, etc." For protection, the Cairo man revealed that he had ordered a "bullet-proof bulkhead around her forecastle and also iron-plated the pilot house." Lt.-Commanding Gwin, who originally captured her, thought that the new little light draft gunboat would be "equal to any emergency that may occur." A total of 30 officers and men would be detailed to the boat, under the command of First Master Jason Goudy, who commanded the prize crew that returned the craft to Illinois from Alabama waters in May. That evening, acting under Pennock's orders, the *Alfred Robb* departed Cairo for Pittsburg Landing on the Tennessee River. Master Goudy would be expected to employ his rebuilt craft, in actuality the first tinclad, to protect Union interests in the considerably more shallow stream.[7]

"Tinclad" was a misnomer born of the popular press and the need in some quarters to differentiate the small, shallow-bottomed, swift, and lightly armed boats from the larger, ponderous ironclads and monitors. Tinclads, of which the *Alfred Robb* was the first, were not clad in tin. Although most of the seventy-six riverboats remodeled into this heterogenous group had some light protection, mostly metal, several, like Master Goudy's command, had wooden bulkheads and only some iron for protection. For compactness of location, let us here complete our review of the weapons system that will dominate the remainder of this book, the U.S. Navy light draught.

The light draught river gunboats called tinclads were all converted from former merchant boats, some brand new. No two of the vessels were exactly alike and photographs do not exist for most of them. Of the 76 total, 49 were stern-wheelers chosen, like the *Alfred Robb,* for their capabilities in shallow streams; the other 23 were highly-maneuverable side-wheelers. Le Roy Fitch would command both types, though his favorite and flagboat, the U.S.S. *Moose,* was a stern-wheeler. As a whole, the group averaged 150–175 feet in length and carried between six and eight cannon, mostly brass howitzers.[8]

The success of the *Alfred Robb's* makeover, coupled with the fiasco of the White River expedition, caused Flag Officer Davis to put into writing the Western Flotilla's need for light draught gunboats. In a missive famous in the annals of tinclad history and directed to the Navy secretary, the river commander wrote:

> Our recent experience in the navigation of the White River has made it apparent that in order to acquire control of the tributaries of the Mississippi, and to maintain that control during the dry season, it will be necessary to fit up immediately some boats of small draft for this special purpose. These boats will be sufficiently protected about the machinery and pilot houses against musketry. They will be selected for their light draft and their capacity to receive a suitable armament of howitzers, field pieces, or other light guns, and to accommodate the requisite number of men; and, finally, for their susceptibility of protection.

Davis ventured a guess, in his opinion to the cabinet officer, that boats could be had for between $8,000 and $10,000 apiece, provided, of course, that their purchase was entrusted to an officer or someone who knew how to obtain the most for the department's money. A copy of the letter was also sent to Quartermaster General Montgomery C. Meigs in hopes that it would be taken seriously and considered by War Secretary Edwin Stanton, who still controlled the purse strings of the Western gunboat squadron. For comparison purposes, it might be noted that the least expensive Union river ironclad was the U.S.S. *Chillicothe*: $92,960.

A week later, from the Vicksburg vicinity, the flag officer again wrote to Welles, providing a brief overview of the recent White River expedition, which closed with the strong suggestion that:

> If it is the intention of the Government to make use of the rivers as a means of communication, I will venture again to suggest that it can only be done by means of suitable vessels of small draft lightly, but sufficiently protected against rifle muskets.

While the Western Flotilla awaited word from Washington on permission to begin creation of a light draught fleet, Davis and Pennock pushed ahead with the renovation of the former Confederate vessels *Little Rebel* and *General Pillow*, both of which reached Cairo in July. When the Mississippi Squadron ordered numbers painted on the pilothouses of its tinclads in June 1862, the former would become Tinclad 16 and the latter Tinclad 20. The other Memphis-captured Rebel gunboats, *General Bragg* and *General Sterling Price*, were also turned into gunboats, but they were not classified as tinclads.[9]

Following the initial depression in trade caused by Fort Sumter and Rebel activities in 1861, the traffic in Union civilian steamboat services on the upper Mississippi and its tributaries gradually resumed beginning in the spring of 1862. Not only was it relatively safe, but for navigation hazards and Confederate guerrillas, for boats to visit Nashville or Memphis, but hundreds were chartered by the U.S. government to support its western armies. Into the logistical pipeline served by both river and rail, but served best bulk-wise by the former, were pumped all manner of necessities from troops and their animals to arms and munitions, food, medicines, equipment, forage to wounded Yankee soldiers, Confederate POWs, men on leave, captured goods and equipment, refugees, and various kinds of seized contraband, the most contentious cargo of all.

Brig. Gen. Joseph G. Totten had prepared an informational memorandum for use by the U.S. government in June 1861 which indicated that 400 passenger steamers were unemployed and available for hire on the Ohio River and at St. Louis and these were now put onto the payroll as quickly as possible. The steamer bottoms required to handle the massive increase in river business in 1862–1863 was significantly more than was available. New riverboats were built by private investors and even the government. One newspaper reported about the time that Flag Officer Davis was seeking support for the acquisition of light draughts:

Mound City was a construction site which also served as a repair facility and supply depot for the Union's growing western navy. It would outlast Cairo as a naval station, not being closed until the mid–1870s (*Miller's Photographic History of the Civil War*).

> The mania at present is for investment in floating property. Everybody wants an interest in a steamboat. We learn of many happy possessors of cash in sums of from one hundred dollars up, who eagerly desire to be steamboat owners. Youth and men who hardly ever saw a steamboat are tremblingly eager to invest.

Riverfront shipyards, primarily along the Ohio River, but on other streams as well, which were idle in late 1861 were a year later working at full capacity. The principal boatbuilding facilities on the Ohio River were Pittsburgh, Wheeling, Virginia (later West Virginia), Cincinnati; Madison and New Albany, Indiana, and Mound City, Illinois. Evansville, Indiana, Carondelet, Missouri, and other riverbank communities all had men engaged in construction or its equally necessary three–R'ed cousin, repair, renovation, and refitting. The first five cities were also noted for the building or repair of steamboat engines. Louis Hunter, quoting the *Cincinnati Gazette* of June 13, 1863, notes that in the spring of 1863, a total of 105 steamboats were abuilding on the Ohio between just Pittsburgh and Wheeling.

These boats, including several which would be turned into tinclads, became a hot and expensive commodity. Those with stock in new construction made fortunes while those with new craft to sell also did extremely well. "So great was the demand for any kind of bottoms that steamboats six or eight years old, or older, which normally would have been destined only for the breaking-up yard brought prices close to or even equally their original cost." Those private companies or persons who owned the boats could liquidate their entire costs in several months of government service or in six or eight safely made trips down and up river.[10]

The gentleman who was initially tasked with answering Flag Officer Davis' plea of June 28 for "an officer of judgment and experience" to purchase and equip the light draught fleet was Capt., soon Cdr., Joseph B. Hull, who had been in the U.S. Navy since 1813. Hull was named by Secretary Welles as superintendent of gunboat construction at St. Louis in May, but would not take up his post until summer. The aged sailor, who spent most of his 47 nautical years on sea duty, would be assisted by Naval Constructor Edward Hartt, who was sent out from the New York Navy Yard. Hartt would actually superintend the work "in all matters pertaining to the hull, cladding, equipment, and accommodations," making certain that all work was done and inspected in conformity with the let contracts and certify bills for payment.

That we may finish the tinclad creation story, we must move ahead in time beyond the strict operational chronology which might at this point be expected.

Upon his return from his June–July visit to Vicksburg, Flag Officer Davis received a telegram from Cdr. Hull on August 12 indicating that a pair of good new boats was located not far from his St. Louis office. If Davis wanted them, the construction boss was inclined to purchase. They drew 18 and 20 inches, respectively and could be quickly fitted up for service.

On August 15, the flag officer sent Hull a formal response via Quartermaster George Wise. Wise had agreed to drop it off and to discuss with Hull the Davis recommendations, which Wise supported, for the purchase of the two steamers to be used in the anti-partisan war. If Hull and Wise could fully agree on the qualities and Hull was authorized, under Davis' sanction, that of Wise, or whomever, the gain would "render valuable aid to the public service." From his Cairo office, the navy chief wrote his belief that neither boat should cost more than $10,000 each as they stood, "without the removal of anything belonging to them whatsoever."

In the same communication, Flag Officer Davis went on to indicate that Fleet Captain Pennock, who had already outfitted the *Alfred Robb* and *Little Rebel*, had the plans "for strengthening and protecting these vessels in a manner suited to the service" anticipated for them. Also during the day, Davis held a long and productive meeting in his Cairo office with Naval Constructor Hartt. The two talked exclusively on the topic of light draught design and renovation per the Pennock model, which included provision that the cabins be left on and light protections. Davis was completely convinced that Hartt left possessed of "all of the information I can give him on the subject." The flag officer reiterated his urgent want for the vessels, needed to aid in the "suppression of the guerrilla warfare now raging on the Upper Ohio and Tennessee."

Four days later, on August 19, the flag officer was shocked to receive a message from Capt. Wise indicating that, while Hull intended to purchase the steamers, he was planning major changes to them. These included putting the officers' apartments below and protecting the boilers and machinery with double six-foot high bulkheads filled with coal and lightly plated. Davis wrote Hull bluntly:

> My plans were founded upon a knowledge of the manner in which guerrilla warfare is conducted on the banks of the rivers. I trust that in the preparation of these vessels for the service for which at the moment they are so urgently required, no speculative notions are to supplant views founded upon actual experience of war and that these vessels be fitted in the manner I have requested.

The two vessels in question were refurbished at Carondelet, Missouri, in the manner Flag Officer Davis requested. They would be delivered as U.S.S. *Brilliant*, later No. 18, and U.S.S. *St. Clair*, No. 19.[11]

Meanwhile, on September 9, Cdr. Hull informed Fleet Capt. Pennock that authority had been received for the purchase of five more light draughts to be "fitted as Commodore Davis desires for the river service." In his September 12 response, the fleet captain provided the most complete published description of the manner in which Davis and he wished these tinclads worked up. It is worth reviewing the salient parts of that report here with comments on actual practice.

First, it was imperative that the boats be of the lightest draft possible. They were to be armed with a pair of 24-pounder and a pair of 23-pounder or four 12-pounder brass howitzers, an armament which would later be augmented at the request of Lt. Cmdr. Le Roy Fitch. Each howitzer was manned by eight men plus a powder boy or "monkey." Later heavier cannon were placed at the bow, where they proved superior to the short range howitzers; indeed, one veteran of the U.S.S. *Hastings*, No. 15, remembered them as "the only effective guns." Those employed were usually either 32-pounder smoothbores, 9-inch Dahlgrens, or 30-pounder rifled Parrots.

It was important that the engines and boilers be safeguarded against light fieldpieces and the space between them against Minie rifle balls. The shielding was to be carried up 10 to 11 feet from the main deck, which was to be used as the gun deck and which was therefore strengthened to accommodate the extra weight of cannon. Protection was to be sufficiently high as to prevent Rebel troops from firing between it and the hurricane deck from their roosts on high banks. In general, this meant that an enclosed 5-inch thick wooden casemate made of planking, vertical on the sides and usually sloping at the bow and perhaps the stern, was constructed.

In the early 1990s, divers from R. Christopher Goodwin and Associates, working with the Tennessee Division of Archaeology and the private Raise the Gunboats foundation, examined the suspected wrecks of the U.S.S. *Key West* and *Tawah* off the former Tennessee River port of Johnsonville. Their research suggested that, in general, tinclad casemates were unsophisticated structures, with walls constructed of 6-inch planks of various widths, which "merely enclosed the main deck without substantially altering the form of the upper works." Prefabricated sections of the casemates, built in whole or in part to the required specifications of individual vessels, could be bolted into the existing boiler deck structures. In order to lighten ship to make repairs or get over obstacles, light draught captains could, among other measures, simply order their casemates, or parts of them, unbolted and held aboard an accompanying barge until reshipped.

Once a tinclad's casemate was constructed and hung, sheets of ½-inch to 1-inch boiler plate were then riveted to its forward part and on each side adjacent to the engines. Rear Adm. Porter later wrote that his light draughts were "well-protected, except in the hull, with an inch of iron all around the boilers, and an inch in the bulwarks abreast and in front of the boilers, making two inches of iron and eight inches of wood, besides the coal." Gunports were mounted in the front and cannon ports on the sides.

The thickness of the metal protection on the enclosed casemate gave the ship type its nickname of tinclad. Everyone seemed to appreciate almost from the start that these craft were not ironclads; they could not battle shore batteries, heavy field artillery, or other warships or rams. If they did get into a serious fight, casualties aboard might be high. A veteran of the *Naiad*, No. 53, remembered: "This kind of a gunboat was ingeniously contrived so that, while a solid shot would go clear through it, taking only what came in its way, a shell would be carefully and safely nursed on the covered deck until it fully exploded." Acting Assistant Surgeon William Howard of the *Brilliant*, No. 18, asserted in a letter home: "We have no protection and a musket ball would be about as dangerous as a 6-pounder. In fact, these boats are ... mantraps."

If, to preserve light draft, it became necessary to take off a portion of the cabin, Pennock cautioned, Davis desired that at least four rooms on a side be retained, in addition to the small apartment usually found at a commercial boat's stern, for use by the captain and officers. If the required draft could be obtained by placing the quarters amidships, then Hull was to have that done while also fitting up a pair of small rooms on each side of the gun deck. In general, protection for these quarters was minimal, usually about ½-inch of wood. A guard or gallery surrounded the officers' quarters, upon which doors opened from the staterooms. The quarterdeck was located forward of the officers' quarters and here the officer of the watch was stationed. The location received minimal protection during the day from a box built about breast high along the edges and stuffed full of the enlisted crew's hammocks.

In general practice, the Texas, if present, was removed along with the civilian pilothouse; a new and heavily protected (iron plate backed by thick wood) pilothouse was located atop the second deck. Beginning on June 19, 1863, numbers were painted on the tinclad pilot houses, each the approximate height of a man.

In any event, whether retrofitting stern-wheelers or side-wheelers, Hull was to be certain that all officers' quarters were located on the upper decks of the boats and that their main boiler decks be kept "clear of everything except the battery." To help accommodate the changing out of cannon, swinging doors were to be located at each end of the casemated gundeck so that "artillery can be taken on board at one end and off at the other." In fact, the boiler and gun decks also housed the crew, which slept in hammocks slung from hooks in the overhead deck timbers, their galley, and coal used to fuel the boilers. The ammunition magazine and storerooms, or lockers, were in the hold, nearly below the waterline. All decks and internal portions of the vessels were reinforced wherever possible with extra timbers and beams.

"In action," wrote E. J. Huling in 1881, "all the officers and crew were stationed below, excepting the pilots and the commander, with a single aide, who were in the pilot house." From the pilot house, the tinclad's captain could see what was transpiring and relay orders through a speaking pipe to the executive officer on the gundeck, who, in turn, relayed the commands to the men. We would be remiss if we did not digress for a few sentences to acknowledge the role of tinclad pilots.

As was the case since before the time Mark Twain learned the piloting craft from the famous "Mr. [Horace] Bixby," the riverboat pilot was, in the words of Flag Officer Davis, "an essential, intrinsic, and indispensable part of the ship's complement." The navy chief, who thought so highly of these men as to recommend to his superiors that those serving the Western Flotilla all be made officers, went on to point out that "no one ever takes the wheel on board of a Western steamboat for a moment except the pilot, such is our dependence upon them ... they always remain attached to a vessel, and the latter never moves without them at any time." James Edwin Campbell, later governor of Ohio, recalled from his time on the U.S.S. *Naiad* the lot of the tinclad pilots:

> The only men who knew their business were the pilots to whose indispensable service, cheerfully rendered, justice has never been done. The pilot house was known as the "slaughter-pen" and on the tinclads—upon which it was my unhappy lot to serve—it was preeminently the post of danger. It was a matter of history that they freely volunteered for this perilous service knowing that they would be targets for every sharpshooter on the bank, and it was not unusual for a single shell to wound or kill both pilots and to blow the steering wheel in their hands into a thousand fragments; yet they were poorly paid and never had either rank or rating as officers of the navy, nor a recognized share in the Memory of its glories.[12]

The already-mentioned Confederate attempt to undermine Northern logistical efforts with irregular tactics was launched due to a keen understanding of Napoleon's maxim that any army "lives off its stomach." During the U.S. Civil War, as in most conflicts, there were really only two ways in which the invading force could handle its physical hunger: forage within occupied territory or live off its own communication lines, setting up supply dumps and depots en route. Foraging could work during short enterprises, such as the Southern forays into Maryland, Pennsylvania, Indiana and Ohio, but could serve only as a supplement to need during sustained efforts like that 1862–1863 Union effort which culminated with victory at Vicksburg.

During the War Between the States, a variety of mathematical formulas was developed in an effort to determine how much transport capability was required to deliver necessary supplies to every fighting man and animal. Each of these was based on the provision of a fixed depot, at a river landing or railhead.

Several methods of transport were available to the opposing forces in 1861–1865. First among these was the six horse- or mule-drawn wagon, each of which could carry up to one ton of goods. Using one formula, the supply of a 100,000 man army, with its attached cavalry and artillery, ten days out from its supply base "would be computed at 10,975 wagons utilizing 68,850 draft animals." Additionally, wagons often broke down and forage for the animals had to be transported in the same vehicles, thereby cutting down on space available for supplies. Obviously, something better was required or required in combination.

Railroad trains, of which the Union possessed an abundance in the area north of the Mason-Dixon line, offered significant bulk delivery advantages over wagons and were, wrote Alan Aronson, the "optimal" method of supply delivery. They could haul large amounts of supply over land which frequently corresponded to an army's advance route and could do so in a timely fashion. They made it much easier to open or expand large supply depots, such as the one at Johnsonville, Tennessee, on the Tennessee River. On the other hand, and particularly during the period we are discussing here, railways everywhere were vulnerable to natural obstructions and weather. Many were single-track lines which could accommodate only so many trains daily. Additionally, creeks and gullies had to be bridged, viaducts maintained, track laid and repaired, tunnels cut, and rockslides cleared. Added to these worries were Confederate marauders, mostly mounted. "Ripping up railroad tracks and bringing down bridges," Lawrence M. Smith wrote recently, "became prime military missions during the Civil War." Still, every flatcar could transport at least two wagons (and other such gear as could be fitted aboard). Mathematicians calculated that, with efficient rolling stock available properly loaded, "a single railroad could accumulate provisions for an army of 300,000 to 400,000 for four to five days within a 24-hr. period."

Water transport was the most efficient way for the North to move supplies in large quantities. This was particularly true in the Western theater where roads and railroads were both fewer and highly exposed to Rebel action or the whims of nature. One Ohio River steamboat, it was estimated, could carry 500 tons of cargo, which translated into sufficient rations and forage for a 40,000 man army and 18,000 animals. Two hundred and fifty wagons or 125 rail flatcars would be needed to haul the same amount. For the fiscal year ending July 30, 1863, Capt. Charles Parsons presented a comparison on the use of the rivers and railroads in handling subsistence, ordnance, medical, and quartermaster stores: by railroad, 193,023 troops and 153,102,100 pounds of goods; by river, 135,989 troops and 337,912,363 pounds of goods.

Tennessee's two great rivers did not show complete favor to the invader because, due to geography and navigational hazards, they were only navigable so far south and were, at their closest point, at least 12 miles apart. During parts of the year, both were too low to permit heavy traffic. Below Nashville, Yankee troops had to march or take the train; between Nashville and Johnsonville to the west, goods could flow by road or rail. Sometimes, as at Chattanooga in 1863, pack mules meant salvation. Without water access, other less efficient transport modes had to be employed, but whenever possible, rivers were preferred. As Maj. Gen. William T. Sherman put it, "I am never easy with a railroad which takes a whole army to guard, every foot of rail being essential to the whole; whereas they can't stop the Tennessee [he was writing about that stream in the source for this quote] and each boat can make its own game." Wagon trains and railway trains could be captured, destroyed, or delayed by roving soldiers; steamships were seldom stopped save by nature or fairly heavy field cannon.[13]

The Mississippi River tributaries the Ohio, Tennessee, and Cumberland were natural highways leading straight into the heart of the Confederacy, with Nashville on the Cumberland becoming the Union's greatest supply depot. Other riverfront logistical centers, including those at Memphis and Johnsonville, were established along the other streams, but Tennessee's capital remained the Union's greatest Western supply hub throughout the war. As the remainder of this book will be concerned with actions on those three rivers, let us here provide certain background about them and the communities along their banks, some of it compiled by Le Roy Fitch himself.

The Ohio River begins at the confluence of the Allegheny and Monongahela rivers at the Point in downtown Pittsburgh and flows 981 miles to join the Mississippi at Cairo, Illinois. It flows through or along the borders of six states, and its watershed encompasses 14 states. The Ohio carries the largest volume of water of any upper tributary of the Mississippi. In fact, it typically carries a much greater volume of water than the upper Mississippi.

From Pittsburgh, the Ohio flows to the northwest through western Pennsylvania before making an abrupt, almost 180 degree, turn to the south-southwest at the state line with West

Virginia (Virginia until 1863), where it then forms the border between that state and Ohio. The stream then follows a roughly southwestern and then western course between Ohio, Indiana, Illinois, and Kentucky until it joins the Mississippi from the east at Cairo. At its mouth, the Ohio is wider than the Mississippi itself. In 1863, the Ohio, at low water, had an average depth of 30 inches over the bars, most of which were sandy and not dangerous.

Interestingly, the original Virginia charter went not to the middle of the Ohio River, but to its far shore so the entire river was included. Wherever the river serves as a boundary between states—Kentucky and Virginia, now West Virginia, on the south and Ohio, Indiana, Illinois and Kentucky, also on the south, the river essentially belongs to the two states on the south that were later divided from Virginia. Due to its role as a natural geographic dividing line between North and South, the Ohio River was earlier seen as the watery stripe dividing free states and slave states.

In addition to Pittsburgh and Cairo, the Ohio River has a number of historic communities along its banks. Those in Virginia (now West Virginia) include, in alphabetical order, Huntington, New Martinsville, Paden City, Parkersburg, Weirton, and Wheeling. Also to the south, in Kentucky, we have Ashland, Brandenburg, Caseyville, Concordia, Covington, Henderson, Lewisport, Louisville, Newport, Owensboro, Paducah (with a population of 4,000 in 1863), Smithland, Stephensport, Uniontown. Louisville, 369 miles from the mouth of the Ohio, was founded at the only major natural navigational barrier on the river, the Falls of the Ohio. These were a series of rapids where the river flowed over hard, fossil-rich limestone beds. The first Ohio River locks were built here before the Civil War to circumnavigate the falls; the Louisville and Portland Canal was 2.5 miles long, 50 feet wide, and its lock could pass a boat through which was 180 feet long and 49.7 feet wide. The Cumberland Bar, near Smithland, marked the mouth of the Cumberland River.

To the north in Ohio, the riverbank towns include Belpre, Cincinnati (the "Queen City"), Gallipolis, Ironton, Marietta, Pomeroy, and Steubenville. In Indiana, Amsterdam (now New Amsterdam), Clarksville, Derby Landing (now Derby), Enterprise, Evansville (with a direct rail line to Indianapolis), Fredonia, Grandview, Jeffersonville (terminus of the Jeffersonville and Indianapolis Railroad), Leavenworth, Madison (terminus for the Madison and Indianapolis Railroad), Mauckport, Mount Vernon, New Albany, Rockport, Rome, Tell City, and Troy are the leading Ohio River communities while those in Illinois are Brookport, Elizabethtown, Golconda, Metropolis (with a population of 400 in 1863), Mound City, home of the naval base, and Shawneetown. The distance from Cincinnati to Cairo by steamer in 1861 was 550.7 miles.[14]

The Tennessee River is the largest tributary of the Ohio River. It is approximately 650 miles (1,046 kilometers) long, covers 41,000 square miles, and drains portions of 60 Tennessee counties and seven states. It is formed at the confluence of the Holston and French Broad Rivers on the east side of Knoxville. From Knoxville, it flows southwest toward Chattanooga before crossing into Alabama. The Flint and Elk Rivers enter at the great bend of the river as it loops through north Alabama, eventually forming a small part of the state's border with Mississippi, before returning to the Volunteer State. Flowing north again through the Western Tennessee Valley, the Duck River (fed by the Buffalo River) enters south of New Johnsonville (the original Johnsonville was lost to the Tennessee Valley Authority dams of the 1930s), while the Big Sandy River joins not far from Paris Landing. The final part of the Tennessee's run is in Kentucky, where it flows into the Ohio River at Paducah, some 12 miles west of the mouth of the Cumberland River. In 1863, the Tennessee River averaged about 1,420 feet in width. The wooded banks were mostly flat and overflowed at high water. High hills were situated about 1–2 miles back of the banks.

Of the three rivers discussed here, the Tennessee saw the least use by antebellum steamboat companies. Two huge natural obstructions gave those who employed the river considerable pause and halted others from considering the prospect. A huge 30-mile long gorge cut through Walden's Ridge at Chattanooga while, in North Alabama the Foot of Big Muscle, the Muscle Shoals, began a half mile beyond Florence. This was a series of obstructions almost 40 miles long. It was made up of shifting gravel bars, rapids, snags, rock reefs, and a narrow channel which often fatally wounded boats. Of the Foot or head of navigation, Le Roy Fitch in 1863 wrote that "only four foot at the highest stages of water [was] ever known." During the war, Union gunboats were forced to guard the Tennessee River, above and below Muscle Shoals, because the great river could be readily crossed by Confederates in many spots.

The Duck River Sucks, 134 miles from the mouth of the river, were considered very dangerous due to its extremely crooked channel and the strong current over its rocks. At low water, these shoals were considered by Fitch to be "one of the most favorable places for locating a battery on the river." This and the other named natural obstacles played such a significant role in Northern river naval strategy that, when Admiral Porter divided the rivers under his command up into districts in 1863, he created two districts to cover the Tennessee, one above Muscle Shoals and one below.

The Tennessee River as far as the Muscle Shoals at Florence, Alabama, has a number of historic communities along its banks, though not as many large towns as are found along the huge Ohio. These, with 1863 populations as provided by Lt. Cmdr. Fitch, include: in Kentucky, Paducah (population 4000), Birmingham (population 200), Aurora, and Callowaytown (disappeared by 1870). Locations of interest in Tennessee include Pine Bluff, Buffalo Landing, Paris Landing, New Portland, Reynoldsburg, Fowler's Landing, Perryville and East Perryville (population 30), Marvin's Bluffs, Brownsport, Cedar Creek, Decatur, Carrollville, Clifton (population 300), Point Pleasant, Cerro Gordo, Coffee's Landing, Savannah (population 500), Pittsburgh Landing, and Big Bend Landing. Eastport was the major Mississippi community on the river in the 1860s. Alabama towns include Chickasaw, Waterloo, Tuscumbia, and Florence (population of 1,000).[15]

The 687-mile long Cumberland River miles starts in Letcher County in eastern Kentucky on the Cumberland Plateau and flows southeast before crossing into northern Tennessee; it then curves back up into western Kentucky, running parallel as it does with the Tennessee River. It drains an 18,000 square mile watershed and runs north into the Ohio River at Smithland, Kentucky. The Lower Cumberland, which winds through highland valleys and ridges, runs 192 miles from Smithland to Nashville and has an average width of 600 to 700 feet. Burnside, 358 river miles above Nashville, was the head of low-water navigation on the Upper Cumberland. The Cumberland Valley between Burnside and Carthage, Tennessee, is about a mile to a mile and a half wide, with the river varying in width from 550 to 600 feet. At the time of the Civil War, the river banks were "generally very thickly wooded with heavy hills overlooking the banks." When the Cumberland began to fall, "the water recedes so fast that there is great danger to being caught," wrote Lt. Cmdr. Fitch in 1863. The stream frequently rose and fell "with such rapidity that a difference of from eight to twelve feet in 24 hours" was "of no uncommon occurrence."

At Carthage, above which the tinclads did not travel, the valley and the river widen south into the Central Basin, and the river eventually re-enters the Highland Rim about 14 miles below Nashville. Steamboat navigation on the Upper Cumberland was confined to the higher water periods from December through May. In 1863, the river, according to Lt. Cmdr. Fitch, averaged about 600 feet in width "inside the trees" which lined its banks.

At least 10 major shoals obstructed the Lower Cumberland, with the most challenging being the 4.3 mile long obstacle formed of gravel bars and rocky ledges and collectively known as Harpeth Shoals. In the early 1860s, boats had "great difficulty" getting above Harpeth Shoals, about 160 miles from the mouth and 35 miles from Nashville. At low water, the Cumberland River was not navigable for boats drawing over 15 inches, that being the average depth of Harpeth Shoals. The Upper Cumberland between Carthage and Burnside was impeded at low water by 16 shoals and bars. At almost any time, the river became very narrow in making the turns and frequently boats got very much broken up," Fitch reported in 1863. "In making the trip to Carthage," he continued," boats frequently are compelled to lower their smokestacks and then suffer much from having their upper works much broken up by the branches of trees." In the summer, naval coverage of the Cumberland was all but impossible. Fitch observed that the stream was "so low during the summer and the bars so frequent and close as to prevent an effectual patrol, even had we all the boats for it alone."

Among the towns and cities on the Cumberland River in Tennessee and Kentucky between Carthage and Smithland which may be mentioned in our narrative are the following: in Tennessee, Ashland City (near the head of Harpeth Shoals, some 33 miles below Nashville), Betsytown (at the foot of Harpeth Shoals), Carthage, Clarksville (a major port due to Harpeth Shoals, which blocked access to Nashville below at low water), Cumberland City, Dover (near Fort Donelson) Gallatin, Gratton, Lebanon, Nashville, Palmyra, Rome, Watkins; in Kentucky, Canton (where the Cumberland River conflict began on Oct. 18, 1861, in a skirmish between Col. Nathan B. Forrest and the U.S.S. *Conestoga*), Rockcastle, Eddyville (site of a large Union supply depot), Eureka, Iuka, Kuttawa, Pickneyville, Smithland, which was something of a boomtown during the conflict, and Woodville.

Lt. Cmdr. Fitch gave his superior (and us) few notes as to his impressions of these towns, the most important of which were Nashville ("The Star of the Cumberland"), Clarksville (today, the state's fifth largest town), and Smithland ("the first town on the bluff," located a mile upstream from the mouth of the Cumberland). He did, however, note, in a March 17, 1863, review of the river itself that:

> Palmyra, between Donelson and Clarksville, and Beatstown [Betsytown] Landing, at Harpeth Shoals, are the most noted guerrilla haunts. I have burned and destroyed all the stores or houses near the shoals frequented by guerrillas.[16]

Upon his delivery of the *General Sterling Price* to Cairo, Lt.-Commanding Le Roy Fitch disappeared from the operational naval record for approximately a month, during which time he was undoubtedly granted leave to visit Logansport. During his absence, the Union's guerrilla problem intensified. A major target was the Louisville & Nashville Railroad, a 186-mile, single-track span which ran south from the Ohio River perpendicular to a number of rivers, including the Cumberland. The three-year old L & N, built mostly through demanding border state countryside, featured many long bridges and trestles. "Few railroads," wrote historian Bennett H. Young, "were ever built that offered better facilities for destruction by cavalry raids." It was from February into July a target of a daring cavalry leader whom Fitch would face in 12 months—John Hunt Morgan. Due to the fragility of the railroads in the

Five. Tinclads, Logistics and Rivers

Nashville region, particularly the L & N artery to the north, the Ohio River and its Cumberland River connection were now seen as the Union Army's principal Western logistical chain inland of the Mississippi. Protecting this route would soon fall squarely upon the shoulders of the Indiana sailor.[17]

While he was in Indiana, however, two other developments, which would both also soon impact the Hoosier, occurred on July 16. On that date, the U.S. Congress passed important legislation affecting the naval establishment. By Public Law 152, *An Act to Establish and Equalize the Grades of Line Officers of the United States Navy*, the whole matter of rank for line officers, which was a problem for some time, was cleared up. Nine officer grades were authorized, which were relative in rank to those in the U.S. Army, including that of rear admiral (replacing flag officer; equal to major general), lieutenant commander (replacing lieutenant commanding; equal to major), and ensign (replacing master; equal to second lieutenant). The legislation set up a new pay scale and rationalized the rank equivalencies between army and navy officers. The same day, Public Law 154, in just two paragraphs, transferred the Western Flotilla from the War Department to the Navy Department (effective October 1).[18]

CHAPTER SIX

Guerrillas and the Nashville Lifeline, August–December 1862

WHEN LE ROY FITCH, NEWLY-APPOINTED to the rank of Lieutenant Commander, returned to the Western Flotilla base at Cairo, Illinois, from leave at the end of July 1862, he found that almost no change in ground positions between the Union and Confederate field armies had occurred in the squadron's operational area in his absence. On the other hand, combat, in many locations, had largely degenerated into a highly vehement low intensity conflict between Rebel guerrilla-raiders and Northern forces.

While Maj. Gen. Don Carlos Buell and Gen. Braxton Bragg maneuvered, irregular warfare throughout the entire Mississippi region grew even more intense than that experienced by Col. Graham Newell Fitch in Arkansas. During July, both of those famous Rebel raiders, Brig. Gen. John Hunt Morgan and Brig. Gen. Nathan Bedford Forrest, unleashed mounted and costly large scale cavalry attacks on Northern logistical targets, principally railroads supporting Buell's crawl toward Chattanooga or Yankee re-supply into Nashville from Louisville. Meanwhile, local partisans and guerrillas, working behind the lines, co-operated with these and other CSA cavalry units in mounting attacks on Yankee lines of communications. Simultaneously, they also furnished the regulars with sanctuaries and bases, intelligence, food, horses, forage, and manpower.

In Tennessee, Federal patience with what historian Stephen Ash has called "the unabating hostility and stiff-necked defiance manifested by Middle Tennesseans," came to an end. Military governor Andrew Johnson, who assumed his post earlier in the year believing that his fellow citizens had been tricked into rebellion by traitorous leaders and that a policy of benevolent governance would bring the "erring and misguided" people to their senses and back to the Union, was disabused of this considerate notion within months of his Nashville arrival. Maj. Gen. Buell, who had ordered his occupation forces to govern with tolerance and restraint, was equally disillusioned. The guerrillas were not a few hardcore infiltrators from outside the region; they were homegrown. Those who ambushed Union personnel "were men and boys who killed by night and hid among their kinfolk and neighbors by day." The support given them, for the most part, was not coerced but freely provided. The attempt to win these people to the Union by forbearance and even some good deeds did not succeed; the policy, which Rear Adm. David Dixon Porter later called one of "milk and water," was replaced with harshness.

One of the first tactics employed by Federal authorities in Tennessee in the counterguerrilla conflict was the same as that announced by Graham Newell Fitch in Arkansas. Per an edict published far and wide from the office of Governor Johnson and from the headquarters of what became the Army of the Cumberland, Tennesseans were informed that attacks on Union soldiers or supply lines would have significant consequences. In the neighborhoods (approximate or specific) where assaults occurred, Yankee troops would march in, take suspected leaders, sympathizers, or wealthy supporters into custody, and demand payment for damages. If payment was not forthcoming, the property of the detainees could be confiscated or buildings (homes, stores, barns, etc.) destroyed. As we shall see, the U.S. Navy adopted this same policy. Historians like Ash have suggested that this form of brutal civilian treatment, coupled with other similar policies such as sympathizer banishment or the arrest of guerrilla family members, somewhat defused the irregular war. If so, that was in the distant future. In the summer of 1862, as would be the case for another two years, the lands transversed by the Ohio, Cumberland, and Tennessee Rivers were not only battlegrounds for uniformed armies, but "a turbulent arena of civil strife where every man and woman was a combatant, every neighborhood a battleground."

When the Army's Western Flotilla became the Navy's Mississippi Squadron in October 1862, it also received a new leader, the colorful David Dixon Porter (1813–1891). Porter not only endorsed the tinclad concept, but expanded the number of available light draughts. He divided his command into districts, retaining Lt. Cmdr. Fitch in that which encompassed the Ohio, Cumberland, and Tennessee Rivers. Like Davis, Porter largely took reports from the Logansport sailor and seldom interfered in his operations, providing behind-the-scenes support when Fitch's convoy methods were challenged by U.S. Army officers. After the war, Porter appointed Fitch an instructor at the U.S. Naval Academy and later spoke highly of the "gallant officer" in his histories and other writings (Library of Congress).

Morgan, "the Thunderbolt of the Confederacy," in his 1,000-mile, July 4–28 "First Kentucky Raid," successfully disrupted the Yankee timetable for moving troops south, while gaining supplies of his own and boosting local Rebel sentiments. Over $1 million in damage was caused to Federal property and over a thousand bluecoated prisoners were taken. The cavalry chief at this time won the derisive Yankee title of "guerrilla," even though his stated purpose was not to attack individuals or private property indiscriminately. Until his death in Greeneville, Tennessee, in 1864, Morgan would always hate that "foul aspersion."

Morgan's activities in the Bluegrass "land of milk and honey" were matched the same month in Tennessee by Brig. Gen. Forrest. The latter's strikes disrupted Maj. Gen. Buell's moves toward Confederate positions at Chattanooga by hitting hard at the Northern rail center at Murfreesboro, southeast of Nashville. This victory, in the words of Frank Cooling, "set the whole region on edge." Forrest and his troopers remained at large in the Nashville area for the entire month and Federal soldiers (who were mostly infantry) were unable to catch the fleet cavalrymen. Buell wired Washington: "The enemy has thrown a large cavalry force, regular and irregular, upon our lines throughout Tennessee and Kentucky." There was even fear in some Northern quarters that, if it could be isolated, Nashville might be forced to surrender.

The twin Morgan-Forrest achievements led the Yankees to begin fortifying their outposts, rail bridges, some river crossings, and even the city of Nashville. The raider triumphs also held up acquisition of additional bluecoat control over portions of Middle Tennessee, encouraged the already-sympathetic local populace, and led to increased attacks by insurgents on various targets, most especially transportation, by irregulars. Still, for Southern sympathizers in Nashville like the Yankee occupiers, the result of these activities meant that food supplies would begin to run low in short order as railroads to the North were blocked and the Cumberland River fell.

Irregular forces led by lesser-known heartland partisans also executed pin-prick raids on Ohio River communities. Leading a group later known as the 10th Kentucky Partisan Cavalry, Adam R. Johnson defeated a group of Union soldiers at Madisonville, Kentucky, and captured the town of Henderson on July 17. Johnson, a surveyor by profession, operated from sanctuaries in Union County, Kentucky, that allowed easy access to Federal posts and transportation on the Ohio, Cumberland, and Tennessee Rivers. Employing a pair of ersatz cannon fashioned from stovepipes, Johnson crossed the Ohio River and scared many defenders away from Newburg, Indiana. Johnson, thereafter known as "Stovepipe" Johnson, did not dally, quickly ending his demonstration and returning to Kentucky. Meanwhile, two companies of Indiana volunteers, armed with a pair of real cannon, departed for Newburg from Evansville aboard the steamer *Eugene* just as soon as the first distress wire arrived.

Indiana governor Oliver P. Morton, on July 19, wired Cairo naval base chief Cmdr. Alexander M. Pennock: "Henderson, Ky., taken by rebels. Evansville and Newburg are threatened." Although Morton

"Stovepipe" Johnson (1834–1922) was the first major Confederate irregular leader to challenge Capt. Pennock and Lt. Cmdr. Fitch on the Ohio River in the summer of 1862. In July 1863, he would command one of the brigades of Brig. Gen. John Hunt Morgan during the Great Indiana-Ohio Raid (Johnson, *The Partisan Rangers of the Confederate States Army*, 1904).

wanted a gunboat sent, Pennock, running activities on the upper rivers in the absence of Flag Officer Charles H. Davis, who was down the Mississippi, had none to spare. Over the next two days, the energetic fleet captain scraped together a makeshift flotilla, comprised of the receiving ship *Clara Dolsen*, armed with four howitzers, the *Rob Roy*, aboard which were 125 base sailors and 200 men from the 63rd Regiment of Illinois Volunteers, and the tugboat *Restless*, also armed with a howitzer. Led by Pennock in person (his only fleet command of the war) on the *Dolsen*, aboard which "the greatest enthusiasm was manifested by all," the little armada steamed up to Evansville, arriving on August 21. Next day, U.S. forces, taken across the stream by Pennock's boats, reoccupied Henderson.

On August 23, reports arrived indicating that "guerrilla" forces had taken over Uniontown and were poised to cross over to Mount Vernon, Indiana. Pennock's craft and troops under Maj. Gen. John Love, Indiana Legion, next secured Uniontown. The Pennock group was near Shawneetown, Illinois, on July 23 patrolling against attack from the Kentucky side of the river when a wire was received from Quartermaster George D. Wise. Irregulars, the logistics man noted, were poised to attack Cairo from the Kentucky shore opposite. Splitting his force and dispatching the troop-laden *Rob Roy* back to Henderson, Pennock pushed back down to Cairo with the *Clara Dolsen* and *Restless*. By the time they arrived, the enemy had withdrawn. Maj. Gen. Love wrote to the commander expressing the "gratitude with which the citizens of this locality will regard the prompt cooperation of yourself and your officers in this emergency, which threatened their security."

The overall Southern raider-guerrilla effort across the upper South would result in additional reprisals against the populace and deepening enmity on both sides. A clergyman named George R. Browder, a Kentuckian who lived on the shores of the Cumberland north of Clarksville, recorded the sentiments of others when he noted the many "small bodies, called gurellias [sic], coming in and scouring the county, and yet not in force enough to hold it." He went on to confess to his diary: "I fear guerilla warfare more than the shock of vast armies in battle array" because the irregulars "are never still—life, liberty and property are not safe an hour." At the same time, regular forces were once more on the move; on August 28, Braxton Bragg and his 30,000-man strong Army of Tennessee began moving north from southern Tennessee and from Knoxville toward the Ohio River, via Kentucky.[1]

The internecine North-South struggle was no less ferocious on the rivers and riverbanks. For sailors and those ashore alike, the accessibility of one combatant or victim to another was intimate. Men were often separated by only a few yards between boat and shore. This proximity occasioned physical and psychological consequences that sparked fear and hatred on both sides. The nearness of Northern steamboat operators and passengers, or tinclad bluejackets, allowed for frequent and sharp exchanges with Confederate raider-guerrillas. These firefights were not always decisive for either side. Additionally, Southern civilians and slaves were often startled and downright frightened to find light draught gunboat tars the first Yankees in areas where good roads did not exist. Over a hundred years later, Michael J. Bennett put into words the sentiment which was obvious to many riverside citizens of the Confederacy. "Southerners viewed gunboats and their crews," he concluded, "as akin to a Viking invasion, spreading fear and instability."

By the summer of 1862, most Confederates well knew that they had no commercial or military boats on the upper rivers and that all steamer traffic profited their enemies. Federal steamboats could carry not only goods, but, as Union fleet captain Pennock's Ohio River expedition demonstrated, troops as well. This realization of vulnerability occasionally bordering on helplessness, coupled with apprehension and abhorrence, helps to explain the upsurge in animus and in attacks upon Western river steamers. Employing speed, tricks, and surprises, plus armament ranging from masked cannon batteries to shotguns, guerrillas increasingly pelted both civilian craft and naval warships. A later historian of the Tennessee River voiced the Confederate point of view as it applied to these brown water operations:

> All river traffic offered a completely legitimate target. The rivers were controlled by the Federals. To a Confederate, soldier or civilian, there was nothing innocent and nice about a steamboat, armed or not.... That boat was carrying either soldiers or supplies, and its presence meant war and death to the South. If women and children were on board, they were where they had no business to be; and of course, their presence could not be detected in advance of an attack.... Every boat—in one way or another was a Federal boat—and it ought to be stopped, captured, burned, or driven back. Therefore, the Confederates, despite the utmost in the way of retaliation, continued to stand behind cottonwoods, or any other convenient point, and to shoot at boats of all sorts.

This Southern philosophy and approach to Northern logistical interdiction would intensify in August and the months ahead into 1864. It would remain for Union naval leadership to create its own counter raider-guerrilla strategy and to introduce those specific tactics necessary to counteract this Rebel scourge. Meanwhile, "in country" Northern military and naval men adopted the mentality that anyone who shot at them from riverbanks or other positions besides forts or formal lines of battle were guerrillas—whether in uniform or not. Guerrilla warfare, as Cmdr. John A. Winslow put it in June, was "barbarian warfare." It was uncivilized and was unworthy of quarter and would be so prosecuted. In the end, however, if the irregulars could not be defeated, perhaps at best they could be contained.

The need for viable light draught Union river patrols that Flag Officer Davis, with the support of other theater commanders, were seeking since at least June was fully demonstrated by his fleet captain's Evansville expedition in late July. Indeed, Cmdr. Pennock, in his report of the Ohio River cruise, offered two closing observations: 1) there was "but little Union feeling on the Kentucky shore"; and 2) the interests of government and the safety of steamers navigating the Ohio require that light-draft gunboats should be kept moving up and down the river." Pennock's actions and reports, lauded to Navy secretary Gideon Welles by Flag Officer Davis on August 6, together with continuing newspaper reports of how "guerrilla warfare was becoming more serious and travel on the Ohio River was extremely hazardous," and "the bold manner in which guerrilla warfare is carried on at the present time on the Tennessee River" now led directly to creation of a "squadron of small vessels to suppress the active guerrilla movements on the Ohio and Tennessee Rivers."[2]

Upon his return to Cairo from below, Flag Officer Davis fell ill with the same fever that touched so many of his officers and men near Vicksburg and Helena since July 4. This was perhaps malaria. For three weeks in early August, he slowly convalesced in a bed in Pennock's quarters. Upon his recovery and prior to his departure back down the Mississippi aboard the refurbished gunboat U.S.S. *Eastport* in the van of the other heavy units of the Western Flotilla, Davis kept his earlier promise to Le Roy Fitch. Back in his June 15 congratulatory letter on the raising of the *General Sterling Price*, the flag officer had promised not to forget the young Hoosier: "I shall be happy, when an occasion offers, to show my just appreciation of the manner in which both ... intelligence and industry were displayed on this occasion."

Having informed Secretary Welles of his intention on August 19 and his fleet captain the night before, Flag Officer Davis created a special light draft squadron on August 21; later sailors and historians would nickname it the "mosquito squadron." Allowing that the "gunboat service of the upper rivers has suddenly acquired a new importance," Davis officially placed the new command under Pennock's "special care." Lt. Cmdr. Fitch was made squadron executive and gunnery officer, which, in effect, gave him on scene operational control of the unit subject to direction from his seniors, Davis and Pennock. Fitch was to send his reports to Cmdr. Pennock, who would read them and react, giving any necessary orders, and then detail the highlights to Davis "from time to time."

The need for fast reaction along the rivers was now absolutely vital. For example, in a combined guerrilla-regular cavalry operation just the previous day, Adam "Stovepipe" Johnson's 10th Kentucky Partisan Cavalry and Thomas G. Woodward's 2nd Kentucky Cavalry, together with two companies from Forrest's 1st Kentucky Cavalry, captured Clarksville, Tennessee, on the Cumberland River; they would hold the town for 29 days.

The Logansport sailor was given the U.S.S. *General Pillow*, largest of the three available small warship conversions, as his flagboat. It became his duty to enforce naval discipline upon the men of the entire mosquito group and, employing his ordnance expertise, to take "pains to render the officers and men efficient in the use of the howitzers and small arms." In his written order, Davis put on paper a sentiment he doubtless personally addressed to this young man of long acquaintance: "I rely upon your zeal and ability, already well known to me, to conduct this service in such a manner as will result in the suppression of this barbarous warfare and the chastisement of those engaged in it." Fitch would undertake his first patrol in just two days.[3]

On August 23, Lt. Cmdr. Le Roy Fitch took the *General Pillow* to Paducah, Kentucky, and on up the Tennessee River, intent upon conducting an anti-guerrilla sweep. Unhappily, the start of his almost three years continuous and indomitable service was immediately frustrated by low water which prevented passage above Duck River. Several days later, the U.S. transport steamer *W. B. Terry*, under Master Leonard G. Klinck, left Paducah, hoping to rendezvous with Fitch. She, too, could not pass the Duck River shoals and so determined to return, hoping perhaps to meet the *General Pillow* en route. Her retreat was halted at sundown on August 30 when she ran aground. Next morning before she could be freed, the steamer was attacked by Rebel troops under Capt. T. Alonzo Napier and James B. Algee. Although she was protected by two 6-pounder field guns and 17 men from the 81st Ohio Volunteer Infantry, the 200 determined men in gray quickly forced her surrender. Once the Confederates were transported across the river and the *Terry's* passengers were put ashore, Klinck, his crew and the soldiers, were put into a raft and the steamer was burned.[4]

Rumors being rife that Paducah would be attacked, the *General Pillow*, low on coal, returned to that port on September 4. Leaving her to guard the Blue Grass community, Lt. Cmdr. Fitch returned to Cairo aboard a commercial steamer to bring up the *Alfred Robb*, then undergoing repairs. Upon reporting to Capt. Pennock the next day, he was pleasantly surprised when his superior pointed out that the newly-captured steamer *Fairplay*, which had arrived at Cairo from Helena on August 31, was already being converted into a tinclad. The earliest light draught for which a photo exists, the side-wheel *Fairplay* was constructed in 1859 at New Albany, Indiana, to participate in the cotton trade. She was 138.8 feet long, with a beam of 27 feet and a draft of 4.9 feet. Her two engines and two boilers permitted a top speed of 5 mph upstream. A pair of 12-pounder smoothbore howitzers were placed aboard, along with two rifled 12-pounder howitzers.[5]

A captured Confederate side-wheel steamer converted into a tinclad, the *Fairplay*, in September 1862, became Lt. Cmdr. Fitch's first flagboat. She was one of the few warships to remain under his control for the remainder of the war, participating in such engagements as the February 1863 Battle of Dover and the December 1864 Bell's Mills fights near Nashville. Sold out in August 1865, she was redocumented as *Cotile* and provided civil service until broken up in 1871. The only image of the boat was captured by Bell & Sheridan of Franklin Street, Clarksville, Tennessee, and is from a collection once owned by probable crewmember Thomas R. Burton (Naval Historical Center).

Work on the *Fairplay* was completed by the evening of September 5. In the predawn darkness of September 6, two infantry companies were embarked aboard the warship, which then left harbor for up river. Reaching Paducah a short time later, the blueclad reinforcements were dropped off and Fitch took the opportunity to meet with local commanders and the captain of the *General Pillow* to review guerrilla alarms. Reports continued to circulate about various real or imagined raids, which were now "very annoying along" the Ohio River; the most pressing concerned a foray by troops under Maj. Gen. Simon B. Buckner, CSA, against the locks at Spottsville, Kentucky. To prevent potentially serious harm to the regulatory machinery, the Western Flotilla's newest unit quickly shoved off and proceeded on up the Ohio. Very shoal water at Cumberland bar prevented the *Fairplay* from proceeding further and it would take a week before passage could be completed.

In the meantime, Indiana Legion Col. John W. Foster, in a military practice which would become more frequent than river war historians have recorded, took over a 50-ton stern-wheel steamer, put a field piece and troops aboard, and rushed to Spottsville. The interim gunboat *Lou Eaves* and her men were able to drive off the Rebel marauders, but not before several tons of rocks were thrown above the upper gate, causing much damage. Fitch, who would imitate the Army practice on occasion, impressed for hire the light draft steamer *Cordelia Ann* on September 1 much as Col. Foster had the *Lou Eaves*. Arming her with a spare howitzer and placing her under command of the *Fairplay's* second master, George J. Groves, Fitch sent his auxiliary up to Caseyville, Kentucky, to punish irregulars reportedly firing at passing steamboats. The Hoosier's instruction to his subordinate required both stealth and firmness:

> In approaching Caseyville, be particular to keep your men hid from observation and use every precaution to disguise the true character of the boat and expedition. Should you be fired into at Caseyville, or any resistance offered, destroy the place at once.

The outcome of the Caseyville gambit is unknown with no contact the probable result. On September 12, Fitch was able to get the *Fairplay* over the Cumberland bar and steam up toward Shawneetown. Near that location, the navy man spied a small 50–60 member band perceived as guerrillas and quietly attempted to put a landing force behind it, thereby trapping those people on the bank between the bluejackets and the tinclad. Unfortunately due to low water, this ploy didn't work. As the sailors prepared to go ashore, they were spotted and the Confederates fled. The *Fairplay* threw "a few shell after them" and went ahead with the landing. Once ashore, the 20 sailors pushed inland some three miles and ransacked their enemy's camp at Cypress Lake. They also took over a riverbank house and made five men captive; as nothing could be proved against them, they were released.

As part of what was turning out to be a flag-showing cruise in damp, chilly and illness-inducing weather, Fitch made it a point to pause at all the intermediate towns en route to Evansville. Stopping at Uniontown on September 16, which he found quiet, the Hoosier sailor informed the mayor and local citizens that he was the new man representing the Union on the Ohio River and that he "would hold them and their property responsible for all guerrilla depredations within 10 miles either up or down the river." After taking aboard a new pilot, the *Fairplay* arrived at Evansville on September 17 with its port engine out of repair, a pump valve malfunctioning, and a large sick list.

Historian Davidson later summed up what became for gunboat commanders both a common observation and usual claim. "Guerrillas," he wrote, "never made a stand against superior forces. When the gunboats landed troops, the guerrillas withdrew or dispersed, and hence gunboat commanders were always able to say that they had 'driven off' or 'broken up' guerrilla parties." Low water, ship repairs, and the need to allow his men to recuperate now forced Fitch to pace the Evansville riverbank until September 29. All he could do was insure by wire that the *Alfred Robb* guarded Paducah while the *General Pillow* cruised between that city and Smithland. He, like everyone else in the port, undoubtedly read with interest newspaper accounts of the horrifically bloody battle of Antietam, fought in Maryland on September 17. Closer to home, they undoubtedly wondered what would happen in the contest between Gen. Bragg and Maj. Gen. Buell, now that the former had that very day captured Mundfordville and was poised to enter Louisville.[6]

On October 1, the Western Gunboat Fleet, brought into being by Cmdr. John Rodgers and Flag Officer Foote, under the jurisdiction of the War Department for operations on the western waters, was officially transferred to the Navy Department and renamed the Mississippi Squadron. Cmdr. David Dixon Porter was jumped several grades to be appointed acting rear admiral and ordered to relieve Rear Admiral Davis, commander of naval forces on the western waters since June. The changeover in top squadron leadership did not occur that day as Porter was still en route from Washington, D.C., conducting inspections along the way. When he reached St Louis on October 13, the new squadron leader was able to examine the rebuilding of the U.S.S. *Signal*. He heartily endorsed the light draught concept and, the same day, asked Navy secretary Gideon Welles to quickly boost by ten the number of tinclads available to his fleet. They would all be fitted with 24-pounder howitzers.

Rear Adm. Davis, meanwhile, availed himself of his remaining tenure to clean up as much squadron business as possible. Among the details not overlooked, as noted in an October 2 report to Navy secretary Welles, was rank title revisions. In the shortly-to-be approved Davis list, for example, all first masters in the Western Flotilla were appointed USN acting volunteer lieutenants, third masters became acting ensigns, etc. Another letter to Welles of the same day praised the work of Lt. Cmdr. Fitch on the Tennessee and Ohio.

The first of the new tinclads available were the stern-wheelers U.S.S. *Brilliant* and U.S.S. *St. Clair*, both of which were purchased by the War Department on August 13. The two departed Carondelet, Missouri, for Cairo on September 25. Slightly heavier, Acting Volunteer Master Charles G. Perkins' 227-ton *Brilliant* was constructed at Brownsville, Pennsylvania, earlier in the year. She measured 154.8 feet in length, with a beam of 33.6 feet. Before her cannon were shipped, her draft was 1.10 feet forward and 2.4 feet aft, though official records would show her with an overall five foot draft. Employing two engines and three boilers, *Brilliant* could make 6 mph steaming against the current. Her initial armament consisted of two 12-pounder rifles and two 12-pounder smoothbores. The 203-ton *St. Clair*, also an 1862 model, was built at Belle Vernon, Pennsylvania, and measured 156 feet long by 32 feet wide; her draft both forward and aft was 2.4 feet. Captained by Acting Volunteer Master, later Acting Volunteer Lieutenant, Jacob S. Hurd, she was powered to an unknown speed by two boilers and probably two engines. Her 66-man complement existed to work two 12-pounder rifles and two 12-pounder smoothbores. Both boats were sold out in 1865 and enjoyed short postwar careers, the former as the merchant *John S. McCune* and the latter as *St. Clair*.

The *Brilliant* was commissioned at Cairo on October 1. Together, the two stern-wheelers reported to Lt. Cmdr. Fitch at Evansville on October 14. Also reporting aboard the *Fairplay* at this time was Acting Surgeon Samuel L. Bolton. Bolton, whose wife was a close friend of Mary Smith Fitch, would be a frequent visitor at Fitch's table.

By this time, Gen. Bragg's Kentucky visit had been cut short by the Union victory at Perryville on October 7 and Confederate troops subsequently retreated back toward Tennessee. A Southern enterprise which had begun with hope of glory ended in hesitancy and withdrawal. The Kentucky incursion caused great consternation in Union circles as well. Maj. Gen. William S. "Old Rosy" Rosecrans succeeded Maj. Gen. Buell on October 23 and within five days, the Rebel Army of Tennessee was back at Murfreesboro.

On the irregular front, "the most sustained and serious threats to the Union hold on the lower Cumberland," wrote Richard Gildrie in 1990, "originated south of the river." Specifically, the most worrisome points were the Yellow Creek district in southern Montgomery County, Tennessee (about 13 miles southwest of Clarksville bordering Dickson County), and the Dickson County seat of Charlotte. To the northeast and northwest of the town were the two main attack positions from which Confederate forces would plague Cumberland river traffic and the Union Navy over the next months: Harpeth Shoals and the community of Palmyra.

As noted in our review of rivers at the end of the previous chapter, the Harpeth Shoals on the Cumberland River northeast of Charlotte were natural obstructions beyond which steamboat traffic could not pass at times of low water. The rocks forced civil and naval craft to proceed cautiously even when the river was up. Attacks at points along the shoals would be frequent. Palmyra, to the northwest, sat on a bluff overlooking the river, which gave onlookers from above a beautiful broadside view of approaching river traffic. The Rebels even build entrenchments and gun platforms here, some of which remained for over 140 years. Skirmishes and bombardments would continue in the area even after Lt. Cmdr. Fitch ordered the town burned in April 1863.

When he took over the Mississippi Squadron on October 15, the colorful Acting Rear Adm. Porter found himself with a mountain of administrative and operational concerns and ploughed straight into these with zeal. As he began these new duties, he found that one of the most troublesome problems facing his command was the guerrillas, who were "firing on unarmed vessels from the river banks and at places not occupied by United States troops, when the steamers stopped." It was also widely believed that "large quantities of goods were intentionally landed [along the Tennessee, Ohio, and Cumberland river banks] for the rebels and shipped from St. Louis" by unscrupulous businessmen and agents. Porter would deal harshly with irregular warfare, authorizing or condoning blockades, port closures, patrols, and retaliations.[7]

By mid–October, "nearly every boat ... which landed at the Evansville wharf told of encountering guerrillas." The Evansville *Daily Journal* ran frequent stories of steamer encounters with irregular Confederate forces. For example, an unsuccessful attempt was made to take the *Eugene* at Randolph, Tennessee, while the *D.B. Campbell* was fired on near Uniontown, Kentucky. The newspaper also reported that 20 raiders slipped across the river at West Franklin, Indiana, and helped themselves to skiffs, boats, and horses.[8]

Having reviewed and worked up the men of his new vessels, Lt. Cmdr. Fitch was ready to pounce when the next incident occurred. On October 16, the day after Acting Rear Adm. Porter moved into his new Cairo offices, word arrived at Evansville that men from Adam ("Stovepipe") Johnson's command had forcibly boarded, with shots exchanged, and taken goods from the U.S. mail steamer *Hazel Dell* at Caseyville. The Hoosier sailor immediately had his two new gunboats and the flagship *Fairplay* steaming toward the scene, but once again, low water, coupled with thick fog, slowed his response.

Unable to proceed as quickly as desired, Fitch wrote his own blockade orders from the

"Old Rosy" Rosecrans (1819–1898) commanded the Army of the Cumberland from October 1862 through October 1863, winning campaigns at Stones River and Tullahoma, but losing at Chickamauga. Rosecrans insisted upon having what he considered ample supplies and manpower before making any advance and, to that end, demanded that logistics flow steadily into Nashville via the Louisville and Nashville Railroad and the Cumberland River. Anything which was perceived to interfere with that goal—including Lt. Cmdr. Fitch's convoy system—brought howls of complaint from his headquarters (U.S. Army Military History Institute).

On several occasions during the fall of 1862, the new tinclads of Lt. Cmdr. Fitch's squadron had occasion to take aim on suspected irregular parties on the Kentucky shore on the Ohio River. The depiction here catches the flavor of these shoots, even if it does not correctly illustrate the configurations of any of the Navy tinclads (*Harper's Weekly*, October 11, 1862, via West Virginia State Archives).

middle of the Ohio River on October 17. These regulations, which were sent by passing steamer or other craft to river communities on both banks, suspended all ferries on the Ohio between Evansville and Paducah (except at the towns of Henderson and Smithland). Additionally, masters of all freight and passenger steamers plying between Evansville and Cairo were prohibited from taking aboard passengers and cargo for or landing at any point on the Kentucky shore not garrisoned by U.S. forces, unless absolutely unavoidable. Further, all boats, skiffs, scows, or flatboats found along the Kentucky shore at unguarded locales were subject to destruction along with all goods, merchandise, or other articles of traffic sold or sent to the Kentucky shore which were not authorized by a port or other U.S. official.

Meanwhile, overland runners were able to reach Caseyville ahead of Fitch's tinclads, sounding a warning which permitted Johnson's people "and many of the most prominent aiders and abettors" to escape. When the *Fairplay*, *Brilliant*, and *St. Clair* rounded to off the community on the morning of October 18, detachments from the three, under the command of Second Master George J. Groves from the flagboat, went ashore, surrounded the town, and detained all the Caucasian men they found.

Upon inspection, Fitch found that a few "good" Union men were in town during the raid, but these were forcibly restrained and prevented from warning off the steamer. "The worst and most rabid persons," the sailor later reported encountering were "the farmers living a mile or so from town. They are the ones who have been feeding and keeping Johnson's men, and the ones also who shared the spoils of the late robbery."

Taking a leaf from his half-brother's book, Le Roy Fitch now did exactly the same thing as Graham Newell Fitch had in Monroe County, Arkansas, on June 22: he posted a notice of warning to local inhabitants that they were being held accountable for the assault. The naval Fitch, however, took the process a step further by demanding, on his own authority, that the citizens of Caseyville and those 10 miles inland in surrounding Union County, collectively pay reparations of $50,000 by 10 P.M. that evening. If the "good current money" was not forthcoming, women and children wold be ordered out of town and the whole place burned to ashes.

Perhaps realizing his ferociousness in that his order did not differentiate between those pledging support to the Union and those who did not, young Fitch modified his order on October 19. Payment was reduced to $35,000, due in a week. If the cash was not ready, "the property of all secessionists or sympathizers ... will be confiscated and their houses, furniture, grain, and produce of all kinds destroyed." A guard was posted who insured that, over the next seven days, nothing was removed; meanwhile, a number of men who could not explain themselves were clapped into irons and sent off to Cairo, via Smithland, for further interrogation and processing.

Lt. Cmdr. Fitch had no direct knowledge of Acting Rear Adm. Porter's position on irregular containment when he published his Ohio River blockade and Caseyville broadsides. He only knew that his own injunction concerning steamer landings on the Kentucky shore was "absolutely necessary" and that Union County was "a well-known thoroughfare for guerrillas." Adopting an oft-quoted modern adage about seeking forgiveness rather than permission (an understandable tactic in those days of poor communication, but still, one very career-risky in the 19th Century U.S. Navy), the Logansport sailor wrote to his new boss admitting, "If I took upon myself too much authority and erred therein it was through a desire to do my duty." Thus it came as considerable relief on October 21 when a mail sack arrived for him at Caseyville with a communication from the admiral, who enclosed a copy of his General Orders Nos. 2 and 4 regarding warship operations and anti-guerrilla precautions. "I had already acted according to my own judgment," Fitch recorded and was quite possibly relieved and "happy to say, nearly in conformity," to orders. In fact, Porter, who saw guerrilla warfare as "an outrageous practice," actually wanted a fee 10 times greater than that levied by Fitch and the arrest of all white male citizens not known to be of "good, loyal" character. Porter's General Orders 2 and 4 of October 18 are worthy of mention in some little detail because they provided Fitch and other Mississippi Squadron officers with a blueprint to employ while conducting counterinsurgency operations.

General Order No. 2, which was to be widely posted, published in newspapers, and handed out aboard every steamboat, essentially called for a mini-blockade. Except at points occupied by U.S. soldiers, any boat passing from shore to shore was subject to inspection and its passengers to detainment, along with any goods, merchandise, arms, ammunition, or contraband. After October 25, no vessel could land cargoes at any point below Cairo or at any point between Cairo and Louisville without the express authority from a revenue collection agent or a Yankee military or naval officer. Lt. Cmdr. Fitch amplified the order for his command area on October 26, indicating that vessels required a pass to cross the Ohio

River from Evansville and those with documentation could only do so in daylight (5:30 A.M.–6 P.M.).

General Order No. 4 provided specific instructions for shipboard detail and anti-guerrilla response, and was aimed at preventing Rebel surprise attacks on the light draught gunboats. Specifically, tinclads were forbidden from lying tied up to riverbanks. They were to keep their guns loaded with grape or canister shot, maintain small arms at the ready, and keep protected lookouts posted at all times. At night, steam was to be kept up and a watch kept on deck. At sunrise and sunset, all vessels were to beat to quarters, with guns pointed at the bank and everyone ready for action. No small boats could put into shore unless they were covered by their ship's guns and none could be sent to obtain provisions from any point not occupied by U.S. troops. If men did go ashore, pillaging was not allowed "under any circumstances."

Although pillaging was prohibited, retribution for attack was expected. Porter's view, shared by Generals Grant, Sherman, and several other Northern political and military leaders in the Western theater, bears quoting as they grant both a permission and set a tone for actions which followed:

> When any of our vessels are fired on it will be the duty of the commander to fire back with spirit, and to destroy everything in that neighborhood within reach of his guns. There is no impropriety in destroying houses supposed to be affording shelter to rebels, and it is the only way to stop guerrilla warfare. Should innocent persons suffer it will be their own fault, and teach others that it will be to their advantage to inform the Government authorities when guerrillas are about certain localities.

Despite the grimness of Porter's message, "the countermeasures taken by the Federal commanders," wrote historian Davidson, "never had more than a local effect." As Alfred T. Mahan put it:

> The ruling feeling in the country favored the Confederate cause, so that every hamlet and farm-house gave a refuge to these marauders, while at the same time the known existence of some Union feeling made it hard for officers to judge, in all cases, whether punishment should fall on the places where the attacks were made.

Historian Cooling has summarized the dilemma as a vicious circle facing Fitch and his counterinsurgency colleagues: "supply route interruption followed by local foraging, succeeded by civil disobedience and rising partisan activity, followed ultimately by harsh retribution."[9]

Assaults on Ohio River shipping did not cease after the Caseyville incident. About two miles above Curlew, Kentucky, on October 21, guerrillas, attacking from a thick cluster of woods and brush, shot up the steamboat *Nashville*; one man aboard was killed and another wounded. When the *Nashville* reached her next port, Shawneetown, witnesses could see 16 bullet holes in her pilot house. That evening as he was reviewing Admiral Porter's communications and rounding up suspects, Lt. Cmdr. Fitch received word of this new occurrence sent by messenger from the boat's captain. The Indiana sailor immediately steamed down to Shawneetown, leaving Masters Hurd and Perkins to oversee Caseyville. He convoyed the *Nashville* up to the head of Mississippi Bend, above Uniontown. En route, the steamer was fired into at the foot of Cincinnati Bar; however, the *Fairplay* was close behind and shelled the attackers off. At Uniontown, Fitch sent a report of the events to Fleet Captain Pennock, asking him to advise packet captains that he would gladly provide convoy to steamboats from either Smithland or a point just above Long's Ford.[10]

The Navy's convoy offer could not be implemented for long due to falling water. Back at Evansville by October 24, Lt. Cmdr. Fitch informed his superiors that he would make Evansville his headquarters for the time being, it being equidistant between Louisville and Smithland for purposes of mail and telegraph communications. Next day, Fitch was obliged to wire Cairo that he could not get above Three-Mile Island as the river was down to just 24 inches in depth. The *Brilliant*, meanwhile, went downstream to convoy the steamer *May Duke*, but could not get below the bar at Henderson Island as the water level there was only 27 inches. The *St. Clair*, already below, encountered great difficulty getting past the bar at Shawneetown. On November 1, she was able to start down convoying the *May Duke* and *Marmora No. 2* with 106 government horses aboard. In his instructions to the tinclad's captain, Fitch ordered that he not attempt to cross the bar at Shawneetown if there was danger of the boat grounding.

By November 2, it was necessary to inform Cairo that the water stage in the Ohio had reached a point where it was "impossible for the gunboats to get either up or down the river." The situation was so bad that it would injure the little warships if they were dragged over the sandbars and, consequently, no more trips could be made down river until it rose. This was a big regret as Confederate irregulars were reported as being "very bad between Wabash Island and Ford's Ferry, below Caseyville."

This is not to say, however, that Fitch was without either his increasingly famous initiative or resources. Borrowing back the leaf first demonstrated by Indiana Legion Col. Foster with the *Lou Eaves* in September and simultaneously imitated by himself, the Logansport sailor put an officer, a gun crew, and a 12-pounder howitzer each aboard several ultra light draft mail steamers plying the river. The practice began with the *May Duke* and some men under Acting Volunteer Master Groves. Some months later, the lieutenant commander was able to recall the results with pride:

> Guerrillas on several occasions made so bold as to present themselves on the banks and hail the steamers in, but receiving rather unexpected and severe lessons from the howitzers, soon learned to let the vessels pass unmolested.

Toward the middle of November, all steamers with government contracts were summarily prohibited from ascending Kentucky's Green River, across the Ohio from Evansville. On November 23, the Evansville *Daily Journal* reported that no mail could be sent from Indiana to any Kentucky town except Henderson, Smithville, and Paducah due to "guerrilla problems." The Green River mails were required to go by way of Owensboro. Lt. Cmdr. Fitch found it necessary to issue the edict because he could not get up that stream and unarmed steamers from Evansville and Louisville were transporting their freight right into the guerrilla sanctuaries. "I must say," he later wrote, "I was very much surprised at the loose manner in which surveyors of customs permitted cases of boots, clothing, and the like to pass into the Green River country, it being at the time almost entirely under the control of organized guerrilla bands." The ban could hopefully be lifted when the rivers rose.[11]

Back in the spring of 1862 following the triumphs at Fort Henry and Fort Donelson, Maj. Gen. Buell wrote optimistically to his superiors that, with Nashville as a springboard, his Union army could "operate east, west, or south. All our arrangements should look to a centralization of our forces [in the city]." Now with his successor, William S. Rosecrans, in charge, this axiom was seen as truer than ever from Tennessee to Washington, D.C. As was the case over the past months, keeping the city bottled up and eliminating any Yankee military—or political—incursions from it remained a prime Confederate objective. If it could be overrun or starved out, so much the better. Conversely, building it up as a staging point preparatory to a strike southward was a major Northern goal.

The U.S. Army in Nashville, according to historian Lenette Taylor, faced three major difficulties beyond the CSA cavalry and guerrilla raiders outside town. The local economy, once among the best in the South as noted in Chapter 2, was devastated by the impact of the war and, in the spring, one of the worst floods to sweep over the Cumberland banks since 1847. Prices on the few available goods were very high and shortages were caused by low water in the Cumberland and wrecked railroad tracks north of the city. In mid–November, a correspondent from a Louisville newspaper wrote about the city, which he called "one of the poisoned strongholds of secessia." "Poor old Nashville—dull, dirty and mourning," he informed his readers. "Two thirds of her stores and business are shut up.... People sour and uncomfortable in appearance."

On top of the town's sad physical state, the 24,000 Caucasian residents who did not flee the city were overwhelmingly (about 120 to 1) Southern sympathizers. Former U.S. senator and war governor Andrew Johnson was sent to the state capital by President Abraham Lincoln to restore civil government and return Tennessee to the Union. After giving up on gentle pacification, Johnson attempted to rule with an iron first, employing what most admittedly disloyal citizens regarded as strong-armed tactics. Naturally, he received little popular support. According to his biographer, Paul H. Bergeron, the politician from Greeneville "arrested and imprisoned newspaper editors, local officials, and clergymen—anyone deemed to be a threat." Even had they been Yankee citizens, the residents would not have been aided by Maj. Gen. Rosecrans' military buildup, which restricted the importation of civilian goods in order to give all priority to military supplies.

Finally, and most importantly to this story, the city's tenuous communication lines were just that—tenuous. Large steamboats could not reach the city during the summer river low, while the Louisville and Nashville Railroad and its spurs were easy targets for the Rebel raiders Forrest, Morgan, and others. When they did arrive, L & N rail goods came into town at the station in the so-called gulch west of the state capital, while a rail yard and junction at Edgefield, a small town across the Cumberland, handled traffic with Clarksville, via a connection at the Kentucky state line with the Memphis, Clarksville, and Louisville Railroad. The two were connected by a rebuilt (June 11) 700-foot, fortified suspension bridge and a wooden railway bridge, built in a swing-span design atop massive stone piers still visible today. With the longest draw of any railroad bridge then extant, its center span could be pivoted to allow passage for steamboats with tall chimneys. In October, a pontoon bridge for wagons and pedestrians was constructed of empty ice barges at the middle ferry landing.

The river was the largest avenue into the city for the vast and necessary quantities of goods needed to equip the Army of the Cumberland. Soldiers, animals, food, forage, wagons and harness, clothing and dry goods, camp or garrison equipment, hospital supplies, and even items down to stationery were taken down gangplanks from the boats and dispersed from a large landing off Broad Street and Front Street, present day First Avenue. This levy was supplemented by two others and all would be extremely busy over the next several months.[12]

Maj. Gen. Rosecrans was a careful and deliberate man. Historian Steven E. Woodworth later wrote of him that "he would, over the course of the war, prove himself to be an excellent general as long as his enemy gave him plenty of time to prepare and did nothing unexpected." As part of his preparation formula, Rosecrans knew that transportation was vital. He was appalled at the damage done to the L & N by Rebel raiders over the past weeks and early in his tenure as Nashville's new military chief "came to rely upon the Cumberland River as his principal transportation artery to the North."

Aware that John Hunt Morgan in particular was and probably would continue to be effective against his rail lifeline, Rosecrans recognized that keeping the Cumberland functioning without Southern interference—when water levels permitted—was a matter to be accomplished at all costs. For the 46 days after his arrival, "Old Rosy" waited in Nashville, "a Union island in a Confederate sea," building up his troops and supply strength and waiting for the proper moment to advance.

On November 14, Rosecrans wired Maj. Gen. Henry Halleck in Washington, D.C., seeking additional troops and took the occasion—the first of several—to ask his superior to intercede with the leadership of the Navy Department to request "some provisions for gunboats to patrol the Tennessee and Cumberland Rivers." These patrols, he explained, could help keep down attacks by Rebel irregulars upon river traffic and even go so far as to prevent expected guerrilla attempts to blockade the river by blasting rocks into it. Of course, at this time, the Cumberland was just beginning to rise. From his headquarters at the Cunningham House at No. 13 High Street, Rosecrans was able to sense nature's unfolding favor late on November 20; that night the winds shifted and the clear nights enjoyed earlier gave way to rains so heavy they flooded Nashville's streets. Early next morning, mist covered the riverfront and the Cumberland was up over an inch.

A week later, "Old Rosy" advised Washington that he would undertake an advance upon Bragg's Army of Tennessee "as soon as practicable." First, however, he wanted to make certain that his supply lines were secure. Rosecrans' biographer carefully explained how he "sought to accumulate enough supplies at Nashville so the army could advance, or withstand a short siege." The end-of-year "advance to Murfreesboro and the victory were made possible" by his thoughtful buildup.

At Gen. Bragg's request, John Hunt Morgan, meanwhile, kept the pressure on Nashville and its defenders, striking at points along the railroad and elsewhere. By the last week of November, reports of Rebel sweeps were handed to Rosecrans almost hourly. Not only were Confederate soldiers moving along the edges of Tennessee's capital city, but local irregulars were assisting them—skirmishes between Yankee pickets and Confederate scouts were commonplace. On November 26, three Union regiments were sent (unsuccessfully) to catch a 1,200 man cavalry outfit that crossed the Cumberland River at Harpeth Shoals. By now "Old Rosy" was so agitated that, in an order to Federal troops guarding the L & N, he opined that his troops ought to know all of the settlers around their posts through local patrols. Any interlopers were to be arrested and those unable to "give a good account of themselves" were to be shot or hung from the nearest tree!

It was in this time of confusion, during which Union Army preparations for an advance against Bragg were stalled, that Rosecrans' mid-month petition reached Acting Rear Adm. Porter. The fire-eating Mississippi Squadron CO on November 27 ordered his tinclad warrior, Lt. Cmdr. Fitch, to begin active patrols of the Tennessee and Cumberland Rivers. Claiming that he did not need to give the Hoosier sailor "precise instructions," he did just that, requiring that no means were to be left for Rebels to cross the rivers—"all small boats likely to carry intelligence" were to be destroyed and all Rebel property captured. Although

Porter believed Fitch knew his views on counter-guerrilla warfare "pretty well by this time," these thoughts were summarized in two pithy sentences: "You can never go wrong in doing a Rebel all the harm you can ... I am no advocate for the milk and water policy." A hundred years later in another place of riverine conflict, milk and water would be reborn as "hearts and minds." The Navy boss anticipated that the Evansville-based light draught flotilla would soon have "water enough" to navigate in Tennessee waters. In closing his written command, Porter, who was at that time also concerned with Army plans for Vicksburg, gave Fitch a "left-handed" complement. Acknowledging a continued belief in the Logansport tar's ability to engineer success largely on his own hook, he closed simply: "I look to you to see that quiet is maintained there."

The call for action downstream reached Lt. Cmdr. Fitch at Evansville three days after it was written, just as the *Brilliant* was returning from Owensboro and as Porter surmised, the winter rise was beginning. On December 1, the Evansville fleet, carrying all of the property acquired from the "Rebels" at Caseyville, departed for Cairo. The same day, Gen. Bragg asked Brig. Gen. Morgan to operate once more against Yankee communication lines behind Nashville, while asking Generals Joseph Wheeler and Benjamin F. Cheatham to run diversions south of the city. Having repositioned to an anchorage off Paducah, the *Fairplay, Brilliant, St. Clair, General Pillow,* and *Alfred Robb* made a trip up the Tennessee River beginning on December 4. The five could not ascend beyond Duck River due to the shoals and so returned north. The *Pillow* and *Robb* were left at Paducah and the three larger craft hopscotched back to Evansville.

Late the night before, Morgan's 2,140 troopers crossed the Cumberland River at Purier's Ferry in two leaky flat-bottomed ferry boats. Then in an electrifying surprise December 7 attack that lasted about an hour, the Confederate cavalrymen obliterated Col. Absalom Moore's Union defense (three regiments—two from Ohio and one from Illinois) in Hartsville, Tennessee, on the L & N Railroad. The raiders escaped virtually unscathed back across the Cumberland the next day with thousands of greenbacks worth of captured supplies. The news uplifted Rebel hearts everywhere and depressed their enemy; *The New York Times* cried on December 9: "Nothing could be more disgraceful to our arms than the capture of the brigade of troops in Tennessee."[13]

The Union Army worked quickly to repair the material and political damage done at Hartsville and renewed plans for an advance against the Army of Tennessee. Upstream at Louisville, the rise which had assisted Fitch to reach Duck River at the beginning of the month continued to increase in volume. Deepening levels in the Ohio were seen in the Cumberland and Tennessee. As the streams inched slowly up their banks, a preacher of Confederate persuasion in Shelbyville was heard to pray: "O, Lord, let the rain descend to fructify the earth and to swell the rivers, but O Lord, do not raise the Cumberland sufficient to bring upon us those damn Yankee gunboats."

As the rivers rose, Lt. Cmdr. Fitch, acting with his usual independent zeal, once more stopped all steamers not in U.S. employ from passing up Green River. Fitch had lost patience with U.S. surveyors of ports who would, in the absence of Navy units, pass contraband articles up the waterway, failing for whatever reason to discriminate between forbidden and legitimate trade articles. They could be regulated only if he kept a warship at every port and he clearly did not have a sufficient number of units to do that. Additionally, it was hoped that his action would prevent guerrillas from getting supplies from the Green River area. To further ensure that nature's semi-annual beneficence did not aid the Confederates as the streams continued to swell, Maj. Gen. Rosecrans would issue his own proclamation on Christmas Eve prohibiting all steamboats not under U.S. contract from trading up the Green or Cumberland rivers.

The rumor game was rife on the Ohio River as it was at Nashville; Rebel cavalry and irregular leaders including Forrest, Woodward, Napier, and "Stovepipe" Johnson were all reported in Union County, Kentucky, by mid–December. They were supposed to have 2,000–3,000 men between them, though, as Fitch wrote Cairo, "I suppose the number is exaggerated." Having already ordered the Green River blockade, the Evansville-based flotilla chief confidently believed that he could prevent irregular forces across the Ohio "from other States, and, if the Cumberland rises enough, can also prevent them from sending many articles south." Just to be certain that he could deliver, however, two more light draught gunboats would be required: two for the Cumberland, two for the Tennessee, and three to patrol the Ohio between Paducah and Louisville.

On December 12, Maj. Gen. U.S. Grant, writing from Oxford, Mississippi, informed Rear Adm. Porter that a large cavalry force was reported to be moving from Columbia, Tennessee, toward Savannah, Tennessee. These were troops under Brig. Gen. Nathan Bedford Forest, who had departed for a sojourn into West Tennessee the day before. "Can a lightdraught gunboat get up there at this time," he wondered. Porter informed the Army leader that two tinclads were going up the Tennessee, but could not get above Cuba Ford.

Porter, on December 13, wrote his man Le Roy Fitch at Evansville imploring him to ascend the Tennessee with all of his force. The Tennessee was reported to be rising and Fitch needed to get his boats up it "as far as you can." It was of vital importance to get possession of the whole stream before Forrest got across it, but if he were too late, the Hoosier was to cut off the Memphis native's retreat by stationing his vessels at the different fords. Fitch, who had not yet received his chief's message, prepared to depart the Green River area on December 14 aboard the *Fairplay*, leading the *Brilliant* and *St. Clair* and headed down the Ohio for Smithland, hoping that there would be water enough there to permit him to ascend the Cumberland. The *Brilliant*, detailed to guard the Ohio from Cave-in-the-Rock to Uniontown, would be dropped out of the parade on the way. Stopping into his office at Evansville early next morning while en route, Fitch found Porter's December 13 command. The message changed yesterday's plans and he rushed over to the telegraph office to wire Cairo that he would be leaving for the Tennessee that night and would leave none of his five boats behind. The admiral was advised to wire information or requirements ahead: "Communications will catch me as I pass Paducah."

Elsewhere at mid-month, alarm bells were sounding and the telegraph wires were humming. Brig. Gen. Jeremiah C. Sullivan, commanding at Jackson, Tennessee, advised Porter and Rosecrans on December 15 that Forrest's cavalry was that day crossing the Tennessee at Clifton. If that were true, Fitch would be too late. Meanwhile, Grant informed Porter the next day that Gen. Bragg was also headed toward the Tennessee and called for gunboats. Grant and Rosecrans also wired Maj. Gen. Halleck in Washington, D.C., reporting their concerns and Halleck, on December 17, sent a note over to Navy assistant secretary Gustavus V. Fox urging that gunboats be found to send up the Tennessee.

From several thousand miles away, Navy secretary Welles took time the same day to wire Rear Adm. Porter informing him of the Army's concern and requesting that gunboats be sent up the Tennessee. From the Cairo telegraph office, Capt. Pennock, writing in Porter's absence down the Mississippi steaming toward Vicksburg, telegraphed back advising that

Fitch was en route "and must be there before now." He also noted that the stream was rising slowly and that until it had more rise, boats would not be able to get very far up. Armed with Pennock's slip of paper, Fox, knowing that Porter was stretched, confidently responded to Halleck: "Five light-draft steamers have been refitted and sent up the Tennessee and Cumberland rivers and have entirely put a stop to the guerrillas in that direction."

On December 18, Grant warned Pennock that Forrest and Napier were approaching the Tennessee intent, once across, in driving on Jackson. The military leader advised that the river was four feet deep. Pennock, hoping against hope that Fitch would make it in time, replied that the tinclads drew only three foot and could go all the way up with the rise. "They are only musket proof," he warned. Already on December 16, Le Roy Fitch had taken the *Fairplay, General Pillow, Alfred Robb, St. Clair,* and *Brilliant* in pursuit from the upper Ohio River, but Forrest won the race and crossed the river well before the tinclads could arrive. Forrest's expedition, unlike that described below by Morgan against the railroads, was designed only to cause as much damage as possible. From December 15 to January 3, the cavalryman ranged around the western half of Tennessee, fighting or scaring Yankees at places like Lexington, Humbolt and Trenton, Rutherford, Union City, Huntington and Parker's Crossroads, as well as points up and down the Tennessee River.

Not finding water enough in the Cumberland, Lt. Cmdr. Fitch and Col. William W. Lowe, post commander at Forts Henry and Heiman, came up with the idea of an amphibious raid which might be able to get behind Forrest's raiders. The Fitch-Lowe expedition, vaguely reminiscent of one mounted by Graham Newell Fitch and Augustus Kilty six months earlier, shoved off on December 20. The *General Pillow* was left behind to guard the forts. The tinclads and the troop ships proceeded as high as Duck River Sucks, where the soldiers were disembarked. Leaving the *Alfred Robb* and *St. Clair* with Lowe's transports, the *Fairplay* and *Brilliant* attempted to steam further up the river. The latter two did not get very far before the flagship grounded on Duck River Bar. Once the flagboat got off, both craft returned without getting higher. While thus engaged, Fitch received word (faulty as it turned out) on December 24 that Forrest was actually doubling back on them and headed toward Fort Heiman. Leaving the *Robb* and *St. Clair* to guard the transports, the Indiana sailor "at once" moved down with the *Fairplay* and *Brilliant* to reinforce the *General Pillow* and provide gunfire support in the event the Rebel riders showed up. No sooner had he arrived at Fort Henry than a telegram was placed in his hand from Col. H. Dougherty claiming that the defenders of his Paducah post were about to be assaulted.

Leaving the *Brilliant* at Fort Henry, Fitch rushed with the *Fairplay* back to Paducah on Christmas Day but found that he had been subjected to another false alarm. Still, in those days of great combat near Murfreesboro, as noted below, no report of Confederate activity could be dismissed. Added to his problems was the fact that his flagship's starboard wheel was damaged and was "much out of order." The young officer found himself with a dilemma on his hands as he wrote his superior seeking reinforcement: "The *Robb* and *St. Clair* are guarding Colonel Lowe; can not leave without sacrificing him. The *Brilliant* and *Pillow* are guarding Fort Heiman; if they leave the fort will be defenseless." There were no replacement vessels to send. Capt. Pennock was so short handed that he was forced to confess to another colleague: "There are now three gunboats here requiring crews, and I have none to put on board." Fortunately for Fitch, Col. Lowe abandoned his fruitless quest and returned to Fort Henry, freeing the fort-defending tinclads for service elsewhere.

While Fitch was occupied with Forrest's activities in the Tennessee River country, John

Army quartermasters and Lt. Cmdr. Fitch worked endlessly to meet the logistical demands of the Army of the Cumberland prior to the Battle of Stones River. Here a great armada of steamers are shown at the Nashville levee in December 1862 offloading large quantities of supplies (*Miller's Photographic History of the Civil War*).

Hunt Morgan also returned to the stage. In a "foot-race" predicted by an observant reporter from the Cincinnati *Commercial* on December 13, Morgan, on December 19, once more slipped across the Cumberland River, this time at Gainesboro, and launched what became known as his "Great Christmas Raid" into the area north of Bowling Green. Unsuccessfully pursued into Kentucky by rail-borne Yankee troops from Gallatin under Maj. Gen. Joseph J. Reynolds, the "Thunderbolt" sped ahead capturing Glasgow on December 24, Mundfordville next day and Elizabethtown on December 27. At Muldraugh's Hill near the latter point, he burned down the great 80-foot high, 500-foot railroad trestle. The 400 mile odyssey would be completed, via Bardstown and Springfield, in Tennessee on January 4.

Although the L & N was down again for another five weeks and some $2 million in Yankee supplies were destroyed by Morgan, Rosecrans had stockpiled for about 35 days and was not immediately impacted. By dint of considerable labor, supplies were gotten through that December. A million rations were sent on light transports from the Ohio River. These steamed through the locks into Green River and reached a point where the meals could be offloaded onto trains for the final trip into the Tennessee capital. Additionally, steamers ascended the Cumberland to Harpeth Shoals where their contents were offloaded onto wagons. The wagons then hauled the tons of goods the 24 remaining miles into Nashville.

As the river continued to rise, more supply steamers made it through to Nashville. In Vol. 2 of Miller's *The Photographic History of the Civil War*, there is a two-page photo-spread showing the busy scene along the Nashville wharf on December 18. Unloading munitions and sustenance were the packets *Mercury*, *Lizzie Martin*, *Palestine*, *Reveille*, *Irene*, *Belle Peoria*, and *Rob Roy*. Pictured on the snow-covered landing are barrels of whiskey (distilled for U.S.

Although taken within months of the end of the Civil War, this depiction of steamers at the Nashville levee shows activity little different from that which occurred during the conflict (Tennessee State Library and Archives).

government use) and sugar, hogsheads of molasses to be used by soldiers in their coffee, and myriad symmetrical piles of boxes each stenciled "Pilot bread [hardtack] from U.S. Government Bakery, Evansville, Ind." Yet to be unloaded in the picture are thousands of barrels of flour.

The Cumberland was now sufficiently high to insure that this supply could be safely, quickly, and directly augmented no matter how much damage was done to the railroad. On December 21–22, the Army of the Cumberland reached full strength with the arrival in Nashville of 13,500 more soldiers under Maj. Gen. George H. Thomas. By Christmas Day, Rosecrans had sufficient supplies on hand to sustain his army until February 1. Glorious as Morgan's foot-race was for the history of Confederate arms, it did not halt the flow of men and goods into Nashville by rail or water nor further divert the Army of the Cumberland from finally moving out. In fact, it has been written that among the reasons Maj. Gen. Rosecrans now sought action was his knowledge that two of the most feared Confederate cavalry chiefs, Morgan and Forrest, would not be available to screen Bragg, while other Rebel troops, under Maj. Gen. Edmund Kirby Smith at Knoxville, were actually moving toward Mississippi. These developments, like the rise in the Cumberland, were seen as a huge tactical plus. "We must therefore close in on them as rapidly as possible," "Old Rosy" announced.[14]

On Boxing Day, December 26, 1862, the Army of the Cumberland departed Tennessee's capital city headed south. "Fight, I say," was "Old Rosy" Rosecrans' order and thus his 43,400 bluecoats set off to attack 37,712 available Confederate grayclads at Murfreesboro, Tennessee. The contest began at Stone's River north of the city on December 31 and the cannon fire could be heard all the way back in Nashville. The great battle, fought in very rainy weather, see-sawed back and forth across fields and cedar brakes until January 4, 1863, when the Army of Tennessee, out of supplies and initiative, retreated southward in the direction of Shelbyville and Tullahoma. Rosecrans' exhausted troops held fast in their hard-won winter quarters at Murfreesboro as the Northern government and press lauded the Pyrrhic victory as a great triumph rather than, in actuality, the near run thing it really was against an opposing force 17 percent smaller. Neither Morgan, Forrest, nor Fitch had any direct role in the mighty clash, which cost both sides heavily. The three, together with Brig. Gen. Joseph Wheeler and other participants, would resume their dueling in the new year.[15]

CHAPTER SEVEN

Fighting Irregulars and Guarding Convoys, January–June 1863

ALTHOUGH NEITHER U.S. NAVY LIEUTENANT COMMANDER Le Roy Fitch or such of his Confederate raider nemeses as John Hunt Morgan, Nathan Bedford Forrest, and "Stovepipe" Johnson were directly involved in the December 26–January 4 Battle of Stone's River, one force of Confederate cavalry did have a role with immediate and sustained consequences for Indiana's tinclad warrior. On December 29–30, several thousand butternut riders, under Maj. Gen. Joseph "Fighting Joe" Wheeler, rode completely around the Army of the Cumberland as it marched toward Murfreesboro, wreaking destruction on its supply train. Wheeler, who at age 26 was a year younger than Fitch, was able to destroy parts of four wagon convoys, obtain fresh remounts for his men, and carry off enough arms to outfit an infantry brigade. "Seven hundred prisoners and nearly a million dollars' worth of property was the penalty paid," wrote a later reviewer.[1]

News of the supply train fiasco was wired to Cincinnati and Louisville on December 30, along with requests that new succor, upwards of a million rations, be pushed down to Nashville as quickly as possible. With the roads between Nashville and Louisville seriously damaged by inclement weather and the railroads in disrepair, Department of the Ohio commander Maj. Gen. Horatio G. Wright and his Kentucky-based deputy, Brig. Gen. Jeremiah T. Boyle, even before Wheeler's raid, realized the importance of getting those additional supplies to Maj. Gen. William S. ("Old Rosy") Rosecrans, by water if possible. On Sunday evening December 28, Wright wired Fleet Captain Alexander M. Pennock at Cairo wanting to know if the navy could spare any gunboats to convoy transports up the Cumberland.

On December 29, Wright ordered Boyle to get the roads repaired and to place goods aboard Ohio River steamers and send them down to Nashville via the Cumberland River. Not knowing whether the water artery into Tennessee's capital was navigable or not, Wright that Monday again telegraphed the Navy seeking help. Capt. Pennock was informed that

Brig. Gen. Boyle was applying to Lt. Cmdr. Fitch at Evansville for assistance and was asked to render what aid he could or to instruct Fitch "to do so if he is under your command." Not taking any chances and not knowing who among his navy colleagues worked for whom, Wright simultaneously sent a message to Fitch telling him that Boyle would be requesting that "you or Captain Pennock, or both," supply convoy taking supplies up the Cumberland to Nashville.

The telegraph lines and other means of communication to Cairo were uncertain in winter and Capt. Pennock finally received Wright's request to furnish convoy on December 31. The fleet captain, in turn, delegated his light draft flotilla leader to offer whatever aid he could.

At the same time, Brig. Gen. Boyle wrote directly to Fitch at Paducah indicating that boats with government stores were leaving immediately. "One hundred and fifty wagons in rear of General Rosecrans, loaded with provisions, destroyed by rebels," he added, rendering "it all important to get provisions up." As if that requirement was insufficient to provide the Hoosier's five tinclads full employment, Col. William C. Lowe at Fort Henry telegraphed Captain Pennock at year's end indicating that Brig. Gen. Grenville M. Dodge, commander of the 2nd Division at Pittsburgh Landing on the Tennessee River, also needed rations. Lowe had supplies to send to him, but all other communications to Dodge save for the river were cut off.

Dodge, whose command tenure extended back to the previous October, was specifically charged by his superior, Maj. Gen. Ulysses S. Grant, with patrolling rear areas, "restoring the railroads and keeping them running, fighting off guerrillas and pushing supplies forward to the troops at the front." Grant likewise wired a request from Holly Springs, Mississippi, that the navy additionally convoy the Pittsburgh Landing relief ships. Pennock on January 1 messaged his subordinate and asked him to help out with this case as well. "Much left to your discretion," he confided, while warning him not to get caught by falling water in either the Cumberland or Tennessee.[2]

Even as the Battle of Stone's River continued on New Year's Day 1863, Lt. Fitch, aboard his flagboat, the *Fairplay*, led the *Alfred Robb*, *Brilliant*, and *St. Clair* up the Ohio River to Smithland from Paducah. Upon his arrival, he was forced to advise Capt. Pennock that the water levels in the twin rivers were so low that his gunboats could not ascend the Tennessee or get up the Cumberland to within 35 miles of Nashville. Any supply steamers would have to stop at Harpeth Shoals and offload some their cargoes to lighters sent down from Nashville. If they could not pass, wagons would be required for the rest of the trip into town.

Perhaps even more distressing, the Indiana sailor found that his starboard wheel flanges had now broken off entirely, necessitating dockyard repairs. Although advised by Pennock to avoid a distant trip if he could for now, Fitch thought he should take the opportunity of low water up the rivers to get the *Fairplay*'s damaged wheel repaired. As he prepared to depart Smithland next morning, the commander wired his superior the news that the water in the Cumberland was beginning a gradual rise and asked after the readiness of Maj. Gen. Wright's transport fleet.

Fitch's flotilla rounded to off the mining town of Caseyville, site of the previous years' ransom episode, early on January 3. Once that messy job of coaling was completed, the *Fairplay* would go on to Madison, Indiana, to complete her repair, while the other three steamers returned to Smithland to co-operate with the Army. As with just about everything else during this trying time, nothing could be quite that easy. At the telegraph office, the navy man found a message from Maj. Gen. Wright reemphasizing the utmost importance of getting supplies to Nashville without delay and indicating that, if absolutely necessary, a Harpeth transfer was acceptable. "I rely on you not only for convoy, but for getting the transports as far up as possible," he concluded. Fitch wired back promising convoy and such other support as he could provide.

More disturbing than the major general's prompting was the local coal situation. The gunboat commander found, upon his application, that the product of the community's Tradewater coal mines was monopolized by others. In need of fuel, Fitch seized the facilities and took what he needed to fill the bunkers of his craft. Once they were finished, the *St. Clair* and *Brilliant* departed for Smithland, there to stand ready to protect any military boats choosing to risk the possibility of a Cumberland rise. While the *Fairplay* steamed toward Madison, the *Robb* remained at Caseyville in possession of the mines and oversaw the loading of a large coal barge for later use by the tinclads on the Cumberland.

Very late on January 4, the *Fairplay* arrived at Madison. Earlier, the *St. Clair* and *Brilliant* rounded to off Smithland ready to provide convoy in Fitch's absence to the Army's chartered transports. Aboard the latter was Acting Assistant Surgeon William W. Howard, who had joined the navy the previous October 1 and who, despite several threats to resign, would remain on duty until November 9, 1865. His letters home would, unlike those of the Fitch brothers, be preserved and would provide a first hand review of many forthcoming gunboat activities on the Cumberland and Tennessee Rivers. Also that day, further south, the fighting at Stone's River ended. The costly but strategically insignificant battle did, however, bring, in the words of historian James M. McPherson, "a thin gleam of cheer to the North."

After the fight, Confederate forces, surrounded by a friendly population, did not actually move that far away from the Yankees; their camps, with a comparatively short supply route beyond, would be located at Shelbyville (30 miles south of Murfreesboro), Tullahoma (18 miles from Shelbyville), and at Chattanooga. The Army of the Cumberland went into winter quarters around Murfreesboro, with its supply lines stretching back via Nashville to Louisville. Massive numbers of Union casualties were now returned over the roads from the battlefield to Nashville. Although many filled the city's hospitals, plans were made to evacuate the most seriously wounded by steamboat back up the Cumberland and Ohio to Louisville. Also, writing from Holly Springs during the day, Maj. Gen. Grant again asked Capt. Pennock to send gunboats up the Tennessee, to which plea the busy fleet captain replied indicating that he would do his best to accommodate the army man come the rise.

The *Fairplay* went on the ways at Madison bright and early on January 5. It would take 16 days to complete her repairs. In that time, the crew was all busy or on leave. The flagboat's officers and noncoms included, in addition to Fitch: Acting Assistant Surgeon Bolton; Acting Volunteer Lieutenant Groves; Acting Volunteer Ensign J. C. Coyle and Thaddeus Conant; Acting Master's Mates Washington C. Coulson, John Revell, and Isaac Summons; Acting Engineers Robert Mahatha, G. S. Collins, Charles Egster, and William Bell; and Acting Carpenter Thomas Manning.

At 4 P.M. that afternoon, the year's first big Cumberland River supply convoy departed Evansville with rations for Rosecrans' army. The 14 steamers, later increased to 18, picked up their naval escort while passing Smithland and their essential cargoes reached the Nashville landing on January 8. The passage was not easy.

En route, Confederate riders were constantly seen on bluffs and in the woods. The *Brilliant* and *St. Clair* sailors fired at them with their Enfield rifles, while shells were sent after the grayclads from the tinclads' bow guns. Aboard both boats, most of the officers usually congregated in the open on the spar decks forward, according to Surgeon Howard of the *Brilliant*. On one occasion, as the doctor's boat was turning, a noise was heard coming from the direction of the left bank of the Cumberland. It was a volley of what was believed to be over 100 minie balls that made all exposed crewmen rapidly dive for cover. Howard, in writing home about the incident some time later, believed it a miracle that the men on his craft were not hit. "One ball went directly over my head and through the chimney—and then through the other chimney, and two struck the pilothouse." The potentially disastrous attack, which the healer labeled "vicious," was a surprise because the Rebel perpetrators left their horses behind and crept up to the edge of the riverbank before shooting.

About four of the convoy's steamers, lighter than the others, paddled on ahead, hoping to get to and over Harpeth Shoals before dark. They were shot into along the way and, being unable to get over, were considered fortunate not to be captured before the tinclad group arrived.

As the two light draft gunboats hovered at the head of the shoals that evening, crews from the heavily-laden steamboats unloaded or crossloaded freight to sufficiently lighten their craft to pass over the obstacle and continue on to Nashville. Cargoes left behind would be strongly guarded until they could be retrieved by other steamers or wagons sent from the capital city. While the *St. Clair* and *Brilliant* were thus engaged, the *Alfred Robb* towed a barge filled with 10,000 bushels of coal down to Smithland.

Maj. Gen. Grant's assistant adjutant general, John A. Rawlins, informed Col. Lowe at Fort Henry, on January 6, of a reported large number of "flat boats and other craft for crossing the Tennessee." Lowe was instructed to "therefore please request the gunboats, which are reported to be up the river, to use every means for their destruction, that the enemy may be prevented from crossing into West Tennessee and Kentucky—they should proceed up the river as far as the water will permit." Grant, who also wanted Capt. Pennock to supply escort for troop steamers to Vicksburg from Memphis, wrote again on January 9 reminding the hard-pressed fleet captain: "There is no gunboat in Tennessee River above Fort Henry. There is 10 feet water and rising." Pennock replied laying out, not for the first time or the last, his situation with respect to available vessels. Two tinclads [*Brilliant* and *St. Clair*] were up the Cumberland convoying Rosecrans' supplies; two [*Alfred Robb* and *General Pillow*] had orders to ascend the Tennessee in response to Grant's request "with rise," and the fifth, *Fairplay*, was undergoing repair. "I have no others to send," he told the future president and those he did have were "only bullet-proof."

On January 10, Fleet Captain Pennock wired the *General Pillow*'s commander, Acting Volunteer Ensign Joseph Moyer, at Paducah demanding he rapidly take aboard a supply of coal from the army. His boat and Jason Goudy's similarly topped-off *Alfred Robb* were then to steam up the Tennessee and provide assistance to the U.S. military in any fashion necessary and not to leave that stream until further ordered. Late that evening, Maj. Gen. Rosecrans fired off the first of several complaining messages to Washington, D.C., directly to Navy secretary Gideon Welles. In order that the army and navy in his area could be made to co-operate and because he had "not as yet been able to communicate but once," "Old Rosy" asked if the USN's top man would personally put him into communication with the commander of the gunboats. Three days later, Welles responded, pointing out that, in case the general was unaware, the Western gunboats were now under the command of Rear Adm. Porter at Vicksburg. Ever the gentleman, Welles suggested Rosecrans communicate with Pennock, the senior officer available in the area, assuring him that the navy would cooperate with him.

The enhanced exchange of Union army-navy command and control messages came about as the result of an orchestrated effort launched by Confederate Gen. Braxton Bragg to keep his Yankee opponents occupied and less interested in trailing his forces out of the Murfreesboro area. Rosecrans, for his part, was under tremendous pressure from Washington to pursue. The politicians and generals on the banks of the Potomac apparently did not understand, as "Old Rosy's" biographer put it, that "the victory ... did not alter the fact that Rosecrans lay deep in enemy territory." The champion of Stone's River conjectured that the Rebel government in Richmond would stretch heaven and earth to send his opponent reinforcements and supplies and would soon try again to regain the ground lost in Middle Tennessee. To guard against this concern, the major general commanding reshuffled troops in the Nashville-Murfreesboro region and demanded more supplies and men from D.C. and the Midwest.

Based on their experiences against him since the previous fall, the Confederates, for their part, knew that Maj. Gen. Rosecrans was a precise man. He always looked after his principal base city, taking every precaution to guard its access and demanding extraordinary materiel and manpower support from his superiors and those around him before he would advance far from it. "Old Rosy" could also be paralyzed by strikes on his supply routes, now as in the weeks before Christmas. To maintain that kind of pressure on his foe, to keep him from moving either east or southwest, and to punish the one accessible Yankee activity most likely to divert Rosecran's attention away from him, Bragg sent his most mobile forces to renew their assaults on Union lines of communication. He also benefited from a widely-circulated piece of disinformation: the corps of Lt. Gen. James Longstreet would soon be transferred west from the Army of Northern Virginia. Unhappily for him, his command was beset with internal dissent and, through the upcoming spring, "the only offensive operations that the Rebels could conduct were raids, led by officers who were outside of Bragg's staff."

To the north of Nashville, Brig. Gen. John Hunt Morgan and his men rode toward Kentucky after crossing the Cumberland above Gallatin. His aim was not only to forage, but to further damage the Louisville and Nashville Railroad. Further south, Maj. Gen. "Fighting Joe" Wheeler and two cavalry brigades hit the Nashville and Chattanooga Railroad and attacked wagon trains slogging between Murfreesboro and Nashville. The worried Rosecrans sent soldiers to counterattack and to attempt to guard these local land routes.

Also, on January 13, Maj. Gen. John Pemberton, at the request of Gen. Joseph E. Johnston, assigned his cavalry units to join with those of Maj. Gen. Earl Van Dorn. As he informed Gen. Bragg, beneficiary of the enhanced horse troop, two days earlier, Johnston wanted Van Dorn "to cover your left by preventing Federal troops from going from West to Middle Tennessee." From Tupelo, Van Dorn would commence a "long ride" which would cross the Tennessee River and come to attract the attention of the Army of the Cumberland and the U.S. Navy.

In this cold, damp January, Rosecrans' entire logistical apparatus hinged on the Cumberland River, the depths of which were becoming daily more navigable. Although it was true that Yankee forces, like his own, would try to live off items taken from the local countryside, Bragg knew that, if he could damage the Federal supply and evacuation convoys, he might gain both success and opportunity. Attacking boats steaming up and down the Cumberland could not only divert Northern forces from his pursuit but cause notable supply hardship for units and organizations in need of replenishment in Nashville and Murfreesboro. For the Rebels, any dissention or finger-pointing this might bring between officers of the Union army and navy would be a bonus. Brig. Gen. Philip H. Sheridan, as quoted by William Lamers, summed up the logistical difficulties which the tired Army of the Cumberland would face:

> The feeding of our army from the base at Louisville was attended with many difficulties, as the enemy's cavalry was constantly breaking the railroad and intercepting our communications on the Cumberland River at different points that were easily accessible to his then superior force. The accumulation of reserve stores was therefore not an easy task.

Over the next several weeks, Wheeler and Forrest, together with local guerrillas, would threaten (the operable word being "threaten" not "damage") "Old Rosy's" water logistics to a point where the Yankee military leader, due partially to Rebel successes, partially to poor communications, and partially to his own demanding nature, not only questioned the support of his U.S. Navy colleagues, but proposed building his own gunboats and armored transport auxiliaries. Much of Army's angst fell on the heads of Alexander Pennock and Le Roy Fitch, who, nevertheless, professionally maintained both their cool and their convoys.[3]

Several of the steamboats to reach Nashville in the inaugural convoy were fitted up as hospital ships for the turn around trip north. When the first evacuation convoy left the city for Louisville on January 11, these craft carried approximately 2,000 wounded Union men. Other boats carried hundreds of Rebel prisoners up both the main rivers and the Green River. On one occasion at mid month, the Evansville *Daily Journal* later reported, the steamers *Mattie Cook* and *Hettie Gilmore* were diverted from Evansville to Bowling Green to return Confederates. Back at the Indiana town, the prisoners spent the night quartered on the Canal Bank before shipping out to Cairo aboard the transport *Courier*. Before long, a huge fleet of steamboats was chartered to haul provisions up river to Maj. Gen. Rosecrans. "What few boats were permitted to run on private account," wrote Evansville steamboat historian Milford Miller, "carried capacity cargoes. Of the steamboats that passed down the river, few returned, for the government pressed them into service."[4]

In mid-month before Fitch could get back from Madison, Rebel raiders enjoyed significant success in attacking Union vessels in the area around the Harpeth obstruction. The winter weather, in addition to the navigational difficulties of the river, may have played a role. All around the weather was freezing and blowing and the towns and countryside were covered with snow. In the words of Kentucky soldier Marcus Woodcock, "everything wore a dreary aspect."

En route to Nashville on January 13, the transport *Charter*, loaded with hay, corn, and commissary stores, was jumped by Capt. Dick McCann's guerrillas at a point near Ashland, five miles on the Nashville side of the shoals. The cargo was destroyed and the boat burned. The whereabouts of Maj. Gen. Wheeler's cavalry was unknown in Nashville at this time and so it was deemed safe that day to dispatch three hospital boats, the *Hastings*, *Parthenia*, and *Trio*, down the Cumberland, each flying hospital flags for identification. In fact, it was no more safe on this snowy day for these vessels than it had been for the *Charter*. Operating near the shoals was an entire brigade of "Fighting Joe's" troopers, under Col. William B. Wade.

In January-February 1863, troops under Maj. Gen. Joseph Wheeler CSA captured and burned a number of steamers on the Cumberland River, including the *Hastings, Parthenia,* and *Trio.* This depiction suggests something of the manner in which the deeds were done (*Annals of the Army of the Cumberland,* 1864).

The *Hastings,* first in line, had aboard 260 wounded bluecoats under the protection of Chaplain Maxwell P. Gaddis, 2nd Regiment, 2nd Ohio Volunteer Infantry. Spied from shore at a point at the head of the shoals, some 30 miles from Nashville and 35 miles from Clarksville, the boat was ordered to halt by a number of Confederate Wade's men brandishing arms. Unable or unwilling to respond, the *Hastings'* civilian pilot turned the boat over to the parson, the military's senior representative aboard. Gaddis called over to the shore that his ship was loaded with Murfreesboro casualties and couldn't stop. The Rebels responded with musket fire. Resigned to compliance, Gaddis ordered the boat put into the river bank, but its slow turn in the swift current was mistaken by Wade's men as an effort to escape. Two rounds from the Confederate's horse artillery slammed into the vessel before it could ground. As the *Hastings* touched, Wade's men, many intoxicated, jumped aboard and set to looting from both the boat and its passengers. It was at this point that the *Parthenia* and *Trio* were similarly taken.

Unbeknownst to both Gaddis and Wade, the three steamers were also transporting cotton. When this was discovered, Wade, who was inclined earlier to parole at least one of the boats, ordered all of their passengers ashore so that he could burn the three and their baled cargoes. Gaddis, with pistols leveled at him, stood up to Wade and refused to order his men off, demanding that Wade first get an order signed by Wheeler. Somewhat surprisingly, Wade complied and a messenger was sent off to find the boy leader. The major general sent the man back with orders to parole the *Hastings* and all of the Yankees, provided Gaddis promised to burn the cotton when he reached Louisville. Gaddis agreed, but before the *Hastings* could depart, yet another strange incident occurred.

As Wade and Gaddis were concluding their parole discussions and preparations to get the *Hastings* under way were being made, the U.S. Army converted gunboat *W. H. Sidell*, an old ferryboat outfitted with a field piece and minimal protection, rounded a bend and headed toward them. Named for a Nashville assistant quartermaster and commanded by infantry Lt. William Van Dorn, the *Sidell* might have been able to change the outcome of the Wade capture—if Van Dorn was able to fight. As the Rebels ran to their cannon, the impromptu warship swung into the Cumberland's opposite bank and, shortly thereafter, signaled its intention to surrender. The amazed Col. Wade ordered the boat to come across and, once under his control, her cannon were thrown in the river. Van Dorn's men were sent aboard the *Hastings*, which was finally permitted to cast off after her surgeon, Luther D. Waterman of the 39th Indiana Volunteer Infantry, signed a written parole. As the boat gathered way, torches were placed to the *Parthenia*, *Trio*, and *W. H. Sidell*.

As might be imagined, a considerable hurrah of glee or public uproar, depending upon your allegiance, was occasioned over Col. Wade's success. Gen. Bragg reported that Wheeler was "hotly pursued by a gunboat [*W. H. Sidell*], which he attacked and captured, and destroyed her with her whole armament." Nashville post commander Brig. Gen. Robert B. Mitchell, on the other hand, hurriedly wrote to Maj. Gen. Rosecrans at Murfreesboro: "The rebels are burning everything on the river. There are at least four more freight boats destroyed." Rear Adm. Porter first heard of the incident while reading captured Confederate newspapers downriver at Vicksburg. He was hopeful that it was not one of his gunboats or a squadron-protected convoy that was lost. If it were and Fitch, whom Porter did not know was at Madison, had gone up with only one vessel, he "disobeyed his orders as I directed him never to let one vessel go alone, and always to have two vessels together." As Rebel accounts were known to not always be reliable, Porter wisely elected not to place confidence in the report.

On January 14, the commander of the Army of the Cumberland telegraphed Secretary of War Edwin M. Stanton admitting that Rebel cavalry had done "great mischief" (because, he suggested, his own was out numbered four to one) and launched a verbal campaign seeking additional horsemen. Rosecrans went on to say that he also required "some light-draught transports, with bullet-proof boilers and pilot-houses, immediately."

Many newspapers reported the Rebel success and even U.S. Navy secretary Welles, from his office on the other side of the Allegheny Mountains, felt compelled to inquire of Rear Adm. Porter concerning the burning of the gunboat on the Cumberland River. Porter, who knew how his military colleagues were prone from time to time to arm steamers, wrote back to his boss on January 29 assuring him that the boat was not one from the Mississippi Squadron. With a certain amount of intra-service glee, Porter noted that "the army undertakes sometimes to get up an impromptu navy, which generally ends up getting them into difficulty."[5]

From his headquarters at Murfreesboro, the pensive Maj. Gen. Rosecrans now began a new push to force the navy to come to his aid. With Rebels on every side of him seemingly on the attack against every wagon and steamer that moved, Rosecrans and his people were receiving all kinds of reports, most false, about not only Longstreet and partisan activities, but about allies as well. For example, on January 17, the general's chief of staff, Calvin Goddard, wired Capt. Pennock that Maj. Gen. Halleck, in Washington, D.C., had reported to "Old Rosy" that the navy possessed "15 light gunboats at Cairo." The major general commanding, he went on, wanted Pennock to put the craft into service "immediately on the Cumberland River to patrol, etc." and wanted the names of the boats and their captains. The next evening, "Old Rosy" himself wired Cairo asking that Pennock send "a couple of good gunboats" up the Cumberland "to destroy means of crossing as high up as Somerset." How soon could that be done? he wondered.

Somewhat flabbergasted at the army's assertions and demands, the fleet captain wrote back to Maj. Gen. Rosecrans on January 19 indicating that Goddard's information was grossly incorrect. On top of a deficiency in gunboat numbers, the squadron was also sorely pressed for new crews—it had none and the men on one ship were down with fever. Besides, Rear Adm. Porter made the decisions on what vessels should be assigned where and he was below at Vicksburg believing that he had previously posted to the Cumberland and Tennessee all the force he could spare. Rosecrans' requests would be forwarded to him.

Not one to take no for an answer, Maj. Gen. Rosecrans opened a further correspondence with Pennock and, seemingly, almost anyone else in authority in the U.S. Army who would accept his post on the matter of convoy protection. In response to the "light-draught transport" comments in Rosecrans-Stanton exchange of January 14, Quartermaster General Montgomery C. Meigs, who was already dealing with the Tennessee-based general regarding his cavalry wants, now had to resolve this demand as well.

Upon receipt of the January 14 message from Stanton, with the secretary's covering note asking that "measures be taken to provide such transports as rapidly as possible," Meigs took the Rosecrans request around to Assistant Secretary of the Navy Gustavus Fox at the Navy Department and to Maj. Gen. Halleck for consultation. Informing Stanton of the consensus, Meigs wrote to Rosecrans on January 19 advising him to stick to Army affairs and not start building armed auxiliary steamers. The Navy, he wrote, was in the business of building light draught gunboats and "for the Army to enter the market would only delay them in preparing those" being converted. Besides, wartime shortages would prevent the military from getting the necessary boats and conversion items "even if we could get the material."

Brig. Gen. Meigs, a master at dealing with interservice army and navy egos and squabbling since at least the time of the creation of the Western Flotilla in 1861, held that a "proper co-operation" between the naval flotilla and the Murfreesboro-based military commander "would prevent the Rebels from crossing the Cumberland and interfering with his supplies by that river." From his experiences with Rodgers and Foote early on, he knew that "transports cannot contend with [the Confederate riverbank ambushers]," and that "[g]unboats alone can carry them through safely." The head quartermaster suggested that Secretary Stanton request such co-operation from the Navy secretary. He also sent almost identical letters of explanation and recommendation for co-operation to Rosecrans, suggesting twice in two sentences that no vessels should "move without convoy." On a technical note, the quartermaster general followed all of this up with notes to his own western men, Col. Robert Allen, the chief quartermaster at St. Louis, and Capt. W. Jenkins, the quartermaster in charge at Louisville, advising that they pile cargoes, hay bales, grain, coal, or even dirt around the vulnerable points on the steamboats they were sending to Nashville.

Late the same day, Secretary Welles, having been approached by Secretary Stanton on the convoy question, bluntly wrote Pennock: "General Rosecrans desires a naval force to protect the transports in the Cumberland: Can you not send vessels for that purpose?"

As if to add physical emphasis to "Old Rosy's" pleas, another steamer was lost on the

19th. The previous day, a 19-boat supply flotilla departed Evansville for Nashville, picking up its Cumberland River escorts *Brilliant* and *St. Clair* as it passed Smithland. Among the merchantmen in the convoy was the brand new steamer *Mary Crane*, which was loaded by the quartermaster at the Indiana port with a cargo that included: 134 barrels of beans, 50 barrels of sugar, 448 barrels of flour, 10 barrels of molasses; 226 barrels of pork, 35 boxes of candles, 50 boxes of soap, and 300 bags of corn. At Betsy's Landing, near Harpeth Shoals, she dropped out of formation to refuel. While the needed cords of wood were being taken aboard, the boat was captured by men from a partisan ranger battalion captained by D. W. Holman. Within minutes, the pilot was dead, the cargo was destroyed, and the *Mary Crane* was ashes.

Because steamers were at this time free to assemble for protection or operate independently, their safety could not be guaranteed. The two tinclads and the 28 survivors made it to Nashville later in the day without further losses. This is not to say that there was no opposition. Horsemen and men in the trees fired on the boats from the banks, forcing the tiny warships to several times shoot back with their howitzers. Sailors on the vessels used riles as well. Surgeon William Howard on the *Brilliant* noted: "Saw one of our men drop a 'grill' out of his saddle very prettily. He was just on the rise of the bank."[6]

The incident which seemed to push Maj. Gen.. Rosecrans over the edge insofar as his reaction to perceived naval inadequacies came the following day. It demonstrates that mistrust and confrontation between the Union army and navy was not confined to the higher ranks.

January 20 at Nashville began with "weather like spring—birds singing, clear sky, etc.," according to Surgeon William Howard on the U.S.S. *Brilliant*. As was their practice upon arrival with a convoy, Acting Volunteer Lieutenant Jason S. Hurd, commander of the *St. Clair*, and Acting Volunteer Lieutenant Charles G. Perkins, skipper of the *Brilliant*, made application for rations of Nashville post commander Brig. Gen. Robert Mitchell. As the gunboats were under direction of the navy, the two were not compelled by regulation or order to check in with the general commanding the post when they arrived with steamers—though perhaps by courtesy it might have been wise to do so. Mitchell, who was feeling the pressure from all of the raider activity surrounding his fortress city, chose to take offense and notified the sailors that they could not draw provisions until they personally came in and made a verbal report. Consequently, the two went over to Mitchell's office and, after a review of protocol, noted that they had but three days of provisions left and if the general continued to refuse to sign off, they would have to haul back to Smithland before the return convoy was formed up. Mitchell relented and then speedily composed a message to "Old Rosy" reporting the incident. Rosecrans angrily endorsed Mitchell's communiqué and sent it along to Secretary Welles, with a copy to Secretary Stanton.

In his cover letter to Stanton, Rosecrans could not pass up the opportunity to dig his spur deeper into the growing inter-service rift by revealing his feelings concerning perceived naval insufficiency. Having been informed several times that the navy would "co-operate" with him, the Murfreesboro commander wanted to "know just what co-operation to expect." Maybe a superior officer could be stationed at Nashville so that the two men could "concert measures." He was hoping for a good working relationship with Capt. Pennock, but had wired him twice without reply. Couldn't these webfeet understand, he wondered, that "if the boats run independently of his wishes, they were not only of little use for the purpose for which they were sent, but endanger their own safety and that of the transports they convoy"? Besides, the general also wanted to use them to destroy ferriage on the Cumberland above Nashville. Rosecrans really didn't want to command the boats, but for them to be efficient, a "hearty co-operation" with the navy was "indispensable."[7]

The fact of the matter at this point in time was that physical communications between Rosecrans' more-or-less static military posts, the naval station at Cairo, and the constantly moving Union gunboats was, the telegraph not withstanding, seldom instantaneous. Additionally, other difficulties with which the army was not always familiar had a way of complicating such good intentions of "hearty co-operation" which existed. For example, Lt. Goudy's *Alfred Robb*, having completed its earlier mission, was at Fort Henry on January 21, wishing to comply with the Pennock-relayed military request to ascend the Tennessee. Unhappily, she, like the *General Pillow*, was out of coal; until the two were resupplied, they could not move. A frustrated Goudy, who did not know the whereabouts of his Cumberland River colleagues, sent blind wires to Captains Hurd and Perkins: "The services of one of the boats is needed in Tennessee River as soon as possible." In hopes of finding them one place or the other, the wires were sent to the telegraph stations at Fort Donelson, Smithland, and Paducah. Fortunately, Lt. Cmdr. Fitch and the *Fairplay* returned to Paducah that same day, found the wire, and dispatched coal before departing up the Cumberland that evening. He did not know that his boss, Capt. Pennock, was anxious to speak with him about army-navy relations; "I can not reach him," the Cairo boss reported next day.[8]

The exchange between Maj. Gen. Rosecrans and Capt. Pennock continued in Tennessee as Rebel raiders rode about and, further north, plans were unfolding to send down the corps of Maj. Gen. Gordon Granger. It also continued between Tennessee and Washington, D.C. On January 22, the Cairo station chief revealed to the Murfreesboro commander that most of the new light draughts were ordered down the Mississippi to support Rear Adm. Porter. Of the remainder, three were in the Cumberland and two in the Tennessee, leaving only two boats at his disposal. One of those at his base on the southernmost tip of Illinois was under smallpox quarantine. The other, assigned as protector of the place, had so little "motive power as to stem the current." Pennock admitted that she might be sent, but there were insufficient sailors available to man her. The flag captain, who knew that Fitch was back and could bring resolution for Rosecrans, recommended that the army communicate with the *Fairplay*'s commander. "He will cooperate and give all the aid he can," Pennock advised.

In a telegram from Murfreesboro, "Old Rosy" suggested his own remedies. Couldn't the smallpox boat [*Silver Lake*] at Cairo be cleaned and sent, he wondered. It probably could, but not instantly. As to crew for that boat or the station guardboat *Little Rebel*, the general was perfectly willing to "furnish a detail of men if necessary." These would, of course, be landsmen untrained to navy ways. Finally, no doubt thinking of the *W. H. Sidell* and other makeshift auxiliaries, Rosecrans suggested Pennock just procure a number of steamboats, barricade them with protective items, put some cannon aboard, and send them up the river. The army would even detail men to man these as well. "Please do the best you can for me," Rosecrans concluded, "as to gunboats."

Not content to rely on Pennock's best and apparently unwilling to make any effort to locate Fitch, Rosecrans also wired Maj. Gen. Halleck late that evening: "I need gunboats to be sent up the river to destroy all means of crossing." The Tennessee was 25 feet deep. Still, Capt. Pennock, the general went on to complain, said he had no tinclads to send, could not crew the two he had, and did not seem receptive to the suggestion of army-manned auxiliary gunboats. Rosecrans' message found its way from Halleck to Gideon Welles, who, despite his vast appreciation for Pennock, was, like Halleck, Stanton, Meigs, and Fox, growing weary of the inter-service bickering out on the Tennessee streams.

A telegraph from Secretary Welles to Cairo on January 23 reminded the fleet captain once again that it was "imperative that more gunboats should be sent in the Cumberland and Tennessee Rivers to protect the transports." To help resolve the matter, the Navy secretary promised to transfer 200 bluejackets from the east within the week. Meanwhile, Capt. Pennock was to send the Welles telegram to Rear Adm. Porter by a fast steamer. Maj. Gen. Halleck immediately informed Rosecrans that Assistant Secretary Fox had just told him that an express boat was steaming to Vicksburg from Cairo with orders (actually, just a copy of the Welles-Pennock wire) for Porter to immediately send more gunboats to the Cumberland and Tennessee. Until help could arrive from Porter, Rosecrans was advised to look for aid from Pennock and to hold out an olive branch by again offering him "details of soldiers to man his boats."[9]

On January 24, Capt. Pennock, perhaps with some relief, wired Maj. Gen. Rosecrans that he was sending the U.S.S. *Silver Lake*, "lightly-manned,"—she shipped 28 men aboard as well as "a case of smallpox"—to the Cumberland River that day. The 236-ton wooden stern-wheeler was constructed at California, Pennsylvania, in the summer of 1862 and was purchased at Cincinnati for $21,000 on November 16 for conversion into a Mississippi Squadron light draught. The steamer was 155.1 feet long, with a beam of 32.2 feet and a six foot draft. Her two engines and two boilers made her capable of a speed of six knots. For offense, she was armed with six 24-lb. brass Dahlgren howitzers. *Silver Lake's* remodeling was completed and she was commissioned on Christmas Eve, with Acting Volunteer Lieutenant Robert K. Riley in command. Through thick and thin, the vessel would remain on the Cumberland or Tennessee throughout the war.

At Cairo, the *Little Rebel*, detailed to watch over the magazines and mortar boats, was relieved so she could undergo repairs. Her place as station guardboat was taken by the newly-available stern-wheeler *Springfield*, the engines of which were of "such small capacity" that the tinclad could not stem the current. Built at Cincinnati during the summer of 1862, the *W. A. Healy* was purchased for the U.S. Navy at that city on November 20 for the price of $13,000. The wooden, 146-ton craft was renamed *Springfield* on December 5, while she was undergoing conversion, probably at the shipyard of Joseph Brown. *Springfield* was 134.9' long, with a beam of 26.11' and a depth of hold of 4.4'. Equipped with two engines, each with a diameter of cylinder of 10" and a stroke of 3.6', plus two boilers, she could reportedly steam upstream at 5 mph—a figure Capt. Pennock soon disputed when he informed Admiral Porter, "she is slow, but will do something." On January 8, the new warship received her armament of six 24-pounder brass Dalhgren howitzers and, on January 12, she was commissioned, Acting Volunteer Lieutenant Henry A. Glassford in command. Like the *Silver Lake*, she would remain on the upper rivers throughout the remainder of the war.

Capt. Pennock, who might be excused if he thought there was some king of co-ordinated army scheme to put pressure on him, on January 24, received yet another plea for naval escort, this one from the U.S. Army's chief quartermaster at Louisville. That snowy day, Capt. W. Jenkins informed the Cairo office that Quartermaster General Meigs in Washington, D.C., had directed him to send a wire from the Kentucky office asking Pennock in Illinois to insure that a convoy to Nashville was provided for several steamers waiting at Fort Donelson. The fleet captain was to find two gunboats "at once" to guard the transports and these were then to be kept running back and forth between Dover and the capital city picking up vessels ascending from Fort Donelson on no particular schedule. This, Jenkins seemed to think, would "save much time and a great deal of expense." In fact, this idea would form the nub of an operational dispute with the military and the civilian steamboat operators that Le Roy Fitch, with backing from Porter and Pennock, would soon have to resolve.

At the same time, Pennock, delayed from conducting a personal inspection of the Cumberland River, was still not in communication with Lt. Cmdr. Fitch, and badly needed a reliable report upon the stream's requirements. Lt. Cmdr. Seth Ledyard Phelps, whom the fleet commander had known since he had brought the Confederate *Eastport* to Cairo as a prize the previous February, was tapped to serve as his eyes. Phelps was dispatched with the U.S.S. *Lexington* on January 25 to conduct a survey and provide a non-biased assessment. The heavily armed timberclad, active on the western rivers for over a year, had arrived four days earlier as escort to a convoy of Confederate prisoners taken in the successful January 4–12 Union campaign against the Post of Arkansas.[10]

While the telegraph wires hummed between Murfreesboro, Nashville, Cairo, and Washington, D.C., in mid to late January, Lt. Cmdr. Le Roy Fitch, beginning on January 22, attempted to upgrade the organized operational tactics of Cumberland river convoys. As others discussed various points of inter-service policy or procedure, he also oversaw the work of his subordinates engaged in reconnaissance patrols up the Tennessee River. It was during this time that he perfected a process for naval convoy which would be followed, with modifications, by the U.S. Navy in later conflicts.

According to historian Rod Paschall, U.S. Army officers have planned convoys for nearly 200 years. In the 1800s, these were essentially infantry and cavalry escorts provided for wagons or river craft that traveled back and forth between a logistical base and the rear area. Because of the locations served, these supply convoys were different from supply trains, transport that accompanied troops. The army mission was one of protection and doctrine advised dividing the escort into advance, main-body, rear, and flank guards. In World War I, Paschall writes, the Allied navies also employed convoys. In these, escort craft surrounded the merchant or troop ships; the most important vessels were centered inside the defensive ring, and the whole convoy proceeded at the pace of its slowest ship. The process was refined in World War II. Escort tactics in the 19th and 20th centuries, as now, are "essentially defensive." In and of themselves, "they do not win wars."

Borrowing somewhat from army doctrine and inventing some of his own, Fitch created lengthy water parades that were majestic, often noisy, but usually well-organized entities designed to ensure "perfect safety" by keeping all transports within covering distance of the escorts' cannon. He was, in fact, establishing what the 1944 *War Instructions of the United States Navy* in its Chapter 6 called "Cruising Dispositions." These largely defensive arrangements required: a) protection against surprise in any form; b) security for the whole force and component parts thereof through mutual support; c) ready transition to approach, contact or battle disposition; and d) provisions for rapid and certain transmissions of orders and information. This regiment was not then an easy process—just as it wasn't in the world wars of the 20th century. The Cumberland River was "very narrow, crooked, and swift" the young convoy commodore later reported; it was impossible to put more than two steamers abreast.

For increased power and protection should one become disabled, it was not unusual for the protected Cumberland steamers to be lashed together "two and two." Fitch placed the slowest vessels (usually towboats with barges) in the van of his columns, with the most valuable cargoes in the center, and the swiftest boats in the rear. The gunboats were dispersed along the line, always with one in the lead and one in the rear. Sometimes in strong current, one or more of the lighter escorts might be lashed to heavy transports. As noted in the wake of the *Hastings* affair, Rear Adm. Porter required a minimum of two tinclads for the escort of any merchant group. In his letter, the Hoosier officer did not mention a common practice remarked upon by Surgeon Howard in a letter home—towing slower vessels and other dirty work, such as helping to free stuck boats. As the *Brilliant's* medical man put it: "If there does happen to be any slow boat without power enough to draw a sitting hen off her nest, we offer her aid, comfort, and support."

The time required to complete a naval convoy cycle was one week. The days were taken up with actually achieving the round trip, coaling the escorts, cleaning boilers and making small repairs, and finalizing arrangements for starting the next fleet down.

Over the next month, this process would be refined, permitting Fitch to offer convoy protection, anti-ferriage patrols up beyond Nashville, and a weekly visit to the Tennessee River. By the beginning of February, Capt. Pennock, who was in agreement with the Hoosier's sailor's scheme as it was being carried out, was able to confidently inform Maj. Gen. Rosecrans that arrangements were in place that allowed the Cumberland River tinclads to "leave Smithland or Fort Donelson every Monday to convoy loaded transports and to return with those which have discharged cargo."

In mid–February, when at Nashville, Lt. Cmdr. Fitch sat down in his cabin to compose a letter to Maj. Gen. Rosecrans in which he presented the clearest report available on the tactics employed for one of his Cumberland River convoys. It is worth skipping ahead a bit in our chronology to review these formations. Noting that he was charged with guarding three rivers, Fitch acknowledged that he was taking a chance by withdrawing all five of his boats from the Ohio River to concentrate on the Cumberland and Tennessee. The Logansport officer reiterated that he ran a convoy from Smithland to Nashville once a week on Mondays. Upon his arrival at Tennessee's capital, two boats were detached to patrol up beyond the city to and above Carthage while the return convoy was being arranged. This disposition of limited assets allowed the convoy commodore to remain in constant communication with all of his boats and, in the event of an emergency, to concentrate them at any given point. At the same time, flatboats and ferries were swept off the rivers per the army's requirement and time was left to make a trip every week or so up the Tennessee River. Anticipating Rosecrans' continuing demand that naval vessels be stationed both above Nashville and below, Fitch pointed out the cardinal fact of tinclad life. His boats were only musket-proof and could not stand up, one-on-one, against Confederate horse artillery. On the other hand, so his thinking went, several together, by enfilade fire, could "drive off a very heavy field battery." Further, if he were to leave two steamers above Nashville, he would only have three left and these were insufficient to guard the large convoys primarily because the Cumberland was so narrow and the transport line so long. "The enemy," he wrote," could make a dash, capture and set fire to a transport before a gunboat could reach the place if there were only two or three convoying."[11]

Having left for Nashville almost immediately upon his January 22 return from Indiana, Lt. Cmdr. Fitch, guarding a big convoy of 31 steamers and eight or 10 barges, encountered the *Brilliant* and *St. Clair* in the area near Dover. The tinclads of Acting Volunteer Lieutenant Hurd and Perkins were coming down with a return fleet from the foot of Harpeth Shoals.

Both convoys halted while their shepherds communicated and revised their steaming plans. The Indiana sailor immediately directed that the warships of his two subordinates break off and join him. The transports, en route to Louisville from Nashville, were now, as those with him had been, below significant danger. Thus they could be bound down out of the Cumberland unescorted. With an enhanced escort, Fitch ordered the big Nashville-bound fleet to resume churning toward the intermediate port of Clarksville.

As the fleets got up steam and began upstream, time permitted the convoy commodore to run ashore to the telegraph office and wire Capt. Pennock. The lengthy communication reported that his present convoy comprised some 30 vessels, "which makes a very long line to be convoyed with only three boats." Could he not have more escort craft? Almost as important, Fitch, believing that he would, at some point, have to contend with enemy batteries placed where the river channel was most narrow, expressed a need to augment his boats' armament. Could not both the *Brilliant* and *St. Clair* each be provided with a 32-pounder of 27 cwt. he wondered. He reminded his boss that he had already sent a request from Paducah for two more 12-pounder howitzers and a 30-pounder Parrott rifle for the *Fairplay*. The ordnance enthusiast assured Pennock that the heavier guns could be easily worked on the tinclads. Unable to contact the *Alfred Robb* over in the Tennessee River, the Hoosier assured his chief that he would be "down to Smithland" as soon as he could get his present charges up and back from Nashville.

While the Logansport native's fleet was ascending towards Clarksville, great billows of smoke pouring from its collective chimneys, Lt. Cmdr. Phelps' *Lexington* was in the Cumberland on January 26 where she met a steamer sailing independently. The vessel had been fired upon by Confederate artillery at Betsytown Landing, a point some 20 miles above Clarksville. Phelps, perhaps remembering his time upstream early the previous year, determined to extract satisfaction for the affront. Pushing on up past Clarksville in the dark, the timberclad, early the following morning, reached the riverbank location described by the civilian craft's pilot. There a landing party went ashore and burned a storehouse supposedly used by Rebels as a "resort and cover."

With his armed reconnaissance completed, Phelps was returning to Clarksville when Rebel cannoneers, firing a couple of Parrot rifles from shore, hit the *Lexington* three times "without injury." She quickly returned fire with her big 8-inch guns and, as Nashville post commander Brig. Gen. Mitchell put it in his telegram on the event to Maj. Gen. Rosecrans, "we succeeded in driving the rebels out." The offending Confederate artillerymen were among those handling the six field guns of Maj. Gen. Wheeler's combined regular army division. Made up of an 800-man brigade led by Brig. Gen. Nathan Bedford Forrest and another, with 2,000 soldiers, under Brig. Gen. John Wharton, Wheeler's force was tasked by Bragg with the interruption of Union navigation of the Cumberland.

Observed from the *Lexington* as well as from shore, the Fitch convoy reached Clarksville toward dusk on January 27 and anchored for the night. There the Indiana commander met with Acting Volunteer Lieutenant Hurd and Perkins, as well as many of the steamer captains, explaining that the rest of the trip was potentially dangerous. To lessen the chances of Confederate attack, the convoy would leave at midnight and proceed under cover of darkness. It would be closely maintained and the three escorts would always be available, with one in the van, one in the center, and one in the rear. Lt. Cmdr. Phelps, joining in the discussions, not only learned the tactical situation from Fitch and his lieutenants, but agreed to lead the convoy into Nashville.

Seven. Fighting Irregulars and Guarding Convoys (1863)

To assist in guerrilla suppression at the end of January 1863, Capt. Alexander Pennock temporarily placed the timberclad *Lexington* under the command of Lt. Cmdr. Fitch. One of the Western navy's first three warships, she was the largest and most heavily armed craft the Indiana sailor would command for any extended period during the Civil War (his sojourn aboard the *Neosho* in late 1864 was very brief) (*Official Records of the Union and Confederate Navies in the War of the Rebellion*, Series I, Vol. 25).

Col. Sanders D. Bruce of the 20th Kentucky Infantry, post commander at Clarksville, reported the fleet's arrival to Maj. Gen. Rosecrans. One steamboat, he noted, had continued on toward Nashville without stopping. It was noted that Confederate raiders were on the south side of the Cumberland, near the shoals; their force was reckoned at 5,000, with eight pieces of artillery. The butternut cavalry had been "collecting such supplies as the country affords." Rebel horsemen could be seen on the south side of the shoals, though Bruce kept a strong picket force on his side of the shoals. Brig. Gen. Mitchell informed Rosecrans headquarters a few hours later that the fleet, with four gunboats, was on its way up that night.

While Fitch and Phelps were occupied on the Cumberland River during the day, Acting Volunteer Lieutenant Jason Goudy's two boat escort completed its convoy of the steamer *Raymond*, and a barge filled with army stores, up the Tennessee River to Chickasaw, Alabama. Later at Hamburg Landing while on his return, the captain of the *Alfred Robb* wired Capt. Pennock seeking assistance. Rebel forces, he wrote, had planted batteries over him at two places ahead: five cannon, supported by an estimated 2,000–3,000 cavalry, were 13 miles ahead at Savannah, while four well supported guns were at Clifton, 55 miles downstream. If Cairo could direct any gunboats to cooperate below, they were needed quickly as it was

Goudy's intention for his boat and the *General Pillow* to try to fight their way out of the river while protecting their transports.

Upon receipt of this disturbing communication, the fleet captain walked over to the Cairo telegraph office to respond to his lieutenant, advising Goudy that it would be too dangerous for him to move without aid, but that there were no gunboats available to send from Cairo. Perhaps Maj. Gen. Rosecrans could send land forces to cooperate, Goudy was advised. Pennock did wire both Lt. Cmdr. Fitch and Phelps in care of Acting Volunteer Lieutenant Riley and the *Silver Lake* at Smithland. It is probable that the station chief realized, even as the *Alfred Robb's* commander did not, that, with the Nashville convoy at least 125 miles away up the Cumberland, little immediate help would come from the commanders of the *Fairplay* or *Lexington*.

Whatever the reason (weather, a deficiency in the original intelligence, or changing Confederate intent), Goudy did not have to fight his way back to base at Fort Henry. Without damage or incident, his charges were safely returned by 6 P.M. on January 28. There he found an order from Lt. Cmdr. Fitch requiring that the *Alfred Robb* come around to the Cumberland as soon as she could coal at Paducah. Anticipating increased Rebel blocking activity on the Cumberland, the Indiana sailor decided to gamble that the Tennessee would remain pacific and to strip that stream to reinforce his Smithland-based flotilla. The *General Pillow*, the other tinclad in the Tennessee, was permitted to steam up to Cairo from Fort Henry for repairs.

Brig. Gen. Mitchell reported to Maj. Gen. Rosecrans on January 28: "Fleet passing Shoals at 1 P.M. without interruption." The convoy made Nashville that evening without, as Phelps put it in his report to Capt. Pennock, "so much as a musket shot having been fired upon a single vessel of the fleet." The *Lexington* remained at Nashville only long enough to coal before returning to Cairo, where she arrived after dark on January 29. As if anticipating at least one of the findings of the Phelps review, Rear Adm. Porter wrote to his fleet captain earlier in the day concerning the matter of escort on the Cumberland and Tennessee. Pennock, Porter directed, was to inform Lt. Cmdr. Fitch and the others tinclad skippers of the mosquito fleet that they were never to permit any vessels to proceed independently up the rivers. Any boats refusing convoy must be forced to participate and while under navy protection, all boats were to conform to any rules the convoy commodore deemed necessary to enforce.

After conferring with Capt. Pennock early on January 30, Lt. Cmdr. Phelps wrote out what he told his superior verbally. The main points of his report were exactly those Pennock, Fitch, Porter, and others realized for some time, but which the army and the civilian contractors were unwilling to recognize or appreciate. Rebel forces were thick on both the Cumberland and Tennessee Rivers. They had a number of guns "with considerable covering force" along the eight to 10 miles of Harpeth Shoals, as well as near Savannah on the Tennessee River. The remedy Phelps saw was not exactly in keeping with Fitch's request of Pennock for more boats and heavier guns for those he commanded, but was held a happy substitute. The captain-designate of the *Eastport* believed the Confederates would not stay away from attacking howitzer-equipped tinclads, but would back off from assaulting any fleet guarded by the big guns of a heavier boat. He recommended that the *Lexington* be sent to Fitch and, further in reinforcing Porter's order, reiterated just how important it was that no steamer be permitted to run on either of the twin rivers without a naval escort. In conclusion, Phelps had no doubt that, "with the aid of the *Lexington*, Captain Fitch will be able effectually to protect all the government vessels in those rivers."[12]

Seven. Fighting Irregulars and Guarding Convoys (1863)

The Nashville return convoy being assembled, Fitch and his gunboats led it down river on January 30. During the day, Capt. Pennock wired a message ahead for his convoy chief to pick up at Fort Donelson. Supplies would await the tinclads at Smithland. Unhappily, there were no Parrott rifles or 27-cwt. 32-pounder available; he did have 32-pounder of 33-cwt. and howitzers to offer. These guns would be sufficient, but would not be retrieved before early February.

Coming down to the head of the Cumberland was, as Fitch later remembered, quite heated. "We were greatly annoyed by rebel sharpshooters from behind the trees." These were "soon dispersed" and the vessels rounded to off Smithland on January 31, a day after the *Alfred Robb* arrived from Paducah.[13]

For Fitch and the Smithland escort group, the final day of the month began with the welcome news from Acting Volunteer Lieutenant Goudy that, despite his earlier suspicion concerning batteries, "nothing very serious" was going on up the Tennessee River. The Hoosier commander, anticipating another big convoy coming from Louisville for Nashville and one to bring back down, was relieved to wire Capt. Pennock: "no danger of either river being blockaded by the rebels." Although a smallpox epidemic was reported at Paducah, Fitch had no choice and sent the *Alfred Robb* and the *St. Clair* to that town to bring back to Smithland the coal barge the *Robb* had dropped off earlier.

During the last two weeks of January, the 12,000 men of Maj. Gen. Gordon Granger's Army of Kentucky were assembled at Louisville. This was a huge command, in fact a division of the Department of the Ohio, which was destined to become the Reserve Corps of the Army of the Cumberland. It comprised 20 infantry regiments, four cavalry regiments, and four artillery batteries. At the city's wharf, an armada of 28 transport steamers was ready to receive these men and their equipment. Early on the morning of January 31, soldiers started to clamor aboard their assigned vessels while wagons, once they were taken apart, "were lugged on board and packed in the hold and between decks." Many of the untried men were, as they boarded, probably as expectant as John M. King of the 92nd Illinois Volunteer Infantry:

> We were to have a long boat ride down the Ohio and up the Cumberland Rivers, where we could ride by day and night, view all the beautiful scenery and catch a glimpse of four or five states, one of which would be our dear old state of Illinois. We could watch the sunbeams, stars and moonlight sparkle, glitter, and dance on the waves of those beautiful rivers.

It would take two days to get everything and everybody aboard the grand fleet. Starry eyed, a few of the thousands of recruits could "dream of what would follow."

Those soldiers and commanders "in country," as well as many elsewhere, possessed some ideas—or fear—as to what might be expected as the transports steamed into Tennessee, with the chief concerns being weather and navigation plus Confederate opposition. Maj. Gen. Wright wrote Capt. Pennock from Cincinnati and noted once more "the importance to the army service of keeping the line of the Cumberland River between its mouth and Nashville constantly open to the use of our steam transports." To make certain that the Rebels would not interfere, Wright requested the navy "assign to that portion of the river an ironclad gunboat, plated with sufficiently heavy iron to resist field artillery, to assist in the above object." Recognizing the Army's dependence on the gunboats, the squadron fleet captain was able to comply with the request almost before it was made. Though no true ironclad was available, the *Lexington*, with her giant cannon, was seen as the next best thing. Pennock was relatively certain that her presence would secure what the Ohio general desperately wanted: "the safe passage thereon of the many transports engaged in furnishing any supplies."

So it was that, on the month's last day, Capt. Pennock, in a letter to Rear Adm. Porter, confirmed that he had on his own hook, due to the Cumberland River emergency and based upon the succor appeals of Welles and Rosecrans, temporarily ordered the *Lexington* to Smithland, along with the repaired *Silver Lake*. Knowing that it would be some time before he could get approval from his superior then off the Yazoo River—and still stung by Welles' implied criticisms, the fleet captain sent the timberclad with "orders to report to Lt. Cmdr. Fitch, to whom I have suggested the propriety of assuming the command of her until she is detailed for other duty." Taking control next morning of the largest and most heavily armed craft he would command for any extended period during the Civil War (his sojourn aboard the *Neosho* in late 1864 was very brief), was, undoubtedly, a very gratifying moment for the 27-year-old officer. Pennock also informed the Navy Department of his arrangements, noting them in the cover letter provided with a copy of the January 30 report by Lt. Cmdr. Phelps that recommended the *Lexington's* transfer in the first place.[14]

As February began, Brig. Gen. Forrest's contingent, coming over from Columbia, reached Palmyra. There his men were concealed and his guns masked. A rendezvous was affected near the town with Maj. Gen. Wheeler, who was seeking the most favorable position from which he, Wharton, and Forrest could challenge Yankee shipping. Union forces, under Brig. Gen. Jefferson C. Davis—no relation to the Confederate president—were, meanwhile, sent by Maj. Gen. Rosecrans to bring the young Rebel's people to battle. The main body of Wheeler's outfit was nearly surrounded in the Eagleville vicinity on January 31, but managed to escape.

There did not appear to be a good attack location for the Rebels. Besides, Wheeler was now convinced that his enemies had divined his intentions and had also stopped dispatching transports up or down the Cumberland. In this, he was only partially correct. The bluecoats did by this time know he was loose in the area, but their reactions did not extend to the river. Steamers were still plying the waterway, but now most were under naval protection and convoys sailed far more infrequently than independent steamers. On top of this, gunboats and army patrols had eliminated all of the miscellaneous ferry boats above Dover, making a Rebel river crossing impossible.

Additional problems for the Confederate raiders were the weather, forage, and intelligence on local defenses. The former was bad and the latter two absent. The most difficult challenge facing Wheeler was a lack of rations and ammunition. Forrest's cavalry carried only about 15 small arms rounds per man with a total of 45 cannon rounds; Wharton's brigade fared only slightly better: 20 shots per man and 50 artillery rounds. Cumulatively, these adversities were seen by Wheeler as necessitating a fast decision either for action in or retreat from the area. Despite a strong protest from Forrest, Gen. Bragg's cavalry chief elected to launch an assault on Fort Donelson; or, more correctly, the fortified nearby hamlet of Dover. If, as he postulated, the place could be captured and held, his people might better interdict Federal shipping.[15]

Fort Donelson, the scene of the great battle of February 1862, was a year later still covered by leavings from that miserable fight and for that reason, the fortifications were abandoned. Easier and more attractive for Union forces to maintain was the town of Dover which, since the fall, was garrisoned by the 83rd Illinois Infantry, under Col. Abner C. Harding, along with elements of the 5th Iowa Cavalry. Four 12-pounder cannon were also available, courtesy of Battery C, 2nd Illinois Artillery, along with an ex–Confederate 32-pounder brought over from the fort's unused water batteries. All the big guns and most of the 750 soldiers were assigned to prepared rifle pits or battery emplacements dug south and east of the town; Dover, itself, was 600 feet south of the Cumberland and was surrounded by deep natural ravines on its north side. Despite a series of false alarms, Harding, and his superior, 5th Iowa Cavalry commander Col. William C. Lowe, at Fort Henry, suspected Confederate forces known to be in the area might attempt something.

On February 2, the Confederates started their movement toward Dover, with Forrest traveling along the river from Palmyra by way of the Cumberland Iron Works. The same day, Col. Harding sent a telegram to Col. Lowe indicating that Forrest, with 900 men and cannon, were at Palmyra intent upon blocking the Cumberland. Just to be certain, he proposed an amphibious expedition be run up toward Palmyra the next morning. The transport *Wild Cat* would be employed and the rest of the day was taken up with reinforcing her decks with hay bales and placing two 12-pounder aboard.[16]

While Confederate raiders and Dover defenders gathered or prepared down on the Cumberland, troops, animals, and supplies from Maj. Gen. Granger's corps were, meanwhile, being loaded aboard the transports at Louisville on February 1 as the weather grew colder and colder. Among the vessels in this steamer fleet were the *Robert B. Hamilton*, *James Thompson*, *Capitola*, *Poland*, *Empire City*, *Horizon*, *Ella Faber*, *Hazel Dell*, *Diadem*, *John A. Fisher*, *May Duke*, *Dove*, *Ollie Sullivan*, *Freestone*, *Huntress*, *Shenango*, *St. Cloud*, *Adelaide*, *Arizona*, *Lady Franklin*, *Science*, *Golden Era*, and *Tempest*. The latter was home to the 92nd Illinois and diarist John M. King. The men were packed on the boiler decks, with animals and coal, while officers were given the cabins above. Cotton bales were employed as bulkheads to protect boilers and engines, while boiler iron was secured around vulnerable pilothouses. "These shields," King remembered, "were about the size of half a hogshead, but longer and so thick that a musket ball could not penetrate them."

Granger's boats were, in the words of diarist King," loosed from the shore" at two A.M. on February 2 and steamed down the Ohio. One of the winter's coldest nights was clear, King later wrote, with a bright moon. Looking aft, the observer noted that the water in the *Tempest*'s "track glistened in the moonlight and it resembled fire so much that it was hard

"Fighting Joe" Wheeler was a year older than Lt. Cmdr. Fitch. He and his men came up against the Indiana sailor directly only once, in the February 1863 Battle of Dover. That July, he was given command of all cavalry in the Confederate Army of Mississippi. Thereafter, Fitch was left to contend with the West's two other noted irregular leaders, John Hunt Morgan and Nathan Bedford Forrest (U.S. Army Military History Institute).

to believe it was not." Granger himself would write Maj. Gen. Rosecrans reporting that his column was finally away: "After perils by land and water, negroism and abolitionism, worthless quartermasters, and vexation of every kind and description."

Sometime before dawn on February 3, the great procession of Yankee army troop boats reached Smithland. The craft hauled up to take on additional coal at first light for the arduous journey up the Cumberland and King of the 92nd Illinois was able to record his impressions of those he saw ashore. "Here," he wrote, "sailors and loafers congregated to lounge and loaf, tell vulgar stories, chew, smoke, drink, and talk politics!" The few hours of coaling were completed and it was time to shove off under the protection of all six of Lt. Cmdr. Fitch's gunboats: *Lexington*, *Fairplay*, *Brilliant*, *St. Clair*, *Alfred Robb*, and *Silver Lake*. Not withstanding the navy, many of the green soldiers aboard were fearful of roving bands of Rebel riders. They were afraid that the riders would attack individual boats by aiming "first to kill the pilot." After that, the enemy could "let the vessel run aground, then after pillaging it, they would burn it."

While Granger's fleet was refueling at Smithland, Maj. Elijah C. Brott of the 83rd Illinois, with two infantry companies, was boarding the *Wild Cat* at Dover for an excursion up the Cumberland toward Palmyra to check on reports of Rebel raiders. Earlier, a small group of 5th Iowa cavalry was sent up by road toward the iron works. It was to act in conjunction with Brott in what was planned as a repeat of the White River envelopment tactics used by Col.. Graham Newell Fitch in June 1862. Before the steamer could shove off, however, a civilian rode into the town warning Col. Harding that Wheeler was at the works; the warning was too late to save the cavalrymen, who were captured.

By 1:30 P.M., Confederate forces were surrounding Dover and Col. Harding was sent an ultimatum from Maj. Gen. Wheeler demanding unconditional surrender. Harding, who was able to wire Lowe seeking aid, replied that he wouldn't surrender the post without a fight. He was also able to send away the town's noncombatants aboard two steamers. Simultaneously, the colonel dispatched the *Wild Cat* with orders to seek out gunboats and bring them to the town's relief and sent messengers to Col. Lowe seeking reinforcements.

Once it started, the combat, which is described by Cooling and other historians and is captured in the pages of the army and navy *Official Records*, continued throughout the afternoon. Wheeler's men mounted determined attacks, skillfully employing their cannon and limited ammunition. Although Yankee infantry was pushed back and the Confederates, at one point, occupied the entire western half of Dover, the Rebel assaults were, in the end, repulsed by the determined Northern defenders. Upriver at Nashville, however, officers at Union headquarters were disturbed by a rumor making the rounds that elements of Wheeler's cavalry were crossing the Cumberland at Harpeth Shoals and making ready to attack Gallatin. The rumor was false.

As dusk fell that cold, snowy winter evening, the Confederate leadership met to consider options. Given his lack of ammunition and the fact that Col. Harding would not surrender (a second ultimatum was sent and refused—Harding did not reveal that he was nearly out of ammunition as well), and realizing that Federal relief was en route, Wheeler decided "that it would be better to retire." In darkness, his men undertook an orderly withdrawal to a bivouac area some four miles south of Dover.[17]

"We could faintly hear the cannonading away up the river at a great distance," diarist King recalled. He and the 92nd Illinois men aboard the transport *Tempest*, as well as soldiers on the other boats being convoyed by Lt. Cmdr. Fitch's six gunboats, were aware of the Dover fight early in the afternoon of February 3. Entirely by dint of Yankee luck, the Granger fleet was only 24 miles downstream from Dover when it was located by the *Wild Cat*. As the procession continued, Harding's steamer and the flagship *Fairplay* made rendezvous and Fitch received the colonel's message sent some hours earlier at the beginning of the battle. Harding's note was brief: his pickets had been driven in, he was being assaulted in force, and he needed immediate assistance.

Lt. Cmdr. Fitch instantly made signal to the other gunboats, ordering that they all push on up toward Dover "with all possible speed." The transports were left to follow "as fast as possible." As has been pointed out, 24 miles is not a great distance by 2007 standards. That is the roundtrip distance daily commuted by the author in about 40 minutes total driving time (admittedly on rural roads in Greene County, Tennessee). But, in 1863, in the current of the Cumberland River, aboard gunboats with a speed of 4–6 knots (5–8 mph), 24 miles was a long way off. Still, the Hoosier escort chief, determined to attempt a rescue, ordered his warships to steam up at forced draught, with coal shoveled into the boilers as quickly as possible.

The trip to Dover took Fitch's flotilla about five hours. A short distance below the town, the *Fairplay* spoke another steamer, the captain of which cried that the place was entirely surrounded and could not hold out much longer. Pushing on up, the gunboats arrived off Dover about 8 P.M. The encircled Col. Harding and his men were found, Fitch later remembered, holding off overwhelming numbers from small breastworks back about 300 yards from the riverbank.

In composing his report next morning, the Indiana sailor offered a rare insight into the command difficulties of those first post-arrival moments. "For a minute or so, I was at a loss as to where to begin," he confided to paper, "as I could not get word from our forces, the enemy then holding the ground between them and the river." With no intelligence at all as to Confederate dispositions, he decided he could at least "let off a gun up the ravine" to give Union forces "encouragement by letting them know that assistance was at hand."

Two other pieces of luck now fell the Federal way. "Just then the moon shone out bright," the Indiana sailor recalled. At the same time, an officer from the 83rd Illinois arrived at the riverbank, having secreted himself through Rebel lines at the sound of the *Fairplay's* howitzer. The man was taken aboard and pointed out the enemy positions. The main body of Confederates was formed in line of battle through the graveyard at the west end of the town, about 700–800 yards from Col. Harding's positions, with its left wing resting in a ravine leading down to the river and possibly extending almost to the river bank. Ironically, just as Fitch was receiving this briefing, troopers from the 5th Iowa Cavalry lead elements of Col. Lyon's relief column from Fort Henry were preparing to engage an 8th Texas Cavalry roadblock five miles west of town, which rapidly disappeared.

It was perfectly obvious to the men aboard the gunboats that Rebel forces were not expecting them. While moving close inshore to make it easier to rake nearly the entire length of the enemy line, the sailors could hear Confederate soldiers talking in the darkness. In position, all six gunboats opened fire up the exposed ravine, into the graveyard, and into the valley beyond—almost every location known or suspected of holding southern troops, active or reserve, and horses. "The rebels were so much taken by surprise," Fitch reported, "that they did not even fire a shot, but immediately commenced retreating." So well directed was the naval bombardment that they departed precipitously and "could not even carry off a caisson that they had captured from our forces, but were compelled to abandon it, after two fruitless attempts to destroy it by fire."

"I was enabled to throw shell right in their midst," Fitch rejoiced. Once the main body was dispersed, the *Alfred Robb* and *Silver Lake* were stationed abreast of Dover to throw random shells and to prevent Confederates from returning to carry off their wounded. The *Fairplay* led the *Lexington*, *St. Clair*, and *Brilliant* above to shell the roads leading out toward the east. Believing that other retreating Rebel units would follow the river for some distance, the *Lexington* and *St. Clair* were sent on up to shell the woods along the riverbank, primarily to harass and annoy any southerners choosing that exit. The *Fairplay* and *Brilliant*, meanwhile, lay opposite the upper ravine and tossed howitzer shells up the various roads. Except for harassment fire, the gunboats ceased fire at 10 P.M. An hour later, Col. Harding sent word that the Confederates were completely gone from around the town. The gunboats were then positioned to provide night guard over the roads approaching Dover.

Fitch honestly believed that, in the words of Admiral Mahan, his arrival occurred with the Union garrison *in extremis* and that his intervention turned the tide in favor of Dover's defenders. Thereafter the naval officer—and the U.S. Navy—always maintained that his men were right to "claim the honor of dispersing" Maj. Gen. Wheeler's forces "and saving Fort Donelson." Indeed, his officers and men "were very glad to have a shot at these river infesters, having been somewhat annoyed by them on previous occasions." While the Logansport officer also acknowledged that much of his late evening firing "after the enemy broke" was random, he and his men had "the gratification of knowing that scarcely a projectile went amiss, and out of the four hundred and odd reported killed and wounded," the gunboats "could claim their share."

Exact losses are still not known and discrepancies at the time were, especially for the Confederates, quite huge in relation to the numbers engaged. Federal losses were 11–16 dead, 40–60 wounded, and 40–60 MIA-POW; the admitted tally by Brig. Gen. Wharton was 16 killed, 60 wounded, and eight MIA-POW, with approximately 200 total killed, wounded, MIA-POW for Brig. Gen. Forrest. Federal estimates of Rebel losses, like those quoted by Fitch ranged from 160 to 200 killed, 600–800 wounded, and 40–50 MIA-POW.

When all was said and done, however, the sailors were very gratified to know—or believe—that, by their actions, the Confederate force was "cut up, routed, and despoiled of its prey by the timely arrival of the gunboats and that Col. Harding and his gallant little band were spared to wear the honors they had so fairly won." A number of soldiers agreed. For example, Eugene Marshall of the 5th Iowa Cavalry, who was in the lead detachment that battled the Texas cavalry, was most appreciative of Fitch's arrival. Without the tinclads, Marshall was convinced that the Confederates would have prevailed; he was later quoted by Frank Cooling in his *The Legacy of Fort Donelson*, as acknowledging that otherwise "the enemy force was too strong."

Fitch's report was widely circulated in Northern circles and was published in several large city newspapers, including *The New York Times* on February 16. It undoubtedly did him much good at a time when Maj. Gen. Rosecrans and the army were criticizing his convoy operations, although there were those then and now who were not as convinced as he of the effects of his timely arrival. Col. Harding was not effusive in his written praise, noting to Col. Bruce at Clarksville on the morning of Feb. 4 that his men, together with Col. Lowe's troops and the gunboats, "got about 200 of them [Confederates]." Conversely, Surgeon William Howard from the U.S.S. *Brilliant* wrote in a letter home: "They were out of ammunition and would have had to give in, so Col. Harding said, in 15 minutes if we had not come up." Robert R. Mackey, writing in 2004, defends the tinclad warrior, proclaiming that "Fitch's vessels demolished the attacking Confederates, pouring shot and shell into the massed Confederate ranks as they prepared for a final assault on the works."

In his *The Army of the Cumberland*, Henry M. Cist is almost neutral, but does acknowledge: "In the latter part of the engagement at Dover, Harding was aided by the fire from six gunboats which were acting as convoys for a fleet of transports convoying reinforcements to Rosecrans' command." As might be expected, "Fighting Joe" Wheeler's report was contemptuous of the tinclads' effort. Having decided to retire from the field at 8 P.M., his men moved off in an orderly manner. At that point, "the gunboats commenced a heavy fire, without any effect whatever and without causing a man to increase his gait from a slow walk."

Fitch admirer Byrd Douglas conceded in 1961 that the Indiana sailor "did not arrive during the attack on Fort Donelson [Dover] in time to render any real assistance." His craft "ineffectively shelled the retreating Confederate troops." In his review of the battle in 1994, Terry Wilson admits the considerable disagreement as to the effect of Fitch's 28 cannon. His assessment is probably the most balanced: "If the naval gunfire did not force the Confederates off the field, it did solidify Harding's somewhat tenuous position."

The night of February 3–4 was very cold with considerable snow in the Dover area. The Union transports, which had made their way up in the absence of naval cover—some racing one another, arrived at the landing about noon on February 4. Many of the soldiers crammed aboard were allowed ashore to stretch their legs, to help with the immediate recovery, to participate in the many funerals, and to hear tales of the gallant defense. King of the 92nd Illinois counted 150 graves. The handful of Union soldiers were "boxed in as good boxes as could be had." Each soldier was buried "good and deep, and after each box was lowered and dirt thrown in, a squad of men fired three volleys in honor of each" as a sort of funeral service. At all these graves, boards were set with names and numbers (where known) and dates. The Confederates, on the other hand, were picked up from their death locations, loaded into wagons, and buried in the cemetery shelled the previous night without benefit of boxes or ceremony in holes large enough to accommodate two bodies.

Elsewhere, surviving Union combatants displayed war souvenirs, some taken from Rebel dead, while visitors from the troop boats noticed that Col. Harding's headquarters was blasted full of bullet and cannon holes. Also ashore for a casual inspection from the U.S.S. *Brilliant*, U.S. Navy surgeon William W. Howard spied a house on a nearby hill that "was so full of holes, that it was difficult to tell where the doors and windows were and this is no exaggeration." All day, the visitors walked the streets of the tiny (500 people before the war) community. Michel Andrew Thompson, a soldier of the 83rd Illinois who was there for the fight, observed the newcomers: "They all express themselves surprised to think how in the world we sustained against such powerful odds and held the post so successfully."

The combined naval and merchant fleet remained off Dover on February 5. Some men preferred to remain aboard while others continued their visit, some to hospitals, some to the old Confederate works at Fort Donelson, and others around the town, though not outside its environs where the enemy ranged. That evening, Lt. Cmdr. Fitch advised Capt. Pennock at Cairo that all the boats would depart for Nashville at dawn.

While Union soldiers and sailors were policing and visiting around the Dover area and congratulating themselves on their stout defense, Maj. Gen. Wheeler and Brig. Gen. Forrest retreated south, through Charlotte and on over the next days to Centerville, on the Duck River. The ground pursuit by the men from the commands of Colonels Lowe, Harding, and others was ineffective in the snow and cold; the nearly frigid Confederates were able to escape across the icy stream after volunteers swam over and returned from the far side with a ferry. A concise evaluation of the battle was rendered some years later by Cumberland River historian Douglas. "It is doubtful if the capture of Fort Donelson [Dover] could have resulted in a complete blockade of the river, but it would have had a tremendous psychological effect upon the people of the south." At the same time, it would have had "a most depressing effect at this particular time upon Rosecrans, who thought he was facing a disruption of his entire line of supplies and communications."

On the morning of February 6, Maj. Gen. Granger's troop convoy, guarded by the navy tinclads, steamed slowly up the Cumberland River toward Nashville. The size of the group was increased by the addition of 17 transports which had arrived the previous day. The civilian boats were "lashed together two by two" one passenger recalled, a formation held as the craft passed Clarksville, "a pretty town" notorious in the eyes of 92nd Illinois soldier John King as home to a group which, besides being "secessh," had made "the world nastier and filthier by raising and shipping large quantities of that weed called tobacco," a product that "boys love to eat, chew, and smoke and they learn to swear and become lazy, filthy loafers." The convoy reached Nashville about 4 P.M. on the afternoon of February 7, though many of the transports were not unloaded until the next morning.

Although the regular Rebel riders were gone, partisans and guerrillas, among them the 2nd Kentucky Cavalry (CSA) of Col. Tom Woodward, remained behind to harass and annoy Union communications. For the next month, Woodward hovered around Cumberland Furnace and joined with local men in making attacks at both Palmyra and Harpeth Shoals. The area from which these people operated was considered not only a safe spot for irregulars, but a protected river crossing point. Wheeler, Forrest, and Wharton may have failed to take Dover, "but the Rebels still effectively controlled the southerly banks of the lower Cumberland River and thereby remained a potent threat to Union supply lines." Rosecrans was not wrong to be concerned, but with Dover in Federal hands, Fitch and his gunboats could continue to move his supplies almost "at will during the balance of the navigable season."[18]

As the troops from Granger's transports found their way in, around, and through the city of Nashville on February 8 and arrangements were completed for the return convoy to Smithland, the *Fairplay* and the *Alfred Robb* ascended about 20 miles up the Cumberland to the mouth of Stone's River. Several flatboats and ferries were destroyed during the outing, but those farther up the smaller stream were safe from the gunboats in shallow water. Later in the day, having returned to the Tennessee capital city and found the steamers ready, Lt. Cmdr. Fitch led them back downstream. Late that night, Col. Lowe at Fort Henry, in a routine telegraph to Maj. Gen. Rosecrans' headquarters, noted the fleet's passing.

All six Navy gunboats and the convoy from Nashville completed the return to Smithland without incident on the morning of February 9. As the civilian steamers continued upstream toward the Ohio River, Lt. Cmdr. Fitch hurried up the bank from the *Fairplay* and over to the telegraph office to send three messages to his superior, Fleet Captain Pennock. The first was exultant. "I have the honor to report my return from Nashville," he wrote, "having landed in safety at that place with some 45 steamers. This makes 73 steamers and 16 barges we have convoyed safely to Nashville since the river has been navigable for our boats." If the first convoy, which was offloaded at Harpeth Shoals, was counted, "we have taken through to Nashville over 100 steamers, all deeply loaded." This was, indeed, a remarkable achievement; not one vessel in the Hoosier's care was lost or even badly damaged.

Putting his joy of achievement aside, Fitch got straight to the business of preparation for the next round of convoys. The coal supply available for his tinclads was nearly exhausted and permission was sought to purchase the contents of two more 10,000-bushel barges. Pennock wired back his permission for one. He also asked whether his deputy still wanted the howitzers and 32-pounder he requested the previous month and about which he had informed Rear Adm. Porter two days before. Yes, Fitch replied. He had dispatched the *St. Clair* for the guns even before coming ashore. The *Silver Lake*, with its lingering smallpox cases, was ordered to Paducah to drop them off at the hospital. If they could not be accommodated there, her captain would wire Pennock for instructions and permission to visit the facility near Cairo. If that were to happen, Fitch implored his chief to please return the gunboat, minus its sick, "without a moment's delay."

When the *St. Clair* arrived at Cairo early on the 10th of February, Acting Volunteer Lieutenant Hurd was forced to put her under repair with leaky boilers and fire fronts in need of repair. Station chief Pennock wired Smithland to let Fitch know that he would try to have the tinclad completed by the evening of the 11th. Also during the day, the Indiana officer received two messages from Murfreesboro.

In the first, Maj. Gen. Rosecrans' chief of staff, Calvin Goddard, informed Fitch that the army police chief, Col. William Truesdale, had discovered some ferriage in Stone's River and, in his superior's name, commanded the navy to send a gunboat to Stone's River forthwith to destroy it. Truesdale would provide a guide if the navy would stop by Nashville and pick him up on the way upstream. Fitch, who had just visited Stone's River earlier in the week and knew about several small craft he couldn't get at due to water depth, was furious. In a note scribbled on the back of the telegraph (and reproduced in the Navy Official Records), he wrote: "If Colonel Truesdale knew the whereabouts of those flats, it was his duty to destroy them."

The second telegram came from Maj. Gen. Rosecrans. Confederates were rumored coming up from Mississippi and the general wanted the Smithland navy chief to get "three gunboats and four transports up the Tennessee in 10 days to intercept [Gen. Earl] Van Dorn." He would supply infantry to accompany the expedition. "Please answer," "Old Rosy" demanded. Fitch, who would shortly begin endorsing his telegrams from the army with the date of receipt, did not get this message until February 17 and so no response arrived from him that day in Murfreesboro. Rosecrans, once more choosing to believe that his webfoot partners were preparing to let him down, now decided to try to get top level authority to take over command of the gunboats himself.

At 4:30 P.M. on February 11, William S. Rosecrans wired President Abraham Lincoln directly seeking control over those U.S. Navy gunboat patrols and operations which impacted upon the activities of the Army of the Cumberland. As he put it:

Information in the possession of the commanding general and post commanders must be promptly acted upon. It is, therefore, absolutely necessary to have the gunboats which cooperate in that work directed to report to and receive instructions from the general commanding, or, in his absence, the commanders along the river districts. The officers commanding gunboats express a willingness to cooperate with the department, but in order to make their aid effective and prompt, such arrangements should be made.

Lincoln, who was used to receiving all kinds of unusual messages from his generals, called Secretaries Stanton and Welles, plus Maj. Gen. Halleck, to a meeting to discuss Rosecrans' "river patrolling" dispatch. The chief executive obtained a promise from the three to do "their very best in the case," but wired "Old Rosy" back informing him that he would not take the matter into his own hands. He couldn't, he explained, "without producing inextricable confusion."

On February 12, as Capt. Pennock was sealing packets containing copies of Lt. Cmdr. Fitch's reports on the Dover affair and the success of the Cumberland River convoy operations for posting to Secretary Welles and Rear Adm. Porter, a biting telegram was sent from the Navy Department. Pennock was bluntly directed by Secretary Welles to "order the senior naval officers on the Tennessee and Cumberland Rivers to put themselves in communication with General Rosecrans and to afford every assistance in those rivers. He complains of the want of cooperation on their part." Welles had forgotten that Fitch alone carried the portfolio for the twin rivers and the Ohio as well.

At Smithland that day, Le Roy Fitch was ignorant of the fact that Maj. Gen. Rosecrans both wanted his aid and was stirring up the Washington politicos in an effort to obtain it. The Hoosier officer started another large convoy up the Cumberland even though the *St. Clair* had yet to return from Cairo. To ensure there would be no delays, he wired ahead to Col. Harding at Dover to have the steamers that had come in independently and were lying there prepared for departure. They were to have steam up and be ready to start up the river as soon as they saw the *Lexington* at the head of the parade. It was too late to move by the time the convoy reached Dover and, unhappily, all was apparently not ready as Fitch requested.

It was February 13 when Fitch, who was already planning one of his regular trips up the Tennessee, may have become aware of the army's requirements on that stream. The rumors of Maj. Gen. Van Dorn's movements were no secret. That morning, the convoy chief wired Fleet Captain Pennock noting that his charges would move out that evening and that he would return as soon as possible. "How much water in the Tennessee?" he wondered. The *St. Clair*, by then returned to Smithland, was ordered to follow on up without delay.

At Murfreesboro, Maj. Gen. Rosecrans was almost simultaneously wiring Capt. Pennock, pleading that two gunboats be sent up the Tennessee as far as Florence to halt Van Dorn, who was expected to cross the river at that point or at Eastport. To the west at Memphis, Maj. Gen. Stephen A. Hurlbut, the post commander, sent a similar message to Pennock. He only wanted one gunboat and pointed out that Van Dorn was delayed by Federal cavalry.

As the U.S. government-chartered steamers and their naval escorts churned up the Cumberland on February 14, civilians—or others—watching from the riverbanks must have found the sight awe-inspiring. Surgeon Howard on the *Brilliant* tried to describe the majesty of a similar passage in a letter home to his wife: "*Lexington* in advance, 64s [gun caliber]—then five transports, *Fairplay*, 24s and 12s—then five transports, *St. Clair*, 24s and 12s—five transports, *Brilliant*, 24s and 12s—5 transports, *Silver Lake*, 24s and 12s—five transports, and *Robb*, 12s.

At Cairo, Pennock telegraphed Maj. Gen. Rosecrans informing him that Fitch and all six of his gunboats were en route to Nashville with a big convoy. The general was advised to contact the navy man there; Fitch, Pennock noted, had instructions to cooperate to the extent of his ability. At the same time, Pennock sent a telegraphic copy of his Rosecrans communication to Fitch, in care of Brig. Gen. Mitchell at Nashville. It confided: "have asked him to communicate with you and informed him that you would cooperate to the best of your ability."

The Cumberland River convoy reached Nashville without incident on February 15. There, Lt. Cmdr. Fitch found his superior's telegram of the 14th plus two from Rosecrans. The Army of the Cumberland CO insisted that it was vital for the navy to send two gunboats on regular patrol between Nashville and Carthage to keep the Rebels, as reported, from building their own gunboats while two others should regularly patrol between Dover and Nashville. Rosecrans, who apparently developed something of a blind spot in his ability to read Capt. Pennock's telegrams, did not understand that there were simply not sufficient tinclads available to patrol and convoy in the manner he desired. Still, as Fitch wrote in his endorsement on the back of the telegram, "the boats are now patrolling the river between Donelson and Nashville in the most effective manner, at the same time giving convoy to transports."

As Fitch was preparing to depart Brig. Gen. Mitchell's headquarters, another wire came in from Capt. Pennock. Handed it by a telegraph operator, the Indiana sailor opened it to read of a new crisis out on the Tennessee. Early that morning, Maj. Gen. Hurlbut wired Cairo that Maj. Gen. Van Dorn was crossing at Lamb's, Bainbridge, Florence, and Seven Mile Island on flats. The army leader in Memphis believed it would take the Confederates 10 days to get across the Tennessee and, if Pennock could send a gunboat up that stream quickly, it could "cut his column in two." After acknowledging the wire, the fleet captain immediately sent it on to Fitch, asking that his subordinate dispatch (he really meant lead) two gunboats if possible to the Tennessee and to cooperate with the army "to the extent of your ability." The tinclad warrior was to watch the water level in the stream, making sure that he and his boats were not caught.

Sometime on February 16, Fleet Captain Pennock bundled up copies of all the army and Washington telegrams received over the past several days and sent them off to Rear Adm. Porter, along with a report on general Cairo station matters. Among the latter was notice that the *Springfield* was being sent out to Smithland that evening to reinforce the upper fleet.

Meanwhile at Nashville, an anxious, but stationary Maj. Gen. Rosecrans wired Lt. Cmdr. Fitch wondering why he had not heard back from him regarding the subject of his "patrol" telegram of the previous day. "Will you not communicate with me," he ranted for the operator to take down. The Hoosier officer, who had already left town, could not immediately reply. Increasingly agitated, the Department of the Cumberland's commanding general, who could not say what might be "the preventing circumstances," again felt himself compelled to vent his frustration with the navy upon the Cairo station chief. What was going on out on the rivers he wanted to know; "none of the gunboat commanders" had stopped by the Nashville office to check in or had wired reports nor provided "any idea as to what they proposed to do or not to do.... Were it not for the hope of some more effectual cooperation," he wrote, "I should at once purchase common transports and try to use them to patrol the river above Nashville at least." Pennock replied simply that Fitch had gone down the river with the Nashville return convoy and told the general that he could telegraph him at Clarksville or Paducah.

Before Fitch departed downstream, he had the foresight and took the time to write a long letter to Rosecrans explaining the convoy and patrol system then being operated upon the Cumberland, details of which were noted earlier in this chapter. The convoy chief revealed that he would be taking his command up the Tennessee as soon as he could, as he had reports indicating that Rebel forces were setting up strong batteries at Tuscumbia Landing and Savannah. A Rebel gunboat was also supposed to be under construction in the area. He closed by adding a final observation and a request. Unescorted steamers passing down were often fired into, several as recently as a few days earlier, because they were easy targets for guerrillas. Could not the theater commander use his executive power to halt all steamers under his supervision from running up or down without convoy, "as they are liable to be captured and burned." The young sailor diplomatically concluded with the hope that his arrangements "would meet with your approbation" and that his few warships could give "general satisfaction and security."

In the dawn hours of February 17, upon receiving and reviewing Fitch's letter, Maj. Gen. Rosecrans telegraphed back: "your letter received this evening; the arrangements very satisfactory." He also hoped the navy man would be able to quickly move up the Tennessee River. Fitch found this communiqué upon his arrival at the Smithland telegraph office later that afternoon. He immediately replied to the army chief at Murfreesboro indicating that he would be taking four gunboats up the Tennessee before first light next morning. If Rosecrans wanted infantry sent with his craft, they should be waiting for him at Fort Henry. Acting Volunteer Lieutenant Henry A. Glassford, who had arrived off the Kentucky base around lunchtime with the *Springfield*, would take charge of the next convoy up to Nashville, with the *Silver Lake* in company. It should be quite safe as, in the convoy chief's estimation, "the guerrillas along the Cumberland had become pretty well thinned out."

Well before dawn on a wet and dreary February 18, Le Roy Fitch sent a telegram to Capt. Pennock announcing his departure "for up the Tennessee" and then, after coaling, made steam with the *Lexington, Fairplay, St. Clair, Brilliant*, and *Robb*. At the same time, Maj. Gen. Rosecrans wired Brig. Gen. Dodge at Corinth suggesting that he send troops over to Hamburg to meet Fitch upon his arrival. While the five Yankee gunboats were moving from the Cumberland, via the Ohio, into the Tennessee, the Cairo station chief received Secretary Welles sharp and rebuking telegram of February 12. The harried fleet captain reported back to Washington that Fitch was under orders to cooperate and that Rosecrans, based upon the copy of his telegram of February 17 enclosed, appeared to be pleased.

The tinclads paused at Paducah before daylight. Surgeon Howard aboard the *Brilliant* was given an hour to travel into town, wake up the medical director of the local hospital, and get the boats' sick admitted to hospital and make certain for their arrangements. The five little warships then puffed their way to a stop at Fort Henry where their youthful leader went ashore for the latest intelligence. Although no telegram was waiting and there were no troops for him to board, Fitch did learn that Van Dorn was supposedly crossing the Tennessee. Rushing back aboard the *Fairplay*, he signaled full steam. Just above the site of Cdr. Foote's victory a year earlier, the little force met a rise which enabled it to ascend quickly on up without hindrance from rocks or sandbars. On February 10–16, Maj. Gen. Van Dorn and his 7,500 cavalry crossed the Tennessee, mostly above the Great Muscle Shoals, with a few getting over on the flat at Florence. Fitch later observed that he could not possibly have gotten at the grayclads even had he been to their crossing points nor could he have prevented them from making their rendezvous with Brig. Gen. Forrest at Columbia.

About this same time, a small Union force mounted a daring little raid of its own, gaining one of the North's few successful military surprises that month in the Federal anti-insurgency conflict. On February 19, intelligence was received by a scouting party from the 3rd Michigan Cavalry, headquartered at Lexington, Tennessee, that noted guerrilla leader Col. John F. Newsom and his men were staying across the Tennessee at Clifton. Having found and refloated a sunken flatboat and mounted a small deception designed to convince local spies that they had returned to base, Capt. Cicero Newell took 60 of his fellow Grand Rapids troopers across after midnight and surrounded Clifton before dawn, February 20, doing in the weary grayclad pickets. Upriver, the gunboat fleet, which had tied up to the shore for the night, got underway at 3 A.M.

In a furious dawn attack upon the sleeping, but fast-responding Rebels at Clifton, 3rd Michigan Cavalry Capt. Newell was wounded in the left leg and succeeded in command by Capt. Frederick C. Adamson. After a short time, 54 Confederates were captured, including Col. Newsom, who was shot in the left arm. Horses and small arms were also taken and the rest of the "guerrillas" had fled. When the battle was done, the town was set ablaze.

With smoke rising from the several burning structures, the U.S. Navy tinclads came around the bend from Fort Henry. Looking through his telescope, Lt. Cmdr. Fitch observed Capt. Adamson signaling him to land. Once ashore, the navy leader and the army officer conferred on the Michigander's raid. Adamson feared a Rebel counterattack and asked the navy to get his force, the Confederate prisoners, and the captured property, including the horses, back across the river. Fitch agreed to all the soldier's requests before inspecting what was left of the community. He then took the time to interview a number of prisoners. Among these the naval officer found two who wished to join the Federal gunboat service. Determining that they were Southern conscripts yet to take the oath, he agreed, in light of the Western navy's pressing manpower needs, to grant their requests. While Fitch and others from the gunboats reviewed the area trying to learn of other local enemy activities, Surgeon Howard dressed the wounds of Adamson and also of Col. Newsom, who was paroled and released.

Later that afternoon after all of the prisoners, whom Howard described in a letter home as "the most ragamuffin collection that can be found," were distributed around the gunboats. Lt. Cmdr. Fitch next took Capt. Adamson and 40 Michigan cavalrymen aboard and steamed up to Eagle Nest Island seeking another reported group of Rebels and a cache of stores. Neither were found, but the *Fairplay's* port wheelhouse "got somewhat smashed" during the landing on the island. Finally, after dark, the tinclads were able to land Adamson and his men on the west bank of the Tennessee, from whence they proceeded back to Lexington. The gunboats continued on upstream. Eyes were peeled for enemy guns and men along the shores. "They are good marksmen," Surgeon Howard admitted of the Confederates, "and if they fire from planted guns, we stand a chance to be well pounded as a ball from a 12-pounder would go through us like so much paper."

Still receiving reports that batteries were being erected at Tuscumbia Landing, the tinclad task force halted briefly at Cerro Gordo before noon on February 21. There a squad of men was sent ashore to acquire some dressed lumber, which was skillfully employed to repair the *Fairplay's* damaged wheelhouse as she and her companions steamed upriver. By and by, the flotilla reached Pittsburg Landing, scene of the previous April's ferocious battle, where Fitch communicated with Brig. Gen. Dodge at Corinth asking him to send cavalry to participate with the gunboats against the batteries reported at Tuscumbia Landing. The horsemen, in a maneuver becoming textbook for joint operations, were to swing in behind the Rebel guns while the tinclads kept them occupied from the river. Dodge, who would years later oversee construction of the Transcontinental Railroad, readily agreed.

The weather all day was very "stormy and bad" and Fitch knew it would be impossible to reach Tuscumbia Landing before dark. There being no good or safe intermediate points to tie up for the night, his group came to at Chickasaw, south of the Tennessee state line, at 3 P.M. The five warriors cast off the next morning and steamed upriver looking for the batteries which reports and rumors insisted had been planted. Perhaps expecting some huge emplacements akin to those that would later be seen in the World War II film *The Guns of Navarone*, Fitch and all of the U.S. Navy sailors were sorely disappointed when they came to off Tuscumbia Landing. The batteries which had grown in size and fueled so many imaginative rumors stretching back to Nashville turned out to be exactly two fieldpieces. When the Confederate gunners saw the tinclads approaching the landing, they hitched up and moved back into the town—straight into the outstretched arms of Brig. Gen. Dodge's forces, which reached the scene at the same time as the navy. The cannon were taken and that concern ended.

Steaming on, the Yankee gunboats reached Florence before noon. No additional batteries were found anywhere en route; however, guerrilla cavalry, like Indians in mid–20th Century western movies, were seen along the hills between Chickasaw and Florence. As the flotilla landed at Florence, observant Rebel pickets were briefly seen across the river.

One of the concerns bothering both Maj. Gen. Rosecrans and the U.S. Navy were constant reports circulating since the first of the year that enterprising Rebels in the upper Tennessee River area were planning to repair for possible gunboat service a steamer named *Dunbar*. The 213-ton side-wheeler was sunk in Cypress Creek in early 1862 to prevent her capture by Federal gunboats after the South's Fort Henry fiasco. Not much was known about the craft except that she was probably built in Brownsville, Pennsylvania, in 1859 and home-ported at Pittsburgh before the war.

Better weather came with the dawn on February 22. In an effort to "sink the *Dunbar*," Fitch sent the *St. Clair*, *Brilliant*, and *Robb* up the Tennessee River about six miles to the foot of the Big (Great) Muscle Shoal. The boat was reported to be there and the Indiana sailor hoped to catch her. Unfortunately, as he later reported, the Confederates, who had received benefit of the stream's rise three or four days earlier, succeeded in getting the *Dunbar* above the shoals where the gunboats couldn't reach her. On the plus side, all hands had the satisfaction of knowing "she can never get below again" as the river would soon be falling.

While his three stern-wheelers were away, Lt. Cmdr. Fitch, in the pilothouse of the *Fairplay*, was amazed to see a "squad of guerrillas" come right down on the hills opposite of Florence to observe activities aboard his ship and the *Lexington*. Three 8-inch shells from the timberclad quickly sent them to cover. Meanwhile, a longboat from the *Fairplay* discovered a hidden flatboat, which was as speedily destroyed. Brig. Gen. Dodge was contacted and agreed to send a force to catch the Florence guerrillas.

As soon as the *Dunbar* expedition returned from above, the five Union warships started back down the river. The vessels stopped at various places all the way to Paducah to take aboard refugee families, about 40 in all, and their few possessions. Additionally, the tinclad sailors gathered up 80–90 bales of cotton "belonging to Squire Cherry, a good Union man, who was fearful of its falling into rebel hands." Stopping briefly at Paducah, Fitch turned his prisoners over to the local post commander and sent the refugees ashore with their goods before continuing on to Smithland, which he reached at mid-day on February 24.

Stepping ashore to the telegraph office as he done so many times before, the Logansport

Seven. Fighting Irregulars and Guarding Convoys (1863)

officer found three telegrams awaiting him from Capt. Pennock. The first brought the welcome news that two coal barges had been left for his boats, which were sorely in need of refueling. It also asked for a fast telegraphic review of the Tennessee River "proceedings." The second asked that Acting Volunteer Master James Marshall be detached from the *Lexington* to personally bring Fitch's written report to Cairo. The third asked that the *Springfield* be sent to Cairo as well. The Hoosier officer responded immediately promising to send Marshall, the *Springfield*, and his report as soon as possible and, in the same wire, recapped the highlights of his week-long voyage.

Fitch did not know, neither did Rosecrans nor Pennock, that the day before Rear Adm. Porter wrote to Secretary Welles from the Yazoo River expressing his outrage over the "aspersions" the Murfreesboro army chief and others were casting against the officers and men of his upper river command. "General Rosecrans is very exacting," concluded Porter, "and at times imperious, forgetting what is due to the Navy Department, which is straining every nerve to carry out the wishes of the War Department." The Mississippi Squadron chief, who developed most cordial relations with Grant, Sherman, and a host of other Union generals, had come to realize, as did Fitch, Pennock, Halleck, Meigs, and maybe even Secretary Welles himself the truth of historian Steven Woodworth's later assessment that Rosecrans had developed a "practice of denouncing others for miscues that were often his own."

Porter simply could not understand how Rosecrans and Company would dare to complain about the shortcomings of Pennock, Fitch, and the handful of available tinclads when the "army at Nashville, some 50,000, do nothing to keep open the line of communications between that city and the mouth of the river." Cataloging his concerns about perceived army failings in the cooperation game, including a belief that the army did not credit Fitch for his timely arrival at Dover, Porter used his message "to show how unjust these army generals are in their complaints." It was hoped, by the admiral, that the head of the navy would understand that he and his people were doing all possible and that his outspoken memo was necessary to avoid the appearance that he was "assenting to the charge of not cooperating heartily." Gideon Welles wrote back endorsing Porter's "general course" and noting that his feelings were appreciated, as was "the vigilance, energy, and efforts of the whole force, etc." One wonders how Pennock and Fitch would have regarded the sincerity of the secretary's response if they had seen the "etc."

After dinner on the evening of February 24, perhaps in his cabin aboard the *Fairplay*, Le Roy Fitch penned his narrative of operations up the Tennessee River. Early the next morning, he added a postscript additional report. Sealing both documents, he saw off Acting Volunteer Master Marshall and the *Springfield*. He then turned his attention to coaling his ships and having their boilers cleaned in preparation for the next Nashville convoy. Meanwhile, over on the *Brilliant*, Surgeon William Howard summed up the entire Tennessee River trip in one sentence of a letter home: "We have gone up the Tennessee River to Florence and some 60 miles above to the Muscle Shoals and we have seen no batteries."[19]

Within two days of the end of the Tennessee River expedition, the *Fairplay*, *Lexington*, *Silver Lake* and *Brilliant* were guarding another large convoy up to Nashville. This they brought into the Tennessee capital city without incident early on March 1, allowing post commandant Brig. Gen. Mitchell to wire Maj. Gen. Rosecrans that the "fleet arrived this morning—26 transports and four gunboats." Several hours were taken for routine repairs, and then the *Fairplay* and *Brilliant* "started up the river to look for things." It was expected they might go up 200 miles or more, but at least the weather was delightful. Previously, it was "frightfully changeable: rains in torrents, etc." Finding that the river was up some 20 feet, no levees could be seen; indeed, no landmarks were visible that were noticeable on the previous visit. Such swollen and swift waters would, in and of themselves, be extremely hazardous for anyone contemplating a crossing. As a result of this finding, the two craft ceased their unproductive patrol when but 60 miles up en route to Carthage. They returned to Nashville after dark and continued on upstream to join the *Lexington* and *Silver Lake*, already protecting a convoy to Smithland.[20]

The seemingly endless demands for protection from the army generals picked up again on the first day of March. Maj. Gen. Rosecrans was apparently no longer completely satisfied with the Fitch convoy and patrol scheme agreed to two weeks earlier. Thus he renewed discussion on the matter with a pair of telegrams to Capt. Pennock. In these, he acknowledged that he was now in regular communication with Lt. Cmdr. Fitch, but that more boats were required in order that additional supplies might be more swiftly moved while the Cumberland was high. Patrols of the river above the city were also required. The next day, Pennock wrote back that he had no boats to spare, but that he would forward the messages down to Rear Adm. Porter.

On March 2, Rosecrans and Fitch launched into a weeklong telegraphic exchange. "Boats 12 days from Louisville, loaded with horses and stores much needed, lie at Donelson waiting convoy," wrote "Old Rosy." "Please see that they get in as soon as possible." The next day, the Murfreesboro-based army leader reemphasized his point that transports should not be detained at the forward assembly point at Fort Donelson for "want of convoy." A large number had assembled there over the past couple of days and were waiting for the gunboats. The items they carried were needed without delay. Further, couldn't the army have some gunboats at its disposal to regularly patrol the river above Nashville?

There may have been a certain validity to Rosecrans' concerns. Huge weekly convoys were not the best way to smoothly restock the Nashville depots. The time and problems of unloading the steamboats and reassembling return fleets for Louisville were significant. As men labored quickly to get goods off the steamers, the various boxes and so forth had to be stacked until carts and wagons could haul them to warehouses. On top of this, "Old Rosy" did achieve unity of command over the land garrisons established to protect the river route. That his "army of 29,000 men on this river [was] doing nothing," in the view of Rear Adm. Porter, "to protect the whole line of river against the guerrillas" was a debatable point. Because he did not personally control the running of the convoys, Rosecrans found it difficult to guarantee his men and contract workers open and safe navigation of the Cumberland. Being, as he was, under pressure to keep Confederate forces away and prepare and mount a new campaign south, the harried general continued to agitate the joint service support issue.[21]

With navy rank equivalent to that of a major on Rosecrans' staff, Le Roy Fitch can be excused for perhaps not appreciating the difficulties, real and otherwise, of a man operating at the senior strategic level of his own chief, Rear Adm. Porter. On the other hand, he probably had hoped that the army people at the top in Murfreesboro and Nashville were acquainted with the patrol and convoy arrangements agreed to by Rosecrans on February 17. He might also have desired a better understanding on their part of the difficulties of shepherding dozens of transports up and down the unpredictable Cumberland in the face of Confederate ambush. Finally, he desperately wanted the army to understand that it could not send transports upstream willy-nilly in ones and twos and expect him to guard them to Nashville in such fashion.

Now disabused of all three expectations, an obviously frustrated Fitch sent two telegrams back to Rosecrans on March 3, one each on the matters of upper river patrol and convoy. In the first, he reported: "I cannot possibly station gunboats permanently above Nashville. I am ordered to keep two always together, besides to make the trip above once a week." Further, he warned of intelligence that Rebel general Earl Van Dorn was expected to strike at the river supply chain at Dover or Palmyra and naval forces were required below to watch out for him. In the second, he stated that it was, frankly, impossible to get more than one convoy through safely per week because he simply did not have "boats enough to do it." For that reason, transports had to unavoidably lay over a day or two at Fort Donelson, because they "come dropping in one at a time just after the fleet starts for Nashville." Of course, there would be no detention if the originating officer, Brig. Gen. Boyle, would simply "send them in fleets from Louisville once a week." Fitch concluded that he understood the fragility of horses and the need for their speedy delivery, but he could not, without endangering them, "hurry the boats up during the heavy flow of drift[wood]" in the swollen Cumberland.

While at the telegraph office, the Indiana sailor also asked the operator to send a dispatch to Brig. Gen. Boyle reinforcing what he told the major general and pleading for that officer in Kentucky to send the transports from Louisville once a week in a single fleet. "Can not the boats load with the stores and provisions and when all ready, take the horses on board and all leave together?" he wondered. As the craft from Louisville dropped in at Smithland or Fort Donelson one at a time after the big naval convoys left up river and because of the standing general order that they could not proceed without gunboat protection, the steamboats had to lay over two or three days. "This makes it bad for the horses," Fitch acknowledged. The navy did not have enough gunboats on the Cumberland to escort steamers individually and could guarantee safely only with weekly convoys. "I care not how large the fleets are," the officer concluded.

Maj. Gen. Rosecrans did not buy Fitch's explanations and, as was his practice, sent a wire of concern to Maj. Gen. Halleck on March 5 for transferal to Secretary Welles. "Something must be done to secure convoys for our boats or this army will be without supplies," was the word from Murfreesboro. "We have gained nothing by the high river in subsistence for the last 10 days, because our convoys are detained," Rosecrans wrote. If he couldn't get any help, maybe, going back to an old theme, he ought to have some gunboats made up on his own. Halleck, who was still joined with Quartermaster General Meigs in battling Rosecrans over other logistical and materiel concerns, received the message late on March 6. It was the same day Le Roy Fitch and his four gunboats took the month's second big convoy into Nashville and made yet another patrol up the Cumberland River to Carthage. Twenty-four hours later, as Halleck was passing the Rosecrans wire to the civilian head of the U.S. Navy, Fitch was headed back up to Smithland where he arrived on March 8.[22]

As might be imagined, Secretary Welles was not particularly happy to hear again from Rosecrans and Halleck on the subject of Cumberland River convoys. Only 20 days had passed since he had scolded Capt. Pennock on the same topic. This time, however, the Navy chief did more than urge the Cairo station chief to try harder in support of the army. This time Pennock was authorized "to purchase a necessary number of suitable boats and arm and equip them." Moreover, Cdr. Hull could be asked to assist in choosing and outfitting the craft and the fleet captain did not have to wait to get these orders from Rear Adm. Porter. "The Department wants prompt and energetic steps immediately taken," the cabinet officer concluded, "to give the necessary protection to the transports of General Rosecrans."

Welles' telegram reached Pennock on the afternoon of March 8. At 9 P.M. that evening the Cairo station chief wired back informing Washington that, although "suitable boats are hard to find," he would purchase steamers for the reinforcement of the upper fleet. Could not the department send additional officers and men for the squadron as a whole? "We must obtain them by some means, or we can not man another boat." Finally, he revealed, he was leaving from the telegraph office to immediately travel up to the mouth of the Cumberland River for a Smithland summit. There he would personally examine the condition of his mosquito fleet and give further instruction, "if necessary," to Lt. Cmdr. Fitch.

Pennock and Fitch met throughout the day at Smithland on March 9, during which time both men inspected the available units of the latter's fleet. Four boats, *Lexington, Fairplay, Silver Lake,* and *Brilliant* were temporarily laid up; the former was scaling her boilers while the latter was under repair. All would be ready and coaled in time for the next convoy, scheduled three days hence. Fitch was apprised of Rosecrans' Washington telegrams and Welles' February 12 wire of "complaint of a want of cooperation." Pennock, who later told Porter that he had "no doubt that he [Fitch] has done everything possible in his power," directed his subordinate to compile a full report on all of his operations and the circumstances surrounding them.

Both officers then discussed the tactical problems caused by Brig. Gen. Boyle's refusal to send down his steamers in large groups. Pennock was convinced, as he later wired Maj. Gen. Rosecrans, that "convoy can be had and empty vessels brought down once a week, provided there is strict compliance with Captain Fitch's arrangements." The conference doubtless concluded with a conversation on the overall lack of manpower available to the Mississippi Squadron, the forthcoming addition of more tinclads, and anticipated upcoming missions which would stretch Fitch's administrative and operational efficiency to the limit. It is quite possible that the fleet captain and the convoy commodore discussed the latter's idea for a geographical division of responsibilities.

That evening, Capt. Pennock, who would return to Cairo at first light, opened several new messages received by dispatch boat from Rear Adm. Porter. One of these contained various situational reports and new, more specific instructions for Lt. Cmdr. Fitch. The intelligence of proposed Confederate action along the Tennessee was extracted and was similar to that provided by special War Department commissioner Charles A. Dana to Secretary Stanton on March 20.

Maj. Gen. Rosecrans, Dana reported, ordered Forts Henry and Heiman abandoned and leveled as he no longer believed their manning essential. What troops were stationed there could be transferred to and better employed at Fort Donelson, which was being rebuilt to accommodate up to 3,000 men and 14 cannon. Before this could be accomplished, Confederate troops occupied Fort Heiman. Out in Memphis, VI Corps commander Maj. Gen. Hurlbut received information on the matter from Brig. Gen. Alexander Asboth, a one-time Hungarian freedom fighter who was now post commander at Columbus, Kentucky. Both men, especially the latter, believed Heiman a key to Columbus as well as Paducah. In anticipation of a consequential U.S. Army move back to Heiman, Porter wanted Fitch on the Tennessee.

Porter's orders for the Indiana sailor were amplified by the fleet captain:

> You will have to keep a good watch soon on the Tennessee River. The enemy's plan is to fall back upon Tennessee with all the forces they can raise, and deal Rosecrans a crushing blow. Now we must keep all the vessels you can spare up the Tennessee as high as they can go. The chance is the enemy will cross over somewhere as high up as Decatur [AL]. At all events get

all the information you can, and be ready to meet them. In relation to the Tennessee River, it is necessary to have for the present two light-draft gunboats there, with good men in command. I do not think the rebels will attempt to cross into Tennessee if we have two boats at Decatur, another at Waterloo. Both these points command important railroads.... The rebel army is stationed at Stevenson, just above Decatur, and going too high up might get the gunboats in trouble. The time has come when we must begin to drive the rebels off the banks of the Tennessee.[23]

Next morning as preparations were launched for the Tennessee River voyage and repairs were pushed on his vessels, Lt. Cmdr. Fitch deputized Acting Volunteer Lieutenant Hurd to lead the next Nashville convoy. A wire was sent to Maj. Gen. Rosecrans informing him that Hurd would be coming up with a smaller-than-usual group of transports, but that he would ascend beyond to Carthage, water-level permitting. Fitch would be making another trip up the Tennessee, but he remained happy to render any possible assistance. The army commander could, if necessary, contact him at Smithland before his departure or talk to Hurd at Nashville upon his arrival.

Interestingly, far up the Ohio River in Cincinnati, Maj. Gen. Wright was simultaneously writing to Col. Lewis B. Parsons, then acting quartermaster of that city, about a message received from Rosecrans a couple of days back. To aid the supply situation of the Army of the Cumberland, "Old Rosy" directed Wright to send to Nashville 10 million rations over the next three weeks. To do this, Wright cut orders for every steamboat available to be pressed into the service. Unhappily, unless steamers were returned more speedily from the Cumberland River, it would, he thought, be impossible to fully carry out these wishes. The shipments were not made in the time frame desired.

Now back at Cairo, Capt. Pennock wrote a lengthy report on his Smithland visit for delivery down to Rear Adm. Porter. Every effort was being exerted on his part to acquire the additional warship reinforcements Fitch required, but manning them would, unless the situation changed, continue to be a problem. It was in this report that the Cairo station chief officially brought up his recommendation of dividing the upper fleet "into two parts— one for the Cumberland River and the other for the Tennessee—Lt. Cmdr. Fitch commanding the former and a commissioned officer of the Navy, of experience and judgement, the latter." Given the pending increase in the mosquito fleet's size and capabilities, the importance of constant vigilance for the Cumberland convoys was thus reinforced as well as the need for attention to operations miles away up the Tennessee.

The *St. Clair, Alfred Robb,* and *Springfield* duly picked up the Louisville transports on the morning of March 12 and steamed on upstream. The same day, Maj. Gen. Hurlbut ordered Brig. Gen. Asboth to reoccupy Fort Heiman. As he stepped off, Asboth wired Capt. Pennock asking what the navy could do to help and wondering if the "gunboats from Smithland [are] already ascending the Tennessee?" Actually, Fitch's boats had yet to depart. In the meantime and in anticipation of possible trouble, the fleet captain decided to send the brand new ironclad U.S.S. *Tuscumbia*, under Lt. Cmdr. James W. Shirk, up the Tennessee to add her firepower if necessary. The giant craft, which would gain a reputation as one of the most poorly built of all Mississippi Squadron gunboats, was commissioned that very day.[24]

On the 13th of March, the refreshed *Lexington, Fairplay,* and *Brilliant* commenced a patrol up the Tennessee River. Stopping in at Paducah for messages, Lt. Cmdr. Fitch found a telegram from Maj. Gen. Rosecrans asking that "every species of craft" that could get Rebels across the river be swept clean. Meanwhile, the general also wired Capt. Pennock reinforcing his demand for Cumberland convoy protection by revealing that he would "arm three transports to aid 'till you can arrange for us." Rear Adm. Porter informed Secretary Welles next day: "The entire Mississippi banks have been alive with guerillas, and we have successfully guarded every point and driven them; and my object is to keep them away. As fast as the vessels are bought and fitted they are now sent to the Cumberland and Tennessee."

Coming around from Cairo, the *Tuscumbia* had already departed Paducah leading a troop transport. Fitch and his boats were handed orders to follow the ironclad. Although the *Tuscumbia* had a design speed of 10 mph, she was actually slower going upstream than the *Fairplay* and was quickly overtaken by the smaller warships. Within a short period, the five vessels were joined by two additional troop steamers carrying Brig. Gen. Asboth, his men, and artillery.

The Tennessee River was very high at this time and, as was the case in February 1862, Fort Henry was largely flooded out. Fort Heiman, across the river on higher ground, was dry, but actually unoccupied. On the morning of March 14, a number of Rebels along the banks fired on the Yankee armada as it approached, "but the first shell from the gunboats made them run." Several local citizens later reported Confederates were lurking about "outback in the country." Asboth's soldiers reoccupied Fort Heiman without opposition under the guns of the fleet.

Next day, the tinclads *St. Clair* and *Alfred Robb* arrived and began checking crossing points in a series of regular daily patrols. Simultaneously, the *Fairplay* (with Asboth aboard), *Lexington*, and *Brilliant* began a 94-mile search up toward Perrysville, Tennessee, sweeping away all manner of river craft, including flats, ferries, and scows. Among the locations passed during the four day round trip were New Portland, Reynoldsburg, and the mouth of the Duck River. Unhappily, the river was beginning to fall and would not allow the gunboats to go up as far as Decatur.

Still, it was a pleasant voyage for the most part and, as Surgeon Howard later pointed out: "The weather is commencing 'summery'—trees budding out and birds singing." On the way down river, Lt. Cmdr. Fitch was able to catch up on much paperwork, including authorship of the long and detailed report of his operations since the previous December 16 requested by Fleet Captain Pennock, a report on the difficulties of navigating the Cumberland River, and a tabulated chart regarding towns, distances, water depths, and populations of, together with sundry remarks about, the Tennessee River.[25]

Leaving the *Alfred Robb* and *St. Clair* to patrol the Tennessee, the Logansport native returned to Paducah with the remainder of his upper flotilla, arriving off the Kentucky town on the evening of March 18. Having stewed over the revelations of army dissatisfaction made known to him by Pennock almost 10 days earlier, Fitch decided to write a long letter to Porter designed to show, as he put it, "whether I have acted with a desire to cooperate or not." The Indiana sailor was concerned that Maj. Gen. Rosecrans had telegraphed negative statements regarding his Cumberland River convoy service to the Navy Department and wished his chance to state the facts of the matter as he knew them. The missive included copies of letters and telegrams he sent and received.

After detailing the difficulties of both the river and the convoy process, the escort commodore went on to state his accomplishments. "Since the river has been navigable," he began, "I have sent convoys through regularly once a week, and never once has there been a steamer reported to me for convoy that has not been taken through safely.... Since the

Seven. Fighting Irregulars and Guarding Convoys (1863)

gunboats have been on the river," he added, over 180 steamers and some 30-odd barges (all laden with Government freight) have been taken through safely to Nashville.... Before the arrival of gunboats in the river," he concluded, "it was blockaded by the enemy; it has not been since."

His defense of action report, together with those composed while traveling back up the Tennessee, were forwarded later in the day to Rear Adm. Porter, who chose not to reply directly. However, the flag officer undoubtedly accepted his subordinate's statements as he quoted from them in reports of his own. Indeed, on March 14, Porter, who trusted both Pennock and Fitch and had long since made up his mind on the convoy matter, again reassured Secretary Welles: "We are doing all we can for General Rosecrans, and will, as we have heretofore done, keep him supplied."

Lt. Cmdr. Fitch augmented his March 17 summary report to Porter on March 21. Writing from Smithland, he noted that the Cumberland River continued "very quiet" as did the Tennessee, where he intended to spend a greater portion of his time. That stream, which he was recently up, still needed "very strict watching." Unless the transport fleets suddenly became much larger, it was anticipated that Acting Volunteer Lieutenant Hurd and four gunboats would be sufficient to guard the Cumberland convoys. Next morning, the *Lexington* departed for up the Tennessee, where she joined in the patrols of the *Silver Lake* (which Fitch called "one of the best light draft boats I have here just now") and *Alfred Robb.*

On the morning of March 27, a new expedition, designed to catch or disperse irregulars along the riverbanks and to stop illicit trade and traffic, was undertaken from Fort Heiman. To assist in the enterprise, 150 soldiers, under the command of Lt. Col. Chaucey Griggs, were taken aboard the three boats as part of an amphibious landing force, the second component of which would comprise tinclad sailors led by the *Lexington's* executive officer, Acting Volunteer Lieutenant Martin Dunn. Several times Fitch ordered men put ashore to check out locations where intelligence indicated guerrilla infestations might be present. Nothing was found and the little task group continued steaming up the Tennessee toward Savannah.

With information provided by friendly locals, quite possibly African Americans, the Indiana sailor learned that an active cotton factory was, at the very least, indirectly doing Confederate business from a place about four miles inland of Boyd's Landing. The place would have to be approached cautiously, as troops from Col. Nathaniel N. Cox's 10th Tennessee Regiment (C.S.A.) were believed stationed only two to three miles away. The entire complement of bluecoated soldiers led by Griggs and 50 Yankee tars under Dunn went ashore and made it to the mill without incident. Upon arrival, cordwood breastworks were thrown up across the road and several people were questioned about what went on in the facility.

The mill was apparently run on shares with surrounding country people and the material produced was said to be sent from friends among them to aid Rebel soldiers in the field. The company books were clear and contained no entries sufficient on their own merit to warrant the factory's destruction. Consequently, Fitch, who did not regularly fire Southern property for the sake of destruction, decided to "effectively prevent its doing more work." Acting Volunteer Lieutenant Dunn's men, guarded by the army troops, disassembled the factory, removing the plant's running gear, pistons, cylinder heads, brasses, and "all like portable portions." A pair of mules and wagons were pressed and hauled the machinery down to the river bank, from whence it was loaded aboard the *Lexington*. The mules, wagon, and a pair of horses caught nearby were retained as lawful prizes.

Another guerrilla hangout was reported a short distance above Boyd's Landing, about three miles inland. This time, Fitch, stretching his legs, went with Griggs and his men to a plantation owned by one Mr. Dillihunty. The owner claimed that he recently purchased the farm from a man U.S. forces were seeking, but that he personally had never conducted any traitorous business on the place and had even taken the oath of allegiance. Reviewing the man's story, Fitch grew dubious. Mr. Dillihunty could not back up his claims with papers and, unlike most Northern sympathizers, was not harassed by his guerrilla neighbors in any way. Further, several suspicious white men were seen on the property (at least one of whom was identified as a Confederate irregular). The Logansport officer, unable to prove culpability but unwilling to take the man at his word, confiscated 25 bales of cotton ("to be held 'till he proved his loyalty") and several horses.

The *Lexington*, *Robb*, and *Silver Lake* steamed on up to Chickasaw, Alabama, at the foot of the Colbert Shoals. The falling Tennessee was only five foot deep at the shoals, making it impossible for the timberclad to proceed. The *Lexington* was tied up opposite Waterloo and Acting Volunteer Lieutenant Goudy was ordered to take the other two boats upstream for a quick, but thorough reconnaissance, returning by daylight the next morning. As the *Robb* and *Silver Lake* paddled up the Tennessee, they were able to capture one Confederate irregular, five horses, and a number of enemy carbines. However, as the tinclads approached Florence, they found heavy, cannon-equipped Rebel forces on both sides of the river. They also saw that repairs were started on the Florence bridge. The aggressive Goudy attacked the Confederate camp on the left bank for an hour and a half and later claimed to have dispersed its occupants. With a heavy gale blowing across the river, uncertain currents, and falling water, he elected not to cross over and repeat his assault, especially since he was unable to ascertain the caliber of the guns which might be awaiting him, though he thought he faced a 24-pounder and some field pieces. Goudy departed the area, rejoined Fitch, and together the three warships began downstream.

On his way back toward Fort Heiman, Lt. Cmdr. Fitch learned of yet another Southern sympathizer, a man named Hays, who owned a farm which was notorious in its provision of supplies, especially foodstuffs, to irregular forces. Lt. Col. Griggs and Acting Volunteer Lieutenant Dunn took their landing force back to his barns, which were actually located about three miles from his house. There they pressed three of Hays' mules and a wagon and used them to carry off about half a ton of bacon and all the corn that could be carried. "Col. Griggs took charge of the bacon, as the army at Fort Heiman was short of supplies."

During the return from Florence, the Fitch task group was not only shot at by people on the river banks, but also stopped to pick up and transport approximately 60 refugee families. From interviews with these folks, the lead naval officer drew the conclusion that "all men along the river above Fort Henry must be either disloyal in sentiment or actually engaged in the rebel cause." No one expressing the least loyal (to the U.S.) sentiments was permitted a moment's peace, safety in their homes, or the unharrased cultivation of their farms. Fitch was quite surprised at how many young Caucasian men were supposed to be fleeing Confederate conscription and decided that he could no longer offer them free passage, though their families would be assisted. Given that both the U.S. cavalry and the gunboat service were in need of manpower, he ordered his captains on the twin rivers to no longer pick up able-bodied young white men. "If they love the Union better than rebellion now is the proper time to show it," he held. "They must either take sides one way or the other ... I deem it high time that some of these loyal refugees were showing some proofs of their loyalty." Fitch's hard line netted about 10 new crewmen for his boats, along with another 30–40 for the cavalry.

Fitch's flotilla returned to Fort Heiman on the last day of March. There the bluejackets bid farewell to Lt. Col. Griggs and his men. The results of the voyage were also tallied: eight guns (cavalry carbines), 25 bales of cotton, 15 horses (three broke loose and escaped at Fort Heiman), 12 mules (one shot through the thigh and left at Heiman), two wagons, and eight prisoners. Additionally, at least 20 new flatboats were destroyed. Several were found up creeks in warehouses hidden under piles of corn. Over on the Cumberland, Acting Volunteer Lieutenant Hurd was preparing to guard a convoy of 2,000 troops earmarked by Maj. Gen. Rosecrans for the Tennessee a day earlier. Hurd, who had hoped to wait for his superior to return, departed Smithland for Dover under direct prodding from Capt. Pennock. He would not find Rosecrans' troops as the general changed his mind and did not be send them after all.

Brig. Gen.. Dodge reported to Army of the Cumberland chief of staff Brig. Gen. James A. Garfield at Murfreesboro that the tinclads were unable to drive out the enemy or silence his heavy batteries at Florence, confirming that the *Lexington* was unable to get above the Colbert Shoals. He further noted that the enemy was building bridges east of Savannah and north of Florence as well as constructing flatboats all along the stream from Florence to the mouth of the Duck River and holding the line of the Tennessee between those points.

While returning to Paducah with the *Lexington*, *Alfred Robb*, and *Silver Lake* on April 1, Le Roy Fitch also realized that his light draughts had not accomplished their Florence mission and that there was a need for another trip upstream. Just as soon as there was a slight rise, he would take all of his boats up and mark those open accounts paid by capturing the Rebel force on the Tuscumbia side at Florence. He took the initiative of writing up his strategy—a variation on what was becoming the standard tactic for river-ground envelopment—and sending it to Brig. Gen. Dodge in hopes of winning his cooperation for a joint operation. Fitch reported to Rear Adm. Porter from Smithland on April 2, that his plan would have him

> get forces from General Dodge, take the infantry over Colbert Shoals, land them at Tuscumbia Landing, let the cavalry come in on the Tuscumbia road, and while the forces are getting in the enemy's rear, I will push on up with four or five of the lightest draft boats and engage them in front.

Farther south in Murfreesboro, Brig. Gen. Garfield was simultaneously informing Maj. Gen. Granger, at Franklin, of the emerging Tennessee River developments. His review was closed with an ominous suspicion: "There seems to be a considerable force at Palmyra." Before the navy could go back up the Tennessee, the fleet slated for the trip would have to return to the Cumberland and deal with the town Fitch had earlier called a "noted guerrilla haunt."[26]

Palmyra, Tennessee, is located on the Cumberland River 27.2 miles upstream from Dover and 10 miles below Clarksville. Host to an important prewar steamboat landing, it was founded as Blountville in 1797. That year the U.S. Congress designated the town the "first official point of entry in the West." Elements of Maj. Gen. Wheeler's force had congregated there before the February attack on Dover as the place, one of the highest to overlook a straight portion of the river, offered such a wonderful position to shoot down from its bluff into approaching Union shipping. At the beginning of April, Woodward's 2nd Kentucky Cavalry (C.S.A.) plus local irregulars and at least three cannon were once again located there to interdict Yankee transport.

By this time, Northern logistics officials, military and civil, had become somewhat complacent with the operation of their Louisville-Nashville-Louisville supply train. After all, some 180 steamers and 30 barges were safely escorted up the river from Smithland or Fort Donelson in convoys to Nashville on January 24 and 28, February 7, 15, and 20, and March 6 and 15. Rations sufficient for an advance had, by now, reached Murfreesboro. The major sticking point, at least officially, to a new Federal move south was the provision of adequate numbers of efficient Union cavalry.

Having stood out from Smithland on March 31, the gunboats *St. Clair* and *Fairplay* arrived at Fort Donelson on April 1, where they took several waiting transports in hand and proceeded upriver, reaching Gower's Island on the morning of April 2. Guessing there was no danger ahead, Acting Volunteer Lieutenant Hurd, the escort commander, signaled the steamers to go on to Nashville while he took his two warships back to Fort Donelson to pick up additional incoming transports and towboats. From the site of the ferocious February battles, Hurd gathered up the new group and headed up the Cumberland late in the afternoon, with the *St. Clair* at the head of the column and the *Fairplay* at the rear. Unhappily, Hurd, one of Fitch's most "brave and efficient" officers, miscalculated his convoy's cruising disposition. He would also fail tactically in the fight which followed.

Lt. Cmdr. Fitch, as noted earlier, always chose to place his slowest vessels in the van, with the most valuable in the center and the fastest in the rear. This allowed for the line to be kept closed up and for one gunboat to always be within supporting range of another. Acting Volunteer Lieutenant Hurd placed his most valuable boats up front and his slowest at the rear, making it impossible for the pokey *Fairplay* to remain within support distance. The line as it proceeded up the Cumberland included the steamers *Eclipse* and *Lizzie Martin* lashed together, the *St. Clair*, the transport *Luminary*, the towboats *C. Miller* and *J. W. Kellogg* each with a barge drawing 7.5 feet of water, and the *Fairplay*. Hurd, who had encountered no enemy activity while passing Palmyra on earlier trips, was concerned about his deeply-laden barges and did not suspect an ambush.

At 10:30 P.M. this fleet approached Palmyra when, off the bluff immediately above that town, it was fired into by an elevated enemy battery comprising a depressed 6-pounder Parrott rifle and a 12-pounder smoothbore cannon. Paired as they were, the *Eclipse* and *Lizzie Martin* were an easy target for the Confederate gunners—who missed badly damaging either largely because the two were already too far upstream in the dark to be easily targeted.

Unhappily, the *St. Clair* and the *Luminary* were only about 400 feet from their attackers, who now gave them their full attention with cannon and small arms. The *Luminary* was struck by numerous Minie balls; however, it was the *St. Clair* which took the brunt of the assault. Acting Volunteer Lieutenant Hurd, his guns run out, was unable to elevate his howitzers sufficiently in his location to hit the guns up on the bluff. Still, he fired away and, as he put it in his official report, "the contest was spirited for a short time." It was also all one-sided, with the tinclad struck by small arms, canister, and at least six shells, one of which went through her deck and struck her supply pipe, letting all the water out of her boilers and making the boat unmanageable. *St. Clair* went dead in the water, but fortunately, the undamaged *Luminary* heeded Hurd's hail, came alongside, and took the warship under tow.

Executive officer Acting Volunteer Master George W. Fouty, one of the mosquito fleet's most popular and devoted officers, got out of a sick bed to go to his battle station as soon

A veteran Cumberland River gunboat, the *St. Clair* was disabled by enemy artillery near Palmyra, Tennessee, on April 3, 1863. She was towed out of danger by another gunboat, and was eventually repaired. The incident resulted in the ultimate application of Col. Fitch's doctrine; the town of Palmyra was burned to the ground in retaliation (Naval Historical Center).

as the fighting began. During the largely one-sided fight, he was badly hurt when a 6-pounder elongated shot came through the *St. Clair's* bulkhead and shattered his right knee. When the wounded tinclad, under tow of the *Luminary*, reached Fort Donelson, Fouty was, after examination aboard by the post surgeon, immediately transferred ashore to the hospital. Acting Volunteer Lieutenant Hurd attempted to wire Lt. Cmdr. Fitch at Smithland, but the telegraph lines to that post were down. He did get a message through to Capt. Pennock while Col. William P. Boone, in command at Clarksville, informed Nashville and Murfreesboro of the attack. There was genuine relief that the two vessels were not captured. The repairs which could be made to the *St. Clair's* supply pipe were so imperfect that she could not safely steam on her own. Col. Lowe graciously ordered the *J. W. Kellogg* to tow the gunboat back to Smithland, where she arrived at 9:30 P.M. on April 4.

Several days later, Acting Volunteer Lieutenant Hurd was forced to accept the displeasure of his superior, whose guidance included a catalog of the volunteer lieutenant's battle mistakes: poor convoy arrangement; a decision (made after his supply pipe was cut) not to anchor and fight back until the *Fairplay* could come up and then using the combined firepower of the two to drive out the Rebels; and a failure to understand that, had he again been compelled to drop down, the current and the availability of towing assistance would have aided him. Following his perceived success at Dover in February and the work of the ironclads at Arkansas Post, Fitch held a supreme confidence in the day-or-night superiority of naval tactics against riverbank cavalry and cannon. Later, particularly at Johnsonville and Nashville, he would come to appreciate their limitations.[27]

Capt. Pennock and Lt. Cmdr. Fitch did not at first realize what happened at Palmyra. The former received Hurd's Fort Donelson wire and immediately sent one of his own to Smithland asking Fitch, who had just returned to that rendezvous, whether he had heard anything of the attack. The Hoosier officer was in his office while the *Lexington* was being coaled preparatory to another ascent of the Tennessee. Upon receipt of his superior's wire, he got up and went to message back that the telegraph into his town from Dover was not working and so he had no information.

Fitch did, however, take the opportunity to send Pennock two housekeeping telegrams. In the first, he informed the fleet captain that the *Silver Lake* would soon need major repairs. Her gun platforms had all given way and her casemate recoiled in with the guns. Still, he couldn't part with her; "will have to fight her a little longer if casemates all give way." In the second, he praised Acting Volunteer Lieutenant Goudy and Hurd as his "best officers" and asked that they both be given newer boats. Pennock replied indicating that the new tinclads *Argosy*, *Covington*, and *Queen City* would be arriving at Smithland shortly and they could take their choice between the latter two.

The 219-ton *Argosy* was constructed at Monongahela, Pennsylvania, in 1862 and purchased for the upper river squadron on March 24, 1863. The stern-wheeler was 156.4 feet long, with a beam of 33 feet and a depth of hold of 4.6 feet. Powered by two engines and three boilers, she could reportedly achieve a top speed of 5 mph. Converted in the remarkably short time of a week, the tinclad was armed with six 24-pound brass howitzers and two 12-pound rifles and authorized a crew of 71 officers and men. *Argosy* was placed in commission on March 29, Acting Volunteer Master William N. Griswold in command.

The *Covington No. 2*, a 224-ton side-wheel ferry, was built in 1862 and purchased on February 13, 1863, from Samuel Wiggins at Cincinnati, Ohio. The craft was 126 feet long, with a beam of 37 feet and a depth of hold of 6.6 feet. Her power plant is unknown but must have consisted of a minimum of two engines and two boilers. Converted at Cairo, Illinois, she was armed with four 24-pound brass howitzers and two 30-pound Parrott rifles and was authorized a crew of 76. When the new fleet addition was commissioned as *Covington* a few days later, Acting Volunteer Lieutenant Hurd would be in command.

Another ferry built at Cincinnati at the beginning of 1863 and purchased from Samuel Wiggins on February 13, *Queen City* was a 212 ton side-wheeler. Her dimensions and power plant are unknown, but were probably similar to those of the *Covington No. 2*. Upon conversion, she was armed with two 30-pounder Parrott rifles, two 32-pounder smoothbores, and four 24-pounder brass howitzers. Acting Volunteer Lieutenant Goudy placed this warship into commission on April 1.[28]

When Lt. Cmdr. Fitch at Smithland finally received word from Acting Volunteer Lieutenant Hurd late on April 3, he immediately ordered all of his captains to prepare for departure. They had already coaled and were, in fact, making last minute preparations to start back up the Tennessee in the morning. Rushing to the telegraph office, he wired Capt. Pennock his news on the assault and also noted "Plenty of fun in other river, as I understand no troops to be convoyed Tennessee just now.... I leave in 10 minutes for Palmyra with all the boats. Will whip them out," he continued. "Please hurry up our other boats. We need them now." The Cairo station chief quickly messaged back: "Go ahead and whip them out on both rivers." Reinforcements would come as quickly as possible, though the men on the new boats would require constant drilling.

Overnight, the USS *Lexington*, *Brilliant*, *Alfred Robb*, *Silver Lake*, and *Springfield* steamed upriver intent upon retaliation for the convoy attack by Confederate guerrillas. Downriver from Dover, the warships encountered the *Fairplay* and the crippled *St. Clair*, under tow of the *J. W. Kellogg*. During the ensuing mid-river rendezvous, Acting Volunteer Lieutenant Hurd made a preliminary report aboard the *Lexington* while other officers and men not on watch or asleep learned what they could of the Rebel assault. Hurd reviewed the particulars of the attack as he knew them, the enemy's positions and guns, and of the wounding of Mr. Fouty. Lt. Cmdr. Fitch ordered his exhausted subordinate to take his vessel down to Cairo for repairs. Although Hurd would receive the reprimand already noted, he also received a new command.

The *Fairplay* joined the avenging fleet, which continued up to Fort Donelson where it arrived during the morning of April 4. There the latest intelligence was sought and final preparations for a visit to Palmyra were completed, including the placement of hay bales around the boilers of the five tinclads. When ready, the fleet proceeded on up, arriving at Palmyra—Surgeon Howard called it "the cursed spot"—late that Saturday afternoon. Several transports, waiting at Fort Donelson for escort to Nashville and perhaps with soldiers aboard, were allowed to accompany the fleet to within a safe distance of the town. They were closely guarded by three of the tinclads. Although the men on the warships were "beat to quarters" and every cannon was ready, no enemy battery or forces were found.

As demonstrated at the Tennessee River cotton factory the previous week and as we have seen in earlier episodes, Lt. Cmdr. Fitch was still somewhat opposed to the more draconian aspects of Federal anti-guerrilla policy then being employed, including "the wanton destruction of property." Many of the men of his command, having experienced a constant peppering from the riverbanks for weeks and now having learned of the fate of "poor Fouty," had no such qualms. Surgeon Howard on the *Brilliant* seemed to speak for most of the bluejackets now off Palmyra: "every town harboring Rebel sympathizers should be burned" because the irregulars did not believe in a fair fight—"they hide in the bush, shoot and run." If it were left to Howard and his fellow tars to set Federal counterinsurgency policy, they would "make this accursed Reb country a howling wilderness, and trust in the goodness of the Lord that it might be peopled by a better race in the future."

As it was, Fitch agreed that, in this instance, the destruction of Palmyra was justifiable. As he had been telling his superiors for some time, "it was one of the worst secession places on the river." Every Federal believed that "unarmed transports had been fired into from doors and windows of the houses in the town." So it was that the *Lexington* landed opposite the town and a detachment was sent on shore, in charge of Acting Volunteer Master James Fitzpatrick from the timberclad, with orders to burn every building in the town. Fitzpatrick was to make certain that his men did not "remove or pillage a single article," because everything was to be torched as an object lesson. As Fitzpatrick and his landing party spread out, several men, perceived as stragglers from the enemy battery, broke from their concealment and tired to run away. They were fired upon and one was killed, with a second wounded and others taken prisoner. Once the work of retribution was completed, the gunboats "left the town of Palmyra by its own light" at moonrise. There was real satisfaction among the sailors; as Howard put it, "it was clean work—every building was in flames and falling." The task group commander, in a mission-ending telegram to Capt. Pennock, was matter-of-fact: "burned the town; not a house left; a very bad hole; best to get rid of it and teach the rebels a lesson." Writing more than 130 years later, Nashville judge Brandt reaffirmed what many Middle Tennesseans were long taught: Fitch's raid "ruined" Palmyra.[29]

Anticipating Union Navy retribution, the Confederates, according to those captured at Palmyra, hitched up their guns and retreated toward Harpeth Shoals shortly after the *St. Clair* attack. The exact destination, as the bluejackets learned, was Betsytown Landing, another notorious guerrilla hangout, some 32–33 miles upstream beyond Clarksville and Hinton. Determined to catch the bushwhackers, Fitch took his fleet up the Cumberland toward it. At Clarksville on April 5, the navy chief and local post commander, Col. Boone, agreed to make the pursuit amphibious. A number of infantry and cavalry from the post, led by the colonel personally, were loaded aboard the tinclads, and the expedition, again with the civilian transports trailing at a safe distance under escort, steamed upstream overnight.

The soldiers were landed a few miles below Harpeth Shoals in the forenoon of April 6 and moved on their suspected enemy while the gunboats steamed up to Betsytown Landing to attract attention with a bombardment from the river. Once more, this was the familiar plan of attack, the same one which was employed at Tuscumbia Landing during the late February Tennessee River expedition. If he could keep the grayclads occupied, it was hoped that Boone's men could sneak up behind them and capture the offending cannon or that they would withdraw directly into the path of the arriving Federals. The scheme was foiled in the end because Fitch's opposition learned of his approach and was able to retreat again, this time from their camp, two miles back from the river, toward Charlotte. Cavalry from the gunboats pursued about six miles up the Charlotte road, but elected, because of the small size of the force, not to pursue deeper into hostile country. The withdrawal of Col. Woodward's force to join Forrest's main body near Columbia and the burning of Palmyra would bring only about a month of relaxation in the Confederate war on Federal transport in Middle Tennessee.

The Cumberland River was now rapidly falling and it was simply too risky to take the huge *Lexington* over the shoals. Believing he had accomplished all that was possible in pursuit of the Palmyra ambushers and needing to ready his next foray up the Tennessee, the Indiana sailor sent the accompanying transports on up to Nashville under protection of the *Brilliant*, *Alfred Robb*, and *Silver Lake*. No incidents were reported prior to their arrival about midnight. The *Lexington*, *Springfield*, and one transport remained behind to re-embark Boone's troops which arrived back at the river from their pursuit about 10 P.M. The soldiers were returned to Clarksville while the timberclad and *Springfield* made the long run back to Smithland, arriving late on April 6. Nothing but smoldering ruins were seen by the warships as they passed the rubble of Palmyra.[30]

Immediately upon his return to the main Cumberland gunboat rendezvous, Lt. Cmdr. Fitch reported to Capt. Pennock that the Cumberland was clear and inquired after the *St. Clair*, as well as the new *Queen City*, promised to him earlier. The fleet captain replied: "Congratulations on your success.... Keep the Cumberland clear of the enemy. Go ahead and clear the banks of the Tennessee." The two tinclads would not, however, be able to report to Smithland for the best part of a week.

Downstream at the same time, Brig. Gen. Mitchell at Nashville informed Murfreesboro that the gunboats were planning to depart downstream at 3 A.M. the next day, despite an order from Maj. Gen. Rosecrans that they await his orders. "They seem to pay no attention," the post commander remarked, though, in their defense, he acknowledged "the river is falling rapidly and large boats may be caught here."

At some point on April 9, a pair of small steamers, both transporting sutler's stores, arrived at Fort Donelson while the *Brilliant, Alfred Robb,* and *Springfield* were taking a return convoy to Smithland. Refusing to wait for the tinclads to come back and thus to join in the next escorted passage, the two set off together next day up the river to Nashville. Both were captured and destroyed. When he heard of the matter, Fitch was frank in his summation. "As far as the boats were concerned," he wrote Rear Adm. Porter on April 15, "there was no one to blame but themselves." Their captains "paid the penalty of disobedience of orders by having their boats burned."[31]

Continuing to require gunboat assistance, officers of the U.S. Army, in addition to Rosecrans, occasionally took it upon themselves, as we have seen earlier in this story, to commission makeshift gunboats. The army leadership at Clarksville, no doubt impressed with the work of Fitch's flotilla in the recent pursuit of the Palmyra belligerents, decided it needed an armed craft to help him check those troopers from Col. Woodward's CSA unit marauding around Harpeth Shoals. Consequently, the ferryboat *Excelsior* was taken in hand, its vitals were barricaded with hay bales, and a couple of field pieces with their gun crews were put aboard. The soldiers then "used her as a gunboat." During the week of April 10, Brig. Gen. Garfield was informed on April 15, the steamer convoyed part of a transport fleet above the shoals. It also stopped to recover a cannon from the wreck of the military gunboat *W. H. Sidell* and dispersed a rebel band that was waiting at the shoals to fire on any unprotected boats, even managing to capture several of its men.[32]

While Fitch and his Cumberland River flotilla were actively engaged in the pacification of Palmyra, another larger enterprise, with a far less happy ending for the Federals, was beginning to unfold: the Streight Raid. The Indiana sailor would attempt to support the first mounted incursion of Confederate territory by a large force of mounted bluecoat infantry and find himself mixed up with not one, but two of the most unusual Yankee outfits of the conflict.

Fifty-first Indiana Volunteer Infantry commander Col. Abel D. Streight was an energetic, original thinker who, like others in his army, was disappointed that the Union had, thus far, been unable to match in effectiveness—or glory—the disruptive behind-the-lines raids of such Confederate saddle wizards as John Hunt Morgan and Nathan Bedford Forrest. At the same time, Maj. Gen. Rosecrans, under continuous pressure from Washington, D.C., to move south, badly wanted to advance, but as bloodlessly as possible. "It occurred to his fertile mind," John Wyeth later wrote, "that if he could secure the destruction of the two important railroads leading from Chattanooga—one to Atlanta and the other to Knoxville—about the time he could force Bragg" south out of Tullahoma, Chattanooga would be cut off.

Streight, like Rosecrans and others familiar with the region, knew that Dalton was a key Confederate rail hub where tracks met connecting Chattanooga and Atlanta. That Georgia junction was vulnerable, so the colonel believed, to a large mounted party riding east through the local mountains from Russellville or Moulton, which in turn could be reached from the Tennessee River at Eastport. If he could capture Dalton and other Northern troops took the railroad center of Tuscumbia, a link in the line connecting Corinth and Chattanooga, easy Rebel transportation into Tennessee would be terminated. Gen. Bragg would have to retreat and Chattanooga could be swiftly taken.

The Hoosier officer also knew that there were pockets of Union sympathizers behind the lines in north Alabama who were in need of succor and encouragement, and who might be as helpful to his foray as southern loyalists in places like Montgomery County, Tennessee, were to the Rebels. It was true that the north Alabama country featured few roads and little forage, but that in turn could be spun into an advantage if there was local assistance, the proper mounts, and timely inter-unit coordination. Naturally, Streight would make the thrust to Dalton, leading a newly-formed Independent Provisional Brigade, that others would derisively label "the Mule Brigade."

Streight sold his idea to Brig. Gen. Garfield, Department of the Cumberland chief of staff, who persuaded the commanding general that the Indianian's concept possessed significant merit. Garfield wanted to take over the force and lead it himself, but "Old Rosy" refused the future president permission and the execution of plan was left to Streight, who received Garfield's enthusiastic support. Indeed, cavalry commander Brig. Gen. David S. Stanley later remarked that the chief of staff "had no military ability, nor could he learn anything, yet he persuaded Rosecrans that with four regiments of mounted infantry, one could ride through the Confederacy." On April 7, Streight received orders to travel up to Nashville and there to speedily assemble his command "for an expedition to the interior of Alabama and Georgia for the purpose of destroying the railroads in that country." He would lead some 2,000 "men of well-attested pluck and endurance" from his own 51st Indiana, plus the 73rd Indiana, the 3rd Ohio, the 18th Illinois, and two companies from the 1st Middle Tennessee Cavalry (U.S.A.), made up of north Alabamians.[33]

Aside from its audacious concept, the Streight project is primarily remembered for the mounts the men were supposed to ride: mules. These animals, it was believed, would be more adept in the hilly country of north Alabama and perhaps easier to feed. Whether or not that may have been true, the animals he had to choose from in Tennessee's capital were young and unbroken or suffering from equine distemper. Still many of these, together with the men, were loaded on steamers and, under convoy of the *Excelsior,* sent up to Palmyra on April 11. There near the "black and charred ruins" of the town, a training and mule-breaking exercise was held the next day. The empty transports were, meanwhile, sent downstream and around via the Ohio to the Tennessee. From there, they proceeded toward Fort Henry, where they were to meet Streight's command, which on April 13 began marching overland the dozen or so miles from the Cumberland. Of the mounts in hand at the beginning of the trek, 40–50 were so sick that they had to be left behind and a dozen died within miles of the start. Thus the colonel and his men were forced to strip the land en route of every available mule. Many quality animals were found, but most were shoeless.

While the Indiana colonel and his men rode or dragged their mounts toward Fort Henry, another unusual group was preparing to play a role in this story. The Mississippi Marine Brigade, led by Brig. Gen. Alfred W. Ellet, was the same outfit which fought in the June 1862 Battle of Memphis. The amphibious command was transferred to the U.S. Navy the previous November and Rear Adm. Porter, like Rear Adm. Davis, found it less than a desirable subordinate command. In fact, on April 2, Porter wrote to Welles: "The time has passed when a marine brigade would be of any service on this river, the guerrilla warfare having been put to a stop by the watchfulness of the gunboats." A letter to the Mississippi Squadron chief from Maj. Gen. Grant on April 4 caused him to send Ellet's people on another mission.

Seven. Fighting Irregulars and Guarding Convoys (1863)

Writing from his headquarters near Vicksburg, the commander of the Department of the Tennessee informed Porter that Confederate movements in North Mississippi and Middle Tennessee compelled him to ask for the marine brigade as reinforcements in holding the line of the Tennessee River. Grant's intelligence from the Corinth area was that both his own forces and those of Maj. Gen. Rosecrans would be attacked "with a powerful cavalry force" even before the Streight project could be launched. Ellet was dispatched to the Tennessee to co-operate with Brig. Gen. Dodge and Streight and to destroy all ferryboats, flatboats and other means that the Confederates might employ to get men across the stream. In an April 9 report to Secretary Welles, Porter noted that Ellet and the gunboats were en route to the Tennessee. "This is all we can do for General Rosecrans," he concluded," and it is all he should require, or would require, if he will advance his troops as far as the Mussel Shoals."

While en route to Eastport, Lt. Cmdr. Fitch received from Capt. Pennock on April 12 a copy of the orders sent to Brig. Gen. Ellet, in which was contained the sentence: "I am pushing a strong force of gunboats up the Tennessee River and your vessels will be able to lie securely under the protection of their guns." It was by this copy and the fleet captain's enclosure with it that the Hoosier officer learned that he was leading that "strong force" and would use it to cooperate both with Ellet and the army. Although Fitch knew before Palmyra that he was returning to the Tennessee, he did not previously know about the presence of either Ellet or Streight.

The same day, Maj. Gen. Rosecrans informed Maj. Gen. Hurlbut that Streight was en route to Eastport (though he had yet to depart). He asked the Memphis commander for his assistance with "this great enterprise, fraught with great consequences," primarily in eliciting further supportive cooperation of Brig. Gen. Dodge. It was anticipated that the XVI Army Corps' 2nd Division, with support from Ellet and Fitch, could whip the Tuscumbia-based Confederates. As cover to his real mission, Streight's brigade would join in the endeavor, before peeling off to "go directly to its main object—the destruction of the railroads." In a similar message to Maj. Gen. Halleck that day, "Old Rosy" reported on his concerted work with Hurlbut in getting the project away. "If this succeeds, rebels must be driven into Georgia." He added: "River low and falling; weather fair."

All the U.S. Navy vessels which could be spared were employed on this duty and Lt. Cmdr. Fitch was instructed to remain up the river as long as possible. It was, after all, the beginning of spring when the height of the waters, already low at shoal spots, were very unpredictable and rises could not be counted upon. His orders from the admiral were, as he put it in a note delivered to Brig. Gen. Dodge on April 16, "Go down as the river falls." Conversely, "of course, I ascend as it rises." The Tennessee, as Rosecrans had told Halleck, had been low for some time and it remained impossible to say whether a rise would occur that would permit the gunboats to get over Colbert Shoals. If it did, and Rosecrans' force did not arrive for whatever reason, the navy was ready and it was hoped that Fitch and Dodge could achieve significant results on their own at Florence or Tuscumbia Landing.

As his contribution to the forthcoming enterprise, Fitch employed the *Lexington* and the new *Argosy*, *Covington*, and *Queen City*, "four of my best boats," which together could also carry about 2,000 infantry. The *Covington* and *Argosy* were left at Fort Henry to convoy Ellet and Streight's transports, while the *Lexington* and the *Queen City* pushed up. Although the Hoosier had left the remainder of his mosquito fleet in the Cumberland to convoy transports back and forth to Nashville, he knew that his combinations were such that reinforcements from their number could be quickly called in for a short period if necessary.

While the two tinclads remained off Fort Henry and Fitch steamed upstream, Streight marched overland and reached Fort Henry on April 14; the next day, the transports sent ahead from Palmyra arrived. Brig. Gen. Ellet, who was not in any particular rush, stopped at Cairo to repair his transports and also arrived at Fort Henry on April 15. Further south that Wednesday, Brig. Gen. Dodge and his soldiers arrived at Burnsville. Two days were required to load Streight's men, 1,250 mules, and 130,000 rations, the latter to be shared with Dodge. That Streight did not have all the mounts he required could be made up, the colonel believed, as his force moved through the enemy's country. Upon learning about that idea, Dodge concluded it was "a fatal mistake."

Brig. Gen. Dodge, with 5,500 infantry and cavalry, arrived at Cook's, just west of Great Bear Creek, itself some 12 miles east of Eastport, on April 16. There he received a communication from Lt. Cmdr. Fitch, but no word from Streight and Ellet. The enemy was found reinforcing Tuscumbia Landing.

On April 17, the same day that Ellet's rams, Streight's transports, and the two escorting gunboats, *Covington* and *Argosy*, departed Fort Henry, Dodge's advance elements crossed Great Bear Creek and marched 13 miles toward Tuscumbia. His Confederate opposition, Col. Philip D. Roddey's 4th Alabama Cavalry brigade, was driven from Great Bear Creek to Caney Creek in a spirited offensive that cost 100 bluecoats and a captured field piece. With no word from Streight, the general ordered his men concentrated back at Great Bear Creek where they would wait until the Mule Brigade and additional reinforcements arrived.

Fitch, meanwhile, took his two boats up toward Eastport that morning, planning to patrol between the Duck River and Chickasaw, before rounding to off Eastport on the evening of April 18. When the *Lexington* and *Queen City* arrived at Eastport, they found Rebel cavalry exchanging fire with a small squad of Union troops. "Shelled; drove them off," the Logansport sailor wired Cairo just after dawn on Saturday.

Fitch was rather exasperated that neither Ellet nor Streight had yet shown up. "Is the river [Mississippi Marine] brigade coming to assist us?" asked the young officer in his April 19 communication to Capt. Pennock. "If so, it had better hurry up!" Unbeknownst to the navy commander, Ellet and Streight did not see eye to eye on the urgency of the mission. Ellet, who obviously hated hauling mules, decided to fulfill the letter of Rear Adm. Porter's orders by stopping hither and yon along the way up to destroy flatboats, ferries, canoes, etc.

At Clifton on April 18, Ellet promised a group of distressed Union sympathizers, burned out of their homes by 300 Rebel irregulars, that he would retaliate, but fortunately for the already-delayed Streight timetable, the marine offered vengeance later. Col. Streight's fleet made it upstream to Savannah that evening. On the morning of April 19 as Fitch was at the Eastport telegraph office asking after Ellet, the Hoosier colonel's transports, with Ellet and Fitch's two gunboats, were approaching. Before they arrived that evening—four days after the time agreed upon for the combined movement to step off—a brief stop was made at Hamburg Landing in anticipation of a message from Brig. Gen. Dodge. None was found and another hour was lost.

When Streight and Ellet arrived at Eastport after dark that Sunday, the colonel rushed into a conference with Dodge that would go on until midnight. As the leaders talked, the many unhappy mules were put ashore into a makeshift corral. The noise and ruckus damaged the evening air to a point where sharp-eared Confederates from Col. Roddey's brigade, hovering on the outskirts of the Federal camp, were alerted. In the dark of early morning, a number of these horsemen stole into the Yankee corral, according to Forrest biographer

Wyeth, and stampeded the mules. Brig. Gen. Dodge later wrote simply that through the carelessness of one of the officers supervising the unloading, "200 strayed away." Whatever the reason, by daylight, over 400 of the best mounts were gone and two days would be required to recapture those which could be caught. Streight remained convinced he could find adequate numbers of replacement stock lower in the Tennessee Valley.

The mule delay was the second incident, after the leisurely ascent from Fort Henry, in a series of unfortunate occurrences that proved mortal to the Streight expedition. At this point, it was learned that Alfred Ellet did not, in fact, have orders to report directly to Grenville Dodge, though he pledged cooperation with the railroad builder. On the plus side, many were cheered to when told that, on the night of the 16th, Porter's ironclad gunboats successfully ran by the Confederate artillery at Vicksburg.

On April 21, Lt. Cmdr. Fitch was forced to inform the army and Capt. Pennock that his gunboats could not get over the shoals. Indeed, the deep draft amphibious boats of Brig. Gen. Ellet were forced to steam back downstream that very morning, departing after a significant portion of Eastport mysteriously burned to the ground. His mission of army support had thus far largely failed. Brig. Gen. Dodge, in his after action report, would attribute some of the blame for the eventual outcome of the Streight project on the failure of the amphibious force commander to initially shepherd the strike brigades to Eastport in a timely manner.[34]

Finally on April 22, Dodge and Streight started their drive on Tuscumbia. Falling water

Famed railroad builder Glenville Dodge (1831–1916) commanded the 2nd Division of the XVI Corps in the spring of 1863. He cooperated closely with Lt. Cmdr. Fitch during the latter's February expedition up the Tennessee and during Col. Abel D. Streight's failed "Mule Brigade" expedition of April–May (Library of Congress).

compelled the *Lexington* to start back down river that Wednesday as well. Before departing Eastport, Fitch ordered his three light-draughts to remain with the army transports until either Brig. Gen. Dodge returned from his mission or the water fell below 5 foot on the shoals. Hurrying ashore, he wired Rear Adm. Porter, informing him that all was quiet. Dodge was about 18 miles beyond Bear Creek he believed and intelligence told him that the Rebel batteries were removed from Florence and that the railroad bridge there was still not repaired. The 3,000-or-so Confederate troops believed to be at Tuscumbia Landing were there primarily to guard large quantities of bacon and corn being shipped across the river above Mussel Shoals to Gen. Bragg's army.

Despite a spirited defense by Col. Roddey, Tuscumbia Landing fell to the Union about noon on April 23, with Florence captured shortly thereafter. At the former place, Dodge found ready for shipment the bacon and corn mentioned by Fitch. "Gave it all to the flames," the general later reported.

On Wednesday and Thursday, the *Lexington* cruised down the river ahead of Brig. Gen. Ellet's fleet. Ellet, for his part, was asked by Brig. Gen. Dodge to make a demonstration at Savannah as a diversion to his own movement toward Tuscumbia and Florence. Rather than honoring the request, the amphibious leader elected to steam slowly down toward Clifton, putting men ashore on both sides of the river to destroy Confederate mills, stores and other property and to "liberate" any reachable cotton bales, horses, or mules.

All of the noise along the Tennessee, from Streight, Ellet, Dodge, Fitch, Roddy and others did not go unnoticed at Gen. Bragg's headquarters. On April 23, the Confederate leader wired Brig. Gen. Nathan Bedford Forrest at Spring Hill and directed him to travel over, link up with Roddy, and put an end to the Streight-Dodge incursion. Within three days, a battery plus the 4th, 9th, 10th, and 11th Tennessee brigades (C.S.A.) would be across the Tennessee (at Brown's Ferry, near Courtland, Alabama) ready to dispute Dodge's further advance. Another brigade, the 8th Tennessee, was sent along the bank of the river to create a diversion in the Union rear. On Sunday, April 26, Streight and Dodge separated at Tuscumbia. Streight and his men slipped away into north Alabama headed toward Russellville, Georgia. Dodge began his attempt to deceive Forrest's men by acting as though he were headed toward a linkup with Maj. Gen. Grant.

The arrival of the famed Confederate raider into the story was the final stroke of bad luck to befall the Streight project. Forrest and his men were not fooled by the Dodge ruse and weaved into a relentless pursuit of the Hoosier colonel that did not end until the 1,446 surviving officers and men of the Independent Provisional Brigade were all cornered and taken on the Alabama-Georgia line on May 3. Neither Dodge, nor Ellet, nor Fitch were in any position to assist and Streight could not get free of his dogged pursuer who, in one of his most celebrated exploits, captured an entire Yankee force three times his size.[35]

A day after Dodge and Streight took Tuscumbia Landing, Ellet and Fitch were themselves drawn into a fight with Confederates secreted on the banks of the Tennessee River. Among the enemy units now unleashed against the Union river invaders was a battery of four fieldpieces belonging to Maj. Robert M. White's 6th Texas Cavalry (CSA). White, a native of the area, had placed his guns at Green Bottom Bar, on the Duck River Shoals just above Waverly Landing, intent upon catching Union steamers coming his way and maybe even shooting up a gunboat or Mississippi Marine Brigade ram. River pilots had long considered this stretch "one of the worst in the river navigation," making it an ideal spot for an ambush.

His first target was Acting Volunteer Master William N. Griswold's brand new light draught, *Emma Duncan*, later known as the *Hastings*, or Tinclad No. 15. The *Emma Duncan*, which had once had a field piece aboard and served briefly as a quasi-army gunboat, was built at Monongahela, Pennsylvania, in 1860 and was purchased from J. Batchelor and others at Cairo on March 24 for $39,000. The 293-ton side-wheeler was 173 feet long, with a beam of 34.2 feet and a hold depth of 5.4 feet. She possessed two engines, three boilers, and was armed with two 30-pounder Parrott rifles forward, two 32-pounders aft, and four 24-pounder brass howitzers in broadside.

Hiram H. Martin was one of the new crewmen aboard, recruited with his friend Robert

Wheeler at Chicago on April 1. Both men were sent to the receiving ship *Clara Dolson* at Cairo and hence to the *Emma Duncan*, which Martin later recalled was a "mosquito boat, only protected against bullets." On April 7, Rear Adm. Porter ordered the warship's name changed to *Hastings*, but that moniker did not initially stick. Within a fortnight, the boat was altered and ready to go to war. Actually, "ready" is not the correct word; "available" might better suit. The *Emma Duncan*, like most of the new tinclads, was, in the words of First Class Fireman Martin, "hardly in condition for service and the crew consisted mostly of green men unaccustomed to service of that kind." Captain Griswold, who had briefly skippered the *Argosy* before turning it over to Acting Volunteer Lieutenant Edward M. King, was placed in command. It would be his responsibility, with assistance from men like the chief engineer, "Mr. Watson, an old River Engineer and a very fine man," to turn his crew into fighting bluejackets.[36]

Griswold's new command was ordered to reinforce Lt. Cmdr. Fitch. After departing Illinois, she steamed up the Ohio River to Paducah, past which she immediately steamed up the Tennessee. The *Emma Duncan* was at general quarters, engaged in its first general exercise in "enemy country," as it approached Green Bottom Bar about 2 A.M. on Friday, April 24, her second night out. As the boat slowed in anticipation of the obstruction, she was fired into by the four guns of the Texas battery. The enemy, as Fireman Martin recalled, "was peppering it into us hot and heavy." The *Emma Duncan* "commenced turning around so that the guns first on one side and then the other could be used."

One early shot (shrapnel) came in forward through the iron sheathing, struck the No. 1 Parrott gun portside, and exploded, mangling the arms of three men so badly that their hurt appendages had to be immediately amputated. The men were all new hands who had shipped at Chicago with Fireman Martin.

The *Emma Duncan* engaged by the light of gun flashes in the dark for a short time. That was the only way the men aboard the gunboat could guess where their enemy was. "But we were a good target for them," Fireman Martin remembered, "as they could see the lights from our furnaces and on the boat." The cannonading continued for about 45 minutes until the riverbank force ceased firing. The tinclad went to full steam and shelled the woods at every nearby suspicious point, but there was no return fire as the Confederates had withdrawn.

Losing touch with the Rebels, Griswold's bloodied command proceeded upriver, checking damages. Upon examination, it was found that the *Emma Duncan* was hulled seven times. In addition to the terrible first shell, it was determined that another came in aft and burst over the heads of the second division. No one was hurt, but the hammock carline and the cabin floor were torn away. Others hit the wheelhouse, but did little damage. Still others badly cut up the light work of the cabin and wardroom.

Late on the 24th, the *Emma Duncan* met the *Lexington*, coming down ahead of Ellet's fleet, and Griswold reported his shot-up craft for duty. Taking a boat over to the timberclad, the master reported his encounter with the unknown Rebel force. Fitch immediately ordered the newcomer to take station astern as the two ran down toward Green Bottom Bar "in hopes of catching the rebels at or near the same place." The Yankee warships reached the bar toward dusk, but there was no enemy activity to be seen. With the *Lexington* short of fuel, the two put down to Fort Henry where the big-gun unit spent most of the 25th coaling.

After supper on April 25, the *Lexington* and *Emma Duncan* steamed back up to the foot of Green Bottom Bar where they anchored about midnight. Guards were posted and a sharp lookout was maintained until dawn. At first light on April 26, a search for the enemy was made but again, nothing was found. Lt. Cmdr. Fitch then directed that the two proceed upriver to meet and communicate with Brig. Gen. Ellet. As the pair paddled on, the tinclad kept station about a mile behind the timberclad. At one point after the *Lexington* had passed, a ferry flat attempted to run out of a hidden creek and make it across the river. Too late. The *Emma Duncan* came upon it and destroyed it just as its occupants jumped out and scurried off into the woods. The cruise, made rather leisurely because a good lookout was kept for the enemy along the right bank, proceeded without incident until the two gunboats came within about a mile of Duck River Shoals, where they met the ram *Monarch*.

The same gunners who had fired into the *Emma Duncan* were now taking aim on the other Ellet rams, *Autocrat*, *Diana*, and *Adams*, as they maneuvered their way into and through the swift current of the shoal's narrow channel. Fieldpieces and rifles raked the wooden boats with canister and Minie balls sending splinters flying into the air but doing remarkably little damage to the boats' heavy oak planking. The rams, unable to round to or back out of the channel, pushed on over the bar taking punishment. It was later reported that while running this gauntlet the pilot house of the *Autocrat* was struck 80 times by rifle balls while six entered the bulwarks of the *Diana*. Canister shot struck, but fell harmlessly into the river.

Coming upon this fiery duel, Lt. Cmdr. Fitch pushed over the Green Bottom Bar and met Ellet's fleet at the head of the shoals, where it was engaging the Texan battery, firing back at it with its onboard field pieces and small arms. The *Lexington* moved into good range and opened fire with her 8-inch guns. Fitch took the battery side of the river to cover Ellet's craft while raking the bank. "The brush was so thick I could not see the enemy's guns, yet the smoke enabled me to fire directly at them," he later recorded.

As soon as the big timberclad rounded the point, the Confederate gunners went into something of a panic. After sending a parting shot toward a brigade boat, Maj. White ordered his gunners to limber up and make off. A few sharpshooters were left behind to take potshots at the boats and attempt to impede any Yankee response.

It was White's misfortune to engage the Mississippi Marine Brigade on one of the few occasions in which that amphibious force actually was able to make a landing and fight as everyone acquainted with it had hoped it could. Once clear of the shoals, the boats went into the bank, lowered their gangplanks, and out came mounted marines. The Rebels, confused that Ellet's craft did not turn out to be the "cattle boats" expected, were pursued. In the ensuing skirmishes, which lasted in some cases out to a distance of 12 miles, nine Confederates and two marines were killed, plus a number of horses. Major White was found at his nearby farm bleeding to death from a mortal wound. Other horse marines stopped off at the plantation owned by the noted partisan chief Col. Thomas Woodward and consumed a banquet that had just been set out to celebrate "the capture of the Yankees."[37]

Once the marine brigade had largely returned to the Tennessee and been mustered back aboard its boats, Fitch took his leave of Ellet about 11 P.M. With the *Emma Duncan* and the *Monarch* in company, the *Lexington* steamed on up to Eastport, reaching that town about noon on Sunday the 27th. There he received a message from Brig. Gen. Dodge indicating that his troops were in possession of both Tuscumbia Landing and Florence and asking that the navy remain as long as possible. As the water level was still dropping, the Logansport officer sent the transports below Big Bend Shoals, keeping the *Lexington*, *Queen City*, and *Emma Duncan* at Eastport another day, hoping to hear more from Dodge.

When no additional news arrived from his army colleague on April 28, Lt. Cmdr. Fitch took his five gunboats and nine transports down to Hamburg Landing where the river was a little deeper. Finding no way to communicate with Brig. Gen. Dodge from that point, he sent the light draughts *Covington* and *Emma Duncan* back to Chickasaw to wait once more on messengers from the general. With no further word from Dodge having arrived by the early morning of April 29, the Chickasaw tinclads went down to Hamburg Landing. At 11 A.M., the fleet descended the river to Fort Henry "to return no more." Aboard the transports were the balance of all rations brought out earlier, save for some of bread and meat taken by Dodge. The five gunboats returned to Smithland on May 1.[38]

By the beginning of May 1863, the number of tinclads available to the Mississippi Squadron had grown significantly. The following units, some recently added, were listed in the monthly report made to the secretary of the Navy: *Forest Rose, Linden, Marmora, Rattler, Signal, Cricket, Curlew, Juliet, Prairie Bird, New Era, Argosy, Brilliant, Covington, Queen City, Champion, Alfred Robb, Hastings, St. Clair, Silver Lake, Springfield,* and *Fairplay*. Of these, the last eleven named were up the Tennessee and Cumberland rivers convoying transports. Rear Adm. Porter and Capt. Pennock, who championed the light draughts, were busily buying and outfitting every one Secretary Welles authorized.

Flowers and dogwood trees were not, in the spring of 1863, the only things to bloom in Middle Tennessee or, for that matter, throughout the Western theater. Plans were renewed for great military achievements on both sides and Confederate raiders, regular and irregular, were out in force busily visiting points in the countryside and on the rivers. In Nashville and other southern towns garrisoned by northern troops, civilian oaths of allegiance and a closer scrutiny became more common. Counterguerrilla activities by Yankee forces were enhanced and this included the Union's Mississippi Squadron.

On March 9 at the time of his Smithland meeting with Lt. Cmdr. Fitch, Fleet Captain Pennock wrote to Admiral Porter suggesting that the upper fleet be divided into two parts. Pennock was rapidly adding additional light draught boats and the Logansport convoy master was stretched to the limit of his powers in dealing with the Army's support demands on the twin rivers. Pennock's idea was to have one task force under Fitch cover the Cumberland and ensure the supply convoys to Nashville which, even with the falling water, would prove important as Maj. Gen. Rosecrans continued preparations to move. The other unit, under an experienced but as yet unnamed officer, would take over the boats operating up the Tennessee.

Pennock's plan found favor with Porter, who directed Lt. Cmdr. S. Ledyard Phelps to head up the new division, at least temporarily, on April 15. Phelps, then waiting to take command of the giant ironclad *Eastport*, was highly regarded by both the admiral and the Cairo station chief because of his Tennessee River experience and his administrative capabilities. Phelps could not immediately take up the post because he was filling in as Cairo commander for an ill Pennock. Indeed, the former commander of the *Lexington* was spending so much time at the tip of Illinois these days that his wife and Mrs. Pennock (close friends) purchased a Mound City home for the two families to share. Upon his return from Eastport, if not before, Lt. Cmdr. Fitch was advised of his change in responsibilities.

Capt. Pennock had recovered sufficiently by the beginning of May so that the Phelps was free to assume command of his new division. On May 4, he and Fitch met at Paducah to discuss assets and cooperation and to amicably divide the 12 available gunboats (11 tinclads and the *Lexington*) between themselves. When the Indiana sailor departed that evening for the Cumberland, his force consisted of the *Lexington* (flagship), *Fairplay*, *St. Clair*, *Brilliant*, *Silver Lake*, and *Springfield*. Fitch's long-time able lieutenants, Hurd of the *Covington* and Goudy of the *Queen City*, remained with Phelps, leaving Glassford of the *Springfield* to become his most trusted subordinate. As certain as there would be new adventures, so too would there be new crews to recruit and train; Fitch, Acting Volunteer Lieutenant Glassford, and others would have their hands full sooner than they might have expected.

Early February to the beginning of May was one of the most frustrating and, simultaneously, exhilarating four month periods yet experienced by the commander of the Mississippi Squadron's first light draught flotilla. Le Roy Fitch had provided safe escort for the largest convoy yet sent from Louisville, via the Cumberland River, to Nashville—indeed, one of the biggest to transverse that waterway during the entire war. Countless other steamers owed him their safe arrival to or from the Tennessee capital. He had rendered important support to the beleaguered garrison at Dover, though maybe not in as decisive a manner as reported 143 years ago. He battled guerrillas on both the Cumberland and Tennessee Rivers, eventually burning the Confederate choke point of Palmyra, and supported the U.S. Army, the Mississippi Marine Brigade, and the few harassed Union sympathizers living along the riverbanks. He was called upon to defend himself against charges of inefficiency in his stewardship of naval support on the twin rivers and, in the end, lost administrative control over one of them in a move which actually rearranged his workload. As the rivers fell and the days lengthened, great challenges loomed and his greatest triumph lay just ahead.[39]

Chapter Eight

Morgan, May–July 1863

THE FIRST FOUR MONTHS OF 1863 were a time of both frustration and success for 28-year-old Lt. Cmdr. Le Roy Fitch, senior officer of the Cumberland River division of the U.S. Navy's Mississippi Squadron. Months of grueling convoy duty and almost constant antiguerrilla sweeps in often-nasty Tennessee weather had dominated that period as Fitch's responsibilities grew far in excess of those originally given him by Rear Adm. Davis in 1862. The return of prime military campaign weather in May, an upswing in Confederate raider and irregular activities, and the increasing availability of light draught gunboats dictated that an administrative readjustment be made. Squadron commander Rear Adm. David Dixon Porter wanted to make certain that the Department of the Cumberland, under Maj. Gen. William S. Rosecrans, received all the supplies sent for an advance south. Through the late winter and early spring, Fitch successfully managed to organize his small flotilla so as to always have a protective or fighting presence at key points at crucial times. Now the navy's top man in the Western Theater wanted his chief convoy commander to devote his full attention to succoring the army.

At the order of his superiors early in May, Fitch turned over a third of his wide-spread command, the Tennessee River, to colleague Lt. Cmdr. S. Ledyard Phelps. Discontinued was the constant challenge and strain of being prepared to move anywhere in a circuit from Carthage, Tennessee, down the Cumberland to Smithland, Kentucky, around in the Ohio River to Paducah, and then up the Tennessee River all the way to Muscle Shoals, Alabama, and back or to any point along the way including many between Cairo and Cincinnati. Fitch did not know it, but on May 13, wheels were put into motion which would see his authority enhanced again very soon. Fleet Captain Alexander M. Pennock, who was authorized to purchase three ultra light draughts for the Upper Ohio River, wrote to Secretary Welles seeking a suitable officer to put in charge of that portion of the fleet.

He also did not know, nor did his superiors or many others until later, that this week actually marked the beginning of Brig. Gen. John Hunt Morgan's great raid into Indiana and Ohio. During this time, the famed cavalry leader, was formulating plans for his undertaking, reasoning that a diversion north of the Ohio River could stall the everywhere anticipated move south by Maj. Gen. Rosecrans and another, aimed at Knoxville and East Tennessee, by Cincinnati-based Maj. Gen. Ambrose Burnside. The scheme, as it was secretly developed, called for a sweep from the Bluegrass State across the Ohio River at Brandenburg, 38 miles below Louisville, then a long ride across the southern counties of Indiana and Ohio, and a return to Kentucky through Virginia. According to historian Lester V. Horwitz, Morgan "got his idea from a Union colonel, Benjamin H. Grierson." Given the time frame, that may be possible, though I would suggest the boldness of Col. Abel D. Streight's work might also have been inspirational.

Finding an appropriate spot to get back across the river was key to the entire Southern plan and so men were now dispatched to the area of the Upper Ohio River as high as Blennerhassett Island to examine the fords. Particular attention would be paid to those between Pomeroy and Portland, Ohio, especially at a place called Buffington Island. A low river in eastern Ohio, easily passable by foot or horse, was vital to Morgan's schemes. According to his brother-in-law and chief of staff, Col. Basil W. Duke, in an 1891 *Century Magazine* article, this requirement was recognized all along as one of the "chief difficulties of the expedition that might prove really dangerous and insuperable." Thus the depth of the Ohio River would play a much more important part than most recognize.

On May 15, a week after the Union defeat in the Battle of Chancellorsville, the Union Navy's revamped Cumberland task force, which continued to be based on Smithland, Kentucky, was still engaged in patrol and convoy work, even as the river fell and the excitement of the previous months died down. The big timberclad *Lexington*, with its 8-inch cannon, and Fitch's favorite tinclad, the side-wheeler *Fairplay*, carried out their duties between Dover and the mouth of Harpeth Creek, with occasional trips down below Dover. The light draughts *St. Clair*, *Brilliant*, *Silver Lake*, and *Springfield* patrolled between Dover and Gower's Island. By the middle of the month, things were so quiet that Fitch planned to send the *Springfield* over to Cairo to have her fire fronts repaired.

About this time, Acting Assistant Surgeon William Howard of the U.S.S. *Brilliant*, in a letter home, revealed that his craft and one or two of the others had taken a convoy up to the foot of Harpeth Shoals with the river rapidly falling. A number of steamers, with barges of coal and hay in tow, were unable to get over the obstructions, where the water was only about five foot deep. These went aground, requiring the *Brilliant* and her consorts to help them off. The deeply-loaded vessels then went to Clarksville where they lightened their loads. "Many of the boats that went upriver will, if the river does not rise, have a summer at Nashville," Howard reported.

At Fort Donelson where several of the boats headquartered, the gunboat crews faced what Howard believed was "a rather precarious style of living, having to depend upon the country people for 'grub.'" Local food prices were exceedingly high, by the standards of that day: butter, $.50 a pound; eggs, $.25 a dozen; chickens $3 each.

Spring on the river brought not only nicer weather and the blooming of blackberries, honeysuckle, and other vegetation, but what the *Brilliant's* medical man called "the sickly season." His boat's commander, Acting Volunteer Lieutenant Charles G. Perkins, took ill at Fort Donelson and was sent home. The Cumberland was, in the doctor's opinion, "a fearfully poor place for a sick man." Many sailors wished to transfer away from the climate and some officers, failing that, wished to resign. Rear Adm. Porter, with continuous manpower problems, refused to grant furloughs or accept resignations while the fate of Vicksburg remained unresolved.[1]

On May 20, Porter issued General Order No. 20, the official decree outlining his divisional administrative plan for the Mississippi Squadron. Doubtless based upon Capt. Pennock's original March suggestion for the upper rivers, this blueprint created six geographical sections. Each would be led by a divisional officer, a trusted regular navy officer, who commanded a certain number of named vessels. Division Five was the Tennessee River under Phelps; Fitch had Division Six comprising the Cumberland and Ohio rivers as far as the Falls of Louisville. Their vessels, like those in the other new districts, were responsible for patrol, convoy, and other work within the assigned boundaries. It was understood that vessels within a district could not leave station without the authority of the district leader, who would also approve all acquisitions (except money) and forward on all communications from their subordinates to Cairo.

The squadron leader's decentralized district plan worked well, though from time to time he was called upon to provide some amplification. In General Order No. 84 of August 20, Porter fleshed out his May outline with specific instructions, primarily for the information of new gunboat commanders. These rules were:

- When commanders are ordered to repair to any point, they are to report to the commander of district, get his orders, and take their stations. It will be their duty to report by first opportunity any thing of importance that may occur. They are not to leave their stations, except to patrol a short distance above and below, and to prevent the passage of rebel troops or munitions across the river. Ferries must be regulated so that no improper persons will pass to and fro.
- Cultivate good feelings with the inhabitants, and allow no improprieties to be committed by officers or crew.
- Pay particular attention to all general orders.
- Warn all passing vessels if there are guerrillas about, and convoy them past danger, if not too far from the station.
- No vessels are to be delayed for convoy.
- Make all reports to commanders of divisions, who will sign all acquisitions, etc., or if too far off, send all requisitions to Capt. Pennock at Cairo.
- Notify the commander of division when short of coal and provisions. If the station is too far from the commanding officer, report by letter, and remain at the station until the divisional commander is heard from.
- As the dispatch vessels go down, find out when they will return, and have the sick and their accounts ready to go up in her.
- When an officer is very sick, he will be sent at once to Memphis hospital without further order than that of the commander.
- The gunboats will never tie up at the bank for night, but lie at anchor ready for anything. Be careful that torpedoes are not drifted down on the vessels, and guard the approach of boats. Never anchor exactly on the same place, but shift position often.

Having provided these general rules, Rear Adm. Porter did not often interfere with the routine work of his district commanders. When, for example, Lt. Cmdr. Fitch was once again pressed by the army for additional convoy support in the fall of 1863, Porter, unlike Pennock, did not travel up to Smithland to check on matters, not did he call the Indiana sailor down to Illinois for a meeting. Instead, he simply issued corrective orders or case-specific instructions (usually by telegraph) from his office or his flagship, the *Black Hawk*, at Cairo.

All of his officers, particularly such battle-tested leaders as Fitch, were given the necessary authority to carry out their responsibilities, were supported in their actions, and, for the most part, were not second-guessed. "It is difficult to determine the importance of Porter's district policy in Union naval control of the rivers," wrote a group of distinguished scholars in 1986, "but the evidence strongly suggests that it was effective and efficient."[2]

On the same day that his superior divided up the squadron, Fleet Captain Pennock wrote Rear Adm. Porter that there was an urgent need for light boats on the Upper Ohio River. Two of the steamers which Secretary Welles had earlier authorized the Cairo station chief to purchase at Cincinnati were already in hand with acquisition of the third expected within days. One of these would be commanded by Acting Volunteer Lieutenant Henry A. Glassford, who was being sent to the Queen City forthwith. Ordnance and ordnance stores for the three were being dispatched there as well so that there would be no delay in outfitting the newest tinclads. Pennock was not the only one anticipating trouble. When Maj. Gen. Burnside took over the Department of the Ohio in March, Maj. Gen. Henry Hallek told him from Washington, D.C., to expect stepped up Confederate raiding activity in Kentucky as soon as the roads were passable. Burnside, whose organizational brilliance would be highlighted during the upcoming Morgan adventure, began in mid–May to closely coordinate intelligence on irregular and other raider activities.

Also for that Wednesday we offer this account of the outcome of a sale. "Cases come up sometimes which are rather puzzling in their character," Rear Adm. Porter told Secretary Welles in relaying the tale of the matter two weeks later. Upon his return to Smithland from his first March cruise up the Tennessee, Lt. Cmdr. Fitch had aboard the *Lexington* a number of prisoners, some cotton, 23 horses and mules, and two wagons. Capt. Pennock asked that the Confederates and the cotton be sent over to Cairo, but gave his subordinate the option of keeping or disposing of the livestock and vehicles as he saw fit. The Hoosier sailor held on to them, thinking that they might be put to work in support of his rendezvous. However, by the middle of May, it was obvious that the idea just wouldn't work. Fitch attempted to find a prize or Treasury agent to take them off his hands, but could not. He could probably have turned them over to the army, but some of the horses would have been rejected. As most of the beasts were in pretty good shape, he suspected the military officers "would have apprised those they wanted at about one-third their value."

So it was that on May 19, the captured horses, mules, and wagons were auctioned off at the Smithfield market center. It might have been something of a sight seeing a Kentucky auctioneer and a Union naval officer in full uniform on the same platform. At any rate, the proceeds were $1,372, of which $25 was taken as expenses for the animals' upkeep; $1,347, a nice sum in 1863 dollars, was turned over to the *Lexington's* acting paymaster, Thomas C. Doan, to lock in the ship's strongbox. Fitch wrote Porter the next morning asking what to do with the cash; Porter told Fitch to receipt the money to the Treasury Department, and the Navy secretary may have chuckled, who knows.

By May 28, six days after Maj. Gen. Ulysses S. Grant launched the climactic siege of Vicksburg, the water level in the Cumberland had fallen to such a low point that Lt. Cmdr. Fitch could no longer employ the *Lexington*. The drop in the level to 3.5 feet at Ingram's Shoals and only 30 inches at Harpeth all but guaranteed that the waterway would be quiet and largely free of Confederate attacks, even though the leafy new foliage along the banks gave the grayclad shooters better cover than they had enjoyed in months. Keenly aware of Rear Admiral Porter's constant need of reinforcements, Capt. Pennock ordered her returned to Cairo for basic repairs prior to her rotation below to Vicksburg. A replacement light draught was promised; Fitch sent the big timberclad away and returned to his old flagship, the *Fairplay*. Within a week, the Logansport native would write that the navigation on the Cumberland was "about closed," as his boats could not get above Eddyville, Kentucky.

Fleet Captain Pennock telegraphed the Indiana sailor on May 31 that he was being tapped to take charge of the upper rivers in addition to his present Cumberland command. Fitch was to quickly make arrangements for his Cumberland river fleet to operate temporarily in his absence and to report to Cairo for instructions. No one knows for sure why the Logansport doctor's brother was chosen for this duty. Several factors probably contributed, including a lack of suitable mid-level regular naval officers available from the East as well as Fitch's own experiences and his availability in the next district down from the upper Ohio, Kanawha, and Big Sandy Rivers. Later that day, after digesting these new orders and talking to those of his captains in port, he sat down to pen a brief report to his superiors concerning his departure arrangements. The *Fairplay*, *St. Clair*, and *Brilliant* were left to patrol the river from its mouth up, while the *Silver Lake* and *Springfield* were on patrol and convoy duty to Clarksville. Taking his document and personal belongings, the Hoosier quit his Smithfield office and rode the dispatch boat to Cairo.

As the Cumberland River continued to fall behind the departing officer, the rapid turnaround of its convoys and, indeed, their sheer size began to fall off. Still, supplies continued to get through to Nashville by that stream, as well as by a significantly rejuvenated—and protected—railroad system. Tennessee's capital city, along with such towns as Clarksville, were under tight Northern control. Although military points or Union sympathizers in the surrounding areas might be hit by Confederate raiders or irregulars, the town centers were secure. The private shipment of goods in or out of Nashville was still very uncommon; however, the vast and increasingly protected logistical apparatus that made the town a key Yankee supply dump was also helping to increase its population. Not only were refugees drawn in, but hundreds of laborers, African American and Caucasian, found work at such spots as the warehouses and waterfront. Others assisted in the city's medical, transportation, supply and even its entertainment businesses. Nashville had changed in many ways since Le Roy Fitch first began running convoys to it; its growth and bustle would continue without interruption while he was away.[3]

After arriving at Cairo on June 3, Lt. Cmdr. Fitch met with Capt. Pennock to discuss the upper river situation, as well as his increased responsibilities for those streams plus the Cumberland. As was now a practice between the two men, Fitch, who had some recommendations to make concerning the distribution of his boats "to insure more safety and better patrols," was encouraged to write down his ideas and turn them in to the fleet captain for review and dispatch down to Rear Adm. Porter. That night in his quarters the Logansport officer composed a lengthy memorandum, written, as he pointed out, "as I will, of course, be held responsible to the admiral."

Fitch's patrol plan would allow two boats, the *St. Clair* and *Brilliant*, to cruise the 61 miles between the mouth of the Cumberland and Shawneetown Bar. The *Silver Lake* and *Springfield* would paddle 77 miles back and forth between Shawneetown and Scuffletown bars. The *Fairplay* would patrol the 169 miles between the Scuffletown and Louisville. When available, the three new boats at Cincinnati would cover the upper rivers while the *St. Clair* and *Brilliant* would also watch the Cumberland as high up as they could safely run.

In effect, the Logansport native was establishing a chain of gunboats capable of regular support and communication one with another. By this arrangement, the craft could patrol back and forth over specified sectors, with the worst of the bars located at the end of each. They could therefore run on their regular stations, communicating with each other at the ends of their lines. This scheme would permit the boats in the Ohio to keep in communication with Cairo and permit a regular means of drawing supplies from headquarters. Indeed, Fitch was proud to suggest that his plan could cut expenses and delays of employing "outside transportation" because "we then have a perfect line of our own from the upper boats down."

It was understood that the *Fairplay* would ply the longest route and not have a consort, as was required by the admiral's standing orders, but she would be so located as to always be within easy range of assistance. Additionally, she could swing down and join a lower patrol if desired, or be joined by one of the Upper Ohio boats should necessity dictate. Fitch hoped that Porter would make an exception for her. Meanwhile, until he heard otherwise, the *St. Clair*, *Brilliant*, and *Springfield* would be left at the mouth of the Cumberland while the *Fairplay* and *Silver Lake* were detailed to make one trip up the Ohio to Uniontown. The voyages would allow preliminary patrols to be maintained pending the squadron commander's decision on his recommendations, while allowing the boats' pilots to "note the water."

As he turned in his report and prepared to board a steamer for Cincinnati, Lt. Cmdr. Fitch, whose enterprise had taken him to the banks of the Ohio starting almost a year earlier, was concerned. "From present indications," he concluded to Pennock, "I anticipate as much, if not more, trouble on the Ohio this year than we had last, unless it is looked to in time." In this observation, he echoed the beliefs of Halleck and Burnside. If Rear Adm. Porter would approve his plan quickly, he could immediately get his boats into position "before the water is too low, and before we hear of some steamer being fired into."

Pennock whole-heartedly endorsed his officer's recommendations and sent them down to Porter for approval.[4]

Eighty Confederate soldiers from Capt. Thomas Henry Hines' Company E, 9th Kentucky Cavalry (C.S.A.), all dressed in Federal uniforms, began a covert six-day reconnaissance on June 8 of potential routes Morgan could take to the Ohio River and beyond and to determine what kind of support the raiders might expect from Northern anti-war and peace factions. Although the group got as far as Seymour, it was quickly discovered and doggedly pursued. Once they made it north across the Ohio River, they were surprised to find themselves being tracked, indeed, hounded by the Indiana Home Guards, whose reputation had previously bordered on the ridiculous but who would make a reputation for themselves chasing Morgan.[5]

From the naval rendezvous at Cincinnati, Lt. Cmdr. Fitch, over the next several weeks, kept an eye on developments along the rivers. Word came in from the army, by telegrams from various quarters, and from the local press, as well as from steamers coming and going. Thus the Hoosier heard of disturbances and fighting in Kentucky and Tennessee, including Maj. Gen. Rosecrans' march and various raids Union and Confederate, plus the confusion surrounding the advance of Gen. Lee's army toward Pennsylvania. The papers were also filled with stories of opposition to the war in certain Northern political constituencies, including his own Indiana, and speculation as to what that might mean in the months ahead.

At the navy's Cincinnati headquarters, the Indiana seaman also learned that the new tinclad *Naumkeag* was caught above the Blennerhassett shoals near Parkersburg and was unable to get down. It was originally intended that she descend to join Rear Adm. Porter's fleet at Vicksburg and be replaced above by one of the new Cincinnati units. However, these were not yet available and she was required to remain into June, even as the water fell. The new commander of the Upper Ohio hoped there would be a rise that would shortly allow her over the sandbar. It was, after all, raining heavily in Kentucky and Tennessee.

The *Naumkeag* was one of a group of light draughts acquired at the beginning of the second quarter for service on the twin rivers of Kentucky and Tennessee. Constructed at Cincinnati early in the year, the 148-ton stern-wheeler was purchased from her owner, Allen Collier, for $32,000. The new squadron addition was 154.4 feet long, with a beam of 30.5 feet. Her depth of hold was 4.6 foot and, deeply laden, her draft was 5.6 foot. *Naumkeag* was powered by two engines, with a cylinder diameter of 14.5 feet and a stroke of 3.6 feet. Her armament comprised two 30-pounder Parrott rifles in the bow and four 24-pounder brass howitzers in broadside. The tinclad's conversion at Cincinnati, under the direction of Acting Chief Engineer Samuel Bickerstaff, was completed at the time of her commissioning on April 16.[6]

Having assembled most of the force he would later take north, Brig. Gen. Morgan took it to a staging point at Alexandria, Tennessee, on June 11. One of his officers, the 11th Kentucky's Maj. James Bennett McCreary, future governor of Kentucky, described the location in his diary as "a country once fertile and rich, but now desolated and barren by the cruel hand of war." It was from that point that the Confederate saddle wizard planned to cross the Cumberland and launch his raid, which if successful, would, hopefully, slow Yankee moves south.

John Hunt Morgan, who would end his mission in frustration, started it out aggravated. The colorful Kentuckian became involved in the wasteful necessity of trying to catch and end a mounted Federal incursion — one far more successful than that attempted weeks earlier by Col. Streight in north Alabama. Col. William P. Sanders' 1,500 men, dispatched by Maj. Gen. Burnside, had traveled in the rain south towards Knoxville. The Sanders raiders, who delayed the start of Morgan's own activities by almost two weeks, destroyed three vital bridges in East Tennessee plus significant stores of supplies, while defeating a brigade of Rebel troops under Maj. O. P. Hamilton near Kettle Creek, Kentucky. Morgan was unable to catch Sanders before he slipped back across Yankee lines, or, as Major McCreary put it, "went back without making a fight."[7]

On June 13, Lt. Cmdr. Fitch reported to Rear Adm. Porter, via the Cairo station, that the fire-front liners were being replaced on the *Springfield*. At the same time by simply reporting the location of his other four tinclads in the lower part of the Cumberland River, he reminded his superior that he had yet to receive a reply to his June 4 patrol recommendations.

In addition to Ohio and Cumberland river operational details, Fitch was also engaged in the conversion, outfitting, and manning at Cincinnati of the three steamboats he was sent to superintend. The work was nearly complete and he was joined in it by Acting Volunteer Lieutenant Glassford, also recently arrived from Cairo. Recruitment was not considered an immediate problem. A new national draft for the army was starting and the Hoosier believed "fear of the draft will drive them into the Navy." Still, there were many men in the boats, as Surgeon Howard had previously pointed out to his wife, whose terms of enlistment or other commitment were set to expire in August. Were these to be discharged?

The ships' ordnance was delivered earlier from Cairo by the squadron ordnance officer,

Lt. Cmdr. Oscar C. Badger, in his last Western assignment before his June 9 transfer to the Bureau of Ordnance in Washington, D.C. It was left to Fitch to see the howitzers installed and, as might be expected from a man with his long-standing interest in that gun type, he was very particular in their placement.

As he checked the workmen attaching the thin armor and mounting her cannon, the tinclad warrior may have taken a moment to reflect on the dimensions of the U.S.S. *Moose*, destined to be his flagboat for the remainder of the war. Like the *Naumkeag*, she was a new locally-constructed 189-ton stern-wheel steamboat which Captain Pennock had also purchased for $32,000. The latest fleet addition was briefly documented as *Florence Miller II* before her acquisition into Union service on May 20. The vessel was 154 feet, 8 inches long and 32 feet, 2 inches wide at the beam. and had a 5 foot draught. Her depth of hold was 4.6 feet and, deeply laden, her draft was five foot. The *Moose* was powered by two engines, each with a 14 inch cylinder diameter and a stroke of 4.6 feet, and two boilers. Once outfitted with armor and six 24-pounder smoothbores, it was said the *Moose* could produce a flank speed of six knots in calm waters. That speed was over a knot faster than the *Fairplay*.

Fitch's new command was armed with six Dahlgren 24-pounder brass howitzers. Interestingly, she also came equipped with a pair of long "grasshopper" spars on her bows. If she happened upon a narrow shoal, these could be fixed into the obstruction. Then, steaming ahead at full power, the gunboat could quite literally pole vault herself forward as many times as was necessary to pass. This "grasshopper" transit, sometimes known as "walking the boat," would be employed within the first month of the tinclad's christening and must have been something to see. No one today has seen either such propulsion or the *Moose*. Unhappily, that vessel is perhaps the most important ship of the Civil War Union navy, save the *Monitor*, for which no widely-known photograph exists.

One of the three feared Confederate cavalry leaders of the Western theater against whom Lt. Cmdr. Fitch was on guard, John Hunt Morgan (1825–1864) of Kentucky led numerous mounted raids into his home state prior to his famous northern incursion. Captured at the end of July 1863, he later escaped from the Ohio State Penitentiary and commanded the Rebel Department of Southwest Virginia. He was surprised and killed at Greeneville, Tennessee, on September 4, 1864 (West Virginia State Library).

By June 14, work on the first of the super light draught tinclads was completed. That evening, Lt. Cmdr. Fitch reported to Rear Adm. Porter that she would be placed into commission at the Cincinnati wharf the following morning. The same day, Confederate Maj. Gen. Joseph Wheeler, having heard of a plan to strike Louisville from Brig. Gen. Morgan, went with him to see Army of Tennessee commander Gen. Braxton Bragg, seeking permission for its execution.

Bragg gave his authority for a small force of about 1,500 to raid up through Kentucky and hit the river port (which had not been and—as it turned out—would not be attacked during the war). Neither Bragg nor Wheeler suspected at the close of the conference, as Col. Duke learned within the hour, that their colleague had a hidden agenda in seeking raid authority.

Morgan had no intention of stopping. After fighting his way up through Kentucky, he would cross the Ohio. Even though the Army of Tennessee needed additional cavalry in the Tullahoma fight, the six foot tall Kentucky-born cavalier thought his plan better. If it worked, he could distract the Union army and take the pressure off Bragg by causing the enemy to pull back and chase him within its own lines. In the process, he could add to the destruction of Union communications by downing telegraph wires and tearing up railroad tracks. He was assured, as part of the concept's due diligence, that the waters at the well-known Buffington Island ford would be extremely low in the summer of the year—two feet or less. An elderly woman had supposedly pointed out that there had been no high water in the Upper Ohio for 20 years and only twice in the past 60 years. Given that quirk of summer, he would come off of his track below Portland, Ohio, and move over to the far beaches, just a few miles north of Ravenswood, Jackson County, in what, on June 20, would be West Virginia. Once over, the horsemen could perhaps link up with Lee in Pennsylvania.[8]

Bright and early on June 15, the crew was mustered on board and, in an impressive, if brief, ceremony, the new tinclad U.S.S. *Moose* was commissioned. The first of three thick logbooks was started with an entry indicating that the weather was "clear and pleasant." In addition to Fitch, the ship's muster roll included Acting Volunteer Master John H. Rice, the executive officer; Acting Volunteer Ensign John Ravell, the drillmaster; Acting 2nd Assistant Engineer Charles McMillan; Acting Assistant Surgeon Abner Thorp, counterpart of letter writer William Howard on the *Brilliant*; Acting Master's Mates Charles W. Spooner and Johnson M. Tusker, plus other petty officers and ratings.[9]

As the new hands aboard the *Moose* began to learn their stations and routines, farther south, by June 18, John Hunt Morgan was able to convince his superiors, Bragg and Wheeler, to boost the number of horsemen in his raiding party from 1,500 to 2,000, actually 2,460 in the final tally. Bragg wanted the men to be Kentuckians, who could stop off along the way and recruit soldiers for the Rebel cause. The unit was divided into two cavalry brigades. The 1st, under Col. Duke, comprised the 2nd, 5th, 6th, and 9th Kentucky and the 9th Tennessee regiments. The 2nd, under Col. Adam R. "Stovepipe" Johnson, was made up of the 7th, 8th, 10th, 11th, and 14th Kentucky regiments. Two mobile horse units of Capt. Edward P. Byrne's Kentucky Artillery were attached. That with the 1st Brigade comprised a pair of 3-inch Parrott rifles while that with the 2nd Brigade included two 12-pounder howitzers, not unlike those aboard the U.S.S. *Fairplay*. Some of the men, like John Weatherred, called these guns "the bull pups." One source suggests the big gun unit was more formidable, giving it four Parrotts and one bronze howitzer. Whatever the artillery makeup, the overall force was the largest Morgan ever lead.[10]

On June 19, in General Order No. 65, Rear Adm. Porter required that every light draught in the Mississippi Squadron be numbered for identification purposes. Every tinclad would have a number two feet tall neatly painted in black on the forward sides (front, port and starboard) of its pilothouse. The numbers assigned to the vessels under Lt. Cmdr. Fitch were: *Moose*, 34; *Fairplay*, 17; *Brilliant*, 18; *St. Clair*, 19; *Springfield*, 22; and *Silver Lake*, 23.

After departing Paoli, Indiana, the same day, the secretive Capt. Hines and his men made for the Ohio River with Hoosier militiamen following. Upon reaching the banks, the Southerners took over a small tug and were gathering way to cross the river on board when they were intercepted by a troop-laden armed steamboat, the *Izetta*. Unable to flee, Hines gave his men the option to surrender or swim across to the Kentucky shore with him. Twelve men, including Hines, took to the water while those choosing prison provided covering fire, shooting into the steamer as it attempted to run down their buddies. Infantrymen on the boat killed three swimmers before turning away under the hail of bullets; Hines and his men vanished into the woods while those left behind raised a white flag in surrender. The episode, together with Morgan's pursuit of Sanders, put the entire Federal establishment in the region on alert.

Although Morgan spent the next two weeks preparing his command to step off, Federal forces from Brig. Gen. Henry M. Judah's 3rd Division, XXII Corps, Department of the Ohio, were also made ready. Brig. Gen. Edward Hobson, the son of a steamboat captain, had his 2,500 man 2nd Brigade (comprising mostly cavalry and mounted infantry) along the north bank of the Cumberland near Burkesville and Marrowbone. Brig. Gen. James M. Shackelford had 1,800 men of his 1st Brigade (attached from the 2nd Division) at Somerset, while Judah took personal charge of 1,200 men from his own 1st Brigade. Unfortunately for the Yankees, too few men from these units were assigned to guard the Kentucky fords close to Burkesville, Scott's Ferry, and Turkey Neck Bend. Unlike the first two, the latter spot on the rain-swollen stream was a particular favorite; Major McCreary penciled in his diary that the location was a "fertile and pleasant valley 'flowing with milk and honey' on the Cumberland River."

While carpenters aboard the light draughts of the Mississippi Squadron scampered to paint numbers on their pilothouses, and work on the *Reindeer* and *Victory* was concluded at Cincinnati, great military strides were underway farther to the south and in the east. It was at the Andrews farm at Turkey Neck Bend on June 23 that many of Morgan's men learned of their forthcoming ride into the Bluegrass State. "For many weeks the intended raid in Kentucky has been much talked about," confided Maj. James McCreary on paper, but now it was a "certainty."

Also on June 23, Maj. Gen. Rosecrans, after considerable preparation and much prodding from Washington, moved out of Murfreesboro headed south toward Bragg. In skilled maneuvering lasting almost 10 days, the bluecoats, in very wet weather, forced their opponent back upon his base at Tullahoma. With Rebel horsemen under "Fighting Joe" Wheeler providing a screen, the Army of Tennessee withdrew toward Chattanooga.

"Old Rosy" entered Tullahoma, 80 miles from his starting point, on July 1. In what was undoubtedly the high point of the Northern general's career, he had lost fewer than 600 men while inflicting 2,000 Confederate casualties, including 1,634 POWs. Many miles to the north on the Cumberland River, Yankee patrols reported "from 5,000 to 7,000" Confederate troops massing across from the fords at Burkesville.[11]

At about the same time that Rosecrans was completing his triumphal entrance into Tullahoma, Morgan and his men began their legendary campaign by crossing the Cumberland River near the Tennessee and Kentucky border. The Great Indiana and Ohio Raid, as it became known, was one of the most famous exploits of the Civil War. In three weeks of hard riding, the audacious horsemen would cover almost a thousand miles in the northernmost penetration of any Confederate force in the entire war. The populations of two leading Midwest states would be panic stricken and over 10,000 Yankee soldiers (mostly untrained) would be led on a merry and frustrating chase that would, for all practical purposes, end at a small island in the Ohio River.

On July 2, Morgan's command reached the Cumberland, which was very high. The next day, small improvised flatboats and canoes were employed to get most of the troopers and their supplies over the flooded river. Many horsemen, however, disrobed and swam their horses across, hanging on to their tails. Small numbers of Union pickets shot at the transfer, but made no impact and were, in fact, scared off by numbers of Confederates "naked as jay-birds" attacking out of the river. Only about two Rebel horses were lost and all were across by 1 P.M.

Brig. Gen. Hobson's 2nd Brigade, the principal Yankee unit scheduled to block the route

Morgan's Great Indiana-Ohio raid of July 1863 was one of the more colorful episodes of the Civil War and, from a military viewpoint, completely useless. Crossing the Ohio River at Brandenburg, Kentucky, Morgan's force proceeded eastward through southern Indiana and Ohio but was blocked by Lt. Cmdr. Fitch at Buffington Island from returning south (*Battles and Leaders of the Civil War*, Vol. 3).

between Burkesville and Columbia, had been shifted west toward Glasgow. Even though the Yankee military establishment suspected he would come to visit, the gate into the Bluegrass State was left open and Morgan entered, scattering the 300 cavalrymen from the 3rd, 8th, and 9th Kentucky Cavalry Regiments (U.S.A.) he encountered near Burkesville. At the same time, up on the Ohio River, the *Moose* undertook her shakedown cruise, paddling toward Louisville, with all aboard ignorant of their own forthcoming great adventure.

Morgan and his men galloped off that July 3 to create the diversion which Bragg and Wheeler believed they would confine to Kentucky. The first objective was Columbia, 20 miles north of Burkesville, which the two brigades reached about 3 A.M. on July 4. The whole force "bivouacked in the road" for the next two hours. At sunrise on Independence Day, the Confederates moved up against 200 fortified Union soldiers from the 8th and 25th Michigan Volunteer Infantry Regiments under Col. Orland H. Moore guarding the Rebels' Green River bridge of choice at Tebb's Bend. These determined Yankees, in a nasty firefight, not only prevented the horsemen from employing their initially-chosen sally point, but forced them to move off a mile and use another ford they located during the fighting. Still, Columbia was taken, with a number of men from each side killed, including Col. David W. Chenault of the 6th Kentucky. In these same hours, but hundreds of miles east, Gen. Lee's men were advancing upon the Pennsylvania farm community of Gettysburg.

Further north at Louisville, the alert Lt. Cmdr. Fitch was making general preparations to battle Rebel irregulars—any irregulars. "I anticipate trouble all along the Ohio this summer," he wrote to Rear Admiral Porter, "but hope to be able to meet and check the guerrillas at every point."

The Hoosier's picket force of tinclads was spread out along the Ohio in anticipation of Rebel activities and disturbances, while also providing something of a coast guard and emergency towing service for vessels that might get hung up on obstructions. The *Springfield* patrolled the Ohio River from Louisville to Scuffletown Bar, while the *Fairplay* and *Silver Lake* moved back and forth from Scuffletown Bar to Shawneetown Bar. The *Brilliant* and *St. Clair* covered the distance between Shawneetown Bar and Smithland, Kentucky. The heavy rains of late would, Fitch believed, bring a rise. If it came, those two boats could make an immediate patrol and convoy up the Cumberland.[12]

Victory was achieved by the Union at both Gettysburg and Vicksburg on July 4, a day on which salutes rang from every vessel in the U.S. Navy. Although the navy was not in the Pennsylvania fight, it had a major role at Vicksburg. The Mississippi Squadron also turned in another noteworthy performance during the day. Eight-inch projectiles from the U.S.S. *Tyler* helped the Union Army win a convincing triumph in the Battle of Helena, Arkansas. In Kentucky, Morgan, having already suffered 71 casualties, made a fast breakout from Columbia, a day ahead of General Hobson, whose troops now included some mounted infantry.

In this time of decisive Union success, Brig. Gen. Morgan, slogging his way north through Campbellsville and Newmarket on Saturday, found that his advance was no piece of cake. Serious resistance was met, particularly from Lt. Col. Charles S. Hanson's 20th Kentucky Infantry (U.S.A.) at Lebanon on July 5. After a seven hour battle, during which Morgan's younger brother, Tom, was killed, the town was taken. The surviving Union troops were taken with the raiders as they departed.

In torrential rain the Southern warriors, with their prisoners, "double quicked" north eight miles to Springfield. There the POWs were paroled and, once Morgan was gone, Hanson, who knew Morgan and whose brother was a Confederate general, wired Burnside alerting him to the Rebels' strength. Elsewhere, the telegraphic service between Louisville and Nashville was down for the whole day and the regular rail service between the two cities did not run.

From Springfield, Morgan's Confederate horsemen pushed on all night to Bardstown, riding in at daylight on July 6. The Rebels rested near Bardstown for a few hours before moving on to capture a train near Lebanon Junction on the Louisville & Nashville Railroad. Morgan was well aware he was being pursued; his telegrapher, George A. "Lightning" Ellsworth, in an early example of "communications or signals intercepts," read the Yankee wires at Lebanon Junction and other points using portable equipment. Throughout the incursion, Ellsworth played a major role in helping the Rebel raider to keep ahead of his pursuers as long as he did.

Also on July 6, Gen. Bragg's army, which was able to prevent Rosecrans from encircling Chattanooga, reached and entered that city. Farther north at Cincinnati, Maj. Gen. Burnside admitted that Morgan was busy in Kentucky and turned his full attention to ending his sojourn. As quickly as he can be "disposed of, I will start the expedition to east Tennessee," he advised General-in-Chief Henry Halleck on July 6. Despite the fact that he had thus far "done but little harm," it would not do to leave the Rebels in his rear "to break up our railroad communications and capture our wagon trains."

Lt. Cmdr. Fitch, having gotten the *Reindeer* into service, oversaw the commissioning later in the day of the last of the super light-draughts, the *Victory*. As both would serve with him for some time, they are worthy of profile here.

Wearing the number 35 on her pilothouse, the 212-ton *Reindeer* was a new Cincinnati-built stern-wheeler which was purchased into the northern navy for $29,750. Although she would not officially be commissioned until July 25, the boat was now ready, but like the two other newly converted Cincinnati tinclads, failed to attract the attention of a photographer, then or later. *Reindeer* was 154 feet long, with a beam of 32.9 feet. Her depth of hold was five foot and, deeply laden, her draft came to six foot even. She was powered by two engines, each with a 16-inch cylinder diameter and a five-foot stroke; steam came from three boilers. Under the command of Acting Volunteer Ensign Amasa C. Sears, the craft was the "racehorse" of Fitch's three Cincinnati boats; her official speed upstream was listed at eight knots, two knots faster than the *Moose* and three quicker than the *Victory*. Six 24-pounder Dahlgren howitzers comprised her battery; much later she would also be given a pair of 30-pounder Parrott rifles.

Weighing in at 160 tons, the *Victory* was the smallest of the three Queen City-constructed boats Capt. Pennock purchased in May and, costing $25,000, the least expensive. The craft, originally documented as the *Banker*, was 157 feet long, with a 30.3 foot beam. Her depth of hold was 4.2 feet and her deeply-laden draft was just five foot. Equipped with two boilers, she also had two engines, each with a 1.1 foot cylinder diameter and a 4.6 foot stroke. The warship wore No. 33 on her pilothouse, carried six 24-pounder howitzers on her gun deck, and was commanded by Acting Volunteer Ensign Frederick Read.

Factoring in information provided by Capt. Hines, John Hunt Morgan had earlier determined that Brandenburg would be his Ohio River crossing point and now headed northwest toward it. The Meade County community was not garrisoned by Union troops. Many of its citizens were Confederate sympathizers, and the spot offered easy access to the stream through a break in the line of low hills in back of the riverbank. Although his main column, made up of cavalry, servants, wounded and hangers-on, cannon, and supply wagons, was almost three miles long in a straight march, Morgan's descent on that town was masked by small units, or "flying columns," broken off and sent out to create diversions. A company went off in the direction of Harrodsburg, suggesting that Morgan was not, after all, moving toward the Ohio River. Another feint, led by Capt. William J. Davis, the 1st Brigade's assistant adjutant general, popped up between Louisville and Frankfort. This ruse would be unusually successful, but Davis and his men could not rejoin their commander before he crossed the Ohio. Local citizens and their press were confused as to what direction the raiders might take. Morgan would use this zigzag, splintering-off tactic over and over in Indiana and Ohio, finding that it often worked to confuse Union commanders.

The Chicago *Tribune* and Louisville *Journal* reported on July 7 that Morgan was approaching; the next day, they cried a warning that he was about to hit Louisville. Two days later, rumored reports were printed that Morgan, himself, was seen in the city in disguise. Many local citizens and defenders were taken in by these reports, though the most outlandish were discounted. In fact, Morgan's main body was continuing on to Salt River and Garrettsville, which they reached on the evening of the 7th.[13]

While his tiny detachments deliberately made deceptive mischief elsewhere, Brig. Gen. Morgan and most of his men pounded on toward Brandenburg. In preparation for their arrival at that town, Col. Duke sent Captains Samuel B. Taylor and H. Clay Meriwether, with

The Confederate raiders were a colorful group who each wore such dress and uniform portions as desired. Skilled horsemen—some said horse thieves as well—these troops rode hundreds of miles through the Northern countryside above the Ohio River, from which Lt. Cmdr. Fitch kept tabs on their movements (*Harper's New Monthly Magazine*, August 1865, via West Virginia State Archives).

about 100 soldiers from Companies E & H of the 10th Kentucky, rushing off ahead from Springfield to find a ford. Morgan, perhaps in his grief from the death of his brother, did not realize that the rain through which he and his men were traveling made the Ohio a far more formidable stream than the Cumberland or Green they had just passed over.

Simultaneously, "Lightning" Ellsworth managed to confuse Maj. Gen. Burnside as to their directions and destination, though he did not fool Hobson, the steamboat captain's son, who learned from stragglers that the river was Morgan's goal. Cutting loose from his supply wagons, the brigadier and his men rapidly headed toward the Ohio River and made up the ground separating them from the Confederates. By 7 P.M. on July 7, Hobson and Morgan were only 12 miles apart, but at that point, Hobson stopped at Rock Haven and wired ahead, hoping to get a gunboat to join him in a co-ordinated attack. None was available and rather than risk a night fight for his tired troops, the Northern general rested his forces.

The flurry of speculative and erroneous newspaper reports about a Confederate descent upon Louisville also caused Lt. Cmdr. Fitch to deploy his boats for that city's defense. The rash of Morgan-sighting stories that the general's small units occasioned appeared in most of the big city newspapers along the river and throughout Indiana, Illinois, and Ohio. Indeed, the naval commander would later complain about the sheer number of press reports and the fact that, amidst the confusion, they were initially his only source of information.

As the raid intensified, the Cincinnati newspapers issued special editions every few hours; the night Morgan rode around the town, there were hourly issues. Ironically, Morgan and his officers, like Fitch, received much of their information by reading the work of local reporters. The Hoosier sailor also could not obtain helpful reports from people on the south side of the Ohio; the "citizens living on the Kentucky shore, and knowing the rebels' whereabouts, take good care not to inform us, but rather to inform the guerrillas of our moves." Morgan, for his part, was often misled by those Indiana and Ohio citizens encountered in his path.

Upon hearing of the supposed Rebel push on Louisville from sympathetic rivermen and then reading of the movement, which he later learned was only a feint, Fitch knew that his gunboats could not prevent the enemy from coming into the city from its rear or land side. Thus he prudently moved to protect the Louisville and Portland Canal, at the Falls of the Ohio. By his direction, Acting Volunteer Master Joseph Watson's U.S.S. *Springfield* did not complete her patrol down to Brandenburg, but rather moved up to and lay off Portland, Kentucky, at the foot of canal. There she was to remain unless her captain heard of enemy activity at some point within his patrol area. If he did, Watson was to move to that hot spot immediately. Meanwhile, the Sixth Division commander posted the *Moose* and *Reindeer* at the upper end of the canal.

Earlier in the day, Col. Duke's point companies reached the wide and swift moat between Kentucky and Indiana, where they met Capt. Hines and seven of his surviving men. Hines, Taylor, and Meriwether agreed that the Ohio River, "800 to a thousand yards wide" (about 2,500 feet) at the chosen crossing site, was too high to ford. So, instead, the grayclads determined to catch a ride. Secreting themselves in the alleys leading to Brandenburg's steamboat landing, the men waited for the first likely steamer to appear. Soon the Anderson & Louisville transport *John T. McCombs*, built at Freedom, Pennsylvania, and homeported at Pittsburgh, hove into view, and was hailed by Confederate sympathizer and local resident N. B. Stanfield. Patience was paramount and the Southerners waited until she had come in and thrown down her stages preparatory to boarding passengers. They then struck quickly and seized the 260-ton, three-year old stern-wheeler, putting her passengers and crew—except for two cooks, a fireman and an engineer—ashore (after first robbing them). The boat was eased back out away from the wharf boat and into an upstream bank, where her captors planned to attract another unsuspecting boat with fake distress signals, a violation of international law.

By supper time, the second necessary craft had been caught. She was Capt. James H. Papper's brand new side-wheeler *Alice Dean*, just purchased by her equally fresh owners, the Dean family of Cincinnati, for $42,000. En route from Mound City to Cincinnati, she was taken after she came into the bank to offer assistance and her pilot saw Capt. Taylor's armed men emerging in a show of force from hiding behind the Texas deck. The two boats were lashed together and run back to the Brandenburg wharf, where they were cabled. Without a shot having been fired, sufficient transport for Morgan's main force was secured. The *Dean's* passengers and sailors were also relieved of their valuables and ushered off to find different conveyance or billets. The *McCombs'* cooks prepared supper for the Confederates and the two closely-guarded boats were held together for the night.[14]

Just after midnight on July 8, Morgan, his horsemen, and artillery began pouring into Brandenburg. This arrival did not go unnoticed across the Ohio. Lt. Col. William J. Irvin, a Home Guard officer in charge of 100 militiamen from Mauckport, Indiana, the next downriver town three miles west, was able to send off reports of the Confederate buildup just across from him in Kentucky. More than that, he became determined to repulse—or at least delay—the Rebels, should they, in fact, elect to move over. As Morgan's artillerymen were placing their big Parrotts on a commanding hilltop location not far from the Brandenburg courthouse and smaller guns lower down the hillside, Irvin found a cannon of his own. He then commandeered a steamer to haul it down opposite Brandenburg.

The pressed craft was the 207-ton side-wheeler *Lady Pike*, built at Cincinnati in 1860 and homeported there. The gun was an old 6-pounder with neither a carriage nor a caisson, but that did come with a few cannonballs. Lt. Col. Irvin and his men lashed it securely into a "borrowed" farm wagon and loaded it aboard the steamboat. Under cover of a thick river fog, the *Lady Pike* made her way down to Morvin's Landing on the north bank of the Ohio opposite Brandenburg. There she offloaded the cannon and 30 soldiers, untrained artillerists all from Leavenworth, Indiana, before returning downstream. Irvin and his people moved under cover and waited to make out the captured *Alice Dean* and *John T. McCombs* on the other side of the Ohio River. They were aided by light from flaming gas wells north of Brandenburg that illuminated the night sky—and the enemy activity.[15]

Under cover of the blanket of fog rapidly dissipating from the Kentucky shore, the *Alice Dean* took over the first group of dismounted Confederate horsemen, the 2nd Kentucky. Although several scouts with Capt. Hines were aboard, the horses were left behind to be sent across later. As men from the 9th Tennessee prepared to board the *John T. McCombs* for the quick hop over to Indiana, a 6-pounder shot smashed into the steamboat's Texas deck, near her pilot house. Grayclad soldier John Weatherred, who was aboard, later wrote in his diary that the shot "made a hail against the boat." Rifle balls also peppered the pilothouse. Cavalryman A. R. Yeiser of the 10th Kentucky observed that "it was worth a monkey show to see the fat pilot dodging." A second cannon round ploughed into a group of riders on the river bank causing them to scatter. Peering across the river from behind a fence which ran along its bank, Confederate riflemen saw their enemy, hiding behind haystacks and houses firing their muskets and working with an unusually-mounted cannon.

Up near the courthouse, Morgan's Parrotts fired back at the spot where smoke from the Yankee was drifting away; lower down, sharpshooters also shot across the stream. Dismounted troopers from the 2nd Kentucky and 9th Tennessee, minus their horses, literally ran aboard the two steamers as Morgan ordered an assault landing made on the opposite shore. After the two regiments assigned to the task were loaded and had shoved off, the Parrotts lifted their fire—at which point Lt. Col. Irvin's men resumed. The oddly-mounted Northern cannon was able to get off only one more shot. After the fast crossing, the Confederates "hit the beach" and took the offending piece, chasing away its crews and defenders. Within "about 5 minutes" of their arrival, the advance party signaled back across that all was well. Irvin had retreated two or three miles "into the bushes back from the river" toward Corydon "and got away," allowing the ferrying job to continue.

About the time that Morgan was preparing his men to board the two captured steamboats and Lt. Col. Irvin was bracing to offer a defense with his 6-pounder, Acting Volunteer Ensign Watson on the U.S.S. *Springfield* received word of the Confederate appearance on the river. His dark warship, wearing the number 22 on her pilothouse, moved down to investigate. As he neared the town of Brandenburg around 9 A.M., he was fired on by infantry from the Indiana shore, but did not return the complement. Her progress was watched by Brig. Gen. Morgan and others and Col. Duke later described her approach:

> Suddenly checking her way, she tossed her snub nose defiantly like an angry beauty of the coal pits, sidled a little toward the town, and commenced to scold. A bluish-white, funnel-

shaped cloud spouted out from her left hand bow and a shot flew at the town, and then changing front forward, she snapped a shell at the men on the other side.

When she was about a mile away from the town landing, the *Springfield* came under fire from Morgan's Parrotts, followed by his lesser cannon. Morgan was determined to sink the tinclad as rapidly as possible because her arrival, far more than Irvin's opposition, jeopardized his entire plan. Every minute she survived, his ferry was halted and Brig. Gen. Hobson's pursuing cavalry neared. The crossing could not be abandoned; if it were, half the Rebel force would be stranded on the Indiana shore.

Acting Volunteer Ensign Watson was just as aware of the stakes as was John Hunt Morgan, then watching the gun duel from the high vantage point of the back yard behind the old Buckner house. Morgan's host, Col. Robert Buckner, was a War of 1812 veteran and a relative of Maj. Gen. Simon B. Buckner, commander of the Confederate Department of East Tennessee. For the next hour and a half, the small howitzers of Watson's craft deliberately bombarded enemy troops on both sides of the Ohio River, while also engaged in a running duel with the larger Rebel field guns. The navy boat could not harm the Parrotts because of their greater range and elevation, but it could make them expend precious ammunition. Watson skillfully handled his stern-wheeler and avoided being hit, and, in the process, managed to delay the Confederate river crossing.

Everyone on both sides of the river who dared watched in utter fascination as the tinclad unloaded her wrath on the Confederates, primarily in and around Brandenburg. According to historian Horowitz, one shell hit the levee and killed three horses. Another went through the kitchen of a local judge, hit the town stable, and buried itself in a hill. Yet a third plunged down through the Meade Hotel to its first floor. In all, more than 50 rounds were estimated to have been fired into the town.

Running low on powder and shell, the *Springfield* withdrew above Brandenburg to wait for infantry support. Two boatloads of bluecoats, some 500 in number, duly arrived. Expecting that the Northern troops would engage from the land side, Watson returned and began firing upon Morgan's embarkation just before the noon hour. Once more the Parrotts replied. Unsupported by the army and within a few shells of ammunition exhaustion, the scrappy Watson realized that he could not alone break up the Rebel crossing. Minutes after starting his second Brandenburg sweep, he retired a second time and steamed up toward New Albany to contact his superior, Lt. Cmdr. Fitch, and to escort additional Yankee troop boats which had already started down.

The troop boats were apparently the *Elk* and *Grey Eagle*. The former was pictured by Arville Funk as a gunboat, while the second was a steamer with elements of the 71st Indiana Volunteer Infantry and the 23rd Indiana Battery embarked. The *Elk* was later said to have put a shell or two into the *Alice Dean* before the two craft withdrew to Louisville. Between them, Irvin with his enthusiastic if untrained militiamen, Watson aboard his tiny gunboat, and the army steamers stopped the forward progress of Morgan's great enterprise for several hours, giving Brig. Gen. Hobson and Fitch a chance to close the distance gap.

Watson's actions won high praise from Le Roy Fitch, who defended his subordinate against uninformed suggestions that he might have run past the Parrotts and tried to capture the *Alice Dean* and *John T. McCombs* on his own hook. The unsupported *Springfield* would have run a huge risk of being disabled, Fitch told Rear Adm. Porter. Besides, even if she were successful, the little tinclad did not have the speed to catch either of the larger river packets making away. The Rebels could simply have outdistanced the *Springfield* and, at their leisure, have run the two boats ashore and burned them. Trained to anticipate the worst, Watson, his boss revealed, potentially faced an even scarier scenario than damage to his boat or the destruction of the steamers. What if Morgan's people had chosen to load some hogsheads of tobacco aboard their prizes as shields and chase down the *Springfield*, boarding her with overwhelming numbers. Fortunately, Fitch did not have to deal with such a fate for Watson's command; he would have to face that problem 14 months later during Nathan Bedford Forrest's Johnsonville campaign. In Fitch's professional opinion, the *Springfield's* captain had "acted very prudently in remaining above the batteries."[16]

Although Fitch was pleased that the *Springfield* had steamed to the spot promptly, he was later forced to acknowledge that she was not alone equal to the emergency. The Indiana sailor did not know about Lt. Col. Irvin's defense or of the *Elk* and *Grey Eagle*.

It was about noon on July 8 when Lt. Cmdr. Fitch received Acting Volunteer Ensign Watson's wire reporting the capture of the *Alice Dean* and the *John T. McCombs*. Just hours earlier having learned from Pittsburgh that a rise might be coming down, he fortuitously dispatched Acting Ensign Sears with the *Reindeer* up the Ohio above Parkersburg to assist the *Naumkeag* over the shoals. Once she was free, both craft were to steam down to Jeffersonville.

Alerted to the Morgan threat, the bulldog sailor sprang into action, quickly putting together a blockade strategy that would eventually lead to the successful containment of the Rebel raiders. Ordering Acting Volunteer Ensign Rice to get the flagboat ready, Fitch rushed to the Cincinnati telegraph office and sent three telegrams. The first two went to Evansville, where the *Fairplay* and *Silver Lake* were instructed to move up the river at once. The second message was sent to his superior, Capt. Pennock, at Cairo advising him of the situation—the wire arrived simultaneously with one from Maj. Gen. Burnside. Fitch promised the fleet captain that a gunboat from Louisville—his *Moose*—would be at Brandenburg within two hours while two others were starting from Evansville. After inspecting the Brandenburg location, all three boats would return to Louisville where they could be contacted.

Leaving the Queen City telegraph office for the *Moose*, Fitch conferred with Acting Volunteer Ensign Read, commander of the *Victory*, ordering him to join him in the chase. Both men realized, as they hurried aboard the quickly-converted warships, that their crews were made up almost entirely of new recruits. These men were new musters and, except for a few ratings, were quite unfamiliar with shipboard routine. Indeed, the men aboard the *Victory* were so green some had only just come aboard and most did not even know their stations. But, as Fitch undoubtedly informed Read and definitely told his own superiors later, "I determined to do the best with them I could."

Steaming in line with the *Moose* in the van, the two boats proceeded from Cincinnati toward Louisville at their best speed. Downriver, the *Alice Dean* and *John T. McCombs* ferried Morgan's men across from Brandenburg all afternoon and into the evening. As the Confederate soldiers awaited their turn on the steamers, most took time to reflect and some enjoyed the vision of the evening sunset. As midnight approached, lead elements from Brig. Gen. Hobson's pursuit came near and even engaged some of Morgan's rear guard. A thick river fog descended, however, cloaking the crossing of the last Rebel troops.

The *John T. McCombs* was left at the Brandenburg wharf boat, more or less undamaged. Her captain was a prewar friend of Col. Duke, who promised to spare the packet. Just before the witching hour on the moonlit night, the last grayclad soldiers, cannon, and horses were offloaded from the *Alice Dean* and headed up towards the camp established a little earlier at Frakes Mill, six miles north. Before quitting the river, the rear guard fired the steamboat, which was cast adrift to burn out. Not all of the *Dean* was consumed before she sank nearby at Buck Creek on the Indiana side of the Ohio. As late as 1942, historian Holland remarked that part of her hull was still visible in the muddy river just below the landing.[17]

Upon his arrival off Louisville on the morning of July 9, Lt. Cmdr. Fitch went ashore and, for the first time, learned that the Confederate force that struck the river at Brandenburg was no mere detachment, but Morgan's entire force "numbering something near six thousand men." If he put two and two together concerning the Rebel's intentions, he may have been further discouraged to learn that the river was reported falling at Pittsburgh and that recent arrivals from that city had noted only "two feet at Buffington and Blennerhassett"—an ideal fording level. Would there be a summer rise, he wondered. While at Louisville, Fitch read a wire from Capt. Pennock approving of his arrangements and granting him permission to undertake the chase as he saw fit. To assist, Pennock sent up the more heavily armed *Queen City*.

The excitement of the day greatly inflated the Southern numbers. No matter the size of the enemy force or the condition of the river, however, the intrepid navy man elected to literally push on. Time was of the essence; Fitch feared that the notorious Rebel raider, "with batteries on shore and two captured boats armed with infantry," might try to take the *Fairplay* and her consort by surprise. Despite the shoal water, the *Moose* and *Victory* pushed over the falls by noon and churned across the slight current of the Ohio toward New Albany, about 15 miles away.

The *Springfield* came to off the Indiana ship-building town a few hours before Fitch and Read. As the *Moose* approached, she hauled close to Watson's battle-tested command and "spoke her." In those few moments, Fitch heard the essentials of what would later be contained in Acting Volunteer Ensign Watson's written report. A line was then passed to the *Springfield* and she was taken under tow. Together the three gunboats made for Brandenburg as fast as possible.

Brig. Gen. Hobson arrived at Brandenburg on the morning of July 9. There the *John T. McCombs* was commandeered and sent back to Louisville for additional troops. When she returned with several other side-wheelers, their troops were dropped off on the Indiana shore. The steamers then began to ferry over the men Hobson brought up through Kentucky. The transfer was not unlike that executed by the raiders the previous day and would take over 12 hours. Hobson's Ohio landing would not be completed until about 2 A.M. Confederate Maj. McCreary, part of Morgan's rear guard, observed, "as I moved up the hills of Indiana, the enemy moved down the hills of Kentucky."

Firmly on Yankee soil, the Southern horsemen moved off to capture, after a stiff fight with 450 militia, the former (1816–1825) state capital of Corydon. There at lunch in the town's hotel, the raid commanders learned for the first time that Gen. Lee had been defeated at Gettysburg the week before. The Cincinnati *Daily Inquirer* that evening received for publication next morning a telegraphic report from its Indianapolis correspondent. It began: "Morgan's forces consisting of infantry, artillery, and cavalry, and numbering between 6,000 and 8,000 crossed into Indiana and captured Corydon. Our forces are falling back."

By the time, Lt. Cmdr. Fitch and his gunboats arrived at Brandenburg between 5 and 6 P.M. that afternoon, Morgan was off to the northeast in the Indiana countryside and Hobson was still sending his cavalry across to chase him. Although the Hoosier navy officer was disappointed, indeed, "mortified," that he could not then get at the Rebels, he was relieved when, about a half hour after his own arrival, the *Fairplay* and *Silver Lake* came in safely with a convoy of seven steamers. Their crews neither heard nor saw anything of the Southerners.[18]

"Invasion of Indiana" read the headlines in the *Cincinnati Gazette* on July 10. Morgan, with "four to eight thousand cavalry," was reported to have crossed the Ohio and was marching on Jeffersonville and New Albany "where tremendous quantities of Government stores are located." When Morgan rode into Salem that day, he was faced with a choice: turn north and take Indianapolis (which was more lightly defended than he knew) or continue east roughly paralleling the river. The latter path was chosen. By midafternoon, the Confederates were about 25 miles ahead of the trailing Hobson.

Everyone intuitively knew that the intrepid Southern horsemen would have to recross to make good their escape and the river was at that time fordable at several points above and below the Falls of the Ohio. To make certain that Morgan's job was not made any easier, the Sixth District commander issued a July 10 general order prohibiting unarmed steamers from running below Madison, Indiana, without convoy. He would make certain that gunboats offered protection from there down while boats from Evansville would handle convoy chores for any transports ascending up above Fredonia.

Elsewhere, Indiana's governor, Oliver P. Morton, was actively and diligently working to aid the Union defense. In addition to calling up male citizens into the home guard and placing Maj. Gen. Lew Wallace in charge of his state's protection, he thrice wired Fleet Captain Pennock at Cairo. On July 9, the politician informed the navy man, as Fitch had done earlier, that Morgan was across, giving the Confederate troop level as 6,000. Next day, he telegraphed again, asking that Pennock send every spare man and boat he had up as he expected Morgan's incursion was just a pinprick and that he might be caught when, as expected, he re-crossed the Ohio at Owensboro or below. A little later, the governor wired saying that Morgan had changed direction. In any event, the Hoosier chief executive confidently believed that Morgan could "certainly be taken."

It was during this time that the raiders gained a reputation for plundering. Claims commissioners in both Indiana and Ohio would later hear how Morgan's people robbed goods from private homes, swiped clothes and valuables, and looted stores at crossroads and in small towns. In retaliation, local citizens shot into Rebel foraging parties or fanned out to take word of the raiders' location to the militia.

Such actions heightened the hysteria in Indiana and Ohio. In turn, the resistance, organized and unorganized, to Morgan's incursion intensified. A number of Confederates were genuinely surprised at the terror shown in this response. They were also reading Yankee newspapers. "The citizens seemed frightened almost to death, for Federal papers have published the wildest tales about us," commented Major McCreary in his diary. Cavalryman Weatherred also wrote, "the numerous papers of Indiana were telling the people that Morgan's men were killing women and children and burning houses and destroying everything." This was not the case, but "it scared the people almost crazy, consequently, they all or most of them left home." Before the raid ended, the governors of Indiana and Ohio mobilized over 115,000 home guardsmen, all of whom were charged with guarding key communities, bridges, rail and supply centers, and with harassing Morgan however possible. By July 10–11, McCreary was recording that the invaders had fought with old and young men "decrepit, white-haired age and buoyant, blithe boyhood."

The Confederate, in columns or small groups, were often targets for farmers shooting from concealment. At one point, Brig. Gen. Morgan even issued an order, reminiscent of that given by Graham Newell Fitch in Arkansas the year before, that the homes of anyone caught bushwhacking be destroyed. It was, however, the Confederates' need for replacement mounts which caused the greatest uproar. "Horse stealing is the order of the day with the raiders," wrote a *Chicago Tribune* reporter in Indianapolis. "We learn that they have already stolen from six to seven hundred head, all fine animals." When General Hobson's men, in hot pursuit, needed horses, they often had to settle for the worn-out jades Morgan left behind. Although there were occasional excesses, Morgan was, on the whole, no more destructive during his raid than, for example, Hoosier Col. Streight had been in gathering up mules in Middle Tennessee. Still, he did take over 2,000 horses during his time in the Buckeye State.[19]

Following Morgan's escape from the Ohio River, Lt. Cmdr. Le Roy Fitch was saddled with one of war's most recurrent problems—faulty information. No one knew for sure where the Confederates were at any given time or where they might appear next. Interviews with citizens were not altogether reliable. Officers of the Federal army, regular or volunteer, either did not know where the Rebels were (which was usually the case) or believing they knew, seemed to "think it beneath their dignity to inform or communicate with a naval commander." Frustrated in his personal efforts to obtain independent intelligence, the Hoosier sailor was forced to rely on accounts in the panic-stricken press or occasional telegrams from the Cincinnati office of Maj. Gen. Burnside.

Faced with an intelligence gap, young Fitch now drew from his professional training and his own guerrilla-fighting experiences to make his own estimates. Reflecting on the skimpy evidence at hand, he guessed that Morgan would be "hemmed in" by Yankee militia "in the center of a circle ... with the river running around him." Basing his strategy on that thesis, the commander decided that his best move was to post a string of gunboats along the Ohio to guard as many of the accessible crossings and shallow fords as possible.

Not knowing where the Confederates were headed on July 9–10, the Logansport native sent the *Fairplay* and *Silver Lake* on night patrol back and forth the 21 miles from Brandenburg to Leavenworth, Indiana. The *Victory* and *Springfield* were asked to do the same, covering the 38-mile distance from Louisville down.

The next morning, the navy learned that Morgan was headed roughly north. Acting on this news, Lt. Cmdr. Fitch sent the *Fairplay* and *Silver Lake* to patrol the 121 miles between Louisville and Cannelton. The *Moose*, *Springfield*, and *Victory* proceeded to and above Louisville, with the former stationed at Madison to receive dispatches. The naval officer asked Maj. Gen. Burnside to send word to both Madison and New Albany when the whereabouts of Morgan became known.

Down on the Ohio on July 11, Lt. Cmdr. Fitch was still receiving all kinds of conflicting reports. "It seems to be the impression," he wrote Rear Adm. Porter, "that Morgan is moving in two directions, the main body of his force moving up in the direction of New Albany." Unless the Hoosier sailor could get accurate intelligence concerning the Rebels' exit destination, the "Thunderbolt of the Confederacy" could "come in and ride across in less than an hour." "I have to get word of him in time to enable me to meet him," Fitch cried.[20]

In "a nice piece of work," Morgan continued to "baffle" Federal calculations by sending flying columns to various Indiana locations. Digesting the assorted location notices, a consensus on Morgan's destinations was reached in various quarters by July 11. As noted in

Another long-time Cumberland River gunboat, the *Silver Lake* participated in the February 1863 defense of Dover, the pursuit of John Hunt Morgan, and the Bell's Mills engagements of December 1864. Sold out of service in 1865, she was converted into a side-wheeler and was renamed *Mary Hein*. The ex-warship was burnt out in Louisiana's Red River in February 1866 (West Virginia State Archives).

the Cincinnati papers, those spots were Jeffersonville, Madison, and New Albany. Acting upon this inaccurate conclusion, the *Springfield* and *Victory* were dispatched above the Falls of the Ohio to patrol between Louisville and Madison. Maj. Gen. Burnside, having heard from Brig. Gen. Jeremiah Boyle at Louisville, informed Brig. Gen. Orlando B. Willcox at Indianapolis later in the day "that the gunboats sent from Louisville up the river are engaged near Madison, which indicates that the enemy are trying to cross there."

In fact, Morgan was weaving back and forth through southeast Indiana, taking the time to burn bridges, plunder supplies, and destroy rail tracks. Just as he would until he were well into Ohio, the butternut commander sent his "flying columns" out on deception missions, which scared locals nearly out of their wits. Towns and their surrounding areas visited or about to be visited included Salem, Canton, New Philadelphia, Vienna, Lexington, Paris, Dupont, Rexville, and Summersville. The gunboats were watching and ready, but not engaged.[21]

Although the Southerners were not moving on the Union supply bases, one of their previously detached units did attempt a linkup. After scouting Louisville and creating a fuss, the 180-man force of Capt. William J. Davis had orders to steal a boat and meet Morgan at Salem, Indiana. Davis chose the early morning of July 11 to effect his crossing of the mustard-colored river. He and his men were soon sighted near Twelve Mile Island (12 miles above Louisville) by a pair of vigilant tinclads. Moving up fast, the *Victory* and *Springfield* "met this gang and shelled them back." Although a few troopers made it over from Dixie, many were just entering the river when the tinclads arrived; these received "a very severe shelling before they could get up the bank again." Federal skippers Read and Watson saw this skirmish as a great victory over troops who were obviously Morgan's reinforcements. In truth, 45 Confederates did get over; the rest were scattered and some were captured on the island. From these, the navy men heard that Morgan was near Memphis, Indiana.

Lt. Cmdr. Fitch heard of Davis' repulse while the *Moose* was near Louisville. The flagboat immediately pushed upstream above the Falls of the Ohio, with her commander thinking he might also have a chance to engage should any more Southerners from the still-unidentified force try to get past the island. By the time the light draught arrived, however, there were no Rebels left to shoot at. Once he had taken reports of the one-sided fight from his subordinates, Fitch sent the *Springfield* and *Victory* upstream to hunt for flats and skiffs while he returned to Louisville.

As soon as the *Moose* anchored off the Kentucky city, the Indiana sailor immediately ran ashore and wired the good news of the Confederate repulse to Maj. Gen. Burnside and to his superiors, Porter and Pennock. Fitch confided to the former that he had grown more confident of "being able to meet Morgan."

While waiting for responses from the three ranking officers, Fitch posted a pair of reports to Rear Admiral Porter. In a postscript to his second document, the Logansport officer, doubtless caught up in the excitement of the moment, proclaimed that "the whole river appears to be infested by guerrillas all at once. I expect there will be very lively times here this summer."

About 12:45 P.M., the Department of the Ohio army chief acknowledged Fitch's message, placing Morgan near the Hoosier town of Vernon; another telegram followed with news that the Confederate advance was really toward Madison. On the other hand, it was possible, Burnside conceded, that "he may turn and try to cross below Louisville." The military man with the famous sideburns promised to communicate by telegraph any information received on the enemy's movements.

Unable to obtain any response from navy headquarters at Cairo, Lt. Cmdr. Fitch departed Louisville for Cincinnati in midafternoon. Unhappily, he also had no word on the progress down of the *Reindeer* and *Naumkeag*. He could only presume by their absence that they were "doing good service perhaps a little farther up the river."

The *Moose* reached Madison, about half way between Louisville and Cincinnati, on July 12. There her commander stepped ashore to mail Rear Adm. Porter a supplement to his previous day's reports giving the latest details on the supposed size of the force (1,500) that *Victory* and *Springfield* had faced down. There he also received a wire from Maj. Gen. Burnside informing him of Morgan's latest moves and suggesting the possibility that the Confederate might try to get back across the river at Madison. "Please look for him there," the theater commander directed.

A little while later, Acting Volunteer Ensign Watson received a message from the general asking that the *Springfield* be moved to Lawrenceburg to protect that place and Aurora, four miles below. Burnside told the tinclad captain that the army had heard of the possibility that the Confederates might attempt a crossing between those towns.[22]

By July 13, the *Naumkeag* had gotten over the shoals and, with the *Reindeer*, had come down from the Parkersburg area. The two made rendezvous with the *Moose* near Madison early that morning. After the warships reached that town and Lt. Cmdr. Fitch took their captains' reports, he went ashore to confer with Lt. Cmdr. George Brown. The former skipper of the U.S.S. *Indianola* was able to give him "more positive information ... than any place yet during the chase." After the meeting, Fitch returned aboard the *Moose* and signaled most of his vessels upriver toward Aurora and Cincinnati. The *Naumkeag* was left to work with Brown.

Farther south that day, Rear Adm. Porter sent a summary review of the Vicksburg campaign to Navy secretary Welles. Porter, receiving regular reports on the Morgan chase from Fitch and Pennock, once more expressed his support for the Indiana sailor, while reviewing his earlier activities. "The war on the banks of the Tennessee and Cumberland has been carried on most actively," he wrote. "Lieutenant-Commanders Phelps and Fitch have each had command of these rivers and have shown themselves to be most able officers. I feel no apprehension at any time with regard to movements in that quarter."[23]

While the Navy maintained its surveillance, John Hunt Morgan pushed his men steadily eastward in "an enormous horserace." Although he was followed by thousands of volunteer, militia, and regular troops who did slow him down somewhat, his movements went roughly according to plan and the Federals were still confused as to his destination. A swathe of burned bridges, wrecked tracks, looted stores, and alarmed Hoosiers were left behind.

This is not to say that the opposition to the incursion was lessened; if anything, the raid seemed to further boost a protective defense of the homeland mentality not previously exhibited on such a scale by Northern citizens. All of the guardsmen and regular Union soldiers engaged in whatever fashion in this act of collective midwestern patriotism benefited alike from the largess of their fellow citizens. Constantly cheered, they were offered, at every corner and stop, fresh victuals and other forms of refreshment.

Leaving Vernon, the Confederates, who continued to take their refreshment by force, proceeded on to Dupont and Summersville. On the evening of July 12, Maj. Gen. Burnside wired Brig. Gen. Boyle at Louisville asking him to "notify the gunboats" that Morgan was evidently making for Aurora or Lawrenceburg, maybe even Cincinnati. Later, he urgently demanded that Boyle "have all the light-draught gunboats hastened up to this part of the river at once." After calling in his flying columns and opposed only by small groups of Indiana "squirrel hunters," Brig. Gen. Morgan arrived at Harrison on the Ohio line on July 13. By this time, he had lost nearly 500 men killed, wounded, or POW.

Out on the Ohio River, Le Roy Fitch kept on Morgan's right and made ready to kill or capture the wily Rebels when they struck "his" river. The Logansport native received reports that Morgan was moving northward and eastward, headed either toward the *Moose* at Aurora, or 15 miles back, still riding north. Fearing that his enemy could arrive on the river between Aurora and Cincinnati or even at Cincinnati, he moved up in that direction with the *Moose* and *Springfield*. The *Victory* and *Reindeer* were stationed between Aurora and Lawrenceburg.

Thinking critically and trying to anticipate his opponents' moves, the Hoosier sailor also made calculations to handle Morgan should he advance other than was initially imagined. By now he had gained an advantage that was unexpected. Heavy rains in the West Virginia mountains over the past several days had caused the river level in the Pittsburgh area to rise rapidly and the surge continued downriver. This unseasonable rise, estimated at five and one-half feet in some sections, had allowed the *Naumkeag* to steam down. More importantly for the Union forces, it would allow navy tinclads and, if available, troop streamers, to range much farther upriver than usual.

Thus, the U.S. Navy's strategy was to block all possible river crossings and to catch the Confederates attempting to get across the now-swelling river. If, for example, Brig. Gen. Morgan should make a retrograde movement and strike at Madison or hit the river either a short distance above or below that town, it was anticipated that the *Naumkeag* and local resources could provide a check. The two boats at Aurora were also quite capable of operating above or below if necessary. If Cincinnati were found safe and no other information was available, the flagboat would find a coal barge loaded with 500–600 bushels and tow it downstream at once.

In the Queen City, thousands of volunteers were called up to begin training as home guard to repulse Morgan, whom even the dullest must have known was headed their way. On top of this, Maj. Gen. Burnside, at his headquarters in the Burnet House on the north side of Third Street above Vine, now had another worry. Although the local newspapers would not begin detailed coverage of the event until July 15, major draft riots had broken out in New York City. It was feared that the new conscription law, which Ohio's provost general started enforcing the month before, could cause disruption in many Northern cities, Cincinnati among them. If trouble started, the former Army of the Potomac chief might need soldiers to police unruly mobs. Fortunately for him, there were no riots in Ohio or Indiana.

Once more masking his move, Morgan sent out another feint along with false messages composed by telegrapher Lightning Ellsworth. Then, avoiding the garrison at Cincinnati, the Confederate horsemen rode through the northern Hamilton County suburbs during the night and came to Williamsburg, 28 miles away, late the following morning—a march of 90 miles in 35 hours. "After this Gilpin race, we rested," bragged Maj. McCreary, "by capturing a train on the Little Miami and a considerable number of prisoners."

Morgan's plan now called for an escape back across the river to the new state of West Virginia. To that end, he steered his men southeast "for the great bend of the Ohio at Pomeroy" still visible on any roadmap today. Along the way, the Confederates captured so many prisoners they had no choice but to "break their guns and parole them." In Kentucky, Brig. Gen. Judah, whose men waited a day and a half without success to cross the flooded Green River, gave up their direct overland pursuit and moved by rail to Louisville to take up the chase from the decks of transport steamboats. Brig. Gen. Boyle was directed to make the transfer happen and to make certain that the steamers had sufficient coal to reach the Queen City and perhaps beyond.[24]

Escorted by tinclads, Brig. Gen. Judah's troop transports arrived at Cincinnati from Louisville on July 14. Now that the Ohio had risen, he could, after boarding some 500 fresh horses, push up relatively fast on the steamers. Meanwhile, other Union cavalry forces were sent rushing by train toward Bellaire, Ohio (across the river from Wheeling). Elsewhere, home guardsmen continued to harass the raiders. Not only did they take pot shots at them, but they also blocked roads by felling trees and tore down bridges (or removed key planks from them). Morgan's people had, themselves, felled trees and destroyed bridges in an effort to stop Hobson. At Jasper, Ohio, they knocked out a vital bridge which held up the Yankee advance for five precious hours. But now, most of the tree felling and bridge busting was done by Buckeyes, who knew which roads the enemy had to travel. Rebel horseman John Weatherred wrote in his diary that Morgan's "advance guard of 4 or 5 hundred had to carry axes with them to cut the timber out of the roads." Morgan's initial offensive was beginning to look to some like a race for survival.

During that Tuesday, the "Thunderbolt of the Confederacy" headed toward Ripley, Ohio, hoping to make a river crossing at that town if conditions were right. Conditions were not right. The Ohio was up and a horde of militia surrounded the town like wasps guarding their nest. Lt. Cmdr. Fitch later told Maj. Gen. Burnside that if soldiers could have forced Morgan onto the river at Ripley, "I could have held him there for a week." With Brig. Gen. Hobson gaining and only 10 miles back, Morgan and company, perhaps sensing that gunboats might arrive off Ripley, rode straight east toward Buffington Island.

About one-quarter mile at its widest point by 1.2 miles long, oval-shaped Buffington Island, unlike Island No. 10 in the Mississippi, survived both nature and the Civil War and today is still located close to the Ohio shore opposite the mouth of Little Sandy Creek, between the communities of Sherman, West Virginia, and Portland, Ohio. On the Buckeye side, Dry Run Creek empties into the big river at the southern tip of the island. Although it extended farther north in 1863 than in 2006 due to dredging, Buffington was always considerably smaller than the better known Blennerhassett Island, about 25 miles upstream. Today, West Virginia, which owns the spot, is 1,000 feet away, while Ohio is only 200; in 1863, when there were no locks and dams, the distance was less. When the river is high, as it would be on July 18–19, 1863, a narrow chute separates the island from the Buckeye State; at other times, as Morgan had hoped, the water could be so low it wouldn't slosh into a knee-high boot. Today's river improvements insure that there is usually a chute.

Originally referred to as Amberson's Island, after John Amberson, a late 18th century squatter, the little dot acquired its present name in the early 19th century from its first owner, Joel Buffington, who farmed it. The head of the 150 acre island blocked the current somewhat and silt and sand piled upon it forming a bar over which people could walk (ford) at low water. The

Brig. Gen. Henry Judah (1821–1866) commanded the 3rd Division, XXII Corps, Department of the Ohio, at the time of Morgan's Raid. During the Union pursuit of the Southern riders, he commanded his own 1st Brigade, while Brig. Gen. Edward Hobson led the 2nd. Overall command of the Federal response was handled by Maj. Gen. Ambrose Burnside in his best command performance since before the disastrous Battle of Fredericksburg (December 1862) (Library of Congress).

atoll accordingly became part of an early transportation route and was important in those years because of the ford, which lay on an angle northwest to southeast from Ohio to the West Virginia shore. Located 43 miles below Parkersburg and 35 below Marietta, the island served as a station on the Underground Railroad prior to the Civil War. After the War Between the States, it became a late 19th Century picnic and swimming area. In the 20th Century, it hosted hunters and, most recently, commercial gravel interests.

By Wednesday, July 15, as he approached the Ohio River and the planned reentry into Dixie, Brig. Gen. Morgan had grown overconfident. He failed to send out flying columns to distract his rapidly converging enemy; indeed, he seldom sent out scouts. Although he knew that Hobson was somewhere behind him in hot pursuit, he did not know about Judah and he continued to believe what he was told a month earlier, that the Ohio would be too shallow for gunboats. Besides, if any showed up, they would be at a terrible disadvantage when matched against his Parrotts. Although the information was readily available, unfortunately for him, no Rebel spy or sympathizer had warned Morgan that the *Moose* and her simultaneously-completed Cincinnati-built sisters were super light draughts. They may not have been heavily armed, but they were extremely light and maneuverable.

After postponing preparations for his own east Tennessee campaign, Maj. Gen. Burnside at Cincinnati coordinated the Morgan pursuit as though he were a symphony director. This was his finest performance since his ouster as commander of the Army of the Potomac after the Fredericksburg debacle the previous December. Indeed, his coordination of the Union side of the entire operation reminds this writer of the organization demonstrated by British Admiralty leadership during the 1941 hunt for the Nazi battleship *Bismarck*. Sifting through available information, accurate and inaccurate, Burnside worked the telegraph wires like a harpist, making them sing as required to all Northerners involved, military, naval, or civil. It was his orders and messages that brought up and co-ordinated troops and home guardsmen, sent the pursuers to certain locations, reassured politicians, informed editors, and moved not only steamboats but also gunboats.

While Union land forces followed Morgan, the gunboats played their defensive role as well. With all commercial river traffic closed and most of the flatboats, skiffs, and scows destroyed or out of the water, the warships could concentrate on two major duties: guarding possible fording sites and convoying troop steamers. They also assisted in other ways. The *Moose*, on July 14, put into Ripley and there speedily offloaded several crates of small arms ammunition for Col. James P. Fyffe's Brown County militia.

On the evening of July 15, Brig. Gen. Judah sent a telegram to Lt. Cmdr. Fitch, which was passed on just after midnight from the Maysville, Kentucky, telegraph office. In it, he asked that the navy ready itself to convoy troop steamers, with cavalry and a little infantry, up toward Pomeroy and Gallipolis "as may be directed." Brig. Gen. E. Parker Scammons, commander of the 3rd Division of the VIII Army Corps based at Charleston, West Virginia, had ordered two brigades based at that community to prevent an invasion of the Kanawha Valley. These were the men Judah had in mind. The first, commanded by future U.S. president Col. Rutherford B. Hayes, comprising the 23rd Ohio and the 13th West Virginia Volunteer Infantry, would depart immediately aboard two steamboats from Charleston up the Kanawha River tributary of Loop Creek. The second brigade was made up of the 12th and 91st Ohio Volunteer Infantry, and an artillery battery and it would follow shortly thereafter.

That evening at West Union, Ohio, which is northeast of Manchester not far from Ripley, a young lady named Lena began a letter to her mother which she finished four days later. One paragraph is particularly germane to our story:

> Morgan must be caught now—Burnside's Army have followed him from Tennessee and it will be a hard thing for him to escape; a line of gunboats moves along the Ohio, with thousands of soldiers to keep the Rebel horde from crossing the River, and couriers are constantly passing from our Army to them [the USN] with orders which way to move.

By July 16th, Burnside had divined that Morgan's goal was Buffington Island and thus began to draw closed the great net that was cast around the invading Southerners from land and water. Increasing their own pace, the pursuing Yankee riders chased the Confederate horsemen relentlessly. Over the next two days, Hobson's men would follow the enemy through Sardinia, Winchester, and Locust Grove.

At Cincinnati, the army had hastily gotten up its own makeshift gunboat, the *Magnolia*, to assist in guarding the waterfront of that town. That vessel, mounting a single Parrott rifle at her bow and protected with captured Southern cotton bales, was home to a Queen City militia unit known as the Guthrie Grays. The boat, minutemen and all, was offered to Lt. Cmdr. Fitch by Maj. Gen. Burnside on July 14. Upon inspection, Fitch determined that her draft was too deep and that she would not do to augment his fleet.

However, another steamer, the much lighter *Allegheny Belle*, was available and her captain, Master Nat Pepper, son of the captain of the late *Alice Dean*, and pilot, John Sebastian, were most eager to join the hunt. With military approval, the cotton and cannon were transferred to her from the *Magnolia*. Anxious for a measure of revenge, Pepper would leave Sebastian to run the boat while he served as a volunteer gunner. Task group commodore Fitch now had five tinclads and an auxiliary with which to continue the chase. "This might have been considered an extravagant use of boats," he later wrote, "but the river was so low and fords so numerous that a less number might not have met with such a favorable result."

Early on July 16, Lt. Cmdr. Fitch's patrol had reached Manchester, upstream from Ripley, Ohio, and Maysville. There he wired Maj. Gen. Burnside the information that at least a portion of Morgan's command had passed through Georgetown the day before and had driven in the Ripley pickets. They then moved on through Decatur and spent the night at West Union. "As well as I can judge," he confided, "Morgan is still moving on to the eastward." Fitch had hoped that Morgan would try to get back across the Ohio at Ripley and was disappointed that he now appeared "to be making for the mountains." "The prospects now look rather dubious," he warned. Morgan could strike the river at some point beyond the reach of the gunboats, "as the river is now falling very rapidly."

The blockade master received two telegrams from Cincinnati that Thursday. In the first, Burnside, echoing Judah's telegram, officially requested the gunboats proceed to Pomeroy and Gallipolis, convoying Brig. Gen. Scammon's cavalry and infantry brigades. "I trust to you to check the enemy at Pomeroy and Buffington Island until our men get up," he wrote in the second. The Ohio Department chief expressed every confidence in the young naval officer: "I am sure you will not allow them to cross if you can prevent it."

As added insurance, Col. William R. Putnam at Camp Marietta was ordered to send down two companies of state militia, with two artillery pieces, to guard the Buffington ford. These men were recent recruits being mustered into the 18th Ohio Volunteer Infantry by Capt. C. L. Wood. Burnside stressed Putnam's people lose no time, to carefully move down to the island on a steamboat ("under no circumstances must you allow your boat to fall into the hands of the enemy"), and to destroy all means of crossing found. If Morgan was already turned toward Marietta, they should go back quickly and assist the defenders of that town, helping to make certain that the Rebel did not get over at Blennerhassett's or seize the Marietta bridge. Acting on his own hook, Col. Putnam also sent 145 infantrymen on up to guard the steamers at Mason City.

On July 17, Maj. Gen. Burnside wired Maysville ordering the captain of the dispatch boat *Imperial*, T. J. Oakes, to rush copies of the army's instructions to Lt. Cmdr. Fitch. His commands were also to be sent by courier to Hobson and Judah. Burnside, given the information provided by Fitch and others, believed Morgan might make an attempt to steal boats and get across the Ohio at Portsmouth. "Instruct gunboats to keep sharp lookout at Portsmouth and other places," his message read, "where steamboats are lying, to prevent capture." Simultaneously, the morning edition of the Cincinnati *Daily Enquirer* reported that the Ohio River at Buffington was but 30 inches deep.

During the day, Capt. Wood's volunteers arrived from Marietta on the Ohio shore opposite Buffington Island aboard the small steamboat *Starlight*. The craft was pressed into service so quickly that it was still towing a barge filled with some 3,000 barrels of flour. Upon arrival, the tow got stuck on tree stumps partially hidden by the deepening water. After climbing atop the high ground overlooking the crossing, most of the two companies were put to work building rough fortifications and situating their cannon. When they were finished, they were to spread out and pretend to be a much larger force. At the same time, Wood directed others to lighten the grounded barge by unloading its cargo. Once freed, the boat and its tow anchored farther out in the river. There they were not only safe from Morgan, but also ready to speedily withdraw Wood's men if the need arose.[25]

From the Queen City, the Federal navy, as requested, escorted the soldier-laden transports of Brig. Gen. Judah upstream to Portsmouth. There they were to meet an infantry brigade of 1,850 men that Burnside had sent down earlier. As the three regiments of blue-coated cavalrymen disembarked from their two dozen steamers to chase the Rebels overland, Judah asked Lt. Cmdr. Fitch to guard the nearby river sector as far upstream as possible. Portsmouth was, after all, a major contributor of manufactured goods to the war effort.

Morgan was 25 miles north en route to Buffington Island. Judah, whose intelligence-gathering was far superior to Morgan's, moved to Pomeroy, from which he wired good news to Burnside. The enemy was advancing into Meigs County, which is essentially a boot-shaped Buckeye peninsula, surrounded on three sides by the Ohio River, which juts down into West Virginia. "Moving thus, Morgan is in a trap, from which he can't escape."

Actually, the Confederates could have gotten away had they been willing or able to move farther upstream before attempting to cross. Apparently, Brig. Gen. Morgan was not briefed upon or did not yet appreciate that the water level in the Ohio was rising. He certainly did not know then that the navy had gunboats able to run "on a drop of dew" and that several of these had moved up as far as they already had. But even these could not have gotten at the Rebels had the horsemen gone over a few miles farther up, say at Reed's Landing (today's Reedsville) or near Parkersburg. There the water would have been far too shallow for gunboat navigation.

Honoring the army petition and building upon his own planning, Lt. Cmdr. Fitch now made his final strategic deployment of the pursuit, establishing a blockade some 40 miles in length around Pomeroy. Steaming north against the increasing current of a fortuitous rise, his six warships were "distributed" at those transit locations which might prove most inviting to the raiders. In all, four major and a number of minor fords were patrolled. The *Victory* and *Springfield* were posted to guard Pomeroy, Wolf's Shoals, and the crossing at Belleville. The ford at Eight Mile Island was covered by the *Naumkeag* while the *Reindeer* watched over the crossing at Goose Island. The *Moose* and *Allegheny Belle*, in company with the dispatch steamer *Imperial*, patrolled even further upstream.

In addition to coverage from the water side, the Union now had two major land columns of cavalry and mounted infantry converging upon Morgan. Throughout the 17th, Brig. Gen. Hobson's men followed from one direction while those of Brig. Gen. Judah closed along the lower river roads. Hobson's cavalry visited Jaspur, Piketown, Beavertown, and Jackson while Judah's troops saw Minersville and Syracuse while pushing on Pomeroy. Out on the river, Lt. Cmdr. Fitch, still not receiving the best of intelligence, believed that Morgan would threaten Pomeroy. In the end, he did not, but, instead, passed within a few miles of the river town. As the Logansport officer later remembered, the Kentucky general thus "threw himself into a position where, by marching not over 10 miles, he could strike the river at four different fords, the two extremes being by river nearly 40 miles apart."

Of course at the time, the Pomeroy threat was not a certainty and so the lengthy blockade was maintained. After all, the Southerners, in their two-state ride, had often been in large river bends, where, just by marching four or five miles in one direction or another, they "could have struck several fords, which, by water, would perhaps be 15 or 20 miles apart." All of those fords "in the rear, ahead, and intermediate" had to be protected from Buffington Island back to a point eight miles below Pomeroy.

Coming up by steamer from Loop Creek under orders from Brig. Gen. Scammon, the brigades of Colonels White and Hayes reached Gallipolis on the morning of July 18. The future president's 23rd Ohio and the 13th West Virginia, finding that Morgan was beyond them, pushed their steamers on toward Pomeroy where the Southerners, according to Yankee intelligence and local reports, were planning to cross the river. Hayes' dismounted soldiers deployed in line of battle to block them.

The Rebels maneuvered around Pomeroy, engaged in a brief skirmish with militia and Hayes' troops, and reached Chester, 18 miles from the Ohio River, at midday on July 18. Hayes and his soldiers, meanwhile, embarked back aboard their transports and steamed up the Ohio toward Buffington. They would not arrive in time to join the fight.

Morgan and his men rested for two hours at Chester before moving straight down the old Chester coach road toward their ultimate goal, the shoals above Buffington Island. Three hours later, Brig. Gen. Judah and his men arrived at Pomeroy, where they halted only briefly before pushing on to Buffington, via Racine. While at Pomeroy, Judah interviewed a captured Confederate who thought that Hobson had given up the chase. Additionally, he testified that Morgan, who now knew of Fitch's pursuit, expected he could "manage the gunboats with his 10-pounder pieces."

About 4:30 P.M., the pursuing Brig. Gen. Hobson received a telegram from Col. August V. Kautz of the 2nd Ohio Cavalry, who with a brigade that also included the 7th Ohio Cavalry, was at the Meigs County community of Rutland. In it he reported upon Morgan's Pomeroy engagement and went on to further opine: "They are supposed to be marching for Buffington Island, about 25 miles from here, where they will try to ford the river. It is too high, however, and the gunboats are on alert." Late in the day, Maj. Gen. Burnside sent a wire to Ohio governor David Tod reviewing the armed circle drawn around the raider. "I don't see how he can well get out," he opined, "if the gunboats do their duty."

Exhausted after their hard flight, scared after running a gauntlet of Meigs County guardsmen firing at them from the hills overlooking the road, and reduced in numbers, the raiders halted about 8 P.M. They now found themselves in possession of an extensive corn and wheat field at the northern end of a small two-mile-long valley, itself a little above Portland. Anchored by Buffington Island in the south where a road was cut in from Pomeroy, the valley floor was skirted by 700–800 foot high hills and woods on its north and east sides. The hills then and now slope down into the valley coming to within about 700 feet of the river where they meet cliffs. Scouts reported back to Morgan, Duke, and Johnson that the hoped for ford across the Ohio was flooded and a chute had opened between the mainland and the island. Additionally, earthen Yankee fortifications, manned by an unknown number of soldiers, were built above the crossing point.

Brushing aside subordinate recommendations to abandon the wounded and swim over with the remainder, Morgan took the decision not to try to ford the river in darkness. The command had no "trusty" guides and there was a very real risk that they could miss the ford altogether. He also elected not to take on the Marietta area militiamen waiting for them. Instead, artillery was unlimbered on the highest elevation in the east commanding the Pomeroy road and preparations, including the construction of some rafts, were made to cross at sunup. "The night was very dark," raider Weatherred wrote in his diary, "we remained all night holding our horses by the bridle reins."

Sensing that they were the only thing standing between the desperate Confederates and freedom, the Athens County and Washington County volunteers were also quite pleased with Morgan's pacific decision. Conceding that discretion was the better part of valor and appreciating that their role had been played, Capt. Wood's Ohioans elected to leave during the night. While the majority quietly retreated aboard the *Starlight*, others rolled the unit's two cannon over into a ravine so that the Confederates could neither taken or use them. Fortunately, the river level was higher than usual and the apprehensive Rebels chose not to interfere. When all were on board, the bluecoats, some of whom were performing deck or coal handling chores for the first time, withdrew back toward Ravenswood. With their departure, the ford was left open. By failing to tackle the green troops and capture the steamer, Morgan's troops lost a golden opportunity to escape across the river.

Before dark on the 18th, Hobson's men came down toward the Ohio through Manchester, Vinton, Winchester, Rutland and Chester while Judah took his Michigan and Indiana cavalry across country toward Portland. Neither Hobson, nor Judah, nor Fitch knew the exact location of the other. Even though more than 6,000 Union troops were closing in on him, Morgan apparently didn't know for certain that any large force was nearby. Later, after the raid, Brig. Gen. Judah wrote that Col. Duke revealed to him that he "could not have been more surprised at the presence of my force had it dropped from the clouds."

Intensely aware of his duty, Le Roy Fitch took it upon himself to handle any crossing Morgan and his horsemen might try to make at Buffington. "I had determined to cut him off at all hazards," the Hoosier later remembered of his decision to take responsibility for the final leg of the chase. Despite the Ohio's increased rise it was still actually fairly low and it was still necessary for the Hoosier to warp and grasshopper his gunboat upstream even with its shallow draft. This tiresome process was often employed by commercial riverboats in dry times or shoal locations. It involved sending out the boat's yawl with a strong hawser which was fastened to a stout tree or anchored to a rock or other point upstream. Once secure, the crew, employing the capstan and aided by the paddle wheel, pulled the line, dragging the boat over the delaying obstruction. Assisted by a tow from the dispatch steamer *Imperial*, as well as its own grasshopper spars, the gunboat passed over Letart's Falls, named for an early 18th century French fur trader and the nearby West Virginia and Ohio villages, and other shoal or swift water obstructions before reaching the blockade's van position.

A few hours before the Confederates reached the crest of the nearby shore, the *Moose*, towed up by the *Imperial*, anchored off Little Sandy Creek Bar, below Buffington Island on the West Virginia shore. Here it was sighted by Rebel outriders sometime later. It was dusk and a night crossing of the bar at the foot of the island would have been risky. Fitch elected to pause; neither he nor Morgan knew that the Buffington ford, now five to six foot deep, was clear of any enemy presence. As was the practice under long-established squadron standing orders, steam was kept up so that the vessels could move quickly if necessary. In the predawn darkness, the *Allegheny Belle*, the packet outfitted at Burnside's order and placed under naval authority, also came up and dropped anchor.

Hastily-made Confederate plans to get across the Ohio at daybreak now began to unfold. Leaving their horses behind, 110 men were first sent across in a flatboat and four skiffs in the wee hours to the West Virginia side. In the new state, they were organized into two companies and ascended the riverbank, up the bluff, and into the bushes from which they were to cover and protect the rest of Morgan's command as it came over. These men would see the entire ensuing battle over on the west bank and later escape.[26]

Unwilling to ford his command, including his wounded in horse-drawn ambulances and wagons, in the dark, Brig. Gen. Morgan found himself entirely surrounded on the morning of the nineteenth and outnumbered nearly four to one. He had only two choices: fight or surrender. In addition to the *Moose* and *Allegheny Belle*, the land forces of Hobson and Judah were closing in from Ohio's interior. Those of the former were rushing southeast on the Chester road, while Judah continued north from the river. The Battle of Buffington Island ensued when the advance elements of the Union army came up from Pomeroy about six in the morning, an hour after sunrise, and Morgan, refusing to quit, fired on them. The volley and charge by the 5th Kentucky Cavalry (C.S.A.) brought the Southerners initial success, which was short lived.

The Union Navy, already on hand, was momentarily stalled. At two o'clock that Sunday morning, Fitch, wishing to move closer, had ordered the *Imperial* to tow him up slowly into the narrow chute separating the island from Ohio. Unfortunately, a dense fog set in over land and river making it too dangerous to proceed and forcing the two streamers to reanchor. Ashore, Brig. Gen. Judah also decided to make a reconnaissance and was caught in the fog. He and his small accompanying force found themselves surrounded and, before he could make his escape in the morning, several of his soldiers were cut off or captured, along with his single small cannon.

Lt. Cmdr. Fitch, uninformed except in general of the army's movements, knew nothing of the impending battle until the officer of the deck awoke him at 7 A.M. with news that musketry was rampant a little ahead off the port bow. The Indiana sailor quickly ran from his cabin to the pilothouse and ordered the *Moose* and *Imperial* to get underway. Fitch also hailed Pilot Sebastian on the *Allegheny Belle*, ordering that, in going through the chute ahead, the auxiliary remain close to the flagboat in case the *Moose* was disabled. If she were, Sebastian was to take hold of her and pull her out, or tow her through. The *Imperial*, third in line, already possessed such orders.

Sounding along the way, the bluejackets were able to con their vessels over the bar "fairly into" the chute between the island and the State of Ohio. Churning slowly ahead through white mist toward the head of the island, the steamers were soon greeted by a hail from shore. Easing in, the *Moose* picked up Capt. John J. Grafton, Brig. Gen. Judah's volunteer aide-de-camp, who escaped capture by shooting the Rebel cavalrymen who seized him, but then lost his way. The soldier was able to give Fitch his first indication of what was going on ashore, as well as the relative positions of the opposing forces as the horse soldier last knew them. As the two men spoke, the fog suddenly started to dissipate.

Morgan's men, fighting with their backs to the river, had enjoyed a brief triumph in pushing back Brig. Gen. Judah's lead elements, but this changed when the reformed Federal line, spearheaded by the 5th Indiana Cavalry in its center, outflanked the 5th Kentucky. Meanwhile, advance units of Brig. Gen. Hobson's force charged in from the west with more pouring into the valley from the Chester road. The battle would eventually cover about three miles on ground running from above the two-street town of Portland to about two miles below.

It was at this point that the men aboard the Yankee river craft saw butternut soldiers headed toward the northern riverbank so quickly that Fitch thought they must be charging him. They had a couple of pieces of artillery (a 20-pounder Parrott and one of Weatherred's "bull pups") with them and the sailor quickly imagined that the Rebels were about to plant them on the bank at the head of the chute to block his progress. To disabuse them of any such idea, he immediately opened fire on the squad with his two bow guns. The Confederates, who were not able to load and sight their field pieces in time, wheeled and ran for cover, firing their rifles as they fled. All were probably, if we may be allowed an understatement, greatly surprised to encounter a Yankee gunboat where they had been repeatedly told none could go.

With the *Imperial* behind, the *Moose* pushed on through the chute and got above the head of the island, nearly opposite Morgan's left flank. From that spot, she yawed just enough to open fire over the high river bank with her three port broadside howitzers, which were elevated to their maximum angle. The relocated Rebel field guns threw a few shells at the two boats, "but their aim was very bad." The rounds either went over or burst short and a little ahead." Thick smoke mixed with the last evaporating mists.

Back from the river, the battle intensified when bluecoat soldiers, mainly cavalry, encouraged by the navy cannonade, joined the attack, rushing onto the plateau between the river and the high ridges which rise a mile inland. By 9 A.M., the fog was gone and Northern units, with a big numerical advantage, began to pummel the Confederate defensive line in the cornfield. The 2nd Ohio and 8th Michigan charged and, to quote the excited prose of Brig. Gen. James Shackelford's later report, horsemen from the 8th, 3rd, and 1st Kentucky Regiments (U.S.A.) hit hard: "With drawn sabers gleaming in the bright sunlight and a yell that filled the foe with terror, they rushed upon him and he fled at their approach." The charge caused the Confederates to "fly in wild consternation," and their shock was further intensified by other attacking U.S. cavalry regiments: the 7th and 11th Ohio, 7th and 9th Michigan, 11th and 12th Kentucky (U.S.A.), 5th Indiana, and 14th Illinois. The 17th Illinois Mounted Infantry and the 2nd Tennessee Mounted Infantry (U.S.A.) had arrived on horseback, Henshaw's (Illinois) Independent Light Artillery and most of the 11th Michigan Battery provided artillery support, and the foot soldiers actually present on the battlefield were from the 23rd Michigan Volunteer Infantry.

The Confederates were not the only ones discomfited that morning. Without gunfire spotters and unable to see what was occurring so as to direct his green gunners, Lt. Cmdr. Fitch was never quite sure where his own 24-pounder shells were landing. Both Yankee and Rebel soldiers later agreed on the confusion the shells caused as they roared in overhead. On one occasion, Brig. Gen. Hobson and his staff, standing on a hill overlooking the conflict, were fired upon. One of the men, aide-de-camp Lt. Henry C. Weaver of the 16th Kentucky (U.S.A.), wrote some years afterwards that "a shot or two caused a hasty transfer of headquarters." Unaware of just where the shells were landing, the newspaperman aboard the *Imperial* later recorded simply that "an extensive scattering took place." Although Fitch remained basically ignorant of the changing bluecoat maneuvers ashore, his fire upon the Rebels was deadly. Col. Duke cursed what he believed was more than one tinclad and "heartily wished that their fierce ardor, the result of a feeling of perfect security, could have been subjected to the test of two or three shots through their hulls."[27]

Overwhelmed by the Union cavalry charges and subjected to bombardment by the *Moose* plus a Union battery on a nearby hilltop, the contest now went against the Southerners. Although Col. Duke was able to hold the line, just barely, the contest was going so badly that a large group of raiders tried to make a break. Shielded by Duke's rear guard plus the howitzer and Parrott on the north bank, many of Morgan's men speedily descended a steep ravine toward the river at a point about a mile and a half above the head of the island. From here they tried to escape along the stream over a pathway Hobson believed impassable. This hasty and desperate push was, however, exactly the event the Hoosier sailor had been dreaming about throughout the 10-day, 500 mile pursuit.

On the enemy's left flank at a narrow place along the river road, the *Moose* opened on the protective Confederate cannon. After a few shots from the bow pieces, the Rebel gunners fled, allowing her to turn her attention toward the men on foot and horseback. The *Allegheny Belle*, which was following Fitch, also opened on the Confederates as soon as the flagboat had cleared the chute and the auxiliary had room to fire clear of her. Her contribution was provided by gunners from the 11th Michigan Battery, employing a few of their embarked 6-pounder field pieces in addition to the Parrott strapped to the bow back in Cincinnati.

Ashore, Col. Duke despaired. "A shell struck the road throwing up a cloud of dust," he remembered. His men panicked as the "gunboats raked the road with grapeshot." Lt. Henry Weaver observed: "The thundering tones of those monsters, together with the terrifying shriek of the shells as they came over the heads of the enemy, completed the rout already begun." Ridding themselves, in many instances, of both clothes and arms, numerous Confederate soldiers tried to make it across the "swift waters rippling over the sand shallows of Buffington Bar and plunged into the angry and powerful currents of the flooded Ohio River."

Seeing Morgan's column about one-third over the crossing, Fitch called down the voice pipe ordering Ensign Rice to have the portside gunners shift fire to the men in the water. The first shell landed at the head of the column, which immediately began to turn back. As they did so, the tinclad moved in so close that the Rebels could not retreat back up the ravine. "Finding our shell and shrapnel too uncomfortable for them," the Southerners broke into a rout up the beach in a line which led directly away from the *Moose*. About 30 Confederates made it across in the confusion.

Hemmed in by the high bank on one side and the river on the other, many men threw down their arms and clawed their way up the bank and headed for the woods. The escape was difficult as the whole area was covered in trees, shrubs, and other brush, some prickly. Col. Duke later remembered that "the hiss of the dreaded missiles increased the panic." Left behind on the beach were the two cannon, transport, camp equipage, "and the like." One of the carriages, "in which Morgan was said to be riding," was upset by a shell and its two horses were wounded. In all, according to the tinclad's logbook, the navy was responsible for making prizes of two artillery pieces, 20 horses, six carriages and buggies, a quantity of dry goods, four kegs of powder, plus canister, shot and small arms. During her part of the action, the *Moose* had expended 29 HE shells, 10 shrapnel, one canister, and 100 rounds of small arms cartridges.

Unable to land the warship because of his desire to pursue the remnant of the scattered band up the river, Lt. Cmdr. Fitch stopped just long enough to dispatch a boat on shore to insure possession of the cannon. The landing party was directed to have the trailing *Imperial* haul the pieces farther down the river to a safe spot where they could be guarded until taken aboard. It was expected that Brig. Gen. Judah's men would look after the Rebels dislocated in the rear. Mr. Horowitz has asserted in his exemplary campaign history that Fitch now stopped to have one of the captured cannon "placed on the deck of the *Allegheny Belle*." There is no indication, in the gunboat's logbook or any contemporary newspaper article or official document, that such an action occurred at this time.[28]

After what seemed like hours of fighting but really was not, Basil W. Duke, Morgan's brothers Richard and Charlton, and about 700 from the weary rearguard gang of "horsethieves, cut-throats, and nondescripts" were POWs by noon. A number of men were captured on the West Virginia side of the river by elements from Col. Hayes' 23rd Ohio. Another 57 Rebels were killed in the fighting, with 63 wounded; three Union officers and eighteen enlisted men paid the ultimate price, with an unknown number hurt.

The Battle of Buffington Island, which some still wrongly regard as a naval battle, was, however, nothing less than a disaster for the outnumbered raiders. Still, a naval mop-up was required as Morgan and his remaining effectives retreated. After the Buffington shooting stopped, the *Moose*, now towed by the *Imperial* and joined by the *Allegheny Belle*, stood upriver. They were followed by Brig. Gen. Scammons' troop-laden riverboats. Meanwhile, Col. Hayes' steamers made for Hockingsport, 14 miles above Buffington.

A significant body of Rebels, indeed, most of the 2nd Brigade, under Col. Adam "Stovepipe" Johnson, with Morgan along, escaped the Buffington melee and were last seen headed north along the riverbank, out of sight to the Yankee soldiers. These approximately 1,100 men were retreating towards Reed's Landing, 20 miles north, from whence they hoped to cross into West Virginia. Lt. Cmdr. Fitch determined to prevent their escape. As the Yankee boats progressed, the desperate Southerners, in their lightning retreat, could be seen from time to time inland of the Ohio. The *Moose*, even under tow was able to keep almost ahead of the confused column in something of a one-side running fight. Whenever practicable, she threw occasional shells over the riverbank toward it. Morgan and company reached a point above Reed's Landing about dusk.

Sometime in early morning, after forcing a local ferryman, John Randolph, to guide them along an old Indian trail to the best fording spot, the Southerners began wading across the head of Belleville Island, which lay just below the Wood County, West Virginia, village 18 miles south of Parkersburg. As the first dozen men were wading over in the swift current, three reliable scouts, on the scene by order of Parkersburg-based Capt. A. V. Barringer, not only saw the Rebels, but "the smoke from a boat about 2 miles below, which was reported a gunboat."

The spies were quickly chased by the fording grayclads and lost sight of the river; as they withdrew, the scouts sensed the boat had "continued forward and heavy firing was immediately heard."

Although some drowned in the rush of men and the flooded river's swift current, 280 men, several stark naked, reached the safety of the east bank of the Ohio before the *Moose* and *Allegheny Belle* came rushing up the channel. Among them was telegraphic warfare specialist George "Lightning" Ellsworth. Again the Confederates, for the most part, were driven back by cannon fire, with a few more men and several horses lost.

Col. Johnson made it across on a skiff and later remembered the scene. Reminiscing later, he reviewed a climactic moment as he neared the safety of the West Virginia shore:

> By this time the gunboats were on us, and the soldiers gathered on the bow looked down on us with guns in hand. Helm [Capt. Neil], believing they were going to shoot, pleaded with me to jump into the river, but knowing the skiff would sink, I paddled with all my might toward shore.... All this time there was not a shot fired at us and not a single shell was thrown on that side of the river. This was an act of humanity I am glad to record.

It is probable that Fitch, remembering the accounts of his older brother and Rear Adm. Charles Davis concerning the previous year's *Mound City* disaster, purposefully ordered that the struggling men in the water not be shot.

According to Capt. Oakes of the *Imperial*, at least three horses were captured and taken aboard his steamer. Fitch's actions at Belleville once more kept Morgan on the north shore. "It was Fitch's navy and army task force that prevented Morgan's escape at Belleville," one reviewer has noted. "If he had not been there, Morgan would have passed over to safety with more than 1,000 of his force."

Foiled in his crossing at Belleville, Morgan, who had gained the middle of the shell-splashed Ohio River only to rejoin the stranded members of his command, headed west and farther up the shore toward Hockinsport hoping to get over there. The *Moose* followed and the effort was not made. Later, Brig. Gen. Scammon's men would be landed at a point between Hockinsport and Lee Creek.

Fortunately for the almost 300 Confederates who made it across earlier, there were no Federal troops waiting for them. Instead, they found support in the area from a few families with Confederate sympathies. These provided some clothing and horses. Not all of those reaching West Virginia fled immediately. Near the Wells farm, on the upper side of Lee Creek two miles above Belleville, 16-year-old Foster Wells, whose four other brothers were serving in the Confederate army, met Stovepipe Johnson and some of his troopers, hoping to guide them to safety. Before departing with Wells, one butternut squad prepared an ambush for the hated navy steamers.

As the unsuspecting Yankee warships passed Lee Creek, the raiders on the Wood County shore fired two volleys of musketry at them from a range of less than 20 yards. Amazingly, only two Union tars were slightly hurt in the ambuscade, one on the *Moose* and one on the *Allegheny Belle*. Accepting the challenge, the *Moose* replied with her starboard battery, killing nine of the bushwhackers. With their guns elevated to fire over the riverbanks, the tinclad and her auxiliary began a general bombardment of the area, concentrating on the roads leading inland. There was no return fire.

Many of the Northern shells passed over the Wells homestead with some cutting limbs from the tops of surrounding shade trees. This "shoot" marked the last Confederate resistance the gunboats encountered. Long before the final naval shell exploded, the Rebel east bank survivors were directed to the Elizabeth Pike and hills leading to the Little Kanawha Valley. Some time later, the men, traveling 200 miles via the West Virginia mountains via Sutton and Lewisburg, would pass into Virginia from Salt Sulphur Springs. They went three days without food and had extremely blistered feet upon arrival.

The *Moose* and *Imperial*, which had proceeded up to the foot of Mustapha Island, found the water upstream increasingly shallow with far too many shoals. Additionally, the river was now falling and the navy was presently upstream of the Rebels, who had already turned back into the Ohio hills. Thinking it best to depart, Lt. Cmdr. Fitch took the *Moose* and her consort back to Reed's Landing where they were able to find and load several additional steeds. The two steamers then returned to Buffington Island. The *Allegheny Belle*, which had patrolled the reaches upstream between the island and Belleville during Fitch's Belleville ascent, continued that mission for several more days.

Back at Buffington by early evening, the *Moose* continued through the chute and anchored at the foot of the island. The *Imperial*, following behind, stopped at the head of the island and took aboard the cannon, carriages, and other items prized in the morning. When the last bluejacket came aboard, the steamer likewise made down through the chute and, as darkness fell, tied up. Aboard his flagboat, the Indiana sailor wrote out a brief report of his actions to send off to Cairo at the first opportunity.

The *Imperial* was sent on ahead to Cincinnati on July 20 with dispatches for Rear Adm. Porter, Maj. Gen. Burnside, and Capt. Pennock, along with the booty loaded the night before; she would arrive two days afterward, having made several intermediate stops. At one point, Capt. Oakes sent Fitch's report ahead by wire to Pennock at Cairo.

On July 21, the fleet captain forwarded it on to Secretary of the Navy Gideon Welles. Later in the day, he also sent it to Rear Adm. Porter, along with a report on Cairo naval station activities. In his cover, Pennock wrote: "Lieutenant-Commander Fitch has been following Morgan with great activity since he crossed into Indiana, and his efforts have at length been crowned with success." Years later in his *The Naval History of the Civil War*, Porter offered his thoughts on the Morgan chase. "It was a novel sight," he wrote, "a flotilla of gunboats (very 'gallinippers') in pursuit of a land force. It was in every respect a new feature of the war."

At Portland and Pomeroy on that Tuesday, the POWs and their guards, many from the 8th Michigan Cavalry, were loaded aboard two steamers for Cincinnati. The *Starlight*, with several of the Marietta volunteers still on board, and the *Ingomar*, with the Guthrie Grays also as guards, took Morgan's men on the first leg of their journey to prison camp beginning the following morning. The *Moose* provided convoy. The steamers halted at Maysville to await the *Navigator*, which was coming down with lately captured POWs under guard of soldiers from the 45th Ohio Infantry. Over the next several days, more prisoners would be sent down aboard the steamboats *Henry Logan*, *Imperial*, *Tariscon*, *Golden Era*, *Marmora*, *St. Louis*, *J. H. Done*, *Ida May*, and *Odd Fellow*. They would be covered by the U.S.S. *Reindeer* and *Naumkeag*.

When the *Moose* and her charges reached the Queen City at dusk on Friday, July 25, the prison boats were anchored in midstream until a suitable guard could be organized to take the POWs ashore. People assembled on the landings, wharves, balconies, house and store tops, and any vantage point on both sides of the Ohio River the next morning to view the humbled Southern horsemen. When all was ready, the Confederates were loaded aboard trains and sent north, the officers to Johnson Island in Lake Erie and the enlisted men to camps at Chicago and Indianapolis.

Pursued relentlessly by Union cavalry or otherwise blocked by Ohio militia, Morgan's men were hounded upstream toward the northeast to McConnelsville and Old Washington as they tried to escape into Pennsylvania. "From this time, for six days," wrote Col. Duke later, "it was a continual race and scramble." Beginning with the capture of 300 men by Brig. Gen. Shackleford's riders near Eight Mile Island in the Ohio River (opposite Cheshire, Ohio) on July 20, the Confederates lost dozens, sometimes hundreds, of their remaining troops to their enemy daily. Finally, with just 364 officers and men left, Morgan was cornered in Columbiana County. At a point between Salineville and New Lisbon, Ohio, near Beaver Creek just west of East Liverpool, he surrendered on July 26. He was less than 90 miles from Lake Erie. When Fitch received word that the "bold raid" was truly over, he lifted the blockade of the Ohio River fords.

Assuming that Morgan's Raid was a good idea following the delayed beginning caused by Col. Sanders, the "Thunderbolt of the Confederacy" made several key errors toward the end of its execution which doomed the foray to failure. The brigadier failed to send out scouts or gather proper intelligence and did not know or appreciate the size of the noose being drawn about him. He certainly did not allow for the gunboats or a change in the depth of the Ohio River. In the final days before the descent upon Buffington, the Rebels halted and slept; true they were exhausted and needed to let stragglers catch up, but some critics suggest they should have pushed on so as to have reached Portland on the morning of July 18th instead of the evening. A day's advantage over the pursuers would have been a huge help.

When they arrived at the place they expected to cross, Morgan's troops had an ambulance and carriage train two miles long with sick and wounded, many of whom might have been able to travel but were otherwise slowing the column significantly. They had also retained all of their field cannon. Rather than take on the Marietta militia in the dark or capture the steamer *Starlight*, the force rested. It has been suggested that, even had the steamer gotten away or not been present, bonfires could have been built on each side of the river to guide the party as it crossed in the dark and fog; some would have drowned and equipment, including the cannon, might have been lost, but the majority of the force, it has been argued, could have escaped. The *Moose*, anchored at the foot of the island, might have tried to come up, but the water being as it was, she could also have grounded.

Although Maj. Gen. Burnside skillfully maneuvered his people, especially his cavalry, there could still have been a successful exit for the Rebels. In the end, Morgan and most of his men, having turned the countryside through which they passed against them and "effectively cowed down sympathy with rebels," simply didn't have either the stamina or the luck to get away.

The value of the weather and the Union Navy's river squadron in repulsing Morgan's raid into Indiana and Ohio is hard to overestimate. It was an unexpected rain in mountains far removed from the hot, dusty hills of southern Ohio which caused the rivers to swell, permitting the gunboats to get much farther up the river than the Southerners could have expected. Further, the Yankee sailors had the foresight to come up with extremely light draught tinclads whose 24-pounders were, as the embedded Cincinnati journalist told his readers, "the most accurate and effective gun in the service for operation against exposed bodies of men." The capture of the Confederates came none too soon as receding water in the Ohio would soon have closed the opportune window and prolonged hot weather would again prohibit upstream gunboat operations. "The lapping waters and not the pursuing Federals were ... in the end," wrote historian Holland in the 1940s, "disastrous."

Coupled with his incredibly poor meteorological fortune, Morgan had the great misfortune to come up against Le Roy Fitch. With little actual knowledge of the Rebels' dispositions, the Logansport native had organized his forces in a most successful manner. Morgan was no mere guerrilla lurking on the riverbank, but a capable regular army opponent. His modern biographer, James Ramage, gives Fitch high praise. Displaying rare determination in his pursuit, the Northern Kentucky University historian wrote in 1986, Fitch overcame great obstacles and hazards "with the tenacity of a bulldog—he was an unrelenting foe." Capt. Oakes of the *Imperial*, a civilian onlooker whom came to appreciate the navy man's tenacious determination, was convinced that "credit of this defeat of Morgan is due entirely to the gunboats."

The importance of the Confederate foray north was portrayed differently in various locales and in succeeding years. Following upon the disasters at Gettysburg and Vicksburg, the "bold raid" was portrayed in the July 16 issue of the Richmond *Enquirer* as "the only actively aggressive operation in which our forces are engaged." According to Morgan's adjutant, S. P. Cunningham, the Southern riders wounded 600 Federal soldiers, paroled another 6,000, destroyed 34 vital bridges and 60 different stretches of railroad tracks, burned army depots and military and civilian warehouses, and tied down over 120,000 militia in Indiana and Ohio. The estimated value of the burned bridges, destroyed railroad equipment, telegraph wires, and military stores was placed at $10 million. On July 28, the Chicago *Tribune* told its readers that the raid had cost the Confederacy over 4,000 men and horses, but had released for other duties over five times that many Federal troops, not counting Hoosier and Buckeye minutemen. The most recent historian to profile Ohio's history, Andrew R. L. Cayton, dismisses the Morgan episode as doing "little serious damage beyond frightening people." The naval historian Bern Anderson was more blunt: "Except for the alarm and consternation it caused, his raid was pointless."

Whatever the tangible significance of the raid, the outcome brought the greatest official praise Lt. Cmdr. Fitch would ever receive. In Washington, D.C., on July 27, the well-pleased Navy secretary, Gideon Welles, took the time to personally write out and sign a letter of commendation for Fitch. As it was the highest accolade this Indiana sailor ever received from his government, it is reprinted here in full:

NAVY DEPARTMENT, *July 27, 1863*

SIR: Since your attachment to the Mississippi Squadron it has been gratifying to the Department to observe the commendable zeal, as shown by reports to it, displayed by you in the execution of the duties to which you were intrusted.

In affording convoy on the Tennessee and Cumberland rivers, in punishing and dispersing the guerrilla bands which infested banks of those streams, and in your timely and important assistance to the Garrison at Fort Donelson when attacked on the 3d of February last by the rebels under General Wheeler and others, you have acted with promptness and reflected credit on the naval service.

Your recent pursuit of the flying guerrilla Morgan, following him upwards of 500 miles, intercepting him and frustrating him in his attempts to recross the Ohio, capturing his train, a portion of his guns, and routing his band, all of which materially crippled his strength and led to his final capture, gives additional evidence of your zeal and ability and reflects additional credit on the service and yourself.

The Department takes pleasure in expressing its appreciation of your meritorious service, and thanks you and those under your command for your many blows to the rebellion and active measures for the perpetuation of the Union.

Very respectfully, etc., GIDEON WELLES
Secretary of the Navy

Three days after the Logansport native saw Welles' congratulatory letter, Maj. Gen. Burnside heralded the "efficient services" of Fitch in achieving the "brilliant success of the engagement." "Too much praise," he wrote Rear Adm. Porter from Cincinnati, "cannot be awarded the naval department at this place for the promptness and energy manifested in this movement." Brig. Gen. Jacob D. Cox, District of Ohio commander writing from the same place, noted: "The activity and energy with which the squadron was used to prevent the enemy recrossing the Ohio, and to assist in his capture, was worthy of the highest praise."

It is unknown whether Fitch ever saw the messages from Burnside and Cox. Later, on August 10, Rear Adm. Porter acknowledged receipt of the twin communications in a letter to the former and offered: "I appreciate highly the compliment to Lieutenant-Commander Fitch coming from yourself." The squadron commander was pleased "that those under my command should be of service to the Army, and I am sure that they will never fail to be so from want of inclination."

There is no indication, in published or unpublished documents, that Porter directly expressed this sentiment or his appreciation to the Logansport officer at the time. It is rather certain that Fitch was aware of his superior's sentiments, as expressed in his July 13 Vicksburg campaign summary. In 1886, Porter wrote: "But for the energy of Lieutenant-Commander Fitch, Morgan's enterprise would doubtless have been disastrous to the people of Indiana and Ohio and disgraceful to the United States Government, which had taken so little pains to guard against such incursions."[29]

The excessive rains of early summer 1863, which had drenched Maj. Gen. Rosecrans at Tullahoma and boosted the water level in the Ohio River, also caused a temporary reversal in the usual seasonal drop of the river stages in the Cumberland. In fact, the deluge kept the Cumberland navigable until late July and permitted the U.S. Quartermaster Department to push thousands of extra tons of supplies into Nashville on dozens of extra steamer runs.

The surprisingly wet month also permitted Fitch to keep the *Brilliant* and *St. Clair* actively employed in convoy. On July 16, during one of their Nashville turnarounds, the pair had the honor of receiving Tennessee governor Andrew Johnson, Maj. Gen. Rosecrans, his chief of staff and future U.S. president Brig. Gen. James A. Garfield, and their staffs aboard for a full review. The general and his assistants had come to Nashville for several days specifically to visit the governor and to review the forts and support facilities of Tennessee's capital. Decked out "gaily," and wearing their best uniforms, the officers and crew of the *Brilliant* and *St. Clair* gave the governor and the army theater commander a full salute. Even after the top figures departed to examine military facilities, other military personnel remained aboard for a considerable period "inspecting things." So far as is known to this writer, this visit by Governor Johnson and "Old Rosy" was the first recorded reception provided to any political leader or army theater commander aboard any boat of the Sixth District.

At month's end, the *Naumkeag*, which was previously en route to the Mississippi River, was detached from the Upper Ohio flotilla and sent to Cairo for duty below. At the same time, in rotating order, the *Springfield, Silver Lake,* and *Fairplay* underwent needed repairs and were returned to their regular Ohio River patrols.[30]

CHAPTER NINE

Chattanooga, August–December 1863

With the Morgan raid over and the Cumberland River fallen to its usual summer levels, the vessels of the Sixth Division of the Mississippi Squadron returned to their normal patrol stations by the beginning of August 1863. The man in charge, Lt. Cmdr. Le Roy Fitch, kept a watchful eye over river commerce in his area of responsibility from his headquarters in Cincinnati, while also overseeing the operations of the U.S. Navy rendezvous in the Queen City. Although there are no records to prove it, it is also possible that Fitch may have taken an opportunity to return home to Logansport, Indiana, for a spot of leave.

Just as June and July were unusually wet and rainy in parts of the Midwest and Upper South, so August now adopted the more usual demeanor for that area—dry and hot. On land, dust was everywhere men marched, while the gunboat men faced a significant decline in the water levels of every stream. August was thus a time of great military weather, perfect in many ways for the movement of large bodies of troops. With Union victories at Gettysburg and Vicksburg, about the only spot where at least some Northern progress was not seen appeared to be East Tennessee. That was about to change; until Christmas, the name of one Volunteer State town would dominate news from the Western theater—Chattanooga.

Located in the Cumberland Mountains on a great bend in the Tennessee River not far from the Georgia border, Chattanooga, with a population then of about 2,500, was an important railroad junction and communications center. Gen. Braxton Bragg, who had retreated into the town in July, enjoyed a well fortified position impervious to frontal attack. Therein he also oversaw valuable Confederate ordnance, quartermaster, and commissary depots, as well as several hospitals. The goal of capturing the place was high upon the Union "to do" list for months, but a combination of factors had thus far prevented its achievement. Maj. Gen. William S. Rosecrans, hoping to repeat his virtually bloodless success at Tullahoma, was working up plans for another strategic envelopment, one which might again cost the Union less in men and treasure than a big battle. Whoever held Chattanooga held the entry key to Atlanta. To the end of gaining this asset, Rosecrans elected to conduct his advance

Nine. Chattanooga (1863)

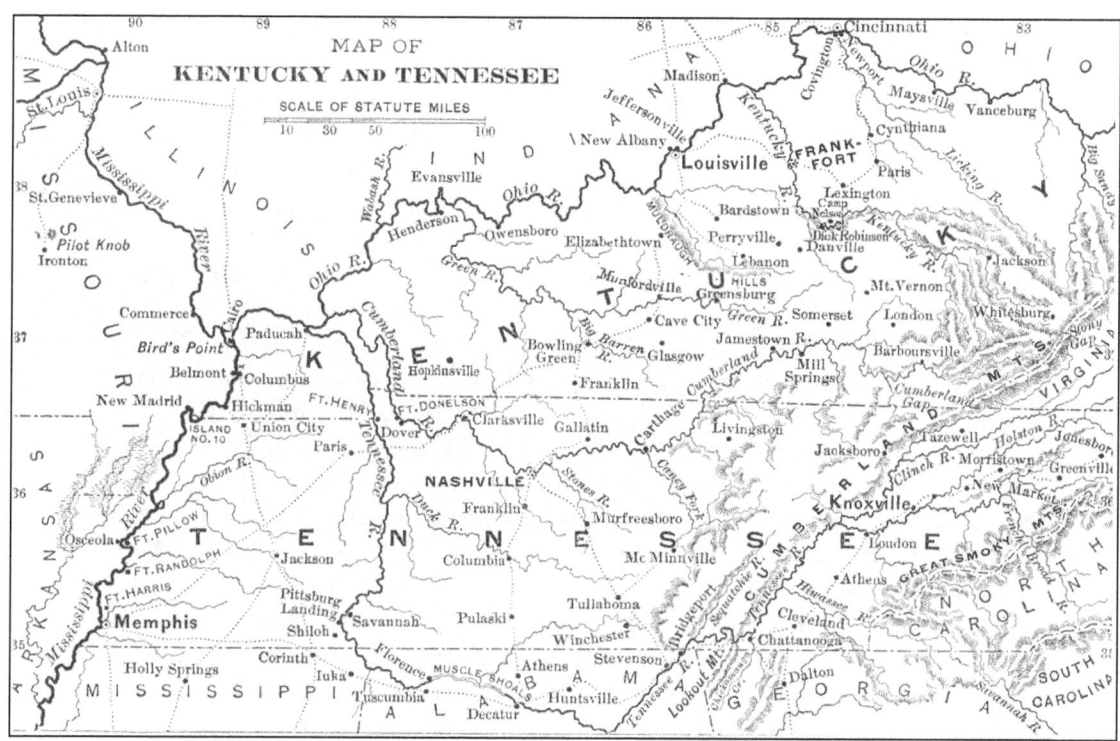

In the fall of 1863, Union focus in the West was shifted toward Chattanooga, Tennessee, and northeast to the city of Knoxville. Lt. Cmdr. Fitch would be asked to support the Federal effort in this arena by stepping up his convoys into Nashville and by overseeing the construction of a fleet of tinclads for the Upper Tennessee River (*Battles and Leaders of the Civil War*, Vol. 1).

west of the city in order to take full advantage of the railroad, which ran to Bridgeport and Stevenson, Alabama. It was anticipated by Bragg that the Yankees would come from the other direction, east, so as to maintain communication with Union troops momentarily expected in Knoxville.

Locked into something of a perceived pattern (at least in the eyes of Washington), the Army of the Cumberland found itself with a case of the "slows," again over the matter of supplies. This time, Rosecrans' logistical situation really was a nightmare. The countryside of middle and east Tennessee had been virtually stripped of food and fodder by bluecoats and grayclad soldiers. Although "Old Rosy" had mounds of supplies in Nashville, the terrain over which it would have to be transshipped was awful and famished. Time was required, he believed, to accumulate yet more provisions and it was hoped that corn might ripen.

The Muscle Shoals prevented direct steamboat access up the Tennessee River into Chattanooga. Once goods reached supply depots at Stevenson or Bridgeport by rail from the Tennessee capital, they had to be sent across the Tennessee and then on to Chattanooga by wagon. The routes available were over one of three roads cut through the northern end of Lookout Mountain, the largest of three ridges that slant southwest across the borders of Tennessee, Alabama, and Georgia. These roads were steep and windy and were often in disrepair. All Northern transport was subject to attack by Maj. Gen. Joseph Wheeler's Confederate cavalry and irregulars even as workers tried to keep the railroads and roads passable.

Indeed, Rosecrans found it necessary to post nearly 20 percent of his 80,000 men to guard supply routes.

On August 5, Maj. Gen. Henry Halleck, the general in chief in Washington, sent preemptory demands to both Rosecrans and Maj. Gen. Ambrose E. Burnside requiring that they advance and gain control of the upper Tennessee Valley. Despite grave concerns, both cut orders to break camp on August 15 and the twin campaigns against Chattanooga and Knoxville, the center of Union sympathy in east Tennessee, began. It is not our purpose here to follow either operation in detail. In the first instance, they were long, confused campaigns, which saw initial Confederate success and Northern anguish (e.g., Battle of Chickamauga) followed by sieges (both Chattanooga and Knoxville) before victory. From a naval perspective, most of the tactical support in the Chattanooga campaign was provided by the Mississippi Squadron's Seventh District, under its able leader, Lt. Cmdr. S. Ledyard Phelps, or by the U.S. Army itself. From the standpoint of this biography, the Cumberland River played an indirect, though substantial logistical role. In the winter of 1863-1864, efforts were made to send supplies upstream above Nashville. Naval operations on that river below Nashville continued under the direction of Lt. Cmdr. Fitch and are chronicled here with reference to the larger picture.[1]

On August 16, Rear Adm. David Dixon Porter returned to the naval base at Cairo, Illinois, from a 10-day visit to New Orleans that included stops at various points along the Mississippi River. Two days later, he issued a new general order (No. 80) outlining a change in naval districts made necessary due to "the additional length of river to be looked after." Lt. Cmdr. Fitch's Sixth District now became the Eighth. As before, divisional officers reported directly to Porter. Vessels from one district were not to be ordered away by superior officers except for emergencies. Specific details of district operation were released the following day.

In mid-August, seven vessels were assigned to the Eighth District. These included: the *Moose* (Lt. Cmdr. Fitch) in the Upper Ohio River, the *Brilliant* (Acting Volunteer Lieutenant Charles G. Perkins) in the Ohio and Cumberland, the *Fairplay* (Acting Volunteer Master George J. Groves) in the Ohio River, the *Reindeer* (Acting Volunteer Lieutenant Henry A. Glassford) and *Victory* (Acting Volunteer Ensign Frederick Read) in the Upper Ohio River, the *Springfield* (Acting Volunteer Ensign Joseph Watson) in the Ohio River, the *St. Clair* (Acting Volunteer Lieutenant Thomas B. Gregory) in the Cumberland River, and the *Silver Lake* (Acting Volunteer Ensign Joseph C. Coyle) in the Ohio River. The reader may recall that *Brilliant* and *St. Clair* had guarded Cumberland convoys while the remainder had joined in the Morgan chase. Now all protected or patrolled key points serving both the escort and coast guard functions while always on the lookout for guerrillas.[2]

Union army forces captured Knoxville on September 2 and Chattanooga seven days later. The same day Maj. Gen. Rosecrans entered the big Tennessee town, Confederate president Jefferson Davis ordered about one-third of Gen. Robert E. Lee's infantry, from the corps of Lt. Gen. James Longstreet, west to reinforce Gen. Bragg's Army of Tennessee. When those men got off the train, the Confederates actually outnumbered the Army of the Cumberland by 20,000 soldiers. Employing this superiority, the Southerners attacked and, on September 19–20, won the Battle of Chickamauga outside the city. Rosecrans was forced to retreat into Chattanooga over the next two days. The railroad center now became a true fortress city under siege. The name of the game here for the next couple of months became supply chain logistics.[3]

Rear Adm. Porter, Lt. Cmdr. Fitch and the men of the U.S. Navy in the West were aware of developments in the great Tennessee campaign largely from newspaper reports, copies of correspondence, reports from officials and civilian river men, and telegrams from various officers. Porter had access to the St. Louis papers and it is almost certain that Fitch saw those papers from Louisville and his home port of Cincinnati, though he certainly did not have as much high-level communication with army leadership as his commander. Chattanooga and the twin rivers were not the only theater concerns for which Porter bore responsibility. He also needed to make certain that the entire Mississippi region down to New Orleans was kept open and that guerrillas and partisans did not wreak havoc on shipping in such spots as the White River.

To provide assistance deeper within Porter's realm of responsibility, two of the tinclads of the Eighth District were ordered south in mid–September, the *St. Clair* and the *Springfield*. Both were to depart their stations and stop by Cairo for dispatches on the way to take up their temporary assignments. They would not be missed. As Lt. Cmdr. Fitch would note in his monthly report, the water in the Ohio River was so low and the availability of coal so poor that his tinclads were moving "only occasionally when necessity requires."

Based at Smithland, Kentucky, the *St. Clair* had no difficulty in obeying her orders and she was quickly off on October 1, along with the *Argosy* from the Fourth District, to reinforce the First District, under Cmdr. Robert Townsend, at Donaldsonville, Louisiana. The *Springfield*, drawing 30 inches of water, was not so lucky. On the way down from Evansville, she grounded on Battery Rock, at Shawneetown Bar, on September 20. That shoal, for a distance of some 200 yards, had only 25 inches. Ensign Watson's under-powered command, with chimneys so badly in need of repair that they were "about to fall down," was stuck and could not get off. The enterprising hero of the Brandenburg fight with John Hunt Morgan made his way back to Evansville on a civilian boat and described his dilemma in a wire to Lt. Cmdr. Fitch at Cincinnati.

When the Indiana sailor received Watson's telegraph, he advised his subordinate to obtain a lighter or a flatboat and to offload into it everything that could be safely transferred. He informed Cairo of the *Springfield*'s delay and of his advice. On September 26, Watson informed Rear Adm. Porter that he had obtained the suggested lighter and, after having all of his goods and stores taken off into her, was able to lighten ship sufficiently to get off the rock. His boat was undamaged and, after re-loading, she resumed her trip the next morning. The *Springfield* also joined the First District, but, unlike the *St. Clair*, she would be back in the Eighth by mid–November.[4]

The Ohio River remained at a low stage during the remainder of September and into the first part of October. The *Moose* was docked at Cincinnati following a run up from Louisville while the *Fairplay* remained at Louisville, bound by shoal water. The *Silver Lake* was at Evansville, no longer able to operate her regular patrol from Scuffletown Bar to Shawneetown Bar. Unable to steam regularly from Evansville to Shawneetown Bar and below, the *Brilliant* held station at Henderson, Kentucky. None of the boats below Louisville were able to run their regular patrols for some time.

The situation was no better on the Cumberland River. Supplies moving from Louisville to Nashville were slowed by rail and water just at a time when they were urgently needed. The Louisville and Nashville (L & N) Railroad was unable to send more than 20 cars of goods per day. Meanwhile, the low water stage meant that steamers from Cincinnati and Louisville had to halt at Clarksville. There their cargoes were offloaded onto a pair of small steamers which could negotiate Harpeth Shoals. This unhappy situation would continue until the water rose. Some supplies made it through. For example, on September 28, a shipment of goods originating in Louisville passed through Nashville en route to Chattanooga; it included 24,000 shirts, 5,000 blankets, 26,000 pairs of socks, and 5,000 axes. But other shipments were lost. Especially discouraging was the October 1 assault by "Fighting Joe" Wheeler's cavalry on Union quartermaster columns in the Sequatchie Valley. Rebel troopers destroyed 350 army wagons and 40 private sutlers' wagons and captured over a thousand mules. The same riders sacked the town of McMinnville next day.

Writing from Knoxville on October 5, Maj. Gen. Burnside warned Brig. Gen. Jacob D. Cox at Cincinnati of an unusual plot to free Morgan from the Ohio State Penitentiary. According to a captured horseman, a Rebel cavalry force from Tennessee would shortly capture a steamboat on the Ohio River, cross the stream, and quickly proceed to Columbus to release the Confederate Thunderbolt. Knowing the scheme unlikely, the bewhiskered general, nevertheless, sent it along with a copy to Lt. Cmdr. Fitch. The Cincinnati general and the tinclad commander both received word of the "improbable expedition" on October 10, at which point, the latter wrote back to Knoxville advising of his nautical precautions and hopes "that should such an expedition be set on foot that, with the hearty cooperation of the two branches of the service, the rebel participants may find comfortable lodging with Morgan and his followers." No such plot unfolded; however, Morgan did escape within the month.[5]

On a more important note, Navy secretary Gideon Welles, later in the day, wired Rear Adm. Porter asking if the water was deep enough in the Tennessee River to allow USN protection of supply transportation as far as Florence, Alabama, or Eastport, Mississippi. His telegraph opened a lengthy period of naval cooperation with the army in support of the Chattanooga and Knoxville objectives. Before replying, Porter called upon Acting Volunteer Master Edward M. King at Paducah, Kentucky, to provide a quick assessment of conditions. The commander of the tinclad *Key West* (No. 32) reported that the water level in the Tennessee was low but slowly rising and that, in the Ohio between his post and Smithland, at the head of the Cumberland, there was but 28 inches. Employing King's data, Porter replied to Washington that, although the Tennessee was rising, he could not get a gunboat even 45 miles above its mouth.

This situation changed for better and worse over the next two weeks as Maj. Gen. William T. Sherman began moving reinforcements from Memphis east toward Chattanooga. It rained heavily during the first two weeks of October, turning roads into mud cordons and further delaying supply shipments. At one point, King informed Porter that the river was up 4 feet and it was "raining smartly." At another time, Porter was forced to inform Welles that there was less water in the Ohio "than has been known for some years" and that there would be no rise of any consequence in any of the rivers until mid-November. Still, Sherman's veterans continued their advance and the general ordered quartermaster Col. Robert Allen send a ferryboat down from St. Louis to transport his army across the Tennessee at Eastport.

With the rail connection between Nashville and Bridgeport still in poor shape due to Rebel raids and rain, the supply chain from the North to Chattanooga was in desperate straits. Confederate activities outside Chattanooga had, by October 8, reduced the number of operational and passable supply routes into the city to just one. By the middle of the month, with Gen. Bragg having largely cut off the Tennessee River, wagon teams making it to Chattanooga from Bridgeport were traveling a 60-mile circuitous and dangerous road. Without a better logistical arrangement than that, the Army of the Cumberland was doomed.

On or about October 17, Secretary of War Edwin Stanton, with President Lincoln's blessing, appointed Maj. Gen. Ulysses S. Grant head of the Military Division of the Mississippi. Among Grant's first moves was the relief of Maj. Gen. Rosecrans from command of the Army of the Cumberland at Chattanooga and his replacement with Maj. Gen. George H. Thomas. The decision was quickly taken to supply and reinforce the new commander's army in steps. Step one required the forwarding to Nashville of goods and supplies being gathered at Louisville. This would be done, under the direction of now Brig. Gen. Robert Allen, who had moved his headquarters to the Kentucky city from St. Louis. Items arriving by rail and water would fill the warehouses of Tennessee's capital. This accumulation could then be pushed on to Chattanooga in step two, movement by rail from Nashville to Bridgeport and then to Chattanooga.

In the eastern tip of Tennessee, Burnside's IX and XXIII Corps skirmished all month with Rebel forces from Kentucky through Cumberland Gap to Loudon and from Jonesboro, Greeneville, the Rogersville and Morristown areas to Maryville. Logistics were vital to these Yankees as well and Maj. Gen. Grant determined that both of his subordinates would have as much succor as could be provided. A way would also be sought to send materiel up the Cumberland to a point where it could be hauled overland to Knoxville.

The depth of the river at Nashville on October 18 stood at 22 feet and it was decided that waterborne transport directly to the city could resume. Next day, Brig. Gen. John A. Rawlins wrote to Maj. Gen. Sherman from Louisville on a variety of topics. A sentence in the communication of interest here reads:

Deeply involved in the Western theater since the Battle of Belmont in 1861, U. S. Grant (1822–1885) was the victor at Forts Henry and Donelson and at Vicksburg. Following Rosencrans' defeat at Chickamauga in September 1863, Grant was called in to secure Chattanooga. Grant, like Rosecrans, had little appreciation for the difficulties of Fitch's convoy requirements and demanded that physically-impossible supply missions be operated. In March 1864, he was promoted to the rank of lieutenant general and went east to become Union general in chief. Prior to his departure, he suggested that a fleet of light draught gunboats be built to protect commerce on the Upper Tennessee River (National Archives).

"The Chiefs of Departments for the West, at St. Louis, Missouri, have been instructed to shove forward by the Tennessee and Cumberland rivers, when they rise, supplies for the troops operating on the Chattanooga and Tennessee lines." Sherman was also advised that Rear Adm. Porter was closely monitoring the stages of both rivers and would "the moment there is a sufficient rise in either, send in his Gun-Boats, and as far up as possible, for the convoying of supply-boats and protection of navigation."

Maj. Gen. Grant, at Nashville, while en route to Chattanooga, and Maj. Gen. Burnside at Knoxville also kept their eyes on the stream's supply possibilities. At 12:30 A.M. on October 20, the Knoxville commander sent a lengthy telegram to his new superior at Tennessee's capital setting forth the disposition of forces in his Department of the Ohio. After a litany of units and their locations, Burnside reviewed his supply situation, concluding with a sentence which would come to have a significant impact on the mission of Lt. Cmdr. Le Roy Fitch: "I have already taken steps to repair the road from Clinton to the mouth of the Big South Fork on the Cumberland to which point stores can be transported by water as soon as that river becomes navigable which may not be 'till January."

From Cairo later in the morning, the Mississippi Squadron commander was able to wire Washington that the water was rising significantly in all theater rivers because, he was told, it was raining heavily in Virginia. As he expected the rise would be permanent, Porter took the action of ordering as many gunboats as possible into the streams. The seasonal dry spell offloading and reloading and other dangerous processes necessary to avoid the rigors of Harpeth Shoals and other Cumberland obstacles could now, it was hoped, be abandoned.

Also that day Quartermaster General Brig. Gen. Montgomery C. Meigs, then in Louisville, wired Secretary Stanton with news that steamers had started from the Kentucky city for Nashville with forage and supplies. "The Navy Department should order gunboats at once into the Cumberland," he added, "to convoy and protect our steamboats."

The army's quartermasters were now sending an ever-increasing amount of goods, which were stockpiled both in the state capital's warehouses and at Carthage. Some percentage was sent by rail to Chattanooga and some would eventually be forwarded to the

Having worked with Navy officers on Western gunboat matters since the summer of 1861, Quartermaster General Meigs (1816–1892) was often impatient with the logistical flow up the Cumberland to Nashville. This was particularly true in November 1863 when several complaints were lodged, on behalf of his subordinates, with Rear Adm. Porter concerning the convoy system of Lt. Cmdr. Fitch. Porter supported the system of his Indiana sailor. Responding to Maj. Gen. Grant's proposal, Meigs, in January 1864, made the Navy Department contact which resulted in orders being cut for Rear Adm. Porter to have gunboats constructed for the Upper Tennessee River (National Archives).

mouth of Big South Fork and then hauled overland to Burnside in Knoxville. To guard the increased influx of supply steamers required a reintroduction of the strict and regular naval convoy system last seen in the spring.

Acting Volunteer Master Coyle's *Silver Lake*, off Evansville, was the first Eighth Division craft to receive a telegraphic order from Rear Adm. Porter demanding an immediate departure for the mouth of the Cumberland. With his tinclad drawing 32 inches, the volunteer faced the unhappy task of sending a telegraph back to Porter indicating that he could not proceed without the most heroic efforts. The small rise of a week earlier did not affect the depth of water at Shawneetown Bar and he could not get over without lightening the ship of her guns, ammunition and stores. Additionally, several points beyond his location to the mouth of the Cumberland had only 27 or 28 inches. Lt. Cmdr. Fitch at Cincinnati also received sailing orders about the same time as Coyle. Fitch wired back that he expected smooth steaming through the canal that skirted the Falls of the Ohio as the river was rising above. He had also heard that the Cumberland was at a good stage and hoped to shortly reach Smithland, via the usual Ohio River stops.

Three boats from Phelps' Seventh Division were sent up toward Eastport on the Tennessee next morning. Grant reached Chattanooga on October 23 and the next day Maj. Gen. Sherman, at Iuka, Mississippi, took over the Department of the Tennessee. Porter promised his close friend to line the Tennessee "with gunboats" and keep his communications from being interrupted "if there is water in the river." The advance elements of Sherman's army, along with 600 wagons and 4,000 animals, had begun crossing the Tennessee with the aid of the navy in midmonth and all would be over by the early days of November.

While Acting Volunteer Master Coyle made preparations to join his divisional commander upon his arrival, Fitch's three super light draughts also departed Cincinnati for Smithland on Wednesday morning, October 21. Although the *Moose*, *Reindeer*, and *Victory* were able to proceed without difficulty, the *Fairplay*, the former flagboat, was delayed by shoals at Louisville. The Hoosier officer believed that she would be down soon, however, in the short run, her failure to join the parade was viewed in a positive light. It was best, Fitch messaged Rear Adm. Porter, that one boat should remain in the Ohio until it had risen to a point where fording was not possible. "After the river rises," he concluded, "there is little chance for guerrilla successes."

Ever anxious in support of his supply lines, Quartermaster General Meigs on October 22 sent a wire directly to Porter asking him to "please give orders to the gunboats to convoy" the steamers with quartermasters' and other army stores en route to Nashville from Louisville. Porter certainly planned to do just that as soon as Fitch and his boats arrived. The navy would shift its primary focus back to the Cumberland from the Mississippi River and even the Tennessee to insure that supply boats would safely reach that primary railhead most directly linked to Chattanooga and Knoxville.

From Chattanooga on October 27, Maj. Gen. Grant wired Lt. Col. Charles L. Kilburn of the Cincinnati QMD depot asking if he had forwarded any rations downriver to Nashville. The busy Grant asked Kilburn to please advise Col. Thomas J. Haines at St. Louis of what action was taken from the Queen City and to request, in Grant's name, that Haines "send in the same way rapidly while the river is navigable."

In the meantime, the trip made south by Fitch's gunboats from Cincinnati was unbelievably rough. The anticipated Ohio River rise was not as deep as the optimistic Cairo-based Rear Adm. Porter had hoped. As the three modern tinclads from the big Ohio port city passed the veteran *Fairplay*, Fitch halted his procession long enough to turn over to her commander, Acting Volunteer Master Groves, a quantity of provisions and clothing for her crew. The short-handed ship's company was also increased by a few new recruits that Fitch brought down from the Cincinnati receiving ship. From there, the smoothness of the trip deteriorated.

The first chartered transport from the Queen City loaded for Nashville started down with Fitch. En route, the tinclads passed several steamers from Louisville loaded with government stores. They also encountered others that were disabled in trying to get down over very shoal and narrow channels. These had to be towed, along with their barges, by the *Moose, Reindeer,* or *Victory*. To get over or through the many shoals blocking progress, the Indiana sailor had on several occasions to supervise the removal of everything of consequence from the boats into lighters. Then, just as in the case of the *Springfield* back at the end of September, once the obstructions were passed, the craft were reloaded. At other times, those emptied transports provided tow to the gunboats and other steamers. Warping was employed when advantageous, but not grasshoppering. Steaming mostly on 26–27 inches of water, "scarcely enough for the very lightest mail boats to run," the small fleet reached Evansville on October 30 without serious injury (there was some damage) or accident. "I never saw the river in a worse stage of navigation," the Logansport native telegraphed Cairo.

Having been joined by the *Silver Lake*, Fitch's group headed for Smithland on Halloween. It was noted that a small rise was following them down, but it was not expected to amount to much by the time it arrived below Evansville. It was hoped that the naval steamers could quickly force their way up to their old rendezvous of just a few months back, but the task group leader was not too concerned. The river's depth affected everyone and he confidently predicted: "I do not think there will be many transports [from the Ohio River] ahead of me." When the naval vessels stopped at Caseyville to coal, one or two of the accompanying boats steamed on, reaching Smithland some eight to 10 hours before Fitch. These were not detained there, but moved on up.

While Fitch's warships were steaming the last miles toward their destination, Grant, Burnside, and Halleck were all discussing the possibilities of the Cumberland above Nashville as a logistical route to Knoxville. Previous thinking concerning the transfer of goods from Nashville to Chattanooga and then up the Tennessee to Knoxville was seen as impractical. On October 29, Halleck wired Grant that the railroad from Nashville could not supply both Chattanooga and Knoxville. "Cannot supplies for Burnside be sent up the Cumberland to Burkesville [Kentucky] or above on flats towed by light steamers," he wondered. After all, Burkesville was only a hundred miles northwest of Kingston, to which goods could be hauled overland "on a hard mountain road" and then forwarded up the Tennessee River the 35 miles to Knoxville.

The next morning, Grant suggested to Halleck that Carthage was probably "the best point." From there supplies could be sent across, via Sparta and Crossville, to Kingston and forwarded to Knoxville. Just to be sure, he wired Burnside asking him if he could "get supplies from Carthage if sent there by boat." The Knoxville commander did not immediately reply, but his counterpart, Maj. Gen. Thomas commanding at Chattanooga, now chimed in. His full and optimistic description provides an interesting review of geographic opportunities and challenges that failed to take into account the exigencies of weather, river stages, or Southern irregulars:

The best wagon route for General Burnside to supply his army at Kingston will be from a depot at Carthage. The road from that place to Kingston runs along the eastern bank of Caney Fork through a fine forage region from Carthage to Sparta.... The road from Carthage to Kingston is graded and runs over a barren region generally hard gravel and firm. The Caney Fork is also navigable as far as Sligo Ferry in the winter, which will decrease the land transportation to about sixty miles.

There were now a large number of unprotected transports operating in the Cumberland River as traffic from Louisville had increased significantly. Writing from Chattanooga on November 1, Maj. Gen. Grant increased the pressure on his downstream logistical operatives to ratchet up their activities. Lt. Col. Kilburn at Cincinnati was told: "Colonel Haines and yourself should get rations to Nashville by water while the Cumberland is up. I did not want Haines to send any by way of Louisville, but thought the Ohio might be navigable below the mouth of the Cumberland when not so above."

The next morning, Haines replied, informing the theater commander that, as Fitch had learned, "the Ohio River cannot be used for the present." Col. Haines was asked to send stores, via Cairo, up the Cumberland. On November 3, Kilburn again wired Grant to say that a small rise was currently in the Ohio at Cincinnati and he was taking advantage of it to load and send off smaller boats. "Will use every exertion to send you stores by water," he promised. Haines, he reported, had indicated that he would "send stores if the Cumberland gets high enough and that he would let Kilburn know as soon as boats could get through from Cairo.

Grant was not pleased with Col. Haines and, with Kilburn's telegraph in hand, burned off a pointed directive to his man in St. Louis: "Have you sent any stores via river to Nashville. I wish you to send all you can, while the river is navigable. Answer!" At the same time, the commanding general at Chattanooga wired his assistant adjutant general, Lt. Col. Theodore S. Bowers, at Nashville demanding that he "ascertain if any provisions and other stores have yet reached Nashville by boat and if more are on the way and inform me."

Col. Haines wired his superior back early on November 4 admitting that he had "sent no stores up the Cumb'd" but that he would that day, reemphasizing that Kilburn at Cincinnati was getting goods off on the new Ohio River rise. At Tennessee's capital, Lt. Col. Bowers sent Maj. William R. Rowley to the telegraph office to report that eight light boats had arrived "since the first inst. Loaded with forage and Commissary Stores ... a number are reported on the way up."

"It was obvious," wrote Tennessee state historian Walter T. Durham years later, "to any dock watcher" in Nashville that volume was up. This waterborne industry was also soon an article of interest to area partisans and guerrillas. Of the eight steamers that reached the capital landings on November 1–2, three were badly shot up while passing the village of Davis' Ripple. Although bullet holes on the boats were everywhere, none of the crews were wounded.

Way to the south in a story well-known but outside of the scope of this work, the army opened a "cracker line" with improvised locally-built steamers from Bridgeport to Chattanooga. The immediate threat of starvation for the Union defenders of the town was eliminated. However, the need to enhance the supply situation, including the number of draft animals, remained. This recovery would be slow and would have no immediate impact on the activities in the Eighth District of the Mississippi Squadron. The supply of Knoxville, on the other hand, would become a major task.

Back on November 3, while Maj. Gen. Grant was exchanging telegrams with Kilburn, Bowers, and Haines on downstream logistical issues, Maj. Gen. Burnside sent both Grant and Maj. Gen. Halleck a telegram which would come to have a direct impact upon Lt. Cmdr. Fitch. Burnside reported that it would not be possible to pick up goods at Carthage because most of his wagons had already been sent up to Camp Nelson in Kentucky for stores. The Knoxville commander suggested an alternative. "If the Cumberland is sufficiently high to allow boats to go to mouth of Big South Fork," he opined, "it would be well for some of the light draft gunboats and steamboats to tow up to that point a million of rations on flats." Once the supply flats were in place, they could be tied to the shore, covered with tarpaulins, and guarded by troops he would send until a wagon train could be gotten together.

Help and support for the merchantmen plying the Cumberland was on the way. The four Union Navy tinclads passed the mouth of the river late on the 4th of November and anchored at Smithland the next day. They were greeted by a single transport, the *Dove*, waiting for convoy to Nashville. Neither Fitch nor anyone connected with the U.S. Navy knew that plans were jelling which might require them to steam way up toward the head of this dangerous river.[6]

Stepping ashore at Smithland on the morning of November 5, it must have seemed almost like old times for Le Roy Fitch. Returning after his Cincinnati sojourn to take possession of his previous headquarters, the Logansport native was informed by army officers and probably merchants, and maybe the mayor, that guerrillas were operating between Smithland and Fort Donelson. Walking with some of them to the telegraph office, he composed a message for Rear Adm. Porter announcing his arrival and his departure next morning on his first fall convoy upstream. Patrols would be established as soon as possible, he promised his chief and those around him, and transports would be sent through as fast as a turnaround schedule could be implemented. He did require some assistance from the naval station.

At this point, the *Brilliant* and the *Victory* were in need of immediate work and missed the first cycle. The former not only needed calking and straightening up, but also her stern had settled. It would probably be necessary to send her to drydock at Paducah as soon as the ways there were clear. The boilers of the *Victory* were leaking so badly that she could not make much steam. Could boilermakers from Cairo, Fitch inquired of his superior, travel to Smithland as soon as possible in order to put things right?

Farther south at Chattanooga that morning, Maj. Gen. Grant wired Knoxville advising that he would seek an immediate opinion as to whether rations could be sent up the Cumberland per Maj. Gen. Burnside's suggestion. While the operator was sending that message, the commanding general composed a second to Lt. Col. Bowers in Nashville, ordering that he send Maj. Rowley out to make inquiries concerning the stage of the Cumberland above the city up to the Big South Fork. If it was navigable, Bowers was to see the city's newly-arrived chief quartermaster, Col. James L. Donaldson, and make arrangements for the transportation, on barges towed by light draught steamers and convoyed by gunboats, of 300,000 rations of salt meat and a million of other rations. Once the goods were aboard and well covered with tarpaulins, the boats would go up, leave their barges, and return.

While his lieutenants readied the *Moose*, *Reindeer*, and *Silver Lake* for departure up the river, Fitch met with the local quartermaster, Capt. Hanson Rasin. Rasin asked that Fitch convoy the *Dove* to Fort Donelson or, if possible, to Nashville. Fitch told him, as he had Porter, that his boats would depart at 7 the next morning and that the *Dove* and such craft as arrived that night would be protected. Having caught up on the news of the region and the river, the convoy commodore retired to his quarters to prepare new general orders for the governance of his operation and as a warning to the populace through whose midst he and his charges would pass.

General Order No. 10 was addressed to inhabitants living along the banks of the Cumberland River, where it had become impossible to tell from appearance Union friend or foe along the shores. Due warning was given that the banks near places where steamers were molested had to be kept clear. The citizens were warned that the gunboat captains possessed orders to fire at every person seen loafing through the woods or standing on the banks at suspicious places or near where boats had been shot at. Harkening back to the message first delivered by his older brother in Arkansas the previous year, Fitch bluntly cautioned that inhabitants would be held responsible for maintaining peace and quiet (law and order) within their immediate neighborhoods. By this he meant specifically that, while it may not be in their power to prevent depredations, it was possible for them to notify steamers or the gunboats concerning the presence of guerrillas.

After handing over this document for copying and distribution, the Eighth District leader turned his attention to the mechanics of convoy organization, something at which he was already very skilled. General Order 12 was written for the succinct instruction of the captains and pilots of steamers under convoy and had three major tenets. First, when steamers left any place under convoy, they were then, and until landed at the place of destination, entirely under the control of the senior naval officer attached to the convoy, who was held personally responsible for each and every steamer leaving port with him. Next, it needed to be understood that no one could interfere with or take boats out of the fleet without the direct permission of the senior naval officer, whether the fleet was under way or halted. Finally, steamers with freight to land or take on at Dover, Clarksville, or other places, were to make known that requirement to the senior naval officer before the convoy sailed, so that arrangements could be made for appropriate stoppage of the lengthy parade.

Late that afternoon, Lt. Col. Bowers at Nashville had his information concerning the upper reaches of the Cumberland River and went to the telegraph office to report to Chattanooga. "Navigation is practicable to Big South Fork," he announced. While there were no barges, a number were expected to arrive within 24 hours. Four million rations were on hand and six steamboats were lying at the wharf. There was only one army gunboat fit for service at Nashville. "Would it not be well," he inquired, "to send an officer by steamboat tomorrow ... to ask the Navy for additional gunboats?" Bowers' telegram makes it clear that the original idea at higher army echelons was to send a convoy up to Big South Fork protected by army and not navy gunboats. It was only after Bowers cautioned that all he had was one improvised gunboat, the *Newsboy*, and that there were insufficient other military boats available that a call to the Mississippi Squadron was contemplated.[7]

Knowing his superiors' continuing appreciation for counterinsurgency initiative and very certain of their anti-guerrilla stance, Lt. Cmdr. Fitch released his general orders at the same time on November 6 that he wrote to Rear Adm. Porter enclosing copies of them in expectation of their approval. Fitch reminded the squadron commander that it was his experience (as it was undoubtedly that of other river convoy commodores) that idle men along the shores often fired into passing steamers. These apparently unarmed folks stood quietly on the banks and often waved at the gunboats. But then, "no sooner are the gunboats out of sight than they turn right around, pick up their guns, and fire into the next steamer coming along." These few sentences convey as well as, and better than most, the simple truth of the irregular war on western waters. The attacks were a terrible annoyance to the Yankees, but could not halt their logistical enterprise. They could best be handled, the Hoosier observed, by ridding the banks entirely.

Fitch believed that "all good Union people had been driven out by the Rebels long since." Thus it should come as no surprise that he, like others in the Federal service, thought that a strong offense against irregular forces and their civilian backers was the best form of defense. Besides, as he put it, "if I were to commence and burn every town (except Dykesburg [Dycusburg]) and house along the river between here and Nashville, I would not do more than justice." The Hoosier sailor was certain that his gunners were accurate and discerning enough not destroy innocent people or hamlets with shot thrown amiss. When they fired, it was expected that they would probably only hit molesting personages, bushwhackers, guerrillas, and the like. Such whiffs of canister, to paraphrase Napoleon, would keep down by force the worst elements of a people whose "sense of honor is very limited."

During the night, four additional transports arrived at Smithland from Louisville, including the *Nightingale*. The five steamers and three gunboats departed the Kentucky rendezvous at 7 A.M. on November 6. As the craft paddled upstream, great clouds of black smoke rising from their chimneys, Maj. Gen. Grant at Chattanooga was in communication with Rear Adm. Porter at Cairo. "Can you not send one or two more light draft gunboats to Nashville," the army leader wondered. "I want to send some steamboats with rations by south fork of the Cumberland ... they cannot go without convoys ... there is an absolute necessity that rations should be sent by this route." Grant then wired Lt. Col. Bowers informing his Nashville adjutant that he had messaged the admiral about the special convoy and ordered that preparations to send the steamers quickly get underway.

As Fitch's convoy was passing down on November 7, word was received from friendly locals that a party of 15 to 20 irregulars had fired into the steamer *John A. Fisher* only a mile and a half or two miles below Dover. Her captain, William Strong, was wounded and now faced a long convalescence at his home in Nashville. The convoy commodore was furious when he heard of the attack and the fact that nearby Union soldiers did not intervene. "This is a sample of the energy displayed by the land forces up this river," he stormed on paper.

Fitch may not have known or appreciated that army lethargy was, for now at least, institutionally induced. Prior to the Battle of Chickamauga, Maj. Gen. Rosecrans withdrew a number of rear area garrisons altogether and stripped others of their most important antiguerrilla tools, their cavalry troopers. These men were now front line reinforcements. The removed soldiers were not replaced and thus the troops at Fort Donelson, Clarksville, Smithland, and other points had all they could do just to hold their own positions, let alone venture out. As historian Cooling later pointed out, given that development, "naval convoys again became the most effective method for ensuring that supplies reached distribution points for the field armies."

Communication during the trip was most often between the sailors and men on shore or other boats. Whistles were often employed for signaling. The telegraph was extremely undependable and it is not likely that much news was received from it. While en route, the naval officers were all surprised to learn that the attacks from shore so far reported were largely made by bands of 15–20 insurgents using rifles and shotguns. "If we are not annoyed by batteries soon," Fitch reported, "it will be a wonder." It was also discovered that a guerrilla meeting place was being regularly maintained at a location a mile or two back of where the town of Palmyra once stood. With bitter memories of that town, the gunboat men resolved to revisit the area soon and break up the rendezvous.

The naval-escorted convoy grew during its long, slow passage to between 10 and 15 steamers, which were sent on once they were safely over Harpeth Shoals and near the capital city. Fitch did not actually go all the way to Nashville, electing to return from Clarksville to Smithland and bring up additional transports. Leaving about 8 A.M. on November 9, the tinclads made a stop at Fort Donelson, where the convoy commodore sent a report of his activities to Rear Adm. Porter. During that first week of November, the Indiana sailor later reported, upwards of 25 to 30 additional transports also made the trip up.

As Fitch weighed anchor for Smithland, he was forced to draw the conclusion that the river was quickly falling and would be low again for about a week—as low as it had been in October. Still, he hoped one or two more large convoys could be pushed above Harpeth before the Cumberland fell. "I will have as much as I can do during low water in convoying to the foot of the shoals."

He might have added that his gunboats not only provided protection, but acted as towboats for stuck steamers and offered other kinds of coast guard or police assistance throughout the convoy treks, voyages which were necessarily and painfully much slower during periods of low water than high. It was common knowledge in squadron and river circles that such shepherding of merchantmen was a hallmark of Fitch-led convoys and was for almost a year. Congestion at key points and boats bunching up at inopportune spots, delays occasioned by assembly tardiness, off-loading and reloading problems, especially at the shoals, all led to frustration.

The Logansport native's zeal to push additional convoys through before the water stage sank further now almost got him into some hot water with Union theater commander Grant, then at Chattanooga, over, of all things, a lack of eagerness to provide cooperative assistance. The episode, as it unfolds in the pages of the army and navy Official Records, is one of confusion, lack of clear communication, misunderstanding, and, perhaps, some want of inter-service good will. Old concerns and army complaints resurfaced again as quartermasters and others worried about meeting the requirements of the demanding Military Division of the Mississippi supreme commander.

It will be recalled that, on the morning of November 6, Maj. Gen. Grant wired Rear Adm. Porter asking for light-draught gunboats to guard a special supply mission he was preparing to send up to Maj. Gen. Burnside. While Fitch's tinclads, out on the Cumberland, were moving with their charges upstream from Smithville toward Clarksville, the army's theater commander miles away had ordered the shipment by steamer and barge of those stores accumulated at Nashville and Carthage to the head of the river's navigation at Big South Fork.

Before noon that Friday, Grant informed Lt. Col. Bowers in Nashville of the Porter communication and ordered him to make certain the convoy was ready, issuing "any order necessary to secure this result in the promptest manner." It was understood that any such Bowers directives were to have the same impact as if they came personally from Grant. The colonel's deputy, Capt. Sidney A. ("Sid") Stockdale of the 103rd Illinois Volunteer Infantry, was to handle the details and when the convoy was cleared for departure, Grant and Burnside were both to be notified. Burnside was also alerted and told that "if the Cumberland does not fall before barges can be got ready and loaded, they will go."

At 6 P.M., Bowers wired back his belief that a trip could be made, but it would have to be made without towed barges because the Cumberland was narrow and filled with sharp turns. Even small steamers were having trouble in the Burkesville area due to falling river levels. Low water in the Ohio River prevented the arrival of commissary supplies from Cincinnati. However, large shipments were coming from Louisville and by rail from St. Louis. Bowers continued to believe that the Cumberland above the capital city was passable and that, once the convoy reached the Big South Fork, it would remain until Burnside's troops could arrive and take charge of the stores.

Nine steamers were available at Nashville to support the Burnside mission. Capt. Stockdale and the quartermasters were quickly at work. Dock workers, assisted by soldiers, labored around the clock to load the steamers with 300,000 rations of salt meat and a million other rations. At the same time, the army gunboat *Newsboy* was made ready to join the escort. She was outfitted with a second 12-pounder gun and additional artillerists were detailed to work it. The craft was also coaled, victualled, and given every other manner of necessary succor.

On November 7, Maj. Gen. Grant wired Lt. Col. Bowers agreeing that if the barges couldn't go, the mission should still be attempted with the stores all piled aboard the steamers. Bowers replied that the transports would be ready by midnight and would depart the next day as soon as the navy gunboats arrived. The adjutant had learned that three tinclads were "at Clarksville on their way up."

Rear Adm. Porter on Sunday morning November 8 informed Grant that four gunboats were available at the mouth of the Cumberland. Fitch had been on the stream for some time, he added, pushing convoys through, one of which was en route to Nashville even now. By the following morning, the last-minute details were all handled and the military and charter boats assembled for Burnside were ready for departure upstream. All that was required was for Fitch and his convoy to show up. After that, the mission would be turned over to the Indiana sailor and the steamers could leave with the navy man in charge.

The arrival of the tinclads and their convoy was expected hourly on Monday. There was surprise in military circles when, by 4 P.M., the gunboats still had not arrived, although a number of merchant steamers had come to the wharf. A half hour later, Lt. Col. Bowers, tired of waiting, gave Capt. Stockdale a letter and ordered him to ascend down the river and find "the naval officer in charge of gunboat flotilla" that was thought was lying between Nashville and Clarksville. Bowers was certain that, whomever the officer was, whether Fitch or a subordinate, he would hurry on up after talking to Stockdale and reading the message.

As noted, the Eighth District navy commander, who was within a few miles of Nashville, but did not know of the army's expectation, turned back for Smithland about noon on November 9. Making good time with the current, the *Moose*, *Silver Lake*, and *Reindeer* dropped anchor off their Kentucky rendezvous about 1 A.M. on November 10. Upon immediate inquiry, the division leader found that no further progress had been made with either the *Victory* or the *Brilliant*. Both remained unavailable. To help compensate for this shortcoming, orders were passed for the *Fairplay* to come down from the Ohio at her first opportunity. The flotilla commander acknowledged receipt of a telegram from Rear Adm. Porter and wired him back announcing that additional steamers would be sent up to Nashville later in the day, probably about 7 A.M., the traditional convoy departure time. The river was falling, he added.

Before breakfast, still unaware of the army's need for him in Nashville, Fitch wrote out a further amplification of his convoy rules in General Order 13 for circulation to his subordinates. "Every officer in charge of a convoy," he directed, must take the name of every vessel leaving port with them or joining the fleet; also the number of barges or flats in tow." The object was to make a more complete record of convoys going up and coming down; all rolls were to be sent to the divisional commander at the completion of each cycle.

Having completed his paperwork, the Logansport officer looked forward to taking the rest of the day off to indulge his passion for duck and wild goose hunting. He'd had no liberty since departing Cincinnati and, with many fowl in the air, a fat fresh bird for dinner would be a welcome change. Acting Volunteer Lieutenant Glassford was looking after the three-boat convoy now leaving for upstream, there was no mail from Cairo or Mound City, and his bluejackets were engaged in their normal in-port routines under the watchful eyes of their officers. Fitch had no inkling that he was about to run into the front end of a buzz saw of army complaint. It would continue for several weeks with an intensity the likes of which he had not felt since his lashings from Maj. Gen. Rosecrans the previous winter.[8]

At the Nashville wharf, the army gunboat *Newsboy* was placed under Capt. Stockdale's orders and, at sunset on November 9, departed down the river. The craft reached Clarksville at 11 P.M. without "having seen or heard of the gunboats." There the army man first learned that the navy tinclads had already returned downriver and were not coming to Nashville. After reporting this development to Lt. Col. Bowers and acquiring a fresh pilot from the disabled army gunboat *Hagan*, the *Newsboy* shoved off and went looking for the USN.

On the morning of November 10, Bowers telegraphed Maj. Gen. Grant informing him that Stockdale did not come across either a Nashville-bound convoy or any navy warships. The captain continued in hot pursuit through the night. He would not give up until he had made contact and gotten definite information.

No gunboats were overtaken or met by the *Newsboy* until she was within about two miles of Smithland. At that point, she made rendezvous with the *Reindeer* and *Silver Lake*, headed toward Nashville with the convoy that had departed from the Kentucky base that morning. Stockdale was told by Acting Volunteer Lieutenant Glassford aboard the former that divisional commander Fitch's U.S.S. *Moose* was lying opposite the town. Paddling on, the *Newsboy* landed above the flagboat at 2 P.M. Stockdale was soon thereafter given permission to board the *Moose* and state his business. Once on the warship's deck, the Nashville envoy was shocked to learn, probably from XO Rice, that "Captain Fitch had gone into the woods gunning." He wouldn't be back until evening.

Stockdale had no option but to return to his boat to await the naval officer's return. At 6 P.M. he went back aboard the *Moose* where he found that Fitch had still not rejoined his command. Finally, at 7 P.M., the Indiana sailor came back aboard and the two men were quickly in conference. It is doubtful that the navy man even changed clothes so "immediate" was Stockdale's business—and we do not know the results of his hunt.

Without hesitation and possibly with some formality, the army captain gave the *Moose*'s skipper the letter from Lt. Col. Bowers. The communication authenticated Stockdale's identity and the reason for his call. It took only a moment for Fitch to read the message which stated that a transport fleet with commissary stores had been prepared and was waiting for naval escort up the Cumberland from Nashville to the mouth of the Big South Fork. It went on to say that Maj. Gen. Grant had telegraphed Rear Adm. Porter on the matter and that it was "of the highest importance that there should be no delay."

Having heard that the tinclads were in the vicinity (then believed to be Clarksville), Stockdale was dispatched to find them in hopes that they could furnish the necessary convoy.

No doubt invoking Grant's name again, he verbally asserted his belief that the entire supply run hinged on Fitch providing help at once. Taking the issue a bit further, he asked Fitch as to "whether or not he had received any intimation from Admiral Porter" that help was so urgently needed at Nashville. The seaman replied that he had not, primarily because neither the mail or telegraphic communications were regularly getting through.

Walter Durham, in his history of Civil War Nashville, asserts that the Hoosier officer was "content to blame falling water and the poor state of repair of some of his few gunboats for his inability to fulfill Grant's requisition." As we have seen, Fitch was not content about much of anything when it came to the war, least of all the seriousness of his role as convoy chief of the Cumberland. This after all was a fellow who had gone so far as to sell horses to the navy's benefit and then worry about whether he had handled the sale proceeds correctly. It is true that he did have certain physical problems with two of his few boats and had no extras to spare, but these concerns paled in comparison to what he perceived as his prime directive: to provide escort for steamers moving up the river from Smithland to Nashville and back. He hoped to get a second convoy, even then starting to assemble nearby to his anchorage, through before the water stage fell again. He would start down with it when the second necessary escort, the *Fairplay*, arrived from the Ohio in a day or so.

What Grant, Bowers, and Stockdale were now seeking was a special operation outside Fitch's mandate or instructions, one which would make it very difficult to properly run the regular convoys up and down the river. Before taking on the dangerous extra job and thereby violating his superior's long-standing orders regarding convoy escort, he wanted clarification and authority from Rear Adm. Porter, which he was willing to seek. The Hoosier promised Stockdale he would wire Cairo and would let the army man know the response the following morning. Stockdale, and by telegraphed inference, his superior, Bowers, regarded the convoy chief as too wary.[9]

Fearing that Fitch would not convey the importance of Bowers' letter and would, instead, give the gathering Nashville convoy priority, Capt. Stockdale left the meeting aboard the *Moose* and had himself rowed across the river to Smithland where he hiked to the telegraph office. There he wired his chief, reporting his conversation and Fitch's word to contact Cario. He also asked what to do should Fitch receive a negative response from the admiral. He informed Lt. Col. Bowers that the naval officer would "do nothing without orders from Admiral Porter." Bowers replied telling Stockdale to continue hounding Fitch until he agreed to provide the requested escort and then wired Grant for affirmation of his action.

The district commander, who could not let the matter drop even if he might have wanted to, went to the Smithland telegraph office as promised, but he could not get through to Porter. After returning to his vessel, Fitch put the finishing touches on a new code of whistle signals to be employed during convoys and thought of an alternative way to get in touch with his superior. It would require Stockdale's help.

Sometime in early evening, say about 8 or 9 P.M., a messenger from the *Moose* went aboard the *Newsboy* with word that Lt. Cmdr. Fitch, too, had gone to the telegraph office, but had no luck in reaching the admiral. The Hoosier, not content to discount the army request until he knew for certain what Porter wanted done, invited Stockdale to his flagboat and there told him his idea.

If the soldier would take Porter some messages (including a copy of his signal codes) and a dispatch seeking instruction concerning Grant's wishes, Fitch would provide the *News-*

boy with an Ohio River pilot to guide him to Cairo. Stockdale, in the words of his report, "cheerfully assented." The flotilla chief quickly wrote out a cover letter to Porter saying that, although he had tried to get through by telegraph on the matter of the Bowers letter, he could not. Therefore, he was taking the extraordinary step of sending Stockdale as an emissary in hopes of an early response.

Stockdale departed Smithland at 10 P.M. on November 10 and reached Cairo at 4 A.M. on November 11. He "immediately waited on Admiral Porter on board the flag-ship *Black Hawk*." After giving the squadron leader Fitch's cover letter and a copy of the Bowers message, the junior army officer explained to the bearded sailor how important the Grant mission was to Burnside's future. Porter, according to Stockdale, "expressed much surprise that the gunboats had not already been furnished agreeably to General Grant's request." He did not know or acknowledge or both that Fitch, while moving back and forth on the river, may not have received the request. In any event, Porter sat down and immediately wrote out orders for Fitch to send a pair of gunboats to Nashville forthwith and, in future, to render Grant "all assistance possible without waiting for orders." In this particular case, he was to do everything possible to supply Burnside.

The U.S. Army captain was back aboard his own gunboat at 5 A.M. and headed back to Smithland. While his deputy was en route, Lt. Col. Bowers received a blunt response from Maj. Gen. Grant to his question of the day before: "You are right in sending Stockdale until convoys are obtained. If gunboats do not accompany our transports, there will be no use in sending them." The *Newsboy* was back at the Kentucky navy rendezvous by noon. Capt. Stockdale immediately retired aboard the *Moose* and handed Fitch the admiral's directive.

During the morning, the Eighth District commander made his own plans to furnish the requested escorts, if, as he had written in his cover letter to Porter, "you so desire it." Although we do not know the content of the Monday telegram Fitch received from Porter, one can only infer from its acknowledgement that it was received. Whether it was the only one received that day is unclear. Capt. Stockdale, in his official report, claims to have seen a wire dated November 9 at Smithland and that it clearly directed "Captain Fitch to report two gunboats to the commanding officer at Nashville without delay." Whether such a document actually existed, how the messenger came to view it, or whether it read as Stockdale asserted remains a mystery. The larger question, of course, is why would Fitch, who to this point appears to have been nothing less than a fire-breathing, straight-shooting bulldog, have engaged in such a sham? What did he have to gain by sending Stockdale to see Porter if he had thought for even a moment that the man might return with orders repeating the instructions he already had while exposing him as a liar in the process?

In the absence of written records, we can only guess at possible answers to these questions. First, it appears to this writer simply impossible that Fitch would have ignored his duty for a day or two of hunting. Did Rear Adm. Porter react to the original army request in something of a round-about fashion or did he actually and directly order Eighth District tinclads on the mission? Were the instructions provided clear or, quite possibly, not received at all. Rather than sending specific orders, did Porter instead leave the matter of initiative in this case to his subordinate, a man well-tested and knowledgeable in the ways of the Cumberland—and the army? If Fitch had received instruction to proceed above Nashville, did he choose to ignore it because he knew the water level in the Cumberland farther up would at that time be too low for any relief convoy to get through? Was Fitch personally needed to lead an expedition or was the army seeking navy participation in a project the leadership for which could be delegated?

If the army had communicated with Fitch directly, it would not only have saved time, but the naval officer would "know exactly what to do." I am inclined to believe, as he later wrote to Maj. Gen. Grant, that he did not know of the first (November 6) request. We choose to believe him when he wrote: "As it was, I was compelled to send to Cairo to know the admiral's wishes." Whether he received a directive on November 9 as clear as Capt. Stockdale claims, we do not know. As events revealed, the Logansport native possessed a much clearer picture of river conditions in his district than did his military colleagues. It is possible that he did not act immediately because he was certain that the Burnside trip could not be made and if he rushed to Nashville to undertake it or had Acting Volunteer Lieutenant Glassford take it, the next supply convoy to Nashville itself might not get up.

Fitch, who like other junior officers in Porter's command were savvy enough to exercise some caution and avoid stepping on the admiral's toes (especially in matters that involved his friends Grant and Sherman), most likely never read Stockdale's report in which he mentioned the squadron commander's surprise. In the end, Porter, despite his closeness to Grant, was uncritical of his subordinate, did not reprimand him in any fashion, and continued to support his resolute convoy expert. As in the past, Fitch found a way to get the information and permissions required and subsequently did his duty well. This level of support from Cairo would be important in the days ahead when additional concerns surfaced from such important logistical personages as Brig. Gen. Allen and Meigs.

At 2 P.M. on November 11, the *Newsboy* weighed anchor for Nashville. Stockdale had in his pocket orders for Acting Volunteer Lieutenant Glassford and a message for Maj. Gen. Grant, to be sent via Lt. Col. Bowers. In the latter, Fitch asked if the army, in future, would please communicate with him directly concerning its needs for assistance from the gunboats on the Cumberland or Ohio Rivers. He repeated his claim not to have known of Grant's request until Stockdale showed up at Smithland. If Grant, Bowers, and others would make their wishes known to him, the Hoosier would, if it were within his power, comply with them "with all my heart."

At 4 A.M. on November 12, the *Newsboy* overhauled the *Reindeer*, *Silver Lake*, and their convoy at a point in the river 12 miles above Fort Donelson. Stockdale went aboard the former and handed Fitch's orders to Glassford. The convoy leader, in turn, assured the army man that his two gunboats would arrive at Nashville the following morning and that he would check in with Lt. Col. Bowers as directed. The *Newsboy* continued up the river and, after a stop at Clarksville to change pilots, returned to Nashville that evening.

The next morning, as the *Fairplay* was arriving at Smithland, Bowers wired Grant informing him of Stockdale's interview with Porter. The admiral, in fact, received Grant's November 6 message and directed his subordinate to send the requested escorts at once, but Fitch didn't get the order. Porter told Stockdale that he had, by the message sent back with him to Smithland, directed the Eighth District commander to furnish Grant "all the gunboats you require from time to time without waiting to consult him." Fitch, said Bowers, wrote that he would hereafter "afford you prompt cooperation." In the telegram, the assistant adjutant general acknowledged that the river was too low for the trip to be made at this time, but once again offered assurances that it "will be up again in a few days." Just to make certain, he promised to send the *Newsboy* upstream the following morning "to ascertain particulars."[10]

At the end of October, Capt. John W. Donn of the U.S. Coast Survey, ordered west from Baltimore, was attached to the staff of Army of the Cumberland chief engineer Brig. Gen. William F. "Baldy" Smith at Chattanooga. So it was that when that leader moved to Nashville, Donn accompanied him and was available to undertake, at Lt. Col. Bowers' request, the Newsboy reconnaissance on November 13. Moving up to Carthage, Donn reviewed his instructions. He was to find a water route for the transportation of supplies to Knoxville, which was then being supplied by way of Chattanooga over a long and circuitous route or by way of Camp Nelson and Cumberland Gap. Every stream flowing into the Cumberland from the south was to be examined and Donn would write a report on their navigability.

Proceeding up from Carthage, Donn found that the army's gunboat drew too much water for Caney Fork, the first stream to be examined. He subsequently returned and obtained a smaller steamer, which drew only 14 inches, and resumed his mission. About four miles from the mouth of the fork, Donn's craft became stuck in the first rapids. After several attempts to remove or get by the obstructions, the boat, freed at last, returned to Carthage. Capt. Donn subsequently talked to everyone he found knowledgeable in that town on Caney Fork and discovered that the stream was a succession of rapids all the way up to Sparta—75 miles above its entrance into the Cumberland. As there was nothing more that could be done in the way of a waterborne relief expedition until the river rose, Donn returned to Nashville.[11]

The *Fairplay* arrived at Smithland on November 12 and, true to Acting Volunteer Lieutenant Glassford's word, the *Reindeer* and *Silver Lake* anchored at Nashville next day, perhaps in time to see off Capt. Donn. On November 13, the *Springfield* came to at the Kentucky rendezvous. With two more tinclads joining his *Moose*, Lt. Cmdr. Fitch could almost, though not quite, afford to leave the *Reindeer* and *Silver Lake* at the Tennessee capital waiting to cover the stalled Burnside expedition. The boilermakers requested from Illinois were hard at work on the *Victory*'s problems and it was expected she would be ready to rejoin the command within a few days.

Until the river rose, it would not be possible to take the division's coal barge down to Fort Donelson as Fitch had hoped. The mail between Smithland and Cairo was still very irregular and the telegraph was seldom in working order. This news was sent to Rear Adm. Porter via another steamer on November 15 as the Indiana sailor prepared to depart upstream with another convoy. This message would be the last from Kentucky until the Hoosier returned on November 21. Although there might not be much to say, Fitch promised to write his superior at every opportunity.

At Chattanooga during the day, a disappointed Maj. Gen. Grant wired Knoxville advising that the waterborne supply expedition was on hold. "Boats have been laying at Nashville," he informed Maj. Gen. Burnside, "loaded with rations to take to Big South Fork ever since you asked to have them sent there, waiting for convoy." The theater commander was miffed that he had to send all the way to Cairo for orders "before gunboats could be got." The tinclads duly arrived at Nashville and would take the convoy up by the first rise—but no one knew when that would occur. In the meantime, efforts would be made to send goods overland.

The *Moose*, *Springfield*, and *Fairplay* were headed up the Cumberland with their charges when a new round of concerns was raised by the army about Lt. Cmdr. Fitch's convoy operations. The first was a dispatch from Quartermaster General Meigs. Sent on November 13, it charged that steamers were not getting through as quickly as they should. On November 16, another complaint from the army about Fitch's convoy work was dropped on Rear Adm. Porter's desk, this one from both Meigs and Brig. Gen. Allen.

On the latter date, Meigs sent over to the Mississippi Squadron commander a copy of an irate telegram from the army's top quartermaster at Louisville. The quartermaster general, who had been in the west since almost the beginning of the Chattanooga siege, provided almost no amplification except to say that it was the sort of thing his November 13 memo was based upon. The concern in the Allen message speaks for itself:

> The quartermaster at Clarksville reports to me that transports have waited six days at Smithland for a convoy. I am tired of writing on the subject to Cairo. The Navy Department gave formal official advices that they were prepared to convoy all vessels up the Tennessee and Cumberland rivers.

Porter, who, primarily through the person of Fleet Captain Alexander Pennock, went through this sort of army criticism of Fitch's convoy system 10 months earlier, sent copies of the Meigs documents, along with his own cover letters or telegrams, on to the Eighth District commander for reply, both on the 13th and the 23rd. His subordinate thus received a chance to counter the charges and Porter once more undoubtedly believed that would take care of the matter.

On November 17, Maj. Gen. Grant wired Maj. Gen. Burnside at Knoxville asking, on behalf of Col. Donaldson, the Nashville quartermaster, whether or not the supply-laden steamers, that were waiting a rise, should be sent to Celina, at the mouth of Obey's River and thence by road thereby saving "one hundred and fifty (150) miles difficult river transportation." A little later in the day, it was learned at Chattanooga that Burnside was engaged with Confederate general Longstreet. Grant informed Donaldson of that development. The next day, Grant telegraphed Brig. Gen. Meigs at Bridgeport revealing his belief that "rations for General Burnside could not be sent now even if there was water enough in the Cumberland until the result of present movements by Longstreet are known." Given the Confederates' activities, Grant decided it was better to unload the boats rather than to keep them in a constant state of readiness.

Rear Adm. Porter received a telegram from Fort Donelson on November 20 noting that Fitch's return to Smithland was delayed. While coming back from the foot of Harpeth Shoals, a number of steamers were found aground and waiting to get over shoals. The *Moose* stopped for these, providing assistance and helping them along. The *Springfield* was then left at the foot of the shoals, guarding and lighting boats over, while the *Fairplay* patrolled between Fort Donelson and Clarksville. At the foot of Ingram's Shoals, six or eight steamers were found with barges unable to get over the obstruction. The *Moose* stood guard while the *Brilliant* went to engage other boats to come up and "light them up." After the shallow draft vessels arrived, the *Brilliant* was left on guard duty between Line Island and Ingram's Shoals helping boats over. All was otherwise quiet on the river and a "good rise" was expected within a few days. The flagboat would be back at Smithland by November 22.

With telegraphic reliability at Smithland still as questionable as it was at the time of Capt. Stockdale's visit, Fitch did not find any messages from Porter awaiting him upon his return late on November 22. He did not know that a message from the admiral was sent that day, with copies of the concerned quartermaster correspondence enclosed. Fitch did, however, find the *Victory* ready for duty. Before turning in, the Hoosier officer wrote his commander a lengthy report detailing his latest trip. There were no guerrilla disturbances; however, irregulars were causing U.S. Army units to suffer from the cold. The bluecoats, who were out of coal, could not readily obtain wood as irregulars kept local farmers from taking their saleable wood to them or down to the river.

To assist in guerrilla control, the Hoosier put forward a plan to create special landing parties for his district, built around additional 12-pounder howitzers he was requesting of Porter. Once organized, these units could be sent from his boats "to break up guerrilla parties forming and encamped some 2 or 3 miles from the river." These, he probably thought, were just the sort of groups which might help with restoring the wood trade. If the admiral agreed to the concept and sent along 10 more boat howitzers, Fitch could have two wheeled guns and 30 men per boat or, if necessary, a consolidated division of 12 to 14 pieces of artillery and about 200 small-arms men. "With this force, I can readily break up or disperse any guerrilla band now along this stream." Fitch, with his special affinity for howitzers and amphibious operations, continued to push this plan. Whether or not he believed it at the time, this was, of course, as Frank Cooling later put it, "precisely what the Mississippi Marine Brigade was supposed to be all about." Fitch had seen the MMB in action on the Tennessee and may have thought he could employ its best attributes on a smaller scale.

Early on November 23, the *Victory* departed Smithland to relieve the *Brilliant*, which, while functional, remained in a poor state of repair. After seeing off Acting Volunteer Ensign Read, Fitch walked over to the telegraph office where he found two telegrams from Rear Adm. Porter. One granted him permission to send the *Brilliant* to Cairo for repairs. The second was less welcome. It was the one sent on November 13 concerning his conduct of convoys up the Cumberland to Nashville. Reading through it, the Indiana sailor may have felt himself experiencing a case of déjà vu. He did not know that he would be bombarded on the matter several more times before the day was over.

Fitch immediately sat down and wrote out brief responses, which he wired to his superior. In the first, he promised that the *Brilliant* would be sent to Cairo as soon as she could depart Ingram's Shoals. *Victory* was en route to relieve her and, if all went well, the damaged tinclad would be in Illinois by late Sunday evening. In his response to the memo of the 13th, it was noted that "there has not been a single steamer detained an hour on our account. They are sent through as fast as they arrive." The boats were not stacking up at Smithland and the only reason any were slowed was "on account of water." Quartermasters were sending steamers up "too deep to get over the shoal."

The two return telegrams concerning operations were followed by one reporting that a dispatch from Porter, expected the previous day, had not arrived. This message closed with another assurance: "I am ready to convoy any number of boats. Boats do not have to wait on us five minutes." Fitch, at the Smithland telegraph office, did not know that the missing message and another was in a mail sack which was even then being sent aboard the *Moose*. Later in the morning, a second telegram on convoying arrived from the *Black Hawk*.

When he got back aboard the *Moose*, Fitch wrote two more reports to be sent to his superior via the afternoon mail boat. In the first he addressed the matter of convoys and his concern with telegraphic communications. After acknowledging receipt of the two earlier convoy-related wires, he reassured his commander that he was, as he had said in his morning telegram, ready at any moment to convoy any number of boats to Nashville or above. Boats were sent through as fast as they arrived and there was not a moment's detention on the part of the navy. Could there be something wrong with the telegraph, he wondered.

"The messages do not get through as soon as they might." At certain times, the Eighth District chief was up the river where telegrams could not reach him. Even at those times, Porter and the army need have no fear in regard to convoys, "for the boats will be taken under our charge before they reach any points of danger, and will not have to wait here a moment for convoy."

After putting the letter into an envelope, the Indiana sailor turned his attention to reviewing his immediate plans in a second report. He would leave that evening or in the morning for Nashville with another convoy expected from the Tennessee River. The water in the Cumberland, as he reminded his boss, was now very low and it required a good deal of vigilance "to keep all smooth." Still, the river was supposed to be rising at Harpeth Shoals. If that were the case, the coal barge might soon be towed up to Fort Donelson. Over most of this next week, no gunboats would be at Smithland as they would all be busy upriver. Still, Porter was advised, mail and dispatches would be sent up aboard various steamers and telegrams would be forwarded through to Fort Donelson, Clarksville, or Nashville. If there were no difficulties, the *Moose* should be back at her Kentucky anchorage by the 27th or 28th.

All of the next day until late in the afternoon, Lt. Cmdr. Fitch paced the deck of his flagboat waiting for the Tennessee River convoy to appear. During the day, he had heard from the *Victory* that guerrillas were attacking Jackson's woodyard, located three miles below Fort Donelson. In order to relieve Acting Volunteer Ensign Read so that he might attend to them, it was necessary for the *Moose* to weigh anchor and start down that night. A telegram to this effect was sent to Rear Adm. Porter, with assurances that his departure would not detain or endanger the fleet coming up from Eastport.

Upon his return from the telegraph office, the Hoosier sailor wrote out a slightly fuller report to be sent to Cairo by mail boat. In it he again assured the admiral that the *Victory*'s relief would not detain the army convoy. Fitch would either have a boat below all danger, ready to receive them, or he would be there himself. In either case, the steamers could push up as soon as they arrived. "I will get them safely through to Nashville," he promised.

These reports were sent off just as a new mail sack came in. When Fitch opened it, he found yet another communication on convoys sent by Porter the previous day. It enclosed copies of Meigs' dispatches and Allen's telegrams. The convoy commodore was asked to once more answer renewed army charges of convoy inefficiencies. He resolved to write out his defense during a quiet moment on the next convoy run. It is unclear whether he also received the news that, during the day, a division of Union troops had captured the summit of Lookout Mountain, near Chattanooga.

The next day, men from the Army of the Cumberland stormed Missionary Ridge. At the same time, the flagboat and *Victory* escorted a convoy toward Nashville. While most of the fleet was detained below Ingram's Shoals, three boats steaming independently farther ahead managed to get over and waited for the Fitch convoy to appear. After sizing up the situation, the Hoosier officer left the *Victory* to guard the steamboats that had not gotten over. Fitch elected to push on to Harpeth Shoals, providing protection en route to those steamers that passed the first obstruction.

Before taking his leave of Acting Volunteer Ensign Read, Fitch completed some hours of work spent composing a response to Rear Adm. Porter's message of November 23, the one to which he had appended letters of concern from the quartermasters Meigs and Allen. After reviewing his progress since the 21st of October, the Eighth District commander once more proclaimed his record, indicating that no boats were forced to wait "even 10 minutes," as all were put through as fast as they arrived. "If the quartermaster at Clarksville or General Allen says that boats have been detained by us six days," the logbooks of his boats and testimony from their officers would prove "their statements to be incorrect."

Warming to his defense, the 28-year-old recited a number of problems which might have given the army concern, many of them occasioned by its own corporate forgetfulness or lack of understanding of river conditions. These were among the navy man's worries occasioned by his military colleagues: 1) the number of steamer sailings at present was so high that there were, in effect, 50 steamers to one gunboat; 2) steamers were sent up with no regularity, one at a time or perhaps one every two hours, making it impossible always to have a gunboat in waiting to give them immediate convoy; 3) due to poor management or want of knowledge, transports were started up the river more deeply laden than there was water in the channel, often with two or three equally overweight barges in tow; 4) even if the channel were deep enough for the overloaded, it was not wide enough; 5) it was these overly-heavy boats which had to be unloaded and lighted over the shoals, and if any boats were detained, it was these big ones engaged in the unloading and reloading process; 6) the deep-drafted boats also caused the navy delays as guardboats had to be posted, taking away from the number of tinclads available for escort duty; 7) the guards had either to flag down other boats to offload the overweight or wait until word reached a port where smaller vessels could be hired to come up and do the job under contract.

The frustrated Fitch, stung by the renewed criticisms, pointed a finger at the army gunboat service. If steamers were being held up a week at Smithland as the quartermasters contended, why did not the Clarksville quartermaster send the improvised military gunboats to convoy them up? "He had two all the time belonging to the army and subject to his orders," Fitch noted.

"It is certainly very discouraging to work as hard as we have to aid and assist the army, and to receive, on their part, only complaints in acknowledgement," Fitch concluded. The officer promised to continue to do everything he could to promote the public interest and would "leave it to time to show whether we have been blamed justly or not by the army."

This brief was sealed and readied to pass to the next dispatch steamer headed downstream. During the night, the tinclads were unexpectedly detained by shoals. Fitch, perhaps not wishing to state the obvious, had spoken of neither river conditions nor weather in that response to Porter which concerned Meigs and company.

Among the three steamers waiting to join the Fitch parade as it passed by on Thursday was the *Duke*, then at anchor off Canton, "usually a safe place." The town was not safe this day, however, as a group of guerrillas from Hopkinsville, being chased by Union horsemen, struck the river just before the *Moose* appeared. Blasts of cold winter wind now apparently blew the civilian steamer's stern into the riverbank and minutes later, a number of irregulars appeared, jumped aboard, and forced the craft to take them to the opposite shore. The raiders rifled the ship's safe and confiscated a barrel of sugar before escaping. Actually, the Eighth District commander believed the officers of the *Duke*, which craft had charged the government exorbitant towing prices the previous year, were in league with the enemy. "Unfortunately, nothing can be proven just now," he confessed, "but I may yet catch her." Later, Fitch would not be surprised to learn that the three boats were warned of the approach by the irregulars and that two of them had moved to be closer to the *Victory*. The *Duke* remained and was "ready for the guerrillas." The captains of the two steamers which had moved did not warn Fitch or Read.

Other Confederates attempting to cross in the vicinity of the *Duke* were not so fortunate and, like Morgan at Buffington earlier, were forced back by shells from the *Moose* as she now appeared and caught them. Taking the *Duke* under her wing, the tinclad continued upstream. Meanwhile, a group of irregulars, that had earlier passed within a mile of Fort Donelson but had not been sighted, fired on the steamers being guarded by the *Victory* below Ingram's Shoals. A few shells from the tinclad encouraged their rapid departure.

At Line Island, Fitch found his old flagboat, the *Fairplay*, shelling another irregular party, or maybe "a party of the same gang of guerrillas" that had supposedly taken over the *Duke*. The two tinclads nosed into the bank, from which Fitch sent detachments from both ashore to chase the Confederates. The locals were pursued about five miles in the direction of Waverly, but were not caught. The boats did not have the force to follow them farther inland so the sailors withdrew.

The situation in the great town below Nashville on the Tennessee was resolved by November 27 when Maj. Gen. Sherman happily wired Memphis commander Maj. Gen. Stephen A. Hurlbut: "We outwitted Bragg and drove him off Missionary Ridge." Unsupported by Longstreet who was still outside Knoxville, the Confederate leader took his men away from Chattanooga and back to north Georgia. The Union crisis in position and supply for the fortress city was resolved. Grant, according to veteran Ralsa Rice, expressing the sentiment of many, was now considered "invincible."

Back at the northern border of the Volunteer State, the Cumberland River was now rapidly rising. The *Moose* returned to Smithland briefly on the evening of November 27. After sending a short telegram to Rear Adm. Porter along with a fuller report placed in the mail, Fitch returned to his flagboat and weighed for Ingram's Shoals to relieve the *Victory*. Once the two tinclads made rendezvous, the *Victory* was permitted to run her convoy, which was already mostly over the obstruction. The *Moose* towed a pair of partially-filled coal barges up to Fort Donelson, where they were left for use of the convoy escorts, and continued on guarding the few steamers which had not passed up with the *Victory*.

Lt. Cmdr. Fitch was briefed at Nashville on the status of the Burnside relief expedition, which was still on hold. Despite pressure from Grant, Porter, Bowers, and Stockdale earlier in the month, the river, perhaps as Fitch anticipated, had conspired with winter to temporarily halt the supply project. The *Reindeer* and *Silver Lake*, still waiting to provide escort, were reassigned to Clarksville for patrol and perform convoy duties above Fort Donelson. The Indiana sailor departed for back downriver. He was pleased to find during his return to Kentucky that the river had reached "a good stage, falling slowly." As he passed over Harpeth Shoals, he found the water had reached a depth of about 10 feet.[12]

The *Moose* dropped anchor at Smithfield on December 2. At the telegram office, Fitch, who was still hoping to hear that the *Brilliant* was en route, found a communication from Rear Adm. Porter, to which he responded with a brief summary of his latest upstream mission. A longer report was left to reach Cairo by boat. With it was enclosed a tabulation of all Cumberland convoys for the month of November (after the 6th) completed the day before. A total of 108 boats, 24 barges, and 60 pontoons were guarded up the Cumberland without a single loss. No manner of obstruction (including a river that was low most of the time), deep-drafted steamers and barges that required lighting by other boats, guerrillas, and even a half-hearted job action by pilots seeking hazardous duty pay had impeded the Hoosier's convoys.

Fitch did not know it, of course, but Porter that very day sent a lengthy report on operations "lately carried on up the Tennessee and Cumberland rivers" to Navy secretary Welles. "The gunboats," he wrote, "have been extremely active and have achieved with perfect success all that was desired or required of them."[13]

Although Chattanooga was out of danger as the new month dawned, Knoxville was still invested by Lt. Gen. Longstreet. The cold Tennessee nights were often wet and the days dreary; the hours of daylight were shorter now than at any other time in the year. Still, from a nautical viewpoint, this climate was preferable to the hot, disease-ridden summers and low water. The Cumberland River convoys, shepherded by the tinclads of Le Roy Fitch's Eighth Division, continued without letup as the river stage increased. The siege of Knoxville was raised by December 7 and Longstreet's Confederates retreated thereafter deep into Dixie. The problem of getting supplies to the Union troops in Knoxville continued, as did the army's desire to push goods up the narrow but now-deeper Cumberland to Big South Fork. For the next couple of weeks, improvised steamers from Chattanooga would head up the Tennessee toward Knoxville, but their capacity was insufficient to meet that garrison's requirements.

On December 9, the *Moose* was at Fort Donelson where she had taken charge of three steamers loaded with private freight. The matter of private vs. public cargo being sent from the north to Nashville was a matter of concern to the navy, the army, and to merchants for some time. The previous rule was that no private freight could be carried aboard steamers, but Rear Adm. Porter gave his permission for two of the boats to drop small packages off for the garrison at Hopkinsville. No other private freight was permitted by Fitch to land elsewhere as he protected the trio upstream. Choosing to err on the side of caution and concerned about possible new rules on private trade with which he was unacquainted, he telegraphed Cairo for instructions before departing downriver.

Later in the day, Maj. Gen. Grant again messaged Porter on the matter of Cumberland River convoys. Being anxious to get a very large stock of provisions, forage, and quartermaster stores to Nashville, the theater commander was anxious that the steamers hauling it be both protected and expedited. Admitting that he did not know the best way to accomplish the two-tailed goal, he suggested that the admiral's Mississippi River course might prove the most advisable. There, the general noted, the river was divided into "beats" and each warship patrolled its "beat" every day, rather like a big city policeman. If that concept were transferred to the Cumberland, steamboats would be safe to pass however and whenever dispatched without convoy. In any event, Grant did not believe any gunboats would be required below Fort Donelson.

Grant appointed Col. Lewis B. Parsons the army's chief quartermaster of western river transportation on Wednesday, giving him an immense responsibility. All accounts for charter of steamers were ordered to his office for examination and settlement. Parsons, who would shortly streamline the way in which the government did business with steamer companies, received full authority to set rates for the transportation of troops and of freight. Under his direction, to quote Quartermaster Meigs, "all the resources of the immense steamboat interest of the West were brought to contribute to the regular, prompt, and abundant supply of the armies operating on the Mississippi and its tributaries."

It was this Col. Parsons, sensing perhaps the weight of the task he had been given, who delivered the major general's letter and spoke at length with Porter concerning the merits of the patrol concept advanced by the admiral's close friend. The station-keeping, anti-convoy idea, Parsons confided, was also supported by Brig. Gen. Allen at Louisville, who also advocated that the convoy system be scrapped in favor of a patrol system. Porter, who knew that Fitch had some success with assigned stations for counterinsurgency work in the summer past at low water on the Cumberland and Ohio and during the Morgan chase, passed Grant's letter on for review. Before changing a system of guardianship which he knew was not really broken, he wisely sought his subordinate's comments on the merits of "beats" for convoy protection.

Before leaving, Parsons also reviewed with the admiral his concerns over the navy's prohibition of private freight on the Cumberland River. Porter promised to lift the prohibition and order Fitch to stop halting such shipments. Parsons returned to his office, convinced that, once the water in the Cumberland was high enough, he would push "forward to Nashville vast stores of supplies at moderate rates." In the process, he knew he would have an ally in Brig. Gen. Allen, as well as Col. Donaldson, supply master of the Tennessee capital, and in his officer in charge of river transportation locally, Capt.. F. S. Winslow.[14]

The *Moose* was at Smithland on December 10. Fitch was in the habit of taking his tinclad back to the Kentucky rendezvous on a weekly basis not only to obtain communications but to "show the flag," so to speak, of a naval protective appearance at the river mouth. Increasingly, however, he had come to feel the need to spend more time upstream near the shoals where he could more effectively assist in sending through the great number of boats carrying government freight.

The Indiana sailor also had reports that many small guerrilla squads were hovering and collecting along the rivers. He was anxious to obtain additional howitzers for his craft so that he could put landing parties ashore to chase off bushwhackers. The *Brilliant* was still not down and her presence was sorely missed. Consequently, the *Springfield* assumed the guardianship of Smithland with the particular task of halting private steamers. Even though the river was "pretty low" again, that stage was not expected to persist much over a week.

Convoy work continued without fanfare through the remainder of December. Two dozen steamers were tied up at the Nashville docks on December 11, a number which swelled, in two days, to 35. All in the depot city were treated to a loud cannon salute on December 14 made, according to the next day's Nashville *Daily Union*, in honor of "recent victories of the national arms." The weather was now turning cold and severe. Large scale military operations in the Tennessee theater ceased, with all others limited to patrols and support missions.

Also in this period, Lt. Cmdr. Fitch mounted two amphibious attacks upon suspected guerrilla meeting places. In the first instance on December 17, a landing party was sent ashore opposite Seven Mile Island. It went out back of the bank about two miles and destroyed a distillery owned by a certain Dr. Lyle. The spot was, intelligence reported, being employed as a rendezvous for irregulars who were firing into river steamers. Several mounted men, "guerrillas" according to the navy, escaped the seamen. A second distillery, belonging to a Nolan, was destroyed five miles back of Palmyra the next day. Irregulars were said to have stayed at the place the night before. One wonders what impact such raids really may have had upon the ability of determined irregulars to gather—other than to perhaps have slightly slowed their libation preparation.

Orders were received aboard the *Moose* on December 19 for the removal of a quantity of pig iron from a great pile at the foot of Harpeth Shoals. Porter's ore would initially be stored in one of the two Fort Donelson barges for removal to Smithland once its coal was used. Later, it would be hauled down to Smithland in small lots aboard the tinclads. Fitch informed his chief in a confirming telegram that the river was at a good stage. Upon his return to Smithland the next day, the Hoosier found a letter from the admiral allowing so-called private boats up the river, so long as they conformed to the rules of strict convoy.

On December 21, Maj. Gen. Grant transferred his headquarters to Nashville, leaving Maj. Gen. Thomas in charge of the Department of the Cumberland at Chattanooga. The same day, Grant wired Maj. Gen. John Foster, Burnside's Knoxville successor, advising that he was "pushing forward everything possible for you with all rapidity." The pledge would be repeated the next day.[15]

On December 22, Fitch received a request from Grant, via Nashville's chief quartermaster, Col. Donaldson, for a gunboat to conduct a reconnaissance up the Cumberland to Big South Fork. Acting with alacrity, the convoy commodore immediately detailed his chief lieutenant, Acting Volunteer Lieutenant Glassford, to carry out the mission. Glassford was told to take the *Reindeer*, which was prepared to conduct such a role earlier in the month, to Nashville to learn the mission parameters from the commanding general himself. Fitch offered his subordinate only general instructions, choosing to leave most operational details to the enterprising volunteer. The *Reindeer*'s commander was warned to be very cautious, not to venture where there was insufficient water depth, and above all, not to be caught above shoals. The tinclad was needed back in good shape as soon as possible.

A former railroad executive, Lewis Parsons (1818–1907) was named chief quartermaster of western river transportation in December 1863. Parsons established rules and regulations for military logistical use of the western rivers, including the manner in which steamers were chartered. Parsons' impatient desire to force as many goods into Union supply depots as possible often resulted in letters of complaint to naval officers concerning convoy and escort matters (Library of Congress).

The *Reindeer* anchored at Nashville on December 23 and Acting Volunteer Lieutenant Glassford immediately went ashore to confer with Maj. Gen. Grant. The cigar-chomping general told the volunteer naval officer that his mission had three objectives: the convoy of supply steamers to Carthage, determination of the existence of any supplies of coal which might be barged down to Nashville, and a general reconnaissance as far upstream as possible — hopefully the whole 400 miles to the head of steamboat navigation at Big South Fork.

Meanwhile, Fitch wrote to Rear Adm. Porter advising him of his arrangement. It would have been possible, he confessed, to send a second boat as well; however, such an action would cause delay, if not danger, for the transports then under convoy below the Tennessee capital. The army could use its oak-covered gunboats in support of the *Reindeer* if it so chose.

It was Christmas week; several high-ranking Northern military leaders, such as Maj. Gen. Sherman, went home to celebrate. The navy's work on the Cumberland ceased only briefly. At Nashville, the men of the *Reindeer*, making ready for their expedition, were perhaps granted selective liberty to attend services at one of the city's many churches on Christmas Eve or Day. Maj. Gen. Grant wired Maj. Gen. Foster at Knoxville informing him that "two steamers here with three more to arrive loaded with stores for you." Upstream at Smithland, Lt. Cmdr. Fitch was on duty. It is not known whether his family was present with him or if it remained in Logansport. The latter is probable.

Early on Christmas Day, Maj. Gen. Foster telegraphed his superior that army depots were finished at Carthage and at Point Isabella at the mouth of the Big South Fork and that everything was ready for the receipt of stores. It was hoped that Point Isabella could be supplied first, but if that was not possible, the goods could be offloaded at Carthage and placed under guard. Maj. Gen. Grant replied informing the Knoxville chief that two steamers loaded with subsistence stores were prepared to leave that morning for Carthage under "charge of gunboats and guards."

Also on December 25, a boarding party from the U.S.S. *Moose* went aboard the steamer *General Siegel* to conduct a search for contraband goods. A number of lots of wines, brandies, and other suspicious items not on her manifest or reported to customs were found and the Eighth District chief consequently ordered her seized until he could personally investigate.

At some point in the day, perhaps after his Christmas dinner, Lt. Cmdr. Fitch also wrote a report to his superior entitled "Regarding the Suggestion of Major General Grant, U.S. Army, in the Matter of Protection of Transports." Penned in response to Porter's inquiry of December 10, Fitch's memo began with another reminder to the admiral that he was processing boats through as fast as possible. "But the army," he added, "seems to wish boats to go through entirely independent of us." If that were the case, Fitch was willing to try Grant's plan "as we will not then be held responsible."

The Hoosier bluntly indicated his belief, probably held for some time, that Maj. Gen. Grant simply did not understand "the shape and condition of the river here," otherwise he would not have made such a request when steamers were already being convoyed "without a moment's delay." If the general's plan were put into place, all the tinclads would have to do was patrol and convoy the private boats. On the other hand, such a scheme would certainly give Fitch more time "to get our men more perfectly drilled in exercise on shore."

As the winter afternoon darkened, these communications were placed into a mail sack and were sent aboard the steamboat *S. C. Baker* for Cairo.

On Boxing Day, Fitch wrote another detailed report to Rear Adm. Porter, this one outlining a skeleton organization for a landing party of small-arms men for his district. The document followed up on his earlier idea and detailed the formation of what was, in fact, a mini–Mississippi Marine Brigade. The plan was rich in detail down to and including the names of people from the different boats who were to be in charge of various parties. He was hopeful that the squadron commander would grant permission to assemble his group.[16]

Upstream that December 26, the U.S.S. *Reindeer*, with Army Lt. John S. Roberts' military steamer *Silver Lake No. 2* in company, departed Nashville for Carthage on the reconnaissance of the Cumberland River requested by Maj. Gen. Grant. In addition to the two warships, three transports, the *Hazel Dell*, *Mariner*, and *Hartupee*, went along with 140 sharpshooters and three officers from the 129th Illinois Volunteer Infantry embarked. Also along, though not mentioned in official reports, was Capt. John W. Donn of the U.S. Coast Survey. The little task group chugged and puffed the 150 miles from Nashville to Carthage without incident, arriving off that town just after noon on December 28.

Acting Volunteer Lieutenant Glassford interviewed a number of local citizens and soldiers and then went to the telegraph office to send a long wire to Grant. In his message, the volunteer naval officer reported that a large quantity of excellent and already-mined coal, maybe half a million bushels, was lying on the bank in the vicinity of Olympus, in Overton County, about 50 miles from the mouth of Obey's River. His informants believed barges could take it out if the army first cleared the area of local irregulars. During the night, Glassford discerned the possibility of a considerable rise in the river's depth which boded well for their endeavor.

After conferring with Lt. Col. A. J. Cropsey of the 129th, Glassford, the overall group commander, determined that 100 soldiers would be left to guard the transports while they were unloaded at Carthage. Cropsey and 40 of his best men transferred aboard the *Reindeer* and *Silver Lake No. 2* at daylight on the morning of December 29. Before their departure, Glassford and Cropsey were warned that a part of Jackson County, south of the Cumberland and Overton as far east as the Obey's River, was a hotbed of guerrilla activity. This well-merited reputation would be fully appreciated by the two officers as they passed through.

The Cumberland River above Carthage winds northeast with a shape something roughly akin to a pair of W's end to end. The progress of the noisy, smoky gunboats was easily observed by residents and as easily communicated. As the craft approached the Jackson County line, irregulars turned out in significant numbers, perhaps as high as 200, to contest their intrusion. Their leaders were believed to include Oliver P. Hamilton, John M. Hughs, Champ Ferguson, and Robert V. Richardson. As Acting Volunteer Lieutenant Glassford later put it, the "whole region seemed roused." Choosing the tops of precipitous bluffs or cliffs, bands numbering from 10 to 15 men up to 75 to 100 concealed themselves in the thick timber or behind rocks and boulders waiting to loose volleys of small arms fire on the steamers.

The *Reindeer* and *Silver Lake No. 2* were taken under fire five times on the 29th. At Ray's Ferry, a party of 15 or 20 men shot into the gunboats; the ambushes were repeated by 15 or 20 men at Flynn's Lick, 40 or 50 at Gainesboro, 15 or 20 at Ferris woodyard, and at Bennett's Ferry, 2 miles below Celina, by 80 to 100.

The Confederates' positions, Glassford later reported, "availed them nothing, however, against the guns of this vessel and those of the *Silver Lake No. 2*; they were completely shelled out of them whenever they let us see them after a few volleys." Lt. Col. Cropsey allowed as how the Rebels "manifested much zeal and skill," but were no match for the gunboats which quickly dislodged them with shot and shell "in fine style under the supervision of Captain Glassford." So well positioned was the enemy that his flight after each attack was easy. Cropsey did not land his sharpshooters or attempt any kind of foot pursuit.

This is not to say that the Rebel assaults accomplished nothing. The stacks and upper works of the *Reindeer*, which were already damaged by all of the trees and low-hanging brush through which she was passing, were perforated with bullet holes. Additionally, the bulkheading on the boiler deck, always weak and defective, was almost destroyed by the firing of the howitzers. Considerable repair, if not replacement, would be required before the officers could again occupy their quarters. Damage to the *Silver Lake No. 2* is not recorded, though it is probable that she was also riddled. Although the Army sharpshooters apparently had no luck against the bushwhackers, no Yankee soldiers or bluejackets were killed, but two were wounded.

While passing Gainesboro, Acting Volunteer Lieutenant Glassford toyed with the idea of stopping to destroy the place much as his superior, Lt. Cmdr. Fitch, had torched Palmyra earlier in the year. The town was supposedly a notorious rendezvous for irregulars and Rear Adm. Porter was on record as having ordered it destroyed. Still, Glassford had learned, quite possibly from Maj. Gen. Grant, that Governor Andrew Johnson wanted to build a military post in the community and would need the town's buildings. For that reason alone, Gainesboro survived. The residents of other small hamlets en route were intimidated by the gunboats, which threw shells at them, according to historian Byrd Douglas, "on the theory that 'guerrillas' [among them] were sniping at the boats."

After what Capt. Donn later called a hundred mile or more "running fight with guerrillas," the two gunboats reached the mouth of Obey's River. There a quantity of loose coal was found, partially burned by the Confederates. It was a small portion of a partially-burned cache of 500,000 bushels that was dumped in 1861. The pile had been partially transferred up the 50 miles from an interior coal mine near the town of Olympus. Lt. Roberts' boat, now almost out of fuel, was ordered to stop and coal from the piles while the *Reindeer* provided cover and gave Capt. Donn a chance to examine the navigational features of the stream. While this was occurring, Acting Volunteer Lieutenant Glassford noticed a certain uneasiness among the people on shore and decided to back off into mid-stream to investigate. A half mile downstream, he came upon the head of a mounted guerrilla band approaching toward the coal dump. Apparently the Rebels believed both boats were in Obey's River, jammed among the branches of the trees that overhung the banks and scooping up the precious fuel. Any idea of an attack on the part of the horsemen was "dispersed with a few rounds of shrapnel and canister."

Moving into Union County, the gunboats found the populace well disposed towards the United States, with many on the bank cheering them instead of shooting. The gunboats crossed over the Tennessee-Kentucky state line and reached Creelsboro, Kentucky, about 12:30 P.M. on December 30. There Acting Volunteer Lieutenant Glassford took stock of his magazine and recorded his expenditure thus far: 57 rounds of shell, 62 rounds of shrapnel, three rounds of canister. If need be, he could continue fighting, ahead or on the way back, with the 81 rounds of shell, 75 rounds of shrapnel, and 48 rounds of canister which remained. There was just 65 miles to go before the expedition reached the mouth of the Big South Fork.

Then forward progress ceased. The weather changed significantly late on December 30, becoming extremely cold. Overnight, the level in the Cumberland declined by four feet, giving unmistakable signs of a fall. Having determined that there would be no coal barges available for towing to Nashville before the February rise, the mission commander elected to return down stream. Leaving the *Silver Lake No. 2* as guard boat at Carthage, Glassford, with Cropsey as passenger, returned to Nashville on January 3, 1864.[17]

Eighteen sixty-three closed for Lt. Cmdr. Le Roy Fitch as it began with action by his flotilla on the Cumberland River in support of the U.S. Army. This busy period was filled with danger, excitement, success, and some setbacks for the Indiana sailor. When taken together, these 12 months were probably the best—and professionally most-stressful—the 28-year-old would ever experience. Never again would he receive the thanks of his government or know the thrill of concluding such a successful combination as the one he had put together on the Ohio River in July. Still, there were a few more big adventures ahead, including brief command of an ironclad monitor in the last major battle in the Western theater.

CHAPTER TEN

Building a Fleet, Fort Pillow, and a Second Summer on the Ohio, January–September 1864

As 1863 turned into 1864, the Civil War in the west was pretty much on hold due to a severe winter, the worst prolonged spate of bad weather experienced during the entire conflict. Lt. Cmdr. Le Roy Fitch was shepherding a convoy up the Cumberland River from Smithland, Kentucky, to Nashville as Acting Volunteer Lieutenant Henry Glassford returned from a reconnaissance of that stream above the Tennessee capital. The latter mission had been delegated by Fitch, at the order of Maj. Gen. Ulysses S. Grant, commander of the Department of the Mississippi, to examine the possibility of running supply convoys to the head of navigation at Big South Fork. At the same time as Glassford's expedition was underway, Grant, beginning on December 26, undertook his own inspection trip, checking the condition of his men, their garrisons and supplies. "The Army of the Ohio had been getting supplies over Cumberland Gap until their animals had nearly all starved," and the general wanted to find out for himself "if there was any possible chance of using that route in the spring, and if not to abandon it."

Grant's route, by steamboat, railroad, and horse, took him over a rough, rectangle-shaped route from Nashville to Chattanooga to Knoxville to Lexington, Kentucky, and back to Nashville by January 12. "It was an intensely cold winter," he remembered years later. "The thermometer being down as low as zero every morning for more than a week while I was at Knoxville and on my way from there on horseback to Lexington, KY." Of particular immediate interest to Fitch and Glassford when informed was the degree of difficulty the theater commander found in his six-day ride from Strawberry Plains, near Knoxville, to Lexington. The badly-cut up and frozen road over Cumberland Gap was so strewn with broken wagons and dead animals that Grant was reminded of his arrival at Chattanooga just weeks earlier.

The need was obvious to the Ohio-born general that Fitch's Eighth District of the U.S. Navy's Mississippi Squadron, together with his own army gunboats, would have to oversee supply convoys to the Big South Fork. "I am satisfied," he wrote to Maj. Gen. Henry Halleck on January 15, "that no portion of our supplies can be hauled by teams from Camp Nelson." The chief general in Washington was informed that "on the first rise of the Cumberland, 1,200,000 rations will be sent to the mouth of the Big South Fork." The road from that point to Knoxville was better than that over the Cumberland Gap. Until that goal could be accomplished, the troops in the East Tennessee citadel would have to live off the land and on what little could be sent by rail and up the Tennessee by improvised steamer from Chattanooga.[1]

An early effort was made to get supplies by river to Carthage. However, the same irregulars that menaced the reconnaissance of Acting Volunteer Lieutenant Glassford at the beginning of the year continued to contest the U.S. Army's logistical passage. On January 24, Lt. Cmdr. Fitch wired Rear Adm. Porter from Smithland informing the Cairo-based squadron commander that he was departing for "up the river" that very night. Word had been received that the transports at Carthage were in danger from guerrillas and the "Army gunboats not sufficient to protect them." The *Silver Lake* would be left as station boat at the Kentucky base to receive orders and guard the coal barges. Fitch would be back as soon as possible.

Fitch arrived at Nashville aboard the U.S.S. *Moose* on January 26. Going ashore to army headquarters, he conferred with Brig. Gen. Eleazer Paine, Lt. Col. Theodore S. Bowers and others and then confirmed to Porter that "the exigency of the service at the present moment requires that we should take some little risk, as the army above need supplies very much." From information coming into the Tennessee capital that morning, it seemed "that the entire population of Jackson County" was rising to prevent the transports from getting through. The Hoosier officer believed his old foe, John Hunt Morgan, was behind the resistance; "I believe it is thought that this will be Morgan's first endeavor to cut off supplies." Fitch secretly relished a rematch. "I trust that for our benefit," he wrote Porter, "the enemy may stick to his purpose."

As the Union Navy's top Western convoy commodore prepared for the expedition, the *Newsboy* returned to Carthage carrying a few soldiers and, more importantly, information that a thousand others would follow. Meanwhile, Fitch, who was not exactly certain of what he faced in Jackson County, was relatively certain of the condition of affairs which he left behind. "I have got the guerrillas pretty well cleared off the river from Nashville down to Smithland" and believed there was really no significant danger from them on that stretch at this time. He did not mention that cold weather probably helped his counterinsurgency efforts. Still, "to guard against any accident," he was leaving three good boats in the lower part of the Cumberland: *Fairplay*, *Silver Lake*, and *Springfield*.

Next morning, the *Moose, Reindeer, and Victory*, the tinclads especially acquired as super light draughts to handle shallow streams, departed for Carthage. The river was falling very slowly, but it was hoped that there would be no danger as it was expected to rise again in a day or so. It was possible, if a rise did not occur, that the Eight District commander might be detained above a week or two, but that was not considered a likelihood given the expected wetness of the season.

The convoy reached Carthage without incident late on January 27. There they found eight steamers loaded for Point Pleasant and the Big South Fork, along with the army gunboats *Newsboy* and the *Silver Lake 2*. After a brief conference in which he stressed how important it was to get provisions through to the forces at Big South Fork who needed them badly,

Ten. Building a Fleet, Fort Pillow, and a Summer on the Ohio (1864)

Fitch left Glassford in charge of the convoy, giving him also the *Victory*. The *Reindeer*, though still hurting from her previous mission, would be ample with the *Victory* and the two army boats for the convoy. Any more, the Indiana sailor judged, would, owing to the narrowness of the river, "be in the way." Believing it would be a week before there was sufficient water to let the convoy over the shoals, Fitch took the *Moose* back to Nashville, where she arrived on the morning of January 29.

From Nashville, Lt. Cmdr. Fitch sent a detailed report of his visit to Carthage on to his superior at Cairo. The *Moose* then steamed down to Smithland where she arrived on the last day of the month to find new orders from Rear Adm. Porter, dated January 24, requiring his immediate return to Nashville. Reviewing his Carthage trip in four short sentences of a six-sentence telegraph, the Hoosier informed Porter that he would coal and immediately proceed back up to Nashville at flank speed.[2]

Weather had a significant impact on logistical operations up and down the Cumberland in the first two months of 1864. During January and early February, ice clogged the Ohio River in the Cincinnati-Louisville area making it very difficult—in some cases, impossible—to push through stores and rations to Nashville in large quantities. At Evansville, ice nearly crushed the army's harbor-defense boat *Lou Eaves* and brought a lull in navigation so profound as to allow ice-skating across the river. Although climate conditions also caused a dwindling in guerrilla activities, still, Maj. Gen. Grant was impatient that the supply chain not fail. On January 15, he wired Brig. Gen. Robert Allen in Louisville advising that, until the rivers were navigable, available rail cars could be used to forward forage rather than rations.

By February, both railroads and river from Chattanooga were avenues of supply to Knoxville, and that post was hanging on with minimal succor. Acting Volunteer Lieutenant Glassford's Cumberland convoy above Carthage was, with difficulty, making its way through toward Big South Fork. Brig. Gen. Paine's punitive expedition killed 33 Rebels and captured 63, but most of the butternut irregulars avoided fighting and hid in the hilly terrain. The sweep, though less than fruitful, was followed by continued gunboat patrols and supply runs to the Burnside Point area into the summer.

The arrival of goods from the north into the main Nashville depot had, on the other hand, slowed to an alarming point by mid-month. On February 11, Maj. Gen. Grant telegraphed Brig. Gen. Allen complaining that "supplies are only reaching here to supply daily consumption. Cannot a large amount of stores be forwarded while the river is navigable?" The theater commander's wire was only one of several sent that Thursday, all of which would, sooner or later, have an impact upon the activities of Lt. Cmdr. Le Roy Fitch.

Upon receipt of Grant's message, Brig. Gen. Allen, the Louisville supply chief, responded with a litany of goods shipped by river from his port and New Albany over the past 10 days. Included in the tally was 13,000 barrels of flour, two million pounds of pork and bacon, 500,000 pounds of bread, 3,200 tons of hay, 34,000 bushels of corn, and 50,000 bushels of oats "all independent of shipments" by the railroad. Three times that amount of grain was en route from St. Louis. Every boat "within our reach, with the boats returning from Nashville and such others as we may be able to procure," would, within the next 10 days, be put on the Nashville run.

Col. Louis B. Parsons, chief quartermaster of western river transportation, was also in frigid Louisville and joined in the discussion with Nashville. He reminded Grant that "it is really only 11 or 12 days since the ice gorge broke so boats could get out at all. There were few boats here or at Cincinnati then, but they were scattered everywhere." Now that the Ohio was passable, nearly 40 boats at the two cities were loaded or were in the process of being loaded for Nashville, with some taking on a second load from Evansville. Parsons went on to confirm for his superior a problem which Lt. Cmdr. Fitch, as convoy shepherd, had been facing all winter: "With the present low stage of the river, none but small boats can get over Harpeth Shoals." The number of boats available was currently limited and barges were being sought. Still, once everything was organized, Parsons was confident: "With a little rise in the river, your levee will soon be covered with stores."

To make certain that the Nashville levee was, indeed, ready, Maj. Gen. Grant, on February 24, once again suspended all private freight shipments on the Cumberland. Fitch, who had only recently received his admiral's instructions to guard the renewal of this traffic, was probably not displeased. Three days later, all of the private freight handlers working at the Nashville wharf were directed to transfer their operations across the river to the Edgefield levee or to move on up to the Nashville landing located above the waterworks. Brig. Gen. Allen's stepped up delivery schedule required the city's major wharves be able to easily handle military shipments.[3]

While these developments were unfolding, another Army plan to develop secure and more plentiful transportation was unfolding on the Tennessee-Alabama border.

The reader will recall how, as related in Chapter 7, Maj. Gen. Rosecrans in January 1863 had proposed the building of several light draft army gunboats or the armoring and arming of transport steamboats (the 20th century classification "armed merchant cruiser" comes to mind). These vessels, which would have supplemented the Navy's hard-pressed Cumberland and Tennessee River escort warships, were not built at the time, largely because of opposition from Secretary of War Edwin Stanton and Quartermaster General Montgomery C. Meigs, who deferred the building of river escort vessels to the USN. Although the army did convert several steamers, like the *Newsboy*, into gunboats, Rosecrans' idea of gun-decked craft did not get off the ground—at least not immediately.

"Old Rosy" Rosecrans was gone from the Department of the Cumberland by mid–October 1863, with Maj. Gen. Grant following him in, determined to raise the siege of Chattanooga and to provide victuals and other stores to his soldiers both in that town and up the Tennessee in Knoxville. Expanding on the groundwork laid by Rosecrans, the Union Army opened the "cracker line" into the Chattanooga, employing a crudely-built flat-bottomed steamer named for the town. Constructed at Bridgeport, Alabama, by army assistant quartermaster and Detroit native Capt. Arthur Edwards, the Lake Erie shipbuilder and mechanic Mr. Turner, and a number of carpenters and other army personnel, the *Chattanooga* opened a hazardous Tennessee River supply run on October 29 through the winding channel of the Narrows, with its swift currents, to Rankin's Ferry, where her cargo was off-loaded into wagons for the final trip to the besieged city. Her trip opened a new chapter in Tennessee River military transport and launched the chain of nautical events which brought Lt. Cmdr. Le Roy Fitch into the story.[4]

As the *Chattanooga* engaged in her early logistical feat, Assistant Secretary of War Charles A. Dana, a Rosecrans critic, remained in Chattanooga continuing to send, as he had for weeks, a series of updating telegrams to Secretary Stanton in Washington. Dana, together with U.S. Grant, were convinced of the value of the upper Tennessee River in the logistical chain to Knoxville. Quartermaster General Meigs already had plans to increase the number of steamers on the stream and all three men recognized the importance of protecting

Ten. Building a Fleet, Fort Pillow, and a Summer on the Ohio (1864)

To support the supply requirements of Chattanooga and the Upper Tennessee River, the U.S. Army began building a fleet of light draught steamers at Bridgeport, Alabama, in the fall of 1863. Lt. Cmdr. Fitch was detailed by Rear Adm. Porter to offer his expertise and advice to the construction chief, Capt. Arthur Edwards, in the fall of 1863 and spring of 1864 (National Archives).

them. Capt. Edwards' boatyard, opened at Bridgeport, below Chattanooga, rapidly constructed thirteen boats, "four of which were partially iron-clad." The feat was regarded by Col. Parsons as "worthy of record among the remarkable incidents of the war."

Although some rightly credited "Old Rosy" with the gunboat notion, it was Dana, who, in the absence of the controversial commander, was able to dust off the concept and bring it back to life. Many times in Civil War reporting, it is difficult to find the exact document in which an idea was launched (or in this case, re-launched). This time, we have it— a November 4, 1863, report from Dana to Stanton. While reviewing the transportation situation for his chief, the one-time managing editor of the *New York Tribune* put the whole matter into one sentence: "I suggest that gunboats of very light draught should be provided for this part of the Tennessee."

By the beginning of 1864, two different plans were afoot to provide transport and gunboat services on the upper Tennessee. The first was revealed to Rear Adm. Porter in Col. Parson's January 5 letter concerning the lifting of the navy's embargo on private steamers entering the Cumberland. The army would attempt to get two small steamers, the *Alone* and *Convoy #2*, that Parsons was about to purchase at St. Louis, up the Tennessee and over Muscle Shoals to Chattanooga. Other steamers then being constructed at Bridgeport would also serve on the upper stream.

On January 10, Porter, no fan of stern-wheelers, advised the army's river transport quartermaster to build side-wheel vessels and not to employ tubular boilers. Indeed, it was recommended that the purpose-built craft be equipped with very large boilers and large cylinders. At this point, Porter believed that Parsons was discussing steamers which would be built at Bridgeport by Capt. Edwards. These were the thirteen referenced above as being worthy of record. Work on this fleet required that Edwards, who initially had neither mechanics nor local material with which to work, obtain all of his machinery and most of his other material from manufacturers on the Ohio or in St. Louis. The orders had then to be transported 600–800 miles overland by already over-taxed railroad trains.

The following week, Maj. Gen. Grant weighed into the matter, strongly endorsing Quartermaster General Meigs' plan for the construction of armed steamers. By this time, Meigs, with a thousand other logistical matters on his mind for armies fighting in both the east and west, had also consulted with Norman Wiard, proprietor of a New York shipyard. Under government contract, Wiard had undertaken, starting in October, to built four shallow-draft gunboats for use on the bays, rivers, and sounds on the East Coast. Plans were actually drawn for the vessels and made available to the War Department, along with a pamphlet describing their layout.

On January 15, Meigs showed a copy of the Grant letter to Assistant Navy Secretary Gustavus V. Fox and, as they did a year earlier, the two men talked over the army's latest gunboat idea. Fox advised Meigs to send over a copy of the Grant memo, along with a note asking that it be forwarded to Rear Adm. Porter "with such instructions as may be proper." Meigs was nothing if not a whirlwind and immediately complied. To further launch the gunboat concept, Meigs went back to his office and sent to Capt. Edwards at Bridgeport a copy of the Wiard pamphlet. Edwards was then building several new steamers for use by the army. While in Louisville at Christmas time, Meigs had contracted for engines for two side-wheelers and four stern-wheelers. The next day, Friday, he wrote to Lt. Col. Langdon C. Easton, chief quartermaster of the Army of the Cumberland and Edward's superior, at Chattanooga on the matter.

The Easton letter spelled out Meigs' thinking on the two plans then under consideration. It would not be possible, he believed, to float steamers over Muscle Shoals from the lower to the upper Tennessee. He knew of the two steamers were already being fitted out in St. Louis to make the attempt, but the quartermaster general was not optimistic that the river would rise to the height necessary to let them pass. Knowing that Grant was "very desirous of having some gunboats on the upper Tennessee"—and by that he meant proper gun-decked craft, not *Newsboy*-type improvisations—Meigs was quite specific as to the layout he wanted. He knew from his talks with Fox that the USN would furnish armament and officers.

Meigs ordered Easton to instruct Edwards to finish at least two of his steamers—one each side-wheeler and stern-wheeler—on the general plan outlined in the Wiard blueprints. The hulls would be built after the style of the already-finished *Lookout* and the side-wheeler currently on Edwards' stocks, but their cabins, yawls, derricks, and other accessories plus armament would be prepared and arranged for a crew per Wiard's plan.

On January 18, Navy secretary Welles forwarded a copy of the Grant letter which Meigs had given Fox out to Rear Adm. Porter at Cairo. The commander of the Mississippi Squadron was authorized to extend whatever aid was within his power "toward arming and manning the boats to which Quartermaster Meigs refers." Porter, who was making extensive prepara-

Top: Captain Edwards' boatyard constructed several supply steamers to support the logistical needs of Federal forces in the Chattanooga area. Four are lined up at the bank in this photograph, along with a coal barge anchored in the stream abreast of the *Lookout* (second in line) (U.S. Army Military History Institute). *Bottom:* The *Lookout*, like many Western steamers, carried a field piece manned by a U.S. Army gun crew. In a pinch, such vessels could be used as naval auxiliaries (National Archives).

tions for his own expedition to the Red River area of Louisiana, ordered Lt. Cmdr. Fitch to go to Alabama and review Capt. Edward's gunboat-building enterprise and to render whatever assistance was required. The *Moose* dropped anchor at Nashville on February 5 and her commander rushed to the telegraph office to wire his superior that he was en route. Valise in hand, the Indiana sailor boarded a train and set off for Bridgeport. The trip would be the first of at least three the Logansport officer would make beyond his district boundaries this year as squadron inspector or fireman.[5]

Lt. Cmdr. Fitch was one of the highest ranking, if not the senior, naval officer to visit Bridgeport thus far in the war. Who met the Indiana sailor at the Alabama community, whether Col. Easton or Capt. Edwards, both or neither, is unknown. It is clear that he consulted with his U.S. Army quartermaster colleagues, who undoubtedly showed him around. At Edwards' Tennessee River shipyard, Fitch saw a pair of stern-wheelers which were just about ready to begin transport service. Both were 140 feet in length with 23 foot beams and depths of hold of 3.5 feet. One of the craft, the one furthest from being finished, had been christened *Missionary*.

The Hoosier seaman was also impressed with a large side-wheeler that was ready to be launched as soon as the water rose high enough to permit it. She was, with a 175 foot length and 27 foot beam, just right for use a transport, but was too large for a gunboat. Engines from the *Dunbar*, that notorious ex–Confederate steamer which Fitch had chased up over Muscle Shoals the previous spring, would outfit the new craft, which could be ready for service within four to six weeks.

The army officers told Fitch of the dire need for transports on the upper Tennessee, boats far more sophisticated than the little *Chattanooga* of the Cracker Line. They explained that the army would remain in the southern Tennessee citadel for some time and that goods would flow by river from that point, as well as Nashville and Carthage, into east Tennessee. Rail and road supply would, of course, continue as possible or appropriate.

The navy consultant and his army guests reviewed the Wiard plans which Capt. Edwards had received from Quartermaster Meigs. It was readily apparent that the draft, for a double-ender gunboat, would be totally inefficient on the Tennessee or Cumberland. Among other blueprint failures quickly ascertained, the guns were all unprotected and their crews totally exposed. As Fitch later wrote Porter, Yankee tars aboard such craft "could be picked off to a man by guerrillas from either side of the river." The Wiard concept was rejected in favor of the tinclad idea already in service.

With these points in mind, the Cumberland convoy chief offered several suggestions to the military builders. First, two boats, for which frames were about to be set up, should be finished as gundeck tinclads. Those now finishing should be completed as transports. The two boats to be built as gunboats would be side-wheelers. It was expected that they would both have dimensions of 160 foot length, 25 foot beam, and four foot holds. The pair should carry as light an armament as possible, in order that they could also carry freight if necessary.

For security and morale effect, Fitch strongly suggested that the *Missionary* be completed as a hybrid gunboat-transport. To accomplish that end, he suggested that she be outfitted with a pair of 12-pounder howitzers on boat carriages, which could be manned by 12 men, two boys, and with a master's mate serving as detail commander. This would not, he argued, detract from her qualities as a transport, but would demonstrate the precedence of a gunboat. When the two being purpose-built were completed, the *Missionary*'s two guns could

Ten. Building a Fleet, Fort Pillow, and a Summer on the Ohio (1864)

be removed and sent to one of them. It was anticipated that the vessel would be ready for temporary service, with her guns in, within a fortnight.

Fitch, as noted earlier, was something of a howitzer aficionado and had considerable experience in arming and manning naval vessels. Rear Adm. Porter wanted his insights on both construction and ordnance placement as they impacted the Bridgeport gunboats and the army's request that the navy handle matters of armament and crewing. The Hoosier was not bashful in supplying his superior with detailed recommendations, which, based on his discussions with Edwards, he may have worked out during his train ride back to Nashville.

Fitch suggested that the two side-wheeler gunboats carry four guns each, two 24-pounder howitzers (one each in the bow and the stern) and a pair of rifled 12-pdrs. The bow and stern guns could work abaft either beam, ahead and right astern. The two broadside guns could work from two points abaft the beam to within one point of right ahead. Each boat should be crewed by 40 officers and ratings, led by an ensign. It would be simple to transport the men, guns, and ammunition, the Logansport native opined. If they could be sent to Smithland, Fitch could take them to Nashville aboard the *Moose* and send them by rail directly down to the boats.

Upon his return to Nashville on February 7, Lt. Cmdr. Fitch posted his Bridgeport report to Rear Adm. Porter and set off aboard his flagboat for Smithland, with the *Springfield* and *Fairplay* in company. The *Moose* and her consorts stopped in the evening at the foot of Harpeth Shoals to pick up a cargo of pig iron for transport down to the mouth of the Cumberland. While they were loading, a party interested in the iron appeared with a safeguard from Nashville commander Maj. Gen. Lovell Rousseau. Fitch, who had seizure orders from Porter to remove the iron, refused to recognize Rousseau's protection. The Eighth District leader not only continued to acquire the cargo, but left the *Springfield* to guard what was left until he could get up again to finish loading the remainder.

The process of transporting down the iron was completed by February 11. On that date, Rear Adm. Porter passed down the Cumberland, returning to Cairo aboard the flagship *Black Hawk* from an inspection of ironclads at Cincinnati. As he passed Smithland, it was noticed that three tinclads were at the rendezvous, where only one, keeping station, was usually expected. When he reached Cairo later in the evening, the Mississippi Squadron commander asked Fleet Captain Alexander Pennock to wire Fitch first thing in the morning asking why his boats were not out on patrol or escorting convoys. Upon receipt of the telegram, the Indiana sailor immediately replied that the *Moose* and *Fairplay* had just arrived from Nashville and were unloading the last of the seized pig iron. The *Silver Lake*, also in port, was having her boiler patched.

Fitch, still sensitive to any possible criticism that he might not be doing his utmost with regard to convoys and counterinsurgency patrols, reported that the river stage was still too low to get his coal barge up to Fort Donelson. Consequently, it was necessary for his boats to come back to Smithland for fuel. Porter, who had not stopped while passing, and Pennock were reassured: "There are no boats here longer than is absolutely necessary for repairs or to discharge pig iron, and coal."

Upon his return to Smithland on February 14 from yet another convoy run, Fitch found a report from Acting Volunteer Lieutenant Glassford, dated February 9, detailing his progress to Burnside Point, Kentucky, on the upper Cumberland. The mission, which had begun prior to Fitch's visit to Bridgeport, was difficult, but the captain of the *Reindeer* was making progress in seeing the steamers hauled through the shoals, discharged, coaled and prepared for their return. It was anticipated that the army at South Gap would have rations for some time and that the fleet would return downriver within a week on the expected rise. Other than this report and what he had picked up at Bridgeport, Fitch knew little about affairs in Knoxville. Quartermaster General Meigs later reported that the repair of the railroad between Chattanooga and Knoxville during the course of the winter largely relieved the necessity for supply steamers to run between those two cities.

Rumors of guerrilla and irregular activities throughout his area of responsibility continued to reach Fitch at Smithland. He was particularly concerned and on his guard for Rebel activities in Kentucky or attempts to disrupt river traffic along that state's northern border. Guerrilla bands in the western part of the Bluegrass State had also increased their assaults on the local African American population, hoping to damage Union recruitment and cause the Yankees additional loyalty concerns. Farther to the south and west, his old nemesis, Nathan Bedford Forrest, was about to encounter the cavalry of Brig. Gen. William Sooey Smith as it advanced on Meridian from Memphis.

On his way to Bridgeport, Lt. Cmdr. Fitch had asked his superior whether or not he should make a trip "up the Kanawha with a couple of boats to look around." The Kanawha was among the most distant points from Smithland of any in the Eighth District, but the Hoosier officer had not been in that area since the previous July. If he did go, it would be possible to leave everything in the Cumberland "perfectly safe."

Porter had promised Fitch another boat to patrol the upper Ohio and Kanawha and so the convoy commodore did not believe it necessary to send a tinclad from the Cumberland to the Kanawha for any length of time. Indeed, Fitch, in a report of February 14 that accompanied Glassford's to Cairo, suggested a program for optimal employment of the Smithland-based flotilla over the next several months. His proposed program had four points.

First, the Hoosier officer would continue his work of supervision and employ his influence to push forward the construction of the Bridgeport gunboats. These had to be armed and equipped in time to take advantage of the spring rise. Next, he would hold two boats in readiness to run another supply convoy to the Big South Fork. Third, patrols would be continued along the Cumberland from Smithland to Nashville and back. These patrols would coincide with convoy escort. Finally, while the Bridgeport work was being finished, Fitch would make a hasty trip to the Kanawha, would settle up pending divisional matters at Cincinnati, would attempt to recruit as many Ohio River sailors as possible, and then would return to Nashville and personally see to the arming of the Bridgeport boats and their entry into operations. With some exceptions, this is the schedule Fitch would follow for the next several months.[6]

The remainder of February and March was taken up in Lt. Cmdr. Fitch's datebook with fulfillment of the first three points on the program he had submitted to his superior. First in priority, of course, was river patrol and convoy. Despite the order in which he had numbered his agenda recommendations, the convoy commodore knew that his first responsibility was in assisting the army to get its supply steamers through. During February, a total of 178 steamers delivered 35,860 tons of goods to Nashville. In March, the number grew to 213, with 62,666 tons. While these cargos were coming in, Nashville quartermaster Col. Donaldson and his river assistant, Capt. Winslow, had set to work building a third levee at the waterfront and upgrading the original two. This process would be completed by April.[7]

During the first week of March, the U.S.S. *Moose* visited Cincinnati so that her com-

Ten. Building a Fleet, Fort Pillow, and a Summer on the Ohio (1864)

mander might check on the naval rendezvous in the Queen City, as well as local USN recruiting. The tinclad was serviced and Fitch looked into the latest material possibilities for the boats under construction in Alabama. In his absence, the Cumberland convoys and steamboat sailings continued unabated. On March 8, the riverfront and levee, according to the next day's Nashville *Times*, "presented a lively appearance" with almost "fifty boats in port." It was the largest number of transports reported at the Tennessee capital on a single day during the war.

Back at Nashville by the 14th, the 28-year-old again took the train to Bridgeport. Upon his arrival, he learned one of the lessons Capt. Edwards had earlier been taught—shortages could cause delays. Work was halted on the gunboats and transports for several days prior to Fitch's arrival because requisitioned spikes and nails had not arrived.

Still, work seemed to be "progressing as well as could be expected under the circumstances." Rear Adm. Porter's designated consultant was at the Alabama boatyard for the launch of the first steamer, "a beautiful model," which Fitch believed would "compare favorably with any side-wheel boat." It was hoped that when the builders were ready to put up the casemates on the craft, Acting Naval Constructor Charles F. Kendall might visit from Cairo for a day or two to provide direction in the minutiae of fitting chocks, etc.

Taking his leave of the army shipwrights, the Indiana sailor returned to the Cumberland River, from which he wrote to Porter on March 18 informing him of his Bridgeport visit. In that report, he suggested that at least one of the new gunboats, which were all to honor army generals, be named for the admiral. Given that the Quartermaster Department was paying $19,000 per copy for the boats which it would own and only charter to the navy, such a designation for any of them was unlikely.

To maintain cordial interservice relations, Fitch hoped to see Ulysses S. Grant at Louisville at the end of the month, upon the general's return from Washington, D.C. He was not aware that Maj. Gen. Grant, newly promoted to lieutenant general, had been asked by the government to go east permanently. Maj. Gen. William T. Sherman traveled to Nashville on March 18 to relieve his fellow Buckeye as commander of the Military Division of the Mississippi. Sherman had now to plan, with suggestions from his superior, the spring campaign that would begin on May 1 and hopefully take him to Atlanta.

A close friend of Rear Adm. Porter, Sherman had always had a keen eye for the logistical necessities of war. This new advance would be no different in that regard. Years later, he wrote in his *Memoirs*: "The great question of the campaign was one of supplies. Nashville, our chief depot, was itself partially in a hostile country, and even the routes of supply from Louisville to Nashville, by rail and by way of the Cumberland River, had to be guarded." Only a month before on February 22, Maj. Gen. Forrest, the greatest human threat to Sherman's supply apparatus, had defeated Brig. Gen. Smith's command at Okolona, Mississippi, and was now "on the loose" in West Tennessee. Ominously and also on March 18, Memphis District commander Maj. Gen. Stephen A. Hurlbut passed word that: "It is reported that Forrest, with about 7,000 men, was at Tupelo last night, bound for West Tennessee. I think he means Columbus and Paducah."

Union concern over the whereabouts of the elusive Forrest, who reached Jackson on the 20th, now intensified. On March 23, Brig. Gen. Mason Brayman, the army commander of the District of Cairo, sent a note over to Capt. Pennock announcing that he, too, had fresh intelligence. The Rebel raider, with what was said to be 7,000 men, was en route toward Union City, a crossroads town in northwestern Tennessee. If the news was accurate, the

In April 1864, Confederate forces under Brig. Gen. Abraham Buford invested Paducah, Kentucky, bringing a call for assistance from Mississippi Squadron 7th District boss Lt. Cmdr. James Shirk to Lt. Cmdr. Fitch, his friend and 8th District colleague. Shirk had only the *Peosta* and tired *Paw Paw* and was much relieved upon the arrival of the bulk of the Cumberland flotilla (U.S. Army Military History Institute).

navy would be advised that gunboats might have to be sent to guard Columbus, Hickman, and Paducah.

Early the next day, Pennock received army advice that Forrest was, indeed, marching in force upon Columbus and that communication with Union City had ceased. The fleet captain was asked to send a gunboat to Columbus post haste and promised to have one under way by evening. Brayman, already at Columbus with 2,000 men, asked that the vessel report to him at that point as he was readying an expedition toward Union City, even though he suspected the enemy was off toward Paducah. The Cairo-based general came within six miles of Union City on the 26th before he learned of its surrender to one of Forrest's colonels.

Also on March 26, Forrest himself led an attack on Paducah, driving its defenders into Fort Anderson on the Ohio River west of the city. Its commander, Col. Stephen G. Hicks, refused to surrender. The gunboats *Peosta* and *Paw Paw* were instrumental in the Northern defense and their praises were sung in Brig. Gen. Brayman's May 2 official report. Holding the town for 10 hours, the raider helped himself to Yankee horses and stores while burning 60 bales of cotton, a steamboat, and a drydock. He then retired to plan his next adventure.

At the end of the month, Lt. Col. Fitch and Nashville garrison commander Rousseau learned of an expedition from Fort Donelson carried out by the tinclad U.S.S. *Silver Lake*. Col. O. L. Baldwin, 5th Kentucky Cavalry (U.S.A.), commanding that post, sent 50 soldiers aboard the light draught on March 30 to scout the countryside below Eddyville. It was feared that Forrest might be in the vicinity, perhaps even on the eastern side of the Tennessee River.

Ten. Building a Fleet, Fort Pillow, and a Summer on the Ohio (1864)

A group of soldiers from Hopkinsville was met by Baldwin, bringing in eight suspected guerrillas, and they reported the feared cavalry commander was not in the area. In his report to Rousseau, the colonel indicated that all was quiet at Smithland and no force was threatening any position on the Cumberland. He had heard from Fitch that Forrest was, in fact, near Columbus, on the Mississippi River.[8]

As certain as is the spring blooming of dogwood in Middle and Western Tennessee, so too was the fall of the Cumberland water level in that season and, in those years, the renewal of Confederate raider activity upon Union outposts and communications.

It was the declining river stage which caused immediate concern to Nashville quartermaster Donaldson. He needed to stock his depots against the start of Sherman's May campaign and the Cumberland was dropping to a point where there would be but 10 or 12 inches of water on Harpeth Shoals. As this natural drop continued, the supply chief ordered his local railroads to transport only urgently required government stores. Simultaneously, he organized, as had been the practice the year before, a fleet of light-draught steamers to run between the obstructions and Nashville after goods were offloaded from the Smithland arrivals.

As April progressed, Col. Donaldson stationed a hundred yoke of oxen to meet the transport fleets. After all in the convoy had rounded to, the lightest steamboats from the north were literally pulled over the shoals to deeper water in which they could continue to the capital. That "novel feature in river navigation" boosted freight totals by 300 to 500 tons per day. During the final fortnight of the month, heavy rains up and down the stream brought an unusual rise of several feet good for most of the period. It was a "godsend," one "that usually occurs here but once in 10 or 12 years." At Louisville, Brig. Gen. Allen made an extra push to send more tonnage; Fitch's gunboats exerted every supportive effort. When Maj. Gen. Sherman stepped off for Atlanta, Donaldson and his crews were able to feel "free and easy." This euphoria of accomplishment was not one which the enemy wished to last.[9]

On April 4, Maj. Gen. Forrest, writing from Richmond, advised, among other things, that: "There is a Federal force of five or six hundred at Fort Pillow, which I shall attend to in a day or two, as they have horses and supplies which we need." Before the month's first week was over, Forrest launched his Fort Pillow expedition by sending Brig. Gen. Abraham Buford's brigade toward Columbus and Paducah. It was hoped that this move would not only cover Forrest's descent upon Pillow, but might also net additional stores and horses.

A general court-martial was adjourned aboard the U.S.S. *Moose* on April 9 and the boat departed Smithland for Cairo where the trial would be resumed with additional witnesses. Word came to Capt. Pennock and Lt. Cmdr. Fitch from Lt. Cmdr. James W. Shirk, Seventh District commander, on April 11 that Paducah was again under Rebel threat. It was hoped that Col. Hicks might be reinforced. While Brig. Gen. Brayman sent two regiments, Pennock sent Fitch. Before departing back up the Ohio, the Indiana sailor telegraphed for some of the boats from his district to cross boundaries and reinforce Paducah, helping to patrol below that town. The *Springfield* was to remain on station at Smithland.

The *Moose* dropped anchor off Paducah, at the mouth of the Tennessee River, on the morning of April 12. An attack, expected all day, did not materialize by evening. Although the Rebels did not appear, most of Fitch's flotilla did. The *Moose*, *Brilliant*, and *Fairplay* joined the *Peosta* in guarding the town, while the *Silver Lake* patrolled below. Earlier, the *Key West* had been dispatched up the Tennessee with an army convoy.

Much farther down the Mississippi that morning, Fort Pillow, a target for the Western

Flotilla in 1862 and lately a guardpost protecting Federal navigation of the river, was encircled by the main body of Maj. Gen. Forrest's command. The Yankee garrison, made up of approximately 262 African American and 295 Caucasian soldiers or a few more from the 11th U.S. Colored Troop and a battalion of the 14th Tennessee Cavalry (U.S.A.), had a number of cannon and was reinforced by the tinclad *New Era* under Acting Volunteer Master James Marshall, the same man who had served in the *Lexington* under Fitch in early 1863.

During the afternoon, Lt. Cmdr. Shirk wired Capt. Pennock informing him that Confederates surrounded his Kentucky base, but had made no assault. It was speculated that Forrest might also have his sights set on either Columbus or Cairo and maybe even to crossing the Ohio River a la Morgan.

As the afternoon waned peacefully at Paducah, Fitch's tinclads were sent on patrol, joining the available Seventh District units and the *Elfin*, provided by Pennock. The stations assigned were: at Paducah, *Peosta* and *Fairplay*; from Paducah to Metropolis, *Victory*; from Metropolis to Head of Chain, *Silver Lake*; from Head of Chain to Caledonia, *Brilliant*; from Caledonia to Mound City, *Elfin*. The *Reindeer* was under repair and unable to participate. When no assault on the town materialized, Fitch went back to Mound City that evening, leaving *Fairplay* under Shirk's direct orders and his other boats strung out to the south.

When the *Moose* departed for Illinois that night, no one in the Kentucky community yet knew the outcome at Fort Pillow, or even that it had been Forrest's target. The truth was that the post had fallen by late afternoon with Federal losses of approximately 231 to 261 killed and 87–100 badly wounded. A total of approximately 168 Caucasian and just 58 African American soldiers were POW. The large proportion of African American deaths led to charges of a Southern massacre and a debate which rages to this day.

Early on the afternoon of April 13, Brig. Gen. Brayman was informed by Col. William H. Lawrence of the 34th New Jersey Volunteer Infantry and commandant at Columbus that the Rebel Brig. Gen. Buford had demanded the surrender of his post, but was refused. Sending his women and children to Cairo, Lawrence posted a message with them calling for help. Brayman wired Capt. Pennock, and, about 3 P.M., the

Nathan Bedford Forrest (1821–1877) was the most successful of the three leading Western theater Confederate cavalry commanders engaged by Lt. Cmdr. Le Roy Fitch. Maj. Gen. Wheeler had ridden away from his rivers in early 1863 and Morgan was turned back in July. Forrest, however, could not be ignored or overcome. The military genius and his lieutenants regularly outwitted Union army and navy commanders. Fitch, himself, encountered Forrest's command or works during Col. Streight's raid in 1863, at Paducah and Fort Pillow in spring 1864, at Johnsonville in November, and at Nashville in December (West Virginia State Library).

fleet captain sent Lt. Cmdr. Fitch, then in town trying to get his court-martial back into session, to the rescue. The Hoosier officer was reminded that Cairo was also a potential target, as was Hickman, Kentucky. Although he was to have two other boats as backup and was authorized to visit the latter point if necessary, should any of his units not be needed they were to return to Cairo immediately. Pennock, anticipating a Fitch request, made certain that Shirk knew of Fitch's new mission and also ordered him to look out for the Cumberland in the absence of its convoy commodore.

The *Moose*, in company with the *Hastings*, churned down the 19 miles from Cairo to Columbus later on the 13th and found the tinclad *Fairy* already on station. Ashore, the sailor interviewed Col. Lawrence, who told him that the threatening Confederates had retired. The Union officer did not know that his enemy consisted of 150 picked men under Capt. H. A. Tyler, sent by Buford to create a diversion. Lawrence, who felt perfectly able to hold his post, was invited to join Fitch aboard his flagboat where, together, the two men discussed possible options.

A bit later, the tinclad warrior composed a message to his superior, which was sent off aboard a dispatch boat. In it, he noted that all indications were that Paducah, Cairo, or some intermediate point was the Southerners' intended target, not Columbus. It was unnecessary to send any boats down to him from Paducah. Indeed, Fitch asked Pennock to let Shirk know what was transpiring downstream and asked that his colleague also watch the Cumberland. Instead of remaining at Columbus, Fitch intended to proceed down to Hickman, or even Fort Pillow. Although he wasn't sure if the latter point had been invested, the fighting gunboatman could, if it had, prevent Forrest from planting batteries on the river until Yankee troops could arrive to reoccupy the area. In a hasty conclusion, Fitch advised Pennock that Acting Volunteer Lieutenant Glassford was probably ready to move. "Never mind the upper works" of the *Reindeer*, he opined, "Keep him near you, so that you can send his boat where necessity requires."

About this time, Navy secretary Welles received a telegram from Pennock reporting that Fort Pillow had, indeed, been attacked. This atop a Confederate demand for the surrenders of both Columbus and Paducah. The fleet captain reported his order that, if Fitch could be spared from Columbus, he proceed to Fort Pillow. There he would endeavor to shell the Rebels from the fort and to keep the river open.[10]

The steamer *Volunteer* had, meanwhile, been dispatched with ammunition for the gunboat *New Era* at Fort Pillow. News was conveyed to Fitch that Pillow had fallen. The Hoosier, determined to pursue his earlier defensive idea, ordered speed increased. The tinclads would arrive as quickly as possible in order to prevent Forrest from throwing up batteries and cutting off communication with the boats below. As the three craft passed Island No. 26, they spoke the steamer *Wilson*, which had tied up with a heavy tow waiting convoy. She was invited to join the naval party.

The *Moose* and *Hastings*, with the *Volunteer* and *Wilson*, arrived off Fort Pillow on the afternoon of April 14. There they saw the *New Era* shelling a group of Rebels who were setting fire to coal barges at a point just above Coal Creek. One of the barges had been towed to that location by the *New Era* the previous evening. The grayclads "displayed considerable bravery," admitted Fitch, as they fired one barge and pushed it adrift. As she came on, the *Moose* also opened fire in the same general direction as the *New Era* and also moved to communicate with that vessel. The new senior officer on scene learned something of events of the past two days from Acting Volunteer Master Marshall.

Armed with Marshall's information and assuming tactical command of all naval forces in the immediate area, Fitch ordered the *Hastings* to round to and shell the woods along the shore up to Plum Point Bend, where Rebel soldiers were "showing their honesty and bravery" by firing the wood piles along the river meant for steamboat replenishment. The *Moose*, meanwhile, ran downstream and picked up the empty coal barge which had been set adrift from Coal Creek. Men from the tinclad's crew jumped aboard and put out the fire before it could do much damage and it was taken in tow and landed opposite Fort Pillow. The warship then steamed up to Plum Point, saw the *Hastings* pounding men hiding behind several woodpiles, and emptied five rounds of shrapnel from her own howitzers toward horsemen along the shore.

At the foot of Island No. 30, which in those days had a chute on its right side, were a number of civilian steamers which were ordered tied up there by Acting Volunteer Master Marshall when the attack on Fort Pillow began. They were joined by the *Wilson*. Another force of Rebel cavalry was seen, congregating in the area above, preparing to make an attack on these transports. The *Moose*, *New Era* and *Hastings* steamed after the riders, and as the butternut troopers galloped off down the wooded shore toward Ashport, the tinclads paddled after them in line ahead formation, right through the chute, loosing random shots toward the men. The pursuit lasted from about 4 P.M. until dark, at which point the Confederate horsemen faded down the Ripley road.

Having determined that the enemy had not crossed Hatchee River, Fitch knew that Fort Pillow was safe—if smoking—and that the light draught *Silver Cloud* had evacuated most survivors and wounded late the previous day. His tinclads now met the commercial steamers and convoyed all of them, save the *Wilson*, below the fort. Once they were off down the river, the gunboatman's vessels and the *Wilson* returned to Pillow, where the *New Era*, *Moose* and *Volunteer* landed under the guns. The remaining women and children in the fort went aboard the *Volunteer* while 10 additional wounded soldiers were brought aboard the *Moose*, where they could be seen by Acting Assistant Surgeon Thorp. The vessels all tied up to the towhead opposite, about noon, where they lay until dawn on April 15.

Fitch did not know that Confederate forces made their move on Paducah that day, driving in the Union pickets and offering the city a flag of true to remove women and children before attacking. When the hour was up, no assault materialized. Lt. Cmdr. Shirk was ready to do his part, with the *Peosta*, *Key West*, *Fairplay*, and *Victory* offering protection. With Confederate troops reported in the upper part of the town and nearby Jersey, the four tinclads pounded the areas, reportedly driving the enemy back to the local fairgrounds out of range. During the day's action, Confederate riders managed to steal into the city and capture all of the U.S. government horses in town—their major goal—and some belonging to civilians as well.

Just after dawn on Friday, the *Moose* and *New Era* moved across to Fort Pillow and landed. Pickets were sent out a sufficient distance to prevent surprise and to permit a detail to finish burying the dead. Many bodies had been left untouched and the job of interring those already buried had been done poorly.

As that work went on, Lt. Cmdr. Fitch had the opportunity to inspect the works, which he thought were insufficiently commanding to insure an adequate defense. His victory had netted Forrest five or six pieces of artillery, including two 10-pounder Parrotts, which could be used on the river up around Mound City or Cairo. The *Hoosier* reported hearing that all of the African American troops and most of their officers were killed. "There was no

Ten. Building a Fleet, Fort Pillow, and a Summer on the Ohio (1864)

doubt," he asserted, that the Rebels had been successful in their assault because they had violated a flag of truce. That he would contemporaneously report what were rumors circulating on the scene two days after the fight—and have no serious doubt of Confederate perfidy—reflects the advanced state of his own loathing for the Southern insurgents, a feeling which was already common among many of his fellow Northern military and naval officers. Testimony on Fort Pillow events was gathered by Brig. Gen. Brayman and others almost immediately, though Fitch was not one asked to comment. Congressional hearings were held within weeks. There was no real surprise as to the immense and bitter recriminations which followed.

Once the Fort Pillow interments were completed and with the enemy gone from the immediate vicinity, Lt. Cmdr. Fitch believed he should return to Cairo as quickly as possible to provide a first-hand report. Ammunition was passed to the *New Era* from the *Volunteer* and Acting Volunteer Master Marshall was ordered to guard the fort. The *Moose*, *Hastings*, and *Volunteer* departed for up the river.

Just after starting, the trio of Yankee vessels came upon a squad of Confederate cavalry that had camped in the woods near the riverbank at Ashport the night before. The horsemen were shelled as they rode off, but none were seen to fall. While en route later on, the mail and supply boat *New National* from Cairo was met. Heaving to, she sought permission to continue her mission of transporting dispatches to Rear Adm. Porter below. Having already written up his own report, Fitch handed it over to the steamer's captain for delivery with the other mail. By this action and in comments to the auxiliary's skipper, the Indiana sailor certified that it was now safe to pass Fort Pillow.

Upstream at Cairo that evening, Capt. Pennock wrote to Porter providing him with the latest available information concerning events at Columbus, Paducah, and Fort Pillow. "With the able assistance of Shirk and Fitch, I have no doubt of being able to take care of the river and keep it open." No charter or commercial steamers were allowed to depart for downriver "until we hear the condition of affairs from Fitch." Pennock wired the same information to Navy secretary Welles and promised another telegraph as soon as he knew more from his on-scene troubleshooter.

Even farther upstream on the night of April 15–16, a party of about 100 Confederates, hidden out along the shore about a mile above Metropolis, opened fire on the patrolling tinclad *Victory*. The super light draught was not damaged and no one aboard was injured, even as she returned fire.

Upon his arrival in Illinois waters on the evening of April 16, Lt. Cmdr. Fitch dropped off his wounded at the U.S. naval hospital at Mound City and then reported to Capt. Pennock. After discussions with his superior, the well-traveled officer knew he had to put off his plans for an early return to Smithland. The fleet captain, who had a new mission in mind for the Hoosier, meanwhile relayed the essentials of his subordinate's Fort Pillow review in a report to Porter and a telegram to Secretary Welles. In his April 19 report made directly to the rear admiral, Lt. Cmdr. Shirk was highly complementary of the manner in which Fitch "very generously came on with five gunboats of the Eighth District."[11]

Fitch was unable to return to his normal station, from which he had been absent most of a week, because Capt. Pennock sent him off to check out another disturbing report—Rebels had taken possession of the town of Hickman, Kentucky. Located on the Mississippi River, 16 miles below Columbus, the small place was not regularly garrisoned by Northern troops. Accompanied by a detachment of U.S. Marines under Lt. C. H. Stillman, the *Moose*, *Hastings*,

Lt. Cmdr. Fitch, acting as Mississippi Squadron fireman, was sent from Paducah to check out reports that Fort Pillow had been overrun by the forces of Brig. Gen. Nathan Bedford Forrest, CSA. Upon his arrival, the Indiana sailor determined the correctness of incoming Union information. Departing the scene, Fitch's flagship, U.S.S. *Moose* (Tinclad no. 34) came upon a squad of Confederate cavalry that had camped in the woods near the river bank at Ashport. These were shelled in an action not unlike that depicted in this drawing (*Battles and Leaders of the Civil War*, Vol. 1).

and the partially-rebuilt *Reindeer* ran down past Columbus to the seat of Fulton County on the evening of April 19 to "see the true state of affairs."

As the three Yankee warships hove to off the town that was built on the second Chickasaw Bluff running nearly parallel to the Mississippi, they greeted a group of 30–40 suspected rebels on the bank with a single shell. The butternut riders high-tailed it away before the Marines could be landed. The *Reindeer* was dispatched on ahead below the town where Acting Volunteer Lieutenant Glassford landed some men to picket the woods. Meanwhile, Fitch and the leathernecks aboard the *Moose* landed at the town and picketed the roads leading to the north. The Hoosier officer then made inquiries and learned that squads of Rebels this size were in the habit of visiting the town daily. Fitch was also told that "three notorious characters" were loose on Island No. 8.

On April 19–20, the *Moose* ran down to the little atoll, but found that the "notorious" ones had escaped across the stream to the Missouri shore. The tinclad searched down the bank for three to four miles in semi-darkness, but no one was seen. Later, the flagboat returned to Hickman, where more suspicious but fleet individuals were seen prior to her landing. As the sun came up, Lt. Cmdr. Fitch took aboard all Union citizens who wanted to leave and provided a fierce Palmyra-type warning to that percentage of the 1,000 residents remaining:

"If there was even a musket fired at any transport or other boat the town would at once be destroyed."

The Eighth District commander did not believe there were very many loyal citizens in Hickman, but also did not believe that the people he had chased were part of regularly-organized forces, being more on the order of "miserable horse thieves and robbers." Returning to Cairo late on April 20, he informed Capt. Pennock that his landings had no great effect except as a warning. It is perhaps of interest that, when the new tinclad *Huntress* passed the community during her mid–June inaugural patrol, the situation had not changed. Her acting assistant paymaster, Edmund J. Huling, later remembered that Hickman continued to be "subject to great annoyances from guerilla bands, who drove off many citizens." The brigands, if you will, several times "made plundering raids into the town, robbing and burning, it would almost seem from very wantonness."[12]

Dropping the *Hastings* off at Cairo, along with the *Reindeer* which had to finish her refit, the *Moose* departed for Smithland on April 21. Earlier, while Fitch's task group was off Hickman, word reached Cairo that detached parties of irregulars were working the Kentucky shore above and below Shawneetown, Illinois, taking horses and enlisting men. Two steamers had been fired into and there was alarm that the Rebels might cross the Ohio and raid the Illini community. Capt. Pennock asked the Eight District commander to check out these new reports before resuming his regular station.

Following a quick Smithland stop for messages, Lt. Cmdr. Fitch moved on up toward Shawneetown on April 23. The same day Pennock received a petition from a local citizens' committee asking that he send a gunboat to protect the government stores stockpiled in the Illinois town. The fleet captain replied that the *Moose* was already en route; however, by the time the tinclad arrived, the situation had quieted. By April 28, Fitch and his flagboat were finally back full-time at the mouth of the Cumberland. For the month as a whole, the district's tinclads, even with their extracurricular activities, had safeguarded 158 steamboats and barges, of 44,029 tons, down the river to Nashville. In his April 28 summary review of activities during the two weeks of crises, Capt. Pennock lauded his subordinates to Admiral Porter: "Shirk and Fitch have been very active, and have done all that men could do."[13]

The dual advance by Grant and Sherman against the Confederacy, east and west, was launched on May 5. Keeping in mind the logistical and convoy necessities of the latter's Atlanta campaign, Lt. Cmdr. Fitch departed for Cincinnati once more at the beginning of May. Following an inspection of the rendezvous there, he crossed over to Louisville and took the train south to resume his support and supervision of the gunboat construction at Bridgeport, Alabama. Capt. Pennock had authorized the resumption of work per the admiral's instructions and promised any assistance required. Still, the process of outfitting the Bridgeport gunboats was proving far more frustrating and complicated than preparations for the *Moose*, *Reindeer*, and *Victory* the previous July.

Upon his arrival at Bridgeport, Fitch found that, while he had been on the Mississippi, the army quartermasters had three new boats in the water, two of which, called Gunboat A and Gunboat B, had even been on machinery-testing trial trips. A fourth side-wheeler would be launched about midmonth. All would soon have their working engines and would have completed their joiner work. A significant difficulty had arisen, however, due to a difference in opinion over who should handle the conversion work. Capt. Edwards believed that his job was only to fit the boats up as transports and then turn them over to the USN for completion as gunboats. Rather than engage in a lengthy debate over which of them was responsible, Fitch, on his own hook, immediately took total charge of the four boats, subject to an agreement with the army officer that the cost of material and workmen to finish construction would be charged to U.S. Quartermaster accounts. With that understanding in hand, the Indiana sailor contracted for the plating, outfits, and other essentials.

Having all but taken over full supervision of the gunboat project, Fitch now found himself riding the rails back and forth between Bridgeport and points in the north attempting to speed acquisition of labor and materials. Iron for plating was not finished by the army and acquiring it was stalled until the naval officer called upon Brig. Gen. Allen in Louisville. From his one-time critic, Fitch obtained an order to cover everything, even to the outfit. Indeed, the quartermaster told the Indiana sailor to go to Cincinnati, buy whatever he needed there or elsewhere, and send the bills to his Louisville office. The Army had already placed a large order with a Chicago firm for lumber.

Upon his arrival back at the Queen City, Fitch immediately repaired to the offices of Swift's Iron & Steel Co., a leading navy contractor, and ordered the plate needed for the gunboat casemates. Deliveries were to begin before month's end. Another major difficulty was a paucity of ironworkers in Bridgeport—there were none. Arrangements were made to take down to Alabama a number of these men, and their tools, from Swift as soon as possible. Going with them would be USN acting chief engineer William D. McFarland, who was detailed on May 23 to review the condition of the boats and determine the number of engineers needed to help crew them. At the same time, a telegram was received from Maj. Gen. Sherman specifically authorizing the Hoosier to contact Nashville quartermaster Donaldson for transportation. Despite the fact that the railroad was very extended, trains from Louisville and Tennessee's capital would provide speedy transport. Once the outfits were shipped, Fitch could look to the boats' cannon from his Kentucky base.[14]

Back at Mound City by May 26, Rear Adm. Porter had time to reflect briefly upon the Bridgeport boat-building enterprise. In a report to Secretary Welles, he noted that the four steamers were almost ready for service and that he was pushing forward their guns and detailing their officers. Porter recommended that the vessels, built under his direction with Quartermaster General Meigs paying the bills, be named in compliment to "those gallant officers" *General Grant, General Sherman, General Thomas,* and *General Burnside.* The Washington navy chief readily agreed.

Writing from Smithland the next day, Lt. Cmdr. Fitch informed his superior that the Cumberland was falling rapidly, with only three feet of water over Harpeth Shoals. It would not be safe to ship the guns up the river to Nashville, so the Tenth District commander determined to pick them up at Mound City and to run them up to Louisville, from where he would ship them by non-stop rail express to Bridgeport. Arrangements were made for U.S. Army ordnance officers to accompany the howitzers from Louisville south.

With the stages in the Cumberland daily declining, river traffic fell. During May, 65 steamboats and barges were convoyed to Nashville, comprising 15,461 tons. Since February, the tinclads under Fitch's command had guarded the arrival of 15,016 tons of government goods. Among the steamers often seen, towed, helped, or otherwise encountered by the *Moose* and her consorts were the *War Eagle, Shreveport, Prima Donna, Norman, Duke of Argyle; Savannah, Lawrence, Mollie Able, Liberty, Gennie Hopkins, Aurora, Kenton, Prairie State, City of Pekin, Anna, Lilly, Venus, Duke, Alpha, Echo No. 2, A. Baker, J. W. Cheeseman, Ollie Sullivan, Nannie, Nettie,* and *Emma.*

This spring the wharf at Nashville was choked and boats sometimes could not unload

Ten. Building a Fleet, Fort Pillow, and a Summer on the Ohio (1864)

Lt. Cmdr. Fitch and his colleague, Acting Volunteer Lieutenant Henry Glassford, oversaw the construction by Capt. Edwards of four light draught tinclads at Bridgeport. Fitch and Glassford secured the officers, guns, and armor for the vessels, which remained Army-owned. The *General Grant* was commissioned in July 1864 and patrolled the Upper Tennessee River until June 1865. Fitch's last official duty with the Mississippi Squadron was to secure the men and guns returned from these boats (National Archives).

for days at a time. New warehouses were filled and items were often sent by rail or road to other depots, such as those at Chattanooga and Bridgeport. Col. Donaldson later remembered the period:

> Col. L. B. Parsons, Saint Louis, Mo., crowded the Cumberland with steamers and barges, and throughout the winter and spring, the entire energies of the depot here were taxed to their utmost to receive and handle the stores heaped in upon us. For weeks together my levee thronged with transports of all sorts, and a force of at least 3,000 men and from 400 to 500 teams were kept constantly at work—day and night, Sundays and week days—in transferring the supplies to my various depots and store-houses. My estimate is that, for three months or more together, I received and handled daily an average from 2,000 to 3,000 tons of freight exclusive of the amount arriving here by railroad.

"Fitch, who by this time was a veteran of many gunboat engagements," wrote Cumberland River historian Byrd Douglas in 1961, "had worked out and completed a system of convoying which had surpassed anything he had hitherto accomplished for Buell and Rosecrans." That not a single transport was lost on the river during the navigable season "was an accomplishment which should be credited to Fitch."[15]

While en route to Louisville with his ordnance cargo, the Indiana sailor found, to his displeasure if not surprise, that an "indiscriminate traffic with the Rebels in Kentucky" had grown up during the winter absence of the gunboats on the Ohio. Without sufficient boats in his district to guard and watch the many crossings, the only way to halt the abuse of the limited trading privileges issued earlier by the U.S. government was to stop all intercourse. Subject to his superior's approval, Fitch, on June 1, issued a proclamation prohibiting all trade to the Kentucky shore below Cannelton. The warning, similar to those issued earlier in the war, provided for arrests and seizures and noted that, once the tinclads stopped their annual Cumberland runs, no steamers would be allowed in that stream until the fall convoys were resumed.

As the month began and the navigation season on the Cumberland drew toward its close, the boats of the Tenth District began their regular summer cruises on the Ohio. Initially, three boats were transferred from the Smithland rendezvous. The others remained below due to low water, but soon would begin their Ohio River patrols. Meanwhile, the *Brilliant* was assigned the Henderson station, while the *Reindeer* and *Fairplay* cruised between Smithland and Uniontown. It was anticipated that, as Maj. Gen. Sherman was "so far to the front," a succession of raids could be expected all along the Ohio in the months just ahead.

On June 6, Acting Chief Engineer McFarland reported the completion of his inspections at Bridgeport and that he had returned to Cincinnati, where he shipped two of the six engineers the army boats required. The *Moose* was off New Albany, Indiana, that day returning to Smithland, prior to a trip to Nashville from which Lt. Cmdr. Fitch would leave for Bridgeport. In the meantime, Confederate irregulars were "getting very thick again" on the Ohio River below Henderson, Kentucky.

Two days later, the Hoosier officer asked Rear Adm. Porter to have the U.S.S. *General Pillow* blockade the mouth of the Green River in order to prevent smuggling and free up a Tenth District tinclad. Porter rejected this request on June 18. On June 9, Fitch wired his superior from Evansville indicating that the "guerrilla" situation was worsening and that he was personally moving to the Henderson area to "look after them." Acting Volunteer Lieutenant Glassford was deputized to take over the Bridgeport mission. Some of Morgan's men were reportedly operating in the Maysville, Kentucky, area and two tinclads were dispatched to that community to investigate. It would now be necessary to withdraw all of his flotilla from the Cumberland to guard the Ohio, which required protection along its entire length. The same day, Porter telegraphed his district leader from Mound City: "Withdraw all the gunboats from the Cumberland and spread them along the Ohio. Get two gunboats from Captain Shirk if necessary."[16]

With the gunboats at Bridgeport approaching completion, Col. Donaldson ordered Capt. Edwards on June 11 to turn them over to Acting Volunteer Lieutenant Glassford and then telegraphed Maj. Gen. Sherman: "Is this right?" Sherman wired back from Big Shanty, Georgia, in no uncertain terms that the transfer (actually, it was a charter) was approved and furthermore asked that all military officers grant every facility and encouragement to the boat captains. The same day he wrote up his arrangement with the USN in Special Field Order 23 and sent a copy to Porter. The document clearly indicated that the boats had been turned over to the Navy "for better service and discipline," but that they would be supplied by army quartermasters and commissaries of all posts and stations as if they still belonged to the army—which, technically, they did. Further, should any of the gunboat captains require any kind of aid whatsoever, it was to be provided if at all possible. On June 20, a copy of the field order was sent on to Fitch from the *Black Hawk*.[17]

The same day the Alabama gunboats were turned over to the navy, Rear Adm. Porter received a disturbing report from Fitch regarding the increase in irregular activities in the Henderson and Uniontown areas. The cause, as ascertained by the Hoosier through talking with residents, was a reaction to alleged abuses perpetrated by troops of Lt. Col. Richard D. Cunningham's 8th U.S. Colored Artillery (Heavy) out of Paducah. These men were supposedly directed to conscript local African American males along the riverbanks and, in the process, entered private dwellings where they "entered ladies' bedrooms before they were up, insulted women, and plundered and searched generally." If the Cunningham charge were true, it constituted a "gross outrage and disgrace to our cause." Many were also draft evaders, attempting to avoid service in the Union Army. It was also said that Cunningham's men landed from steamboats convoyed by a USN gunboat, a disgraceful charge which Fitch knew to be untrue.

The charges about Cunningham were not unlike hundreds of others made on both sides of the irregular war. The truth of the matter was that the Union was recruiting African American troops on a large scale and that the Confederates did what they could to halt the process. "Guerrilla bands in western Kentucky," wrote Richard Gildrie recently, increased their efforts to intimidate the local African American population. Tales and incidents abounded. As he moved downstream, Fitch found the people along the Ohio River banks so frightened and excited by such incidents that he thought it proper to attempt to send them a communication which, at least insofar as the gunboat service was concerned, might set the matter straight. He may not have realized that, as the author of several threats to burn entire communities, his affirmation that the gunboats were not "cruising up and down the river running off negroes and committing gross depredations" might not be believed. His pledge "not to interfere with, or molest, the persons or property of peaceful and loyal citizens in any way whatsoever" probably did not change many minds.

On June 12, Fitch completed his arrangements for summer Ohio River gunboat patrols and turned in a list of stations. Acting Volunteer Lieutenant Perkins' *Brilliant* was given the task of running from Smithland up the Cumberland to Ingram's Shoals and then on up the Ohio from Smithland to Shawneetown. Acting Volunteer Master Groves' *Fairplay* operated from Shawneetown to Evansville while Acting Volunteer Master Coyle's *Silver Lake* plied between Evansville and Cannelton. Acting Volunteer Master Morgan took the *Springfield* back and forth between Cannelton and New Albany while Acting Volunteer Lieutenant Glassford's *Reindeer* churned the waters between Louisville and Maysville. While Glassford was away, his boat was left in the charge of her executive officer. The *Victory*, under Acting Volunteer Master Read, steamed between Maysville and Pomeroy as Fitch's *Moose* was left free to go where necessary.

Over the next two weeks, the Tenth District flagboat cruised to the vicinity of Owensboro and above, checking on reports of Confederate irregulars operating along the Kentucky shore from Louisville down, and also up the Cumberland. At the same time, the June 1 order restricting trade was extended from Louisville down the Ohio and up the Cumberland. The Nashville *Dispatch* warned steamboat captains that, when plying the Cumberland from Smithland to Nashville, it was safe to put in only at Fort Donelson and Clarksville.

The U.S.S. *Moose* remained constantly on the go attempting, like the other vessels of the flotilla, to keep the banks clear and steamers protected. Guerrillas were quite "annoying" around Maysville, above Cincinnati, but it was anticipated that the super light draughts *Reindeer* and *Victory* could handle them. Late in the period, six boats under requisition and of special interest to Col. Parsons at St. Louis were convoyed by Acting Volunteer Lieutenant Perkins to Nashville.

During the week of June 20, a trap was laid to catch roving bands of irregulars operating back of Uniontown. About 150 Union cavalry were assigned to act in concert with the *Moose* in this combined arms operation, but the Yankee horsemen were not strong enough to overrun the Confederates' regular encampment. That lesson was learned the hard way when they moved against it and found they were outnumbered five to one. On the evening of June 26, the *Moose* set off from Evansville for Uniontown and Caseyville on another sweep.

Rear Adm. Porter received an update on the Bridgeport gunboats from Lt. Cmdr. Fitch, sent by a dispatch boat as he was en route toward Caseyville on June 26. One of the boats had its plating on and was nearly finished, but the others were delayed because the required lumber, ordered by the U.S. Army earlier, had been delayed. It actually arrived at Louisville on that date and Brig. Gen. Allen wired Fitch that it was being railroaded through at once. When it was on hand, Fitch promised that he and Acting Volunteer Lieutenant Glassford would push the others on as rapidly as possible. In the intervening period, he was busily gathering up the different bills he had contracted so that Allen could invoice the boats in proper form. Receipts for the boats would be forwarded as soon as the quartermaster invoices were made out.[18]

After returning to Evansville from Caseyville at the beginning of July, the commander of the Tenth District went over to Bridgeport to consult with Acting Volunteer Lieutenant Glassford on the final outfitting of the army gunboats. Although not commissioned, one of these, the *General Thomas*, the first completed and armed temporarily, had already begun patrolling the Tennessee. Back to Cincinnati by July 14, Fitch wired Porter informing him that most of the boats were fully officered and that two, the *General Grant* and *General Sherman*, would be officially commissioned at the Alabama town next day. All four of the boats would not only have USN officers, but petty officers as well; the remainder of the crews were provided by the U.S. Army. The pair would immediately relieve the *Thomas*, which would then receive its permanent guns and be regularly commissioned along with the *General Burnside*.

When the bills were paid, the four side-wheelers each cost the government $19,000. The dimensions of all four were approximately the same. The 201.5 ton *General Burnside* was 171 feet long, with a beam of 26 feet and a 4.9 foot depth of hold. The 204 ton *General Grant* had identical specifications. With the same beam, a length of 168 feet, and a depth of hold of 4.6 feet, the 187 ton *General Sherman* was slightly smaller, while the *General Thomas*, with the same hold depth and beam, was three feet shorter and three tons lighter than the *Sherman*.

The *General Grant* was commissioned on July 20 under the command of Acting Volunteer Ensign Joseph Watson, transferred over from the Cumberland River tinclad *Springfield*. She was armed with two 30-pounder Parrott rifles and three 24-pounder howitzers. It would be a week before the *General Sherman* was commissioned. When she entered service under the command of Acting Volunteer Master Joseph W. Morehead, her five cannon included three 24-pounder howitzers and two 20-pounder Parrott rifles. The *General Burnside* and *General Thomas* were armed identically to the *General Sherman*. Acting Volunteer Master Gilbert Morton was put in charge of the *Thomas* while Acting Volunteer Lieutenant Glassford, temporarily detached from the *Reindeer*, was named captain of the *Burnside* and Fitch's deputy as commander of the upper Tennessee flotilla.

Fitch and Glassford had the pleasure of knowing that they had midwifed the birth of a fleet. They would also soon learn that the war had moved beyond the point where it could make a significant difference. Both men would be officially relieved of responsibility for any part of the unit on September 29 when Rear Admiral Porter named regular USN Lt. Moreau Forrest commander of the *General Burnside* and of the new Eleventh District. Acting Volunteer Lieutenant Glassford returned to the *Reindeer* on October 1.[19]

As Lt. Cmdr. Fitch was winding up business in Bridgeport and attempting to police the riverbanks within his district, new army quartermaster convoy concerns arose. Much of this came about because of a guerrilla success on July 18 when the *St. Louis*, a 350-ton sternwheel steamer loaded with government supplies and headed to Nashville from Louisville, was captured and burned at Sailor's Rest, the Yellow Creek outlet, about 20 miles below Clarksville. Other attacks on river traffic also occurred, though none so blatant or terminal.

On July 22, Col. Donaldson asked Maj. Gen. Sherman to petition the USN for a gunboat patrol of the Cumberland from Smithland to the foot of Ingram's Shoals. The army gunboats *Silver Lake No. 2* and *Newsboy* were performing such service from Nashville down to Ingram's. When they were not patrolling, the two hauled freight. Next day, Col. Parsons in St. Louis brought up another worry. This one, originating from Capt. Hanson Rasin at Smithland, was forwarded to Capt. Pennock, acting in the absence of Rear Adm. Porter. The assistant quartermaster at the navy rendezvous, a man with whom Fitch had worked earlier, reported that no gunboat had made an appearance off the town in 10 days and over 2,000 tons of government stores were thus unguarded.

Pennock immediately replied to Parsons indicating that Lt. Cmdr. Fitch would station a tinclad off Smithland if it were not needed elsewhere and wondered why a sufficient number of troops couldn't be regularly stationed at the town to protect the quartermaster's stores. Sherman, writing from the field near Atlanta two days later, simply suggested Donaldson contact Fitch or Porter.

It is perhaps interesting to note that Fitch was not the only district commander now faced with army concerns over convoy provision. More prompt convoy service was also being demanded by Col. Parsons of both Lt. Cmdr. S. Ledyard Phelps and James Shirk, commanders of the Seventh and Ninth Districts, respectively. In August, both Brig. Gen. Allen in Louisville and Col. Parsons would become overly demanding on this issue once more to a point where Capt. Pennock would find their communications "to me discourteous, to say the least."

While the army was in correspondence with Cairo, Fitch, in July, made three trips back and forth between his temporary headquarters at Evansville and Uniontown watching the movements of suspected guerrillas and attempting to catch them. On each occasion, different Union cavalry formations were dispatched to cooperate with the Indiana sailor, but, in the words of his somewhat disgusted report, "they have always been themselves defeated and driven off." By the middle to the end of the month, as reports on the progress of the new Bridgeport gunboats came in to Evansville, the stage of water in the Ohio dropped significantly and continued to go down further. Indeed, if the river stage had been the same in 1863 as it were now, there was, Fitch probably thought in reflection, little doubt that Morgan might have made it to West Virginia from Ohio. By July 24, the water level was less than it had been as late as September 1863. At the Indiana summer base, the *Moose* was lightened. With an even more shallow draft, it was hoped she could regularly return and attempt to keep the Uniontown irregulars from doing real damage to Northern shipping or other interests.[20]

As July closed, Col. Thomas Swords, assistant quartermaster at Cincinnati, found himself responding to War Department concerns regarding the low-water patrol of the Ohio River between Pittsburgh and Louisville. The U.S. Army was just as worried as Fitch about guerrilla incursions from Kentucky, some of which had already resulted in the seizure or destruction of several steamboats. Quartermaster General Meigs, familiar with the on-going work of the army gunboats on the Cumberland, authorized Swords to get up a fleet of six light-draught armed auxiliaries to cover that stretch. While these units, similar no doubt to the hastily-provided *Allegheny Belle* of July 1863, Ohio governor David Tod suggested on July 29 that the navy might provide temporary relief.

On July 30, Swords wrote to Capt. Pennock asking if it would be possible to "borrow" one or more Mississippi Squadron boats to patrol the upper Ohio until full navigation of the Cumberland was resumed. Three days later, Pennock wrote back informing the colonel that the USN already had seven tinclads, "expressly adapted for cruising during low water," at work on the Ohio. Their commodore, Le Roy Fitch, would, of course, be pleased to confer with the army as to their best disposition. Tenth District boats, particularly the *Victory*, no doubt obliged military requests as best they could, but, as Meigs reported in his annual report for 1864, the six auxiliaries were duly acquired, including the *Lou Eaves* and *Virginia*, and placed into service.

By August, the water level in the Ohio River was so low that even the super light draught tinclads could seldom move freely or without great difficulty. Much farther south, where the water level was not a problem, the West Gulf Coast Blockading Squadron, under Admiral David G. Farragut, damned the torpedoes and fought the Battle of Mobile Bay on August 5. Maj. Gen. Sherman, who spent the late spring and summer pushing on Atlanta, faced Maj. Gen. John Bell Hood in a series of battles around that city, before skirting around it to attack the railroads at Jonesboro. The great hope in Southern circles for success in the west now hinged on the infliction of damage to Union supply lines north of the Georgia front.

On August 13, Confederates, led by newly-promoted Brig. Gen. Adam "Stovepipe" Johnson, commander of Morgan's 2nd Brigade the previous July, made something of a start on this goal with an appearance in force near Caseyville, across from Shawneetown, Illinois, and along the shore several miles down. Three steamers, including the *Jennie Hopkins*, were captured. These were partially loaded with 275 head of U.S. government beef and were stranded on Shawneetown Bar when taken. During the attack, one crewman was killed. Afterwards, the cattle were all thrown into the river. Most survived by swimming to shore, though those coming up on the Kentucky bank were quickly taken by locals.

Although Johnson's attack force was initially estimated by Union intelligence at 1,500 men, the number was actually closer to 700. Of these, about 100 crossed the Ohio to the north bank between Shawneetown and Mount Vernon, Indiana, and looted on the outskirts of the former.

Once Brig. Gen. Henry B. Carrington in Indianapolis received word of the crossing, he ordered all steamboats to stay clear of the Kentucky shore between Evansville and Louisville and sought help from available Hoosier units and the Indiana Legion. Among the units responding was the 46th Indiana Volunteer Infantry, Col. Graham Newell Fitch's old outfit, which had recently reported to Evansville from a July visit to Logansport. During Sunday, the 46th steamed down the Ohio aboard an old light draught mail boat, reaching Mount Vernon at suppertime. Shortly after midnight, a large railroad ferryboat, capable of carrying

1,000 men and en route from Pittsburgh to the Mississippi, put into the landing, where it was immediately commandeered.

At daylight on August 15, the 46th and another regiment, the 43rd, went aboard the railroad ferry and started toward Shawneetown. There the Rebel rampage had resulted in two days of indiscriminate firing upon all passing steamers. Johnson's men now elected to retire, leaving a small force on the Sabine River. These soon came under intermittent fire from the U.S.S. *Fairplay,* commanded by Logansporter Acting Volunteer Master Groves.

From Cincinnati, the U. S. Army's Northern Department telegraphed the *Reindeer* at Madison and the *Victory* at Louisville later that Monday asking them to steam down. Low water prevented their movement and it was useless to even try lightening them. As Lt. Cmdr. Fitch noted four days later, "Had I taken everything off of them, even to the casemates, there was not enough water for them to get over the bars."

About 2 P.M., the two Indiana regiments reached Shawneetown and, finding no enemy, moved up to the Sabine where howitzer fire was heard. After waving off the *Fairplay,* the ferry put into shore and the troops landed. Although they skirmished inland for a distance, no sizeable body of Confederates was found to engage. The soldiers were reembarked within an hour and the little expedition returned to Shawneetown.

On August 16, after making their escape, the Southerners returned the three captured steamers to their owners for a $1,000 (U.S.) ransom. These were at Shawneetown when the *Fairplay* and 46th Indiana returned from the Sabine River. At this point, the railroad ferry was returned to its civilian crew, and the regiment moved aboard the *Jennie Hopkins,* which would soon become part of a larger movement.

Determined to chastise Johnson's raiders, the Union host, gathering in response, was readied to push off into Webster and Union counties, Kentucky, on a punitive expedition. As he was directing all available Yankee forces to converge on the Mount Vernon, Indiana, area on Monday night, Northern Department commander Maj. Gen. Samuel P. Heintzelman called for additional naval assistance.

Employing five detained steamers, Union field commander Maj. Gen. Alvin P. Hovey, who had participated in the Morgan pursuit in July 1863, crossed the Ohio from opposite Uniontown on August 17. A further wire from the Queen City to Capt. Pennock brought back the unwelcome news that no Tenth District gunboat, not even the *Fairplay,* could be sufficiently lightened to get over Shawneetown Bar to cruise as far below that point as was required. As additional Union troops from Cairo and Shawneetown poured into Kentucky to support Hovey, the soldiers had their first engagement at White Oak Springs, near Morganfield.

From Cairo on August 18, Pennock wired both Lt. Cmdr. Shirk at Paducah and Lt. Cmdr. Fitch at Evansville seeking aid: "It is important to have a boat there to cooperate with the land forces," he told the latter. Shirk could not help and Fitch wired his superior that he would not be able to send any boats except the army gunboats *Lou Eaves* and the smaller *Virginia,* which were put under his command by the Evansville quartermaster. These two improvised craft, sent to cruise below Shawneetown, were the only "gunboats" involved in support of Hovey's expedition, which ended on August 24 with Brig. Gen. Johnson's wounding and capture.

The remainder of the Tenth District boats were on patrol, or, more accurately, attempting to make patrols on a stream so low that the actual tours could seldom be completed. The *Reindeer* was at Madison, where she was about to be hauled out and calked. The *Victory* was stuck at Louisville with orders to proceed to Smithland as soon as the water would permit. The *Springfield* was moving between Cannelton and New Albany, while the *Silver Lake*, scheduled to patrol from Canneltown down to Evansville, was caught by the river stage at Owensboro. She, like *Victory*, had orders to Smithland. The *Fairplay*, which had recently been at the Sabine River with the 46th Indiana, could, as shown, occasionally run between Evansville and Shawneetown, but the *Brilliant*, at Henderson, which was supposed to patrol from Shawneetown to Smithland, could not get down. She would move up to Evansville by month's end for work on her boilers. The *Moose* was at Evansville, where Lt. Cmdr. Fitch likely read of the fall of Mobile on August 23 and perhaps of Hood's abandonment of Atlanta on August 31–September 1.[21]

The remainder of the summer was, for the officers and men of the Tenth District, Mississippi Squadron, largely a repeat of the previous year. Efforts were made to ensure efficient traffic flow at a time of low water and, in September–October, escort and counterinsurgency efforts once again shifted from the Ohio River to the Cumberland, and her sister, the Tennessee. The merchant fleets guarded up the former were now often smaller, due largely to increased reliance on the Nashville and Northwestern Railroad. The well-protected NNR steel route permitted easy transport of essential goods the 75 miles from the Tennessee River port of Johnsonville to the state capital. Despite the completion of the 60-mile long Edgefield and Kentucky link between Nashville and Clarksville around Harpeth Shoals, much traffic was forwarded to the new Johnsonville location, thereby permitting the avoidance of the low-water 185 mile trip through a long and slender route through the heart of a disaffected, if not disloyal, region.

An example of the reduced Cumberland service was seen on August 26 when the *Silver Lake* convoyed just six steamers from Smithland to Nashville. Once in the capital city, the gunboatmen were, as in the past, granted liberty; the city editor of the Nashville *Daily Press* defined USN bluejacket shore activities as "grogging around."[22]

Although two last great military adventures awaited Le Roy Fitch at Johnsonville and Nashville in November–December, the preceding months from mid–August onward were quite routine. Professor James R. Soley summed them up years ago:

> The last months were chiefly occupied in convoy duty and keeping up communications on the Mississippi, in blockading the Red River, and in active operations in conjunction with the army by the fleets on the Tennessee and Cumberland rivers, the former under Lieutenant-Commander Shirk and the latter under Lieutenant-Commander Fitch. Both these officers displayed great energy and resource in an exacting and difficult service, and they were ably seconded by the volunteer officers who commanded the light gun-boats in frequent and hotly contested engagements with the Confederate batteries and troops on the banks.[23]

CHAPTER ELEVEN

Johnsonville, September–November 1864

FOLLOWING MAJ. GEN. WILLIAM T. SHERMAN'S triumph at Atlanta at the beginning of September 1864, the Union high command had next to decide in which direction to send the scrappy redhead. Sherman himself favored a "scorched-earth" ride east destroying Confederate logistics between the Georgia capital and the Carolina seacoast. It would be his intention to emulate—indeed, exceed—his greatest communications foe, Maj. Gen. Nathan Beford Forrest, by encouraging his Army of the Tennessee, made lean, to live off the countryside. "I can make this march and make Georgia howl!" he promised Lt. Gen. Ulysses S. Grant, his superior in far off Washington, D.C. Maj. Gen. George Thomas and 60,000 men could be sent north to guard the Tennessee rear and would act without fear of any Southerner, Hood, Forrest, or whomever. Sherman was particularly contemptuous of the former after hearing warnings that he might make an end around toward his Chattanooga or Nashville supply center. "Damn him," the commander snapped. "If he'll go to the Ohio River, I'll give him rations. Let him go north. My business is down south!"[1]

Gen. John Bell Hood was, indeed, contemplating a visit north in a move historian Bruce Catton called a "strategy of despair, verging on the wholly fantastic, based on the belief that the way to counter Sherman's thrust into the deepest South was to march off in the opposite direction." The Confederate field commander realized he might not be able to reach the Ohio, but he could, if lucky, move "smartly" enough in western and middle Tennessee to defeat Thomas or capture Nashville or do both. Taking the Tennessee capital would not only destroy a major Northern supply depot, but could force Sherman to return to the Volunteer State. If he did not, Hood would be free to range at will, perhaps even venturing east to Virginia and a reunion with Gen. Robert E. Lee.

During September, Sherman and Hood took advantage of fine weather to reorganize their commands for what Benson J. Lossing later called the "vigorous work" ahead. The Union general believed that his opponent would mount a Tennessee offensive. As a precaution, Sherman ordered Thomas to Nashville to guard against any Southern gambit; the major general arrived in the city on October 3. Hood moved over the Chattahoochee and attacked the railroad near Big Shanty, not far from Kenesaw, two days later.

In the next two weeks, the Southern commander marched farther west, trying to lure his opponent out of Georgia while avoiding a decisive battle. Sherman became so convinced of Hood's goal that he once more determined to go the other way and march toward the sea. Lt. Gen. Grant approved his subordinate's Savannah strategy on October 13. Seven days later, Sherman gave Thomas full authority to deal with any Confederate incursion north and sent him reinforcements with which to do the job. Included would be four corps, all of the cavalry units available, less one division, all the troops in all the garrisons in Tennessee, plus two divisions under Maj. Gen. Andrew J. "A. J." Smith ordered to move over from Missouri where they were chasing Maj. Gen. Sterling Price.

To aid in the grand endeavor to lure Sherman out of Georgia by smashing up the Union supply line from the north, Hood, on October 7, called upon his cavalry. In particular, he needed Maj. Gen. Forrest, the man whom Sherman himself had named "the very devil" following his fantastic July victory at the Battle of Brice's Cross Roads in Mississippi. President Jefferson Davis, Maj. Gen. Hood, and everyone else on the southern side hoped that Forrest would be able to further divert the Yankees while the Confederate Army of Tennessee strode into the Volunteer State.[2]

An expert at hit-and-run attacks, as well as a master of traditional cavalry combat, Forrest had been involved in numerous raids and pursuits that won him laurels in the South and a controversial reputation in the north. It was Forrest (and Wheeler) whom Lt. Cmdr. Fitch had battled at Dover in early 1863. The navy man was prefatorily involved with Forrest's activities, both in the expedition leading to the capture of Col. Streight and in the aftermath of the Memphis native's descent upon Fort Pillow. "Breaking enemy communications was one of Forrest's favorite chores," wrote Edward Longacre in 1975.

By October 6, the "devil," also known as the "Wizard of the Saddle," had already made a sixteen-day circuit from Cherokee Station in Alabama as high as Spring Hill outside Nashville assaulting Sherman's supply lines. Confederate hopes that Forrest would, according to Maj. Gen. Jacob Cox, "occupy Thomas' forces so as to create a diversion in his favor" were met. It was during this sojourn that, according to Jordan and Pryor, Forrest first became aware of the Yankee treasure trove at Johnsonville and put it on his target list:

> He also received information, through citizens, that a vast amount of army stores had been collected at Johnsonville on the Tennessee River, the terminus of the Nashville and North-Western Railroad, destined and essential for the Federal forces at Chattanooga and Atlanta. This depot and the bridges on the railroad leading to it, it was likewise his purpose to destroy, if the condition of his horses, on reaching Spring Hill, would warrant him in undertaking it.

During his Middle Tennessee raid, Maj. Gen. Forrest was pursued by numerous Federal troops from Nashville, Chattanooga, Memphis, and even Atlanta. The chase became so close that a major butternut goal, destruction of the Nashville & Chattanooga Railroad, was abandoned. While several of his subordinates made feints to draw off the bluecoats, the "devil" was able to get his command back to safety over the swollen Tennessee River via a cane-covered island which kept the men from view.

Among those detailed after Forrest's raiders was Col. George B. Hoge, who had received orders to move out with some 1,300 soldiers from the 113th and 120th Illinois Volunteer Infantry, the 61st U.S. Colored Infantry, plus four 12-pounders of Battery G, Second Missouri

Light Artillery. From Clifton, Hoge was to move his men by water up to Eastport, Mississippi, and after disembarking, quick march over to the Iuka area and destroy its railroad connections. Unhappily for the colonel, the Confederate leader learned of the plan from scouts, however, and, on October 6, dispatched Lt. Col. David C. Kelley of the 26th Tennessee Cavalry (C.S.A.), with 300 men and several artillery pieces to give the northerners a welcome.

The Confederate greeting party hid behind the crest of a ridge about 600 yards from the river at the Eastport landing. While the Federal troopboats *City of Pekin*, *Kenton*, and *Aurora*, guarded by the tinclads *Key West* and *Undine*, were discharging their passengers that October 10 afternoon, Kelley's gunners and riflemen opened up. Both the latter named transports were hit and set on fire and many men fell into the stream and drowned as the boats cut their cables and fled. The counterfiring light draughts, under the command of Acting Volunteer Lieutenant Edward M. King, were also hit while the *City of Pekin* tried to pick up survivors. Eventually, the little task group was reunited and fires were extinguished. It then retired to Clifton, assessing its losses while en route. Years later in reviewing the episode, Admiral David Dixon Porter, though not directly naming him, insisted that Ninth District chief, Lt. Cmdr. James W. Shirk, shoulder some

Lt. Col. David Kelley (1833–1909) was a Forrest confidant nicknamed "The Parson" from his days as a Methodist minister. Also a physician like Graham Newell Fitch, Kelley led the 26th Tennessee Cavalry (CSA) in the fall of 1864, winning recognition for his artillery work against river craft. It was Kelley whose gunners not only played havoc at Johnsonville in November, but blockaded the Cumberland against Lt. Cmdr. Fitch and two ironclads in December. Kelley was one of the founders of Vanderbilt University in 1873 and ran (unsuccessfully) as the Prohibition Party candidate for governor of Tennessee in 1890 (courtesy Robert Henderson).

of the blame for King's setback. "Sometimes the naval commander of a district, from a feeling of over-security," the former Mississippi Squadron boss asserted in 1886, "sent an insufficient force of gunboats when trouble would ensue and the undertaking became a failure."

Acting Volunteer Master John L. Bryant's *Undine* was a new boat built at Cincinnati the previous year and homeported there under the name *Ben Gaylord*. Purchased by the USN on March 7 for $35,600 and then converted and renamed, the 179 ton stern-wheeler was 10 tons lighter than the U.S.S. *Moose*, but possessed the same battery of eight 24-pounder howitzers. The *Key West* was a 207-ton stern-wheeler which was built at California, Pennsylvania, in 1862, documented as *Key West No. 3*, and homeported at Pittsburgh. She was purchased into the USN on April 16, 1863, for $33,800 and converted. Significantly larger than the *Undine*, the task group flagboat was 156 feet long, with a beam of 32 feet and a 4.6-foot depth of hold. Commissioned at Cairo, Illinois, on May 26, 1863, under the command of since-promoted Acting Volunteer Master King, her armament consisted of six 24-pounder rifled howitzers, two 24-pounder smoothbore howitzers, and one 12-pounder Wiard rifle.

Both the *Undine* and *Key West* would face Forrest's cannoneers again and next time they would not escape. Lt. Col. Kelly would also plague Lt. Cmdr. Fitch at Nashville in just two month's time. Fitch's final Confederate nemesis merits a profile.

The Rev. Dr. David Campbell Kelley was born at Leeville, Tennessee, on Christmas Day, 1833. An 1851 graduate of Cumberland University, in 1853, he, like Graham Newell Fitch, became a medical doctor, graduating from the University of Nashville. That same year he traveled to China as a Methodist medical minister. Nicknamed "the Parson," Kelley began his war service at Huntsville, Alabama, as captain of The Kelly Rangers-Kelly Troopers, Company F, Forrest's Battalion (3d Tennessee Cavalry). It was Kelley whom Forrest asked to pray for the troops at Fort Donelson in February 1862, becoming thereafter, according to Dr. Wyeth, one of the cavalry leader's intimate associates. After the Civil War, the colonel took a D. D. degree from Cumberland University in 1868 and served the Methodist Episcopal Church at Gallatin, Tennessee, and at other towns thereafter in the Nashville area. Kelley was one of the founders of Vanderbilt University in 1873 and served on its board of trustees from 1875 to 1891. Fitch's wartime opponent held numerous posts within his church hierarchy and ran (unsuccessfully) as the Prohibition Party candidate for governor of Tennessee in 1890. Kelley, who died at Nashville on May 14, 1909, "was a vocal force," according to John E. Fisher, "in urging upon whites reasoned and informed views of blacks and relations between the races."

Forrest, as he told his immediate superior Lt. Gen. Richard "Dick" Taylor on October 12, had to his way of thinking "done something toward accomplishing" the goal of destroying Maj. Gen. Sherman's logistical apparatus, but not nearly enough and was "anxious to renew the effort." The question was where he and his horsemen could apply the greatest leverage and secure the greatest return. Like Morgan before the Ohio Raid, Forrest took out his maps and studied the possibilities closely.

The Yankee campaign in Georgia was supplied from Louisville, the north's central point for provisioning its western armies since the beginning of the conflict. There were three major corridors available to bring goods south to such big intermediate Union depots as Nashville and Chattanooga. The first two were old and known: the Cumberland River, the primary route for goods in bulk when it was high, but which was still at a low stage, and the well-guarded Louisville and Nashville Railroad.

The newest and most vulnerable route was one humming along with, to date, virtually no interference: the Tennessee River from Paducah down to the transfer point at Johnsonville and hence east along the Nashville and Northwestern Railroad. Laying down his charts, Forrest determined "to take possession of Fort Heiman on the west bank of the Tennessee River below Johnsonville, and thus prevent all communication with Johnsonville by transports."

Back in May, the Nashville and Northwest Railroad was completed between the state capital and the site of a growing supply depot and arsenal at Johnsonville, 78 miles to the southwest near Reynoldsburg, in Humphreys County on the eastern or right bank of the Tennessee River. A range of hills came down at this point to within 100 yards of the stream and the railroad was required to run several miles along the base of those hills before it reached the river. Previously known as Lucas Landing, Johnsonville was located about two to three miles above the old town of Reynoldsburg. The two communities were separated by the Trace Creek Valley, while Reynoldsburg Island was a few miles south. The area north of the railroad toward Reynoldsburg was flat; all of its timber was cut off for over a mile from the riverbank. The ground on the western or left bank of the Tennessee was heavily wooded and high.

As the Tennessee River, 400 yards wide at Johnsonville with a straight course, was not subject to the annual low water navigation difficulties of the Cumberland, its importance as a supplementary avenue of supply was enhanced. The birth of the facility was marked on May 19 by the one-day turnaround visit of Governor Johnson and several other Nashville dignitaries. Tradition has it, according to the *Nashville Banner* of March 18, 1958, that, when he got off the first passenger train, Johnson climbed up atop a pile of crossties and made a speech naming the base in his own honor.

During late spring, summer, and into the fall, steamers from Louisville, after churning upstream to Johnsonville via Paducah, unloaded their cargoes of stores, clothes, guns, and ammunition almost directly to waiting trains. The NNR tracks, which followed the south bank of Trace Creek, hosted upwards of a half dozen daily trains running in either direction between the base and Nashville. The railroad roundhouse featured a turntable to service freight trains. The bustling installation featured storage yards and rows of warehouses that ran in a 300-yard-wide strip downstream from the railroad wye and turntable as well as houses in the river draws for government employees. Among the facilities was a narrow and a wide transfer building equipped with lifting machinery to unload boats and barges right into the warehouses. Some 800 employees of the U.S. Army Quartermaster Department provided the labor needed to handle the trains, as well as the dozen or more steamers and barges which came to the wharf every day.

Also named for Governor Johnson, Fort Johnson, an earthen redoubt and blockhouse, overlooked the port's landscape from a prominent hill south of the railroad. From here Col. Charles R. Thompson's depot was guarded by 700 untested troops from the 43rd Wisconsin Volunteer Infantry, plus smaller detachments from the 12th, 13th, and 100th U.S. Colored Infantry, the 11th Tennessee Cavalry (U.S.) and 1st Kansas Battery. A total of four 12-pounder Napoleons and ten 10-pounder Parrotts protruded from Fort Johnson or from nearby entrenchments. Johnsonville was also a forward base for Lt. Cmdr. Shirk's Ninth District of the Mississippi Squadron. Four tinclads—*Undine, Key West, Elfin,* and *Tawah,* often commanded by Acting Volunteer Lieutenant King in two-boat task groups similar to those operated by Acting Volunteer Lieutenant Glassford on the Cumberland—made frequent stops at the levy while on convoy escort or patrol. Johnsonville's destruction might not halt Sherman's upcoming March to the Sea, but it could, perhaps, slow it down.[3]

"The movement of the Confederate army through northern Alabama to Decatur and Florence, and thence across the Tennessee River towards Franklin and Nashville was now in full swing," wrote Forrest's biographer, Dr. Wyeth, years later. The "Wizard" was also beginning his mission against the Johnsonville supply depot. On October 16, his advance elements set out from Corinth for various points in West Tennessee. Among the units available to the "devil" on his last independent raid of the war were the division of Brig. Gen. Abraham Buford, Col. Edmund W. Rucker's brigade, and two batteries of horse artillery. These, together with Forrest and the division of Brig. Gen. James R. Chalmers, came together and made their headquarters at Jackson on October 21. There they rested while the command's weary horses were reshod. By the next day, Gen. Hood's main force occupied Gadsden, Alabama.

Just as Hood's advance required Sherman to shift over to a blocking point west of Rome, Georgia, to guard Chattanooga and Atlanta, Forrest's move toward Tennessee was noticed by other Federal authorities, who now made their own preparations. The telegraph wires buzzed with sightings, reports, movement orders and the like. Garrisons at Columbus, Memphis, and Paducah braced for return visits by the butternut horsemen who had come their way earlier. Forrest himself wondered if Union troops might make the same response now as they had in September, coming at him from several directions. He did not know (and may not have cared if he had) that, in Washington, D.C., U.S. Navy secretary Gideon Welles was about to infuse the Mississippi Squadron with new leadership. On October 17, he offered the unit and a chance to regain the title of acting rear admiral to Capt. Samuel Phillips Lee. Lee had been relieved from command of the North Atlantic Blockading Squadron, that was going to Rear Adm. Porter, and was given a week to accept, which he did on October 19.

A Virginian by birth, Acting Rear Adm. Samuel Phillips Lee (1812–1897) was shifted to command of the Mississippi Squadron in October 1864 in order to make room for Rear Adm. David Dixon Porter to take over his old command, the North Atlantic Blockading Squadron. Lee arrived on the Western scene just in time to take reports of the Johnsonville disaster. Low water in the Cumberland River prevented him from personally reaching Nashville to take charge of on-scene naval operations. Consequently, it was Lt. Cmdr. Fitch who fought Lt. Col. Kelley's batteries in December and provided direct support to Union military requirements. It fell to Lee to disband the squadron in April–July 1865 (Naval Historical Center).

While blacksmiths worked their forges and Rebel enlisted ranks were boosted through local recruitment, Forrest's scouts determined that no Federal operations were actively underway against them from any quarter. Yankee cavalry patrols in western Tennessee were recently decreased in order to send riders to North Alabama to watch for Hood along the Tennessee, while the sheer number of Forrest sighting reports coming into army posts and naval bases actually helped mask the Confederate's mission.

On October 20, Maj. Gen. Sherman outlined his trans–Georgia plans for Lt. Gen. Grant in a lengthy telegram. At the same time, he delegated to Maj. Gen. Thomas authority to command troops not only in Tennessee, but those in Alabama, Kentucky, Mississippi, Indiana, and Ohio. These would protect not only those areas, but the communities of Chattanooga and

Decatur as well. Capt. Alexander M. Pennock, temporarily in command of the Mississippi Squadron, now worked to prevent southern reinforcements from making it across the Mississippi itself. Hood's force departed Gadsden on October 22.

On October 24, Maj. Gen. Forrest's horsemen saddled up and broke camp, headed northeast toward the Tennessee-Kentucky line. Meanwhile, James W. Shirk and Le Roy Fitch, on the Tennessee and Cumberland rivers respectively, continued their efforts to provide convoy protection and reconnaissance. Although both were aware that Hood was on the loose and that Forrest had been reported in west Tennessee, neither knew that the Confederate menace, in the person of the latter, would quickly be upon them. Hood arrived at Decatur, Alabama, on October 26, where he learned that Forrest was way up in the north central part of the Volunteer State. The same day, Grant made known his wish that Maj. Gen. William S. Rosecrans, commander of the Department of the Missouri, send all available bluecoat soldiers to Thomas.[4]

With Brig. Gen. Buford's cavalry in the lead, two batteries of Forrest's Cavalry Corps, under the command of Capt. John W. Morton, arrived at the mouth of the Big Sandy River on October 27. After an equestrian reconnaissance for several miles on either side of the Big Sandy's mouth, it was decided to post cannon at the abandoned Confederate Fort Heiman, two miles above Fort Henry, and at Paris Landing, five miles below. This spider trap was laid in such a way that unsuspecting Northern vessels might pass in, but would, in all likelihood, never exit. If the strategy worked, navigation of the Tennessee would be obstructed and communications would be cut off with Johnsonville, 40 miles away.

Under the personal command of Capt. E. S. Walton, Lt. W. O. Hunter's section (Walton's Battery) of 20-pounder Parrotts—the two heavy guns railroaded from Mobile—were placed in the upper fort at Fort Heiman while lighter guns from Lt. J. W. Brown's section (Morton's Battery) of 3-inch Rodmans were placed 800 yards below Hunter on the river bank. A dismounted brigade of cavalry under Brig. Gen. Hylan B. Lyon was deployed as skirmishers. Down at Paris Landing, 10-pounder Parrott rifle sections of both Walton's Battery and Morton's Battery were emplaced, the former at the landing and the second a thousand yards above near the mouth of the Big Sandy. Brig. Gen. Tyree H. Bell's brigade of dismounted cavalrymen were the skirmishers here.

The masked batteries were given the strictest command not to open fire until ordered. The plan was to await fully-laden boats and to leave alone those empty craft returning for new loads. A whole day—and four empty steamboats—would pass before such a target arrived. The first prize snared in the trap was the stern-wheel transport *Mazeppa*, towing two barges and en route from her Cincinnati homeport. She was disabled by the Paris Landing batteries on the morning of October 29 after having been allowed to steam in ignorance past Fort Heiman. Laden with 700 tons of quartermaster's and subsistence stores, the big steamer, whose crew had fled permitting her easy capture, was quickly unloaded and burned. Some of the plunder was sent on to Gen. Hood.

The next morning the surrender of the 110-ton side-wheeler *Anna* was arranged after she had passed Paris Landing and been caught at Fort Heiman. However, before the Confederates could take possession of their prize, her captain ordered up full steam and the vessel turned downstream and headed toward Paducah. When almost out of range, several lucky shots riddled her masthead, pilothouse, and chimneys. Forty miles from Paducah that Saturday the transports *Naugatuck* and *Alice* were both captured at Widow Reynolds' Bar. At the same time, several *Mazeppa* personnel reached the Federal post 10 miles downstream at Pine Bluff and informed its commander of the attack. Lt. Col. T. R. Weaver quickly sent word to Capt. Henry Howland, the Johnsonville quartermaster, who passed it on to Brig. Gen. James Donaldson at Nashville, exclaiming that he anticipated an attack on his depot on Wednesday or Thursday, November 2 or 3.

Hardly was the *Anna* out of harm's way before combat at the Fort Heiman–Paris Landing trap was resumed. The *Undine*, which had escorted the *Anna* to Sandy Island, a point just above the spot where the transport was ambushed, was en route back to Johnsonville when the sound of big guns was heard. The tinclad came back to investigate, cleared for action. And action she found. Bell's brigade and the guns at Paris Landing took her under fire and a contest of wills and iron ensued for most of an hour. The light draught, which was not designed to stand up against heavy cannon, was badly damaged and forced to retire downriver out of range of the guns at either Rebel position. At anchor on the river bend, her crew worked to repair her damages while her gunners fired at the Paris Landing battery as well as Confederate marksmen harassing them from the west bank.[5]

While the *Undine* was so occupied, the 235-ton stern-wheel transport *Venus*, with a barge in tow, came in sight from downriver. Blithely choosing to ignore warning signals from the tinclad, she steamed within range of the Confederate upper battery and was taken under fire. Although not damaged, her captain was killed before she could run past the guns and anchor near the *Undine*.

Paris Landing was reinforced by troops from Brig. Gen. Chalmers' division and sections of Walton's Battery an hour before noon. It being a busy morning for all concerned here, not 20 minutes later, the barge-towing, 251-ton stern-wheel *J. W. Cheeseman* came down the Tennessee. She, too, ignored a warning from the *Undine*, but, unlike the *Venus*, she did not escape. Rebel gunners

Fitch sketched out this map of Confederate and USN positions near Johnsonville to send to his superiors following the destruction of the huge Union supply depot in November 1864. Fitch, who enjoyed art and later entered a painting in a Logansport contest, left only this one official work (*Official Records of the Union and Confederate Navies in the War of the Rebellion*, Series I, Vol. 26).

shot off her steam pipe and otherwise so damaged her that she was forced to run into the west bank and surrender, a useless wreck.

Capt. Morton now received orders from Brig. Gen. Buford to take a section of horse artillery down to the bend where the Yankee vessels were licking their wounds. Once in place, he was to destroy them or force them to steam back under the guns of Fort Heiman or Paris Landing. The day was chilly, with the sun obscured by hanging clouds; still, the sweating and exhausted graycoats manhandled their cannon into place and, just after 3 P.M., opened fire on both the *Venus* and her escort. Musketry from the Tennessee battalions of Kelley and T. C. Logwood was also telling, even though Bryant's howitzers spit canister at them from a distance of less than 100 yards.

The battle between the tinclad and the riverbank continued loudly. Word that Forrest had batteries at Fort Heiman and Paris Landing and that the two Union boats were in trouble between them made it to Johnsonville, via Pine Bluff, later in the day. With this message in hand, Capt. Howland rushed down to the wharf where he found the executive officer of the U.S.S. *Tawah*, Acting Volunteer Master James B. Williams. With the boat's commander, Acting Volunteer Lieutenant Jason Goudy, away at Paducah, Williams agreed to cast off and steam to the rescue.

Goudy, the reader will recall, had enjoyed an active convoy career on the Tennessee River, beginning with the U.S.S. *Alfred Robb* in early 1863. In September of that year, he was promoted into the *Tawah* a 108-ton side-wheeler built at Brownsville, Pennsylvania, in 1859 and first documented as the *Ebenezer* after her owner, Ebenezer Blackstone. Acquired by the Navy for $11,000 on May 9, 1863, and subsequently renamed, the boat was 114 feet long, with a 33-foot beam and a 3.9-foot depth of hold. *Tawah* was armed with two 30-pounder Parrott rifles forward, four 24-pounder howitzers in broadside, and two 12-pounder Wiard rifles at the stern. The uncomfortable vessel was not popular with her crew and was, at best, known as "a miserable ship."

The *Undine* and the Rebel batteries traded iron for nearly three hours, At 3:45 P.M., the steam pipe in the paddle wheeler's doctor room was cracked and filled the engineering spaces with hot gasses that forced the engineer and his men out. *Undine* was now unmanageable. With her ammunition nearly exhausted, Bryant ordered the tinclad headed into the east bank so that as many of her crew as possible might abandon ship. Before quitting ship, the captain, unable to resist further, ordered his guns spiked (two were) and unsuccessfully attempted to destroy his vessel. At 4 P.M., the colors were struck. This surrender was not observed by the Confederates and firing continued for a period. *Undine* was the last U.S. warship surrendered in action prior to the U.S.S. *Pueblo* (AGER-2) in 1969.

The *Venus* was simultaneously taken under fire, but put into the west bank to surrender. With the *Undine* taken intact, as well as the two transports, Forrest's command had possession of three boats that could potentially be put to good service in ferrying troops across the Tennessee River.

Lt. Col. Kelley put two companies aboard the *Venus*, taking prisoner the surviving members of her 20-man armed guard from the brand-new 34th New Jersey Volunteer Infantry, under Lt. William H. Gibson. He then crossed over to the other side where he took possession of the *Undine*. Kelley also, unknowingly, came into possession of the secret USN signal books. Loss of the codes set off something of a panic in Union Navy offices from the Mississippi to Washington, D.C., but there is no evidence that the Confederates who held them knew how to use the codes—or even that they had them.

As Kelley was securing the Confederate prizes, another Yankee gunboat hove into sight from above. This was Acting Volunteer Master Williams' *Tawah* from Johnsonville. Despite the best of intentions, Williams quickly found that he was outgunned by Forrest's artillery. To be on the safe side, the *Tawah* anchored about a mile and a half above, but her long range cannonade had no impact on the Confederates near Paris Landing. Brig. Gen. Chalmers ordered a section of his artillery shifted to handle the newcomer and when those Parrotts opened fire, Williams found it necessary to withdraw.

Meanwhile, under Lt. Col. Kelley's direction, the *Venus* towed the *Undine* down to Paris Landing and a cheering welcome from Rebel troopers. "The Parson," who had directed fire on the tinclad at Eastport, Mississippi, earlier in the month, was pleased to find that, although she had four shell holes in her casemate, the warship was otherwise not seriously injured in hull, machinery, or armament. The barges were emptied and destroyed, as was the hulk of the *J. W. Cheeseman*.

Having missed the action of the previous days, Maj. Gen. Forrest arrived at Paris Landing on the morning of October 31 overjoyed to find that he now had a Confederate "Tennessee River Navy." As plans were made as what exactly to do with this windfall, Capt. Morton was asked to overhaul the *Undine*, make sure her guns were operable, and take charge of the "fleet." The artilleryman agreed to the handle the upgrade, but asked that someone else with nautical experience skipper the gunboat.

The man chosen to take over the former Yankee warship was an experienced Cumberland River steamboat man, Capt. Frank P. Gracey of the 3rd Kentucky. His crew, recruited from his own unit, included several who previously served aboard the C.S.S. *Arkansas*, the ironclad that threatened the Union fleet at Vicksburg in 1862. Another steamboat man, turned horse soldier, Col. William A. Dawson of the 15th Tennessee, took over the *Venus* as "fleet commodore." With Forrest and Morton embarked upon the transport, the two boats made a trial run to Fort Heiman. There the *Venus* was armed with the two 20-pounder Parrott rifles moved down from Walton's upper battery.

The capture of the *Undine* and *Venus* offered Forrest a golden opportunity to mount a co-ordinated attack on Johnsonville. The "Tennessee River Navy" would create a diversion to draw off Acting Volunteer Lieutenant King's tinclads—and any others which tried to interfere—while Rebel ground pounders and artillery assaulted the town, at the very least destroying its stores while perhaps even capturing the giant horde of goods for transfer south. Throughout the remainder of the day, volunteer "horse marines" learned the ropes aboard the boats as preparations were made to move upstream. Fort Heiman, which had not previously played a very big role in the conflict, would be left behind after having proved to the world once and for all that, with a minimum of artillery, Confederate riders could "fight the Federal gunboats on even terms."[6]

Acting Volunteer Master Bryant and a number of surviving *Undine* crewmen made their way to Pine Bluff, arriving at 4:30 on Halloween morning. After reviewing events for Lt. Col. Weaver, reports on the loss of the *Undine*, *Venus*, and *J. W. Cheeseman* were wired by the post commander to Brig. Gen. Donaldson and Capt. Howland, who telegraphed them on to others in authority. In his own message, post commander Col. Thompson was quite emphatic: "Forrest intends to capture Johnsonville and has 4,000 men." Later, when Maj. Gen. Thomas wondered if the Johnsonville commander was up to the task of defending the depot, Thompson wrote: "I have not now, nor have had any idea of surrendering. Will fight to the last if attacked. I feel confident that I can hold the place." Only a few reinforcing troops could be drawn into town from railroad guard duty, while Quartermaster Howland armed his employees.

As the fall sun rose, guerrillas, over on the Cumberland River, captured and burned the chartered 250-ton stern-wheeler *David Hughes* and her barge. This loss of U.S. government stores was recorded at a point 15 miles above Clarksville. Alarm bells now began to sound all along the rivers; Paducah was once more thought to be a major Rebel target. When the tinclad *Curlew* came into Mound City from Louisiana, she was granted one hour in port to discharge the clerk and a passenger of the since-captured steamer *St. Louis* who were picked up at Randolph. Capt. Pennock then hurried her off to reinforce Lt. Cmdr. Shirk. Elsewhere, Brig. Gen. Donaldson in Nashville wired Louisville and St. Louis to cease shipments up the Tennessee and directed additional rail cars to Johnsonville to deplete the depot.

The Confederate threat on the twin rivers occasioned Lt. Col. Weaver, with Acting Volunteer Master Bryant and party, to evacuate his small riverfront post and head overland to Fort Donelson, where the mixed party of bluecoats and bluejackets arrived about 7 P.M. As word of Pine Bluff's abandonment was received at Johnsonville, the *Undine*'s pilot, having escaped into the woods, came into the depot on foot and reported to Col. Thompson and Capt. Howland. *All Hallow E'en* for those at the Tennessee River facility ended gloomily with a first-hand report of the weekend disaster.[7]

The next morning, November 1, Acting Volunteer Master Bryant and those *Undine* crewmen with him boarded the steamer *Cuba* at Fort Donelson and headed down the Cumberland to Smithland. Simultaneously, Acting Volunteer Lieutenant King, with the *Key West* and *Elfin*, arrived at Johnsonville from Paducah. The *Elfin*, the only one of Johnsonville's regular gunboat visitors not yet described, was previously the civilian steamer *W. C. Mann*, purchased from John N. Shunk at Cincinnati for $34,700 by Admiral Porter's agents on February 23, 1864. Converted into a light draught, the 192-ton sternwheeler was 155 feet long, with a beam of 31 feet and a 4.4 foot depth of hold. Armed with eight 24-pounder howitzers, the vessel was placed into commission on May 30, Acting Volunteer Master Augustus F. Thompson, former skipper of the *Paw Paw*, commanding. After a month in the squadron's Seventh District, she was transferred to Lt. Cmdr. Shirk's Ninth District in July.

Also in the hours after breakfast, Acting Rear Adm. Lee, who had informed Lt. Cmdr. Fitch of his arrival by dispatch at 1 A.M. that morning, assumed command of the Mississippi Squadron in a brief ceremony aboard the flagboat *Black Hawk* at Mound City. The new commander's joyful day quickly turned sour. As his predecessor put it, Lee "was not fortunate on his arrival in the West." In his first report to Secretary Welles, the cabinet official who fired him earlier, Lee was forced to acknowledge that the *Undine* and two transports were reported ("but not officially") captured on the Tennessee River.

Fitch and Lee would work hand in glove over the next two months, though it is doubtful that the former enjoyed the same warmth of relationship with his new chief that he had with Rear Adm. Davis and Porter or Capt. Pennock. Lee certainly did not demonstrate any particular faith in the fighting gunboatman, particularly after unavoidably missing what his subordinate enjoyed, a chance for combat in the Battle of Nashville.[8]

With some of the goods from the *Mazeppa* and the two 20-pounder Parrotts transferred to the *Venus* and the *Undine* readied, Forrest's command struck out for Reynoldsburg and Johnsonville this same morning. The general had, unhappily, found it necessary, due to the poor roads and the worn-out condition of his artillery horses, to load the big guns and the

Mazeppa plunder aboard the *Venus*. The weather was damp and miserable. A cold rain plagued the butternut troopers all day and into the night as they marched along the muddy bank working to keep up with the troop-laden boats in the river.

Brig. Gen. Chalmers' men were in the lead with Buford's in the rear; the horse artillery attempted to remain close to the ex–Yankee steamers, which had orders not to get ahead. The underbrush was thick and thorny and the trails available did not always permit easy access to the river. The trek was particularly nasty for the cannoneers, who were, nevertheless, prepared to "drop the trails and begin shooting in defense of the vessels at a moment's notice." At dusk, the Confederates made camp near the wrecked Memphis & Ohio Railroad bridge at Danville.[9]

All Souls Day was particularly busy in local Union circles, as the northern army and navy began to react to the crises on the Tennessee, which Hood was starting across. At St. Louis, "Old Rosy" Rosecrans, who had not forwarded any reserves, received a direct order from Lt. Gen. Grant, sent via Maj. Gen. Henry Halleck, demanding that all available troops in the St. Louis vicinity be ordered to Nashville *posthaste*.

At Nashville, Brig. Gen. Donaldson, informed of developments by Capt. Howland at Johnsonville, went over to see Maj. Gen. Thomas in the early afternoon to report the loss of the *Undine* and the transports, including the *David Hughes*. Thomas immediately wired both Halleck and Sherman relaying the news. Word of the disasters, meanwhile, also reached Lt. Cmdr. Fitch and army post commander Capt. Henry P. Reed at Smithland. The latter wired Brig. Gen. Soloman Meredith, in command of the post at Paducah, who, in turn, copied the message to Brig. Gen. Stephen Burbidge, the man in charge at Columbus, Kentucky.

Maj. Gen. Thomas wasted no time in calling upon the USN that Tuesday. Telegrams buzzed to both Capt. Pennock and Lt. Cmdr. Shirk asking that they lift Forrest's blockade of the Tennessee. When the *Curlew* arrived off Paducah that afternoon, her crew expected to perhaps find the town invested by "the devil's" cavalry corps. Instead, Acting Volunteer Ensign H. B. O'Neill's boat was immediately sent up the Tennessee by Shirk in company with the *Fairy* and *Paw Paw*. The expedition was under the command of Acting Volunteer Lieutenant Goudy, whose *Tawah* was in action against Morton's gunners two days earlier.

Fleet Captain Pennock acknowledged Thomas' telegram at 6 P.M. and promised to send all of the gunboats upriver that he could spare. Meanwhile, Lt. Cmdr. Shirk wired Mound City two hours later reporting that he had dispatched three boats upstream already and was calling upon the Tenth District for reinforcement. Though Forrest may have bottled most of his fleet up at Johnsonville, it was entirely possible for the U.S. Navy to recombine against him through a judicious transfer of squadron elements from the Cumberland, via Smithland and Paducah. Shirk's message, similar to one sent to Maj. Gen. Thomas, was acknowledged at 8 P.M. by Acting Rear Adm. Lee. At the same time, the *Cuba*, carrying Acting Volunteer Master Bryant and his crew, arrived at Smithland from Fort Donelson. There the former skipper of the *Undine* gave Lt. Cmdr. Fitch a first hand account of his encounter with Forrest, as well as the capture of the *Venus* and *J. W. Cheeseman*.[10]

About 10 P.M., a messenger from Smithland brought Shirk's call for help from the local telegraph office to Lt. Cmdr. Fitch aboard the U.S.S. *Moose*, which was anchored across the stream from the town. Although the Tenth District commander, who was even now receiving a description of the crisis from Acting Volunteer Master Bryant, quickly determined to reinforce his neighbor with the boats available, it was too dark to get over the bars at the mouth of the Cumberland. The captains of the *Brilliant* and *Victory*, Acting Volunteer Lieutenant Charles G. Perkins and Acting Volunteer Master Frederick Read, were ordered to get their boats ready to leave in the morning.

Early on November 2, just before departing, Fitch appeared at the Smithland telegraph office and sent a reassuring wire to Maj. Gen. Thomas indicating that he would reinforce Lt. Cmdr. Shirk. The Indiana sailor optimistically opined: "I think there is no doubt that we can reopen the Tennessee." Puffing along as rapidly as possible, his little task group arrived at Paducah later in the day. There the Cumberland convoy commodore immediately went into session with his Tennessee River counterpart. Both men were convinced that Confederate forces might yet attack Paducah. Maybe, they wondered, the enemy really wanted to cripple the upper river gunboat flotillas in order to have free reign over the rivers.

Whatever the "wizard's" motives, he had to be halted and the two naval officers, attempting to "cover all the bases," settled on a plan. Fitch would take his boats up the Tennessee, assume tactical command of all naval craft in the Johnsonville area, and try to stop Forrest if he was there. Shirk would remain behind with the *Peosta*, then under repair, to guard Paducah just in case that town was again the Rebel goal. Once this strategy was settled upon and the two commanders took their leave of one another, Acting Volunteer Master Bryant reported to the Ninth District commander, who heard his story and, per orders already in hand, sent him along to Mound City to report to Acting Rear Adm. Lee. Bryant would be exonerated by a board of inquiry within a few days.[11]

Upstream this day, the Rebel columns moving along the west bank, together with the Tennessee River Navy, made steady and uneventful progress toward Johnsonville—until about 3:30 P.M. that is. The *Venus*, faster than her consort, had, contrary to orders, pulled ahead of the *Undine* and moved out of range of the supporting horse artillery. Moving into a sharp bend in the stream off Green Bottom Bar, some six miles below Johnsonville, her luck ran out. Almost like a train running head on toward a broken trestle, the Parrott-equipped steamer came into gun range of the U.S.S. *Key West* and *Tawah*.

The Yankee tinclads initiated a river reconnaissance from Johnsonville a half hour before this encounter and it is quite probable that the tars on the opposing craft, professional and amateur, were equally surprised to see one another. Recovering quickly from any astonishment, Acting Volunteer Lieutenant King's two boats "made short work of Forrest's sailors," wrote Dr. Wyeth years later. In a 20-minute engagement, the *Venus* was badly damaged and, in an effort to avoid her capture or destruction, she was run ashore. There her officers and crew abandoned her, "without setting it on fire." The *Undine* rounded to "and sought safety in flight," moving, "with shot through her," according to King, under the protection of the Rebel mobile field batteries. Heavy fog and mist and the unknown placement of the southern guns prevented her pursuit. King, whose *Key West* had worked in tandem with the *Undine* earlier, sarcastically noted that "she went down river faster than ever before!"

The capture of the prize boat *Venus* was significant in helping to raise the morale of Johnsonville's defenders. Not only was the transport taken intact, she had aboard Forrest's two largest cannon (the 20-pounder Parrotts), plus two hundred rounds of ammunition and the freight from the *Mazeppa*. After running a gauntlet of musket fire at the head of Reynoldsburg Island, the tinclads returned to the wharf of the supply depot with the *Venus* about 6:30 P.M. Running to the telegraph office, Acting Volunteer Lieutenant King wired Lt. Cmdr. Shirk to report the capture of the steamer and the escape of the gunboat. With the Confederates known to be just over five miles away, a more ominous note was also sounded: "All anxious about this place. Please send up more gunboats at once.... We won't allow this place to fall into enemy's hands, if our forces can prevent, but please send up more gunboats."

While King's message was humming toward Paducah, the task group under Acting Volunteer Lieutenant Goudy finally reached the vicinity below Forts Henry and Heiman. Progress up the river was slowed by the *Paw Paw*. The center-wheeler "was so slow that we were over two days getting up to that place," remembered Acting Master's Mate De Witt C. Morse, alias "Gunboat," aboard the *Curlew*.

Out at St. Louis, Maj. Gen. Rosecrans was equally slow, this time in following his orders to send reinforcements to "Old Pap" George Thomas. Responding to the request from Washington, D.C., "Old Rosy" inquired whether the men he sent were to go by a specific route, take their artillery, ammunition, and regimental trains along, and whether they were to be sent "in driblets" or *en masse*. When Grant learned of Rosecrans' telegram, he quickly ordered his own chief of staff, Brig. Gen. John Rawlins, to St. Louis to end what the supreme commander considered to be a case of stalling.[12]

The next morning, the *Paw Paw*, *Fairy*, and *Curlew* undertook a reconnaissance by fire into the areas surrounding Fort Henry and Fort Heiman, pumping shells at suspicious wooded areas and neighboring hills as they steamed past. "Our shell would not bring a man in sight at either place," noted Mate Morse. As the three were so engaged, the task group under Lt. Col. Fitch came up, allowing the veteran Hoosier to assume overall command. After "speaking" Goudy, Fitch directed that the six boats all drop back and form into a line-ahead order which would permit them to reserve their fire for any batteries which opened upon them. The Tennessee was quite deep at this point and wide enough to permit the tinclads to engage batteries as a fleet without risk of grounding.

When no sign of the enemy was found, Fitch ordered his craft to steam upriver the three or four miles to Paris Landing. Going ashore there, the tinclad warrior found a surgeon tending a number of wounded U.S. sailors from the *Undine*. Some of these men, all of whom were "suffering for want of medicines, etc., " reported that Forrest's cavalry corps was en route toward Johnsonville. They were reported to have some 18–20 artillery pieces which they were hauling overland, as well as the undamaged *Venus* and *Undine*. One of the men, less severely wounded than the others, was taken aboard the *Moose*. Medical supplies and medicines were left with the surgeon by flagboat sailors for the others.[13]

By noon on November 3, Forrest's cavalry and the *Undine*, last remaining vessel of the Tennessee River Navy, had reached the vicinity of Reynoldsburg Island, 3.5 miles below Johnsonville. The island was a major navigational feature that split the river flow and forced upstream traffic to pass it through a narrow chute that hugged the Tennessee's west bank. The river's main channel cut abruptly to the east bank south of the island and impassable shoal water lay to its east. Confederate artillery was placed at the head and foot of the atoll and a new trap was laid for the Union navy.[14]

In an effort to draw Acting Volunteer Lieutenant King's tinclads from Johnsonville into an ambush, Capt. Gracey's *Undine*, still loaded with grayclad troops, twice boldly sortied toward the Yankee depot. On each occasion, King was tempted to go after her, moving the *Key West* down a mile to a point where she came under intense volleys of musketry from the head of Reynoldsburg Island. Sensing his peril, the volunteer lieutenant refused both times to commit to further pursuit. Rather, he retired to the Johnsonville levee and, in the end, elected to anchor and station the *Tawah* with her head downstream, so as to command the channel with her 30-pounders. Having in the meantime received a telegram of encouragement from Lt. Cmdr. Shirk, King returned the wire, reporting that he had the *Undine* in sight below the island and that a battery of Rebel 10-pounders was reported on the adjacent western riverbank. Believing the outpost surrounded and that his boats might be subjected to a commando raid after dark, he once again pleaded: "Send large fleet of gunboats at once, if possible."

In the early afternoon, the King relief force, *Moose, Brilliant, Victory, Paw Paw, Fairy,* and *Curlew,* departed Paris Island for up the river. At the Memphis and Clarksville Railroad crossing, the six came upon a force of 40–50 cavalry foraging. "They were shelled and soon disappeared."

Back at Johnsonville around 4 P.M., Acting Volunteer Lieutenant King wrote to Capt. Howland advising him what action should be taken with regards to the steamers in port in the event of a surprise night attack on the gunboats. The assistant quartermaster was advised to make plans to fire all of the transports to keep them out of Forrest's hands should the Rebels attempt to board and take the navy craft. Howland passed the message on to his assistant, Lt. Samuel W. Treat, who passed it on to all of the masters at the levee along with a warning not to destroy any of the boats until their takeover was imminent.

As the afternoon waned, Maj. Gen. Forrest and his artillery chief, Capt. Morton, stealthily examined the area across the river from Johnsonville seeking firing locations from which to bombard the depot. The western shore was boggy, with only a few bad roads, much underbrush, and a surprisingly wide variety of wildlife. Working covertly in daylight, the two chose behind the levee and east of the low crest on the earthen tongue which separated Trace Creek and the Tennessee. The men could plainly see every detail of the base, 800 yards away, and hear every noise from horses to lifting machinery. Several boats and barges had yet to be unloaded because there wasn't room. The landing and banks were piled high with freight destined for Maj. Gen. Sherman. Indeed, all of the warehouses were full and trains were running "incessantly night and day in removing" the goods. The Federals had no pickets across the river and did not know they were under close surveillance.[15]

Above Turkey Island—or just below Green Bottom Bar—about 30 miles above Fort Heiman, the task group led by Lt. Cmdr. Fitch came upon a large Rebel encampment about 9:30 P.M. The gunboats opened fire in the dark and the shelling, which went on for a time, caused the soldiers to extinguish their campfires. The Indiana sailor believed they might have been driven back, but perhaps "not entirely away, as they could be heard during the night."

Given the narrow places, bad bars, and other navigational difficulties known to be ahead and unsure whether or not any Southern artillery awaited him, Fitch elected not to advance farther. Instead, he dropped down a little below the camp he was shelling and located a point where there was no road by which the enemy could bring cannon on the bank abreast his boats. There, six miles below Johnsonville, his flotilla anchored for the night.

By dark, all of Forrest's troops had arrived and he began to dispose them at key points from which they could bombard the Union depot across the Tennessee. As he later wrote in his official report, the Yankees commanded the position he designed to occupy and so he was necessarily compelled to act with great caution. Having chosen his artillery locations that afternoon, the "Wizard" set to work that night planting his guns. Brig. Gen. Chalmers recorded the disposition:

Colonel Mabry, with his brigade and Thrall's battery, on the right immediately above and opposite to Johnsonville; Colonel Rucker, with Morton's battery and the Seventh Alabama

Cavalry, immediately below and opposite to that place; Lieutenant Colonel Kelley with the Twenty-Sixth Tennessee Battalion and two guns of Rice's battery, opposite to Reynoldsburg, and Lieutenant Colonel Logwood, of the Fifteenth Tennessee Cavalry, with his regiment and a section of Hudson's battery, at Clark's House, still further down the river and about two miles below Johnsonville.

Capt. Thrall's howitzers, at their location about a half mile above the landing, were tasked with resisting Union attacks from upriver, while Capt. Hudson's two guns would hopefully beat back any assault from downstream. The others would smash the Northern depot when the attack began at noon sharp.

While his officers and men worked on their surprise, Maj. Gen. Forrest wrote a dispatch to his commander, Lt. Gen. Taylor. In it, he revealed that he was in front of Johnsonville, where he could see three gunboats, seven transports, "and quite a number of barges." Batteries were placed above and below the boats and the night was being spent fortifying and placing a battery straight across from them. On the morrow, he would "endeavor to sink or destroy them." Forrest, almost prophetically, offered his thoughts on the *Undine*. "We still have the gunboat," he noted, "but she is out of coal." As her furnaces required coal and he was unable to obtain any or run her by Johnsonville, "I may have to burn her." Even if he did not need to do so next day, he would certainly do so "day after tomorrow" before moving off to join Gen. Hood.

When Capt. Morton arrived on the scene early on the morning of November 4, he found the secret work of clearing away the undergrowth and placing the guns well advanced. With Forrest's permission, Morton made a final check of possible positions and found a very suitable spot higher up. The scene which unfolded below him was animated with an "air of complete security." Two gunboats with steam up were moored at the landing, while another plied directly beneath the bluff on which the Confederate artillery chief stood. He could, he remembered, "almost have dropped a stone upon it." Two freight trains were being made up, and a number of barges were being loaded by African Americans.

Morton hastened back to detail his findings to Forrest. The spot was ideal, the gunner pleaded. It was too high for the gunboats to reach without firing over it and the Yankee fort stood on a ridge that was so elevated that its guns could not be depressed sufficiently to hit any Rebel guns. A skeptical general permitted his artillery man to move two 3-inch guns to his "comparatively safe" location. The task, undertaken through mud and thick underbrush, required two hours of back breaking hand transport to accomplish. Once they were placed, Forrest had eleven cannon in close proximity to the huge base and no enemy the wiser. None of the gunboats or transports at Johnsonville or downriver from them would be able to pass Reynoldsburg Island either to escape or to help.[16]

While Capt. Morton was making his reconnaissance, Lt. Cmdr. Fitch got his task group underway and proceeded up the river in the rain the six miles from his night anchorage to the foot of Reynoldsburg Island. From this vantage point, he could see the three Ninth District gunboats above, *Tawah*, *Key West*, and *Elfin*. The *Moose*, followed by the *Paw Paw* and *Fairy*, chosen to accompany because they shipped the guns with the longest range, moved up to the foot of the chute separating the island from the shore.

As the three steamers paddled up, a battery was spotted at the head of the chute; Fitch ordered it taken under fire in order to test the caliber of the Rebel cannon. The Southerners refused to respond; rather, they moved their guns around into a small ravine or behind an embankment. This firing was heard at Johnsonville by, among others, quartermaster Capt. Howland.

In late morning, as the Indiana sailor's downstream gunboats were attempting by their fire to draw out the Confederate horse artillery, one of the gunboats above moved down toward Fitch and made its number, identifying itself as Acting Volunteer Lieutenant King's flagboat *Key West*. King, from a dispatch received via Nashville, knew that his superior had brought a quantity of fixed ammunition and stores for his boats. Unhappily, he was prevented from making a rendezvous with Fitch by a heavy battery placed in the false bend of the Tennessee just above the point. The battery commanded the upper end of the chute and was protected from the *Moose*, *Paw Paw*, and *Fairy* by a skirt of heavy timber on the point below. Acting Master's Mate Morse aboard the *Curlew* later remembered that "seeing the *Key West* stand toward us reminded me of a drowning man reaching out his hand to an idle crowd of cowards."

Perhaps as cover for the Confederates' final bombardment preparations, particularly Morton's activities in digging his battery into a small enclosure, "Commodore" Dawson and Capt. Gracey now chose to run the *Undine* up toward Reynoldsburg Island. Their move was another attempt to lure the Johnsonville-based gunboats under the shore batteries of the two leaders' land-based colleagues, Rice and Hudson. Located as she was on the river below Pilot Knob, the highest point on the west bank of the Tennessee, the former Union gunboat, after shooting a few shells toward Johnsonville, succeeded in provoking the *Key West*, *Tawah*, and *Elfin* to cast off after her.

As the three Union Navy tinclads moved toward him, Gracey ordered his vessel backed downstream under the protection of the Southern land cannon. As the soldier-captain later recalled in a statement quoted in John Latham's book, his attention was drawn astern by wild gestures in the noise made by Ohio River pilot William Weaver in the pilothouse. Coming around that structure, Gracey "saw a sight to make him gesticulate. There were seven of the largest Ohio River gunboats within easy gunshot range." The *Undine* was caught between the guns of Fitch's task group and King's task group, with the former blocking her escape downriver. Gracey and his crew fully realized, as Forrest's own admission confirmed, that they were expendable, but, just before she was lost, perhaps a price might be extracted from the Yankee fleet.

The *Key West* and *Tawah* came up with their former consort and, in a brief engagement, the amateur Confederate sailors were easily outmaneuvered. Still, *Undine* gave as good as she got—for a little while. Then, out of coal, Dawson and Gracey decided the game was over. Still, as they ran the tinclad ashore under the Rebel batteries two and a half miles below Johnsonville, they knew they had accomplished something—Acting Volunteer Lieutenant King's three boats were drawn within range of Hudson's and Rice's gunners.

When the *Key West* approached the battery in pursuit of the *Undine*, she was taken under fire by the shore-based artillerists who pumped thirty-odd shots at her in a space of 20 minutes, two-thirds for effect. The gunboat suffered ten hits through her upper works, seven through her berth deck, and two through the hull, with several guns disabled. *Elfin* was also damaged and the *Tawah* was largely ineffectual because her newly-received ammunition, obtained from Nashville a day earlier, proved too large. Additionally, the *Tawah's* hull began to open along her stem as the result of the concussion of her bow guns. The shelling forced King to back up and return above, with the *Key West* aided by the *Tawah*.

At the same time that the *Moose* started up the chute and the *Key West* started down, volunteers aboard the *Undine* tore up their straw mattresses. Capt. Gracey and several men then spread the spilled mattress contents around the deck and engineering spaces, and sprinkled oil upon them. The boat was headed hard for shore and struck a sandbar in three feet of water, about 75 yards from the head of the island. Gracey and several others applied the torches and jumped into the water. The *Undine* quickly burned down to the waterline, her magazine exploded spectacularly, and what was left of her lodged in the false bend above Reynoldsburg Island. The saga of the Tennessee River Navy was over. All of its surviving amateur sailors were now soldiers once more. Before escaping back across the river that night, they hid out for the rest of the day in the canebrakes that lined the bank.

As he watched the *Undine's* demise, Lt. Cmdr. Fitch understood, from earlier reports, that the Rebels had taken the gunboat intact and knew that she was fully armed when this morning's engagement started. Although he really did not know for certain, but assuming this was the case, the task group commander later told Rear Admiral Lee there was little chance that any of her howitzers were removed by the escaping men and that all of the little cannon were at the bottom of the river.

Aware of the gunfire clash between King and the *Undine*, sailors aboard the tinclads of Fitch's task group pondered whether a push through the Reynoldsburg Island chute, maybe reminiscent of the *Moose's* rush up the Buffington Island slot after Morgan in 1863, might be attempted. "We were every moment expecting orders to advance," Mate Morse later recalled. Capt. Gracey on the *Undine* later wondered: "Why they [Fitch's boats] did not shoot I could not say, unless they were afraid of striking their friends who were in easy range just above me."

Those aboard the *Curlew*, "both officers and men," were particularly anxious to assist, "Gunboat" recalled. Lt. Cmdr. Fitch himself was initially inclined "to try to run the batteries and get above," but soon changed his mind. In operational control of most of the tinclads remaining in the Mississippi Squadron's Ninth and Tenth Districts, the Logansport native was fully aware of the stakes he faced that day and the potential for disaster that awaited any nautical charge. The enemy batteries, narrowness of the channel, shoal water, and the possibility of a damaged vessel blocking the passage militated against any decision to proceed. Forrest had outmaneuvered the USN and the Indiana sailor knew it. Historian Latham later confirmed Fitch's situation: "At the same time, the *Paw Paw, Fairy,* and *Moose* were engaging a Confederate battery at the head of the chute, thus making it impossible for them to ascend the river."

The Hoosier officer afterwards outlined the difficulties he thought he faced in a report to Acting Rear Adm. Lee. The document, reproduced in the Navy *Official Records,* is accompanied by a map, which is not reproduced in the online version of the navy documents provided by Cornell University. It was drawn by Fitch and is the only example of his artwork that has ever been published. Lee was advised that, to pass through the narrow channel to the right of the bar, the tinclads would have had to proceed single file within 50 yards of Hudson's battery. If any one of them was disabled in the swift, shoal water, she would lodge on the head of the bar directly under the Rebel guns, less than 100 yards away. If such occurred, none of the other boats could steam to her assistance, as there was insufficient space to pass up alongside to go on ahead.

"Had there been a chance of my getting through with the loss of only one or two boats and then dislodging the enemy," perhaps remembering the exploit of Capt. Henry Walke at Island No. 10 in 1862 when the ironclad *Carondelet* and the following U.S.S. *Pittsburgh* had accomplished a similar goal, "I should have attempted it." Unlike Walke's exploit, however, Fitch had no land force to render assistance or gain advantage from any success the tinclads might realize and keep the Rebels away permanently. Even if all or any of his six boats got through, they still had to return below again past Reynoldsburg Island by the same chute, at which time it could be expected that Forrest's guns would have been sited to fire into their sterns. "After considering everything and seeing what little chance there was for any of my boats getting through," he later wrote, "I thought it mere folly to attempt such a hazardous move." Indeed, the task group commander believed that, if he made the effort, "not a single boat would have got out of the river."

Thus it was that the rescue attempt some in the Paducah fleet hoped for did not come off. At least three men aboard one of the upper boats were upset at leaving Acting Volunteer Lieutenant King to his fate while a later historian blamed Fitch's reluctance on "his imagination." Once again, the Indiana sailor, as at Dover in early 1863 and with the Cumberland convoys in both 1863 and 1864, was second-guessed.

The *Curlew* skipper, Acting Volunteer Ensign O'Neill, "was a brave little man" whom Acting Master's Mate Morse for one admired. "But he don't wear stripes enough; he offered to run the battery, but they couldn't see that of a lower Mississippi boat." The Tennessee pilot aboard O'Neill's boat, "about the oldest in the business and who can with a pencil trace the whole Tennessee river from memory," was, according to Morse, adamant that the channel past Reynoldsburg Island, even when low, could, under his guidance, "take two or three boats up abreast past the battery."

On the other side of the debate, Haines of the *Paw Paw* "rightly saw that Confederate gunners were only waiting to get the relief ships between the batteries covering the narrow stream and add to the number of their victims." "It seemed hard," Seaman Norman Carr of that boat remembered in a letter home, "to see the Rebs shell our boats so and we could not get them."

While offering historical background in his journal article on Nathan Bedford Forrest State Park, historian Edward Williams emphatically indicates his belief that Fitch and Shirk were overly cautious in their initial response two days earlier, thereby saving "Forrest from a considerable amount of harassment which would otherwise have seriously hampered his next move and made his task very difficult." He further states that the reason the *Moose* was not initially fired upon when she moved up on the morning of November 4 was not because Forrest wished to draw her into a trap, but because Hudson's battery was being moved into position for the forthcoming Johnsonville bombardment. Williams goes on to contend that Fitch was prevented from entering the Reynoldsburg chute "by his imagination more than anything else."

The eastern side of Reynoldsburg Island was obstructed and Fitch was hesitant to "move past the narrow channel to the west ... because he suspected a trap," wrote Forrest biographer Lonnie Maness in 1990. Therefore, he "was content to carry on a long range bombardment." Repeating Williams' claim, Maness advised that the Hoosier was not fired on because the Confederate guns were moved and "Hence, Fitch was stopped more by his imagination than anything else."

There is no other collaboration of Morse's tale regarding either O'Neill or the pilot. Even if the channel or the chute beside the island had not changed naturally in size after the war, with the entire Johnsonville area under water, there is no way now to confirm even an approximation of its width. Without fire control parties or scouts ashore, it was impossible for Lt. Cmdr. Fitch to know exactly what the status of the Rebel batteries may have been unless, perhaps, they returned his probing fire—which they did not. Although Morse and Williams (and Maness) strongly suggest more aggressive action might have been taken by the Ninth and Tenth District commanders, both fail to appreciate the larger "whole district" picture being viewed by the veteran upper river Union navy defenders or their state of mind concerning it.

Maj. Gen. Forrest was universally feared in Yankee circles, afloat and ashore, because of his successes and because of his ability, and that of his lieutenants, to pop up unannounced. Acting Rear Adm. Lee was new and untried on Western waters, while Capt. Pennock trusted Fitch to do the right thing and had not previously been disappointed. Shirk at Paducah and Fitch were growing anxious about an increasing number of convoys, particularly on the Cumberland. Moreover, neither had any way to know, from the various reports reaching them, that Forrest, with thousands of soldiers and rifled cannon, was not repeating, with some variance, his March-April offensive that culminated in the Fort Pillow engagement.

Additionally, Fitch and Shirk knew the thin protection of their vessels. Fitch remembered the fate of the *St. Clair* off Palmyra the year before and both had read reports of the hard knocks taken by the tinclads during the Red River expedition. They probably were extremely sensitive to tinclad vulnerabilities after hearing and reading of the losses of the U.S.S. *Signal* and *Covington* when they came up against rifled field guns near Alexandria, La, back in May. What the lieutenant commanders kept foremost in mind was that they operated only a few boats and could not afford to lose any recklessly. If the Confederate batteries were located as Fitch saw them, then to run the chute under those circumstances would have been far more calamitous than "mere folly."

Hoping to save ammunition and suspecting that he could not "do much execution" due to the intervening heavy timber, Fitch, nevertheless, ordered his three vessels to open a slow and deliberate fire on the offending gunners. This heavy shoot continued without result "until about 11 o'clock, when it ceased." Though not as physically uncomfortable as Capt. Gracey, who was then hiding in the canebrakes along the river bank with the survivors of the *Undine*, the Hoosier officer and his sailors were also unable to take any active part in the events that occurred after lunch.[17]

Following the *Undine* engagement, Acting Volunteer Lieutenant King's three gunboats retired to a position off Johnsonville to protect the transports and supplies. Many in the town, including those aboard King's craft, believed—in error—that the morning's triumph caused Forrest's people to hesitate or perhaps withdraw. The *Key West, Tawah, and Elfin*, moored at the landing, kept steam up, even as their officers and men attended to such regular duties as clothes washing and deck scrubbing. Just to be certain that the Rebels were departed, the damaged *Key West* and *Tawah*, lashed together, pushed off from the dock shortly before 2 P.M. to investigate a report that the enemy was "planting batteries directly opposite, also above and below, our warehouses and levee."

As the tinclads swung out, ten hidden Confederate cannon, all carefully trained on them, "were discharged with such harmony that it could not be discerned there was more than one report—one heavy gun." The cannonade that followed against the river craft and depot facilities was the "most terrific" Capt. Howland, for one, had ever witnessed and was accompanied by volleys of rifle fire. Maj. Gen. Forrest observed that King's gunboats (28 guns) and Fort Johnson (14 guns) returned fire and that about 50 guns were "thus engaged at the same time." Like Howland, the "Wizard" found that "the firing was terrific."

The racket from all this gunfire was easily heard by Fitch's task group above. About 2:30 P.M. as the din increased, the Logansport native took his *Moose* up into the Reynoldsburg Island chute, thinking that Hudson's battery might have been removed and that he might somehow assist King. It had not and opened on the Hoosier's flagboat. After an uneventful 15-minute engagement during which she was unable to dislodge the Southern guns, the *Moose* returned and tied up at the foot of the island. Smoke and the din of combat continued from the direction of Johnsonville throughout the afternoon.

At some point, a messenger from Johnsonville reached Lt. Cmdr. Fitch with word that King's gunboats were actively engaged and fighting desperately. Thus it was believed on the boats above, but without conclusive visual collaboration, that the *Key West*, *Tawah*, and *Elfin* were having somewhat more success against the Rebel batteries than was actually the case. Still attempting to assert some control over the situation, Fitch quickly penned an order to King directing him to "get the transports and the gunboats together, and as a last resort to run the batteries and get below to me, but above all not to let any of the transports fall into the enemy's hands." At Fort Johnson, Col. Thompson was telegraphing Nashville, which promised that the entire XXIII Corps under Maj. Gen. John M. Schofield would soon arrive.

When it was nearly dark, observers reported Johnsonville ablaze and that all of the boats along the levee were on fire. It was impossible to determine "whether the shell fired them or they were set on fire by our forces." It was, however, fairly certain that "the gunboats were among the number we saw on fire." In a report to Acting Rear Adm. Lee, Fitch expressed a belief that Forrest probably couldn't take Fort Johnson, "but his shell or our forces have undoubtedly destroyed everything." How accurate he was would shortly be revealed.[18]

When the Rebel artillerists opened fire, the *Key West* and *Tawah* were headed toward a Tennessee River bend above Johnsonville. The peaceful scene changed, as Capt. Morton later put it, "as if a magician's wand had been suddenly waved over it." The cannonade "continued with one unceasing roar" and, according to Forrest, quickly disabled King's two boats. "In fifteen minutes after the engagement commenced," he remembered, they "were set on fire and made rapidly for the shore, where they were consumed." The *Elfin* likewise was run ashore, fired, and abandoned. The officers and men from the three boats scrambled to the safety of Fort Johnson.

Forrest's batteries, having disposed of the USN guard, "next opened upon the eight transports, and in a short time, they were in flames." Among those thus destroyed were the *Anna*, which Forrest nearly nabbed earlier, the prize *Venus*, and the *Duke*, which Fitch had earlier accused of Rebel sympathies. At 4 P.M., Acting Volunteer Lieutenant King wired Lt. Cmdr. Shirk at Paducah advising him of the disaster. The *Paw Paw* and other boats were below, with batteries above and below them, and unable to intervene. Johnsonville, he warned, could be saved only by a large force and ironclads. Shirk did not receive the telegraph until the next day.

Maj. Gen. Forrest did not know in real time that most of the transports and barges were purposefully put to the torch under the earlier contingency plan designed to prevent their capture agreed to by King and Col. Thompson. The 10-foot-high stacks of provisions stored in the open and on the levee, warehouses, and other facilities were shot up and, by nightfall, "the wharf for nearly one mile up and down the river presented one solid sheet of flame."

At Nashville, Capt. John C. Van Duzer wired a summary of the latest news to Maj.

Thomas Eckert, head of the Federal telegraph service at the War Department and, after the war, assistant secretary of war. The news from the Tennessee capital was bleak. There was no definite information concerning the movement of Hood's main body. Additionally and bluntly, Van Duzer noted that Forrest had "repulsed five gunboats which attacked him and compelled them to fall back down the river," in addition to destroying three gunboats and at least two transports at Johnsonville.[19]

Less than 10 men all together on both sides were killed in action at Johnsonville. The Federal loss in material was estimated at $2.2 million, though one modern historian has estimated that, in terms of the 1990s value of the dollar, the goods destroyed could not be duplicated for less than $20 million. Not counting the value of the *Mazeppa*, Forrest was proud of the fact that, during the course of this unique raid, he destroyed four gunboats, numerous steamers and barges, the 33 artillery pieces on the navy warships, and quartermaster's stores estimated at between 75,000 and 120,000 tons while capturing 9,000 pairs of shoes, a thousand blankets, and 150 prisoners.

Nearly every history of the Johnsonville campaign suggests that the Union commanders in the town, both naval and military, acted too quickly to destroy the boats and supplies. Lt. Cmdr. Fitch, "whose judgment and courage were well proved," according to Admiral Mahan, said that King's three gunboats were well handled, but could not stand up to the heavy guns firing upon them in the uncertain channel. Admiral Porter agreed on the bravery exhibited, but added that "they had been sent on duty that more properly belong to ironclads, and in contending against the enemy's works, their ardor eclipsed their judgment." Mahan, after reviewing the events of the day and noting that Johnsonville was relieved 24 hours later by elements from Schofield's corps, was blunt: "If King had patiently held on a little longer, his pluck and skill would have been rewarded by saving his vessels."

Brig. Gen. Donaldson, in a June 30, 1865, review penned for Quartermaster General Meigs, was equally direct. "I am not prepared to believe," he wrote, "that the destruction of property at Johnsonville was necessary or warranted under the circumstances ... I think," he continued, "there was a want of judgment on the part of the officer who ordered the transports to be fired." Donaldson was ready to contest the view that King and Thompson feared Forrest would capture the transports. "The answer to this is," he observed, "the transports were under his [Forrest's] guns and could have been destroyed at any time." Forrest, a master of placing the "skeert" into his enemy, outfoxed his opponents. "It was fear," Thomas biographer Thomas Van Horne later admitted, "rather than necessity that caused this waste." Porter, when he wrote of the matter two decades later, was equally blunt. "Had he [Fitch] been present [in Johnsonville], his good judgment would have led to a different result."

The real story of the Johnsonville operation was, for the South, one of an opportunity seized too late and, for the North, the loss of a facility that, in the end, didn't matter all that much. Maj. Gen. Sherman had already assembled all of the supplies required for his sortie from Atlanta to Savannah. Indeed, in less than a week, he would cut himself off entirely from the north and "live off the land" of the Georgia countryside. At Nashville, Maj. Gen. Thomas, who received "the truth on the disgraceful affair" from Schofield a few days later, could depend upon both the Louisville & Nashville Railroad and the Cumberland River.

The attacking Southern troops hoped to sever Sherman's supply lines, forcing him to abandon the forthcoming march across Georgia. Able to grasp the big picture, Sherman, in a message to Lt. Gen. Grant, was not overly upset even as he noted "that devil Forrest was down about Johnsonville making havoc among the gunboats and transports." Johnsonville was not rebuilt as a depot; in fact, it was abandoned on November 30. Its wreckage would not be cleaned up for months. Forrest's audacity did not change the Northern logistical situation one iota, but it did further enhance it's author's legend.[20]

Because most of the depot's goods plus the gunboats and transports were destroyed, Maj. Gen. Forrest did not cross the river in force and capture Johnsonville. He had orders to rejoin Gen. Hood and could not have gotten over anyway, having only two small boats from the *Undine*. Besides "the work designed by the expedition" was substantially completed; there was nothing to be gained by ransacking the blazing ruins of the depot or attacking Fort Johnson. Pleased with their success, the Confederates marched six miles away from the depot during the night "by the light of the enemy's burning property." The weather remained wretched, with rain falling heavily and mud everywhere, especially on the roads.

Also after dark, Lt. Cmdr. Fitch wondered what good he could do from his location below the burning town. Simultaneously, he found that the Confederate commander, anxious to press his advantage while covering his withdrawal, was moving some men abreast of him "doubtless with a view of planting batteries." Several of his boats were ordered to fire bursts of canister at the dimly-perceived graycoats, driving them back from the riverbank.

A little while later, the Indiana sailor learned that Forrest was transferring some of his batteries downstream to cut off his gunboats below Reynoldsburg Island. If that occurred, Fitch would be in as much difficulty as was Acting Volunteer Lieutenant King earlier, unable "to contend successfully against heavy rifled field batteries in a narrow river full or bars and shoals." On top of this, a thick fog was developing that would prevent the craft from running if necessary. To avoid the possibility that, due to the low stage of water, the Rebels might be able to get cannon into a position from which to destroy one or more of his command, it was decided to drop down. At 10:30 P.M., the six units in Fitch's task group came to off Fort Heiman for the night.

The following morning, November 5, Maj. Gen. Forrest returned to the Tennessee opposite Johnsonville to personally observe his success by daylight. After a brief artillery and rifle exchange with African American troops across the stream, the butternut contingent headed off to the southwest to join the rest of the cavalry group as it moved toward Corinth, five days away. At Paducah, Lt. Cmdr. Shirk received the wire sent by Acting Volunteer Lieutenant King the previous day and rapidly sent it on to Acting Rear Adm. Lee, respectfully asking that arrangements be made to send an ironclad up the Tennessee when it rose to "clear it out."

Meanwhile, Lt. Cmdr. Fitch's boats spent that Saturday tied to the bank near Fort Heiman. Nearly all were out of fuel and landing parties busily cut cords of wood and hauled them aboard. During the day, Acting Volunteer Lieutenant Glasssford's *Reindeer*, together with the *Fairplay*, joined Fitch, bringing orders for the detachment of the *Curlew*.

On the morning of November 6, the weather turned inclement again. Rain and high winds made life miserable for anyone exposed on the Union gunboats. Fitch, who had planned to start back down the river, was advised by his pilots that the Sunday downpour and particularly the breeze made it far too dangerous to attempt to run the crooked and rocky bars. The commander was advised that, if he proceeded, there was a good chance that one or more of his craft could be lost by striking obstructions. Heeding the warning, the Indiana sailor ordered his group to cease departure preparations and sent out pickets to the hills above Fort Heiman. The men fired on several roving groups of butternut horsemen during the day.

At Cairo before lunch, Acting Rear Adm. Lee sent the first of many wires to Maj. Gen. Thomas. Written in cipher, the telegram announced his assumption of squadron command and promised to always cooperate cordially with the Nashville-based Army boss. The message also recapped what was known of Johnsonville area activities and preparations the navy was making to help prevent enemy reinforcements reaching Hood from over the Mississippi.

Also during the day, Acting Volunteer Ensign O'Neill's *Curlew* departed Fort Heiman for Paducah, "heartily sick," according to Acting Master's Mate Morse, "of the company we had been in." Meanwhile, the first "refugees" escaping the Confederate onslaught reached Nashville and began telling their stories to the local newspapers. Stories would appear in the town's journals over the next three days.

Maj. Gen. Thomas at Nashville finally received Lee's November 6 dispatch at 9 P.M.— 11 hours after it was sent. The theater commander replied immediately, noting that the Johnsonville garrison had reported being able to see the smoke from Fitch's task group, but was unable to communicate with it. He, too, asked the navy boss to assign some ironclads to the Tennessee "when the river gets high enough." Ever optimistic, he prophesized that, together, they would be able to "clear the enemy entirely out of west Tennessee." Even after almost four years of war, the word "ironclad" still had magic.[21]

CHAPTER TWELVE

Nashville, December 1864–January 1865

WHILE MAJ. GEN. NATHAN BEDFORD FORREST was away bustin' Johnsonville, Gen. John Bell Hood's advance into Middle Tennessee was delayed by three weeks. Although Florence and Tuscumbia were occupied, the main army paused to gather supplies and repair the Meridian-Corinth-Tuscumbia railroad. During this time, Union Maj. Gen. George "Old Pap" Thomas was also being reinforced with several corps and cavalry. Among the troops coming his way were two divisions (10,000 men, including four Minnesota infantry regiments) of the XVI Corps, commanded by Maj. Gen. Andrew J. "A. J." Smith, which the Nashville commandant had been expecting ever since they were promised by Maj. Gen. Sherman in late October. Smith was temporarily soldiering in Maj. Gen. William S. "Old Rosy" Rosecrans' Department of the Missouri, joined in the effort to repel the invasion of the Show-Me State by Maj. Gen. Sterling Price. Following the latter's defeat at Westport on October 23, Smith's men were free to reinforce Thomas and were, on November 2, ordered by "Old Rosy" to do so.

As Forrest created havoc among the gunboats and transports at Johnsonville, Smith undertook a grueling overland march covering the 200 miles from Westport to St. Louis. The same bad weather pelting Forrest and Fitch on the Tennessee slowed Smith's men. On November 7, Thomas wired Smith to warn him that the Rebels had blockaded that stream and advised that his men should proceed, instead, via the Cumberland. From St. Louis later in the day, Smith telegraphed Nashville to advise that three regiments and a battery, 2,500 men, was embarked and would reach Paducah next evening. Thomas responded at 10:15 that night reporting that the Cumberland had risen sufficiently to permit Smith to bring his entire command to Nashville via that stream. "I wish you, therefore, to get here as soon as you can," Thomas added. Lt. Gen. Grant's liaison to Maj. Gen. Rosecrans also telegraphed Nashville with the optimistic news that Smith's command was expected to leave St. Louis within three days. The entire Smith transfer was being orchestrated by Capt. Lynn S. Metcalf, the assistant quartermaster at St. Louis tasked with river traffic oversight.

Also on November 7, the mixed Ninth and Tenth Division task force got underway and steamed up the river. Some 10–12 miles above Fort Heiman, Lt. Cmdr. Fitch received intelligence that Forrest's forces were divided and some of them were moving on Paris Landing. Leaving the *Paw Paw* and *Victory* to seek additional information, the Indiana sailor took his remaining boats back to Paris Landing prepared to prevent the erection of a Confederate battery at that point. As with so many other tips received in those years of uncertain communication, this one was erroneous. At 4 P.M., the *Victory* and *Paw Paw* joined the rest of the fleet.

During that Monday, Acting Rear Adm. Lee ordered Lt. Cmdr. Shirk, then at Mound City, to send the *Peosta* to the relief of Johnsonville, telling his subordinate that Nashville was reporting that the stages of both the Tennessee and Cumberland were rising, with the depth of water in the latter up to five foot on the shoals. Shirk, in a meeting aboard the flagboat *Black Hawk*, countered that, while it was raining, the swelling water was still too low to send the heavy tinclad. Lee also informed Shirk that a new system was being put into place to distribute ammunition closer to the places where it was required. In times past, each district was forced to send a boat to Mound City or Cairo for replenishment. The new regiment would be implemented first on the Tennessee and Cumberland rivers.

Lee, who reshuffled commanders and gunboats in his more distant districts by the day's General Order No. 5, was anxious to get as much heavy support into the twin rivers as possible. Contained in copies of the GO sent downstream via the U.S.S. *Sybil* was a requirement that the river monitor U.S.S. *Neosho*, under Acting Volunteer Lieutenant Samuel Howard, be transferred to the Ohio River from the Sixth District. At the same time, the message steamer *Benefit* was sent down to the Memphis naval station with orders that the veteran Pook turtle U.S.S. *Carondelet*, then undergoing engine repair, be sent, under tow, to Mound City "the very hour that her machinery can be turned over." The repair of the Pook turtle *Cincinnati*, which was sunk at Vicksburg the year before and then raised, was approaching completion at the same Illinois base.

The *Carondelet* and *Cincinnati* were

Remembered as "The Rock of Chickamauga," the six-foot-tall Maj. Gen. George Thomas (1816–1870) was deputized by Maj. Gen. William T. Sherman to provide a defense for Nashville in the fall of 1864. During the ensuing campaign which culminated in mid–December, Thomas worked well with Lt. Cmdr. Fitch, while maintaining a voluminous telegraphic correspondence with Acting Rear Adm. Samuel P. Lee. Thomas was very complimentary of naval support during the Battle of Nashville (U.S. Army Military History Institute).

Originally commissioned in early 1862, the Eads-built U.S.S. *Carondelet* was the most famous of all the Union river ironclads. She participated in every major campaign in the West from Fort Henry through Nashville and basked in the glory of her famous passage by the guns of Island No. 10. Noteworthy as she was, she was also among the slowest vessels in the Northern river warship inventory (U.S. Army Military History Institute).

two of the seven Pook turtles constructed at Carondelet, Missouri, in 1861. The sisters, including the *Mound City*, which was on Col. Graham Newell Fitch's 1862 Arkansas expedition, were all but identical, except for the different colored identification bands on their chimneys. By late 1864, all were pretty well worn out, having been in most of the heavy combats of the river war since Fort Henry in February 1862.

Choosing the *Carondelet* as our example, we find a 512 ton steamer that was 175 feet long, with a beam of 51.2 feet and a depth of six foot. She possessed a rectangular casemate with sloped armor (thickest at the front) and a single paddle wheel located amidships toward the stern. Powered by two horizontal high-pressure engines, with a 22" cylinder and six-foot stroke, and five boilers, she could supposedly make a top speed of nine mph. The 251 officers and men aboard were responsible at this time for working a battery that comprised two 100-pounder Parrott rifles, one 50-pounder and one 30-pounder Dahlgren rifles, and three Dahlgren nine-inch smoothbores.

Capt. Henry Walke's boat at Island No. 10, *Carondelet* was the "most famous of all the river gunboats of the Civil War" and, as her first commander put it, "was in more battles and encounters with the enemy (about fourteen or fifteen times; and under fire, it is believed, longer and oftener) than any other vessel in the Navy," including those which went to sea. She was the only one of her class to directly engage a Confederate armor-clad, the C.S.S. *Arkansas* in July 1862. The twice-sunk *Cincinnati* (Fort Pillow, 1862; Vicksburg, 1863) would be ready for Nashville with a battery that included one 100-pounder Parrott rifle and one nine-inch Dahlgren smoothbore, plus four 24-pounder howitzers.[1]

Designed by James B. Eads, the *Neosho*, and her sister the *Osage* were the only sternwheel monitors. Both were laid down at Carondelet in 1862; the former cost $194,757.67 and was commissioned in May 1863. With a "turtleback" design on wooden hulls, both came in at 523 tons. The pair, which both participated in the Red River Expedition, measured 180 feet, with beams of 45 feet and depths of hold of 4.6 feet; each had a single forward-mounted revolving turret and one tall chimney amidships. Both were powered with a pair of horizontal high-pressure engines and four boilers and were designed to steam at a top speed of 12 mph. Armament comprised two 11-inch Dahlgren smoothbores in the turrets, which were shielded by six inches of armor. Armor protection on the sides was 2.5" thick, with 1.25" on the deck.[2]

Out on the Tennessee on November 8, the *Paw Paw* signaled Lt. Cmdr. Fitch that she was nearly out of fuel. Thus when the other boats weighed anchor for above, she was left behind to procure wood. She was also to guard against any Confederate effort to bring in batteries. At White Oak Island, about 15 miles below Johnsonville, the Tenth District commander received some startling news. It turned out that, on the night of the 4th instant, Southern forces had, supposedly, planted a four-gun battery at that point designed to cut off his advance. The location of the island chute, with a swift and narrow channel running under the left bank, would have required the gunboats to pass within 20 yards of the gray-clad cannoneers and all would have been disabled. Fitch felt considerable self satisfaction that he had chosen to drop much farther down that evening. Frustrated that their enemy had held back, the Rebels removed their guns the following morning.

From White Oak Island, the gunboat task force made its way, undisturbed, to Johnsonville. There Fitch learned that Acting Volunteer Lieutenant King and his men had departed for Mound City, via Nashville, the previous evening. After conferring with Col. Thompson, the gunboats departed for Fort Heiman. En route, Fitch, Glassford, and the other boat commanders took the time to examine closely the enemy gun positions of November 3–5.

Not only were the Hoosier officer's original observations confirmed, but he came to believe that "our chances of running the batteries were much less than I had calculated" originally. In additional to the treacherous river, its banks were higher than the hurricane decks of the tinclads and were then alive with sharpshooters, "who would have picked off every man that had showed himself." Leaving the area, Fitch was more convinced than ever that, had he attempted to run the Reynoldsburg Island chute, "every boat would have been destroyed and not a single man would have escaped."

Back at Fort Heiman that evening, Fitch composed a second report for Acting Rear Adm. Lee, sending along intelligence that Forrest was evidently crossing a heavy force above, to stop supplies ascending the Cumberland to Nashville. If that were, indeed, the case—which it wasn't but no one knew for sure—the Logansport native believed it best to withdraw the boats of his division and head back to Smithland to guard the increasing number of steamers headed to the Tennessee capital.[3]

Fitch's task force returned to Paducah on November 9, where the Hoosier sailor stopped briefly by the Ninth District office to drop off his latest report on Tennessee River activities and to ask Lt. Cmdr. Shirk to forward it to Acting Rear Adm. Lee. As Fitch and his steamers paddled into the distance toward the Ohio, Shirk wrote out a brief covering letter to accompany his colleague's document, as well as a short note of his own.

In the cover to the Fitch enclosure, the Pennsylvanian noted that, of his two remaining tinclads, the *Paw Paw* was in such bad condition as to be "utterly worthless." Even though he thus had only one effective vessel, he selflessly begged his commander not to deprive the Tenth District of boats with which to repopulate the Ninth. It was Shirk's opinion that the twin rivers would both need watching for a long time to come and thus it would be best if new warships could be provided. This opinion complemented Lee's own request of the Navy Department for ten new tinclads, which would shortly be approved.

In his own report, Shirk noted that Fitch had, indeed, withdrawn up the Cumberland. The move was made necessary, as Fitch himself indicated, by the need for additional convoy protection even as, "in all probability," Forrest had sent a portion of his forces to blockade that stream as well. Shirk went on to place as positive a spin on developments as possible. Given that it would not be possible to clear away the Johnsonville wreckage for some time, the Tennessee was really not a resupply option. Given that situation, his own lack of boats, and the continuing need to protect Paducah, the present rise in the Cumberland was most fortunate. Still, he warned, since Forrest's late success, "the light draft gunboats will have lost, in his sight, all the moral effect they ever had." To compensate, Shirk was more persuaded than ever of the value of Lee's posting one or two of the ironclads in each of the Ninth and Tenth Districts. With the *Carondelet*, *Neosho*, and *Cincinnati* tasked to those rivers as soon as available, the new Mississippi Squadron commander was already atop the requirement.[4]

Having learned on the evening of November 10 that Fitch's light division had not steamed above Johnsonville, but had, in fact, returned to Smithland, Acting Rear Adm. Lee wired Maj. Gen. Thomas with the news that the Cumberland was now navigable and that army transports should, henceforth, take that river rather than the Tennessee. Indeed, upon his return to his Tenth District base, Fitch had found 40 army steamers awaiting convoy and, in his usual fashion, vigorously set to work organizing a massive nautical trek upstream to the Tennessee capital. Meanwhile, as Lee noted in a wire to Thomas, the navy was pushing to put one ironclad on each of the twin rivers, with a third in reserve convenient to either.[5]

The next day, Brig. Gen. Robert Allen at Louisville telegraphed Mound City asking that Rear Admiral Lee see to the convoy of a large number of army transports to Nashville. These were the boats Fitch found at Smithland and so, being as yet unfamiliar with the initiative of his subordinate, Lee wired Fitch informing him of the Allen request and asking that the Indiana sailor render all of the assistance and protection he could.[6]

U.S. Army headquarters in Nashville, which expected Maj. Gen. Smith in Tennessee by that Friday, continued to wait. Three days later, Smith, who came ahead to St. Louis, wired Maj. Gen. Thomas that his men were still arriving from western Missouri. Almost ten more days would be required before Smith could get his force together and several days more to get them to the Cumberland. The tempo of major arena events continued to otherwise boom as the weather deteriorated and the month progressed. During all of this time, supply steamers continued to be pushed up the Cumberland under direction of Lt. Cmdr. Fitch's tinclad watchdogs.

On November 12, Maj. Gen. Sherman cut himself off from the north and started toward the Atlantic. Two days later, the 25,000 men from the IV and XXIII Corps were at Pulaski to oppose Hood. Confederate forces, beginning on November 19, marched toward Columbia, planning to turn the Yankees out of Pulaski. The Northern field commander, Maj. Gen. John Schofield, evacuated that place on November 22 and moved back toward Columbia, entrenching south of the Duck River. Hood's soldiers came upon Columbia five days later, at which point Schofield moved across the river, destroying its bridges. The Southern campaigner, with help from Forrest and Maj. Gen. Stephen D. Lee among others, managed to start turning the Federals over the next four days so that, by November 29, Schofield was nearly cut off, reaching Franklin only through good luck on November 30.[7]

The convergence of the blue- and gray-uniformed soldiers in middle Tennessee, though occurring in late fall and early winter, was not unlike the coming of a summer thunderstorm to areas of the Volunteer State. Even today, the threatening clouds of such a local tempest can be seen well ahead of time by any attentive person and most folks, after some residence, can almost tell how long it will be from first sightings of various thunderheads until the wind and rain arrives. Unlike the rapid thrust of a raider or guerrilla squall, the movement of the armies of Hood and Thomas was as ominous as such a gathering storm. Telegraph wires, scouts, patrols, shippers, journalists and civilians, like modern day electronic and communications media, all contributed to the pool of threat intelligence and assessment available for review.

As Hood, Thomas, their lieutenants, and others near and far made and remade their observations and preparations for the military deluge on land, the sailors of the Ninth and Tenth Districts, led in person by Fitch, Shirk, and Mississippi Squadron chief Lee, made every effort to control the Cumberland and Tennessee Rivers. The seamen knew a gale of Confederate iron was blowing and that it was their duty to help protect against it. Through close coordination with the army, the Navy could best accomplish its duty by blockading the use of the twin rivers to Union purpose. Specifically, district vessels were tasked to prohibit their crossing or other use by Southern forces, to detect and, whenever possible, defeat Rebel movements, and to guard and facilitate the continuing transfer of men and supplies. The last named goal included the protection of key ports and rendezvous and, as possible, coordination with army quartermasters and railroad chiefs.

While November advanced, the riverine navy's mission intensified. As historian Byrd Douglas later commented, the arrival of Maj. Gen. Smith's army from Missouri remained "of utmost importance" as was the need for cavalry horses. "There was not a mule to be found in Middle Tennessee, let alone a horse." Nearly every steamer coming up the Cumberland brought a few horses, as well as a few advance units of Smith's force, to say nothing of supplies. As Fitch had warned, it now became obvious at both army and navy headquarters that a blocking assault on the Cumberland by Forrest could be disastrous. If Maj. Gen. Forrest could blockade transportation there as he had on the Tennessee, "it might result in the loss of the impending battle with Hood before it was fought."

Lee, Fitch, Shirk and their army counterparts continued to push, directly and indirectly, the buildup of the Tenth District squadron; "above all," this growth "indicates the respect that Thomas, Sherman and Admiral Lee had for Forrest." In order to cope with the powerful rifled batteries the Confederates could be expected to erect along the Cumberland River, Lee wisely strengthened the forces of Lt. Cmdr. Fitch with ironclads. None of the local Union leadership could, however, know that the "devil's role would be confined to support of Hood's main force inland of the rivers. Only a small portion of Forrest's command would threaten Cumberland transportation during the upcoming battle.[8]

On November 12, Maj. Gen. Thomas at Nashville telegraphed Mound City acknowledging Acting Rear Adm. Lee's November 10 ironclad arrangement. He also suggested he might want to send one or more of the heavy craft up the Tennessee to check on Hood's progress, but would give plenty of warning as to their need.

By his General Order 16, dated November 18, Lee redrew the boundary of the Ninth District to include the territory from Mound City to Muscle Shoals and ordered Lt. Cmdr. Shirk to report to him in person with the *Paw Paw* as soon as he could depart Paducah. Two days later, orders were passed for the *Neosho* to steam from Mound City to Smithland, there to report to Lt. Cmdr. Fitch. The *Carondelet*, having meanwhile arrived at Mound City, continued under repair.[9]

Through the month, the divisions of Maj. Gen. Smith marched across Missouri to St. Louis. Early on November 24, Smith wired Brig. Gen. Meredith at Paducah advising that the First Division of the XVI Army Corps and a brigade of the XVII Army Corps was underway to Cairo and that the 3rd Division of the XVI Army Corps was embarking for departure next day. Meredith was advised to send on any other of Smith's men who independently showed up directly by water to Nashville. Smith's late departure had prevented Thomas from implementing an earlier plan to place the soldier's men at Eastport, Mississippi. Instead, Hood was threatening Columbia and according to Col. Henry Stone of Thomas' staff, it now became "an open question whether he would not reach Nashville before the reinforcements from Missouri."

The watch for waterborne reinforcements was now underway in earnest. During the day, Maj. Gen. Thomas personally ordered Col. Arthur A. Smith of the 83rd Illinois Volunteer Infantry, commanding at Clarksburg, to begin advising his office of troopboats passing his post en route to Nashville. Smith wired back that the 7th Cavalry Regiment had passed up at 8 A.M. Across the state at Memphis, Maj. Gen. Cadwallader C. Washburn passed on a requirement that both the 6th Tennessee Cavalry Regiment (dismounted) and 19th Pennsylvania Cavalry Regiment immediately embark for Nashville, via the Cumberland, taking along their horses, camp and garrison equipage.

In addition to convoys guarded by the USN, numerous steamers operated independently on the Cumberland, a few with protection from army gunboats. Near Cumberland City during the day, one of the lone sailors, the *Nannie,* was fired into by "guerrillas" hidden along the riverbank. About thirty rounds struck the boat, but no one was hurt and there was no damage.

Back aboard the steamer *Wananita* at the St. Louis wharf that evening, XVI Army Corps 3rd Division Acting Assistant Adjutant General James B. Comstock advised his unit's brigade commanders that their transport fleet would depart at daylight. The troops, transportation, and batteries were all to be aboard by then.[10]

As Maj. Gen. Smith's command ascended the Ohio toward Paducah on November 25, the Clarksville post commander reported that the steamers *Minnehaha* and *Liberty No. 2* had passed his town, "loaded with troops." For his part, Maj. Gen. Thomas, expecting that certain regiments had departed the previous Wednesday, was still wondering about Maj. Gen. Smith; in a wire to Brig. Gen. Meredith, he inquired: "Have none of General Smith's troops left Paducah yet?" Some were expected to leave later that day, came the reply. It should, of course, be remembered that other forces were arriving in the Tennessee capital by road and rail. Additionally, some people, including prisoners of war and refugees were leaving. As the sun waned, 738 penniless evacuees from Nashville arrived at Louisville aboard the transports *J. K. Baldwin* and *Irene.*[11]

Another troopboat passed Clarksville on November 26, about the same time Nashville commander Thomas wired Maj. Gen. Rosecrans at St. Louis to inquire if Smith had departed the Missouri town and if so when. Assurance was quickly received that the entire command was en route. With Hood threatening Columbia, Thomas was anxious not only about Smith's speed but whether the Confederate general had all of his force (including Forrest) with him. To find out, the army theater commander confidentially telegraphed Acting Rear Adm. Lee asking if any ironclads that "can resist heavy shot" were available and if so, whether they might be sent up the Tennessee River "as far as they can go on a reconnaissance." Lee, in turn, invited Lt. Cmdr. Shirk at Paducah to make the scout; the Ninth District commander asked that the *Neosho* and *Carondelet* accompany his *Peosta*.[12]

Just after dawn on November 27, Lt. Cmdr. Fitch received a telegram from his Cairo-based superior requiring that the *Neosho*, which had arrived at Smithland several days earlier, report to Shirk at Paducah. At the same time, the squadron commander, unhappy with the pace of repairs to the *Carondelet*, sent a messenger over to her commander, Acting Volunteer Master Charles W. Miller, ordering that, Sunday or not, final preparations be speeded up and that the bearer return with an estimate of when she would be ready. Fully expecting that the carpenters, painters, and calkers would be off the boat in a matter of hours and that she would have shipped her ammunition, the admiral signaled the auxiliary *Volunteer*. She was to coal and ready herself to tow the famous old fighting ship to Paducah. Meanwhile, the Ninth District commander received a confidential order to ascend the Tennessee next day, taking with him all of the ammunition and fuel required.[13]

As the *Neosho* steamed into the Ohio, repairs were completed on the *Carondelet*, and final arrangements for Shirk's nautical scout were completed, Maj. Gen. Smith's fleet reached Paducah from St. Louis. Thomas' headquarters was notified that the transports would steam to Smithland the next morning as soon as they had coaled. The major general commanding was also pleased to inform Lt. Gen. Grant at City Point, Virginia, that the usual "skeert" of Maj. Gen. Forrest, was evaporating. Although there was no positive news that the Confederate "devil" had departed Tennessee, he was "closely watched," and Thomas intended to move against Hood as soon as possible "whether Forrest leaves Tennessee or not."[14]

Toward dusk, Acting Rear Adm. Lee learned that Lt. Cmdr. Shirk, in poor health of late, was too ill to undertake the next day's reconnaissance. At 6:15 P.M., the squadron chief sent a wire to Smithland that tersely asked the Tenth District commander, then returning from Nashville, to proceed to Paducah where he would find new orders. At 9 P.M., Acting Volunteer Master Miller of the *Carondelet*, which had anchored abreast the *Black Hawk* three hours earlier, met with Lee aboard the flagboat to receive his orders and packets for Lt. Cmdr. Fitch. At 11:30 P.M., the ironclad steamed upriver under tow of the *Volunteer*.

The orders which were prepared for Fitch did not immediately reach the Indiana sailor and it would be another day or so before he would learn of them. If he had received the original wire, he might have been somewhat surprised at its mysterious shortness. Later, he would learn the reason: Thomas' confidential reconnaissance up the Tennessee River. The Indiana sailor was authorized to take both ironclads or just the *Neosho*, with such other boats from either district as he may desire. The *Volunteer* would steam ahead, towing a coal barge up to Johnsonville for use of the task group. At the scene of recent destruction, the army had promised to build a naval magazine and, once the scout was completed, the *Carondelet* and *Peosta* were to guard the working party. It could not have been anticipated, given the upstream speed of these boats or the construction project, that Fitch would soon be back at Smithland. Time was not plentiful and much of what lay on the pages of Lee's dispatch, then languishing in the dark at the bottom of the mail sack, would never be executed.

In addition to his immediate mission up the Tennessee, the Hoosier officer also learned of his colleague's illness and Lee's decision to have him sit in for Shirk until he recovered and resumed his duties. So it was that, unbeknownst to him at the moment, Le Roy Fitch now assumed tactical command of the USN ironclads *Carondelet* and *Neosho*, as well as the heavy gunboat *Peosta*, the tinclads *Moose* (flagboat), *Fairplay*, *Silver Lake*, *Brilliant*, *Springfield*, *Reindeer*, and *Victory*, plus at least one auxiliary. As the river's historian Douglas confirmed, "these constituted the greatest fleet of gunboats ever to appear on the Cumberland during the War." Although it is not generally recognized, Fitch could, if desired, also call upon available army gunboats, such as the *Silver Lake No. 2* and *Newsboy*. Although he did not hold elevated rank, Fitch now had more operational authority over more heavy vessels than any Mississippi Squadron junior officer since Capt. Henry Walke commanded the squadron's lower division at Vicksburg the previous year. He was also overall commander of more fighting ships at one time than any other junior officer in the history of the entire unit before or after its transfer from the War Department to the USN in October 1862.[15]

The *Carondelet* and *Volunteer* arrived at Paducah at 9:30 A.M. on November 28, where they joined the *Peosta* and *Neosho*. The captains of the three warships conferred throughout the morning. All realized that Shirk was ill, Fitch was incommunicado and that Acting Rear Adm. Lee was coming over from Mound City. While his heavy units were assembling at the Kentucky port, the Mississippi Squadron commander received a telegram from Maj. Gen. Thomas asking that he provide escort to Smith's troop fleet. Immediately agreeing, Lee hoped to head off Fitch and change his mission before his tireless subordinate departed.

The *Black Hawk* landed at the Paducah levee just after noon where the admiral met with Brig. Gen. Meredith. Armed with Thomas' request, briefed on Hood's reported movements and possible threats to the Cumberland logistical chain, and the size of Smith's convoy, Lee had little difficulty accepting Meredith's suggestion to postpone the Tennessee River reconnaissance. After all, Thomas possessed the same intelligence as those officers in Paducah and if it were correct, the voyage up past Johnsonville was unnecessary.

A half hour after visiting army headquarters, the squadron boss wired Smithland asking that the junior officer on duty there notify his chief that Lee was waiting for him at Paducah. When by 2:30 P.M. the Tenth District commander had still not arrived, Lee penned new orders for the Indiana sailor. After expediting the *Carondelet*, *Neosho*, and *Volunteer* on to Smithland and putting aboard the latter named vessel his messages for Fitch, Lee messaged Maj. Gen. Thomas and then returned to Mound City.[16]

The two ironclads, with the *Volunteer*, arrived at Smithland at 7:40 A.M. on November 29 and landed ahead of the U.S.S. *Moose*. The mail sack containing Acting Rear Adm. Lee's dispatches was immediately delivered aboard the Tenth District flagboat. In his cabin, Lt. Cmdr. Fitch read the several messages penned aboard the *Black Hawk* over the previous days and learned in detail of his new command responsibilities. He read the plans for the Tennessee River reconnaissance and the Johnsonville magazine. The latest orders required that he guard the passage of Maj. Gen. Smith's troop and supply boats to Nashville. Once that goal was accomplished, Fitch was to meet with Maj. Gen. Thomas. At the theater commander's pleasure, the Hoosier seaman was authorized to then make the Tennessee River reconnaissance or perform other necessary services on the Cumberland.

It is probable that Fitch was well aware of the details surrounding the urgency of Smith's assembling convoy and was even then completing plans for its escort. The night before army commanders aboard the steamers *Albert Pearce* and *Wananita* sent general orders for the Cumberland journey to their subordinates. All were to proceed carefully in strict observance of the fleet steaming order delivered earlier as well as those for the convoy received from the USN. No one wanted a repeat of the loss of the transport *W. L. Ewing*, which had struck a snag south of St. Louis and sunk, though fortunately not before all of the troops aboard were successfully transferred to nearby boats.

At 10 A.M., just over two hours following the arrival of the ironclads, the *Moose* started up the Cumberland leading the grand parade. Among the nearly 60 troop steamers joining the procession were the *Albert Pearce, Havana, James Raymond, Julia, Lilly Martin, Maggie Hayes, Victory, Marmora, Camelia, Silver Cloud, Arizona, J. F. McComb, Mercury, Financier, Lilly, New York, Lady Franklin, Pioneer, Magnet, Prima Donna, Wananita, America, Thomas E. Tutt, Mars, Omaha, Olive, Silver Lake, Kate Kearney, Spray, Mollie McPike, Prairie State,* and another *Victory.* Interspersed among the transports were the tinclad gunboats, acting as both shepherds and, on occasion, as towboats. Every available light draught of the Ninth and Tenth District was assigned to this expedition, except the *Paw Paw* and *Peosta.* The leading *Neosho* and the *Carondelet*, which brought up the rear, made their best speed; the sureness of their size and armament, if not their immediate proximity to the steamers, made them a viable "distant cover," a term later used for Allied battleship protection of convoys in the Atlantic during World War II.

Trailing huge clouds of smoke from over 50 chimneys, the steamboat parade stretched out over miles of river length and proceeded without incident throughout the day and into the evening. This was the largest troop convoy Fitch had escorted to Nashville since that of Maj. Gen. Granger at the beginning of 1863. Numerous steamers were passed moving downstream and for the most part the weather was pleasant. The first difficulty did not occur until 9:30 P.M. when an overhanging tree carried away and destroyed the *Carondelet's* gig. The tiller rope of the ironclad broke two hours later, forcing her to come to stop to effect repairs.[17]

On November 30, Gen. Hood's army, numbering something less than 16,000 effectives, attacked the 22,000 entrenched Union defenders of Franklin, losing 6,252 men, including six general officers killed. The five-hour battle cost the Northerners approximately 2,300 soldiers. Writing on "the five tragic hours" years later, historian Fisher opined that "Hood had virtually destroyed his army."

In a telegram to Acting Rear Adm. Lee sent about midafternoon, Maj. Gen. Thomas confided his continuing belief that Hood possessed a larger cavalry force than did Wilson and, as a result, the army was "compelled to fall back and concentrate on Nashville." As soon as the cavalry corps could be increased, the theater commander was certain he could drive Hood back.

Believing the ironclads were set to return to Paducah after delivering Smith, Thomas, who had not received Lee's Monday message, asked if he could have them back in the Cumberland on patrol and convoy duty. Fitch would help him make up his perceived cavalry deficiency with river patrols and other reconnaissance missions above and below the city. Before midnight, Maj. Gen. Schofield started yet another forced march, leaving his dead and wounded on the battlefield. All who were able set off for Nashville, 18 miles away.

As the Franklin bloodbath continued, Lt. Cmdr. Fitch was leading the stretched-out Smith convoy up the Cumberland. The heavier vessels steamed more slowly and were often overtaken by lighter units; all were regularly passed by vessels traveling in the other direction. Among the boats making the swiftest upriver passage was a specially-commissioned hospital boat, the *D. A. January*. In Nashville while en route to a reception, Col. James F. Rusling, acting chief quartermaster of the Department of the Cumberland in the absence of Brig. Gen. Donaldson, stopped by to see Maj. Gen. Thomas. The latter happily showed his supply officer a telegram from Schofield claiming to have defeated Hood at Franklin and reporting his withdrawal. Was there news of Smith? Thomas wondered. No, Rusling replied, though he had sent a steamer (probably the army gunboat *Newsboy*) down the Cumberland earlier in the afternoon to hurry the fleet. "Well," the commanding general replied," if Smith does not get up here tonight, he will not get here at all; for tomorrow, Hood will strike the Cumberland and close it against all transports."

Out on the Cumberland, the plodding convoy passed Fort Donelson at noon and Clarksville was reached at 10:45 P.M. Here the *Carondelet* dropped anchor to review her shaky tiller situation, but her respite was brief. An hour later, the *Moose*, with another steamer lashed alongside, came up with the final convoy elements and signaled the ironclad to get underway and follow her up.

It was around midnight when the first couple of troop transports, encouraged ahead by Rusling's steamer and speeding in advance, came to off the city levee. Maj. Gen. Thomas was in a meeting with Maj. Gen. Schofield, who had himself just arrived, and Brig. Gen. Thomas J. Wood at Department of the Cumberland headquarters in the St. Cloud Hotel when the news arrived. The quartermaster colonel had hurried back from his engagement and burst into the room to announce that Smith had at long last come. He, like many other Nashvillians, had heard the joyful whistle calls of the advance steamers. Not long thereafter, the veteran infantryman walked in and was immediately given a bear hug of welcome by the usually undemonstrative Thomas. Following brief handshakes, Rusling departed about 1 A.M., leaving his four superiors on their knees reviewing maps spread over the floor. Smith and several of his officers were among the few coming ashore. Most of the soldiers remained on their troopboats over night.

Also around 1 A.M. on December 1, the *Brilliant* was assigned the duty of towing the *Carondelet* up the Cumberland. Thereafter the old turtle and the *Neosho* continued to plod upstream in pleasant, if cool, weather with various units of the "mosquito fleet" occasionally providing a tow. The steamers of the Smith convoy tied up or dropped anchor at Nashville all night long and throughout the morning.

Also at the first hour of the day, Acting Rear Adm. Lee aboard the *Black Hawk* sent a confidential wire to Lt. Cmdr. Fitch ordering that he continue to patrol the Cumberland and otherwise support Maj. Gen. Thomas rather than return his boats to Smithland. To make certain this order was received and not lost should the telegraph go down, a copy was also sent to Fitch's downstream rendezvous. Another telegram was sent at 1 A.M. to Thomas granting his November 30 request just now received. Lee noted that he expected to send the U.S.S. *Cincinnati* to Smithland in a few days, "ready to operate on either river." A mirrored message was also forwarded to Brig. Gen. Meredith at Paducah.

By noon, the bulk of Schofield's XXIII Army Corps (10,207 men) from Franklin was behind Nashville's fortified line, joining the 14,171 effectives of Maj. Gen. Frank Stanley's IV Army Corps, led by Brig. Gen. Wood. As the day wore on, more men arrived from various Tennessee locations, including 7,541 miscellaneous of Maj. Gen. James B. Steedman's Provisional Detachment of the District of the Etowah from Chattanooga. Each man was no doubt awed by the sight of the city's most prominent structure, the state capitol up atop Cedar Knob.

By dark, the defending force had grown to approximately 60,000, a roughly two to one advantage over the Rebels. Nashville, under Union occupation longer than any other major southern city, now ranked second only to Washington, D.C., as the most heavily fortified town on the continent.

During the day, the Confederate Army of Tennessee, though exhausted and in some cases shell shocked, moved toward the outskirts of the city, traveling up the Nashville and Franklin Pike. Most of the foot soldiers came through the Green Hills area while the horsemen rode to the west.

On the Cumberland, perhaps the most exciting event, if exciting was the right word, recorded in the logbooks of the convoy escorts was an exchange of whistles between the navy tinclads and the army gunboat *Newsboy*. Lying at the bank below the capital town, she appeared to some almost like a one-boat welcoming committee.

With whistles and horns sounding in a continuous din to alert all that the long-awaited reinforcement was at hand, the remaining elements of the nautical procession slowly paddled the final few miles to the Nashville wharves. Having dropped her partner some hours earlier, the *Moose* escorted in the final boats with 5,000 men just before late afternoon darkness. The ironclads *Neosho* and *Carondelet* tied up to the bank below Fitch's tinclad about 8 P.M.

At 9:20 P.M., Thomas wired Acting Rear Adm. Lee at Mound City to let him know that his communication, both by Fitch (who had obviously received it upon debarking and had hand-carried it to the hotel when reporting in) and by telegram of 1 A.M. this date, were received. Thomas was pleased with the navy's dispositions. Acting on advice Fitch gave, the army commander asked if, instead of stopping her at Smithland, the *Cincinnati* might be stationed at Clarksville to make the river "perfectly safe."

Ten minutes later, the Nashville chief telegraphed Maj. Gen. Halleck: "I have two ironclads here, with several gunboats, and Commander Fitch assures me that Hood can neither cross the Cumberland or blockade it. I therefore think it best to wait here until Wilson can equip all his cavalry." In one of the more famous quotes of the campaign, Thomas went on to size up his enemy's chances: "If Hood attacks me here, he will be more seriously damaged than he was yesterday; if he remains until Wilson gets equipped, I can whip him and will move against him at once."[18]

Maj. Gen. Smith's units, now collectively named with several other provisional groups as the Army of the Tennessee Detachment, were debarked from their boats on December 1–2 and were moved into line of battle on a range of hills two miles southwest of town. There they threw up earthworks and settled down to wait, guarding the right of the Union defense. The center was held by the IV Corps under Wood, while Schofield's XXIII Corps was on the left.

First thing that Friday morning, Lt. Cmdr. Fitch sent a telegram to his superior composed the previous night but, which, in the press of business, did not get sent. In it, Fitch reported his arrival and advised that Thomas was well pleased with the movement of Smith's fleet. The Union troops were all drawn into Nashville and the enemy, he added, was close at hand and might possibly attempt a crossing of the Cumberland below the town. To prevent it, the Hoosier had all of his boats arranged, while also maintaining a smooth-working and vigilant patrol down to Clarksville. Echoing his advice to Thomas, which he may or may not have known was passed on as such to the *Black Hawk,* Fitch asked that the *Cincinnati* be stationed at Clarksville, where she could "operate quickly either up or down, as there is telegraph there."

Due to a variety of circumstances including traffic and downed wires, there now began a certain disconnect in the electronic messaging back and forth between Nashville and Mound City, Paducah, and Cairo. Acting Rear Adm. Lee did not receive Maj. Gen. Thomas' evening telegram until sometime on December 2, at which point he immediately replied agreeing to post the *Cincinnati* at Clarksville. On the other hand, the delay permitted him to learn something of the fighting at Franklin. Without complete details on the encounter, the navy man offered Thomas his "sincere congratulations" on what was believed to be a "success."

The Cumberland River leading into Nashville was also busy throughout the day as steamers brought in additional goods, men and horses. When not themselves being replenished in supplies or coal, Fitch's light draughts were constantly in motion. The *Neosho* and *Carondelet* remained tied to the bank, their watch officers duly noting every witnessed activity in their logbooks. At Clarksville, Col. Smith, who had not received instructions to stop sending in his sightings, informed Nashville that three more steamers had passed his post that day "with troops."

Meanwhile, Gen. Hood's 25,000 men were almost at Nashville, having entered Davidson County that morning. Thinking he might draw Thomas into battle, the Southern commander, from his new headquarters at Traveler's Rest on the Franklin Pike, considered that the possibility of a demonstration against the Union garrison at Murfreesboro was in order. This compulsion would remove one infantry division and all but a few of the men Thomas feared most—those from Forrest's Cavalry Corps. The rest of the Rebel army set to establishing their line. As Stanely Horn put it in his review of the wartime city, the Rebel position "stretched from Rains' Hill on the Nolensville Pike across the Franklin and Granny White roads to his main salient on the Hillsboro Pike." Hood's four-mile line was three miles shorter than the outer defenses built by the Nationals around the Tennessee capital. The Confederate left flank was manned by the troops of Lt. Gen. Alexander P. Steward, while Lt. Gen. Stephen D. Lee watched the center and Nashville native Maj. Gen. Benjamin F. Cheatham the right.[19]

As the Confederate Army of Tennessee chose its spots just beyond Union cannon range, its leaders discovered that they had insufficient men to run their 12-mile line completely around the city's two sides and down to the Cumberland River. Specifically, the line halted two miles from the river in the east and four in the west, leaving four of the eight roads into the city wide open. One historian, Steven Woodworth, called this "an atrocious defensive position," while another, Tom Connelly, was equally brutal: "Hood could not have aligned his troops on a worse position." The whole line could, had Thomas chosen, been enveloped on either flank, on the west via the Murfreesboro Pike or via the Harding Pike in the east. Still and all, the length of the lines involved would make Nashville one of the most extensive Civil War battlefields in terms of acreage.

Be that as it was, the 1,500 men of Brig. Gen. James Chalmers' division were ordered by Forrest to operate in the unclaimed spaces that ran about four miles south between the Cumberland River below Nashville and Hood's anchor on the Hillsboro Pike. Specifically, the men were to patrol the Charlotte, Harding, and Hillsboro pikes on the left (west) flank of the army. As part of this deployment and in keeping with Gen. Hood's demand that artillery be placed in the most favorable positions, Chalmers now made one of the most important dispositions of any Rebel commander in the Nashville campaign.

Late in the afternoon, Lt. Col. David C. Kelley was sent to blockade the Cumberland River at the lower end of Bell's Bend. Kelley, who had bombarded river traffic twice in the last two months, positioned 300 men of Col. Edmund W. Rucker's brigade and two 12-pounder Parrott rifles of Lt. H. H. Brigg's section of Capt. T. W. Rice's artillery near Samuel Davidson's house on a ridge beyond a little creek that emptied at Davidson's Landing into the south side of the Cumberland.

This wooded location, which would allow Kelley's gunners to drop plunging fire on any vessels passing below, was opposite an old mill (Bell's Mills) and its landing on the north bank. The Mills and Bell's Landing lay four miles below the town by land. By river, they were, depending upon who is providing directions, anywhere from nine to 18 miles below. The spots were (and are) located at the nearest point to the city in the third large bend in the Cumberland as it comes nearly back of Nashville. By name east to west, the bends are White's, Cockrill's, and Bell's. Hyde's Ferry was a prominent crossing point in the former that Lt. Cmdr. Fitch would employ as a staging area.

Soon reinforced with another two guns, Kelley had a pair in a lower battery and two in an upper emplacement, placed .5 miles east of Davidson's Landing. The new additions were a pair of 12-pounder howitzers from Walton's Battery. Marksmen were detailed in support from points in the hills above and below the artillery. Former Battle of Nashville Pres-

The six-acre Kelley's Point Battlefield forms part of a 13-acre parcel of land nine miles west of Nashville in the community of Bellvue. Located just off the Charlotte Pike exit of Interstate 40, the riverbank site originally hosted Lt. Col. Kelley's cannon during the Battle of Nashville. It was earlier a portion of a larger 60-acre tract of land where giant Lowe's and Wal-Mart outlets now (2007) exist (courtesy Robert Henderson).

ervation Society president Bob Henderson's research finds that subsurface mines (known then as "torpedoes" or "infernal machines") were placed in the river as well. This Johnsonville-like deployment (plus the mines) allowed the "fighting parson" to be largely successful in his mission, even though he had already missed the biggest target of all—A. J. Smith's troop convoy. Still, as historian Byrd Douglas noted, Kelley in the days ahead proved "what even a small force in gifted hands could do to supply lines and all the fine gunboats sent up the Cumberland."

In a 10 P.M. wire to Maj. Gen. Halleck, "Old Pap" Thomas outlined his defensive plans for Nashville. As part of that arrangement, the ironclads and gunboats were so disposed as to prevent Hood from crossing the Cumberland. "Captain Fitch," he added, "assures me that he can safely convoy steamers up and down the river." According to Durham, Thomas had two major concerns about the river: that Confederates be neither able to cross it nor cut off his supplies from below with mobile artillery. Neither knew for certain that their old foe Kelley was even then endeavoring to ensure the latter, though rumors were beginning to come in that the Confederates were putting up cannon along the river in preparation for a night attack.

The vigilant Fitch had one last matter to deal with that evening. At 10:30 P.M., he called Acting Master Miller of the *Carondelet*, together with his Cumberland pilot, to a conference aboard the *Moose*. There the ironclad skipper was detailed to accompany the flagboat several miles downstream with his powerful craft beginning a half hour later.[20]

At 2 A.M. on December 3 with a severe storm threatening, the *Moose* and *Carondelet* tied up in the rain to the north bank below Hyde's Ferry in White's Bend and across from the picket line. This was a commanding position slightly to the right of the Army of Tennessee Detachment. When Fitch returned to Nashville, Acting Volunteer Master Miller had strict orders to assist Smith's troops in any way necessary. The supply steamer *Magnet* came alongside the *Carondelet* and made fast just after 8 A.M. Two hours later, the *Moose*, beginning a series of patrols, rounded to abreast of the ironclad. The turtle's no. 2 gig hauled her captain out to the flagboat to report, allowing a reassured Fitch to steam on. A little while later, the *Carondelet* moved 500 yards upstream while the *Magnet* cast off and also went on up.[21]

While the tinclads plied the Cumberland, Thomas and Lee were again in telegraphic communication. The soldier reviewed his situation for the navy man and added, "Captain Fitch has cheerfully complied with my request to patrol the river above and below the city." At 5 P.M., Lee acknowledged the general's December 2 wire and asked if Thomas would order his telegraph operators to provide him with copies of Lee's orders to Fitch. The first of these was, undoubtedly, one simultaneously sent to the Indiana sailor. By it, Lee reconfirmed his Cumberland patrol orders of December 1, advised that he hoped to bring up the *Cincinnati* in a couple of days, and cautioned his division leader to continue "always to cooperate most heartily" with "Old Pap" and the army.

Nashville army headquarters remained nervous concerning Hood's intentions and grew concerned about the possibility that the Rebels might attempt to cross the Cumberland above Nashville. Feeling it unsafe to trust the courier line between Gallatin and Carthage for information, the commanding general wanted Lt. Cmdr. Fitch, if the river level permitted, to institute a patrol to Carthage "with at least one ironclad and two gunboats." This dispatch, together with Acting Rear Adm. Lee's wire, reached Fitch just as he returned from his morning patrol.[22]

The Hoosier officer quickly honored Maj. Gen. Thomas' request. Acting Volunteer Master Edmund Morgan of the U.S.S. *Springfield* was summoned aboard the *Moose* and was ordered to undertake the spy mission, in concert with the most famous member of the army's Cumberland River gunboat service, the *Newsboy*. That afternoon, the towboat *N. J. Bigley*, chartered to the USQM, was convoyed upstream by the *Springfield* and the *Newsboy*. Their destination was Young's Point, 100 miles above Nashville near Hartsville. The former boat was to retrieve a number of workers from the area, while the others were to note Rebel activities.

Back on the main tributary, the busy steamer *Magnet* again passed the stationary *Carondelet* about 3:45 P.M., headed downriver. At 5 P.M., the patrolling *Moose* came upstream and landed briefly on the south side near the *Carondelet* before moving on up to Nashville. While the boats paddled back and forth on the river, Col. Kelley's battery, farther down on Bell's Bend, made its inaugural attacks.

Responding to warning shots from the bluffs above the Cumberland, the contract steamers *Prairie State* and *Prima Donna* put into the south bank, tied up and surrendered themselves into Confederate hands. Immediately after the two boats, loaded with grain and cavalry animals, were taken and all 56 aboard the two were made prisoner, grayclad soldiers scrambled aboard and led off almost 200 horses and mules. They also pressed "into service the colored women on board who were employed as cooks and chambermaids," to help "liberate" items of value and to scatter and destroy the grain.

The naval supply steamer *Magnet* was fired into as she passed through the Bell's Bend channel and was hit several times. Her captain, a man named Harrol, pushed her beyond the first battery, but, finding another below, gave up and ran into shore, tying up at a point about eight miles below Hyde's Ferry.

In the darkness of early evening, Capt. Harrol suddenly appeared and sought permission to board the *Carondelet*. Obviously shaken, the steamboat captain told Acting Volunteer Master Miller and his guest, Col. Israel Garrard of the 7th Ohio Volunteer Cavalry, how his boat was fired into and crippled near Bell's Mills. After the assault, the captain traveled back to Hyde's Ferry, arriving where the ironclad was stationed about 7:30 P.M. Unable to move on his own without orders, Miller detailed Acting Masters Mate L. W. Hastings to accompany Harrol up to Nashville, where they could raise the alarm with Lt. Cmdr. Fitch.

The *Moose* was not moored long at Nashville when, about 9 P.M., Hastings and Harrol came aboard. Harrol repeated his story. By this time of this interview, the strength of the audacious Confederates had grown in the telling from a few guns to elements of the enemy's entire left wing. This body had, according to Harrol, struck the river and planted multiple batteries on its south side across from the old mills. Fitch, who had passed the location on many occasions over the past several years, was keenly aware of the location and knew it took far longer to reach by water than by land.

Even though it was very cloudy and threatening more rain, Fitch immediately determined to launch a night strike to wrest the two captured boats back from the enemy. He quickly stopped in to see Maj. Gen. Thomas and won his support to either recapture them or force their destruction—in either event, taking the steamers away from the Southerners. A signal was made to the captains of the *Neosho*, *Brilliant*, *Fairplay*, *Reindeer*, and *Silver Lake* at 9:30 P.M. to get up steam and follow the *Moose* downriver at best speed.

Fitch's task group hove to near the *Carondelet* about 11 P.M. and the Pook turtle was invited to join the parade. The *Neosho* took over the Hyde's Ferry station in support of the

Army position, with the *Brilliant* detailed to operate with her (i.e., provide tow if necessary). Fifteen minutes later, Fitch steamed on with his boats arranged in this order: *Carondelet, Fairplay, Moose, Reindeer,* and *Silver Lake.*

At 12:30 A.M. as the ironclad and four mosquito boats approached Bell's Mills, all hands on board the warships were called to quarters. Aboard the tinclads, captains and pilots made close observation from their pilothouses. Down on the gundecks, the eight men of each 24-pounder crew looked to their executive officer for orders and for the young boys or "powder monkeys" that brought them ammunition from the magazine. They did not have long to wait. The boats moved down, as the Indiana sailor put it later, "perfectly quiet, with no lights visible."

Fitch might be excused for that turn of phrase; steamboats were not quiet, but made puffing and chugging noises which were usually quite audible. There is no record that the Logansport native had the time for his engineers to reroute the steam pipes. Before her run past Island No. 10 in April 1862, the engineers aboard Capt. Henry Walke's *Carondelet*, the same "turtle" now with Fitch, had rerouted her exhaust steam aft into her wheelhouse rather than the chimneys. This eliminated the usual puffing sound. What probably masked their approach was the myriad of noises associated with a large city, sounds from the competing armies, general river traffic not yet completely stopped, and the crying of stolen livestock.

Lugubriously coming down darkened (one can almost hear the music played during the enemy battleship advance in John Wayne's World War II film *In Harm's Way*), the *Carondelet*, closely followed by the *Fairplay*, steamed towards Kelley's batteries. The night was cool, cloudy and devoid of natural light and hence the Confederates did not spot the Yankee craft, even though one was as big as a house. About 12:45 A.M. December 4, the *Carondelet* opened with a hail of grape and canister as she passed the main Rebel camp in a hollow back of Davidson's Landing on the south side of the river opposite Bell's Mills. As her guns came to bear, a number of the men aboard could clearly see the *Prairie State* and *Prima Donna* tied up at the bank at Hillsboro Landing, two miles below. This point is about a half mile beyond the present day Commodore Marina on River Road. When the ironclad initiated the battle, the *Fairplay* was a little below the upper battery, with the *Moose* abreast of it, the *Reindeer* about 50 yards above, and the *Silver Lake* behind.

As soon as the *Carondelet* started the fight, Kelley's musketmen poured a heavy volley into all of the boats and began a responsive cannonade. Rebel fire, in the words of Acting Volunteer Lieutenant Glassford, "was rapid and warm." The Pook turtle steamed slowly by the lower battery. After passing, she rounded to and came up within about 300 yards of the Confederates, fired a few shots, then passed up abreast, before dropping back again. The Confederates returned the ironclad's fire for about 20 minutes before falling back; *Carondelet* pumped occasional shells toward the last known Rebel locations until 2:30 A.M. When her gunners took stock of the magazine later in the morning, it was found that 26 rounds were expended.

The thinly-protected *Fairplay* could not possibly stand up to Kelley's rifled field guns and made no offensive effort to do so. Acting in concert with the ironclad, her job was to get quickly past the Rebel gunners and to ensure the recapture of the transports at Hillsboro Landing. Acting Volunteer Master Groves' gunners fired rapidly in passing and turned the bend below out of range. The tinclad did not get by entirely unscathed as Kelley's artillerists assaulted her from their commanding position on the southern bank. One 12-pounder shell passed through the boat, between the main and boiler decks, flying a few inches above the forward part of the boilers and damaging the port engine's escape pipe. The other projectile went straight through the cabin directly beneath the pilothouse. Fortunately neither shell exploded and both exited without causing serious damage. Despite her short time in battle, the *Fairplay* fired a total of 37 rounds of grape and canister.

The smoke from the guns and chimneys, combined with steam and the darkness of a starless night, quickly cut visibility for the mosquito boats. In this most literal "fog of war," the flagboat, in the narrow river bend, was hidden from the craft above and below her. Pilots and officers could see virtually nothing and the fear of collision became palpable, particularly aboard the *Moose* and *Reindeer*. On top of this, the smoke was so thick that, occasionally, the river surface could not be seen from their Texas decks.

Lt. Cmdr. Fitch, fearful of ramming the *Fairplay*, ordered the *Moose* stopped quickly. Acting Volunteer Master Groves of the *Fairplay* also halted briefly before following the *Carondelet* below the bend. At this point, the *Moose* was becoming a plump target for the Confederate gunners, who were firing at her so far on her port quarter that her guns could not be brought to bear to fire back. She was now in great danger and simply could not stay where she was long enough for the smoke to lift. It would also be very dangerous for her to attempt to round to. There was only one option and thus the Hooser officer directed his pilots, John H. Ferrell and George W. Rowley, to back up to a clear spot above the batteries and get out of the thick smoke below.

If the *Carondelet* and *Fairplay* had passed down, rounded to, and were on their way back up, the danger of their running into the out-of-position flagboat was great. At this time, the *Moose* lay at a spot in the river not over 75 to 80 yards wide and directly under the Rebel guns. The Confederates, thankful for such a sitting duck, now gave her their full attention. Fitch's tinclad had to move slowly while backing up, but the craft was so well handled that executive officer Acting Volunteer Master Washington C. Coulson was able to work the guns "with marked rapidity and precision." Fitch believed Coulson's gunnery was the major reason "that in a great measure they were kept silent." ADM Porter afterwards attributed the success to the "great judgement and coolness" of Fitch's vessel management. Most Southern participants attribute the silence to the fact that "Kelley's artillery ammunition was, unhappily, exhausted."

Fitch observed that, although the musketry along the bank and on the hillside, was rather "annoying," the enemy artillery fire, though rapid, was not very telling because it was not well aimed. Still, he admitted, it was a miracle "that amid so many shots and volleys of musketry, we should escape without the loss of a single man and no injury to the boats." By injury, the Hoosier meant major damage. The lucky *Moose* was, in fact, hit three times by shells, two of which could have sunk her. One ploughed into the bread room, close to the magazine, but did not explode. A second, which also did not explode, "struck us fair," her commander later reported. The bullet would have passed out through the bottom, but was deflected by a deck beam and lodged in the rake. Another hit the paddle wheel, but did no damage. As might be expected, the flagboat threw many rounds toward the banks of the Cumberland during the battle. Afterwards, an exact count showed 59 expended.

During the few moments the shore was hidden from the *Reindeer* by the smoke, that tinclad went broadside to the current and drifted downstream toward the flagboat. To avoid a collision, Acting Volunteer Lieutenant Glassford immediately ordered her bow run ashore and then swerved round, stern downstream. Although badly exposed to a raking Rebel fire, the *Reindeer* was lucky as Kelley's men, in their excitement, were shooting high and managed only to knock a few splinters off her paddlewheel. As soon as he could get clear, the volunteer officer ran his tinclad upstream and rounded to, resuming his place behind the *Moose*. By the time these maneuvers were completed, the hour and a half action was over. A check of the *Reindeer's* magazine showed 19 rounds fired.

The *Silver Lake* did not get close enough to actually engage the batteries. She did, according to Lt. Cmdr. Fitch, fire six rounds of canister and helped keep the musketry "silent along the bank above." Perhaps this explains how Landsman Rowland S. True confused the actions of December 4 and 6 in his later account. Still, the Pennsylvanian witnessed what he later called "a grand display of fireworks." He would always remember the "thundering of the mighty guns, the shells screeching through the air back and forth, from one side to the other; sometimes bursting in the air, sometimes in the water throwing the water high in the air."

The first Bell's Mills engagement (sometimes numbered as two separate fights) was not a great victory for either side. It is true that Fitch's task group was able to recapture the two steamers before they were destroyed. The navy man claimed his boats drove the Rebel guns back from the river and that it was his intervention which forced Kelley to destroy most of the prized grain before it could be transported and to free some of their crews. The fight was something of a tradeoff, but, in the end, the Rebels stayed away for less than a day and then, despite several more Fitch visits, closed the Cumberland tight for a week.

At 2.45 A.M. that Sunday, the *Carondelet* and *Fairplay* made fast to the *Prairie State* and *Prima Donna* and towed them across the river. After they were made fast, the *Fairplay* came alongside of them and the *Carondelet* dropped out into the river offering defense in depth. Navy sailors worked with the civilian crews of the two steamers to repair damages and put them in running order. At 4 A.M., the *Fairplay* got underway and proceeded four miles down the river to where the disabled *Magnet* was lying. Her damages were not as great as Captain Harrol had at first feared (and probably described). At 5:30 A.M., the two steamboats above were able to get up steam, but did not depart. Instead, they waited for the *Carondelet*, which had also put down, to return towing the *Magnet*. At 6 A.M., the ironclad, trailed by the *Magnet*, and the *Fairplay*, convoying the *Prima Donna* and *Prairie State*, departed for up the river.

While the ironclad and Tinclad No. 17 were engaged below, the remainder of Fitch's task group had departed upstream at 3:30 A.M. The *Moose* was lashed alongside the *Reindeer* for support and several hours later, the vessels arrived at Hyde's Ferry where the *Neosho* and *Brilliant* were tied up. Fitch informed the captains of the two guardians that the other units were trailing them from below and that they could depart upon their arrival. Meanwhile, the *Moose*, *Reindeer*, and *Silver Lake* continued upriver, easing into the East Bank about eight miles below Nashville. At 10 A.M., the *Carondelet*, *Fairplay*, and the civilian steamers departed with the *Neosho* and *Brilliant*. These vessels arrived at Nashville at 4:45 P.M., about four hours behind the *Moose*.

Also during the afternoon, U.S. 6th Cavalry Division commander Brig. Gen. Richard W. Johnson sent a reconnaissance to investigate the Bell's Mills matter. His men returned to report that, although the Confederates had taken two boats across from that place the previous evening, they were reclaimed by Fitch's gunboats. Local citizens reported that, while enemy pickets were visible, no large force was present.

Fitch made best speed back to Nashville to report the engagement to Maj. Gen. Thomas and to wire an account to Acting Rear Adm. Lee. In his hasty report to the former, made while two of his boats were still down the river, the Indiana sailor passed on intelligence (presumably from liberated former steamboat prisoners) that confirmed that the enemy had established heavy batteries across from Bell's Mills. He was pleased that he had "cleaned out the rebel battery" and taken back the captured steamers, but believed that it was now unsafe for transports to come up from Clarksville.

The Hoosier officer suspected that Hood's left, under the command of Forrest, rested on the Cumberland at that point and believed that he had engaged Buford's brigade. In point of fact, the left did not quite reach the river and both Forrest and Buford were about to invest Murfreesboro. Kelley, the trusted Forrest lieutenant, was in charge of the artillery he fought.

The tireless naval officer asked the commanding general to sound the alarm in a wire to Clarksville. Would he please, Fitch asked, forbid steamers from coming above that place and also prohibit any from departing Nashville "for down the river until the batteries are removed." He did not know that the commanding general had wired Col. Smith at 9 A.M.: "Do not allow any more transport steamers to come up the river until further orders." The Indiana gunboatman closed his message by confiding to Thomas that he planned to go up toward Harpeth Shoals "with the other ironclad [*Neosho*] to make a reconnaissance in force this evening." Thomas succinctly reported the naval action and plan in a late night report to Maj. Gen. Halleck.

Not to be forgotten in the excitement of Bell's Mills-Round One was the joint Army-Navy expedition above Nashville started the previous day. The *N J. Bigley*, the *Springfield*, and the U.S. Army gunboat *Newsboy* reached Young's Point, near Hartsville, about 11 A.M. Sunday. There the *Bigley* took aboard a party of timbercutters and then returned downstream, reaching Tennessee's capital about 7 P.M. First Lt. S. H. Stevens of the Chicago Board of Trade Battery, Illinois Volunteers, who was in charge of the mission, reported to Brig. Gen. Donaldson that the enemy had not been seen and there was no evidence that "he had been upon the river." At the same time, a "heavy force" of Confederate cavalry was reported raiding near Lebanon.

This is not to say the Cumberland was everywhere quiet. At Paducah, where Acting Rear Adm. Lee had just arrived with the Pook turtle U.S.S. *Cincinnati*, Brig. Gen. Meredith received a wire from the Smithland post commander, Capt. Henry P. Reed. It is probable that Meredith and Lee both shared the one sentence note: "Steamer *Mars* reports being fired into by both artillery and musketry eighteen miles this side of Nashville, Ten."

That evening, as hands were at supper, heavy firing was heard back of Nashville. About the same time, Lt. Cmdr. Fitch received a laudatory note from "Old Pap" Thomas, in which the theater commander confused Bell's Mills and Harpeth Shoals. The Hoosier seaman took the opportunity in reply to gently point out the difference, while laying out the reason he had not as yet departed on the reconnaissance promised earlier.

Harpeth Shoals was some 35 miles below Nashville, while Bell's Mills, as noted above, was nine to 18 river miles away (though just four by land) in a great bend of the Cumberland behind the city. Fitch had planned to start off for the former that evening, but when the cannonade back of the town was heard, he "thought perhaps there would be a general attack" and that his boats could assist on the right. "The heavy boats are so slow," he wrote, that if he departed and Hood came on, "I would not have been able to reach here again until tomorrow afternoon."

Again, the Navy's local point man promised to make a downriver reconnaissance as soon as possible. Once he had cleared out the river, Fitch would arrange for regular convoys. In the meantime, "owing to the position of the enemy's left and the crookedness of the river," it was a bad idea to send steamers down and "give the rebels the least chance to disable or capture any more of our boats."[23]

The firing heard by the gunboatmen, and for that matter nearly everyone else in the area, was from the attack made by Morton's artillery and Brig. Gen. Tyree Bell's brigade on Blockhouse No. 3 south of Nashville. The cannonade heralded the fall of one more of the seven small fortifications established to guard bridges along the Nashville & Chattanooga Railroad route to Murfreesboro. Most of these were ordered evacuated, but, with Rebel cavalry about and the telegraph down, the word did not get to the defenders of several outposts. Nos. 1–2 had been taken since Friday.

Between 2:30 A.M. and 3:15 A.M. on the morning of December 5, men aboard the Nashville gunboats again heard "heavy firing on the left of the line," a cannonade which resumed at 8:45 P.M. with the sound of drums and bugles coming from the direction of the Tennessee State House. During the day, Federal artillery blasted the high ground and hills in front of their defense line to remove cover that attacking Confederates might employ. Walter Durham tells us that "the rumble of cannons was heard in Nashville all day long" and that many houses were destroyed.

Lt. Gen. Forrest and Brig. Gen. Buford oversaw the capture of Blockhouse No. 4, near La Vergne, that morning. This anti-transportation campaign had an impact on the outcome of the entire Nashville battle as Hood now elected to send the cavalry leader, with two divisions, to assault the railroad and invest Murfreesboro and its giant defensive supply bastion, Fortress Rosecrans, the largest earthen fort built anywhere during the Civil War. Chalmers and Kelley were left at Nashville, but only 250 horsemen of Col. G. H. Nixon's Consolidated Regiment remained for patrols.

Despite these activities, the general Confederate assault that many within Union ranks had expected for almost a week had yet to occur. Both sides continued to dig and to shoot at one another with cannon and rifle. Kelley was reinforced by the transfer of two more 12-pounder Parrotts from the brigade of Col. Jacob B. Biffle.

Northern newspapers actively opined upon developments. A correspondent with the Milwaukee *Daily Sentinel* reported his belief home for readers to see on December 15 that Hood had "let his opportunity slip" and had given Maj. Gen. Thomas a gift of extra preparation time. The editor of the Nashville *Daily Press* told his readers in the day's edition that he still expected Hood to dash around the city without a fight and make for Kentucky. He would repeat his observation in the issues of December 7–8.

Another consequence of the Confederate activities, albeit a small one which has not been mentioned in the campaign histories, was the postponement of the Bell's Mills–Harpeth Shoals nautical scout promised to Maj. Gen. Thomas by Lt. Cmdr. Fitch. One can perhaps wonder if starting down a day earlier would have made any difference in the Hoosier's ability to break Kelley's blockade.

While Forrest moved toward Murfreesboro and the defenses of both sides were improved around Nashville, Fitch spent December 5 writing a detailed after-action review of the previous two days. This report for Acting Rear Adm. Lee was complete with detailed reports from the commanders of the *Carondelet*, *Fairplay*, and *Reindeer*. Once it was certain that no general attack was in the offing, he also completed arrangements for his departure down the river, as well as a task group visit above the city. The latter was once again necessary because the Rebel cavalry reported at Lebanon the day before was now said to be crossing the Cumberland at Carthage.

In a conference of gunboat captains aboard the *Moose*, Fitch outlined his plans to once again test the strength of the Rebel positions near Bell's Mills. With the Indiana sailor and his chief pilot, John Ferrell, embarked, the most powerful and best protected vessel available, Acting Volunteer Lieutenant Howard's *Neosho* would lead the assault, backed up by the Pook turtle. If their attack was successful, it would permit the tinclads, under command of Acting Volunteer Lieutenant Glassford, to convoy a number of transports on toward Clarksville. While the monitor and the *Carondelet* were engaged, Glassford's convoy fleet would await the outcome some two to three miles above. While this large group was below, Acting Volunteer Master Morgan's U.S.S. *Springfield* and the U.S.S. *Brilliant*, under Acting Volunteer Master John H. Rice (the *Moose* officer who commanded the mission while also filling in for the ill Acting Volunteer Lieutenant Perkins) would ascend the Cumberland on a mission in support of Brig. Gen. J. H. Hammond, the Louisville & Nashville Railroad guardian.

Once the meeting broke up, Lt. Cmdr. Fitch informed the army high command of his plans. Shortly thereafter, Brig. Gen. Whipple, Thomas' chief of staff, wired Col. Smith at Clarksville reporting that gunboats would soon be joining him and that he could then send back the transports waiting off his post for convoy.

Also on December 5, Acting Rear Adm. Lee, then at Paducah with the *Cincinnati*, dispatched orders to Cdr. John W. Livingston, who had taken over as commander of the Mound City station the previous day, to fast forward 100 or more rounds of ammunition for the *Neosho, Carondelet, Moose, Reindeer, Silver Lake, Brilliant, Victory, Springfield,* and *Fairplay*.

Lee moved on to Smithland and hence up the Cumberland later in the day, fully expecting to reach Nashville in a day or so and take over direct command from Fitch. Before leaving Smithland, the Mississippi Squadron commander wired Livingston recommending he purchase all twelve loaded coal barges then tied up off the Tenth District rendezvous. The admiral thought these would be important to upcoming activities on the twin rivers.[24]

Around 4 A.M. on a cold but clear December 6, the U.S.S. *Springfield* and the U.S.S. *Brilliant* dropped down astern of the ironclad *Carondelet* and, after making fast, refueled from the fleet coal barges. At 8 A.M., the two, under Morgan's command, departed for a rendezvous with troops under the command of Brig. Gen. Hammond.

The major navy show got underway at 9:30 A.M. when these boats moved out into the Cumberland and started downstream: the monitor *Neosho*; the stern-wheel transport *Metamora*; the tinclads *Moose* and *Reindeer*, still lashed together; the stern-wheelers *Prima Donna* and *Arizona*; the side-wheelers *J. F. McComb* and *Mercury*; the tinclad *Fairplay*; the stern-wheelers *Financier* and *Lilly*; the side-wheelers *New York* and *Lady Franklin*; the tinclad *Silver Lake*; the side-wheelers *Pioneer* and *Magnet*; and the ironclad *Carondelet*.

The parade moved peacefully on down past Hyde's Ferry and on past Robertson's Island. Fitch, in his correspondence, mistakenly labeled the atoll Robinson's Island. Located on the western side of Cockrill's Bend, the island was correctly depicted on Wilbur Foster's ca. 1871 Nashville map. That chart, showing the three great bends of the Cumberland behind the city, was first reproduced by Bob Henderson in his noteworthy unpublished study. Meanwhile, Brig. Gen. James R. Chalmers ordered Col. Edmund Rucker to push the Confederate defense line from Harding Road to Charlotte Pike and Brig. Gen. Matthew D. Ector extended his brigade across Harding Pike and Richland Creek.

At approximately 11:15 A.M., the *Neosho*'s lookouts spied a large Confederate force nearly opposite Bell's Mills apparently waiting for them. Lt. Col. Kelley's gunners and riflemen,

The river monitor *Neosho* was the principal ironclad gunboat employed by Lt. Cmdr. Fitch to oppose the gunners of Lt. Col. Kelley during the Battle of Nashville. Armed with two giant 11-inch smoothbore cannon in her revolving turret, the shallow draft stern-wheeler received no injury during the December 6 engagement, but was struck over 100 times. For gallantry during the day's action, two men aboard, John Ditzenback and John H. Ferrell, were subsequently awarded the Congressional Medal of Honor (courtesy Robert Jackson via Robert Henderson).

replenished, reinforced, and ready for a fight, wasted no time in opening upon on the monitor from their protected emplacements behind the spurs of hills. An early practitioner of what would be known in World War II as "deception," the "parson" successfully confused his enemy by ordering his mobile artillery to move from spot to spot along the high ground above Davidson's Landing. The ploy convinced the bluejackets aboard the Yankee warships that the Confederates were opposing them with some fourteen cannon rather than the six available.

Signaling Glassford to move back up, Lt. Cmdr. Fitch ordered Howard's pilots to run slow and began returning the fire coming at them from above, abreast of, and below. The *Neosho* went on down abreast of the lower battery, stopped, rounded to, and steamed back until abreast of the middle battery, which was nearly midway between the upper and lower emplacements. At that point, the monitor came to and her 11-inch cannon spat grape and canister at Kelley's gunners, who were now all attempting to sink her. The position, about 20 to 30 yards off shore, was chosen by the Indiana sailor as the best available from which to employ his anti-personnel shells. As he reported later, Fitch had "great faith in the endurance of the *Neosho*," accurately believing this duel would certainly "test her strength."

The battle between the rifled cannon ashore and the giant Dahlgren smoothbores afloat raged on for the next two and a half hours. *Neosho's* turret fired slowly and deliberately and was able to scatter the grayclad infantry and sharpshooters with little difficulty. The elevated

Confederate cannon were another matter and could not be hit from the angle of the river. Kelley's gunners poured a "terrific fire" down upon the Eads-built Union warboat, demolishing all perishable items on her deck, including the flag and signal staffs, leaving the National flag drooped over the wheelhouse. Eventually they shot away the summer pilot house, which caused it to fall over the fighting pilot house, thereby obstructing the view of Fitch, Howard, and the pilots.

Unable to see much, Fitch now ordered the *Neosho* to disengage and steam back up the river. As Stanley Horn put it 90 years later, Kelley was "doing good work and thoroughly enjoying himself with his guns on the river bank."

As the monitor steamed up past the upper battery and while yet under cannon and musket fire, *Moose* pilot Ferrel and *Neosho* quartermaster John Ditzenback scrambled out of the fighting pilothouse, took the national colors from where they lay, and tied them to the stump of the main signal staff, the highest mast remaining. For their action, both men were recommended by Fitch for the Congressional Medal of Honor, then not given to USN officers. Strangely enough, when Acting Rear Adm. Admiral Lee sent in the reports relating to the action on December 29, he recommended only that John Ditzenback be given the award. Still somewhat new to the western theater, he may have been under the impression that Ferrell, as a riverboat pilot, was carried on the rolls as a volunteer officer, and thus did not qualify for the award. Secretary of the Navy Welles, no fan of Lee's, reviewed the case in greater detail and, as a result, also placed Ferrell on the qualifying list. Both medals were authorized under General Order 59, June 22, 1865.

Moving out of range in the bend, the *Neosho* came up with the remainder of her task group, most tied at the bank near Robertson's Island, still in the original order of sailing. Fitch, Howard, Glassford, and Acting Volunteer Master Miller of the *Carondelet* reviewed the action, while tars "cleared all the rubbish off of the *Neosho*'s deck." Fitch and Howard wanted another daylight crack at Kelley and hoped that assistance from Miller's *Carondelet* might help them prevail. On the other hand, it was realized that sufficient Confederate cannon would probably survive the renewed battle to sink one or more of the light draughts or transports if they tried to make it past. As a result, Glassford was ordered to return with the mosquito boats and the steamers to Nashville.

At 3:10 P.M., the transport convoy returned upriver. There is some irony to all of this. The water in the Cumberland near and over Harpeth Shoals was dropping rapidly. Even had the steamers gotten through—or had Kelley not been there—it is probable that they might have been forced back before reaching Clarksville.

As the light draughts and their charges disappeared toward Nashville, the *Carondelet* was ordered to drop down and tie up astern of the *Neosho*. As the monitor's sailors completed their task of tearing off the summer pilothouse and all moveable articles, Fitch and Miller put the finishing touches on their attack plan. The *Carondelet* would follow down and make fast to the bank above the batteries while the *Neosho* went below, drawing the enemy's fire and showing their location to Miller's gunners. At 4:20 P.M., the two ironclads got underway.

The second round of Fitch's Tuesday match vs. Kelley opened at 4:30 P.M. when the *Neosho* steamed below the Confederate emplacements, rounded to, came back, and stopped in midstream as before, about 30 yards off the beach. Having drawn Rebel fire on her way down, the monitor easily succeeded in getting Kelley's men to show their locations to the *Carondelet*, which now joined Fitch in a spirited shelling.

Unfortunately, the Union warships working together still had no great advantage as the high enemy position allowed only one boat to engage the batteries at a time with any effect. That effect was minimal as the ironclads were forced to elevate their guns over the banks to clear them, thus missing the grayclads. Acting Volunteer Ensign Oliver Donaldson, writing in the *Carondelet's* logbook, called the Confederate response "feeble." Fitch himself did not find the contest quite as spirited as the earlier fight and thought his boats disabled two of Kelley's guns, believed to be 20-pounder Parrott rifles (they were 12-pounders). Years later, Landsman True of the *Silver Lake* related a story he had heard of how, at one point, a canister shell from the *Neosho* wiped out an entire Rebel gun crew save for one man. That fellow "pluckily loaded his gun and returned the fire alone."

About 5:30 P.M. as dusk launched another cold and this time cloudy night, the *Neosho* steamed up again, but was saluted by only two Confederate cannon as she passed and none as she continued, giving orders for the *Carondelet* to follow her upriver. Miller rounded to and joined his commander; at 10 P.M., the two made fast to the end of the line, astern of the *Reindeer* and *Moose*. Marveling that the *Neosho* was struck over a hundred times in the day's two battles, "but received no injury whatever," Fitch shook hands with Acting Volunteer Lieutenant Howard and returned to his flagboat. In the most intense big gun duel of the Nashville campaign, "some six or eight men in the turret of the *Neosho* were somewhat bruised and scratched in the face by a shell striking the muzzle of one of the guns and exploding." All other casualties were "too trivial to mention."

After his several engagements with Lt. Col. Kelley, Fitch conceded that his opponent still controlled Cumberland navigation and that the L & N Railroad north was the city's lifeline. As he knew from past experience, naval craft, without enveloping cavalry support, could not defeat rifled artillery dug into the riverbank. Fitch was wise to Confederate antishipping strategy and appreciated that the wily Kelley had carefully set up where he could not be captured from the river as long as Hood's left wing held its position. Until the army was ready to assist, the Indiana sailor decided it was best to induce his opponent into remaining just where he was, rather than perhaps chase him off to place his guns at an even worse spot, say anywhere closer to the Nashville levees. Regardless of how one judges the Hoosier's thought process on this occasion, all were agreed, as Walter Durham put it, that "the halt to navigation added to the siege mentality that recurrently threatened soldiers and civilians alike in Nashville."[25]

The in-port Nashville naval flotilla spent December 7 coaling and mending. Workers swarmed over the *Neosho* patching up her perforated chimney, repairing, replacing, or juryrigging davits, masts, deck structures, and small boats; others tended to her steam pipes, which were leaking badly. A boiler leak aboard the *Carondelet* was also repaired. The wind was slight from the southwest and the day was cloudy, but warm.

The *Brilliant*, sent above Nashville the previous day to assist Brig. Gen. Hammond, returned to the city in the afternoon, while the *Springfield* remained near Carthage. Shortly thereafter, Hammond sent Fitch a letter praising Rice's activity and efficiency in facilitating the army "scout through the country as far as Lebanon." In particular, the brigadier was impressed with the manner in which the tinclads permitted him to cross almost 225 men and horses over the Cumberland and back without accident or injury."

After Rice informed Fitch that no enemy had been sighted on the riverbank from 40 miles above Carthage and with Hammond's letter in hand, Lt. Cmdr. Fitch took Rice's intelligence over to Maj. Gen. Thomas. The weather was changing, the seaman noted as he paced. The wind squalled and it began to rain; within an hour, it became much colder and a piercing north wind replaced the morning breeze.

Acting Rear Adm. Lee arrived off Clarksville this Wednesday afternoon, but shoal water prevented his continuing on to Nashville. The river level had started to fall and would continue to do so for several days yet. According to his biographers Cornish and Laas, the naval leader, unable to personally coordinate his operations with Thomas, now began "an extended telegraphic colloquy" with the army leader. "With three, four, five, or more exchanges per day," Lee, though his command was entirely separate from "Old Pap's," nevertheless "achieved unity of Union command by subordinating his actions to Thomas' needs."

Fitch, who continued to have the commanding general's ear, remained as the on scene navy instrument. Indeed, the first wire passed to Thomas from Lee at 8 P.M. that evening concerned the Tenth District commander: "Where is Fitch? Please acquaint him with my arrival." Meanwhile, chief of staff Whipple received a telegram from Brig. Gen. Allen at Louisville noting that Nashville's chief quartermaster would soon return; Donaldson would also warn of falling river stages.

At 9 P.M., the commanding general wrote Maj. Gen. Halleck reporting that Hood had not increased his strength on the front or above Nashville. He also confirmed that Fitch had attempted to get a convoy down the previous day, but was unsuccessful in silencing the enemy batteries. At that point, Thomas advanced to Acting Rear Adm. Lee an idea that he and Fitch had under discussion. The following morning, so the thinking went, Fitch would take his ironclads back down, reengage Kelley's batteries, and, "with the assistance of the *Cincinnati*, now at Clarksville," would hopefully "clear them out." He would also take a company of soldiers for a reconnaissance. At 9:15 P.M., Thomas sent his first "colloquy" telegram to Lee, acknowledging the admiral's wire: "Captain Fitch is here, and will go down the river at daylight to-morrow morning as far as Harpeth Shoals."

The only major fire in Nashville during the battle period started about 10 P.M. that night and could be seen from the gunboats, several of which noted in their logbooks that it had started in the rear of the statehouse. Of unknown origin, it consumed railroad personnel quarters near the Chattanooga depot on Church Street. It could not be extinguished by firefighters and required the destruction of nearby buildings to halt its spread.[26]

Early on the morning of December 8, Lt. Cmdr. Fitch received information that a force of enemy cavalry had crossed the Cumberland River below the mouth of Harpeth River, which was two miles below the head of Harpeth Shoals at Harpeth Island, a report which he quickly passed on to Maj. Gen. Thomas. The foraging horsemen, moving up the river to strike the Springfield Pike, were represented as being "pretty strong" in number, taking cattle and everything in reach.

A little while later, Fitch also asked Acting Rear Adm. Lee to take the *Cincinnati* up as far as possible; hopefully she could get near the spot. The Hoosier indicated that the water was falling so low that he could not get down as far as Harpeth River. This even if he could get past Kelley, whom he had not tested in two days to see if the blockade remained.

Back in communication with the commanding general, Lt. Cmdr. Fitch informed Thomas that he would take his task group down as far as possible, but did not expect to reach Ashland. He would be departing soon and would not be able to take a company of soldiers as previously requested. It was expected that his vessels might be gone a day or two, though he would try to get back as soon as possible. If he could reach the Rebel crossing point, he would destroy any pontoon bridges found. At all costs, he would attempt to avoid grounding his heavy boats. If he did, Fitch was fully aware that they would "be useless as the river is falling so fast" that they couldn't be freed before a rise.

Upon receipt of Fitch's dispatch, "Old Pap" Thomas, in turn, wired Acting Rear Adm. Lee at Clarksville asking him to check out the information. If it were possible to get the *Cincinnati* up, could Lee not patrol the river between Clarksville and the shoals, destroying any Rebel pontoon bridges found? This was to be in addition to any movement against Kelley.

The two-pronged attack envisioned by Fitch, Lee and Thomas against Kelley's Bell's Mills batteries, together with the anti-cavalry reconnaissance, began at 9:30 on December 8 when the *Neosho*, *Carondelet*, and the lashed together *Moose* and *Reindeer* cast off and steamed down river. At the time he left, the Indiana sailor did not know whether or not his superior would be able to join him with the *Cincinnati*, but he probably had his doubts. Meanwhile, Acting Volunteer Lieutenant Glassford was detailed to take the *Springfield* and *Brilliant* back up the Cumberland above the city on another sweep toward Carthage.

At almost the same time of Fitch's departure, Acting Rear Adm. Lee telegraphed Maj. Gen. Thomas to report that the best pilots at Clarksville had informed him that the water level over Harpeth Shoals was five foot four inches. They advised that the heavy *Cincinnati* could not go up and get over the bars unless she left immediately. Thomas was asked to send an immediate estimate from his people on the prospect of a rise from above. Meanwhile, would he please also let him know if he should convoy down the half dozen or so vessels waiting to come up. A little while later, the Nashville quartermasters warned that the river was not going to rise and Lee wired Thomas to say that he could not stay. Thomas had to let him know immediately what he wanted to do about the transports as he was leaving to avoid having the *Cincinnati* caught above the bars.

When Thomas had a chance to answer Lee's two messages, he asked the admiral to bring the steamers with him. Delivery of this request was delayed. As he waited, the rear admiral visited with the Clarksville harbor master who gave him more bad news. The draft of the *Cincinnati* was too great to permit her to get across Davis' Ripple. Furthermore, and his own pilot confirmed it, unless the Pook turtle was taken back down river to Smithland soon, Lee risked her being stranded for the remainder of the winter. The squadron commander believed he could deal with the Rebel troops then supposedly gathering for an attempt to cross the river, but now knew that he could not join Fitch in a co-operative attack against Kelley's batteries.

As the telegraph wires hummed between Clarksville and Nashville that morning, Fitch's four warships reached Robertson's Island and tied up to its bank in order of steaming. The Hoosier officer was now rowed in the *Neosho*'s gig to the three other ships, going aboard each to confer with their captains. The two ironclads cast off at 11:30 A.M. and, as they continued downstream with the monitor in the lead, their crews were beat to quarters. The tinclads followed much farther back.

About an hour after starting down, the *Neosho* rounded to and turned back up, making a signal that the enemy was across the river. The *Carondelet* went back to warn the trailing light draughts and to remain with them until after lunch. Downstream during this time, Acting Rear Adm. Lee finally received Thomas' early morning wire and replied that he would take the convoy with him and would remain, taking "the chance of wintering here, if you think it justifiable."

The *Moose* and *Reindeer* returned up river at 1:30 P.M. and the *Neosho* and *Carondelet* went back down, the two ironclads steaming on until a brick house, seen earlier opposite Bell's Landing and perceived to be occupied by Confederate troops, came into view. The monitor and the turtle spent the next hour and a half alternatively shelling the place both "vigorously" and leisurely. At 4 P.M., Fitch's two iron monsters proceeded back up the Cumberland to Hyde's Ferry, where they arrived about 7 P.M.

Lee was not able to go up the Cumberland past Davis' Ripple and Fitch could not get above Ashland. This left the Confederates a 17-mile sanctuary free of gunboat interference with any crossing to the north shore and, whether Kelley's guns remained emplaced or not, the falling river below Nashville was blockaded. Although a Confederate crossing in an end run around Nashville concerned the generals in Washington, it was not a strategy then being considered by Gen. Hood.

While the *Neosho* task group was moving upriver, Acting Volunteer Lieutenant Glassford's tinclad expedition returned to Nashville from up the river. Fitch's trusted lieutenant penned a brief report to Maj. Gen. Thomas confirming that there were no Confederate forces operating on the Cumberland anywhere between Nashville and Carthage. On the other hand, he did hear a report, while on the water, that the Rebel Maj. Gen. John C. Breckenridge and 3,000 troops were said to be at Sparta. He could not vouch for its accuracy.

By late in the afternoon, Lee was worried about what might have befallen his subordinate's expedition. Fitch had proposed communicating earlier, but by 4:45 P.M. had not done so, either because the wires were down or because he was not near a telegraph. In noting this concern in another wire to Thomas, Lee asked the commanding general to inform the Indiana sailor that the *Cincinnati* would be remaining at Clarksville. Thomas, who was out on the lines when he received Lee's three dispatches, replied about 45 minutes later promising to give Fitch his superior's message.

An evening exchange of messages brought a further promise from Thomas that he would ask the Hoosier to patrol down to the mouth of Harpeth River, something that neither he or Lee knew to be possible. As a matter of fact, Fitch did twice wire his superior that afternoon and evening, sending copies to Mound City. One told of the engagement, praising the *Neosho*'s endurance, and the second asked for additional supplies of coal and ammunition.

Meanwhile, Thomas' chief of staff, Brig. Gen. Whipple, received a communiqué from the across town headquarters of Cavalry Corps commander Maj. Gen. James H. Wilson. "In regard to the report concerning the presence of a force of rebel cavalry on the north side of the Cumberland," Wilson had intelligence from an officer riding in from Clarksville that day. It was perceived that "only a small force of scouts, not to exceed 50 men, had crossed the river." It was not believed any more had gone over.

At 8 P.M. that evening, Maj. Eckert in Washington, D.C., received an update from Capt. Van Duzer. Although there was no change in Hood's position, a nautical reconnaissance had found a large artillery force on the south bank of the Cumberland, between the capital city and Harpeth Shoals. "One of our gunboats came to grief in exchange of iron at Bell's Ferry," reported the Nashville telegraph operator. Outside his office, the mercury was falling—fast. The north wind continued to howl and the ground was freezing.

That evening, Lt. Cmdr. Fitch let it be known that he would make another reconnaissance upriver the following morning. The Indiana sailor asked Maj. Gen. Smith, via his aide Maj. John Hough, to order Col. Jonathan B. Moore to have a company from his 33rd Wisconsin Volunteer Infantry ready to board the *Moose* as soon as that tinclad appeared the next morning at the extremity of Third Division lines on the river. The soldiers would act as a guard for the boat. Meanwhile, three companies of the 7th Ohio Volunteer Cavalry were also ordered to make a morning reconnaissance down the river toward Ashland, seeking horses and Fitch's Confederates.[27]

Logbooks and soldier memoirs reported that the weather for the previous two weeks in the Nashville area had been cold, sometimes sunny, mild and pleasant, often cloudy. All of that changed for the worse between 8 A.M. and noon on December 9. A cold giant rain set in mixed with sleet and snow and the previous day's wind was now damp and "cutting." The temperature bottomed at about 10 degrees F. In just a few hours, the ground, houses, tents, cannon, gunboats—everything was covered in a sheet of ice. As Capt. Van Duzer told Maj. Eckert, the storm "prevents any movement of our force or of the enemy." For the next five days, the thermometer would not rise above 13 degrees F. Many of the soldiers from both North and South, especially from the South, suffered terribly and Nashville campaign literature is replete with stories of the woe and misery that afflicted both sides.

If any group in the city or without—besides a few privileged souls—did not endure major hardship from the weather in that period, it was the gunboatmen. Steam was, as always, kept up on the majority of the craft and those tars not on deck, coaling, or exposed for other duties were generally relatively warm. Not every ship was immune; the engineers aboard the *Carondelet* blew off steam in order to make boiler repairs.

Additionally, carpenters aboard the ironclads, despite the sleet and snow, were put to work rigging torpedo catchers, also known as torpedo rakes or "devils." Lt. Cmdr. Fitch had some reason to believe Kelley or others had placed "torpedoes" in the river. These devices were actually underwater mines, the "infernal" improvised explosive devices of their day. Union officers had heard and read the stories of these devices and the Hoosier was prudently acting in accordance with Rear Adm. Porter's standing General Order 184 of March 20, which required vigilance against "destructive inventions of the enemy." Both Porter and Lee had practical (and unfortunate) experience with mines and in preparation for a return downriver, both the *Neosho* and *Carondelet* were outfitted with the wrought-iron hooks and logs comprising the available countermeasures system.[28]

The terrible weather halted most military and naval operations in the immediate vicinity, but not all. Acting Rear Adm. Lee took the *Cincinnati* up the Cumberland on December 9 as far as his best pilots would permit, but nothing of interest was seen or heard. This peace was reported to Maj. Gen. Thomas, who replied asking that, if he had any to spare, could Lee have gunboats convoy his cavalry-laden steamers from Smithland to Clarksville. Thomas was asking because Maj. Gen. Grenville M. Dodge at St. Louis had wired indicating that boats had departed for Nashville with fresh cavalry and that their captains "do not like to go up the Cumberland." Anticipating USN assistance, Thomas informed the incoming cavalry that they could "ascend Cumberland River as far as Clarksville with perfect safety" and then disembark and march overland along the north bank. Back from his voyage, Lee replied that that he would have two gunboats at Smithland "prepared to convoy" in a day or two.

In his message to Lee, Thomas had also noted that "I have not heard from Captain Fitch since he started down the river this morning." Beginning just before noon, the *Moose*, in company with the *Reindeer*, did indeed conduct a downstream reconnaissance. They too encountered no significant Rebel presence on the water. Fitch and his tinclads would be constantly on the move over the next several days checking for Confederate activity and acting as a coast guard, as well as an emergency towboat service for steamers within their reach around the city.

Under orders of the previous evening, the horsemen of the 7th Ohio Volunteer Cavalry also conducted a scout, going down a mile below Ashland. "If the enemy had crossed as stated in the communication of the officer commanding U.S. steamer *Neosho*, it is quite probable that I would of heard of it," wrote Col. Garrard. Neither the colonel himself, on an independent reconnaissance toward Clarksville, nor his men coming back from Ashland could determine that more than small bands of deserters had passed. The Buckeye rider was of the opinion "that no cavalry force of the enemy has crossed the river."

Unbeknownst to Thomas, Lee, and Fitch, a slight disruption in the Cumberland supply chain was about to occur. The first alarm bells began sounding that night as the snow in and around Nashville piled up to almost three inches. The inaugural indication was a wire to Brig. Gen. Whipple from Brig. Gen. Meredith at Paducah indicating that Confederate Brig. Gen.. Hylan B. Lyon crossed the Tennessee River at Danville with upwards of 2,500 men the day before. At the same time, Maj. Gen. Stephen G. Burbidge at Bean's Station was warned by Capt. J. Bates Dickson at Lexington that Lyon, with 2,000 men and six artillery pieces, was preparing to cross the Tennessee above Fort Heiman. "Do not put much faith in Lyon's ability to cross the Tennessee and Cumberland," he concluded.[29]

Fear of a Confederate end-run around Nashville had long been a concern of Union commanders. As early as December 5, Lt. Gen. Grant wondered of Maj. Gen. Thomas: "Is there not danger of Forrest moving down the Cumberland to where he can cross it?" The Nashville commandant acknowledged the possibility the next day, but added, "I am in hopes the gunboats will be able to prevent him."

Despite Capt. Dickson's optimism, Forrest's lieutenant, Lyon, had in fact been sent by Gen. Hood on November 21 to make a Cumberland crossing, to capture Clarksville, and, if possible, to destroy the Yankee rail lifeline between Louisville and Nashville. On the evening of December 9, he and his 800 followers reached the Cumberland near Cumberland City, about 20 miles below Clarksville. There the Rebels set up a pair of 12-pounder howitzers under Lt. R. B. Matthews of Gracey's battery. These quickly took the steamer *Thomas E. Tutt*, loaded with grain and carrying Lt. Col. Robert Buchanan of the 7th Missouri, plus two lieutenants and 23 privates. Buchanan and his men were paroled. Other steamers en route up from Fort Donelson that night were fired into in the dark.

Lyon's activities were not widely known to Union defenders on the morning of December 10. At that time, the *Tutt* was employed to ferry Confederate troops to the eastern bank. Later in the day, a fleet of four empty boats departed Clarksville for Smithland. The *Ben Smith*, two hours in advance, was taken and also employed as a ferry. Two of those following turned back when they arrived and saw Lyon's guns, but two others ran the "blockade" and made it to Fort Donelson.

Capt. Isaac P. Williams, assistant quartermaster at Clarksville, was among the first to hear of the depredations and to get off a wire to his superior, Brig. Gen. James Donaldson at Nashville. In addition to confirming the destruction of the *Tutt* and *Ben Smith*, he revealed that the tow boat *Echo* had also been captured. The steamers, together with four barges, were, in Lyon's words, "anchored in the channel and consigned to the flames." Almost instantaneously alerted to developments by his chief quartermaster, Maj. Gen. Thomas ordered Smithland's post commander, Capt. Reed, to hold all boats preparing to ascend the Cumberland until further notice.

Thomas also wanted to know, independently, from Col. Smith at Clarksville whether or not the steamers Williams had mentioned were destroyed. Smith confirmed the situation. Although Lyon had driven in Smith's scouts, it was expected that the Confederate raiders would head into Kentucky rather than attack the river post. Reacting to this suggestion and other information that Lyon planned to burn the railroad bridge at Bowling Green, Thomas ordered all troops railroading to Nashville from Louisville diverted to protect the key crossing point.

Looking out from the St. Cloud hotel, the commanding general saw the wind whipping the freezing snow around from the northwest. Further south, Gen. Hood ordered Col. Biffle's 9th and 10th Tennessee cavalry to Murfreesboro. Although Brig. Gen. Chalmers was able to employ the excuse of bad weather to delay the movement by three days, it will eventually have the effect of reducing Rucker's brigade to just 900 men.

At Mound City, measures were taken to resupply Lt. Cmdr. Fitch. When the Hoosier's wires of December 8 reached Mound City on December 9, Cdr. Livingston had just finished loading aboard the *Benefit* the ammunition ordered sent up to Nashville by Acting Rear Adm. Lee a few days earlier. As escort for the auxiliary, the *Hastings* (Acting Volunteer Lieutenant Joseph Watson) was transferred from her post below Memphis. The *St. Clair* (Acting Volunteer Lieutenant James S. French), fresh from the local repair dock, was also made ready. Under the overall command of Lt. Frederick J. Naile, squadron flag lieutenant and commander of the squadron flagboat *Black Hawk*, the *Benefit* task group weighed anchor for Smithland.

At Smithland by late Saturday, Naile met Acting Volunteer Master Read of the U.S.S. *Victory*, then the most modern light draught available in the lower Cumberland. That ship was detailed to join Naile's passage upriver. Also at that hour, a correspondent from *The Times* of London, relatively new to Nashville, sent off a report on local military matters, which his readers in the U.K. and New York would see 12 days later. The dispatch began: "The situation in Tennessee begins to inspire alarm in Washington. Confederate batteries, 14 miles west of Nashville, effectually blocked the Cumberland, and repulsed all efforts by gunboats to dislodge them." It is doubtful whether Fitch ever saw that story.

Many miles away at 1 A.M. on December 11, the *Benefit*, guarded by the *Hastings*, departed for Louisville, where the transport would transship her cargo and send it on to Fitch via the Louisville & Nashville Railroad. Convoying a pair of chartered steamers towing one coal barge each, Naile's two remaining tinclads simultaneously departed for down the river. Two or three other steamers declined when invited to join the naval parade.[30]

Acting Rear Adm. Lee at Clarksville was advised by "Old Pap" Thomas on that bitterly cold Sunday afternoon (minus 10 F) regarding Lyon's activities. The theater commander was not certain whether the steamers the Rebel raider had employed to cross the Cumberland were still in his hands and asked Lee to "send down the river and recapture the boats and destroy the enemy's force." Within the hour, the naval leader informed Thomas that, from all indications, the boats had been burned and Lyon was across the river, reportedly headed towards Hopkinsville.

As was usually the case with Confederate mounted raider activity, rumors were rife as to where the feared horsemen might strike next. Also on December 11, Brig. Gen. Donaldson sent a note down to Lt. Cmdr. Fitch informing him that the USQM had a number of steamers and barges upriver near the mouth of Stone's River gathering in a supply of wood for Nashville's campfires and fireplaces. Given the intense demand for fuel during the terrible storm now blowing, it was feared that Rebel wood foragers were about to set up a battery and try to capture the craft, taking their prized cords for themselves, or failing that, to destroy them.

The Cumberland was too low and the weather too bad to permit Fitch to send Howard and the *Neosho* on the mission so the Indiana sailor detailed the *Springfield* to deal with the task. Acting Volunteer Master Morgan was cautioned to steer his vessel and shepherd the others so as to prevent the enemy from getting batteries below or abreast. Despite the cold and the strong northwest wind that blew across the frozen landscape, the *Springfield* successfully convoyed the boats below by evening. The Logansport officer later heard that the Rebels actually did set up a battery on the river the following morning, but it was too late to catch the wood boats. Their riders did, however, burn a large wood stockpile.

Toward evening, the Indiana sailor wired his superior at Clarksville stating his need for ammunition and fuel. Lee did not receive the telegram until almost midnight on December 13. Both were probably glad to be on board ship. Sleet had fallen all day, occasionally whipped by 60 mph winds.[31]

All day Sunday and on Monday, December 12, the heavily-guarded Naile replenishment convoy made its way up the Cumberland. En route, the *Black Hawk's* commander made the usual stops and spoke other boats going to and fro. From these, he learned that Lyon's force was headed toward Hopkinsville. The vessels halted at Cumberland City where Naile was informed that Lyon had emplaced a pair of cannon at Paducah and two more near Fort Donelson. He was also told that the Rebels had a cache of ammunition opposite his anchorage. Immediately, a party was sent across to search for it and returned sometime later with a barge containing nine boxes of carbine cartridges and a caisson. As they departed, the men aboard Naile's boats could all see the burnt-out wrecks of the *Echo*, *Ben Smith*, and *Thomas E. Tutt*, plus at least four barges. Before leaving the scene on his raid, Lyon later said, he estimated the value of the property destroyed at about $1 million.

Often wearing icicles, the light craft of Fitch's Nashville flotilla remained active in the cold. The mighty *Neosho* and *Carondelet*, undoubtedly covered in some places topside with frozen snow, remained tied to the bank largely unable to move due to the low river stage. Over on the hills and in the valleys surrounding Tennessee's capital city, the soldiers were chopping down trees for firewood at such an alarming rate that quartermaster Col. Rusling believed it would take a century to replace them. That night, logbook entries reported "considerable picket firing around the line."

Fitch had time early on December 13 to send a request over to the St. Cloud Hotel asking that, if Thomas made any military advance in which he could be of service, to please let him know as soon as possible. The gunboat man did not want to be left out of the big battle everyone seemed to know was coming. With a seaman's eye for climate, the Hoosier offered his opinion that the rain, sleet and extreme cold would soon be a memory, "probably by morning." After all, the wind was no longer blowing cold from the north; it was now moderate and from the east and southeast. The temperature was steadily rising, though it remained cold.

Aboard the *Carondelet* sitting 5 miles from Nashville at a fort with several other gunboats," John Hagerty wrote home from the engine room. "We had a fight with the Rebels on the 5th ... since then the monitor *Neosho* and us attacked the Rebel batteries and drove them back.... The monitor and us then went up to Nashville," he revealed, "and then returned on the 6th and they fired on us again ... a shell from the monitor set a house on fire." The

Confederates had blockaded the river, Hagerty informed his wife, "and no mail can come from Cairo." Although there were gunboats at Clarksville "to help us," they couldn't come up because of the river stage. Like everyone else, the sailor was confident that "our land forces will drive them away ... can hear the pickets firing from both sides ... we are in front of 60,000–70,000 Rebels."

"River low," Fireman Hagerty again told Margaret "Maggie" O'Neil. Indeed, the river was so low that Lt. Cmdr. Fitch could presently move only one of the heavy boats (the *Neosho*). To do that, he would have to drop her down below Robertson's Island with lines—slow, labor-intensive hand work as steam could not be trusted to take her through. If the weather changed even slightly, Fitch would get men aboard her in the morning to begin the task.

Maj. Gen. Thomas, through his assistant adjutant general Capt. Robert H. Ramsey, reassured Fitch that his fighting wish would be granted. In fact, the commanding general had in mind a big role for the gunboats to play in any move that might be made against the enemy "should there really be a change of weather and a rise in the river sufficient to enable you to move your fleet with facility." Two days before his actual advance occurred, Thomas had planned that Fitch's ironclads engage "the batteries on the river below the city" in order to attract their attention while other troops swooped in upon them from behind. Something of a knowing smile may have come to the sailor's face as he read the army plan. This was exactly the same scheme his half brother, Col. Graham Newell Fitch, and Cmdr. Augustus H. Kilty, had agreed upon at St. Charles, Arkansas, in June 1862 and one he had also attempted to utilize several times since.

The commanding general went on to offer the Logansport officer his "thanks for your cordial cooperation heretofore" as well as in the future. Finally, it was asked if the navy might have the river patrolled as high up as Carthage so that any enemy movement in that quarter could be detected instantly.

Lt. Cmdr. Fitch replied to Ramsey as soon as his message was received, promising to watch the river above carefully and to do all he could to fulfill Thomas' wishes. The sailor continued in hopes that they would all soon be cheered by better weather and water prospects. If they would combine to permit, he would "surely give the rebel batteries below sufficient amusement to keep them occupied, and at the same time, try to induce them to bring as many guns on the river as possible."

The supply convoy under Lt. Naile reached Clarksville after dark that Tuesday. Once Acting Rear Adm. Lee had received the *Black Hawk* skipper's report on his voyage upstream, he went over to the telegraph office and sent two cipher wires to Nashville, one each to Lt. Cmdr. Fitch and Maj. Gen. Thomas. Fitch was advised that Lee now finally had, via Lt. Naile, the telegrams he had sent to Mound City on December 8 reporting the *Neosho's* fight with Kelley's gunners. Because his subordinate's telegram was necessarily brief, Lee wondered: "What sort of works and guns did you engage on the 8th, where, and with what effect?" Thomas was advised of Naile's observations regarding Lyon. Both men were promised that Lee would handle getting the next convoy down to Smithland, employing the just-arrived *St. Clair* and *Victory*.

The day's news was telegraphed from Nashville army headquarters to Maj. Gen. Halleck at the War Department around 9 P.M. Although there was no change on his front, the theater commander reported that his planning was finished, the time for defense was over, and he was ready to take the offensive as soon as the weather improved. Maj. Gen. Thomas confirmed that telegraphic communication was reestablished with Clarksville and that he had heard from Lee that the two gunboats and their transports had arrived. Lyon's means of recrossing the Cumberland were destroyed and there was no worry about the L & N as sufficient troops had been detailed to contain the Confederate. Fitch's patrols to Carthage reported no enemy activity and Thomas was "in hopes of a sufficient rise on the river to enable me to use the gunboats in reopening the Cumberland as far as Nashville." His wire would not come into the War Department until 8 the next morning.

Well after dark, Maj. Eckert in Washington, D.C., received his nightly telegram from Capt. Van Duzer. The Nashville operator was pleased to note that the "thaw has begun, and tomorrow we can move without skates!" He did not note that the permafrost of recent days was rapidly being replaced with gooey mud. News of Lyon's Cumberland crossing was relayed, along with the fear that use of the L & N railroad and telegraph might soon be lost. Even so, the news was not too worrisome. "He cannot stay long—not strong enough" was the reported consensus.

"To the utter consternation and dismay of Thomas, Lee and Fitch," wrote Byrd Douglas in 1961, Lyon returned across the Cumberland after his Kentucky sojourn and headed toward Sparta. His desperate ride had little impact on Thomas' supply chain, but did, once again, prove that the current navy blockade of the Cumberland was porous. Although Lyon's well-executed raid turned out to be a ride too little too late, it ever after gave the "what if" school of history reason to believe, as Douglas put it, "that Forrest, with adequate forces, could have dealt Thomas a severe and timely blow if he had been permitted to strike before reinforcements reached Nashville."[32]

The hoped for meteorological change began after midnight on December 14 when the winds warmed. At sunup, a slight rain fell and the entire city was covered until 11 A.M. by a thick blanket of fog. Still, the ground, when visible, was rapidly losing its snow cover, even as men and animals waded in the slush and mud that replaced it. Throughout the morning, as he attempted to spy the land before him and consider those thousands of details a commanding general notes before a big battle, George Thomas still took the time to exchange telegrams with Acting Rear Adm. Lee on such matters as convoy and the roaming Rebel Lyon. Lee would have no physical role to play in the upcoming offensive, but Thomas soothed any sense of absence held by his nautical colleague. There was "no doubt," he wrote, "that the presence of your ironclad at Clarksville prevented Lyon from moving up opposite that place and destroying the transports."

At midday, "Old Pap" Thomas warned his corps commanders to prepare for an offensive according to the plan the high command had discussed throughout the cold snap. At 3 P.M., Thomas hosted a final conference at the St. Cloud Hotel to go over last minute details. Three hours later, Special Field Orders No. 342 were drawn up and dispatched for an all-out advance beginning the next morning as close to 6 A.M. as possible. An attack would be feinted on the Confederate right flank while the positions on their left along Richland Creek would be divided. Among the initial objectives for the offensive in the latter salient was the removal of the Confederate battery across from Bell's Mills.

The major general commanding had a few last details to manage after dinner. At 8 P.M., he wired Maj. Gen. Halleck: "The ice having melted away today, the enemy will be attacked tomorrow morning." Although he regretted not having moved earlier (and doubtless thinking under his breath, that he might have been spared from the barrage of nonstop Washington prodding that had continued the past two weeks), he just did not feel it could have been done "with any reasonable hope of success."

A large number of other orders were also cut, including these two of greatest interest to our subject. At 8 P.M., Capt. Ramsey sent a lengthy note to Lt. Cmdr. Fitch advising him that the enemy would be attacked at an early hour on Thursday morning. If it were possible for the Indiana sailor to "drop down the river and engage their batteries on the river bank," it would be "excellent cooperation." It was "very probable" that Kelley's gunners would be attacked from the rear by Union forces and thus it became "very desirable and necessary that your fire does not injure the attacking force." Perhaps knowing of—but maybe not—the confusion of the *Moose's* bombardment at Buffington Island in July 1863, Ramsey confided that it was the avoidance of friendly fire casualties, as well as the nautical diversion, which had caused his warning of "the proposed attack." Fitch received the communication "about 10 P.M." Early in the evening, Maj. Gen. Wilson's chief of staff, Lt. Col. A. J. Alexander, sent an order from the Union cavalry commander to Brig. Gen. Johnson saying that Fitch would drop down and engage the battery in the morning. Wilson believed, as Alexander indicated, that Johnson could capture the battery if he moved "with rapidity."

At approximately 10:30 P.M., the Logansport native sent for his officers. These came aboard the flagboat over the next half hour and soon all were reviewing Ramsey's communication and making plans for the morrow. The conference aboard the *Moose* broke up after midnight and the naval captains returned to their boats in banks of river mist thickened by campfire smoke. Heavy picket firing was heard from the river in the first hours after midnight.

During the day, Gen. Hood was apprised that Federal forces were amassing on his left flank. Not knowing exactly what Thomas was up to, he passed orders for Lt. Gen. Alexander P. Stewart to dispatch the infantry of Ector's Brigade, under Col. David Coleman, to support Brig. Gen. Chalmers on the Harding Pike. The maneuver allowed Chalmers to shift his force farther left, northwest past Charlotte Pike. That night, he sent a note via a courier to Chalmers warning him to expect an attack on his lines before morning or very early into the morning.[33]

December 15 began cloudy, warm, and extremely foggy. This was a pea-soup fog familiar to residents of the eastern seacoast or London—or the hills of Tennessee in winter. Union ground forces, readied for the start of a great offensive, were nevertheless bugled awake between 3:30 and 4 A.M. and breakfasted. The gray or blackish smoke from campfires, building chimneys, and other burning sites continued to mingle with drizzle, creating a cloud that hung low and prevented visual penetration of more than a few feet. Not only the soldiers, but also the gunboat men wondered if the 6 A.M. advance would occur as scheduled.

Thick haze and mist continued past the starting time, past 7 A.M., indeed, throughout most of the morning. Some Yankee forces stepped off as scheduled and some did not. Maj. Gen. Thomas' plan was largely based upon a great cavalry sweep around the western side of Gen. Hood's army—and mounted horsemen required good visibility. The fog forced the commanding general to wait out the perceptibility problem and led to some confusion in his ranks, including those slated to co-operate with the navy as well as an unplanned march by Smith's infantrymen across the path of Maj. Gen. Wilson's cavalry, elements of which did not get off until about 10 A.M.

There was no puzzlement on the part of Le Roy Fitch. From 6 A.M., the men aboard his vessels were able to hear, though not see, the apparent movement of the U.S. Army. At 7:20, the *Hoosier's* task group got underway in a moderate southern breeze headed down the river with the *Neosho* in the lead. She was followed by the *Carondelet, Moose, Reindeer, Fairplay, Brilliant* and *Silver Lake*. Fitch remained aboard the flagboat which was, together with the others, beat to quarters about an hour later.

Due to the delays and bafflement caused by the fog ashore, the honor of firing the first shots in the actual Battle of Nashville went to the U.S. Navy. This giant engagement was not only the last big clash of arms in the Civil War's western theater, it was the climactic large-scale action for the Mississippi Squadron. Although he did not know it at the time, it was also the last major day of fighting in Le Roy Fitch's career.

It is somewhat ironic to note that, as at Buffington Island in July 1863, Lt. Cmdr. Fitch did not know for certain the location of the Union cavalrymen whom he expected to move in behind the Confederate cannon opposite Bell's Mills. Expecting that they would soon be along, the Logansport native determined to gain the attention of Lt. Col. Kelley's gunners while Johnson's men rode up.

According to the plan worked out on the *Moose* around midnight, Acting Volunteer Lieutenant Howard's *Neosho* was sent down below the batteries about 9:30 a.m The monitor was not to knock out the guns, but only feel their strength, before returning above to report back to Fitch. The light draughts tied up well out of range while the *Carondelet* followed the *Neosho* down, tying up to the bank, probably on the south side of White's Bend near Clifton and Fort Zollicofer, within eyesight and extreme gun range. Howard easily attracted Rebel attention, carefully and deliberately engaging them for approximately 50 minutes. During this time, the Pook turtle above also sent four shells at Kelley's works. Several homes were damaged in the shoot, including the Childress and Stump home in the present Sylvan Park area.

By 11 A.M., the two Yankee monsters had steamed back upstream and were anchored with the tinclads. Howard went aboard the flagboat to report that Kelley had replied with only two guns of four spied and that no Federal cavalry was seen.

After hearing from Acting Volunteer Lieutenant Howard, Fitch was convinced that this time he could easily silence Kelley's cannon and drive them away. Capture, however, and not dispersal, was the plan agreed to with Thomas. Because Brig. Gen. Johnson had not arrived by noon, all hands were piped to lunch. All afternoon, the naval task group "maneuvered around above them" waiting for Johnson's people to reach a desirable position behind the artillery.[34]

Much earlier, at 4 A.M., Brig. Gen. Johnson's 6th U.S. Cavalry Division broke camp and moved along the Charlotte Pike to the outer line of Union fortifications. Then, to put it bluntly, Johnson's horsemen, even though they had been waiting since 6 A.M., simply did not get started by the time the *Neosho* and *Carondelet* finished their shoot. Johnson, who would be breveted for his "success" at Nashville, was the same commander who had once promised to capture John Hunt Morgan—and ended up being captured himself over two years earlier. This time the officer, who was given increasingly more important assignments, had 2,100 men in two brigades, one mounted under Col. Thomas J. Harrison and a second dismounted and commanded by Col. James Biddle.

On the Cumberland River flank before him was an unknown number of Confederates. As it turned out, only about 900 Rebel horsemen of Col. Edmund Rucker's brigade were standing guard along the Charlotte Pike near Richland Creek, with Brig. Gen. James R. Chalmers present. When Gen. Hood had learned that morning that an attack was coming, he had sent Chalmers from Belle Meade Plantation to the area at Charlotte Pike and White

Bridge Road to take command. Five days earlier, Chalmers, by Hood's order, had sent his other brigade, that of Col. Jacob B. Biffle, to the Rebel right wing and now faced a much larger foe with small numbers. Today, the scene of this stand is McCabe Golf Course.

When Chalmers was seen across Richland Creek about noon, Johnson ordered Biddle's 759 horseless soldiers to get over the stream and capture the grayclad barricades atop a ridge behind it. Unhappily, this assault was slowed, at least to a certain extent, because the cavalrymen were unfamiliar with infantry maneuvers, fell over their lengthy sheathed sabers—which no one thought to leave behind—and were unable to wade the creek under fire.

"It was a terrible scene," Confederate Capt. James Dinkins later remembered, "but it brought about a retreat." It was at this point, in one of the great vignettes of Nashville history, that 75-year-old local one-armed Confederate sympathizer Mark Robertson Cockrill (grandson of Nashville's founder and the man for whom the nearby river bend was named) rode onto the scene to rally the butternut soldiers. He survived these heroics, near present day Interstate 40 and Charlotte Pike, waving his father's Revolutionary War musket and his hat with his good hand and holding his horse's reins in his teeth! The senior citizen was reacting to the slaughter that morning by Federal soldiers of his prize-winning herd of Saxony sheep. Fitch and his sailors did not see this gallant, some later said foolhardy, individual charge and if any of Johnson's men were witnesses, they remained silent.

Seeing that Biddle was failing, Johnson next sent Harrison and his men riding ahead beyond their dismounted colleagues. The riders stormed up the slope on the right flank intent upon catching a portion of Kelley's artillery expected, with dismounted men in barricades, to be found at the summit—the guns thought to have been attracted by the *Neosho* earlier. Watching the "gallant charge" from below, Johnson thought his men would quickly capture the battery or "at least, to disperse the supports and shoot down the horses before the guns could be moved." The leading Yankee cavalry unit ran into a stone wall—literally—at the top of the hill and was forced to dismount in order to knock it down.

By the time the Northerners got through the barrier, the Rebel troopers behind had moved off. In the confusion of the morning's activities, the rest of Rucker's brigade, less a few stragglers, also escaped along the Charlotte Pike. The retreat was seen, at least partially, from the Cumberland. Acting Volunteer Ensign Thomas A. Quinn, officer of the deck aboard the *Carondelet*, wrote in the ship's log that "our cavalry charged over the hill and drove the enemy out of his works."

Once Johnson reassembled his brigades, his 6th Division set off west along the Charlotte Pike after Chalmers. The pursuit went about four miles before the Federal cavalrymen once more ran into Rucker's brigade, posted in a strong position of long rail barricades located along a ridge beyond a small creek near Davidson's house overlooking Bell's Landing. This was, in fact, the true location of Kelley's artillery, which could now sweep the pike and the creek bridge. John Johnson of the 14th Tennessee Cavalry, CSA, later remembered that the riflemen, posted along the ridge, were reinforced with cannon.

An energetic attack on the Confederate rear "directly into his works" by Col. Garrard's unsupported 7th Ohio made about 3 P.M. was soon thereafter repulsed with heavy losses. "The rebs have chosen a good position," he messaged Maj. Gen. Wilson shortly after 2 P.M. Thinking himself close enough to the Cumberland for the gunboats to make a difference, Johnson ordered his own advance stopped and sent a messenger to find Fitch and obtain his help. Horseman Johnson remembered that he and his companions were able to repulse "several charges of cavalry" and, even though the gunboats would shell close to their rear, they held "our ground until night came to our relief."[35]

About 3:40 P.M. the *Neosho* and *Carondelet* steamed down the river, rounded to, and began shelling what they perceived to be the Confederate positions. This attempt to enfilade the Confederate line was more noisy than effective. Many aboard the ironclads and among Johnson's troopers were convinced that the Rebels must be suffering great harm from the huge explosions. Private John Johnston of the 14th Tennessee Cavalry, C.S.A., remembered in 1905 that "the gunboats on the Cumberland, though out of sight, threw a number of immense bombs in our direction, which exploded not far in our rear."

According to contemporary and later reviews by Chalmers, Horn, and McDonough, the giant shells caused no damage to the butternut horsemen, but did cut up a lot of nearby private property. The naval bombardment continued for 20 minutes, after which the *Carondelet* led the monitor back upstream. As the darkness of a winter evening approached, reaction to this cannonade was different from the perspectives of the three principles involved: Johnson, Chalmers, and Fitch.

While the navy was in action, interrogated Southern prisoners informed Brig. Gen. Johnson that an entire Confederate cavalry division was in front of him. Stung once by overconfidence with Morgan, Johnson sent a messenger off to Maj. Gen. Wilson seeking reinforcements and admitting he had not captured the guns "for reasons which I can fully explain to you at another time." As it would soon be dark, Johnson stayed put waiting for his superior to send help. Of Fitch's shoot, the horseman believed "the tremendous discharges of his heavy guns contributed largely, I doubt not, to the already serious demoralization of the enemy."

For his part, Brig. Gen. Chalmers was apprised that the Yankees were moving on his rear. Soon they took his headquarters at Belle Meade Plantation. To avoid being cut off, he ordered his men to abandon their present locations and hurry back toward the main Confederate army. At this point, Lt. Col. Kelley limbered up his guns and retired away from the Cumberland, finally shutting down his blockade.

Out on the water, Fitch believed that Kelley had found himself in a bad position and was attempting to remove his guns. He was "too late," the Hoosier officer believed, as "our cavalry closed in and took them with but little resistance." Satisfied that the combined arms objective had thus far "been successfully carried out," the Tenth District commander moved his task group down opposite Bell's Mills, where it tied up to the right bank.

Replanting his cannon about a half mile back from the river near Davidson's landing, Kelley lobbed a few shells toward Brig. Gen. Johnson's cavalrymen and towards the *Neosho*. This behavior was taken as an affront not only to the horsemen targets, but by Fitch and by gunners from Lt. Frank G. Smith's Battery I, 4th U.S. Artillery, located on a hill that overlooked the gunboats. "A few rounds of shell and shrapnel from our heavy guns," together with the land artillery, "soon silenced the Rebels." Although the Indiana sailor also believed this battery taken, it too was not.

The rapid arrival of darkness brought an end to naval maneuvering in the Cumberland off Bell's Mills. "Not knowing the exact position our forces had taken, the firing on our part ceased and the boats were withdrawn a short distance above" the suspected Confederate gun emplacement. Fitch wanted to be absolutely certain that his men did not initiate any friendly fire casualties. At 5 P.M., the gunboats landed at the bank, headed downstream.

Unlike Buffington Island, the location of the battles between Lt. Col. Kelley and Lt. Cmdr. Fitch has been consciously preserved as a Civil War landmark. Known as Kelley's Point Battlefield, these six acres form part of a 13-acre parcel of land nine miles west of Nashville in the community of Bellvue. Located just off the Charlotte Pike exit of Interstate 40, the riverbank site was originally a portion of a larger 60-acre tract of land where giant Lowe's and Wal-Mart outlets now (2006) exist. The Battle of Nashville Preservation Society and its 1990–1994 president, Robert Wayne "Bob" Henderson, Jr., were instrumental in convincing the JDN Realty Corp. to donate the land to the Nashville Metro Department of Parks and Recreation, which holds it as a portion of the city's Brookmeade Park historical greenway. Funds to support the formation of the battlefield park and its markers was provided by the American Civil War Round Table of the United Kingdom (ACWRT-UK).[36]

The day's fighting around the city resulted in a Confederate disaster, despite the late Union start and the coming of darkness. Hood's left wing was collapsed and Thomas was able to order a general advance along his entire line. The Rebels, with their center and right under intense Northern pressure, elected to depart their defenses and move several miles to a new position in the Brentwood Hills. All day long, local citizens, most with Southern sympathies, found spots on the hills behind the battle from which to watch the fighting. One Union officer from Ohio observed the nearly-silent multitudes, remaking that: "No army on the continent every played on any field to so large and so sullen an audience."

At 9 P.M., "Old Pap" wired Maj. Gen. Halleck announcing his attack on Hood's left and his success in driving it from over eight miles from the river below the city. Grayclad fortunes would, in fact, be worse on the morrow as Thomas was determined to attack again. The message was confirmed in the nightly telegraph exchange between Capt. Van Duzer and Maj. Eckert.

About the same time, chief of staff Whipple messaged both Acting Rear Adm. Lee and Lt. Cmdr. Fitch noting that the Confederate left had been turned with many prisoners taken, along with guns, wagons, and Brig. Gen. Chalmers' headquarters chain. Lee replied an hour later with his warm congratulations and Fitch answered more completely. The Indiana sailor noted that "things here are working well," and restating his belief that U.S. forces "had captured the guns in the upper rebel battery on the river." He noted the presence of another battery "back from the river near the landing," which he believed the *Neosho* had silenced.[37]

December 16 was the deciding day for the big battle around Tennessee's capital. When the sun came up, it was foggy again, but not nearly so dense as the day before. The last patches of mist were burned off by 8:30 A.M. and within an hour and a half, local thermometers registered 65 degrees F. under cloudy skies. Anyone standing on the steps of the state capitol building or on surrounding hills (and thousands did) had a panoramic view of blue lines and saw numerous puffs of gunpowder smoke.

As the main battle unfolded farther south, the men on the Cumberland front, not knowing that Chalmers' last defenders, the 7th Alabama Cavalry, had quietly withdrawn during the night, prepared for battle. At daybreak as the fog lifted, troopers from the U.S. 6th Division discovered the enemy's departure and took unopposed possession of the abandoned field.

Under cover of darkness, Col. Kelley and his troops had abandoned their positions on the river, rode through Bellevue, and pushed down the old Sawyer Brown Road to the Little Harpeth River. Eventually, they rejoined Brig. Gen. Chalmers' division near Hillsboro Pike and present day Old Hickory Boulevard.

When he learned of his good fortune, Brig. Gen. Johnson fired off a message to Maj. Gen. Wilson: "We have driven the enemy from this place and [are] following up." This effrontery brought a stern rebuke by one battle student many years later. "With double the strength of Chalmers and the heavy firepower of the gunboats," wrote Stanley Sword, Johnson so bungled "his assignment as to not only allow the enemy to escape with little loss, but to withdraw from his front without knowing they were gone."

As the fog lifted from the river, the *Neosho, Moose, Carondelet, Reindeer,* and *Fairplay* steamed downriver to Bell's Mills. Still not knowing exactly what to expect, Lt. Cmdr. Fitch had his boats cleared for action. Upon arrival at the old battle site, the gunboat men found that Federal forces were in entire control of the area. The shooting part of the navy's war at Nashville was over.

About 10 A.M., Acting Rear Adm. Lee at Clarksville, according to the second number of Vol. 44 of the Army Official Records published in 1894, wired Navy secretary Gideon Welles regarding Thomas' attack of the previous day. The assault "upon Hood's left resulted in the capture of Chalmers' headquarters train, with papers, 1,000 prisoners, and 16 pieces of artillery, with probable loss to the army not exceeding 500 killed and wounded." The Navy Official Records, issued in 1914, inserts the wording "supported by the Tenth Division of this squadron" between the words "left" and "resulted." The author does not know if the compilers of the first set of records left the phrase out or whether it was added later for the sake of propriety and never really existed.

Having accomplished all that he believed was possible in the vicinity of Bell's Mills, Lt. Cmdr. Fitch decided to return to Nashville to make certain that all was safe on the river there and above. His flotilla took their leave of Johnson's men at 11:30 A.M. and steamed back at the bank opposite the city, arriving in the rain at 3 P.M. Throughout their voyage, seamen aboard the boats heard heavy firing on the left of the Union lines.

In his official Christmas Eve report of the battle, Brig. Gen. Johnson claimed that when his men chased Kelley beyond Davidson's on the morning of the 16th, they left behind "a battery of six guns abandoned by the enemy." Informed that the cannon were later "discovered" by a landing party from the gunboats and sent by the sailors on into Nashville, Johnson, nevertheless, felt "entitled to claim these as the capture of" his 6th Division.

Whether, as noted above, these were the guns Fitch believed on the 15th that "our cavalry closed in and took them with but little resistance" or some others is unclear. The Tenth District commander did not, as he had so carefully done at Buffington Island in July 1863, record the disposition of any ordnance either seized or transported by his boats.

Perhaps the brigadier was misinformed and there were no captured guns. Brig. Gen. Chalmers wrote in his report that Lt. Col. Kelley's regiment had gotten away to Brentwood during the night and Lt. Col. R. R. White was able in the darkness to get out a picket in front of the encamped 6th Division while "the infantry and artillery column" passed. Lt. Col. Kelley, as an appendix to Private Johnson's story, wrote in *Confederate Veteran* in 1905 that he had led the men away "without the loss of gun or wagon."

While most of Fitch's command was downstream supporting Johnson, the *Springfield* was left behind at the cross-river Nashville rendezvous. Acting Volunteer Master Morgan had orders to conduct reconnaissance patrols above the city up as far as Stone's River. Although undertaking his runs, Morgan failed to report his findings to Fitch, which "considerably annoyed" the young Indiana officer. Not finding the *Springfield* in port upon his return and thus unclear as affairs on the river east of the city, the Tenth District leader hailed

Acting Volunteer Lieutenant Glassford. The *Reindeer's* captain was asked him to take his boat, *Silver Lake,* and *Fairplay* above to check conditions.

On Christmas Day as the North continued to celebrate good war news, Brig. Gen. Johnson sat down at his headquarters and dictated a lengthy thank-you note to Lt. Cmdr. Fitch. In it, he acknowledged the "promptness, readiness, and efficiency" with which the Hoosier's gunboats had cooperated with the 6th Division "in the attack upon the enemy's left during the recent battle of Nashville." Although he did not know the names of the navy men or boats involved other than that of their commander, Johnson went on to say that he believed "everything was done that could be done on the part of the naval forces to cooperate." Would, therefore, Fitch please accept his gratitude and also convey it to his officers and men.

Upon its receipt, Fitch passed a copy of the message on to Acting Rear Adm. Lee, with a cover letter suggesting that his superior would be gratified to know "that such a letter was written, giving the vessels of the squadron under your command credit." The only direct letter of appreciation the gunboat man received for his participation in the Nashville campaign was received on April 21, 1865. Whatever one may think of Johnson's generalship, his interservice etiquette in this case was first class even if his timing was deficient.[38]

The situation with Gen. Hood's main army deteriorated throughout the 16th to a point where the shattered graycoats rushed pell-mell in sleet and rain not stopping until they were south of Brentwood after dark. Only then were scattered units able to commence their regrouping process. "The night that followed was strangely silent," wrote Walter Durham in 1987, "the last cannonading having stopped at dark with the flight of the rebels."

Weather, weariness, and darkness halted the Yankee pursuit, which would resume the next day. In the two day battle, Maj. Gen. Thomas lost 387 men killed and 2,562 wounded, while capturing 4,462 Confederates. The Confederate commanding general did not know how many human losses he had suffered, but did know he had left 54 cannon behind. As occasional lightning flashes rent the darkness, stragglers could be seen exiting the battlefield, either south or toward Nashville.

Upon reflection, residents of the fortress city would come to appreciate that Hood's rapid decampment south had spared the city from the ravages of urban warfare and street fighting and had ended weeks of concern over the fates of families, homes, and all properties not yet damaged. Still, a majority of citizens had hoped for a different battle outcome. "Nashville's heart was heavy with sorrow," wrote Stanley Horn in 1945. "Mourning was her becoming dress."

In response to a congratulatory note from President Lincoln that morning, "Old Pap" Thomas replied to the commander in chief at some length at the dinner hour. After recounting the manner of his success and the activities of various of his generals, the "Old Roman," as Rear Adm. Porter liked to call him, praised Johnson for driving the enemy from his Cumberland batteries "in co-operation with the gun-boats under Lieutenant-Commander Fitch."

About this same time, Lt. Naile returned to Smithland. The convoy escorted down from Clarksville by the *Black Hawk*'s commander encountered no opposition. The *Hastings, Victory,* and *St. Clair* were sent to watch the lower Cumberland, but saw no sign of the enemy. The next morning, the Smithland post commander, Capt. Reed, confirmed that the "river is now being patrolled with gunboats from here to Clarksville."[39]

The *Springfield,* which was on a river scout above the city, came down and landed below the *Carondelet* at 2:30 A.M. on December 17. Acting Volunteer Master Morgan was immediately called to the *Moose* and reported all was clear above. Despite the positive intelligence,

Fitch, who seldom castigated his officers, found it necessary to censure Morgan "for neglect in this particular and for not exhibiting a little more enthusiasm and energy." Acting Volunteer Lieutenant Glassford's patrol to the Stone's River sector also returned during the night to report all quiet.⁴⁰

Early that morning, Nashville's logistical chief, Brig. Gen. Donaldson, received a brief message from Maj. Gen. Thomas, via his adjutant, Capt. Ramsey. Although short, its impact on the remaining Civil War career of Lt. Cmdr. Le Roy Fitch was significant. In short, it set forth the commanding general's belief that the "Cumberland River is perfectly safe" and his desire that Donaldson "resume shipments on the river to Nashville from below."

After lunch, Maj. Gen. Wilson, writing from a location outside Franklin, informed chief of staff Whipple that "the rebels are in a great skedaddle." The weather was wet and warm. More fog would follow after dark.

That evening after dinner, with Gen. Hood in full retreat, Maj. Gen. Thomas from the field, also near Franklin, wrote to Acting Rear Adm. Lee asking once more for Fitch's services. If feasible, the Tenth District commander should proceed up the Tennessee with one or two ironclads and several gunboats to destroy Confederate pontoon bridges believed near Florence and at the mouth of the Duck River. The Hoosier sailor and his men on the Cumberland may have been reading battle accounts in copies of the local press. The headline of one, the Nashville *Daily Union*, screamed: "The Rebels Completely Routed. They Flee in a Perfect Panic."⁴¹

At Clarksville, Acting Rear Adm. Lee received Thomas' telegraphic request for Fitch's services at midmorning on December 18, 13 hours after it was sent. Upon receipt of Thomas' request, Acting Rear Adm. Lee quickly consulted a chart and found that the Duck River was 147 miles from Florence. The fleet commander knew that he would be in a better position to oversee his subordinate's activities from Paducah and took fast passage downriver. The *Cincinnati* was ordered to follow; her post as station ironclad at Clarksville would be assumed by the *Carondelet*.⁴²

Witnessed by a good crowd of dockworkers and others watching from the bank, the first post-battle return convoy from Nashville to Smithland departed in two waves beginning at 11:30 A.M. The parade was led by the *Neosho*, under tow of the supply boat *Magnet*. The monitor was followed ten minutes later by the *Moose* and *Reindeer*, which led the transports *Metamora*, *Financier*, *New York*, *Prairie State*, *Stephen Bayard*, *Tacony*, *Lilly*, and *Lady Franklin*. At noon, the steamers *Arizona* and *Prima Donna* departed, followed by the hospital boat U.S.S. *Red Rover* and with the *Fairplay* bringing up the rear. All but the sternwheeler *Prairie State*, the side-wheelers *Stephen Bayard* and *Tacony*, and the *Red Rover* were in the December 6 convoy that Fitch wanted to push by Lt. Col. Kelley.

"We open the Cumberland today," Brig. Gen. Donaldson cheerfully wrote to Quartermaster General Meigs in the afternoon of December 18 after witnessing the departure. "Transports here have left under convoy of the gunboats." The weather was cloudy, threatening rain.

Perhaps saluted by the *Newsboy* as it passed the army gunboat, the convoy made its way down the Cumberland throughout the afternoon and into the evening. Beyond Robertson's Island, Davidson's Landing, and Bell's Landing and Mills it steamed, trailing a great cloud of chimney smoke. The sites of recent bombardment could now be safely passed, with damaged homes, busted trees, and shell craters clearly visible.

While Fitch was on the river, his superior wired Maj. Gen. Thomas agreeing to push a suitable naval force up the Tennessee River as soon as Fitch arrived and the thick fog dissipated. If there was water enough in the river, Acting Rear Adm. Lee anticipated that the bridges at the Duck River and Florence would be destroyed, Hood's retreat would be cut off, and Brig. Gen. Lyon, if he were still on the loose, would be prevented from recrossing the Tennessee.

That evening, Thomas received three telegrams from Lee within an hour. In responding, the commanding general suggested that Fitch could probably make it to Florence within six days. Would it be possible for the intrepid officer, he wondered, to pause at Johnsonville or Clifton and pick up a number of troop boats requiring convoy to Florence if such a request were made?[43]

Rain, with a continuous wind from the north, accompanied the Smithland-bound convoy all through the night and until early afternoon on December 19. At 5:30, the boats arrived at Clarksville, and tied up to the opposite bank. While Acting Volunteer Lieutenant Glassford and his fellow escort captains looked to the replenishment of their tinclads, the ironclads remained with slight steam up.

Hurrying ashore to report to Acting Rear Adm. Lee, Lt. Cmdr. Fitch learned from the post commander, Col. Smith, that the Mississippi Squadron commander was already traveling to Paducah. The Hoosier officer was given a packet of dispatches, among which were orders from Lee to follow, prepared to execute Thomas' request for assistance on the Tennessee.

Le Roy Fitch had now been constantly at war for 26 months, almost without a break. In the past month, he had maintained an almost unbelievable personal schedule and must have been nearly exhausted. On top of this, he remained divisional officer for both of the twin rivers and had been away from the business of those units for almost two months. Additionally, the Cumberland was just now fully reopening to trade following several strenuous weeks and it was important to make certain that its convoy system was fully reestablished.

Walking over to the Clarksville telegraph office, the Logansport native sent a brief request to Acting Rear Adm. Lee which may have been among the most difficult of his career to compose. Emphasizing the requirements of his rivers, Fitch asked if he might turn down the Florence assignment. It was the first and only time he turned down the opportunity to steam into harm's way.

When Lee received Fitch's wire aboard the *Black Hawk*, then anchored at Smithland, he found himself with an opportunity to participate, operationally, in the final pursuit of Gen. Hood. The squadron commander readily granted his subordinate permission to remain behind, agreeing to take command of the expedition in person. Instructions were left for the Logansport native, upon his arrival, to arrange all necessary convoys, making certain that there no delays. He would be able to keep the *Moose* as his flagboat; however, several other craft would accompany Lee up the Tennessee, including the *Silver Lake*.[44]

Thomas and Lee, urged on by Washington, D.C., generals and other leaders, pursued the retreating Confederates as they sped back to Alabama. Two days into Hood's retreat, Lt. Gen. Nathan Bedford Forrest took over as Confederate rear guard and provided spirited cover. According to Stanley Horn, the butternut soldiers sang a parody of *The Yellow Rose of Texas*:

> But now I'm going to leave you;
> My heart is full of woe.

> I'm going back to Georgia to see my Uncle Joe.
> You may talk about your Beauregards and sing of General Lee
> But the gallant Hood of Texas played hell in Tennessee.

Acting Rear Adm. Lee's expedition duly proceeded up the Tennessee, destroying flatboats and ferries en route to Chickasaw, Alabama, where it dropped anchor on Christmas Eve. Although no large Rebel formations were encountered, the admiral was confident that he had "destroyed all the enemy's visible means of crossing below Florence." Between December 25 and 28, the remnants of the Confederate Army of Tennessee crossed the river and made for its final rendezvous at Tupelo, Mississippi.

Lee remained on the Tennessee in support of "Old Pap" Thomas until the end of January 1865. With the close of the Nashville campaign, he reported to Secretary Welles that army-navy cooperation in the recent operation had "been of a most pleasing and cordial character." Saluting the admiral with kind remarks equally well earned by Lt. Cmdr. Fitch, Lee's recent biographers conclude: "It is difficult to find anywhere in the history of the American Civil War a better demonstration of combined operations in which the army and the navy worked together with fewer problems and more impressive results."[45]

CHAPTER THIRTEEN

From Brown Water to Blue and Home, January 1865–April 14, 1875

By the end of January 1865, Confederate Gen. John Bell Hood's Army of Tennessee had completed its retreat back across the Tennessee River into Mississippi. Pursuing Union forces, knowing that it was spent, allowed it to melt away, content in the knowledge that their actions since mid–December had all but finished the campaign in the west. Indeed, as historian Richard Gildrie has put it, the massive Union victory "effectively ended the war between the Mississippi River and the Appalachian Mountains." While Hood was in Tennessee, Maj. Gen. William T. Sherman's march to the sea virtually destroyed Rebel ability to send food and fuel to Virginia from the lower South via Georgia. The focus for Civil War military action now turned east, where Lt. Gen. Ulysses S. Grant had besieged the Army of Northern Virginia at Petersburg while Sherman and Rear Adm. David Dixon Porter set about shutting down Confederate succor from the sea by capturing Fort Fisher and Wilmington.[1]

Mississippi Squadron commander Acting Rear Adm. Samuel Phillips Lee doubtless kept tabs on the eastern seaboard activities of Porter, the man whom Navy secretary Gideon Welles had chosen to attack Wilmington rather than himself. He was also, undoubtedly, stung when the U.S. Congress voted its thanks to the army for its role in the Battle of Nashville while specifically refusing to cite the navy role. Further, George Thomas, who had held the rank of brevet major general, was promoted to the rank of major general in the regular army after the campaign while he remained a captain instead of a rear admiral. Although far more formal in his dealings with subordinates than his squadron predecessors Porter or Rear Adm. Charles H. Davis, these disappointments, and others outlined to friends, may also have contributed to what can only be perceived in his writings as a distinctly distant relationship with Lt. Cmdr. Le Roy Fitch, the Nashville fighter who wasn't promoted either, but who did gain headlines with his Bell's Mills combats.[2]

Military action along the western waters subsided almost daily from late January through the conclusion of the war in April. Just as it was reported that Confederate soldiers were deserting from the lines in the east, so too did many disappear from duty in the Tennessee Valley—but not all. "The guerrilla war continued," observed Gildrie, "having a logic of its own, even though the military purposes were negligible." The Mississippi Squadron was gradually altered from a war fighting command to a coast guard force, which handled various police duties, some counterinsurgency activities, and customs inspections. Acting Rear Adm. Lee informed Secretary Welles on February 16 that "quiet prevails on the river," while "trading under Treasury permits is largely increasing."[3]

During the time of the Nashville campaign, Ninth District chief Lt. Cmdr. James W. Shirk was on the sick list. His duties were temporarily assumed by Fitch, who remained responsible for Cumberland and Ohio Rivers covered by his own Tenth District. At the end of December, this close colleague, who had come west with Capt. Henry Walke in September 1861 and had worked with Col. Graham Newell Fitch the following June, sought detachment to a healthier climate. In January 1865, Shirk received orders to assume new duties as navigation officer of the Philadelphia Navy Yard. Lt. Cmdr. Fitch was now the most senior junior officer in the entire Mississippi Squadron.

Shirk's replacement as Ninth District commander was Lt. Cmdr. Robert Boyd, Jr. Prior to coming west, the Maine native had served in the South Atlantic Blockading Squadron. From October 1863 through October 1864, he was aboard the flagship of the West Indies squadron. Boyd began his duties at Eastport, Mississippi, on January 18, taking over from Rear Adm. Lee, who returned to Mound City. The new man was informed that he would have six tinclads with which to undertake a new convoy system agreed to by Lee and Maj. Gen. Thomas. Lee also informed Boyd that "one lieutenant-commander, Fitch, is ordered to [be] sent" and that he should keep up a supply of coal at Eastport "and send the empty barges to Lt. Cmdr. Fitch at Smithland." The Indiana sailor, in addition to his duties as Cumberland River convoy commodore continued to handle the fuel supply for both districts during the remainder of his Kentucky tenure.[4]

When Lee went up the Tennessee in late December 1864 to assist Thomas in the pursuit of Hood's army, he took almost every available boat of the upper river command. When Lt. Cmdr. Boyd arrived at Eastport, the Ninth District comprised the ironclad *Carondelet* and the light draughts *Peosta, Brilliant, Silver Lake, Reindeer, Fairplay, Tensas, Naumkeag, St. Clair,* and *Curlew.* Lt. Cmdr. Fitch was operating his Cumberland River convoys in January 1865 with just *Moose, Springfield,* and *Victory.* During this time, Fitch retained the *Moose* at Smithland as station ship. Here convoys were assembled, the coal barges for the two districts were received and guarded, and communications were centered. Acting Volunteer Master Edward Morgan of the *Springfield* and Acting Volunteer Master Frederick Read of the *Victory* were well acquainted with Fitch's convoy methods and were now, in fact, the river's principal shepherds.

During the last week of January, the *Victory* was sent to Cincinnati to serve on a short special detached duty with Capt. Oscar Bullus. The *Moose* herself, in company with the *Springfield*, made the last trip of the month. At this time, the officers and men of the Tenth District flagboat, in addition to Fitch, included: Acting Volunteer Master Washington C. Coulson; Acting Volunteer Ensign John Revell, D. B. Dudley and Isaac Wiltse; Acting Master's Mates Daniel Molony, O. W. Miles, and W. S. Holden; Acting Assistant Surgeon W. M. Reber; Acting Assistant Paymaster Jason W. Clark; Acting Chief Engineer William D. McFarland; and Acting Assistant Engineers Thomas N. Hall (1st), Charles McMillan (2nd), and J. D. Hedges (3rd). Acting Volunteer Ensign John H. Rice had been promoted to Acting Volunteer Master and transferred as XO of the *Reindeer* while Acting Volunteer Ensign Morgan was promoted commander of the *Springfield*.

Though not as ferocious as in previous years, partisan and guerrilla activities remained one of Lt. Cmdr. Fitch's major concerns. Hit and run attacks continued to be made on shipping at Harpeth Shoals and from the banks near Palmyra's ruins. Many of the raids originated out of western Kentucky and were aimed at rail connections from Bowling Green to Clarksville to Nashville. Guerrillas continued to operate in or near towns and communities up and down the Cumberland. Outrages, such as robberies and shootings, continued.

On January 26, the Indiana sailor wired Cdr. John W. Livingston, commander of the naval station at Mound City, asking for additional tinclads with which to boost the naval force available for use against guerrillas operating on the Cumberland. He also took the precaution of sending the request via the dispatch boat *Volunteer*. It was his hope to resume the ambitious amphibious counterguerrilla program he had run in previous years.

Livingston forwarded the message to Lee the next day and both were in the admiral's hand when he wrote his responses to the commodore and the commander. Livingston was told that there were no more vessels to send Fitch; "he can make out with the three gunboats he now has." It was impracticable to send any more vessels, Lee informed his Smithland-based subordinate. Fitch was to make arrangements with whatever authorities were necessary in order that his present force could secure convoys. Additionally, as Lee saw it, it was not Fitch, but the military authorities that "should take action regarding the occupation of towns by guerrillas." The Logansport native would, nevertheless, keep his "small-arms men" against the possibility that they might be called upon.

Lee may have been somewhat sympathetic to Fitch's petition, though not because of the Hoosier's desire to run additional anti-guerrilla patrols. There remained a standing order that convoys be protected by two boats, as well as a need to provide police and coast guard services from Smithland to Nashville and beyond. There were simply too few boats to adequately operate patrols and the weekly convoy escorts now possible. It would be a month before help would arrive.[5]

The three boats of the Tenth District handled their duties without fanfare throughout February. Weekly convoys operated and patrols were mounted, though far more infrequently than before. Throughout the North optimism was high. There was a belief that the new offensive planned by Gen. Grant would be the last big push of the war. In its wake, Richmond would fall and the war would be over. Not all in the South were of the same opinion. The Richmond *Daily Examiner* ran an editorial on March 1 which opined in part: "We cannot help thinking that 'our friends, the enemy,' are a little premature in assuming the South to be at their feet. There are Southern armies of magnitude in the field, and Richmond , the capitol, is more impregnable at this hour than it has been at any period of the war."[6]

The *U.S.S. Reindeer*, fresh from a Mound City overhaul, was permitted to transfer back from the Ninth District to the Cumberland on March 1. Acting Volunteer Lieutenant Henry A. Glassford, Fitch's long-time associate, was hardly back on the river before he received orders to run a special patrol. Lt. Cmdr. Fitch, on a stop in Nashville late in the month's first week, received a request from Maj. Gen. Thomas to undertake a scout as far up the Cumberland as possible to check on the depth of the river and the peace of the shoreline population.

On March 8, Acting Volunteer Lieutenant Glassford, who seemingly owned a patent on such Upper Cumberland investigations, was invited aboard the *Moose* and given the job. Guerrilla activity in the areas above and below Nashville remained a topic of concern, Fitch informed his subordinate, though details on actual attacks or gatherings remained scarce. The commanding general would like the navy to take a look. The next day, after the *Victory* had arrived at Tennessee's capital with *Springfield* from Smithland, Glassford and Read departed upriver. Fitch, meanwhile, sent off word on the reconnaissance mission to Acting Rear Adm. Lee before setting off with the *Springfield* toward Clarksville.

The Mississippi Squadron flagboat *Black Hawk* passed Smithland on March 11 en route back to Mound City. Acting Rear Adm. Lee was completing an Ohio River trip during which he had inspected the conversion of several steamers into tinclads and the building progress of certain freshwater monitors. While passing the Tenth District rendezvous, he found no gunboats in port and so postponed a stop to consult with Lt. Cmdr. Fitch on an urgent escort request. Back at Mound City on March 12, Lee called the *Alfred Robb* alongside and had her captain take a written order back to Smithland.

At Louisville during his upriver visit, Acting Rear Adm. Lee had a meeting with Maj. Gen. John M. Palmer. The Department of Kentucky commander asked if it would be possible for a gunboat to escort a supply convoy up the Cumberland to Burkesville. The orders which the *Robb* dropped off at Smithland were telegraphed on to Fitch and required that the Hoosier officer handle the Palmer matter. Fitch was to wire Palmer at Louisville in cipher and inform him whether the depth of the Upper Cumberland would permit such a trip and whether or not any gunboats were available to provide cover. He was also to inform the admiral what action, if any, was taken.

While the district commander made his way back toward Kentucky, the *Reindeer* and *Victory* steamed to Wolf Creek Shoals, a point about 40 miles below Camp Burnside, the name given the army camp at Big South Fork. Fitch stopped off at Fort Donelson on March 13 to check for telegrams and found Lee's letter. He immediately replied to his superior, noting that the Acting Volunteer Lieutenant Glassford was already headed upstream. When the two tinclads arrived at Wolf Creek Shoals, they found only five feet of water on the obstructions. With the river rapidly falling, Glassford determined it would be imprudent to proceed further and his little task unit started to descend.

On March 15, Lee informed Fitch that his plan to send Acting Volunteer Lieutenant Glassford up the Cumberland was sound and his instructions were judicious. He also sent along a copy of his General Order No. 48, which enclosed a copy of the March 9 issue of the *Louisville Journal*, which reprinted a fantastic story of local Confederate naval activity as told in that day's issue of the *Chattanooga Gazette*.

According to the newspaper stories, a Confederate torpedo boat, accessory equipment, and a nine man party under Lt. Arthur D. Wharton, C.S.N., was captured by armed citizens near Kingston, Tennessee, on March 5. According to intelligence, the Southern expedition was organized in Richmond in early January and went by rail to Bristol, Tennessee, where a boat was obtained and launched in the Holston River. The boat made it undetected past Federal guards at Kingsport and under the bridge at Knoxville and was not sighted until it was four miles below Kingston. Wharton's mission was to destroy Union commerce and key bridges on the Tennessee River, but he failed before achieving any of his goals. During his subsequent interrogation, it was revealed that he was part of a plan to clear obstructions which would allow Lee's army "to leave Richmond about the 1st of March and retreat in the direction of East Tennessee."

Acting Rear Adm. Lee, who just weeks earlier had largely refused to approve the call of his Tenth District commander for enhanced vigilance, revealed that "the highest military sources" had informed him "that the rebel navy is reported to have been relieved from duty on the Atlantic coast and sent to operate on the Western rivers." Fitch, like the other district commanders who received copies, were to make the report widely available to their officers and men. Additionally, he and they were to "keep an active patrol of the river, and a constant and bright lookout."

All the way up and also all the way back, the *Reindeer* and *Victory*, meanwhile, stopped at all of the important towns and landings on the Upper Cumberland, as well as many farmhouses, to impress upon the people the benevolent intentions of the United States government so long as attacks were avoided. It was expected that a good opinion would be carried back inland. At one point, Acting Volunteer Lieutenant Glassford was informed that a force of 200 irregulars had crossed the river near Celina, at the mouth of Obey's River, on Sunday, March 12, for unknown reasons. That intelligence was passed to the army commander at Carthage and to a camp of woodcutters at Dixon's Springs, 30 miles lower.

Upon his return to Nashville on March 17, Acting Volunteer Lieutenant Glassford reported to Thomas that there was a good deal of suspicion on the north side of the Cumberland that the guerrillas that crossed at Celina, if that they were, had plans to attack the woodmen. He also reported his findings on civilian sentiment, the lack of irregular activity and the stages of the upper stream to Lee and Fitch. The squadron commander, in turn, sent a letter with the dispatch boat mail from Mound City to Louisville telling Maj. Gen. Palmer that his Burkesville supply petition could not be honored.[7]

While bushwhackers continued to attack isolated points throughout the Cumberland Valley, the river convoys from Smithland to Nashville continued, though there were far more independent sailings now that the end of the war appeared imminent. In Washington, D.C., Navy secretary Gideon Welles was among a host of government and political leaders looking ahead not only to peace but to a reduction in the huge Union military and naval force.

Even before the conflict was finished, orders were sent to leaders afloat, ashore, and in the field to cut costs wherever possible. For example, on March 30, Acting Rear Adm. Lee received a communication from Welles ordering that all vessels chartered by the Mississippi Squadron be immediately discharged. In future, their duties would be carried out by squadron boats "least serviceable as gunboats." At the same time, a number of newly finished tinclads joined the fleet. Their presence would be brief.[8]

The final push by the Army of the Potomac against Gen. Lee's lines began southwest of Petersburg on April 1. Meanwhile, in the west, Acting Rear Adm. Lee proceeded to fulfill Secretary Welles' order concerning the replacement of chartered vessels with line units no longer deemed necessary. Richmond fell on April 4, but word of the Union victory was not received in the west until late in the day. At noon the next day, a 36-gun salute was fired in honor of the triumph.

In these heady days of Union victory, unregulated navigation on the Cumberland River was fully reopened and the military responsibilities of the Tenth District were significantly reduced. Resources would be reduced accordingly.

At Nashville on April 7, Lt. Cmdr. Fitch received a terse telegram: "Send *Reindeer* and *Victory* here immediately and expect *Silver Lake*." Acting Volunteer Lieutenant Glassford received the same wire at Smithland. Neither Lee nor Fitch appreciated that Acting Volunteer Master Coyle's *Silver Lake*, then undergoing repair, would be unavailable for some time. The next day, Acting Rear Adm. Lee's General Order No. 57 required the Indiana sailor, and the other nine divisional officers, to "exercise the utmost vigilance and make every effort to prevent the crossing of the Cumberland [or the other rivers] from either side" by rebel officers attempting to flee from the east to the west.

On April 9, as the *Reindeer* and *Victory* were reporting to Mound City, Lt. Gen. Grant meet Gen. Lee at Appomattox Court House and took the formal surrender of the Army of Northern Virginia. News again reached the *Black Hawk* too late for a salute at the customary noon hour.

The next morning, Acting Rear Adm. Lee met with Acting Volunteer Master Samuel Hall during the commissioning ceremony for the new tinclad U.S.S. *Abeona*. There he was informed that Acting Volunteer Lieutenant Glassford was on leave and that the second of the super light draughts to be commissioned in 1863 was being turned into a fast transport and dispatch boat. *Abeona's* captain was ordered to receive the *Reindeer's* battery, ordnance equipment, and most of her crew. Her firemen and coal heavers—African Americans all— would be replaced by seven 2nd class firemen from the *New National*. That boat was one of the chartered vessels eliminated under the March 30th Welles economy and was being replaced as a supply and dispatch vessel by the *Reindeer*. Hall was to finish loading stores and coaling with all practical dispatch, and when ready, to steam to Smithland. There he would report to Lt. Cmdr. Fitch for duty in the Tenth District.

At precisely noon, a 100-gun salute was fired in honor of the Appomattox ceremony. It was repeated at sunset. At this point, no one knew precisely where Confederate president Jefferson Davis and his followers were, least of all the men of the Mississippi Squadron. A belief would soon take hold that they were trying to escape west to continue the war from Texas.

Acting Rear Adm. Lee informed the *New National* commander, Acting Volunteer Ensign J. M. Farmer, on April 11 that he and his men were ordered transferred to the *Reindeer*. The former fighting vessel, which even now was being stripped was to be ready to start transport service on April 15.[9]

On Good Friday, April 14, Lt. Cmdr. Fitch at Smithland received a copy of his superior's General Order 60. Henceforth, his gunboats, like those of several other districts, would not be required to cover the landings by steamboats engaged in lawful trade unless desired by military authorities or the parties making the landings. In short, convoy escort was ended. Any conflicting squadron orders on this point were revoked. Additionally, his need to countersign Treasury and military permits for trade and intercourse was ended. In general, Fitch was to concentrate on coast guard duties. His boats, to save fuel costs, were to be kept underway "under easy steam to preserve a vigilant police of the rivers and protect public and private interests as required."[10]

With her guns and casemates removed, the *Reindeer* began her temporary career as a naval transport also on April 15, along with Acting Volunteer Master Read's *Victory*. At Smithland, Lt. Cmdr. Fitch retained his flagship, the *Moose*, along with the *Springfield*. Acting Volunteer Master Hall's newly commissioned *Abeona* arrived that day, the last vessel to join the flotilla of the Logansport native. Purchased for $37,000 at Cincinnati on December 21, 1864, the 206-ton side-wheeler was 157 feet long, with a beam of 31.5 feet and a depth of hold of 4.5 feet. Her armament consisted of two 30-pounder Parrott rifles, two 12-pounder Parrott rifles, and two 24-pounder smoothbore howitzers. The No. 32, previously worn by the U.S.S. *Key West*, was painted on her pilothouse.[11]

Thirteen. From Brown Water to Blue and Home (1865–1875)

By late Saturday evening or early on Sunday morning everyone in the Mississippi Squadron had heard the awful news from the east. President Lincoln was shot shortly after 10 P.M. on April 14 while watching *Our American Cousin* at Ford's Theatre. He died at 7:22 A.M. the next day. While the nation came to grips with the enormity of the assassination and Vice President Andrew Johnson became president, plans were put in place to honor the late chief executive.

On Sunday, Navy secretary Welles wired all of his squadron commanders requiring them to observe the funeral with appropriate respect. More complete special orders were sent by mail. Acting Rear Adm. Lee sent word of Lincoln's death to all of his commanders. On most boats, including those of the Tenth District, the men were assembled and the official announcement was read, along with the order for mourning. All officers began to wear crape, something which would adorn their uniforms for the next six months.

In accordance with Welles' directive and out of respect for the funeral solemnities of the late president, a variety of actions were taken on April 19 at the Smithland naval rendezvous, as well as aboard all other ships and at shore facilities of the Union navy. Labor was suspended afloat and ashore for the day, while all national ensigns were kept at half mast until after the funeral. At noon, the *Moose*, as flagboat of the Tenth District, joined all other flagships in firing 21-gun salutes. Fitch and all officers and men not required aboard the boats attended special funeral services. Half hour guns were fired during the 12–4 P.M. and 4–6 P.M. watches.[12]

The flagboat *Black Hawk* burned out on the morning of April 22, the victim of a coal oil fire. Although none of the officers and crew aboard were lost, a goodly portion of the Mississippi Squadron's official records for the previous quarter were destroyed. Even though district commanders were asked to send duplicate copies of messages, returns and reports, only a small percentage of the loss could be reconstituted.

In response to an April 23 telegram from Secretary Welles urging the utmost vigilance to prevent the escape of Jefferson Davis and his cabinet across the Mississippi, Acting Rear Adm. Lee directed: "The immediate engrossing and important duty is to capture Jeff. Davis and his Cabinet and plunder. To accomplish this, all available means and every effort must be made to the exclusion of all interfering calls."

The next day, Lee, by special dispatch boats, ordered that each divisional officer was to "live aboard of a gunboat in which he can quickly and readily move about within the limits of his command, to see that orders are properly attended to, and that the duties required of the different vessels of his district are well performed." In the event Fitch or any of his colleagues picked up Davis or any of his followers, they were not to be turned over to military, but were to be immediately sent to Mound City aboard a gunboat.

Maj. Gen. Thomas at Nashville wrote to Acting Rear Adm. Lee on April 27 to say that he had received information that Davis and his followers were planning to make their escape across the Mississippi. The squadron commander laid the highest priority on effecting a capture and ordered all of his divisional commanders "to make a minute report of the dispositions made" to accomplish the "great object."

The following afternoon Secretary Welles and Lt. Gen. Grant forwarded hearsay information on the Confederate president's escape route. Welles advised Lee to continue to watch the Mississippi and its tributaries while Grant thought Davis was headed to South Carolina and eventual escape out of the U.S., maybe via the great river. Lee now began sending reinforcements from the upper flotillas to Memphis and lower points where it was realistically expected that the Davis party might make a run. Among the boats transferred to the pursuit were the *Silver Lake, Brilliant, Ozark, Naumkeag, Tyler, Victory, Neosho, Ibex, Kate, Juliet, Marmora, Colossus, Louisville, Romeo,* and *Abeona.* The acting rear admiral took personal charge from his new flagboat, U.S.S. *Tempest* (No. 1), off the mouth of the White River. Over the next few days, the target search area shifted gradually south to the regions near Grand Gulf, Rodney, or Bruinsburg.

No Mississippi Squadron boat ever came close to intercepting the Confederate president, who never actually made it very far west at all. Jefferson Davis, with members of his Cabinet, reached Abbeville, South Carolina, on May 2. After several more days of fruitless running, Davis, his family and part of his cabinet, were arrested at Irwinville, some 15 miles from Macon, Georgia, five days earlier. Acting Rear Adm. Lee received a telegram from Maj. Gen. Thomas on May 15 announcing the capture.[13]

Aside from that information provided by request of Acting Rear Adm. Lee, little was heard from Lt. Cmdr. Fitch in April. Undoubtedly, part of the reason was that his reports and records on the *Black Hawk* were destroyed. As the quest for peace began, the *Moose* continued her police work. Taking into account occasional dustups such as the Davis chase, the upper rivers were now pacific and fully open to commercial steamboat traffic. Spring was upon the land and with it the certainty that the Cumberland's water stage was in decline. Thus, as was now customary, planning started to transfer operations to the Ohio from a temporary base at Evansville, Indiana.

It is possible to speculate that Fitch at this time may also have sought a transfer or leave, though such an action would not have dulled his sense of responsibility. In any event, the Indiana sailor was by a year the most senior serving district officer in the entire Mississippi Squadron having been master of the Cumberland and Ohio since the summer of 1862. It is somehow fitting then that his Civil War career should end with an account of one last guerrilla skirmish.

Fitch was on temporary duty at Mound City toward the end of April and his executive officer, Acting Volunteer Master Coulson, was in acting command of the U.S.S. *Moose* on the Cumberland River. On April 29, the Tenth District flagboat was lying at the Tennessee Rolling Mills, not far from Eddyville, Kentucky. At 6 A.M. on that date, Coulson was hailed by Acting Volunteer Master Hall of the tinclad *Abeona* and told that 16 guerrillas were reported at Center Furnace, about two miles from the river. Some time later, a courier arrived with additional information concerning an even larger group. Supposedly, 150–200 Rebels, armed mostly with revolvers, were moving on Eddyville, with the intention of crossing the river and sacking the town. The group was supposedly led by a Maj. Hopkins of Brig. Gen. Abraham Buford's Second Division, a part of the cavalry corps of Lt. Gen. Nathan Bedford Forrest. This report was not correct; a review of the officer roster for Forrest's entire command published as the appendix to Jordan and Pryor shows no leader down to company level named Hopkins.

Even though the Cumberland was falling, Coulson got the *Moose* immediately underway and started down the river. Nothing was seen until she reached the head of Big Eddy where, on rounding the point, a large body of armed butternuts was discovered on shore, with two troop-laden boats shoving off for the opposite bank. Upon seeing the tinclad, the men in the small boats began jumping overboard. To halt the *Moose's* way, Coulson stopped her engines and began backing. At the same time, he ordered the forward gun on the upper deck fired and had his armed sailors begin shooting with rifles. Few of the men caught in the boats reached shore, most were wounded, killed, or drowned.

The flagboat's party of small-arms men was then landed and these engaged the disorganized Confederates. Armed only with revolvers, these were no match for the landing force which dispersed most of the party, while killing or wounding 20 men and taking six captives. Additionally, 19 horses, three mules, saddles, bridles, accoutrements, and numerous pistols were also taken.

About 60 Southerners and their leader escaped on the north side of the Cumberland. Deciding it was not prudent to chase them too far inland, Coulson recalled his landing party, took his prisoners and plunder aboard, including the animals, and proceeded to Eddytown. There he informed the local post commander of the crossing, posted a report of the proceedings to Lt. Cmdr. Fitch, and then returned to Smithland.

Although he was not aboard the *Moose* for this fight, Fitch received Coulson's report and gained some satisfaction in knowing that his flagboat had emerged triumphant in the last significant naval counterinsurgency engagement on the western rivers during the Civil War. Returning to Smithland, Fitch reviewed with Coulson the particulars of the operation and spoke with some of the prisoners. It was found that two of those under guard had been impressed by the Confederates as guides. These, together with their mule, were released. The others were retained aboard the *Moose* subject to a decision on their fate by Acting Rear Adm. Lee. The horses, also subject to a disposition decision, were pastured. It was later learned that some of the men who survived and made it across the river were taken by Federal land forces.

Plans to reduce the overall size of the U.S. naval establishment were in full swing by the start of May. On the third day of the month, Secretary Welles ordered the expenses of the Mississippi Squadron reduced as far as possible. To start with, only 25 vessels were to be kept in commission. Any units that belonged to the army or USQM were to be dismantled of naval property and returned. These specifically included the four Upper Tennessee gunboats built under the supervision of Lt. Cmdr. Fitch the year before. The resignations of any officers who wished to leave the service were to be approved. Requests for leave or transfer would also be considered, as long as a sufficient number of officers was retained to man the dwindling number of boats.

Acting Volunteer Master Coulson's full report of the *Moose's* last fight was forwarded to Acting Rear Adm. Lee on May 4, along with a covering letter from the Tenth District commander which summarized the combat and praised the officers and men of the *Moose*. On May 15, Acting Rear Adm. Lee forwarded a copy of Coulson's written report to Secretary Welles and paraphrased its contents from Fitch's cover letter of May 4. Without complement for either Fitch or Coulson, the busy squadron leader mentioned only that the report originated as part of an enclosure from Fitch. This was the last time in his Mississippi Squadron tenure that the Indiana sailor had his name placed before the civilian navy head.[14]

Lt. Cmdr. Fitch was detached from command of the U.S.S. *Moose* effective May 11. An order to this effect was sent to him at Smithland by Acting Rear Adm. Lee, along with a request that he wind up his business at the Tenth District rendezvous. When the Indiana sailor did not immediately appear at Mound City with his flagboat and his papers, a telegraph was sent to him on May 14. Fitch replied: "Dispatch just received. Will leave at once. Just done cleaning boilers."

Although the Logansport native knew that he would soon be leaving Illinois for the first time in a long, but unknown period, he still had almost two weeks of work to put in before his departure. On May 16, he and his colleagues in the Fifth, Sixth, Eighth, and Ninth Districts were asked to provide information for the Bureau of Construction and Repair on the locations of sunken wrecks within their jurisdictions.

Four days later, Maj. Gen. Thomas wrote to Acting Rear Adm. Lee, advising that, in his opinion, there was no longer a reason to keep up the Upper Tennessee River gunboats. These were the four outfitted under the Bridgeport, Alabama, supervision of Lt. Cmdr. Fitch and Acting Volunteer Lieutenant Glassford the previous year. They had already been earmarked as prime targets in Secretary Welles' force reduction order of May 3. The Thomas message also went to Quartermaster General Meigs.

On May 22, Welles wired Lee noting that the "boats of the Quartermaster's Department are the *General Grant, General Sherman, General Thomas,* and *General Burnside.*" The same day, the Mississippi Squadron commander ordered Eleventh District boss Lt. Moreau Forrest to ask Thomas as to which local quartermaster the boats and a few storage buildings on shore should be receipted. Additionally, he was to speedily make crew transport arrangements with Thomas and Lt. Cmdr. Fitch. Within a few days, the general provided a train to take the officers and men to Nashville, together with the ordnance, guns, paymaster's and other stores furnished by the USN. Two towed barges and a gunboat sent by the Hoosier officer returned the sailors and their goods from there to Mound City.

While awaiting orders at Mound City in May, Lt. Cmdr. Fitch was able to handle a few additional details for the Mississippi Squadron and to finish the remaining paperwork of his district. On May 29, Acting Rear Adm. Lee formally realigned his command into three operational districts, First, Second, and Third. Later in the day, the Western rivers war of Le Roy Fitch officially closed when he was detached from the squadron and granted permission to await new orders from his home in Logansport.

The manner in which the 29-year-old naval officer took his leave of Lee and others at the Illinois naval post is unknown. Years later, his previous commander, ADM David Dixon Porter, wrote an appreciation not apparent at the time:

> Although his command was not a large one, this young officer was often mentioned [in dispatches] for gallant and efficient service, and he ever displayed sound judgment, no matter in what position he was placed. His officers and men, inspired by his spirit, were conspicuous for their bravery.
>
> The gallant Fitch never shrunk from the performance of any duty however hazardous. He was always under fire whenever opportunity offered, not owing to chance circumstances, to which sluggards often attribute a man's reputation for heroism, but to a determined will. This gallant officer gained little promotion for his war services, and his highest recognition was a complimentary letter from the Secretary of the Navy on the occasion when he brought about the capture of General John Morgan, the celebrated Confederate partisan leader.

Over the next decade, Porter would remember Fitch and would, indirectly, from his own position of power, make certain that he had at least some active employment when others often had none.[15]

Lt. Cmdr. Fitch returned home to Logansport where he was reunited with his wife, Mary, and two-year old daughter, Marie, as well as other members of the Fitch family. Buds and blossoms seen in Tennessee and Kentucky weeks earlier were now also popping out farther north and the agriculture of central Indiana was well advanced in its annual cycle. The population of Cass County was growing as newcomers, many from ethnic groups such as the Germans, Irish, and Italians, were joined by returning veterans.[16]

Thirteen. From Brown Water to Blue and Home (1865–1875)

The preeminent and most dynamic personality in the U.S. Navy during the remainder of the 1860s was not its single admiral, David G. Farragut, but its only vice admiral, David Dixon Porter. Between May and August 1865, the former commander of the Mississippi Squadron was a member of the board of visitors of the U.S. Naval Academy (USNA), where Capt. George S. Blake, superintendent since 1857, was nearing the end of his tenure. In August, the same month the Mississippi Squadron was discontinued, Porter, who had requested the postwar assignment in 1862, was named the sixth head of the naval school since 1845 (fourth since 1850). He assumed his duties on September 9 and would remain in charge until December 1, 1869.[17]

During the Civil War, the USNA was removed to Newport, Rhode Island, for its protection. There the midshipmen trained first at Fort Adams and then in a single building, Atlantic House, a downtown hotel. During the four years absence, administration, curriculum, and morale all suffered decline. Lessons and practical training were provided aboard the famous old frigate U.S.S. *Constitution*. She was joined in 1862 by the *Santee*, a frigate laid down in 1820 but not launched until 1861, and the yacht *America*, winner of the first America's Cup. The men-o'-war also provided dormitory space. Summer practice cruises continued. Among the warships employed were the sloops of war *John Adams*, *Macedonian*, and *Marion*, the *America*, and in 1864, the steam gunboat *Marblehead*, which would be Fitch's last command. In May 1864, the U.S. Congress passed legislation requiring the return of the academy to Annapolis by October 1865. It also authorized an increase in the number of midshipmen to a complement of 566.

The U.S. Army, which had employed the Maryland facility during the war, moved out of the yard and naval personnel returned. All summer the rundown academy buildings and grounds were restored to a point where they might be used when classes started on the traditional opening day, October 1. The goal would be met, though quarters and facilities would be cramped. Meanwhile, in December 1864, the steam gunboat *Marblehead* returned to Newport after five months of coastal patrol to serve as a practice ship.

The energy employed in resuming USNA activities did not translate to other commands in the American naval establishment during the decades after Appomattox. In 1865, the Northern fleet was the largest and possibly the most powerful in the world, with more ironclads and battle tested officers than all others combined. In the next several years, it was largely dismantled. The United States, with "a navy in decline," would find its oceanic deterrence and war-fighting capabilities inferior to those of many other nations, many smaller. Confused strategic thought, technological change and reactionary Navy Department administration that featured a war between line and staff officers, a general lack of public interest in the USN due to westward continental expansion and internal industrial growth, and legislative indifference were all causes of this nadir.[18]

Lt. Cmdr. Fitch received orders on July 3 to report to Newport and there join the Practice Squadron, U.S.S. *Marblehead* and *Santee*, then preparing to return to Annapolis. The next day, July 4, he caught a train east. About the time he reached Ohio, a brief toast he had penned was read at Logansport's city celebration: "To the President of the United States."

The *Santee*, with midshipmen embarked, returned to Annapolis on August 2 and dropped anchor off Fort Severn. She would continue her duties as a school ship in the upcoming school year, before becoming a gunnery and dormitory ship in 1866-1867. The frigate was joined at the school dock by the *Marblehead*. This was the first time Fitch had

The 691-ton screw gunboat *Marblehead* served off the coasts of South Carolina and Georgia during the Civil War. During her postwar career, the vessel was a unit in the North Atlantic Squadron, occasionally serving with the U.S. Naval Academy Practice Squadron. Lt. Cmdr. Fitch operated the vessel in 1867–1868, taking her as far as the Caribbean. She was not only his final command but the only sail-equipped steamer he ever skippered. This photograph, taken by Byron at New York sometime in 1864–1868, was made after she was armed with all guns mounted in broadside (Naval Historical Center).

returned to his alma mater since his graduation nine years—a lifetime it might have seemed—earlier.

When classes at Annapolis were resumed on October 1, the Indiana native and USNA alumni held the academic rank of acting assistant professor of astronomy, navigation, and surveying. His department chairman was Lt. Cmdr. Robert L. Phythian, himself new to that program in 1865. A New Yorker and one of Fitch's classmates, Phythian's last post had been aboard the giant U.S.S. *New Ironsides*.

New superintendent Porter had great plans for his institution and for the men in his charge. He not only launched a land acquisition and building program, but a reformation of the academic program as well. Having found his faculty composed of 29 civilians and only 10 officers, he began to redress this imbalance during the year. "He recruited as instructors," wrote Lance Buhl, "some of the brightest junior officers in the service." According to Porter's biographer Chester G. Hearn, Navy secretary Gideon Welles "feared the admiral would seed the institution with too many of his wartime cronies." He did so, "but carefully."

By the close of the 1865-1866 academic year, there were 25 civilian instructors and 31 officers at the USNA. A number of these gentlemen had served in the Mississippi Squadron and were acquaintances known to Le Roy Fitch. Among the brown water veterans were: superintendent's assistant Cmdr. K. Randolph Breese, former commander of the flagship *Black*

Thirteen. From Brown Water to Blue and Home (1865–1875)

Hawk; Lt. Cmdr. James A. Greer, former commander of the ironclad *Benton*; Lt. Cmdr. Thomas O. Selfridge, Jr., who skippered the *Cairo* when she was sunk by a torpedo; Seamanship Department head Lt. Cmdr. Richard W. Meade, skipper of the Pook turtle *Louisville* in 1862; the one-time captain of the turtle *Baron de Kalb*, Cmdr. John G. Walker; and Department of Gunnery chairman Lt. Cmdr. Francis M. Ramsay, last commander of the squadron's Ninth District.

During his one-year appointment, Fitch undoubtedly taught mostly surveying classes. As Professor Soley later pointed out, these were "taught by practical exercises, consisting of surveys of the mouth of the Severn River, and the projection of charts." Lt. Cmdr. Fitch was detached from the USNA on May 29, 1866, and allowed to return home to wait for new orders. Several others who had come in with him were also sent to new posts or half pay.[19]

As the American sea service sank in terms of size, number of ships and men, and national attention, its seniority-based officer promotions were few. Additionally, there were simply not enough active duty officer berths to go around. As practiced in the antebellum fleet, the postbellum U.S. Navy returned to a system of reduced pay (well known as "half pay" in the Royal Navy at the time of Napoleon I and before). Under this arrangement, officers who were not required for sea or shore billets were permitted to remain at home or elsewhere until called up, rather like a reserve; their income was actually slightly more than half of the sea duty rate. This system in the American navy was known as "waiting orders." When Le Roy Fitch returned to Logansport from Annapolis, his annual pay voucher at his grade declined from $1,875 to $1,500. When or if he returned to sea, it would jump to $2,343.

There was no limit in regulations as to how long a person could be designated as "waiting orders." The lower the rank, as in Fitch's case, perhaps the more frequent the home watch. Most officers in the U.S. Navy of the late 1860s and 1870s spent at least some time in that category. Among names known to the Indiana sailor who spent lengthy periods on the beach were Rear Admiral Lee (December 1867–April 1868 and September 1868 to February 1869), Commodore Henry Walke (August 1865 to February 1868), and Captain Alexander M. Pennock (March–October 1869).[20]

Following her service at the U.S. Naval Academy, the steam gunboat *Marblehead* arrived at the Washington Navy Yard where she was decommissioned on September 19, 1866. The craft was recommissioned the following month and assigned to the North Atlantic Squadron. On December 14, orders arrived at Logansport directing LCD Fitch to travel to New York and assume her command.

The 507-ton *Marblehead* was not only the last ship that Le Roy Fitch would command, but also a far different type from the *Moose*, *Fairplay*, and his other Mississippi Squadron boats. This was a true deep-water warship, a two-masted screw steamer of the *Unadilla* class, popularly known as the "90-day gunboats" after a building clause in the contracts of the civilian constructors.

One of the 23 vessels in her class, the *Marblehead* was built by G. W. Jackman, Jr., of Newburyport, Massachusetts, and launched at his yard on October 16, 1861. The hull of the craft comprised white oak framing and yellow pine planking, reinforced for longitudinal strength by diagonal iron strapping. When launched, she was 158 feet long, with a beam of 28 feet and a 12 foot depth of hold. Her draft was five foot forward and 7.5 feet aft; fully loaded, it was 10.6 feet. The gunboat's machinery was built by Isaac Stanton and J. H. Mallery of the Highland Iron Works at Newburgh, New York. There were two horizontal, back-action engines, with a 30-inch cylinder diameter and an 18 inch stroke, with two Martin tubular boilers, each with two furnaces.

Like her sisters, *Marblehead* was outfitted with surface condensers and force-draft fans; her coal bunker had a 112-ton capacity. She had two masts and was rigged as a hermaphrodite brig, with two square yards forward and one gaff aft on the foremast and gaff sails on the mainmast. Her armament comprised one 30-pounder Parrott rifle, two 20-pounder Parrott rifles, two 8-inch 63cw smoothbores, and two 24-pounder Dahlgren howitzers. During the war, crews averaged 65 to 100 men. The $96,500 steamer was originally commissioned at Boston on March 8, 1862.

Under the command of Lt. Cmdr. Richard W. Mead, the *Marblehead* gained fame in her engagement with a Confederate battery on John's Island, Stono River, South Carolina, on December 25, 1863. Quartermaster James Miller distinguished himself by continuing to take soundings while under fire and was subsequently awarded the Congressional Medal of Honor.

Fitch read himself into command on December 19 and shortly thereafter the gunboat departed southward. Rated at a top speed of 11 knots upon delivery, the *Marblehead* was certainly the fastest vessel in which the Hoosier officer ever served. Like others of her class, however, this speed declined as the vessel aged. It was said that she and her sisters were good sailors—when they sailed—but were prone to roll heavily.

From the beginning of 1867 through the summer of 1868, the *Marblehead* plied the Atlantic Coast and served in the Caribbean. Although much routine cruising was undertaken in support of American interests, there were several incidents of interest which occurred in that area during this time. In 1867, Marines occupied Managua and Leon, Nicaragua, to protect U.S. citizens while France withdrew support from its puppet government in Mexico in November. In 1868, Secretary of State William Seward, with support from VADM Porter, sought—unsuccessfully—to obtain rights to the Bay of Samana, Santo Domingo (Dominican Republic). Many summer months in both years were taken up, as earlier, with the USNA practice squadron. The ship's cannon were probably fired on a regular basis, but always in practice or salute, never in anger.

After her unmemorable service, the *Marblehead* returned to the New York Navy Yard on August 18, 1868. The crew was paid off and Lt. Cmdr. Fitch was detached on August 17, ordered to report to the commandant of the New York Navy Yard. Ten days later, he was notified that there were no posts available and home would be his next stop. While he returned to Indiana to wait orders, the gunboat was decommissioned on September 4. She was sold at auction on September 30 for $14,100. *Marblehead* was one of the last of her class sold out of service. By the end of the fourth quarter 1868, only 81 U.S. Navy vessels remained in commission.[21]

Throughout the earlier years of U.S. naval history, shore duty for officers occurred on an as-needed basis for undetermined periods of time. By an 1868 general order of the Navy Department, fixed intervals were established for sea duty and shore duty. These were to follow alternately throughout an officer's active career, though it became something of a practice that a shore stop was the final posting. Rear Adm. Davis' biographer called this ruling "the first step in the decadence of the navy which followed the Civil War." Whether it was or not, this directive dictated the next assignment for Lt. Cmdr. Fitch, from sea to shore.[22]

After his detachment from the *Marblehead*, there were no billets available for Lt. Cmdr. Fitch. He returned to Logansport and his family, there to wait orders for two years. This

Thirteen. From Brown Water to Blue and Home (1865–1875)

was the longest period spent away from the U.S. Navy in 17 years. During this time, Le Roy, Mary "Mollie" and Marie lived with Col. Benjamin H. Smith and Mary "Polly" Smith. The Smith home was a large and spacious two-story frame house located on the southeast corner of Court and Bridge Streets.

There is no mention of the naval officer in the Logansport papers of this period; still, we can make several unsupported suppositions concerning his activities during this enforced period of professional idleness. Although the naval officer drew a salary, it is quite possibly that he found employment as a surveyor, which art he had taught at the naval academy. We know that he continued his interest in small game hunting and shooting, eventually becoming vice president of the Northern Indiana Shooting Association.

It was during this period that, Col. Smith, the naval officer's father-in-law, built another home, Mint Julep Springs, across the Wabash River on the south side of Cliff Drive "just west of the Wabash railroad embankment, between it and the river." It was designed by George Bevan and would, upon completion, be a good-sized two-story frame dwelling. A frontal photograph of the home, improved by a rear addition after it became Logansport's first hospital in 1893, appears in historian Will Ball's August 17, 1958, newspaper column.

A shore billet opened for Le Roy Fitch on August 28, 1870, when he was ordered to report to the Pensacola Navy Yard. There he would serve as the executive officer and be in charge of day-to-day activities. His autonomous authority in Florida was similar to that granted for operations on the Cumberland and Tennessee by Rear Adm. Davis and Capt. Pennock in 1862.

There was no significant growth in the Old Navy during the years Fitch was in Indiana. Instead of adopting a proactive national defense position, "the government was," as historian Buhl put it, "content to adopt prewar standards of diplomatic and military policy." By 1870, the sea service was "a third rate establishment at best" and morale was low in the officer corps. The sense of humiliation "was real." Postings remained few and far between, while advancement was nearly impossible.

When Fitch departed for Florida, the organization to which he devoted his life was mired in the doldrums of decline and inefficiency. As historian Stanley Sandler wrote 99 years later, the U.S. Navy

> presented the spectacle of a rather large and very expensive collection of antique unarmored steam sailing vessels, whose captains were forbidden to use their engines except in the direst of emergencies, and who presumably would not have tried their smoothbore ordnance nor risked their matchbox vessels except in similar circumstances.[23]

Lt. Cmdr. Fitch arrived at Pensacola sometime in September 1870. It was his first time back in these Mexican Gulf waters since 1868, when his *Marblehead* had last visited. After reporting for duty, he took the time to examine the grounds, which were actually about five miles from the city. There he found a facility not unlike that first seen from the deck of the *Wyandotte*. The 80-acre yard was enclosed by a high wall on two sides, with the third side being the irregular bay shore.

Approximately 30 buildings supported a depot station that had well served the vessels of ADM Farragut's West Gulf Coast Blockading Squadron during the late rebellion. After its recapture from the Confederacy, the post's facilities were in a shambles. Most of the buildings were destroyed, though the pre-war walks and trees mostly survived. The commandant lived in the single stone house to survive the Southern occupation, while officers were

This sketch depicts the yard as it appeared at the outbreak of the Civil War in 1861. Despite some expansion to accommodate ships of the Union blockade, it was not significantly changed by the time Cmdr. Fitch was in charge 1870–1872 (Lossing's *Pictorial Field Book of the Civil War*, Vol. 1).

quartered in "old kitchens and stables." In fact, the current officers' quarters had actually been servants' quarters prior to the war. When the Rebels evacuated the yard, they placed shells into the fireplaces of the officers' housing and blew them up. A temporary naval hospital was established by Farragut's command and workers from two neighboring villages were employed postwar.

Among the buildings rebuilt, refurbished, or upgraded by 1868 were the commandant's quarters, the commander's quarters (where Fitch would reside), the quarters of the 1st and 2nd lieutenants, the quarters of the surgeon, chaplain, master, naval constructor, assistant surgeon, the quarters of the commandant's secretary and those of the civil engineer. Other functioning buildings included the mold loft and naval constructor's storehouse, the blacksmith, coppersmith, boilershop, and foundry, two bathhouses, the guardhouse and prison, the sawmill and joinershop, the pitch house, the fire house, the office of the chief engineer's office, the armory and chapel, the temporary hospital building, the carriage and forage house, the lime house (used as a shell house and armory building), the ice house, store house, the machine shop, and the blacksmith's shop. The last of 33 structures were two cisterns, the boat gate, the stable, the yard magazine, and the muster office.

In the postwar period, navy yard improvements were made everywhere on an *ad hoc* basis. The Pensacola facility continued to lack heavy machinery and permanent upgrades in the years of tiny congressional appropriations were minor. It would be placed out of commission in 1881 and would remain so until the Spanish-American War almost two decades later.

Still in 1870, many remembered the artistic beauty of the pre-war station, which was laid off into regular squares around and through which were planted evergreen oaks in military precision. The semi-tropical plants and vines which adorned the place earlier remained, adding great beauty. Great pyramid stacks of cannonballs were placed at regular intervals along the streets, particularly along Central and North Avenues.

The characteristic mild weather of Pensacola Bay was a pleasant plus to Lt. Cmdr.'s Fitch's posting to this out-of-the-way location. Mild that is if one discounts seasonal hurricanes.

Although reporter Charles Bliss lauded the area's "climate of unsurpassed healthfullness" in 1894, there were dangers. Among these was disease. In 1863, a yellow fever outbreak forced the Union Navy out of the yard for some weeks.

Hardly had Lt. Cmdr. Fitch undertaken his new duties than he was sent to examination for promotion on October 26. After all, his position and housing required a boost in standing. As was long the practice in the peacetime navy, the Congress of the United States would not confirm an officer's promotion until someone in the desired rank either died or was promoted. So it was the a number of nominations for promotions were announced by President Grant on December 5. Among these was the promotion of VADM Porter to the rank of admiral of the navy upon the death of ADM Farragut. Much further down a lengthy list was the nomination of Lt. Cmdr. Le Roy Fitch to be a commander to succeed Cmdr. William G. Temple, promoted to Capt.

The Indiana sailor received his letter of promotion on December 3, effective back to August 28, the day he received orders to report to Pensacola. The commission arrived on January 24, 1871.[25]

This photograph was taken in late 1870 after Fitch was named executive officer of the Pensacola Navy Yard in Florida. During the postwar U.S. naval force reduction, the executive officers of smaller naval stations were usually the senior officers with no formal commandant named. This was virtually an independent command, the wise operation of which the Hoosier may have learned from his old chief, Capt. Alexander Pennock (Naval Historical Center).

The new commander's Pensacola deployment continued without incident throughout 1871 and into 1872. Vessels arriving at his yard were serviced by a small force that included a mix of navy men and local hires. There is even a possibility that Fitch was able to indulge his passion for hunting during his assignment. In the nearby woodlands, reporter Bliss revealed in 1898, "the sportsman finds deer, wild turkeys, pheasants, quail and other small game."

It was with sadness that the Hoosier officer learned of the death of his nephew Henry Satterlee Fitch, 37, in late May 1871. The son of his older half-brother, who was himself a year older than Le Roy, had enjoyed an active career since attempting to resign as the Memphis quartermaster in January 1863. While waiting for the measure to take effect, the lawyer served as MJR and judge advocate and provost marshal on the staff of Maj. Gen. William T. Sherman until October 1864. His resignation was not actually accepted until January 11, 1865. The new president, Andrew Johnson, appointed Henry the U.S. district attorney for Georgia and Fitch moved to Savannah where he practiced. The first postwar Georgia legislature named him one of the state's U.S. senators in 1868, but the U.S. Congress refused to recognize the election.

The attorney returned to Logansport at the beginning of 1869. Upon his arrival, he gave his father a Tennessee stallion named Eclipse for breeding. During the winter of 1870-1871, he relocated to Chicago to take up the practice of law. Henry was suddenly taken ill in the Windy City on May 23. His condition was wired to his father, but less than two hours after Graham Newell's receipt of the telegram, Henry died. The funeral was held at the 7th and Market Street home of Graham Newell and Harriet A. Fitch at 1 P.M. on May 25. The time frame was such that Le Roy could not attend.[26]

Cmdr. Fitch was detached from the Pensacola Navy Yard on February 9, 1872, and returned to Logansport to await orders. This time he was "on the beach" for only four months. On May 2, he was ordered to special duty at the U.S. Navy Department in Washington, D.C. That service continued for the remainder of the year.

Fitch retired to Logansport in January 1873, probably, wrote former Cass County historian Will Ball in 1960, "because of ill health." There the "small bearded man" joined his family and his father- and mother-in-law at the recently-completed Mint Julep Spring home across the Wabash. We do not know much about the sailor's activities during his remaining years. A very few gleanings can be obtained from the Logansport newspapers, but the picture which emerges is cloudy. We do know that he was not home long before he was faced with another family tragedy. On January 23, his brother, Henry A. Fitch, 28, died at Louisville of spotted fever.

At some point after his return, Fitch became a member of the Cass County Agricultural, Horticultural & Mechanical Association. His passion for hunting and sportsmanship continued as he maintained his membership in the Northern Indiana Shooting Association. He would be remembered as "quiet and unassuming in his manners, but prompt, courageous, and daring when action was required of him."

Many hours were spent creatively by the Logansport sailor over a year or more moving around the rural townships of his local area illustrating scenes with pencil and paintbrush. Perhaps some of this time was spent in the farming district of Harrison Township at or around the location of a crossroads known as "Fitch," where a store and post office were established in 1850 (the post office was discontinued in 1865). George Lease took over the store in the late 1860s and the stop became known as Leases Corner.

In August 1874, Fitch entered a display of oil and other paintings of historic county landscapes and buildings in the Art Hall at the Cass County Fair. For his effort, he won blue ribbons in the categories for best landscape or fancy picture in oil, best watercolors, and best pencil drawings. None of these depictions are known by the author to be extant. Not a politician or physician like his older half brother, Graham Newell, Le Roy passed his remaining years in peace and near obscurity.[28]

Sometime in the winter following his Cass County Fair success, Cmdr. Fitch took ill. He was nursed at home, but his condition steadily worsened, according to the Logansport *Pharos*, over a period of "three or four months" and could not be reversed. Those known to be in attendance at his bedside were members of his family and local friends, as well as Dr. Asa Coleman, Jr., partner of his older half brother Graham Newell and husband to his youngest daughter, Emma.

Father Henry Koenig (pronounced Caney) of St. Joseph's Roman Catholic Church was a frequent visitor. "St. Joseph's," local fourth-generation funeral director Paul Kroeger noted in an electronic interview, "was the ethnic German Catholic Church in Logansport, with names like Spitznagel/Spitznogle, Bauer, Koehne, yes even Kroeger." Kroeger Funeral Home, the remodeled Graham Newell Fitch house, is one of the oldest family-owned funeral homes in Indiana. There were two other Catholic communities in town, "the Irish St. Bridget's Church or the Italian St. Vincent's Church." Cass County historian Thomas Helm confidently wrote in 1886 that St. Joseph's was an "offshoot from St. Vincent de Paul, a considerable proportion of its original membership coming from that congregation." Father Koenig was the church's third pastor, assuming his duties on August 24, 1872, ministering to about 60 families. St. Bridget's was "a further outgrowth from St. Vincent."

The commander was a convert to his wife's religion. When he changed denominations, he broke with the longstanding Fitch family tradition of Anglicanism which stretched back to New York state. The Fitches were well-known Episcopalians in Logansport and were a charter family for establishing that religion in the community. Helm states definitely that "the family of Dr. Grahan N. Fitch ... was the first of which we have now any satisfactory account who were members of this church." The charter document with the Fitch name(s) still hangs in the Parish Hall. Henry Satterlee Fitch was among the first children baptized in the congregation's first official act, August 2, 1840. The large stone baptismal font standing in the back of Trinity Episcopal Church was originally donated in memory of a Fitch family member. The family name is prominently etched on the base of the font, which is one of only two public Fitch remembrances in the city. Harriet V. Fitch, the physician's wife, was in the church's first confirmation class, March 17, 1842.

At the end, it is almost certain that the commander received the Last Rites from Fr. Koenig. Le Roy Fitch died on the morning of Wednesday, April 14, 1875, age 39. In the obituary that appeared in that afternoon's edition of the Logansport *Daily Star*, an anonymous reporter was moved to comment that even citizens of his hometown knew little "of the brilliant career and eminent services of this young officer whose record is thus suddenly terminated." Another, writing for the competing *Pharos*, remarked that the commander "was a genial, warm-hearted man with a host of true friends."

Kroeger Funeral Home's records do not begin until 1875. Mr. Kroeger, from his intimate knowledge of local custom, offers his thoughts as supplement to the bare bones information provided in the local newspaper. "Based on custom," Kroeger writes, Fitch "most likely was buried in a wood casket. He may or may not have been embalmed. His casket was probably made by a cabinet maker but not custom-made for him. As Logansport was a sizable city in its day, caskets were readily available in quantity."

The last opportunity for his family, local friends, and well-wishers to pay their respects occurred at a local mortuary in the hour or so before the deceased's funeral at 10 A.M. on Thursday, April 15. "Most funeral masses would have been at 9 A.M. or earlier—this was the custom until about 20 years ago," wrote Paul Kroeger. Until late in the 20th Century, Roman Catholic priests fasted from midnight prior to saying mass. An early funeral mass allowed the priest to breakfast. The "later time of 10 A.M. may have given the family some hours or so for visitation (prior to the funeral mass), at the mortuary. Open caskets were/are not the custom for Catholic Church funerals. Another possibility for a late mass of 10 A.M. is that there was another funeral at 9 A.M. at the church, so the Fitch funeral was 'the second in line.' The regular daily Mass schedule at St. Joseph's Church was 6:30 A.M. and 8 A.M., so the first funeral could have been at 9 A.M."

After Rev. Koenig said his funeral mass in St. Joseph Catholic Church, Le Roy Fitch was buried in Mount Hope Cemetery north of the city center. He had been dead just 24 hours. Two days later, Mary Fitch formally wrote a letter to notify the Navy Department of his death.[29]

The cause of Cmdr. Fitch's protracted illness remains a mystery, though the exact cause of death was given by Mary Fitch in her 1878 application for a Federal pension. In the document, Dr. Coleman stated that he "treated him for Chronic Diarrhea which resulted in the induration of the walls of the Stomach and Cirrhosis. The immediate cause of death was peritonitis, probably caused by perforation of the stomach or bowels."

In an effort to determine the cause of his decline, both historical and contemporary reviews were undertaken. Local Logansport Health Department death records provide no assistance. We are relatively certain that the cause was not typhoid fever. Such community outbreaks were always reported and, as Stephen E. Towne of the Indiana State Archives advised, the epidemics were "avidly followed."[30]

In a further effort to uncover a reasonable possible cause for Fitch's illness, a layman's review of medical literature was undertaken. The confused findings reaffirmed the reasons why the naval officer then—and we today—relied upon a physician; disease and medical failure is extremely complicated. To help sort out what might have happened, we turned over the slim leads we were able to establish to a learned friend, Thomas F. Beckner, M.D., FACP, for his best analysis. "I think this can be said," wrote the doctor in a July 2, 2006, e-mail to the writer:

> While determining Fitch's exact cause of death is difficult, it can be said that his problems appeared to be primarily gastrointestinal in nature, and were rapidly progressive. If (and we have no information to show this) he was a heavy drinker, he could have died of chronic pancreatitis and cirrhosis, with spontaneous peritonitis as a terminal event. Other causes could have been cirrhosis secondary to hepatitis, a malignant tumor of the colon, cancer of the stomach (fairly common back then,) or some type of colitis, such as ulcerative colitis.

Cmdr. Le Roy Fitch died at his father-in-law's Logansport home on April 14, 1875, age 39. He was buried at Mount Hope Cemetery the next day. His daughter, Marie Fitch, about whom we know next to nothing, died at age 40, on April 28, 1902, and was buried at Mount Hope Cemetery two days later. Mary Fitch died at Washington, D.C., on March 3, 1913, at age 77. She was originally buried at Mt. Olive Cemetery, D.C., but was removed and reinterred at Mt. Hope Cemetery, Logansport, on June 12, 1918, with her daughter and husband under a three-sided stone (courtesy John T. Fitch).

Mary Fitch continued to live at Mint Julep Springs and, on May 5, became administrant of her late husband's estate. On October 17, 1878, she filed a "Declaration for Widow's Army Pension" at Cass County Courthouse on October 17, 1878. This followed by a few months a claim filed by her father for an ancient injury to his left knee. Col. Smith received a pension (#207,137) for $12.50 in March 1882. Under the U.S. Senate resolution of December 8, 1882, Mary received a lifetime annual payment (#2,428) of $25.[31]

Harriet Valerie Satterlee Fitch died at Logansport on May 30, 1881, aged 71 years and eight months, and was buried in Mt. Hope Cemetery. Graham Newell Fitch, who continued to practice medicine, died at Logansport on November 29, 1892, and was also buried at Mt. Hope Cemetery. The doctor and his wife have separate monuments.

Years later, Fitch Street on the west side of Logansport was named in his honor. The boulevard is only about a block or so long. As noted, the imposing home at 711 East Market Street became the Kroeger Funeral Home. The dense, wooded Dr. Fitch farm (Fitch's Glen) west of Logansport on U.S. 24 in Noble Township, in the area along the Wabash and Erie canal known as Kenneth, was purchased at the end of the year by the Casparis Stone Company. The firm became the largest stone crusher in northern Indiana, employing several hundred men to ship tons of product from its quarry. Retired eye doctor Gardner Abner currently resides on the property. Fitch's Glen is "becoming increasingly unknown to younger generations," laments Paul Kroeger, "as there is no roadside sign indicating it. The marking existed only on older highway maps." These three features, plus the cemetery markers and the baptismal font in Trinity Episcopal Church, are the major remaining physical remembrances of the Fitches in Logansport. Neither the senator, his son, or the commander are remembered by plaque or bust.

Upon the death of her father, Col. Smith's Mint Julep Springs was willed to Mary Fitch, who continued to live in the house for some years. In October 1893, it was sold, becoming Logansport's first hospital, St. Joseph's. Marie Fitch, 40, about whom we know next to nothing, died on April 28, 1902, and was buried at Mount Hope Cemetery two days later. Mary Fitch died at Washington, D.C., on March 3, 1913, at age 77. She was originally buried at Mt. Olive Cemetery, D.C., but was removed and reinterred at Mt. Hope Cemetery, Logansport, on June 12, 1918, with her daughter and husband under a three-sided stone.[32]

Except in the pages of those Civil War histories and memoirs touching upon the Western waters (and not all of them), the memory of Cmdr. Le Roy Fitch faded quickly after his death. In his April 1875 obituary in the Logansport *Daily Star*, the writer had been moved to comment that even citizens of his hometown knew little "of the brilliant career and eminent services of this young officer whose record is thus suddenly terminated." That situation hardly improved in the decades which followed. It would require another great war to actively bring his spirit back to the USN he loved.[33]

Following World War I, the United States retrenched its military establishment, much as it had in 1865-1866. As the international situation deteriorated in both Europe and the Pacific during the last half of the 1930s, America began to rearm. When war came at Pearl Harbor on December 7, 1941, the U.S. Navy was not quite as ill prepared as it had been in 1861, though massive building was still required. Numerous fleet units were constructed on an accelerated schedule beginning in 1938—including the first and only vessel to bear the name of Logansport's long forgotten Civil War hero.

USS *Fitch* was one of a group of fast small warships known as destroyers, which did not technically exist when Le Roy Fitch participated in the Civil War. Modern destroyers (DD hull classification) are small, fast warships which can undertake a variety of missions from escort to shore bombardment to patrols. One cannot help but imagine, however, that Fitch would have been quite comfortable with the type, as his light draught steam gunboats performed almost identical duties in his time. His namesake vessel was authorized by act of Congress on May 17, 1938, and, like a Civil War tinclad, she would wear an identifying number, 462. One of the latter *Benson* class ships, she was laid down at the Boston Naval Shipyard on January 6, 1941.

Commissioned in February 1942, the destroyer USS *Fitch* (DD-426) spent most of her World War II years in European waters, often serving in the escort of the aircraft carrier *Ranger*. After serving off Utah Beach during the Normandy invasion, she was converted into a high speed minesweeper (DMS-25) in which configuration she sailed until 1955. Decommissioned in 1956, she was struck from the Navy list on July 1, 1971, and was sunk as a target off the Florida coast on November 15, 1973 (National Archives).

In order to fulfill an old tradition of ship sponsorship by a namesake's nearest surviving female relative, the U.S. Navy, shortly after Christmas 1940, began searching for an appropriate Fitch kinswoman. Newspaper articles reported the quest. Initially, Miss Harriet Fitch, daughter of a Pennsylvania railroadman, was identified. Meanwhile, there was another, Mrs. Madeline Fitch Thomas, a Logansport native who had moved to 1897 South 5th St., Salt Lake City. Mrs. Thomas was, indeed, the late commander's grandniece and was born in "Aunt Mollie's house" before it became St. Joseph's Hospital. She was so identified to the Navy Department by her aunt, Mrs. Melia Copeland. Satisfied that they had found the right candidate, Navy secretary Frank Knox, on April 7, 1941, invited Mrs. Thomas to christen DD-426 at a future date. On May 7, Boston Navy Yard commander ADM William T. Tarrant informed Mrs. Thomas that the launch would occur on June 14.

The news of Mrs. Thomas' choice made the Salt Lake City newspapers. On top of that, it was revealed that she would employ water from the Great Salt Lake in the christening ceremony instead of the traditional champagne. This change in tradition did not sit well with ADM Tarrant, who wrote Mrs. Thomas on May 14 to say that the Navy desired the time-honored custom of a champagne christening. As it was scripted, so it would be; Mrs. Thomas did not take a bottle of brine on the train to Boston.

With pomp, ceremony, and a few speeches, the U.S.S. *Fitch* was launched on June 14. Mrs. Thomas, with her husband, Walter, watching, did smash the champagne bottle across the bow and the hull slid down the ways. DD-426 was put into water almost simultaneously with the adjacent U.S.S. *Forrest* (DD-461), named not for Le Roy's great Confederate rival, but for War of 1812 hero Lt. Dulaney Forrest.

The 1,630 ton U.S.S. *Fitch* was 348.3 feet in length, with a beam of 36.1 feet and an

11.10 foot draft. Her two-shaft geared turbines, with four boilers, provided 50,000 standard horsepower, good for a top speed of 37 knots. Her steaming range was 6,500 miles at 12 knots. As completed, the destroyer had a versatile armament that her namesake would have appreciated. The big guns were five 5 in. 38 cal. (12 cm) dual purpose cannon. Light armament included six 0.5 in (12.7 mm) guns and six 20 mm AA cannon. Ten 21-in. torpedo tubes and two depth charge tracks completed the offensive suite. With 16 officers and 260 enlisted men, DD-426 was commissioned on February 3, 1942, Lt. Cmdr. H. Crommelin in command.

The *Fitch* was assigned as escort for the aircraft carrier *Ranger* (CV-4) on Atlantic and Mediterranean operations between July 1942 and April 1943. In these months, her group three times ferried U. S. Army aircraft from the U.S. to bases in Africa. Additionally, the destroyer guarded the *Ranger* and two escort carriers during the American landings at Fedhala, French Morocco, on November 8, 1942. During the spring and summer, DD-426 participated in Atlantic escort operations, at one point, on September 20, providing transport between Iceland and Scotland for Navy secretary Knox and ADM Harold R. Stark. In the fall, she was reunited with the *Ranger* as she flew her aircraft against German bases in Norway and also supported the weather station at Spitzbergen. From December through April 1944, the destroyer undertook U.S. coastal and Caribbean escort duty and participated in hunter-killer operations in the western Atlantic.

During May, the U.S.S. *Fitch* participated in the great buildup for the Normandy invasion, escorting convoys from Northern Ireland to Plymouth. On June 6, she provided gunfire support off Utah Beach and rescued the survivors of the mined *Corry* (DD-463). Interspersed with Channel convoy work, she returned to the French coastal gunline repeatedly through June 19.

The veteran of operations off northern France went to the Mediterranean in July to participate in the upcoming invasion of the southern coast of that nation. *Fitch* sortied from Taranto, Italy, on August 11 for the invasion of Southern France on 15 August, during which she spotted the fire of the battleship *Texas* (BB-35), as well as firing in the prelanding bombardment. Through the remainder of the summer and fall, she provided escort services in the western Med.

Between November and January 1945, the *Fitch* was converted at Norfolk into a highspeed minesweeper (DMS-25). She then sailed for the Pacific, but before she could enter active service, she was damaged during a training exercise off Hawaii. Repairs at Pearl Harbor required almost five months. Restored, she was able to join the U.S. fleet off Japan on August 6. During the period from August through December, the *Fitch* swept off Japan and in the East China Sea, before returning to America. *Fitch* received five battle stars for World War II service.

The *Fitch* continued to be employed as a minesweeper for the next decade. Homeported at Charleston she was often deployed on exercises along the East Coast, in the Caribbean, and cruised to the Mediterranean in 1949, 1951, and 1953. Again classified DD 462 on July 16, 1955, she also conducted tests in the Caribbean during the year for Operation Development Force. The reborn destroyer was decommissioned at Charleston on February 24, 1956, and placed in reserve. There being no further employment for the veteran, she was struck from the Navy list on July 1, 1971, and was sunk as a target off the Florida coast on November 15, 1973.

After the destruction of the *Fitch* over 30 years ago, no other U.S. Navy vessel was given the name of the Indiana sailor. Once more, his memory literally disappeared back into the history books. In 1875, an anonymous writer in the Logansport *Weekly Journal* called the local hero "a brave and faithful defender of his country." We join in the sentiment expressed then that his "deeds deserve a place in the remembrance of every grateful patriot in the land he periled his life to save."[34]

Notes

Preface

1. Bern Anderson, *By Sea and By River: The Naval History of the Civil War* (New York: Knopf, 1962), p. 196; Mark Grimsley, *The Hard Hand of War: Union Military Policy Toward Southern Civilians, 1861–1865* (New York: Cambridge University Press, 1995), p. 112.

2. Jay Slagle, *Ironclad Captain: Seth Ledyard Phelps and the U.S. Navy* (Kent, OH: Kent State University Press, 1996).

3. Henry Walke, *Naval Scenes and Reminiscences of the Civil War in the United States on the Southern and Western Waters During the Years 1861, 1862 and 1863 with the History of That Period Compared and Corrected from Authentic Sources* (New York: F. R. Reed, 1877).

4. Richard West, Jr., *Mr. Lincoln's Navy* (New York: Longmans, Green, 1957), p. 198.

5. Logansport *Daily Star*, April 14, 1875.

6. David Dixon Porter, *Naval History of the Civil War* (New York: Sherman, 1886; Reprint, Mineola, NY: Dover Publications, 1998), pp.803–804; Byrd Douglas, *Steamboatin' on the Cumberland* (Nashville, TN: Tennessee Book Company, 1961), p. 139.

7. Will Ball wrote a series of columns, "This Changing World," for the Logansport *Pharos-Tribune* and Logansport *Press* in the 1950s and 1960s, with this quote taken from the one published on Oct. 2, 1960.

Chapter One

1. John T. Fitch of Cambridge, Massachusetts, traces his family back 16 generations to William Fytche of Wicken Bonhunt, County Essex, in England. The first Fitch American immigrant was James Fitch who, together with his descendants, have been profiled by John T. Fitch in a large two-volume work, *Descendants of the Reverend James Fitch, 1622–1702* (Rockport, ME: Picton Press, 1999).

2. Biography 1979, "Dr. Frederick." In: John T. Fitch, *Descendants of the Reverend James Fitch, 1622–1702: Vol. II, Generations Six and Seven* (Rockport, ME: Picton Press, 1999), p. 142–143; "History—Encyclopedia: Washington County, New York," Nationmaster.com http://www.nationmaster.com/encyclopedia/Washington-County,-New-York (accessed June 27, 2005).

3. Joe Craig, "A Primer on 18th Century Medicine," *The Northern Campaign: Learn About the Past*, http://www.thenortherncampaign.org/past8.htm (accessed June 27, 2005); Fitch, "Dr. Frederick," in *Descendants*; Thomas Neville Bonner, *Becoming a Physician: Medical Education in Britain, France, Germany and the United States, 1750–1945* (Baltimore: Johns Hopkins University Press, 1995), p. 20; another helpful review of early U.S. medicine and medical thinking is Lester L. King, *Transformations in American Medicine From Benjamin Rush to William Osler* (Baltimore: Johns Hopkins University Press, 1991).

4. Neal Smith, "Villages/Areas," *Welcome to LeRoy, Genesee County, New York*, http://www.rootsweb.com/~nygenese/leroy.htm (accessed June 27, 2005); Susan L. Conklin, "Genesee County History," *Genesee County, New York, Home Page* http://www.co.genesee.ny.us/frameset.html?/dpt/countyhistory/index.html&1 (accessed June 27, 2005).

5. Fitch, "Dr. Frederick," and "Biography 4004, Hon. Graham Newell," in *Descendants*, pp. 559–561; Thomas B. Helm, "Dr. Graham N. Fitch," in *History of Cass County, Indiana* (Chicago: Brant & Fuller, 1886), p. 507; Dean Arthington, "Graham Newell Fitch," Arthington Collection Local Names Scrapbook, Logansport Public Library, n.d., p. 2667.

6. John Fraser, "The Battle of Queenstown Heights October 13, 1812," *Magazine of American History* 24 (September 1890): 203–211; Fitch, "Dr. Frederick," *Descendants*, and "Biography 4007, Egbert Benson," in *Descendants*, p. 562; Henrietta Fitch perished at some unknown date prior to the 1840s. Egbert Benson and his wife, Mary Ann Kynere, had a son named Frederick, who was born at Pekin, Tazwell County, Illinois, in 1840 and died in Logansport on November 7, 1888.

7. Fitch, "Dr. Frederick," in *Descendants*, and "Hon. Graham Newell," in *Descendants*, pp. 559, 561; Indiana University School of Medicine, Ruth Lilly Medical Library, Special Collections Department, "Record No. 19271, Graham Newell Fitch," 19th Century Indiana Physicians Database, http://www.biblioserver.com/19centurydocs/index.php?m=search&id=&ftype=data&q=fitch (accessed June 30, 2005); Stanley B. Weld, ed., "A Connecticut Surgeon in the Civil War: The Reminiscences of Nathan Mayer," *Journal of the History of Medicine and Allied Sciences* 19, 1964:

272–286, cited in Frank R. Freemon, *Gangrene and Glory: Medical Care During the American Civil War* (Urbana: University of Illinois Press, 2001), p. 24; Bonner, p. 175; Edward C. Atwater, "Making Fewer Mistakes: A History of Students and Patients," *Bulletin of the History of Medicine* 57 (1983), 168–171.

8. Samuel Eliot Morison, *The Oxford History of the American People* (New York: Oxford University Press, 1965), p. 475.

9. Andrew R L. Cayton, *Frontier Indiana* (Bloomington: Indiana University Press, 1996), p. 158; Terra Realty, "History of Logansport," *Welcome to Logansport and Cass County*, 1997, http://www.terrarealty.com/relo/churches.htm (accessed June 28, 2005); "The History of the City of Pekin, Illinois." http://www.ci.pekin.il.us/history.asp (accessed June 26, 2005); Fitch, "Biography 4008, Cmdr. Le Roy," p. 562–565; Helm, "Dr. Graham N. Fitch" in *History of Cass County*; in a June 14, 2005, e-mail exchange, Fitch family historian John T. Fitch agreed that it was possible that Le Roy had been named after the New York community; writing in 1950, Will Ball, former president of the Cass County Historical Society in Indiana, cast something of a red-herring shadow upon the Fitch arrival date. According to Ball, Lawrence Cole, who purchased Graham Newell's house upon his death in 1892, had also obtained a copy of Helm's local history with a handwritten alteration in the Graham Newell Fitch profile obviously made sometime before the physician's death. "Some one had scratched out the date 1834 and written in ink the date 1829." Given the death of Polly in New York, this tale is hard to believe. Will Ball, "This Changing World," *The Logansport Press*, April 2, 1950.

10. Ball, "This Changing World," *The Logansport Press*, April 2, 1950; for an excellent and detailed review of Indiana medical practice during the 1830s, the reader is directed to Kathy Mandusic McDonnell's "Medicine of Jacksonian America," *Conner Prairie Organization Homepage* http://www.connerprairie.org/HistoryOnline/jmed.html (accessed June 30, 2005).

11. "Indiana Militia in the Antebellum Era," *Conner Prairie Organization Homepage* http://www.connerprairie.org/HistoryOnline/militia.html (accessed June 27, 2005); Arthur L. Bothura, *History of Miami County, Indiana: A Narrative Account of Its Historical Progress, Its People, and Its Principal Interests*. Vol 1. (Chicago: Lewis Publications, 1914), 204–205; Helm, "Dr. Graham N. Fitch" in *History of Cass County*, pp. 329–330.

12. Helm, "Dr. Graham N. Fitch" in *History of Cass County*; Fitch, "Hon. Graham Newell," in *Descendants*. Graham Newell Fitch was a Democrat and would remain so throughout his political career.

13. Fitch, "Dr. Frederick" and "Hon. Graham Newell" in *Descendants*; Fitch, "Biography No. 6811, Capt. Frederick Fitch," in *Descendants*, p. 142; Terra Realty, "History of Logansport," *Welcome to Logansport and Cass County* [1997] http://www.terrarealty.com/relo/churches.htm, (June 28, 2005).

14. Jehu Powell, *History of Cass County, Indiana* (Chicago; New York: Lewis Publishing Company, 1913), cited in Cass County Historical Society, "Legends," *Cass County Historical Society Homepage*, http://casscountyin.tripod.com/legends.htm>, (accessed June 26, 2005); Fitch, "Hon. Graham Newell," in *Descendants*; Ball, "This Changing World," *The Logansport Press*, August 24, 1958, October 2, 1960; Helm, "Dr. Graham N. Fitch" in *History of Cass County*. Members of the Coleman family later purchased the Graham Newell Fitch home in the city; in 1953, it became the present Kroeger Funeral Home. "Our History," *Kroeger Funeral Home Homepage* http://www.kroegerfuneralhome.com/index/cfm (accessed June 30, 2005).

15. Terra Realty, "History of Logansport," Welcome to Logansport and Cass County, 1997, http://www.terrarealty.com/relo/churches.htm (accessed June 28, 2005); Northern Indiana Historical Society, "Canals," *Northern Indiana Center for History Homepage* http://www.centerforhistory.org/indiana_main4.html (accessed July 20, 2005); the Wabash & Erie Canal was completed in 1853 and, due to floods, the need for constant repairs, and railroad competition, went out of business in 1874. The city of Delphi, Indiana, not far from Cass County in Carroll County, has preserved a portion of its section of the waterway. "General Information," *Wabash and Erie Canal Organization Homepage*, http://www.wabashanderiecanal.org/subpage/interpretive/generalinfo.html (accessed June 29, 2005); additional studies of river transportation in this period include Erik F. Haites, James Mak, and Gary M. Walton, *Western River Transportation: The Era of Early Internal Developments, 1810-1860* (Baltimore: Johns Hopkins University Press, 1975) and Gary M. Walton, "River Transportation and the Old Northwest Territory," in David C. Klingaman and Richard K. Vedder, eds., *Essays on the Economy of the Old Northwest* (Athens: Ohio University Press, 1987), pp. 225–242.

16. Jehu Powell, *History of Cass County, Indiana*, op.cit.; Eric-Jan Noomen, "The Transfer of Napoleon's Corpse," *The Second Page of the Dead* http://www.xs4all.nl/~ejnoomen/story101.html (accessed June 23, 2005).

17. "Indiana: Mrs. Graham Newell Fitch, 1859–1880," in Portraits/Biographies of Regents and Vice Regents to 1874, *Mount Vernon Ladies Association Home Page* http://www.mountvernon.org/learn/collections/index.cfm/pid/333 (accessed June 30, 2005); Ball, "This Changing World," *Logansport Pharos-Tribune* and *Logansport Press*, August 7, October 16, 1960. The tree, regardless of its origin or time of its planting, was eventually blown down in a windstorm and the curved fence built to protect it was straightened. Still, it is reported that twigs from this tree were planted all over town.

18. *The Logansport Journal*, August 3, 1874; William B. Cogar, *Dictionary of Admirals of the U.S. Navy*. Vol. 1 (Annapolis, MD: Naval Institute Press, 1989), 200–201; Aubrey Gardner Wright, "Henry Walke, 1809–1896: Romantic Painter and Naval Hero" (unpublished master's thesis, George Washington University, 1971).

19. Fitch, "Dr. Frederick," in *Descendants*, p. 143; "Hon. Graham Newell," *Ibid.*; Helm, "Dr. Graham N. Fitch" in *History of Cass County*.

20. Helm, "Dr. Graham N. Fitch" in *History of Cass County*; Fitch, "Dr. Frederick," in *Descendants*. Dr. Fitch's obituary appeared in the *Logansport Pharos*, March 20, 1850, and *Logansport Weekly Journal*, March 23, 1850. His remains were later removed and reentered in Mt. Hope Cemetery.

21. Carol H. Foster, "The Requirement for Admission to the Naval Academy: An Historical Review," *U.S. Naval Institute Proceedings* 44 (February 1918): 348; Extract from the United States Naval Academy Roll of the Midshipmen, 1851-1852, provided by Alice C. Creighton, head, Special Collections and Archives, Nimitz Library, United States Naval Academy, May 13, 1997; Fitch, "Commander Le Roy Fitch," in *Descendants*; Sarah Corbin Robert, "The Naval Academy as Housekeeper: Feeding and Clothing the Midshipmen," *U.S. Naval Institute Proceedings* 72 (April 1946): 122; As a colleague later reflected upon the ease of the entrance exams, if they had not been so, he remarked, "many of us would not have followed the Navy as a career." Robley D. Evans, *A Sailor's Log: Recollections of a Naval Life* (New York: D. Appleton, 1901), p. 35.

22. Charles Todorich, *The Spirited Years: A History of the Antebellum Naval Academy* (Annapolis, MD: Naval Institute

Press, 1984), pp. 68, 74, 78–79, 95–96; Cogar, *Dictionary*, I, 184–185. Lt. Craven, who would serve two tours as commandant of midshipmen, is remembered as captain of the U.S.S. *Brooklyn* during the Battle of New Orleans in 1862 and for his unsuccessful effort, along with Capt. Henry Walke, at blockading the C.S.S. *Stonewall* at El Ferrol, Spain, in March 1865. He was promoted to rear admiral in 1866. Cogar, *Dictionary*, I, 36–37.

23. Todorich, *The Spirited Years*, pp. 84, 79, 130; Jack Sweetman, *The U.S. Naval Academy: An Illustrated History* (Annapolis, MD: Naval Institute Press, 1979), pp 39, 42; Fitch, "Commander Le Roy Fitch," in *Descendants*; Extract from the United States Naval Academy Roll of the Midshipmen, 1851–1852, photocopy provided by Alice C. Creighton, head, Special Collections and Archives, Nimitz Library, USNA, May 13, 1997; "Fitch, Le Roy," Entry No. 2080, Abstracts of Service Records of Naval Officers: Records of Officers, 1798–1893, U.S. Navy Department, Bureau of Navigation, U.S. National Archives and Records Service, Record Group 24, Reel 8, January 1846–December 1858 (cited hereafter as Fitch, with reel number and date), also kindly provided in photocopy by Alice C. Creighton, May 13, 1997; James Russell Soley, *Historical Sketch of the United States Naval Academy, Prepared by Direction of Rear Admiral C. R. P. Rodgers, U.S.N.* (Washington, DC: GPO, 1876), p. 101.

24. Todorich, *The Spirited Years*, p. 84, 171–173, 180; Dahlgren is a father figure in American naval ordnance history, responsible for the invention of many cannons, including the boat howitzers which would arm Le Roy's tinclad fleet during the Civil War. Cogar, *Dictionary*, 40–41; William D. Puleston, *Annapolis: Gangway to the Quarterdeck* (New York: D. Appleton-Century, 1942), pp. 73–74; The training ship *Preble* had been commissioned at the Portsmouth Navy Yard in June 1840. Displacing 566 tons, she was 117' 7" long with a beam of 33' 10" and a depth of hold of 15' 6"; her complement totaled 150. She served as the academy ship from 1851 to 1855, 1857 to 1858 and would be burned at Pensacola on April 27, 1863. Paul H. Silverstone, "Dale Class," *The Sailing Navy, 1775–1854* (Annapolis, MD: Naval Institute Press, 2001), pp. 42–43.

25. Sweetman, *Naval Academy*, 47; Todorich, *The Spirited Years*, pp. 119, 125.

26. Todorich, *The Spirited Years*, pp. 86–91; "Acting Midshipman Le Roy Fitch Conduct Roll," 1854-1855 and 1855-1856, photocopy provided by Alice S. Creighton, May 13, 1997. George Dewey, *Autobiography of George Dewey: Admiral of the Navy* (New York: Charles Scribner's Sons, 1913), p. 21.

27. Edward Chauncey Marshall, *History of the Naval Academy* (New York: D. Van Nostrand, 1862), pp. 86, 137; Carroll Storrs Alden and Ralph Earle, *Makers of Naval Tradition* (Boston: Ginn, 1925), p. 229; Dewey, *Autobiography*, pp. 21, 17; Todorich, *The Spirited Years*, pp. 139–140, 150; "Merrimac," in Vol. VI of *Dictionary of American Naval Fighting Ships* (Washington, DC: GPO, 1976), p. 337; Paul H. Silverstone, *Warships of the Civil War Navies* (Annapolis, MD: Naval Institute Press, 1989), p. 27. The American frigate gained immortality in 1862 when, as the Confederate *Virginia*, she dueled the U.S.S. *Monitor* in history's first ironclad combat.

28. Cogar, *Dictionary*, I, 72; Samuel R. Franklin, *Memories of a Rear Admiral Who Has Served for More Than Half a Century in the Navy of the United States* (New York: Harper and Brothers, 1898), p.146; Puleston, *Annapolis*, p. 73; Todorich, *The Spirited Years*, pp. 171, 175–176. After significant shore and sea duty, Green became a rear admiral on June 13, 1870.

29. Fitch, Record Group 25, Reel 8. January 1846–December 1858; Cogar, *Dictionary*, I, 70–72. Superintendent Goldsborough completed his tour at the academy in 1857 and was named a rear admiral on July 16, 1862; during the Civil War, he commanded the Atlantic then North Atlantic Blockading Squadrons, 1861-1862 and served on shore at Washington, D.C., for most of the remainder of the conflict.

Chapter Two

1. The physical portrait of Dr. Fitch appeared in Will Ball's "This Changing World" column in the April 2, 1950, issue of the *Logansport Press*. Information on the activities of Mrs. Harriett V. Fitch and the existence of servant Major is drawn from Dean Arthington, "Harriet V. Fitch," Arthington Collection Local Names Scrapbook, Logansport Public Library, n.d., p. 2668; Henry Clyde Hubbart, *The Older Middle West, 1840-1880: Its Social, Economic and Political Life and Sectional Tendencies Before, During and After the Civil War* (New York: Russell & Russell, 1963), pp. 110, 114; "Colonel Fitch's Election to Senate was Scandal of '50's," Indianapolis *News* (November 18, 1938); John T. Fitch, "Biography No. 4004, Graham Newell Fitch," *Descendants of the Reverend James Fitch, 1622-1702* (Rockport, ME: Picton Press, 1999), p. 559–561.

2. Arthington, "Henry Alvord Fitch," and "Henry S. Fitch," Arthington Collection Local Names Scrapbook, p. 2668–2269; Fitch, Graham Newell Fitch," in *Descendants*; Fitch, personal e-mail, June 14, 2005; Lawrence Kestenbaum, "Index to Politicians: Fitch," *The Political Graveyard: A Database of Famous Cemeteries* http://politicalgraveyard.com/bio/fitch.html#S2Q1DKTZ3 (accessed July 4, 2005); Judge Biddle's profile appears in Vol. I of *The Biographical History of Cass, Miami, Howard, and Tipton Counties, Indiana*, 2 vols. (Chicago: Lewis, 1898) and reprinted on Ronald Branson's *County History Preservation Society Homepage* http://www.countyhistory.com/doc.cass/004.htm (accessed July 4, 2005).

3. *Indiana Herald*, September 19, 1855; Bryan Looker, "Early Cass County," *Cass County Historical Society and Museum Home Page*, http://casscountyin.tripod.com/earlycass.htm (accessed July 3, 2005); for those interested in far greater discussion of Midwestern railroading in this period than the scope of this work permits, the most helpful and interesting review uncovered is Frederic L. Paxson's "The Railroads of the 'Old Northwest' Before the Civil War, "*Transactions of the Wisconsin Academy of Sciences, Arts, and Letters* 18, Part 1 (October 1912), reprinted in Thomas Ehrenreich, *Railroad Extra, 2001* http://www.catskillarchive.com/rrextra/abonw.html (accessed July 3, 2005).

4. "Fitch, Le Roy," Entry No. 1574, Abstracts of Service Records of Naval Officers: Records of Officers, 1798–1893, U.S. Navy Department, Bureau of Navigation, U.S. National Archives and Records Service, Record Group 24, Reel 10, January 1859–December 1863 (cited hereafter as Fitch, with entry number, reel number and date), also kindly provided in photocopy by Alice C. Creighton, head, Special Collections and Archives, Nimitz Library, United States Naval Academy, May 13, 1997; Fitch, "Biography Number 4008, Cmdr. Le Roy," in *Descendants*, p. 562; Arthington, "Mrs. Mary Smith Fitch," Arthington Collection Local Names Scrapbook, p. 2669; Will Ball, "This Changing World," *Logansport Press*, August 17, 1958, June 19 and October 7, 1960. The Smith home was torn down early in the 20th Century. Col. Smith would later build another home, Mint Julep Springs, across the Wabash on the south side of Cliff Drive near the Wabash railroad underpass. It would be willed to Mary and, in 1893, was sold, becoming Logansport's first hospital, St. Joseph's.

5. "Wabash," in Vol. 8 of *Dictionary of American Naval Fighting Ships* (Washington, DC: GPO, 1981), p. 7; hereafter cited as DANF, followed by the volume number, a colon, and the pagination; "St. Mary's," DANF, 4: 250; Paul H. Silverstone, *Warships of the Civil War Navies* (Annapolis, MD: Naval Institute Press, 1989), p. 27; William B. Cogar, *Dictionary of Admirals of the U.S. Navy*, Vol. 1 (Annapolis, MD: Naval Institute Press, 1989), 41–43; Jane Resture, "Jarvis Island," *Jane's Oceania Home Page 2003* http://www.janeresture.com/jarvis (accessed July 4, 2005).

6. "St. Mary's," DANF, 4: 250. Davis' command of the St. Mary's is remembered in the biography by his son, *Charles H. Davis: Life of Charles Henry Davis, Rear Admiral, 1807–1877* (Boston and New York: Houghton, Mifflin, 1899); Howard I. Chappelle, *History of the American Sailing Navy* (New York: W. W. Norton, 1935), p. 120; Robert E. Johnson, *Thence Round Cape Horn: The Story of United States Naval Forces on Pacific Station, 1812–1923* (Annapolis, MD: Naval Institute Press, 1963). p. 105. Other U.S. squadrons of the pre-war years reflected their locations: Mediterranean, West Indies, Brazil, Pacific, and East Indies.

7. William Oscar Scroggs, "William Walker and the Steamship Company in Nicaragua, "*The American Historical Review* 10 (July 1905): 792–811; William Oscar Scroggs, "William Walker, 1824–1860," *1911 Encyclopedia*. http://69.1911encyclopedia.org/W/WA/WALKER_WILLIAM.htm (accessed June 25, 2005); Walker's own narrative, accurate as to details, is *The War in Nicaragua* (Mobile, AL: S.H. Goetzel, 1860, reprint, Tucson, University of Arizona Press, 1985); "Walker's Expeditions," *Global Security Page*. http://www.globalsecurity.org/military/ops/walker.htm (accessed June 25, 2005). The tale of the sea battle between Walker's ship and its Costa Rican adversary, as well as colorful details of the spring battles and the Davis surrender, is related in Edward Wallace, *Destiny and Glory* (New York: Coward-McCann, 1957), pp. 214–231, 237. The entire war is succinctly profiled by Robert L. Scheina, *Latin America's Wars: The Age of the Caudillo, 1791–1898* (Washington, DC: Brassy's, 2003), pp. 220–231, while the most valuable study, both as to its U.S. Navy viewpoint and its rich documentation, remains Francis X. Holbrook, "The Navy's Cross: William Walker," *Military Affairs* 39 (December 1975): 197–203.

8. Johnson, *Thence Round Cape Horn*, p. 109; Holbrook, "The Navy's Cross" in *Military Affairs*, pp. 199–200; *The New York Times*, June 8, 1857. Walker later complained that Davis had not been neutral in his dealings with him, while Davis and Cdr. Mervine were able to convince U.S. authorities that the decision to hold the *Granada* (later turning it over to the allies) prevented her forceable takeover by the French frigate *L'Ambuscade*. The fate of the St. Mary's three lieutenants is largely unknown to this writer, though Lt. McCorkle apparently "went south" at the start of the Civil War. A Lt. D. P. McCorkle is listed by Sharf as in charge of the C.S.N. "ordnance works in Atlanta." J. Thomas Sharf, *History of the Confederate Navy from Its Organization to the Surrender of Its Last Vessel* (New York: Rodgers and Sherwood, 1887, reprint Fairfax Press, 1977), p. 50.

9. "St. Mary's," DANF, 4: 250; Jane Resture, "Jarvis Island," *Jane's Oceania Home Page 2003*; Chester G. Hearn, *Admiral David Glasgow Farragut: The Civil War Years* (Annapolis, MD: Naval Institute Press, 1998), p. 149; Robert C. Suhr, "Personality: Charles Henry Davis' Brilliant U.S. Navy Career was Interrupted, Not Enhanced, by the Civil War," *Military History* 21 (January-February 2005): 74–75. In 1857, William Walker had returned to Nicaragua and tried another takeover; this time the St. Mary's was not involved; the Tennessean was arrested by Cdr. Paulding himself with the U.S.S. *Wabash*; Scheina, *Latin America's Wars*, p. 231.

10. Cogar, *Dictionary*, I, 42; Fitch, Entry No. 1574, Record Group 24, Reel 10. January 1859—December 1863. During the 19th century, a "master in line for promotion," formerly called a "sailing master," was a commissioned officer in the navy who ranked next above an ensign and below a lieutenant but who, unlike a "warrant officer" could be advanced in grade. Aboard a warship, he had immediate charge, under the commander, of sailing the vessel. The rank, borrowed from the Royal Navy, would become today's lieutenant, junior grade, in 1883. Brainy Media, "Master," *Brainy Dictionary 2005* http://www.brainydictionary.com/words/ma/master188291.html (accessed July 6, 2005); "The Origin of the Ranks and Rank Insignia Now Used by the United States Armed Forces, Officers: Lieutenants," *Traditions of the Naval Service* http://www.history.navy.mil/trivia/triv4-5d.htm (accessed July 7, 2005).

11. Chappelle, *American Sailing Navy*, p. 114; *Savannah*," DANF, 4: 364; Silverstone, *Warships*, pp. 127–128.

12. "Savannah," DANF, 4: 364; Fitch, Record Group 24, Reel 10. January 1859—December 1863; Scheina, *Latin America's Wars*, p. 232, 299–301. Among Master Fitch's companions aboard the *Savannah* during this cruise were Lt. John Irwin, later to serve in the West Gulf Coast Blockading Squadron, and Lt. John L. Worden, who would captain the U.S.S. *Monitor* in her battle against C.S.S. *Virginia* in March 1862. Cogar, *Dictionary*, I, 84–85, 212–213.

13. Arthington, "Mary Smith Fitch," Arthington Collection Local Names Scrapbook, p.2269; Hubbart, *Older Middle West*, pp. 146–165, 74–89; Kenneth M. Stamp, *And the War Came: The North and the Secession Crisis, 1860–1861* (Baton Rouge, Louisiana State University Press, 1970), pp. 63, 110, 123, 128–140; Stephen D. Engle, *Struggle for the Heartland: The Campaigns from Fort Henry to Corinth* (Lincoln: University of Nebraska Press, 2001), p. 2; *Harper's Weekly* 5 (March 16, 1861): 116; Thomas B. Helm, "Dr. Graham N. Fitch," *History of Cass County, Indiana* (Chicago: Brant & Fuller, 1886), p. 507; Graham Newell Fitch's activities as a first-term U.S. senator are also covered by Stamp in his *America in 1857* (New York: Oxford University Press, 1990); the Hoosier lawmaker was labeled a traitor by *Harper's Weekly* for, among other things, his participation on the winter 1859-1860 Senate committee with Jefferson Davis and James Mason that reviewed the John Brown raid. *Harper's Weekly* 5 (August 24, 1861): 530.

14. Fitch, Entry No. 700, Record Group 24, Reel 9. January 1859—December 1863; John T. Fitch, personal e-mail. May 9, 2005. In the time between Christmas and the time Le Roy reached Philadelphia, the pressure of the secession crisis which helped ruin his older half brother's Senate career reached an explosive point. State governments in the South had begun a process of taking over—or attempting to take over—the arsenals and forts of the Federal government located within their territory.

15. Fitch, Entry No. 700, Record Group 24, Reel 9. January 1859—December 1863; "Water Witch," in Vol. 8 of *Dictionary of American Naval Fighting Ships* (Washington, DC: GPO, 1981), p. 158; Silverstone, *Warships*, p. 24; Adams to Welles, May 3, 1861, in U.S. Navy Department, *Official Records of the Union and Confederate Navies in the War of the Rebellion* (Washington, DC: GPO, 1894–1922), Series 1, Vol. 4, 154–155 (cited hereafter as ORN, followed by a comma, the series number, a comma, the volume number, a colon, and the page number). *Water Witch* had one 32-lb. cannon.

16. "Wyandotte" in Vol. 8 of *Dictionary of American Naval Fighting Ships*, p. 488; Silverstone, *Warships*, p. 96; Stamp, *And War Came*, pp. 105–106, 175–279; ORN, 1, 4:

118, 210–211; Henry Walke, *Naval Scenes and Reminiscences of the Civil War in the United States on the Southern and Western Waters During the Years 1861, 1862 and 1863 with the History of That Period Compared and Corrected from Authentic Sources* (New York: F. R. Reed, 1877), pp. 1–16; the story of the *Wyandotte's* Pensacola cruise is reviewed in Bern Anderson, *By Sea and By River: The Naval History of the Civil War* (New York: Knopf, 1962), pp. 18–20, and the comment on her summer seaworthiness appeared in Fitch's obituary, *Logansport Daily Star*, April 14, 1875.

17. Cogar, *Dictionary* I, 63–65; Donald L. Canney, *Lincoln's Navy: The Ships, Men and Organization, 1861-65* (London and New York: Conway Maritime Press, 1998), pp. 42–44; Silverstone, *Warships*, p. 125; Dennis J. Ringle, *Life in Mr. Lincoln's Navy* (Annapolis, MD: Naval Institute Press, 1998), pp. 25–26.

18. Richard Webber and John C. Roberts, "James B. Eads: Master Builder," *The Navy* 8 (March 1965): 23–25; C. B. Boynton, *History of the Navy During the Rebellion*, Vol. 1 (New York: D. Appleton, 1867), p. 498; James B. Eads, "Recollections of Foote and the Gunboats," in *Battles and Leaders of the Civil War*, Vol. 1, edited by Robert V. Johnson and Clarence C. Buel (New York: Century, 1884–1887, reprinted Thomas Yoseloff, 1956), 338 (cited hereafter as B&L, followed by a comma, the volume number, a comma, and the page numbers); U.S. Navy Department, Naval History Division, *Riverine Warfare* (Washington, DC: GPO, 1968), p. 21; ORN, 1, 22: 278, 280. The West and Western Rivers in Civil War literature refers generally to the Western theater of operations. See Bruce Catton, "Glory Road Began in the West," *Civil War History* 6 (June 1960): 229–237.

19. Bern Anderson, "The Naval Strategy of the Civil War," *Military Affairs* 26 (Spring 1962): 15; Anderson, *By Sea and By River*, pp. 33–34; John D. Milligan, *Gunboats Down the Mississippi* (Annapolis, MD: Naval Institute Press, 1965), pp. 3–4; Gideon Welles, *The Diary of Gideon Welles, Secretary of the Navy Under Lincoln and Johnson*, edited by John T. Morse, Jr. Vol. 1 (Boston: Houghton, Mifflin, 1911), 242; *St. Louis Daily Democrat*, May 10, 1861.

20. Welles to Rodgers, May 16, 1861, ORN, 1s, 22: 280; Milligan, *Gunboats*; Robert E. Johnson, *Rear Admiral John Rodgers, 1812–1882* (Annapolis, MD: Naval Institute Press, 1967), pp. 156–157; Jay Slagle, *Ironclad Captain: Seth Ledyard Phelps and the U.S. Navy* (Kent, OH: Kent State University Press, 1996), p. 33, 115–150; Walke, *Naval Scenes*, pp. 17–50. Both Phelps and Walke have left detailed accounts of timberclad operations in the fall and winter of 1861-1862.

21. U.S. War Department, *The War of the Rebellion: A Compilation of the Official Records of the Union and Confederate Armies* (Washington, DC: GPO, 1880–1901), Series 1, Vol. 4, 390 (cited hereafter as OR, followed by a comma, the series number, a comma, the volume number, a colon, and the page number); ORN, 1, 22: 297; John Niven, *Gideon Welles: Lincoln's Secretary of the Navy* (New York: Oxford University Press, 1973), p. 378; James M. Hoppin, *The Life of Andrew Hull Foote, Rear Admiral, United States Navy* (New York: Harper and Brothers, 1874), pp. 152–153; Spencer C. Tucker, *Andrew Foote: Civil War Admiral on Western Waters* (Annapolis, MD: Naval Institute Press, 2000), 114–115. The building and outfitting of the City Series ironclads of the Western Flotilla is told not only by Eads in his B&L article, but most completely by the National Park Service historian in charge of salvaging one of them in the 1960s, Edwin C. Bearss. His *Hardluck Ironclad: The Sinking and Salvage of the Cairo* (Baton Rouge: Louisiana State University, 1966), pp. 10–27, and personal interviews piqued my own interest in Civil War naval history and led directly to my first work in the area, *U.S.S. Carondelet,*

1861-1865, (Manhattan, KS: MA/AH Publishing, 1982) and indirectly to this study.

22. Alfred T. Mahan, *The Gulf and Inland Waters*, Vol. 3 of *The Navy in the Civil War* (New York: Scribner's, 1883), pp. 19–21; Charles Dana Gibson with E. Kay Gibson, *Assault and Logistics, Vol. 2: Union Army Coastal and River Operations, 1861-1866* (Camden, ME: Ensign Press, 1995), pp. 65–66; Tucker, *Andrew Foote*, pp. 129–130; documents for the Belmont campaign are provided in ORN, 1, 22: 398–427 and OR, 1, 3: 267–310, while the whole is most recently reviewed by Nathaniel Cheairs Hughes in his *The Battle of Belmont: Grant Strikes South* (Chapel Hill: University of North Carolina Press, 1991); Smith, *U.S.S. Carondelet*, pp. 64–73; the Kentucky political and military developments are covered in Lowell H. Harrison, *The Civil War in Kentucky* (Lexington, KY: University Press of Kentucky, 1975), pp. 14–32, and OR, 1, 4: 179–181; the *St. Louis Daily Democrat*, January 24, 1862, reported on expected sailor life, but cheerful reporter was wrong about the grog—there would be no booze in any squadron commanded by Andrew H. Foote.

23. OR, 1, 4: 362–363, 372–373; R. M. McMurry, *Two Great Rebel Armies* (Chapel Hill: University of North Carolina Press, 1989), p. 142; George Edgar Turner, *Victory Rode the Rails: The Strategic Place of Railroads in the Civil War* (Indianapolis: Bobbs-Merrill, 1953), p. 118; Anne J. Bailey, *The Chessboard of War: Sherman and Hood in the Autumn Campaigns of 1864*, Great Campaigns of the Civil War series. (Lincoln: University of Nebraska Press, 2000), p. 135; T. L. Connelly, *Civil War Tennessee* (Knoxville, TN: University of Tennessee Press, 1979), 13–18; Byrd Douglas, *Steamboatin' on the Cumberland* (Nashville: Tennessee Book, 1961), p. 112; Benjamin F. Cooling, *Forts Henry and Donelson: The Key to the Confederate Heartland* (Knoxville, TN: University of Tennessee Press, 1987), 13–14; *Harper's Weekly* 6 (March 15, 1862): 162.

24. Cooling, *Forts Henry and Donelson*, pp. 29, 42; Ulysses S. Grant, *Personal Memoirs of U.S. Grant: A Modern Abridgment* (New York: Premier Books, 1962), p. 80; Stanley F. Horn, comp., *Tennessee's War, 1861-1865: Described by Participants* (Nashville: Tennessee Civil War Centennial Commission, 1965), p. 29.

25. Allan Nevins, *The War for the Union: War Becomes Revolution* (New York: Charles Scribner's Sons, 1960), pp. 14–15; Stephen E. Ambrose, "The Union Command System and the Donelson Campaign," *Military Affairs* 24 (Summer 1960): 78–86; Cooling, *Forts Henry and Donelson*, xiv; Tucker, *Andrew Foote*, pp. 125–126; the *Conestoga's* fall reconnoiters are covered in ORN, 22 and, more interestingly, by Slagle, *Ironclad Captain*, pp. 143–148, while Rowena Reed also reviews Yankee strategy for Tennessee and the tangled relationships between Halleck, Buell, and Grant in her *Combined Operations in the Civil War* (Annapolis, MD: Naval Institute Press, 1978), pp. 64–84.

26. OR, 1, 3: 317–324; OR, 1, 4:491–492, 504–505, 513. Clarksville on the Cumberland was also occupied. General Polk's wartime career is detailed in Joseph H. Parks, *General Leonidas Polk, C.S.A.: The Fighting Bishop* (Baton Rouge: Louisiana State University Press, 1962).

27. ORN, 1, 22:485–486, 503.

28. Louis C. Hunter, *Steamboats on the Western Waters: An Economic and Technological History* (Cambridge, MA: Harvard University Press, 1949), pp. 219–222, 225, 231, 233–236; ORN, 1, 23: 360; Mark Twain, *Life on the Mississippi* (New York: Harper & Brothers, 1950), p. 83.

29. ORN, 1, 22: 540–615; ORN, 1, 4: 620–639, 861–862; Gibson, *Assault and Logistics*, pp. 67–73; Douglas, *Steamboatin' on the Cumberland*, pp. 118–121; *Cincinnati Daily Gazette*, February 18, 1862; Cooling, *Forts Henry and Donelson*, pp. 57, 128–227; Tucker, *Andrew Foote*, pp. 146–

162; Edwin C. Bearss, *The Fall of Fort Henry* (Dover, TN: Eastern National Park and Monument Association, 1989), p. 26; Bearss, *Unconditional Surrender: The Fall of Fort Donelson* (Dover, TN: Eastern National Park and Monument Association, 1991), p. 35–45; Mahan, *Gulf and Inland Waters*, pp. 26–28; David Dixon Porter, *Naval History of the Civil War* (New York: Sherman, 1886), pp. 144–150.

30. Anderson, *By Sea and By River*, p. 99; Douglas, *Steamboatin' on the Cumberland*, pp. 124–125; Gibson, *Assault and Logistics*, pp. 74–75; M. F. Force, *From Fort Henry to Corinth*. Campaigns of the Civil War (New York: Scribner's, 1882, reprinted Broadfoot Press, 1989), pp. 64–65; Stanley F. Horn, *The Army of Tennessee* (Indianapolis: Bobbs-Merrill, 1941), pp. 99–105. Beauregard's Feb. 7 plans and resultant defensive line summary is cited in OR, 1, 4:861–862, 911, 915.

Chapter Three

1. "Fitch, Le Roy," Entry No. 700, Abstracts of Service Records of Naval Officers: Records of Officers, 1798–1893, U.S. Navy Department, Bureau of Navigation, U.S. National Archives and Records Service, Record Group 24, Reel 9, January 1859–December 1863 cited hereafter as Fitch, with entry number, reel number and date, kindly provided in photocopy by Alice C. Creighton, head, Special Collections and Archives, Nimitz Library, United States Naval Academy, May 13, 1997; John T. Fitch, "Biography No. 4008, Commander Le Roy Fitch," *Descendants of the Reverend James Fitch, 1622-1702* (Rockport, ME: Picton Press, 1999), p. 563–565.

2. Thomas B. Helm, *History of Cass County, Indiana* (Chicago: Brant & Fuller, 1886), p. 507; Will Ball, "This Changing World," *Logansport Press*, April 2, 1950.

3. Philip van Doren Stern, ed., *Soldier Life in the Union and Confederate Armies* (New York: Premier Books, 1961), pp. 14–15; Regimental Association, *History of the 46th Regiment, Indiana Volunteer Infantry, September 1861-September 1865* (Logansport, IN: Press of Wilson, Humphries, 1888), pp. 9–11; Will Ball, "This Changing World," *The Pharos-Tribune and Logansport Press*, October 30, 1960; Fitch, *Descendants*, "Biography No. 6811, Capt. Frederick," p. 141. Frederick Fitch would remain in the 46th Indiana throughout the war, retiring as a captain. Before his death on November 7, 1888, and burial in Mount Hope Cemetery, he would work for one of the Logansport railroads as a baggage handler and watchman. He had three children by two wives; one boy, born on August 10, 1870, was named for his uncle Le Roy, who undoubtedly had a chance to be with the youngster before his own death in 1875. Grand-nephew Le Roy Fitch, who served as a lieutenant in the 160th Indiana during the Spanish-American War, had a daughter named Madeline. She was born in the home of "Aunt Mollie" Fitch, Great-Uncle Le Roy's widow. Madeline later married a man named Thomas, and moved to Salt Lake City. On June 14, 1941, Madeline Fitch Thomas would christen the U.S.S. *Fitch*, named for her Civil War ancestor, at the Boston Navy Yard. Will Ball, "This Changing World," *The Pharos Tribune and Logansport Press*, October 2, December 16, 1960.

4. *Logansport Journal*, December 14, 1861; Regimental Association, *History of the 46th Regiment*, pp. 12–21; Kenneth P. McCutchan, ed., *"Dearest Lizzie": The Civil War as Seen Through the Eyes of Lieutenant Colonel James Maynard Shanklin, of Southwest Indiana's Own 42nd Regiment, Indiana Volunteer Infantry, and Recounted in Letters to His Wife* (Evansville, IN: Friends of Willard Library Press, 1988), pp 88–89. The soldiers spent most of their Cairo duty at Fort Defiance. For a description of the Alexander County river town visited by thousands during the conflict, including the Fitch brothers, see "Cairo," in Paul M. Angle, ed., *Illinois Guide and Gazetteer: Prepared Under the Supervision of the Illinois Sesquicentennial Commission* (Chicago: Rand McNally, 1969), pp. 95–98.

5. Detailed reports concerning the New Madrid-Island No. 10 operation from the viewpoints of both the Union and Confederacy are found in U.S. War Department, *The War of the Rebellion: A Compilation of the Official Records of the Union and Confederate Armies*, 128 vols. (Washington, DC: GPO, 1880–1901), Series 1, Vol. 7 (cited hereafter as OR, followed by a comma, the series number, a comma, the volume number, a colon, and the page number), and U.S. Navy Department, *Official Records of the Union and Confederate Navies in the War of the Rebellion*, 31 vols. (Washington, DC: GPO, 1894–1922), Series 1, Vol. 22 (cited hereafter as ORN, followed by a comma, the series number, a comma, the volume number, a colon, and the page number). The most complete monographic study of the campaign is Larry J. Daniel and Lynn N. Bock, *Island No. 10: Struggle in the Mississippi Valley* (Tuscaloosa, AL: University of Alabama Press, 1996); Spencer Tucker, *Andrew Foote: Civil War Admiral on Western Waters* (Annapolis, MD: Naval Institute Press, 1998), covered the story in chapters 12–13, while many other standard histories detailing the Western Flotilla should also be consulted, including Alfred T. Mahan, *The Gulf and Inland Waters, Campaigns of the Civil War* (New York: Scribner's, 1883), pp.28–39, and John D. Milligan, *Gunboats Down the Mississippi* (Annapolis, MD: Naval Institute Press, 1965), pp. 53–60; activities surrounding the military approach to and skirting of New Madrid in early March from the perspective of Col. Fitch's 46th Indiana are nicely reported in Regimental Association, *History of the 46th Regiment*, pp. 21–27; William L. Shea and Earl J. Hess, *Pea Ridge: Campaign in the West* (Chapel Hill: University of North Carolina Press, 1997); Robert D. Whitesell, "Military and Naval Activity Between Cairo and Columbus," *Register of the Kentucky Historical Society* 61 (1963), 107–121.

6. OR, 1, 7:553; ORN, 1, 22: 493–495, 632; ORN, 1, 23: 153; James M. Hoppin, *The Life of Andrew Hull Foote, Rear Admiral, United States Navy* (New York: Harper and Brothers, 1874), p. 232; Jay Slagle, *Ironclad Captain: Seth Ledyard Phelps and the U.S. Navy* (Kent, OH: Kent State University Press, 1996), p. 185; Tucker, *Andrew Foote*, p. 166; Paul H. Silverstone, *Warships of the Civil War Navies* (Annapolis, MD: Naval Institute Press, 1989), p. 181; Scott K. Williams, "St Louis' Ships of Iron: The Ironclads and Monitors of Carondelet (St. Louis), Missouri," *Missouri Civil War Museum Home Page*, http://www.missouricivilwarmuseum.org/1ironclads.htm (accessed July 12, 2005).

7. James M. Merrill, "Cairo, Illinois: Strategic Civil War River Port," *Journal of the Illinois State Historical Society* 76 (Winter 1983), 242–257; James M. Perry, *A Bohemian Brigade: The Civil War Correspondents, Mostly Rough, Sometimes Ready* (New York: John Wiley, 2000), p. 71; "Cairo," in Angle, *Illinois Guide and Gazetteer*, p. 96; "My Pollard Family: Chapter 2 & Chapter 3, Daniel, the War Years," *My American Family, or ????* Homepage http://freepages.family.rootsweb.com/~ricksgenealogy/e_book.htm (accessed July 13, 2005); George Ward Nichols, "Down the Mississippi," *Harper's New Monthly Magazine* 41 (November 1870), 839.

8. William C. Lytle, comp. *Merchant Steam Vessels of the United States, 1807-1868 "The Lytle List"* (Mystic, CT: The Steamship Historical Society of America, 1952), p. 104; OR, 2, 1:115; ORN, 1, 23: 22–23; Silverstone, *Warships*; George Ward Nichols, "Down the Mississippi," 836. The *Judge Torrence* would be stripped of her stores and sold in an August 1, 1865, U.S. government auction to John A.

Williamson, *et al.*, for $9,100. Refurbished, she was redocumented as the merchant *Amazon*, January 2, 1866, and plied the Western rivers until snagged and sunk at Ozark Island, near Napoleon, Arkansas, on February 19, 1868.

9. Eugene B. Canfield, *Civil War Naval Ordnance* (Washington, DC: Naval History Division, U.S. Navy Department, 1969), p. 21; ORN, 1, 23:104, 280; St. Louis *Missouri Democrat*, February 9, 1862; Slagle, *Ironclad Captain*, p. 199; Scott K. Williams, "St Louis' Ships of Iron: The Ironclads and Monitors of Carondelet (St. Louis), Missouri," *Missouri Civil War Museum Home Page, http://www. missouricivilwarmuseum.org/1ironclads.htm* (accessed July 12, 2005). Although these mortar boats would not in any way prove decisive in operation, they were a topic of concern to President Lincoln, whom, it was recorded, paid attention to "the mortar business." Richard West, Jr., "Lincoln's Hand in Naval Matters," *Civil War History* 4 (June 1958), 181. Washington, Missouri, artist Gary R. Lucy has posted an outstanding detailed rendering of mortar action in his painting "The Battle of Island No. 10, 1862," which we saw July 12, 2005, on his home page, *http://www.gary lucy.com/island.html*.

10. ORN, 1, 22:631–632; "Henry E. Maynadier," in, Mark M. Boatner III, *The Civil War Dictionary* (New York: David McKay, 1959), p. 521; Lieut. S. Y. Seyburn, "Excerpts from The Tenth Regiment of Infantry," *U.S. Regulars Civil War Archives Home Page, http://www.usregulars.com/us-army/10us.html* (accessed July 6, 2005). Maynadier would later comment that the services of his mortar fleet were not "near equal to their cost" in a report which would eventually lead to their retirement; he rejoined the Army of the Potomac in October 1862, was breveted a major general, went on to command Fort Laramie, and died a year younger than Le Roy Fitch at Charleston, South Carolina, Dec. 3, 1868.

"Maynadier, Henry E., maj. gen. U. S. A," *American Biographical Library http://search.ancestry.com/db-abl/P1084. aspx*, (accessed July 12, 2005). In 1861 shortly after his promotion, Capt. Maynadier, "an ardent Union man," had occasion to assist James Morris Morgan, the son of his wife's first cousin, defect from the U.S. Naval Academy, where he was a midshipman, to Alexandria, Virginia, via Washington, D.C. When challenged by a Rebel sentry, the youngster, who was accompanied by the pass-bearing Maynadier, halted a shooting, assuring the guard that Maynadier "was coming south later." Morgan later remembered: "He did ... the same year, Captain Maynadier and I were shooting at each other at Island Number 10 on the Mississippi River." James Morris Morgan, *Recollections of a Rebel Reefer* (Boston: Houghton, Mifflin, 1917), p. 35.

11. Hoppin, *Life of Andrew Hull Foote*, p. 266; ORN, 1, 22: 655–656, 770; ORN, 1, 23: 279; Daniel and Bock, *Island No. 10*, pp. 73–78. As part of Flag Officer David G. Farragut's New Orleans campaign, Cmdr. David Dixon Porter would operate a flotilla of mortar schooners against the city's forts beginning in mid-April. Chester G. Hearn, *The Capture of New Orleans, 1862* (Baton Rouge: Louisiana State University Press, 1995), pp. 178–189.

12. Regimental Association, *History of the 46th Regiment*, p. 25; ORN, 1, 22: 770; Daniel and Bock, *Island No. 10*, p. 88. The campaign is concisely reviewed by Howard P. Nash in his "Island No. 10," *Civil War Times Illustrated* 5 (December 1966): 42–50; William H. Hix to Sarah Hix, April 4, 1862, "Letters from William Hix (Persons)," *76th New York Regiment Homepage http://www.bpmlegal.com/76NY/76personswh.html* (accessed July 12, 2005).

13. Daniel and Bock, *Island No. 10*, 87–141, 148; Mahan, *Gulf and Inland Waters*, p. 34; Tucker, *Andrew Foote*, pp. 180–188; C. B. Boynton, *History of the Navy During the Rebellion*, Vol. 1 (New York: D. Appleton, 1867), I: 549–553;
ORN, 1, 22: 696–718; ORN, 1, 23: 279; Slagle, *Ironclad Captain*, pp. 189–209; Henry Walke, *Naval Scenes and Reminiscences of the Civil War in the United States on the Southern and Western Waters During the Years 1861, 1862 and 1863 with the History of That Period Compared and Corrected from Authentic Sources* (New York: F. R. Reed, 1877), pp. 99–199; Charles Dana Gibson, with E. Kay Gibson, *Assault and Logistics, Vol. 2: Union Army Coastal and River Operations, 1861–1866* (Camden, ME: Ensign Press, 1995), pp. 80–87. St. Louis *Missouri Democrat*, April 7, 1862. Walke's fortress run-by technique would become "almost commonplace on the Western rivers." William H. Fowler, *Under Two Flags: The American Navy in the Civil War* (New York: W. W. Norton, 1990), pp. 171–172.

14. Mahan, *Gulf and Inland Waters*, pp. 36–39; Maj. Gen. Halleck's strategy is discussed by Rowena Reed, *Combined Operations in the Civil War* (Annapolis, MD: Naval Institute Press, 1978), pp. 203–208; Stephen E. Ambrose, *Halleck: Lincoln's Chief of Staff* (Baton Rouge: Louisiana State University Press, 1962), pp. 45–48; Tucker, *Andrew Foote*, pp. 189–194; Whitesell, "Military and Naval Activity Between Cairo and Columbus," 110–111. When Halleck's soldiers finally showed up at Corinth on May 29, Beauregard, Johnston's successor, simply moved down the road to Tupelo. Tucker, *Andrew Foote*, p. 189.

15. ORN, 1, 22: 767–768; Tucker, *Andrew Foote*, p. 190; Regimental Association, *History of the 46th Regiment*, p. 27.

16. ORN, 1, 23: 14–17, 63; *Cincinnati Times*, May 16, 1862; Hoppin *Life of Andrew Hull Foote*, pp. 299, 310–317; Slagle, *Ironclad Captain*, pp. 219–225; Milligan, *Gunboats*, pp. 64–67; Mahan, *Gulf and Inland Waters*, pp. 43–45; Charles H. Davis, *Life of Charles Henry Davis, Rear Admiral, 1808–1877* (Boston: Houghton, Mifflin, 1899), pp. 223–229; Walke, *Naval Scenes and Reminiscences*, pp. 245–276. The Confederate naval commander, J. E. Montgomery, believed that the hour-long contest had been a great victory and boasted of it directly to Gen. Beauregard. ORN, 1, 23:55–57.

17. Anderson, *By Sea and By River: The Naval History of the Civil War* (New York: Knopf, 1962), p. 111; ORN, 1, 23:39, 45–51; *Cincinnati Daily Commercial*, June 11, 1862; Chester G. Hearn, *Ellet's Brigade: The Strangest Outfit of All* (Baton Rouge: Louisiana State University Press, 2000), pp. 3–22, 27–28; Davis, *Life of Charles Henry Davis*, p. 236–238; Regimental Association, *History of the 46th Regiment*, p. 28–29; Walke, *Naval Scenes and Reminiscences*, pp. 270–275; Gibson, *Assault and Logistics*, pp. 101–111. By 1870, Fort Pillow was gone below the surface of the river. One traveler noted "several acres of forest and the remains of the fortifications one day collapsed with more suddenness than did the rebellion and sank beneath the flood. It is but little satisfaction to our curiosity to point to treetops swaying in the current as the spot where this famous fort once stood." George Ward Nichols, "Down the Mississippi," p. 843.

18. ORN, 1, 23: 114–141; *Memphis Argus*, June 6, 1862; *Chicago Tribune*, June 10, 1862; *Cincinnati Daily Commercial*, June 11, 1862; Mahan, *Gulf and Inland Waters*, pp. 48–49; Milligan, *Gunboats*, pp. 73–77; Davis, *Life of Charles Henry Davis*, pp. 237–242; Regimental Association, *History of the 46th Regiment*, pp. 30–31; *New York Tribune*, June 11, 1862; St. Louis *Missouri Democrat*, June 10–1, 1862; Boynton, *History of the Navy During the Rebellion*, Vol. 1, 573–574; Walke, *Naval Scenes and Reminiscences*, pp. 277–297; Slagle, *Ironclad Captain*, pp. 233–241; Warren D. Crandall and Isaac D. Newell, *History of the Ram Fleet and Mississippi Marine Brigade* (St. Louis: Buschart Brothers, 1907), pp. 60–80; Hearn, *Ellet's Brigade*, pp. 30–38; Alfred W. Ellet, "Ellet and His Steam Rams at Memphis," in *Battles and*

Leaders of the Civil War, edited by Robert V. Johnson and Clarence C. Buel, Vol. 1 (New York: Century, 1884–1887, reprinted Thomas Yoseloff, 1956), 456–459, cited hereafter as B&L, followed by a comma, the volume number, a comma, and the page numbers; Charles C. Coffin, *My Days and Nights on the Battlefield: A Book for Boys* (Boston: Ticknor and Fields, 1864), pp. 291–311; Gibson, *Assault and Logistics*, pp. 111–115. Coffin, the noted correspondent for the *Boston Morning Journal* and competitor of Franc Wilkie, was writing as "Carleton." He was highly respected by Capt. Davis and finished this book, based on his 1862–1863 columns, by telling the tale of Capt. Wilcox of the St. Louis and Memphis Steamboat Company's *Platte Valley*. Wilcox was the man who skippered that craft in 1861 as it made the final steamboat trip north up the Mississippi sanctioned by Confederate authorities before they closed the river to Northern shipping. He and his chartered vessel had returned to her original home port as part of the Union fleet train and would be the vessel chosen to take the prisoner-survivors of Montgomery's flotilla back up the river to Cairo.

19. ORN, 1, 23: 121, 126–127, 136, 149; *Harper's Weekly* 6 (June 28, 1862): 410–411; Memphis *Daily Avalanche*, June 9, 1862; George E. Currie, *Warfare Along the Mississippi: The Letters of Lieutenant Colonel George E. Currie*, edited by Norman E. Clarke, Sr. (Mount Pleasant, MI: Clarke Historical Collection, Central Michigan University, 1961), pp. 50–51; Anderson, *By Sea and By River*, p. 114; Regimental Association, p. 30; Ellet, "Ellet and His Steam Rams at Memphis," p. 458; Hearn, *Ellet's Brigade*, pp. 38–40. Charles H. Davis never admitted that his nemesis, Charles Ellet, was first to get a national flag up over the city.

20. Anderson, *By Sea and By River*, pp. 115; ORN, 1, 23: 160–162.

Chapter Four

1. Ulysses S. Grant, *Personal Memoirs of U.S. Grant: A Modern Abridgment* (New York: Premier Books, 1962), pp. 128–129; Francis Vinton Green, *The Mississippi. Campaigns of the Civil War*, vol. 8 (New York: Charles Scribner's Sons, 1885, reprinted, The Blue & The Gray Press, n.d.), pp. 29–30, 34; Donald Davidson, *The Tennessee, Vol. II: The New River, Civil War to TVA* (New York: Rinehart, 1948), pp. 41–43. Navy Secretary Welles was appalled at Maj. Gen. Halleck's lack of action at this time and later reflected, "Halleck was good for nothing then, nor is he now!" Charles Lee Lewis, *David Glasgow Farragut* (Annapolis, MD: Naval Institute Press, 1943), p. 107.

2. William Tecumseh Sherman, *Memoirs* (New York: Penguin Books, 2000), p. 243; Edwin C. Bearss, "The White River Expedition, June 10–July 15, 1862," *Arkansas Historical Quarterly* 21 (Winter 1962): 305–307.

3. U.S. Navy Department, *Official Records of the Union and Confederate Navies in the War of the Rebellion* (Washington, DC: GPO, 1894–1922), Series 1, Vol. 23, 119–121, 134–135, 142–144 (cited hereafter as ORN, followed by a comma, the series number, a comma, the volume number, a colon, and the page number).

4. "General Sterling Price," In Vol. 3 of *Dictionary of American Naval Fighting Ships* (Washington, DC: GPO, 1968), p. 59. ORN, 1, 23: 134–135; Alfred W. Ellet, "Ellet and His Steam Rams at Memphis," in *Battles and Leaders of the Civil War*, Vol. 1, edited by Robert V. Johnson and Clarence C. Buel (New York: Century, 1884–1887, reprinted Thomas Yoseloff, 1956), 457; Chester G. Hearn, *Ellet's Brigade: The Strangest Outfit of All* (Baton Rouge: Louisiana State University Press, 2000), pp.34–35.

5. Charles Dana Gibson and E. Kay Gibson, comps., *Dictionary of Transports and Combat Vessels, Steam and Sail, Employed by the Union Army, 1861–1868* (Camden, ME: Ensign Press, 1995), p. 54; ORN,1, 22:120, 136, 142–144, 208–209, 212. A description of the use of diving suits and pumps in riverboat salvage is provided in Louis C. Hunter, *Steamboats on the Western Waters: An Economic and Technological History* (Cambridge, MA: Harvard University Press, 1949), pp. 119–120. Given the immense age difference between Le Roy and Graham Newell Fitch, it may not be a surprise that Henry S. Fitch was actually a year older than his uncle. On June 20, after another Hoosier soldier, Maj. Gen. Lew Wallace, reached Memphis with his Third Division, Capt. Davis was able to get him to sign off on the repair bill for the five vessels. ORN, 1, 23: 219.

6. Benjamin Franklin Cooling, *Fort Donelson's Legacy: War and Society in Kentucky and Tennessee, 1862–1863* (Knoxville: University of Tennessee Press, 1997), p. 70–73, 219–222; Philip Shaw Paludan, *A People's Contest: The Union and Civil War, 1861–1865* (New York: Harper & Row, 1988), p. 452; J. F. C. Fuller quoted in Richard P. Gildrie, "Guerrilla Warfare in the Lower Cumberland River Valley, 1862–1865," *Tennessee Historical Quarterly* 59 (Fall 1990): 161; in his widely respected recent study *The Uncivil War: Irregular Warfare in the Upper South, 1861–1865* (Norman: University of Oklahoma Press, 2004), pp. 6–7, Robert M. Mackey reviews the fine points in the differences between guerrillas, partisans, and raiders, all of whom have existed, sometimes simultaneously, in history going back thousands of years, quoting Lieber as necessary. The "Lieber Code," reprinted in War Department General Orders 100 (April 24, 1863), *Instructions for the Government of Armies of the United States in the Field*, is found in U.S. War Department, *The War of the Rebellion: A Compilation of the Official Records of the Union and Confederate Armies*, 128 vols. (Washington, DC: GPO, 1880–1901), Series 3, Vol. 3: 148–164 (cited hereafter as OR, followed by a comma, the series number, a comma, the volume number, a colon, and the page number); other discussions concerning Northern efforts to organize a code of legal conduct include Frank Freidel, "General Orders 100 and Military Government," *Mississippi Valley Historical Review* 32 (March 1946): 541–546, and Richard S. Hartigen, *Lieber's Code and the Law of War* (South Holland, IL: Precedent Publishing, 1983). A facsimile reproduction of the actual code can be found in *The 1863 Laws of War: Articles of War; General Orders No. 100; Army Regulations–U.S. War Department* (Mechanicsburg, PA: Stackpole Books, 2005). The literature concerning the "wizards of the saddle," or "guerrillas," as the misused term for insurgents in the "low intensity conflict" of 1861–1865 came to stick, is immense; for a sampling, see Daniel E. Sutherland, "Sideshow No Longer: A Historiographical Review of the Guerrilla War," *Civil War History* 46 (March 2000): 5–23.

7. Mackey, *The Uncivil War*, pp. 28–31; OR, 1, 8: 28, 814–815; OR, 1, 13: 831–832; OR, 1, 16, 1: 300; Gildrie, "Guerrilla Warfare in the Lower Cumberland River Valley, 1862–1865," p. 162; Stephen V. Ash, "Sharks in an Angry Sea: Civilian Resistance and Guerrilla Warfare in Occupied Middle Tennessee, 1862–1865," *Tennessee Historical Quarterly* 45 (Fall 1986): 226–227; Diane Neal and Thomas W. Kremm, *Lion of the South: General Thomas C. Hindman* (Macon, GA: Mercer University Press, 1993), pp. 116–119; Daniel E. Sutherland, "Guerrillas: The Real War in Arkansas," *Arkansas Historical Quarterly* 52 (Autumn 1993): 257–285. General Order No. 17 is cited in OR, 1, 13: 835 and Mackey, *The Uncivil War*, pp. 207–208. Hindman's martial law activities, more than his guerrilla warfare policy, led to his replacement on August 12, 1862. After the war, he became involved in Arkansas reconstruction politics and was shot and killed on Sept. 28, 1868,

"while sitting in his house, near Helena, by an assassin, who shot him through the window." "Thomas Carmichael Hindman," in Mark M. Boatner III, *The Civil War Dictionary* (New York: David McKay, 1959), p. 402; Regimental Association, *History of the 46th Regiment, Indiana Volunteer Infantry, September 1861-September 1865* (Logansport, IN: Press of Wilson, Humphries, 1888), p. 43.

8. OR, 1, 13:421; ORN, 1, 23:161-162 ; Bearss, "The White River Expedition," 305-307.

9. ORN, 1, 23: 162-163; Bearss, "The White River Expedition," pp. 308-309; Rowena Reed, *Combined Operations in the Civil War* (Annapolis, MD: Naval Institute Press, 1978), p. 214. Charles Ellet, Jr., died on June 21, 1862, from the wound he received during the Battle of Memphis. Hearn, *Ellet's Brigade*, p.42.

10. ORN,1, 23: 164-165; Bearss, "The White River Expedition," pp. 312-313; Regimental Association, *History of the 46th Regiment*, p. 34; John D. Milligan, ed., *From the Fresh Water Navy, 1861-1864: The Letters of Acting Master's Mate Henry R. Browne and Acting Ensign Symmes E. Brown*, Naval Letters Series, Vol. 3 (Annapolis, MD: Naval Institute Press, 1970), p. 90.

11. ORN, 1, 23, 165-166, 200-205; OR, 1, 13, 34-35, 103; Bearss, "The White River Expedition," pp. 319-323; Regimental Association, *History of the 46th Regiment*; Jeanie Mort Walker, *Life of Capt. Joseph Fry, the Cuban Martyr* (Hartford, CT: J. B. Burr, 1875), p. 157. Fry, an unknown at this time, would gain international notoriety in 1873 when, as "Captain Fry of the *Virginius*," he and several crewmen were executed by Spanish authorities in Cuba after having been captured during an unsuccessful filibustering gunrunning operation. Robert L. Scheina, *Latin America's Wars: The Age of the Caudillo, 1791-1898* (Washington, DC: Brassy's, 2003), p. 356.

12. ORN, 1, 23: 166; Regimental Association, *History of the 46th Regiment*, pp. 34-35; George N. Gray, "Narrow Escapes: Just a Little Bit of History," *Ironton* [Ohio] *Register*, December 23, 1886, submitted by Donald E. Darby to Sons of Union Veterans of the Civil War Patriotic Recollections, http://suvcw.org/pr/art008.htm (accessed July 12, 2005).

13. ORN, 1, 23: 166-158, 178, 200-204, 692-693; *Cincinnati Daily Commercial*, June 20, 1862; *Harper's Weekly* 6 (July 5, 1862), 419; Gray, "Narrow Escapes"; Regimental Association, *History of the 46th Regiment*; Bearss, "The White River Expedition," pp. 323-330; Walker, *Life of Capt. Joseph Fry*, pp. 159, 163-164; William M. Fowler, Jr., *Under Two Flags: The American Navy in the Civil War* (New York: W. W. Norton, 1990), pp. 184-185; Jay Slagle, *Ironclad Captain: Seth Ledyard Phelps and the U.S. Navy* (Kent, OH: Kent State University Press, 1996), p. 245-248; Alfred T. Mahan, *The Gulf and Inland Waters, Campaigns of the Civil War* (New York: Scribner's, 1883), p.50. It was later recorded that Col. Fitch recovered and retained after the battle the logbook and rebel flag of the C.S.S. *Mauripus*. Acting Master's Mate Henry Browne was one of those killed on the *Mound City*; the entire episode was reported home by his brother. Milligan, *From the Fresh Water Navy*, pp. 92-99.

14. Mahan, *Gulf and Inland Waters*; Brian Hogan, Conrad Bush and Mike Brown, "The 76th New York and the Navy," 76th New York Infantry Regiment Homepage http://www.bpmlegal.com/76NY/76navy.html (accessed July 12, 2005); ORN, 1, 23: 173; Charles H. Davis, *Life of Charles Henry Davis, Rear Admiral, 1808-1877* (Boston: Houghton, Mifflin, 1899), p. 245-246; David Dixon Porter, *The Naval History of the Civil War* (New York: Sherman, 1886; reprinted Secaucus, N.J.: Castle Books, 1984), pp. 173-174. Davis was appointed flag officer and commander of the Western Flotilla on June 17, formally relieving Flag Officer Foote.

15. ORN, 1, 23: 169-170, 174-177, 181, 693 ; OR, 1, 13: 106; Regimental Association, *History of the 46th Regiment*, pp. 35-36; Bearss, "The White River Expedition," pp. 335-339; Winslow is profiled in William B. Cogar, *Dictionary of Admirals of the U.S. Navy*, Vol. 1 (Annapolis, MD: Naval Institute Press, 1989), 211-212. On Sept. 24, 1864, a bit further upstream in this White River vicinity, Confederate Brig. Gen. Joseph Shelby, with fewer than 1,200 men and four pieces of cannon, attacked a fleet of tinclads, capturing U.S.S. *Queen City* while sinking U.S.S. *Fawn* and putting to flight two other would-be rescuers, U.S.S. *Sunbeam* and *Naumkeag*. R. W. Crabb, "Cavalry Fight Against Ironclads," St. Louis *Missouri Republican*, July 3, 1886.

16. ORN, 1, 23: 175-177, 181-182, 184, 693; OR, 1, 13: 106-107; Mackey, *History of the 46th Regiment*, p. 32; Bearss, "The White River Expedition," p. 341; Regimental Association, *History of the 46th Regiment*, p. 41; Davis, *Life of Charles Henry Davis*, p. 248; Charles Dana Gibson, with E. Kay Gibson, *Assault and Logistics, Vol. 2: Union Army Coastal and River Operations, 1861-1866* (Camden, ME: Ensign Press, 1995), pp. 123-125. Davis and Le Roy Fitch knew all about warm weather from their time dealing with William Walker in Nicaragua back in 1857.

17. OR, 1, 8: 117; ORN, 1, 23: 182; Bearss, "The White River Expedition," p. 342. On June 29, Flag Officer Davis took the ironclads *Benton, Cincinnati, Louisville*, and *Carondelet*, and a few miscellaneous boats, downriver from Memphis to a point above Vicksburg for a planned rendezvous with the fleet of Flag Officer David G. Farragut. Men from the two groups met on July 1 and would linger near the Mississippi bastion for about a month. ORN, 1, 23: 235.

18. OR, 1, 13: 108.

19. OR, 1, 13: 108-109; Mackey, *The Uncivil War*, p. 33; Regimental Association, *History of the 46th Regiment*, p. 42.

20. OR, 1, 13: 107-113, 118-119; ORN, 1, 23:183-184, 188-194, 197-198; *Harper's Weekly* 6 (July 6, 1862), 419; Regimental Association, *History of the 46th Regiment*, pp. 36-39; Bearss, "The White River Expedition," 343-362; Robert L. Kerby, *Kirby Smith's Confederacy: The Trans-Mississippi South, 1863-1865* (New York: Columbia University Press, 1972), pp. 32-33; Reed, *Combined Operations in the Civil War*, p. 215; Mackey, *The Uncivil War*.

21. OR, 1, 10:2: 69; Cooling, *Fort Donelson's Legacy*, p. 75; Cornelia and Jac Weller, "The Logistics of Bedford Forrest, Part Two: A Leader of Men," *The Army Quarterly* 121 (October 1991): 429; Noel C. Fisher, "Prepare Them for My Coming': General William T. Sherman, Total War, and Pacification in West Tennessee," *Tennessee Historical Quarterly* 51 (Summer 1992): 79-81; Richard E. Beringer, Herman Hattaway, Archer Jones, and William N. Still, Jr., *Why the South Lost the Civil War* (Athens: University of Georgia Press, 1986), p. 189; Mackey, *The Uncivil War*, pp. 32, 35-36, 170-171; R. Blake Dunnavent, *Brown Water Warfare: The U.S. Navy in Riverine Warfare and the Emergence of a Tactical Doctrine, 1775-1970*, (Gainesville, FL: University of Florida Press, 2003), p. 70; Carole Bucy, *A Path Divided: Tennessee's Civil War Years* (Nashville, TN: Tennessee 200, 1996), p. 5. After the *General Sterling Price* reached Cairo, she was taken in hand for repair and conversion. She was formally transferred to the Navy by Quartermaster Henry A. Wise on September 30, 1862. Although at that time she was renamed *General Price*, she continued to be referred to as *General Sterling Price* in dispatches; she would not complete her refit until March 1, 1863. "General Sterling Price," *Dictionary of American Naval Fighting Ships*.

22. Regimental Association, *History of the 46th Regiment*, p. 44; Will Ball, "This Changing World," *Logansport*

Press, April 2, 1950; *Biographical Directory of the American Congress, 1774–1961* (Washington, DC: GPO, 1961), p. 891; John T. Fitch, "Biography No. 4004, Graham Newell Fitch," *Descendants of the Reverend James Fitch, 1622-1702* (Rockport, ME: Picton Press, 1999), pp. 559–561. Mrs. Harriet V. Fitch also died at Logansport, on May 30, 1881, and is buried next to her husband.

23. ORN, 1, 23: 310, 322.

Chapter Five

1. We will have relatively little to say here about leadership or equipment on the military side of the war of the guerrilla, partisan, or raider except as it may impact upon combat or logistical matters. For helpful reviews of the intricacies of the insurgency war on territories inland of the rivers, readers are directed to the titles contained in Daniel E. Sutherland, "Sideshow No Longer: A Historiographical Review of the Guerrilla War," *Civil War History* 46 (March 2000): 5–23, as well as the two "shadow war" works most important to this study, Robert R. Mackey, *The Uncivil War: Irregular Warfare in the Upper South, 1861-1865* (Norman: University of Oklahoma Press, 2004), and Benjamin Franklin Cooling, *Fort Donelson's Legacy: War and Society in Kentucky and Tennessee, 1862-1863* (Knoxville: University of Tennessee Press, 1997).

2. Mark Twain, *Life on the Mississippi* (New York: Harper & Brothers, 1950), pp. 33–34; George Ward Nichols, "Down the Mississippi," *Harper's New Monthly Magazine* 41 (November 1870): 839; Edmund J. Huling, *Reminiscences of Gunboat Life in the Mississippi Squadron* (Saratoga Springs, NY: Sentinel Print, 1881), pp. 31–32; Adam Kane, *The Western River Steamboat* (College Station: Texas A & M University Press, 2004), pp. 91–93; Louis C. Hunter, *Steamboats on the Western Rivers: An Economic and Technological History* (Cambridge, MA: Harvard University Press, 1949), p. 160; Paul H. Silverstone, *Warships of the Civil War Navies* (Annapolis, MD: Naval Institute Press, 1989), pp.151, 155. Paymaster Huling remembered that, when steamers were taken in hand for conversion into tinclads, the saloon piano was usually retained for the entertainment of the officers, p. 31.

3. Kane, *Western River Steamboat*, pp. 67–80; Hunter, *Steamboats on the Western Rivers*, pp. 133–142; Silverstone, *Warships*, pp. 172–173; Huling, *Reminiscences of Gunboat Life*, p. 29; Fred Brown, "Sultana Burning," *Appalachian Life*, no. 41 (March 2000): 3–4, 8. Coal was the preferred fuel of the Union gunboats. Brig. Gen. Joseph G. Totten pointed out in June 1861 that "Pittsburgh coal is the best. Pomeroy coal nearly if not quite as good (Pomeroy is half way between Pittsburgh and Cincinnati.)" He also noted that there were about 200 coal barges available on the Ohio River, each able to carry an average load of 10,000 bushels. The naval base at Cairo did not have a significant coal depot and the "nearest considerable coal supply above Cairo" was at Caseyville, about 120 miles up the Ohio River. U.S. War Department, *The War of the Rebellion: A Compilation of the Official Records of the Union and Confederate Armies* (128 vols. (Washington, DC: GPO, 1880–1901), Series 1, Vol. 52, Part 1: 164 (cited hereafter as OR, followed by a comma, the series number, a comma, the volume number, a colon, and the page number).

4. Kane, *Western River Steamboat*, pp. 81–82; Hunter, *Steamboats on the Western Rivers*, pp. 72, 167–172, 219; Huling, *Reminiscences of Gunboat Life*, pp. 30–31; U.S. Navy Department, *Official Records of the Union and Confederate Navies in the War of the Rebellion*, 31 vols. (Washington, DC: GPO, 1894–1922), Series 1, Vol. 25, 681 (cited hereafter as ORN, followed by a comma, the series number, a comma, the volume number, a colon, and the page number); Gary Matthews, "'Tinclad'—In Response to: Re: Tinclad (Terry Foenander),'" *Civil War Navies Message Board* http://history-sites.com/mb/cw/cwnavy/index.cgi?noframes;read=1314 (accessed December 7, 2005).

5. Alfred T. Mahan, *The Gulf and Inland Waters*, Vol. III of the *Navy in the Civil War* (New York: Scribner's, 1883), p.51; Silverstone, *Warships*, p. 159; ORN, 1, 23: 76–77, 91, 93, 98. "Alfred Robb" In: Vol. 1 of *Dictionary of American Naval Fighting Ships*, Rev. ed. (Washington, DC: GPO, 1991), p. 179. Columbus, Indiana, native William Gwin, always remembered for his service at Shiloh, commanded the U.S.S. *Benton* in the December 27, 1862, battle at Haines Bluff on the Yazoo River. There he was mortally wounded and died on January 3, 1863. "William Gwin," in Vol. 3 of James Grant Wilson and John Fiske, eds., *Appleton's Cyclopaedia of American Biography*, 5 vols. (New York: D. Appleton, 1888), p. 19.

6. Alan Westcott, "Alexander Mosely Pennock," in Vol. 14 of *Dictionary of American Biography*, 10 vols. (New York: C. Scribner's, 1937), p. 444; William B. Cogar, *Dictionary of Admirals of the U.S. Navy*, Vol. 1 (Annapolis, MD: Naval Institute Press, 1989), 126–127; Lewis B. Hamersly, *The Records of Living Officers of the U.S. Navy and Marine Corps* (Philadelphia: J. B. Lippincott, 1870), p. 54; Jay Slagle, *Ironclad Captain: Seth Ledyard Phelps and the U.S. Navy* (Kent, OH: Kent State University Press, 1996), p. 323; ORN, 1, 23: 267.

7. ORN, 1, 23: 102–103, 115–116. When the Mississippi Squadron adopted its now famous tinclad numbering system on June 19, 1863, the number 21 was painted in large black letters on the pilothouse of the *Alfred Robb*. Silverstone, *Warships*, p. 165. Named an acting volunteer lieutenant on October 1, 1862, Goudy would become one of Lt. Cmdr. Fitch's favorite officers and would rise to command the ironclad U.S.S. *Cincinnati*. He died at Paducah, Kentucky, on March 28, 1865, and was buried with full honors. ORN, 1, 24, 74; ORN, 1, 27: 125; Edward W. Callahan, *List of Officers of the Navy of the United States and of the Marine Corps, from 1775 to 1900, Comprising a Complete Register of All Present and Former Commissioned, Warranted, and Appointed Officers of the United States Navy, and of the Marine Corps, Regular and Volunteer. Compiled from the Official Records of the Navy Department* (New York: L.R. Hamersly, 1901, reprint, New York: Haskell House, 1969), p. 225.

8. Donald L. Canney, *Lincoln's Navy: The Ships, Men and Organization, 1861-65* (London: Conway Maritime Press, 1998), p. 76.

9. ORN, 1, 23: 245–246, 251, 307; Silverstone, *Warships*. For two years before entering the Confederate River Defense Force, the 161-ton *Little Rebel*, built at Belle Verne, Pennsylvania, was known in civilian life as the *R. E. & A. H. Watson*. She was a screw steamer (an unusual type on the upper rivers) with one engine and two boilers. Union workers at Cairo armed her with two 24-pounder howitzers and two 12-pounder rifles. She actually entered service before being purchased from the Illinois Prize Court in January 1863. The 38-ton side-wheeler *General Pillow* had been captured on the Hatchee River on June 9, 1862. She had two engines and two boilers and was outfitted with a pair of 12-pounder smoothbore howitzers. Silverstone, *Warships*, pp. 167, 180.

10. Hunter, *Steamboats on the Western Rivers*, pp. 548–550; St. Louis *Missouri Democrat*, June 2, 1862; OR, 1, 52, 1: 164.

11. Hamersly, *Steamboats on the Western Rivers*, pp. 63–64; ORN, 1, 23: 98, 290, 292–293, 307, 353–354, 379–380. The *St. Clair* was purchased from R. D. Cochran, Robert Finney, C. A. Dravo, Jane and Mary A. Nim-

ick of Allegheny County (Pittsburgh), Pennsylvania, for $19,750; total costs of repairs were $7,554.53. Slightly more expensive, the *Brilliant* was acquired from Albert G. Mason, Joshua Michem, and William Cock of Brownsville, Pennsylvania, for $20,000. ORN, 2, 1: 47, 197.

12. ORN, 1, 23: 353–354, 360; ORN, 1, 25: 596; John M. Latham, *Raising the Civil War Gunboats and Building the Magic Valley History Tower* (Camden, TN: J. M. Latham: Press Pros, 1997), pp. 172–173, 180; James Edwin Campbell, "The Mississippi Squadron." *Ohio Archaeological and Historical Quarterly* 34 (January 1925): 60; Huling, *Reminiscences of Gunboat Life*, pp. 5–7; Rowland Stafford True, "Life Aboard a Gunboat [U.S.S. *Silver Lake*, No. 23]: A First-Person Account," *Civil War Times Illustrated* 9 (February 1971): 39; Mark F. Jenkins, "Tinclads," *Ironclads and Blockade Runners of the Civil War homepage* http://www.wideopenwest.com/~jenkins/ironclads/tinclads.htm (accessed July 29, 2005); "A Tale of Three Tinclads, All Named Argosy," *Mid Missouri Civil War Roundtable Homepage*, 2005, http://www.mmcwrt.org/2005/default0501.htm (accessed July 29, 2005); "The Archaeological Investigations of the Battle of Johnsonville," *PanAm Consultants Homepage*, http://www.panamconsultants.com/PAGE (accessed June 8, 2004); William H. Howard to wife, April 6, 1863, William H. Howard Papers, University of Tennessee Library, Knoxville (cited hereafter as Howard Papers, with date). Pilot Bixby was a real person, a "small, sturdy man" who ruled his craft "dressed in high starched collars, silk neckties, and stickpins." He died in 1910, two years after Mark Twain. Ron Powers, *Mark Twain: A Life* (New York: The Free Press, 2005), p. 78.

13. ORN, 1, 25: 474; OR, 1, 52, 1: 707–708; Alan Aronson, "Strategic Supply of Civil War Armies," *General Histories of the American Civil War* http://members.cox.net/rb2307/content/STRATEGIC_SUPPLY_OF_CIVIL_WAR_ARMIES.htm (accessed March 30, 2000); Lawrence M. Smith, "Rise and Fall of the Strategy of Exhaustion," *Army Logistician*, November-December 2004: 35; Hunter, *Steamboats on the Western Rivers*, pp. 547–556; Benjamin W. Bacon, *Sinews of War: How Technology, Industry and Transportation Won the Civil War* (Novato, CA: Presidio Press, 1997), pp. 75–79.

14. "Ohio River," in *Wikipedia: The Free Encyclopedia*, http://en.wikipedia.org/wiki/Ohio_River (accessed August 5, 2005); ORN, 1, 25: 610–61; OR, 1, 52, 1: 166. In his 1863 Ohio River survey undertaken for Acting Rear Adm. David Dixon Porter, Le Roy Fitch offered some thoughts on certain communities: Cairo, Illinois: "population floating"; Caledonia, Illinois: "small town"; Paducah, Kentucky: "very few loyal citizens"; Caseyville, Kentucky: "guerrillas live in vicinity"; Uniontown, Kentucky: "very disloyal"; Evansville, Indiana: "requires watching"; and Owensboro, Kentucky: "very disloyal and smuggles goods."

15. "Tennessee River," in *Wikipedia: The Free Encyclopedia*, http://en.wikipedia.org/wiki/Tennessee_River (accessed August 5, 2005); Ann Toplovich, "Tennessee River System," in Carroll Van West, ed., *The Tennessee Encyclopedia of History and Culture* (Nashville: Rutledge Hill Press for the Tennessee Historical Society, 1998), pp. 943–945; Stanley J. Folmsbee, Robert E. Corlew, and Enoch L. Mitchell, *Tennessee: A Short History* (Knoxville, TN: University of Tennessee Press, 1969), pp. 12–13; Donald Davidson, *The Tennessee, Vol. II: The New River, Civil War to TVA* (New York: Rinehart, 1948), pp. 1–118; ORN, 1, 24: 59–60. In his 1863 Ohio River survey undertaken for Acting Rear Adm. David Dixon Porter, Le Roy Fitch offered some thoughts on certain communities: Paducah, Kentucky: "very few loyal citizens"; Callowaytown, Kentucky: "two houses"; Paris Landing, Tennessee: "one house and mill"; New Portland, Tennessee: "three houses, Union"; Reynoldsburg, Tennessee: "three families, rebel"; Fowler's Landing, Tennessee: "very bad rebels"; Perryville and East Perryville, Tennessee: "rebels"; Marvin's Bluffs, Tennessee: "two houses, Union"; Brownsport, Tennessee: "iron foundry, Union"; Cedar Creek, Tennessee: "iron furnace"; Decatur, Tennessee: "iron furnace, Union, yet rebel"; Carrollville, Tennessee: "four houses, Union"; Clifton, Tennessee: "rebels town burned February 1863"; Point Pleasant, Tennessee: "three houses"; Cerro Gordo, Tennessee: "deserted"; Coffee's Landing, Tennessee: "hot secesh"; Savannah, Tennessee: "mixed, Union and rebels"; Pittsburgh Landing, Tennessee: "deserted"; Big Bend Landing, Tennessee: "deserted and destroyed"; Chickasaw, Alabama: " eight families, four Union, rest doubtful; Waterloo, Alabama: "all rebels"; Tuscumbia, Alabama: "all rebels back"; Florence, Alabama: "rebels."

16. "Cumberland River," in *Wikipedia: The Free Encyclopedia*, http://en.wikipedia.org/wiki/Cumberland_River (accessed August 6, 2005); Ann Toplovich, "Cumberland River," in Carroll Van West, ed., *The Tennessee Encyclopedia of History and Culture* (Nashville: Rutledge Hill Press for the Tennessee Historical Society, 1998), pp. 227–228; Folmsbee, Corlew, and Mitchell, *Tennessee: A Short History*, pp. 13–14; "Towns of the Cumberland," *Save the Cumberland Homepage*, http://www.savethecumberland.org/towns.htm, (accessed July 21, 2005); Byrd Douglas, *Steamboatin' on the Cumberland* (Nashville, TN: Tennessee Book, 1961), pp. 28–31; ORN, 1, 24: 58–59; ORN, 1, 25: 160.

17. Bennett H. Young, *Confederate Wizards of the Saddle* (Boston: Chappel, 1914), p. 97; Stewart H. Holbrook, *The Story of American Railroads* (New York: Crown, 1947), pp. 123–124; James A. Ramage, *Rebel Raider: The Life of General John Hunt Morgan* (Lexington, KY: University Press of Kentucky, 1986), pp. 61–63, 85–87, 95–97. The standard history of the L & N is Kincaid Herr, *The Louisville and Nashville Railroad, 1850-1963* (Louisville, KY: Public Relations Department, L & N, 1964); reprinted, University of Kentucky Press, 2000). Herr's 402-page work had originally taken the story through 1942 and was published by the railroad in 1943.

18. Canney, *Lincoln's Navy*, p. 141; Charles Oscar Paullin, *Paullin's History of Naval Administration, 1775-1911* (Annapolis, MD: Naval Institute Press, 1968), p. 401; ORN, 1, 23: 389; U.S. Navy Department, *Laws of the United States Relating to the Navy* (Washington, DC: GPO, 1866), pp. 19–23. Under terms of PL 152 and at the recommendation of Flag Officer Davis, Le Roy Fitch was promoted to the rank of lieutenant commander on September 21, 1862; he would physically receive his commission on April 18, 1863. His mentor, Davis, had become an acting rear admiral just six days earlier. "Fitch, Le Roy," Entry No. 700, Abstracts of Service Records of Naval Officers: Records of Officers, 1798–1893, U.S. Navy Department, Bureau of Navigation, U.S. National Archives and Records Service, Record Group 24, Reel 9, January 1859—December 1863, cited hereafter as Fitch, with entry number, reel number and date, also kindly provided in photocopy by Alice C. Creighton, head, Special Collections and Archives, Nimitz Library, United States Naval Academy, May 13, 1997; ORN, 1, 23: 377.

Chapter Six

1. U.S. War Department, *The War of the Rebellion: A Compilation of the Official Records of the Union and Confederate Armies*, 128 vols. (Washington, DC: GPO, 1880–1901), Series 1, Vol. 16, Pt. 2: 136, 197, 727 (cited hereafter as OR, followed by a comma, the series number, a comma, the volume number, a colon, and the page number);

Stephen V. Ash, "Sharks in an Angry Sea: Civilian Resistance and Guerrilla Warfare in Occupied Middle Tennessee, 1862–1865," *Tennessee Historical Quarterly* 45 (Fall 1986): 227–229; U.S. Navy Department, *Official Records of the Union and Confederate Navies in the War of the Rebellion*, 31 vols. (Washington, DC: GPO, 1894–1922), Series 1, Vol. 23, 508, (cited hereafter as ORN, followed by a comma, the series number, a comma, the volume number, a colon, and the page number); Robert R. Mackey, *The Uncivil War: Irregular Warfare in the Upper South, 1861-1865* (Norman: University of Oklahoma Press, 2004), pp. 131–135; Benjamin Franklin Cooling, *Fort Donelson's Legacy: War and Society in Kentucky and Tennessee, 1862–1863* (Knoxville, TN: University of Tennessee Press, 1997), pp. 70–72, 85–91; Richard P. Gildrie, "Guerrilla Warfare in the Lower Cumberland River Valley, 1862–1865," *Tennessee Historical Quarterly* 49 (Fall 1990): 163; James A. Ramage, *Rebel Raider: The Life of General John Hunt Morgan* (Lexington, KY: University Press of Kentucky, 1986), pp. 91–107; John Allan Wyeth, *Life of General Nathan Bedford Forrest* (New York: Harper & Bros., 1904), pp. 83–103; Evansville *Daily Journal*, July 18, 1862; Walter T. Durham, *Nashville: The Occupied City–The First Seventeen Months– February 16, 1862–June 30, 1863* (Nashville: Tennessee Historical Society, 1985), pp. 104–107; Richard Troutman, ed., *The Heavens Are Weeping: The Diaries of George R. Browder, 1852-1886* (Grand Rapids, MI: Zondervan, 1987), pp. 119, 122. Adam R. "Stovepipe" Johnson, *The Partisan Rangers of the Confederate Army*, edited by William J. Davis (Louisville, KY: George G. Fetter, 1904; reprint, Austin, TX: State House Press, 1995), pp. 112–125; Raymond Mulesky, *Thunder from a Clear Sky: Stovepipe Johnson's Confederate Raid on Newburgh, Indiana* (New York: iUniverse, 2005). Governor Johnson's edict on guerrilla suppression measures is found in LeRoy P. Graf and Ralph W. Haskins, eds., *The Papers of Andrew Johnson* (Knoxville, TN: University of Tennessee Press, 1976), V, 374.

2. Michael J. Bennett, *Union Jacks: Yankee Sailors in the Civil War* (Chapel Hill: University of North Carolina Press, 2004), pp. 85–88; Donald Davidson, *The Tennessee, Vol. II: The New River, Civil War to TVA* (New York: Rinehart, 1948), pp. 77–78, 84–85; ORN, 1, 23: 245, 262–265, 305; Milford M. Miller, "Evansville Steamboats During the Civil War," *Indiana Magazine of History* 37 (December 1941), 373. Pilot Samuel G. Sheely, who had served with Lt. Fitch aboard the *General Sterling Price*, also served as pilot for the Pennock expedition.

3. Charles H. Davis, *Life of Charles Henry Davis, Rear Admiral, 1807–1877* (Boston and New York: Houghton, Mifflin, 1899), p. 274; OR, 16, 1: 862–870; Johnson, *The Partisan Rangers*, pp. 104–108, 112–15; ORN, 1, 23: 209, 307–309; Miller, "Evansville Steamboats During the Civil War," p. 373. The U.S. riverine force during the Civil War introduced a new tactical doctrine into brown water warfare—the patrol. Three kinds were initially executed: "day or night general patrols, reconnaissance patrols, or interdiction forays." R. Blake Dunnavent, *Brown Water Warfare: The U.S. Navy in Riverine Warfare and the Emergence of a Tactical Doctrine, 1775-1970* (Gainesville, FL: University of Florida Press, 2003), p. 78.

4. OR, 1, 17, 1: 34; ORN, 1, 23: 332–333; Cooling, *Fort Donelson's Legacy*, p. 114. Certain Ohio outfits were not faring too well at this time; it was elements of the 71st Ohio that had surrendered at Clarksville two weeks earlier. Fort Heiman commander Col. William Lowe and his 5th Iowa Cavalry, known as the Curtis Horse, with a mixed brigade, were able to retake that Cumberland River town on September 7. Gildrie, "Guerrilla Warfare in the Lower Cumberland River Valley," 165.

5. ORN, 1, 23: 309; Paul H. Silverstone, *Warships of the Civil War Navies* (Annapolis, MD: Naval Institute Press, 1989), p. 166; "Fairplay," In: Vol. II of *Dictionary of American Naval Fighting Ships* (Washington, DC: GPO, 1963), p. 385. A joint Army-Navy expedition under Lt. Cmdr. S. Ledyard Phelps captured the Confederate transport *Fairplay* at Milliken's Bend on August 18 before she could offload a large cargo of rifles, cannon, and ammunition. ORN, 1, 23: 294–304, 333; Jay Slagle, *Ironclad Captain: Seth Ledyard Phelps and the U.S. Navy* (Kent, OH: Kent State University Press, 1996), p. 283–286; Edwin C. Bearss, "The Union Raid Down the Mississippi and Up the Yazoo—August 16–27, 1862," in Editors of *Military Affairs, Military Analysis of the Civil War: An Anthology* (Millwood, NY: KTO, 1977), pp. 213–224.

6. ORN, 1, 23: 310, 322, 359–360; Evansville *Daily Journal*, September 10, 1862; Charles Dana Gibson and E. Kay Gibson, comps., *Dictionary of Transports and Combat Vessels, Steam and Sail, Employed by the Union Army, 1861-1868* (Camden, ME: Ensign Press, 1995), p. 205; Davidson, *The Tennessee, Vol. II*, p. 80; Miller, "Evansville Steamboats During the Civil War," p. 373. The *Lou Eaves* was purchased at Evansville by the U.S. Army Quartermaster Department on October 15, 1864, and remained in service through the following June. It was during September that we conjecture that Lt. Cmdr. Fitch and his older and retiring half brother, Col. Graham Newell Fitch, may have met during the latter's return to Logansport. The older Fitch had been one of the first to feel the sting of Confederate guerrillas and was known to support tough suppressive action against them. For details on Col. Fitch's encounters with irregulars in Arkansas, see Chapter 4. On September 24, Flag Officer Davis received word of his promotion to the rank of Rear Admiral, effective July 16. ORN, 1, 23: 377.

7. U.S. Navy Department, Naval History Division, *Civil War Naval Chronology, 1861-1865: Part II, 1862* (Washington, DC: GPO, 1962), p. 100; "David Dixon Porter," in William B. Cogar, *Dictionary of Admirals of the U.S. Navy*, Vol. 1 (Annapolis, MD: Naval Institute Press, 1989), 131–133; Chester G. Hearn, *Admiral David Dixon Porter: The Civil War Years* (Annapolis, MD: Naval Institute Press, 1996), pp. 145, 151–152; ORN, 1, 23: 379–380, 390, 394, 451–452; Cooling, *Fort Donelson's Legacy*, p. 115; Silverstone, *Warships*, pp. 169, 178; "Brilliant," in Vol. 1 of *Dictionary of Ships American Naval Fighting* (Washington, DC: GPO, 1959), p. 157; "St. Clair," in Vol. 6 of *Dictionary of American Naval Fighting Ships* (Washington, DC: GPO, 1976), p. 236; OR, 1, 20, 2: 102–103, 187–188; OR, 1, 52, 1: 10–11. The Battle of Perryville is covered in most Civil War military histories. Our review was taken from Thomas L. Connelly, *Army of the Heartland* (Baton Rouge: Louisiana State University Press, 1967), pp. 243–270, and Stanley F. Horn, "The Battle of Perryville," *Civil War Times Illustrated* 5 (February 1966), 4–11, 42–47. Maj. Gen. Rosecrans is the subject of William M. Lamers' *The Edge of Glory: A Biography of General William S. Rosecrans, USA* (New York: Harcourt, Brace, 1961). Jacob Hurd, who would resign on April 13, 1864, was also one of Lt. Cmdr. Fitch's favorites; Bolton remained with the *Fairplay* until he resigned from the service on December 1, 1863. ORN, 1, 24: 74; Edward W. Callahan, *List of Officers of the Navy of the United States and of the Marine Corps, from 1775 to 1900, Comprising a Complete Register of All Present and Former Commissioned, Warranted, and Appointed Officers of the United States Navy, and of the Marine Corps, Regular and Volunteer. Compiled from the Official Records of the Navy Department* (New York: L.R. Hamersly, 1901; reprint, New York: Haskell House, 1969), pp. 65, 286. Mary Fitch's relationship to Bolton's wife is revealed in a letter home from his colleague, the acting assistant surgeon aboard the U.S.S.

Brilliant. William H. Howard to wife, July 19, 1863, *William H. Howard Papers,* University of Tennessee Library, Knoxville (cited hereafter as Howard Papers, with date).

8. Evansville *Daily Journal,* September 16, 18–19, October 18, 1862; Miller, "Evansville Steamboats During the Civil War," p. 373.

9. ORN, 1, 23: 421–422; 434–438; Cooling, *Fort Donelson's Legacy,* p. 115, 163; Evansville *Daily Journal,* October 27, 1862; Davidson, *The Tennessee, Vol. II;* Alfred T. Mahan, *The Gulf and Inland Waters.* Vol. 3 of the *Navy in the Civil War* (New York: Scribner's, 1883), p.179. The Caseyville assessment, paid largely in goods, continued for months. The first installment was collected shortly after the *Hazel Dell* attack and consisted of about 1,100 bags of wheat, 40 barrels of whiskey, and 10–15 barrels of lard. On December 4, Lt. Cmdr. Fitch visited the community and brought away as part of the reparation payment: 939 bags of wheat, 13 kegs of lard, 35 barrels of whisky, a barrel of meat and one of salt, five half barrels of ale, and "some small boxes of groceries." ORN, 1, 23: 311, 530–531. Promoted to the rank of acting volunteer master on October 1, 1862, George Groves would later command the *Fairplay* and be honorably discharged on December 11, 1865. Callahan, *List of Officers,* p. 235.

10. Evansville *Daily Journal,* October 23, 1862; ORN, 1, 23: 311, 437.

11. ORN, 1, 23: 311, 446, 459, 463–464, Evansville *Daily Journal,* November 23, 1862.

12. Buell's Nashville quote is from Lenette S. Taylor's *"The Supply for Tomorrow Must Not Fail": The Civil War of Captain Simon Perkins, Jr., a Union Quartermaster* (Kent, OH: Kent State University Press, 2004), p. 22, while much of the remainder of this section is based on pp. 19–23 of her work; other details about the city are taken from the Nashville *Dispatch* of August 14 and 22, 1862, the Louisville *Daily Journal,* November 15, 1862, Durham, *Nashville: The Occupied City,* pp. 206–207, and Mark Zimmerman, *Battle of Nashville Preservation Society Guide to Civil War Nashville* (Nashville, TN: Lithographics, 2004), pp. 8–11, 25; the Johnson reference is from Paul H. Bergeron, "Andrew Johnson," in Carroll Van West, ed., *The Tennessee Encyclopedia of History and Culture* (Nashville, TN: Rutledge Hill Press for the Tennessee Historical Society, 1998), p 482.

13. Byrd Douglas, *Steamboatin' on the Cumberland* (Nashville, TN: Tennessee Book, 1961), p. 138; OR, 1, 20, 1: 15–23; Lamers, *The Edge of Glory,* p. 192; Steven E. Woodward, *Nothing But Victory: The Army of the Tennessee, 1861-1865* (New York: Alfred A. Knopf, 2005), p. 246; Ramage, *Rebel Raider,* pp. 128–133; OR, 1, 20, 2: 77, 100–108; ORN, 1, 23: 309, 508, 517. The first direct L & N train from Louisville for some months reached Nashville on November 25; supplies now flowed into the city by both land and water. Nashville *Daily Union,* November 26, 1862.

14. Louisville *Daily Journal,* December 11, 1862–January 5, 1863; Nashville *Daily Union,* December 25, 1862; *The New York Times,* December 15, 1862; OR, 1, 20, 2: 213, 229, 237–238; ORN, 1, 23: 311–312, 626–629, 631, 659; ORN, 1, 24: 56–57; Ebenezer Hannaford, *The Story of a Regiment: A History of the Campaigns and Associations in the Field of the Sixth Regiment Ohio Volunteer Infantry* (Cincinnati: Privately printed, 1868), p. 390; Frank Miller, *The Photographic History of the Civil War,* Vol. 2 (New York: Review of Reviews, 1911), 162–163; William Bickman, *Rosecrans' Campaigns with the 14th Army Corps; or, the Army of the Cumberland: A Narrative of Personal Observations* (Cincinnati: Moore, Wilstach, Keys, 1863), p.121; Ramage, *Rebel Raider,* pp. 135–147; Mackey, *The Uncivil War,* p. 142. Morgan's biographer completely covers the Christmas Raid with OR footnotes saving us the space of citing them here.

The Shelbyville preacher's prayer is found in Lamers, *The Edge of Glory,* p. 194. Out west, a Confederate force under Maj. Gen. Earl Van Dorn did far more damage than Morgan or Forrest, destroying Maj. Gen. Grant's supply base at Holly Springs, Mississippi, on December 20, along with goods valued at between $500,000 and $1.5 million. OR, 1, 17, 2: 508–516.

15. This overview is based on James Lee McDonough's *Stones River: Bloody Winter in Tennessee* (Knoxville, TN: University of Tennessee Press, 1980), pp. 81–216; Bickman, *Rosecrans' Campaigns,* pp. 150–307; Larry J. Daniel, *Days of Glory: The Army of the Cumberland, 1861–1865* (Baton Rouge: Louisiana State University Press, 2004), pp. 201–224; G. C. Kniffin, "The Battle of Stone's River," in *Battles and Leaders of the Civil War,* edited by Robert V. Johnson and Clarence C. Buel, Vol. 3 (New York: Century, 1884–1887, reprinted Thomas Yoseloff, 1956), 613–632 (cited hereafter as B&L, followed by a comma, the volume number, a comma, and the page numbers); Lamers, *The Edge of Glory,* pp. 202–243. Federal losses in the Battle of Stones River were 1,636 killed, 7,397 wounded, and 3,673 POWs for a total of 12,700 or 29 percent of those engaged; Confederate losses totaled 26 percent: 1,236 dead, 7,766 wounded, 868 POW. We've taken these figures from Peter Cozzens' convenient *The Battle of Stones River* (Washington, DC: Eastern National Park and Monument Association, 1995), pp. 47–48.

Chapter Seven

1. Joseph P. Dyer, *From Shiloh to San Juan: The Life of "Fighting Joe" Wheeler* (Baton Rouge: Louisiana State University Press, 1961), pp. 65–68; G. C. Kniffin, "The Battle of Stone's River," in *Battles and Leaders of the Civil War,* edited by Robert V. Johnson and Clarence C. Buel, Vol. 3 (New York: Century, 1884–1887, reprint, New York: Thomas Yoseloff, 1956), 614 (cited hereafter as B&L, followed by a comma, the volume number, a comma, and the page numbers).

2. U.S. Navy Department, *Official Records of the Union and Confederate Navies in the War of the Rebellion* (Washington, DC: GPO, 1894–1922), Series 1, Vol. 23, 665–666, (cited hereafter as ORN, followed by a comma, the series number, a comma, the volume number, a colon, and the page number); U.S. War Department, *The War of the Rebellion: A Compilation of the Official Records of the Union and Confederate Armies* (Washington, DC: GPO, 1880–1901), Series 1, Vol. 20, Pt. 2: 273–274, 296 (cited hereafter as OR, followed by a comma, the series number, a comma, the volume number, a colon, and the page number); Steven E. Woodworth, *Nothing But Victory: The Army of the Tennessee, 1861–1865* (New York: Alfred A. Knopf, 2005), p. 246. An 1851 graduate of Norwich Military Academy, Dodge became a railroad engineer before the war and settled in Iowa. After Fort Sumter, the Council Bluffs resident became colonel of the 4th Iowa Volunteer Infantry and led it in the Battle of Pea Ridge, Arkansas. Later, before this command, he was placed in charge of repairing the Mobile & Ohio Railroad, which ran from Columbus, Kentucky, to Corinth, Mississippi. Herbert Feis, "The War of Spies and Supplies: Grant and Grenville M. Dodge in the West, 1862–1864," in Steven E. Woodward, ed., *Grant's Lieutenants: From Cairo to Vicksburg* (Lawrence, KS: University Press of Kansas, 2001), pp. 183–198.

3. James M. McPherson, *Battle Cry of Freedom: The Civil War Era* (New York: Oxford University Press, 1988), pp. 582–583; ORN, 1, 23: 312; ORN, 1, 24: 5–9, 57; Charles Dana Gibson and E. Kay Gibson, comps., *Dictionary of*

Transports and Combat Vessels, Steam and Sail, Employed by the Union Army, 1861-1868 (Camden, ME: Ensign Press, 1995), p. 228; OR, 1, 17, 2: 832; OR, 1, 20, 2: 296–297, 307–308, 313, 317, 322–323; Robert R. Mackey, *The Uncivil War: Irregular Warfare in the Upper South, 1861-1865* (Norman: University of Oklahoma Press, 2004), p. 173; Thomas L. Connelly, *Autumn of Glory: The Army of Tennessee, 1862-1863* (Baton Rouge: Louisiana State University Press, 1971), pp. 69–79; William M. Lamers, *The Edge of Glory: A Biography of General William S. Rosecrans, USA* (New York: Harcourt, Brace, 1961), 248–249; William H. Howard to wife, March 9, 1863, William H. Howard Papers, University of Tennessee Library, Knoxville (cited hereafter as Howard Papers, with date). Howard would be honorably discharged on December 9, 1865, while Ensign Moyer was honorably discharged on October 12. Edward W. Callahan, *List of Officers of the Navy of the United States and of the Marine Corps, from 1775 to 1900, Comprising a Complete Register of All Present and Former Commissioned, Warranted, and Appointed Officers of the United States Navy, and of the Marine Corps, Regular and Volunteer. Compiled from the Official Records of the Navy Department* (New York: L.R. Hamersly, 1901; reprint, New York: Haskell House, 1969), pp. 278, 396; David Dixon Porter, *Naval History of the Civil War* (New York: Sherman, 1886; reprint, Mineola, NY: Dover, 1998), p. 293; Rosecrans would verbally war with other Yankee officers besides those of the navy, including his superior, Maj. Gen. Halleck, and Quartermaster General Montgomery Meigs. His exchanges are detailed by Alethea D. Sayers in her essay, "The Paper War Between Rosecrans & Halleck," *Civil War Web* http://civilwarweb.com/articles/12-99/paperwar.htm (accessed June 6, 2005). See also Curt Anders, *Henry Halleck's War: A Fresh Look at Lincoln's Controversial General-in-Chief* (Indianapolis: Guild Press of Indiana, 1999), pp. 396–398.

4. Nashville *Daily Union*, January 11, 1863; Evansville *Daily Journal*, January 13–14, 17, 1863; Gibson, *Dictionary of Transports and Combat Vessels*, p. 228; Milford M. Miller, "Evansville Steamboats During the Civil War," *Indiana Magazine of History* 37 (December 1941): 375.

5. OR, 1, 20, 1: 980–984; OR, 1, 20, 2: 322–323, 326, 328; *Nashville Dispatch*, January 14, 17, 1863; Nashville *Daily Union*, January 14, 1863; ORN, 1, 24: 15, 19. On January 14, one of the *Sidell's* gunners made it back to Nashville where he reported that the disaster to his craft had been caused by the pilot leaving his wheel. Lt. Van Dorn was taken prisoner and the rest of the men were paroled.

6. OR, 1, 20, 2: 332, 338–339; ORN, 1, 24: 9–10; Scott K. Williams, http://missouricivilwarmuseum.org/lironclads.htm; Nashville *Daily Union*, January 20, 1863; Evansville *Daily Journal*, January 23–24, 1863; Kenneth W. Noe, ed., *A Southern Boy in Blue: The Memoir of Marcus Woodcock, 9th Kentucky Infantry (U.S.A.)* (Knoxville, TN: University of Tennessee Press, 1996), p. 143; the Meigs-Rosecrans exchange on armed transports is reviewed in David W. Miller's *Second Only to Grant: Quartermaster General Montgomery C. Meigs* (Shippensburg, PA: White Mane Books, 2000), pp. 182–183; Benjamin Franklin Cooling, *Fort Donelson's Legacy: War and Society in Kentucky and Tennessee, 1862-1863* (Knoxville, TN: University of Tennessee Press, 1997), p. 190; Howard Papers, January 20, 1863. The 19th of January was an important, if little appreciated, day in the annals of the Middle Tennessee conflict. That day, the *New York Tribune* reported that Lt. Gen. Longstreet had arrived at Shelbyville, Tennessee, with 13 brigades and had succeeded Bragg as Army of the Tennessee commander. This "confirmation" by a respected Yankee newspaper of a series of rumors circulating since the beginning of the year caused Maj. Gen. Halleck to order Maj. Gen. Wright to concentrate 32,000 troops for the defense of key points in Kentucky, Indiana, and Ohio, and to send a three-division corps under Maj. Gen. Gordon Granger to reinforce Rosecrans. Preparations to hire the 55 steamboats necessary for transport and worries over the safe arrival of the 12,000 battle-untested men would occupy Union military leadership and quartermasters for the rest of the month. Claire E. Swedberg, ed., *Three Years with the 92nd Illinois: The Civil War Diary of John M. King* (Mechanicsburg, PA: Stackpole Books, 1999), 64–74. Robert Allen, who will reappear in this chronicle, was born in Ohio in 1815 and had a distinguished Mexican War resume. In November 1863, he became chief quartermaster for the Mississippi Valley, with Louisville headquarters, a position he held until 1866. Promoted to brigadier general in 1864, he was chief quartermaster of the Pacific from 1866 until his 1878 retirement. He died at Geneva, Switzerland, on August 6, 1886. "Robert Allen," in Vol. I of James Grant Wilson and John Fiske, eds. *Appleton's Cyclopaedia of American Biography* (New York: D. Appleton, 1888), p. 55.

7. OR, 1, 20, 2: 341; Walter T. Durham, *Nashville: The Occupied City—The First Seventeen Months, February 16, 1862-June 30, 1863* (Nashville: Tennessee Historical Society, 1985), p. 219. One of those created an acting volunteer lieutenant the previous October 1 Charles Perkins would resign on March 25, 1865. Callahan, *List of Officers of the Navy of the United States and of the Marine Corps*, p. 430; Howard Papers, January 20, 1863.

8. ORN, 1, 23: 312; ORN, 1, 24: 10–12.

9. ORN, 1, 24: 12–13. In a January 24 follow-up letter to his January 23 telegram, Secretary Welles let Capt. Pennock know in no uncertain terms that "the Department" was not pleased with the way in which the station chief had recently handled relations with the prickly Murfreesboro-based army leadership. "It is expected," Pennock was reminded, that every service possible be extended to military colleagues and, "in an emergency such as that now on the Cumberland and Tennessee rivers, that every exertion will be made to meet it." The hard-pressed Pennock, disappointed with the reprimand but who, nevertheless, carboned his immediate superior with that and all correspondence, would be buoyed a week later by a letter from David Porter. The rear admiral, more knowledgeable of the local scene than the Washington establishment, expressed his complete confidence in his subordinate's ability to "always do what is right." Besides, Porter added, he hoped that Pennock would "take every opportunity to write these army officials and inform them" that the Cairo office did not have information to disseminate concerning squadron activities, that "General Halleck has no control here," and that he [Porter], and nobody else in country, disposed of western navy assets. ORN, 1, 24: 13–14, 18.

10. ORN, 1, 24: 14–15, 192, 472; ORN, 2, 1: 209, 213; "*Silver Lake*" [and] "*Springfield*," in Vol. 6 of *Dictionary of American Naval Fighting Ships* (Washington, DC: GPO, 1976), p. 507, 589–590; Jay Slagle, *Ironclad Captain: Seth Ledyard Phelps and the U.S. Navy* (Kent, OH: Kent State University Press, 1996), p. 322. No sooner had the *Silver Lake* arrived in the Cumberland River, and before she could join Lt. Cmdr. Fitch, than her "doctor" engine broke down, requiring her return to Smithland. Fleet Captain Pennock in Cairo immediately ordered its repair. ORN, 1, 24: 200. Acting Volunteer Lieutenant Riley resigned on February 16, 1863. Acting Volunteer Lieutenant Henry Glassford, on the other hand, would become one of Fitch's most trusted subordinates and would remain with him for much of the war. He was discharged on November 29, 1865. Callahan, *List of Officers of the Navy of the United States and of the Marine Corps*, pp. 220, 463.

Notes—Chapter Seven

11. Rod Paschall, "Tactical Exercises—Mission: Protection," *MHQ: The Quarterly Journal of Military History* 4 (Spring 1992): 56–58; ORN, 1, 24: 24, 38–39, 61, 66; OR, 1, 23, 2: 32; Howard Papers, April 6, 1863; Swedberg, *Three Years with the 92nd Illinois*, p. 64–74.

12. ORN, 1, 23: 312; ORN, 1, 24: 15–17, 19, 21–22; Thomas Jordan and J. P. Pryor, *The Campaigns of Lieut. Gen. N. B. Forrest and of Forrest's Cavalry* (New Orleans and New York: Blelock, 1868), p. 224; Slagle, *Ironclad Captain*, p. 322. Rear Adm. Porter had also anticipated, given the flurry of communications between Washington, Murfreesboro, and Cairo, the need for additional gunboats on the upper rivers. On January 28, he wrote Pennock from the Yazoo River authorizing his retention of the *Lexington* and two light-draft gunboats then at Cairo. "If the army officers would only notify us when they want a convoy, there would be no trouble," he lamented. Next day, 200 replacement sailors arrived at Cairo from New York City per the earlier promise of Navy secretary Welles; all were ordered to crew the ironclads, with none left over for any of the hard-pressed light draughts. ORN, 1, 24: 18, 216.

13. ORN, 1, 24: 20, 31. According to Eugene Canfield's naval ordnance history pamphlet, 32-pounders available to the U.S. Navy during the Civil War were constructed in 27, 32, 42, 46, 51, and 57 hundredweight sizes, a scale under which a hundredweight was 112 pounds. Ordnance men of the time like Fitch and later historians of naval cannon such as Canfield understood the differences: for each degree upward in hundredweight, there was a slight difference in the weight of the gun tube and the length of bore. A 32-pounder of 27-hundredweight had a 3,000-pound gun tube, a 68.4" bore, and could throw its 32-pound shot 1,469 yards at five degrees of elevation. The tube of a 33-hundredweight weighed in at 3,600 pounds and had a 75.1" bore; its 32-pound shot could fly 1,598 yards. Still, to the men in the gun crews, one 32-pounder on its four-wheel common carriage must have appeared much like another. Eugene B. Canfield, *Civil War Naval Ordnance* (Washington, DC: GPO, 1969), pp. 5, 20.

14. OR, 1, 20, 2: 342; OR, 1, 23, 2: 38–39; ORN, 1, 24: 20–24; Swedberg, *Three Years with the 92nd Illinois*, pp. 40–42. Although Fitch had the *Lexington*, he exercised his right to maintain his command chair and writing desk on the *Fairplay*. In working the convoys, he would put the big timberclad, under command of Acting Volunteer Master James Marshall, in the lead and himself occupy a shepherding position with the smaller side-wheeler farther back.

15. OR, 1, 23, 1: 40; Jordan and Pryor, *Campaigns of Lieut. Gen. N. B. Forrest*, pp. 225–227; Thomas B. Van Horne, *History of the Army of the Cumberlands*, Vol. 1 (Wilmington, NC: Broadfoot, 1988), 289; John Allan Wyeth, *Life of General Nathan Bedford Forrest* (New York: Harper & Bros., 1904), p. 146; Benjamin Franklin Cooling, "The Battle of Dover, February 3, 1863, *Tennessee Historical Quarterly* 22 (June 1963): 143–144; Cooling, *Fort Donelson's Legacy*, pp. 192–196; Terry Wilson, "'Against Such Powerful Odds': The 83rd Illinois Infantry at the Battle of Dover, Tennessee, February 1863," *Tennessee Historical Quarterly* 53 (December 1994): 261–264; John E. Fisher, *They Rode with Forrest and Wheeler: A Chronicle of Five Tennessee Brothers' Service in the Confederate Western Cavalry* (Jefferson, NC: McFarland, 1995), p. 29. Acting Volunteer Master Marshall would go on to command the U.S.S. *New Era* and was involved in the April 1864 defense of Fort Pillow against forces led by Maj. Gen. Nathan B. Forrest. He resigned from the service on September 14 of that year. Callahan, *List of Officers of the Navy of the United States and of the Marine Corps*, p. 352.

16. Cooling, "Battle of Dover," p. 145; Cooling, *Legacy*, p. 195; Wilson, "'Against Such Powerful Odds,'" 265; OR, 1, 23, 1:34.

17. OR, 1, 23, 1: 32–41; OR, 1, 23, 2: 41–42; ORN, 1, 24: 15; Robert Selph Henry, *"First with the Most" Forrest* (Indianapolis: Bobbs-Merrill, 1944), p. 123; Miller, "Evansville Steamboats During the Civil War," 375; Swedberg, *Three Years with the 92nd Illinois*, p 46–47. Cooling, "Battle of Dover," 147; Cooling, *Legacy*, pp. 196–199; Jordan and Pryor, *Campaigns of Lieut. Gen. N. B. Forrest*, pp. 228–229; Wyeth, *Life of General Nathan Bedford Forrest*, pp. 147–150; Van Horne, 1, 289–290; Wilson, "'Against Such Powerful Odds,'" pp. 266–268; Nashville *Daily Union*, February 4, 1863. A messenger reached Col. Lowe at Fort Henry about 3 p.m. and within two hours, a relief column from the garrison at Fort Heiman, on the west bank of the Tennessee River, had been ferried over and dispatched toward Dover. Led by Col. William P. Lyon of the 13th Wisconsin Infantry, it comprised units from that regiment, the 71st Ohio Infantry, and four companies from the 5th Iowa Cavalry. Cooling, "Battle of Dover," p. 149.

18. OR, 1, 23, 1: 146–147; OR, 1, 23, 2: 31–45; ORN, 1, 23: 313–314; ORN, 1, 24: 25–27, 30; Nashville *Daily Union*, February 4–6, 1863; Cooling, "Battle of Dover," p. 150; Cooling, *Legacy of Fort Donelson*, pp. 202–204; Wilson, "'Against Such Powerful Odds,'" p. 268; Richard P. Gildrie, "Guerrilla Warfare in the Lower Cumberland River Valley, 1862–1865," *Tennessee Historical Quarterly* 49 (Fall 1990): 168; Wyeth, *Life of General Nathan Bedford Forrest*, pp. 154, 161; Jordan and Pryor, *Campaigns of Lieut. Gen. N. B. Forrest*, pp. 229–230; Swedberg, *Three Years with the 92nd Illinois*, pp. 47–52; Howard Papers, February 5, 1863; Alfred T. Mahan, *The Gulf and Inland Waters*. Vol. 3 of the *Navy in the Civil War* (New York: Scribner's, 1883), p. 181; Henry M. Cist, *Army of the Cumberland*, Campaigns of the Civil War (New York: Charles Scribner's Sons, 1892), p. 141; Mary Bess McCain Henderson, Evelyn Janet McCain Young, and Anna Irene McCain Naheloffer, *"Dear Eliza": The Letters of Michel Andrew Thompson* (Ames, IA: Carter Press, 1976), p. 23; Byrd Douglas, *Steamboatin' on the Cumberland* (Nashville: Tennessee Book, 1961), pp. 139–140; Mackey, *The Uncivil War*, p. 171.

19. ORN, 1, 23: 314–315; ORN, 1, 24: 30–46, 57–58, 318; OR, 1, 23, 1: 152–160, 215–239, 359–362; Robert G. Hartje, *Van Dorn: The Life and Times of a Confederate General* (Nashville: Vanderbilt University Press, 1967), p. 274; Howard Papers, January 20, February 18, 20, 24, 1863; Samuel B. Barron, *The Lone Star Defenders: A Chronicle of the Third Texas Cavalry, Ross' Brigade* (New York and Washington, DC: Neale, 1908), p. 144–145; Jordan and Pryor, *Campaigns of Lieut. Gen. N. B. Forrest*, pp. 246–248; William R. Morris, "The Burning of Clifton," *Wayne County Historian* 2 (June 1989), reprinted on the Civil War Page http://www.netease.net/wayne/burningclifton.htm (accessed March 3, 2004); "Dunbar," in U.S. Navy Department, Naval History Division, *Civil War Naval Chronology, 1861–1865*, Vol. 6 (Washington, DC: GPO, 1962-1966), 223; Ben Earl Kitchens, *Gunboats and Cavalry: A History of Eastport, Mississippi, with Special Emphasis on Events of the War Between the States* (Florence, AL: Thornwood, 1985), p.103; Woodward, *Grant's Lieutenants*, pp. 183–198. The two young men taken prisoner in Clifton who were desirous of joining the gunboat service were personally given the oath of allegiance by Le Roy Fitch at Paducah on February 25; one was assigned to the *Lexington* and the other to the *Fairplay*. ORN, 1, 24: 46.

20. ORN, 1, 24: 47; Howard Papers, March 1, 1863.

21. ORN, 1, 24: 43, 48; Cooling, *Fort Donelson's Legacy*, p. 224; Durham, *Nashville: The Occupied City*, p. 221.

22. ORN, 1, 24: 48–50, 58.

23. ORN, 1, 24: 50, 53–54, 463–464, 472; Cooling,

Fort Donelson's Legacy, pp. 216–217. To grow the fleet needed in the Cumberland and for the Tennessee River enterprise, Pennock sent the Springfield back from Illinois to Smithland. The tinclad, which had been employed at the Cairo station for most of the last month, had probably conveyed the fleet captain to his meeting with Fitch. The Hoosier officer was also authorized to engage a sufficient number of Cumberland and Tennessee River pilots.

24. ORN, 1, 24: 51–52, 472; OR, 1, 23, 2: 136. Designed by Joseph Brown at Cincinnati, the 915-ton Tuscumbia had been launched on December 12, 1862. Brown, who would complete a large number of U.S. Navy contacts during the war, including some for the conversion of tinclads, assembled a vessel with 6-inch casemated sides that was 178 feet long, with a beam of 75 feet and a seven-foot depth of hold. The side-wheeler had four engines and six boilers and, most importantly, was armed with three 11-inch smoothbore cannon forward and two 9-inch smoothbores aft. Paul H. Silverstone, Warships of the Civil War Navies (Annapolis, MD: Naval Institute Press, 1989), p. 155. Born in Pennsylvania on July 16, 1832, the Tuscumbia's commander had skippered the U.S.S. Lexington the previous year and had been up the White River with Graham Newell Fitch that June. He was commissioned a commander on July 25, 1866, and died on February 10, 1873. Callahan, List of Officers of the Navy of the United States and of the Marine Corps, p. 495. Lewis Baldwin Parsons, son of the founder of Parsons College in Iowa, was born in New York state on April 5, 1818. A lawyer by profession, he relocated to Illinois where he practiced law and, in 1853, became president of the Ohio and Mississippi Railroad. From a staff assignment with Maj. Gen. Halleck in 1862 to handle rail and river transportation, Parson's brief by 1864 would include responsibility for all Army rail and water transportation west of the Alleghenies. That coverage would be extended to the entire country a year later. Breveted both brigadier general and major general for service, he returned to the railroad business after the war and died in Illinois on March 16, 1907. "Louis B. Parsons," in Vol. 4 of James Grant Wilson and John Fiske, eds., Appleton's Cyclopaedia of American Biography (New York: D. Appleton, 1888), p. 664; Charles Dana Gibson, with E. Kay Gibson, "Lewis B. Parsons, Union Quartermaster and the System Set in Place on the Western Rivers, 1861–1866," in their Assault and Logistics, Vol. 2: Union Army Coastal and River Operations, 1861–1866 (Camden, ME: Ensign Press, 1995), pp. 535–554.

25. ORN, 1, 24: 53–56, 58–60, 318; Howard Papers, March 21, 1863; Cooling, Fort Donelson's Legacy, pp. 216–217. While Fitch had been up the Tennessee, the U.S. Army had outfitted its own gunboat for supplemental support of its forces at Carthage. On March 17, the Orient convoyed up three steamers from Nashville with 320 tons of rations. Skirmishes were fought with guerrillas all the way up and back, but the four boats, all uninjured, returned to Nashville on March 23. A second four-day round trip was undertaken on March 24, with guerrillas pouring particularly heavy rifle fire into the boats in the 10-mile stretch leading into Rome. Again, no damages were recorded. OR, 1, 23, 2: 162, 172.

26. ORN, 1, 23: 315–316; ORN, 1, 24: 60–65, 71, 472–473; OR, 1, 23, 2: 200; Cooling, Fort Donelson's Legacy, pp. 226–227. As we have noted earlier, most of the territory bordering the Cumberland and Tennessee Rivers was not friendly to the Union; consequently, it would have been possible to uncover many farmers and others aiding the Southern cause. Acting Volunteer Lieutenant Dunn would succeed Lt. Cmdr. Fitch as skipper of the Lexington, but resigned from the service on August 3, 1863. Callahan, List of Officers of the Navy of the United States and of the Marine Corps, p. 174.

27. Lamers, The Edge of Glory, p. 257; Durham, Nashville: The Occupied City, pp. 221–222; ORN, 1, 24: 66–71; Howard Papers, April 4–6, 1863; Cooling, Fort Donelson's Legacy, pp. 226–227. At the time of his return to Smithland, Fitch still had eight prisoners, 23 horses and mules, two wagons, and cotton aboard the Lexington. Capt. Pennock authorized him to keep the animals and wagons if he needed them, send them to Cairo along with the cotton, or dispose of them as he thought proper. The prisoners were sent to the Smithland provost marshal. Fitch kept some of the cotton to protect the boilers of his warships. Fitch temporarily held onto the livestock and wagons. ORN, 1, 24: 73–74; ORN, 1, 25: 151. Fouty's leg was amputated, but he died at the Fort Donelson hospital on April 10. Callahan, List of Officers of the Navy of the United States and of the Marine Corps, p. 202.

28. ORN, 1, 24: 74–75. "Argosy," in Vol. 1 of Dictionary of American Naval Fighting Ships, rev. ed. (Washington, DC: GPO, 1991), p. 367 (cited hereafter as DANFS); "Covington," in Vol. 2 of DANFS (Washington, DC: GPO, 1969), p. 197; "Queen City" in Vol. 5 of DANFS (Washington, DC: GPO, 1970), p. 411; Silverstone, Warships, pp. 166–169. Griswold would shortly be given command of the new Emma Duncan or Hastings; he would be honorably discharged on September 18, 1865. Callahan, List of Officers of the Navy of the United States and of the Marine Corps, p. 234.

29. ORN, 1, 23: 317; Cooling, Fort Donelson's Legacy, pp. 227–228; Howard Papers, April 4–5, 1863. Fitzpatrick would go on to command the U.S.S. Chickasaw and Signal and would be honorably discharged on December 30, 1865. Callahan, List of Officers of the Navy of the United States and of the Marine Corps, p. 196.

30. ORN, 1, 23: 317; ORN, 1, 24: 71–72, 75, 78; OR, 1, 23, 1, 333, 346–347; OR, 1, 23, 2: 212, 219, 240, 253; Cooling, Fort Donelson's Legacy, pp. 227–228; Howard Papers, April 5–6, 1863; Gildrie, "Guerrilla Warfare in the Lower Cumberland River Valley, 1862–1865," pp. 168–169. Back at Smithland on April 6, Fitch wrote out a full report of the Palmyra incident for Rear Adm. Porter. He concluded it with the observation that contingency plans made earlier for the concentration of his entire upper fleet at any one point during an emergency had worked in this case. It was hoped they would be equally as successful should the need arise in the future. On April 8, Capt. Pennock bundled up all of Cairo's telegrams relative to the Palmyra episode and forwarded them down to Porter; four days later, Porter reshipped them Secretary Welles in Washington. ORN, 1, 24: 72–73, 78.

31. ORN, 1, 24: 66, 77; Howard Papers, April 10, 1863.

32. OR, 1, 23, 2: 240. There is no further mention of the Excelsior in the OR; however, at least three army gunboats were active on the Cumberland during the year and she may have been one of them.

33. OR, 1, 23, 1: 281–294; Wyeth, Life of General Nathan Bedford Forrest, pp. 185–187; Gibson, Assault and Logistics, p. 304; Cooling, Fort Donelson's Legacy, p. 251; Lamers, The Edge of Glory, p. 257; David Stanley, Personal Memoirs of Major-General D.S. Stanley, U.S.A. (Cambridge, MA: Harvard University Press, 1917), pp. 131–132; Kitchens, Gunboats and Cavalry, p. 105. The most complete single-volume history of the Streight raid is Robert R. Willett, Jr., The Lightning Mule Brigade: Abel Streight's 1863 Raid into Alabama (Carmel, IN: Guild Press of Indiana, 1999). Also at this time, a highly successful Union cavalry raid through Mississippi was planned and undertaken by the Michigan schoolmaster Col. Benjamin H. Grierson; the strike, as celebrated as Streight's was ridiculed, was the inspiration

for the 1959 John Wayne motion picture *The Horse Soldiers*. Another Yankee gambit, the equally inspired Andrews raid, was a tragic-ending covert raid; it too got a movie, Fess Parker's 1956 *The Great Locomotive Chase*.

34. ORN, 1, 24: 76–77, 79–80, 522–523; OR, 1, 23, 2: 232, 251, 254–255, 264; Wyeth, *Life of General Nathan Bedford Forrest*, p. 188–190; Grenville M. Dodge, *The Battle of Atlanta and Other Campaigns, Addresses, Etc.* (Council Bluffs, IA: Monarch, 1911; reprint, Denver: Sage Books, 1965), pp. 113–117; Chester G. Hearn, *Ellet's Brigade: The Strangest Outfit of All* (Baton Rouge: Louisiana State University Press, 2000), pp.154–156; Cooling, *Fort Donelson's Legacy*, p. 252; Kitchens, *Gunboats and Cavalry*, pp. 105–107. Upon the army commanders' departure inland, Fitch, in his role in the plan, would be left in charge of the transport fleet off Eastport. It would be his decision as to when the water might compel its transfer downstream. ORN, 1, 23: 286.

35. OR, 1, 24, 3, 246–261; Wyeth, *Life of General Nathan Bedford Forrest*, pp. 190–222; Cooling, *Fort Donelson's Legacy*, p. 253; ORN, 1, 24: 87; Stanley, *Personal Memoirs*, pp. 131–132; Jordan and Pryor, *Campaigns of Lieut. Gen. N. B. Forrest*, pp. 278–279; Dodge, *Battle of Atlanta*, pp. 118–119; Kitchens, *Gunboats and Cavalry*, pp. 107–108. Streight's report is found in OR, 1, 23, 1: 281–294, while Forrest's account is in the same volume, pp. 120–121. Dodge, who reprinted both his official report and Streight's in his 1911 book, meanwhile, fell back after taking Tuscumbia Landing and Florence on April 29–30, believing his part of the expedition a success. Also on May 3, Grierson's raiders, pursued but not by the likes of Forrest, made it safely to Union lines at Baton Rouge.

36. ORN, 2, 1: 100; Silverstone, *Warships*, p. 107; "Hastings," in Vol. 3 of *Dictionary of American Naval Fighting Ships* (Washington, DC: GPO, 1968), p. 269; Gibson, *Assault and Logistics*, p. 231; Hiram H. Martin, "Service Afield and Afloat: A Reminiscence of the Civil War Edited by Guy R. Everson," *Indiana Magazine of History* 89 (March 1993): 44. King would remain on the Tennessee River and be caught in command at Johnsonville, Tennessee, when the supply depot there was burned to prevent its capture by Forrest late in 1864. Though court-martialed, he was honorably discharged on July 18, 1867. Callahan, *List of Officers of the Navy of the United States and of the Marine Corps*, p. 314.

37. OR, 23, 1, 1: 278–280; ORN, 1, 24: 86–88, 90–91; Hearn, *Ellet's Brigade*, pp. 156–159; Martin, "Service Afield and Afloat," pp. 45–47; Warren D. Crandall and Isaac D. Newell, *History of the Ram Fleet and Mississippi Marine Brigade* (St. Louis: Buschart Brothers, 1907), pp. 277–281. The three men wounded on the *Emma Duncan* on April 24 were later sent to the naval hospital at Memphis. ORN, 1, 24: 636. Fitch's role in support of MMB craft at Duck River Shoals was not acknowledged by Brig. Gen. Ellet in his reports to either Secretary Stanton or Admiral Porter. The Ellets, as Rear Adm. Davis and Col. Graham Newell Fitch had learned at Memphis the year before, always liked to claim any credit for themselves alone.

38. ORN, 1, 24: 85–88; Dodge, *Battle of Atlanta*, pp. 118–119.

39. Cooling, *Fort Donelson's Legacy*, pp. 258–264; Slagle, *Ironclad Captain*, pp. 329–330; ORN, 1, 24: 658. On May 17, Pennock asked Porter to make Phelps' assignment to the Tennessee permanent. The fleet captain's housemate would remain headquartered at Paducah until December. ORN, 1, 24: 679.

Chapter Eight

1. Jay Slagle, *Ironclad Captain: Seth Ledyard Phelps and the U.S. Navy* (Kent, OH: Kent State University Press, 1996), pp. 329–330; Lester V. Horwitz, *The Longest Raid of the War: Little Known and Untold Stories of Morgan's Raid Into Kentucky, Indiana, and Ohio* (Cincinnati: Farmcourt, 1999), p. 2; Charles R. Rector, "Morgan Goes A-Raiding and Views West Virginia: A Bit of Civil War History," *West Virginia Review* 6 (May 1929): 310; U.S. Navy Department, *Official Records of the Union and Confederate Navies in the War of the Rebellion* (Washington, DC: GPO, 1894–1922), Series 1, Vol. 24, 472–473, 656, 674, (cited hereafter as ORN, followed by a comma, the series number, a comma, the volume number, a colon, and the page number); William H. Howard to wife, May 6, 10, 1863, William H. Howard Papers, University of Tennessee Library, Knoxville (cited hereafter as Howard Papers, with date); Basil W. Duke, *A History of Morgan's Cavalry* (Bloomington: Indiana University Press, 1960), pp. 410–411; Basil W. Duke, "The Raid," *The Century Magazine* 41 (January 1891): 404; Cecil Fletcher Holland, *Morgan and His Raiders: A Biography of the Confederate General* (New York: Macmillan, 1942), p. 217; Myron J. Smith, Jr., "Gunboats at Buffington: The U.S. Navy and Morgan's Raid, 1863," *West Virginia History* 44 (Winter 1983): 98–99. On April 17, Fleet Captain Alexander M. Pennock, the Cairo station chief, informed Admiral Porter that Navy Secretary Gideon Welles had ordered the purchase of three more light draft gunboats for the protection of the Upper Ohio, Kanawha, and Big Sandy Rivers because affairs were very unsettled in that area. The fleet captain recommended that the region become a fleet division and that "an officer of energy and discretion should be placed in command." ORN, 1, 24: 680.

2. ORN, 1, 24: 672; ORN, 1, 25: 124, 377; Richard E. Beringer, Herman Hattaway, Archer Jones, and William N. Still, Jr., *Why the South Lost the Civil War* (Athens: University of Georgia Press, 1986), pp. 191–192.

3. ORN, 1, 25: 132, 139, 141, 145, 160; OR, 1, 23, 2: 162–164, 339–340; Benjamin Franklin Cooling, *Fort Donelson's Legacy: War and Society in Kentucky and Tennessee, 1862-1863* (Knoxville, TN: University of Tennessee Press, 1997), pp. 258–260; Walter T. Durham, *Nashville: The Occupied City—The First Seventeen Months, February 16, 1862-June 30, 1863* (Nashville: Tennessee Historical Society, 1985), 280–281. When Fitch departed for Cairo, he left the *Fairplay* in the capable hands of its executive officer, Acting Volunteer Master George J. Groves. Groves would command the side-wheeler through the remainder of the war and would be honorably discharged on December 11, 1865. Edward W. Callahan, *List of Officers of the Navy of the United States and of the Marine Corps, from 1775 to 1900, Comprising a Complete Register of All Present and Former Commissioned, Warranted, and Appointed Officers of the United States Navy, and of the Marine Corps, Regular and Volunteer. Compiled from the Official Records of the Navy Department* (New York: L.R. Hamersly, 1901; reprint, New York: Haskell House, 1969), p. 235.

4. ORN, 1, 25: 159–160. Hoping to regain the South's initiative in the war, Robert E. Lee's Army of Northern Virginia began a move toward Pennsylvania on June 3 that would end a month later at a little town called Gettysburg. The outcome of the titanic battle fought there, together with the fall of Vicksburg to Maj. Gen. Grant and Rear Adm. Porter, would completely overshadow the romantic Morgan's skirmish in which Fitch was about to become involved. James A. Ramage, *Rebel Raider: The Life of General John Hunt Morgan* (Lexington, KY: University Press of Kentucky, 1986), p. 158; Smith, "Gunboats at Buffington": 98–99.

5. OR, 1, 23, 1: 397; Lowell H. Harrison, *The Civil War in Kentucky* (Lexington, KY: University Press of Kentucky, 1975), pp. 67–68; Horwitz, *The Longest Raid of the War*, pp. 19–21, 43–44; James D. Horan, *Confederate Agent: A Discovery in History* (New York: Crown, 1954), pp. 25–26.

6. ORN, 1, 24: 575. 672–673; ORN, 1, 25: ORN, 2, 1: 156; "*Naumkeag*," in Vol. 5 of *Dictionary of American Naval Fighting Ships* (Washington, DC: GPO, 1970), pp. 24–25; Paul H. Silverstone, *Warships of the Civil War Navies* (Annapolis, MD: Naval Institute Press, 1989), p. 175. There was later some speculation that Morgan's raid was tied to some kind of attempt to rally northern political ("Copperhead") opposition against the war, but this idea is now largely discounted. Ramage, *Rebel Raider*, p. 173. Hines and the remnant of his band captured a passenger train on the Louisville and Lexington Railroad near Christiansburg, Kentucky, at the end of the month. His entire effort was viewed by one historian as simply a "prelude" to Morgan's memorable strike. Cooling, *Fort Donelson's Legacy*, p. 281.

7. Robert R. Mackey, *The Uncivil War: Irregular Warfare in the Upper South, 1861–1865* (Norman: University of Oklahoma Press, 2004), pp. 180–181; OR, 1, 23, 1: 384–393; James Bennett McCreary, "Journal of My Soldier Life," *Register of the Kentucky State Historical Society* 33 (July 1935): 197. Madison County native McCreary became Kentucky governor in 1875. Ramage, *Rebel Raider*, p. 253.

8. ORN, 1, 25: 168, 174; ORN, 2, 1: 151; "Moose," in Vol. 4 of *Dictionary of American Naval Fighting Ships* (Washington, DC: GPO, 1969), p. 434; Silverstone, *Warships*, p. 174; Horwitz, *The Longest Raid of the War*, pp. 3–4, 11; Robert E. Rogge, "Crossing the Line: Bragg vs. Morgan." *Civil War* 11 (March-April 1993): 16–22; Mackey, *The Uncivil War*, p. 32; Ramage, *Rebel Raider*, pp. 159–160; Holland, *Morgan and His Raiders*, pp. 220–223; Duke, *A History of Morgan's Cavalry*, pp. 410–411; Smith, "Gunboats at Buffington": 97, 99; Jean Backs, "Morgan's Raid," *Explore Magazine* (Spring 2001), Ohio Department of Natural Resources Home Page http://www.dnr.state.oh.us/parks/explore/magazine/spsu2001/morgan.htm, (November 14, 2005). No widely known photographs of the tinclad *Moose* exist. So far as this author knows, it has, without his personal verification, been pictured in only one source. Shown as a carte de visite with no backmark and courtesy Marc McLemore, an image of No. 34 was exhibited at the 1999 Mason-Dixon Civil War Collectors show at Gettysburg in 1999 and was reproduced as one of several from that show in a review, "Great Guns: Top Images at the 1999 Gettysburg Show," *Military Images* 19 (November-December, 1999): 13. The process of "walking the boat" is described in Louis C. Hunter, *Steamboats on the Western Waters: An Economic and Technological History* (Cambridge, MA: Harvard University Press, 1949), p. 254, and by Michael Marleau in the "Steamboats.Org Glossary," *Steamboats.Org Homepage*, http://www.steamboats.org/cgi-bin/glossary/guru_glossary.cgi?word=walking_the_boat (accessed December 7, 2005). Morgan was not unaware of three other potential danger points earlier in his raid: getting over both the Cumberland and Ohio and circuiting around Cincinnati. Rector, "Morgan Goes A-Raiding": 310.

9. Logbooks of the U.S.S. *Moose*, June 15, 1863–August 10, 1865, Records of the Bureau of Navigation, Record Group 19, U.S. National Archives, Washington, D.C., June 15, 1863 (cited hereafter as Logbook of the U.S.S. *Moose*, with date). Medico Thorp, recruited on May 15, was honorably discharged on November 1, 1865; Mate Spooner was named an acting ensign on February 12, 1864, and resigned on March 22, 1865, and Engineer McMillan resigned on June 5, 1865. Acting Volunteer Master Rice, who had held his rank since the previous December 30 would rise to command the tinclad *Brilliant* and was honorably discharged on October 26, 1865; Acting Volunteer Ensign Ravell, who had the misfortune to have his named spelled Revell in the Navy's register, had been a mate on the *Fairplay* when promoted on May 8. Resigning for health reasons on February 17, 1865, he is the only member of the *Moose's* crew besides Fitch to be profiled in print. Callahan, *List of Officers of the Navy of the United States and of the Marine Corps*, pp. 544, 514, 372, 460, 458; Mike Fitzpatrick, "Miasma Fogs and River Mists," *Military Images* 25 (January-February 2004): 25–29.

10. Mackey, *The Uncivil War*, p. 278; Dee Alexander Brown, *The Bold Cavaliers: Morgan's 2nd Kentucky Cavalry Raiders* (New York: J. B. Lippincott, 1959), p. 179; John Weatherred, "Wartime Diary of John Weatherred, Bennett's Regiment or 9th Tennessee Cavalry, John Hunt Morgan's Command," edited by Jack Masters, *The Wartime Diary of John Weatherred* http://www.jackmasters.net/we1863.html (accessed April 11, 2005).

11. ORN, 1, 25: 187; Ramage, *Rebel Raider*, p. 167; Michael R. Bradley, *Tullahoma: The 1863 Campaign for the Control of Middle Tennessee* (Shippensburg, PA: Burd Street, 2000), p. 85; Larry J. Daniel, *Days of Glory: The Army of the Cumberland, 1861–1865* (Baton Rouge: Louisiana State University Press, 2004), pp. 265–275; Mackey, *The Uncivil War*, pp. 181–183, 250–251; Horwitz, *The Longest Raid of the War*, pp. 19–20, 44–45; Horan, *Confederate Agent*, pp. 26–28; Ramage, *Rebel Raider*, pp. 162–163; McCreary, "Journal of My Soldier Life," p. 196–197. Maj. Gen. Burnside reported the outcome of the Hines mission in OR, 1, 23, 1: 397–398. The Army Official Records (OR), Vol. 23, Part 1, provide reports on the Tullahoma campaign, which, like Lee's Pennsylvania expedition and its thousands of histories, is really outside the scope of this story, except marginally with regard to logistical aspects or hoped-for scenarios at the conclusion of Morgan's Ohio raid. Gen. Bragg was deprived of two-thirds of his cavalry leadership during his southern withdrawal. Maj. Gen. Forrest was recovering from a personal encounter with another officer, while Morgan had stepped off, headed north. Bragg had expected the latter to withdraw and join him after creating a diversion in Kentucky. N. I. Klonis, *Guerrilla Warfare: Analysis and Projections* (New York: Robert Speller and Sons, 1972), p. 23.

12. ORN, 1, 24: 223–224; U.S. War Department, *The War of the Rebellion: A Compilation of the Official Records of the Union and Confederate Armies* (Washington, DC: GPO, 1880–1901), Series 1, Vol. 23, Pt. 1: 645–647 (cited hereafter as OR, followed by a comma, the series number, a comma, the volume number, a colon, and the page number); Harrison, *The Civil War in Kentucky*, pp. 66–67; Weatherred, "Wartime Diary of John Weatherred"; Alan Keller, *Morgan's Raid* (New York: Bobbs-Merrill, 1961), p. 26; McCreary, p. 196–197; Logbooks of the U.S.S. *Moose*, July 2, 1863. The *Brilliant* and *St. Clair* were, indeed, up the Cumberland on a Nashville convoy during Morgan's time in Indiana and Ohio and consequently played no role in "one of the strangest blockades in naval history." Though Fitch would doubtless have usefully employed their support, this writer would even more dearly have liked to one day been able to read the campaign comments of the *Brilliant's* letter-writing medical man, William Howard, who was then dreaming of a way off the tinclad. Smith, "Gunboats at Buffington": 99; Howard Papers, July 19, 1863.

13. Keller, *Morgan's Raid*, pp. 47, 56, 76–77, 79–80; OR, 1, 23, 1: 634; ORN, 1, 25: 242; ORN, 2, 1: 190, 232; "Reindeer," in Vol. 6 of *Dictionary of American Naval Fighting Ships* (Washington, DC: GPO, 1976), p. 65; "*Victory*," in Vol. 6 of DANFS (Washington, DC: GPO, 1981), p. 512; Holland, *Morgan and His Raiders*, pp. 230–231; Smith,

"Gunboats at Buffington": 99; Backs, Ibid.; Duke, "The Raid": 408; Horwitz, The Longest Raid of the War, pp. 22–39; McCreary, "Journal of My Soldier Life," p. 198; Weatherred, "Wartime Diary of John Weatherred"; Louisville Journal and Chicago Tribune, July 7–8, 10, 12, 1863; Nashville Daily Union, July 7–8, 1863. An Acting Volunteer Ensign since the previous Christmas Eve, Read was named an Acting Volunteer Master on March 5, 1864, and was honorably discharged on September 16, 1865. Sears was slightly Read's junior, having been appointed Acting Volunteer Ensign on January 3, 1863. He, too, would become an Acting Volunteer Master, on March 7, 1864, and would be honorably discharged on August 10, 1865. Read would skipper the Victory throughout the war while Sears would also command the tinclad New Era. Callahan, List of Officers of the Navy of the United States and of the Marine Corps, pp. 453, 488.

14. OR, 1, 23, 1: 659; Logbooks of the U.S.S. Moose, July 4, 1863; Brandenburg Methodist Church Men's Club, The Brandenburg Story: With Particular Reference to John Hunt Morgan's Crossing of the Ohio July 8, 1863 (Brandenburg, KY, 1963), p. 18; Keller, Morgan's Raid, pp. 61–62, 65; Duke, "The Raid": 409; Ramage, Rebel Raider, p. 167–168; Weatherred, "Wartime Diary of John Weatherred"; Adam R. "Stovepipe" Johnson, The Partisan Rangers of the Confederate Army, edited by William J. Davis (Louisville, KY: George G Fetter, 1904; reprint, Austin, TX: State House Press, 1995), p. 144; William C. Lytle, comp., Merchant Steam Vessels of the United States, 1807–1868 "The Lytle List" (Mystic, CT: Steamship Historical Society of America, 1952), pp. 6, 102; A. R. Yeiser, "The Capture of the Alice Dean," Confederate Veteran 23 (July 1914): 364; Louisville Journal, July 9–10, 1863; Horwitz, The Longest Raid of the War, pp. 38–46, 116–117.

15. Lytle, Merchant Steam Vessels of the United States, p. 109; Mackey, The Uncivil War, p. 187; David L. Taylor, With Bowie Knives and Pistols: Morgan's Raid in Indiana (Lexington, IN: TaylorMade Write, 1993), pp. 36–43; Fred W. Conway, Corydon: The Forgotten Battle of the Civil War (New Albany, IN : FBH, 1991), pp. 8–10; Brandenburg Methodist Church Men's Club, The Brandenburg Story, p. 19–20.

16. Mackey, The Uncivil War, p. 187; ORN, 1, 25: 240–246; Holland, Morgan and His Raiders, pp. 232–233; William E. Wilson, "Thunderbolt of the Confederacy; or, King of Horse Thieves," Indiana Magazine of History 54 (June 1958), 125; Yeiser, "The Capture of the Alice Dean": 365; Duke, A History of Morgan's Cavalry, pp. 432–434; Taylor, With Bowie Knives and Pistols, p. 37; Weatherred, "Wartime Diary of John Weatherred"; Arville L. Funk, The Morgan Raid in Indiana and Ohio (1863) (Corydon, IN: ALFCO, 1971), p. 5; Brandenburg Methodist Church Men's Club, The Brandenburg Story, pp. 23–24. There is no record of the Elk in the Official Records, just as there was mention of the activities of Indiana Legion Col. John W. Foster's impromptu gunboat Lou Eaves the previous fall. Both were undoubtedly temporary expedients "gotten up" in the manner of the Allegheny Belle, described below. The Springfield's commander was named an Acting Volunteer Master on September 16, 1863, and was honorably discharged on September 14, 1865. He had previously commanded the U.S.S. New Era. Callahan, List of Officers of the Navy of the United States and of the Marine Corps, p. 572.

17. ORN, 1, 25: 240; Holland, Morgan and His Raiders, p. 234; Wilson, "Thunderbolt of the Confederacy": 125–126; Ramage, Rebel Raider, p. 280; New Albany Ledger, July 9, 1863; Louisville Journal, July 10, 1863.

18. ORN, 1, 25: 239–240; Cincinnati Daily Commercial, July 9, 1863; Cincinnati Daily Enquirer, July 10, 1863; Smith, "Gunboats at Buffington": 102; McCreary, "Journal of My Soldier Life," p. 198; Conway, Corydon, follows the Corydon battle in detail. Pennock sent the Queen City in response to rumors of Rebel fortifications at Brandenburg; upon arrival at Evansville on July 13, the ship's captain, Lt. Cmdr. James P. Foster, who was also commanding officer-designate of the squadron's 2nd District, wired his superior confirmation of the intelligence. Other than playing the part of Evansville guard, neither Foster nor his boat had any active role in the Morgan pursuit.

19. Cincinnati Gazette, July 10, 1863; Chicago Tribune, July 15, 1863; Holland, Morgan and His Raiders, pp. 235–239; Mackey, The Uncivil War, pp. 188–189; Backs, Ibid.; McCreary, "Journal of My Soldier Life," pp. 198–199; ORN, 1, 25: 238–239, 246–248. Although it is now understood that Morgan did not anticipate support from local members of the Northern war opposition ("Copperheads"), there is some indication that he, like McCreary, was surprised by the intensity of local citizen opposition. Ramage, Rebel Raider, p. 173.

20. ORN, 1, 23: 318, 721, 728; ORN, 1, 25: 246–248. Until the danger was passed, Maj. Gen. Burnside strictly enforced the commander's general order. Cleveland Daily Plain Dealer, July 14, 1863. The Ohio River mileage noted here was taken from the "Tabulated Report of the Ohio River," prepared by Lt. Cmdr. Fitch for Rear Adm. Porter later in the year. ORN, 1, 25: 610–611.

21. ORN, 1, 25: 246–248; OR, 1, 23, 1: 726; Cincinnati Daily Gazette, July 10–11, 1863. A brief summary of "Morgan's Ohio Raid," appears in Battles and Leaders of the Civil War, edited by Robert V. Johnson and Clarence C. Buel, Vol. 3 (New York: Century, 1884–1887, reprinted Thomas Yoseloff, 1956), p. 634–635.

22. ORN, 1, 25: 248–250; OR, 1, 23, 1: 728; Keller, Morgan's Raid, pp. 98–105; Horwitz, The Longest Raid of the War, pp. 40, 55–57, 193. Due to a failure with the telegraph system, Fitch had no direction or contact with either Rear Adm. Porter or Capt. Pennock during most of the Morgan chase. At one point, on July 13, the obviously frustrated district commander began a brief update wire to Pennock ("for the admiral") with the beginning sentence, "Was my telegram of 11th from Louisville received?"

23. ORN, 1, 25: 250–251, 277; OR, 1, 23, 1: 728, 736; The Naumkeag was left to guard Madison. The steamer Union, outfitted as an armed auxiliary and armored with hay bales and a pair of Rodman guns, was also on hand under Brown's command. Three months older than Le Roy Fitch, George Brown, a native of Rushville, Indiana, had been held as a POW from February 24 until his exchange on May 25. He would finish the war in the West Gulf Coast Blockading Squadron and rise through the ranks to be appointed a rear admiral on September 1893. He died at home in Indianapolis on June 29, 1913. OR, 1, 23, 1: 723; William B. Cogar, Dictionary of Admirals of the U.S. Navy, Vol. 1 (Annapolis, MD: Naval Institute Press, 1989), 21–22.

24. OR, 1, 23, 1: 735, 738; Ramage, Rebel Raider, p. 175–176; Cincinnati Daily Commercial, July 13–20, 1863; Cleveland Daily Plain Dealer, July 14, 1863; Weatherred, "Wartime Diary of John Weatherred"; McCreary, "Journal of My Soldier Life," p. 198–199; Keller, Morgan's Raid, p. 120; Horwitz, The Longest Raid of the War, pp. 114–162; Mark Rae Schilling, "Morgan's Raid," 45th Ohio Volunteer Infantry Home Page, http://www.homestead.com/ohio45/morgan˜ns.4.html (accessed October 29, 2005). At least one Midwestern journal felt the Rebel advance was bankrupt by this time; "John Morgan's raid is dying away," announced the Chicago Tribune on July 13. Interestingly enough, the New York, Pittsburgh, and Philadelphia papers had very little information on this story and neither did the Wheeling Intelligencer, the closest to the river fights, until the aftermath of Buffington Island; all were content

to print "exchange" reports copied from the Cincinnati or Louisville papers. This is perhaps understandable as *The New York Times*, the New York *Herald*, the New York *Tribune*, and other Eastern papers were busy reporting the great draft riots while the West Virginia journal was intent upon the formation and business of the new state legislature then meeting in its town.

25. Ramage, *Rebel Raider*, pp. 173–175; OR, 1, 23, 1: 747, 760, 766; ORN, 1, 25: 243, 252–253; Cincinnati *Daily Gazette*, July 20, 1863, quoted in New York *Herald*, July 23, 1863; Keller, *Morgan's Raid*, p. 165; Yvonne Sheldon, ed. "Peril in West Union: Ohio Prepares for Morgan's Raiders," *Civil War Times Illustrated* 23 (November 1984): 39; T. Harry Williams, *Hayes of the 23rd* (New York, Knopf, 1965; reprint, Lincoln, University of Nebraska Press, 1994), pp. 153–154; Horowitz, *The Longest Raid of the War*, 157–158, 204–205, 208, 210; Weathered; "Wartime Diary of John Weatherred." Because of state boundaries, Buffington Island is officially part of West Virginia; thus both jurisdictions are able to claim "ownership" of the Battle of Buffington Island, as I learned when I penned my article for *West Virginia History* years ago. The best photographic review of the area and the island remains B. Kevin Bennet and Dave Roth, "The General's Tour: The Battle of Buffington Island," *Blue & Gray Magazine* 15 (April 1998): 60–65. Officially known as the *Allegheny Belle No. 4*, Pilot Sebastian's 143-ton side-wheeler had been built at Pittsburgh in 1859 and was still homeported at the "Steel City." The *Imperial* was a 286-ton side-wheeler that had recently been constructed at her homeport of Cincinnati. Lytle, *Merchant Steam Vessels of the United States*, pp. 6, 89.

26. Hunter, *Steamboats on the Western Waters*, pp. 253–254; Schilling, *Ibid.*; OR, 1, 23, 1: 655–658; 660; 760–761, 770, 773; Horwitz, *The Longest Raid of the War*, p. 114–162; McCreary, "Journal of My Soldier Life": 200; Duke, *A History of Morgan's Cavalry*, pp. 445–446; Williams, *Hayes of the 23rd*, p. 156; ORN, 1, 25: 256; Cincinnati *Daily Gazette*, July 20, 1863, quoted in New York *Herald*, July 23, 1863; Backs, *Ibid.*; Weatherred, "Wartime Diary of John Weatherred." Capt. Wood and his men reported to Brig. Gen. Judah for duty after the Buffington fight and were well complemented; the *Starlight* was given the "honor" of transporting several hundred of Duke's soldiers back to Cincinnati, from whence they would begin their trek to POW camps. In the "for what it's worth department," when the town fathers of Lethart, Virginia, and Lethartsville, later Lethart Falls (Meigs County), Ohio, named their communities in honor of a local pioneer, they spelled his name wrong; it was James LeTort. "Lethart, WV," *Epodunk: The Power of Place* homepage http://www.epodunk.com/cgi-bin/genInfo.php?locIndex=23586 (accessed November 24, 2005).

27. OR, 1, 23, 1: 656; 776; ORN, 1, 25: 656; OR, 1, 23, 1: 641; 677; OR, 1, 51, 1: 207; Boyd B. Stutler, *West Virginia in the Civil War* (Charleston, WV: Education Foundation, 1963), pp. 232–233; Cincinnati *Daily Gazette*, July 20, 1863, quoted in New York *Herald*, July 23, 1863; Rector, "Morgan Goes A-Raiding": 310; Schilling, "Morgan's Raid," *45th Ohio Volunteer Infantry Home Page*, http://www.homestead.com/ohi045/morgan~ns.4.html (accessed October 29, 2005). The battle was named for the island, the only noteworthy geographical feature in the vicinity. The actual infantry-type fighting was contained entirely upon the Ohio mainland and was the only major battle fought in the Buckeye State during the Civil War. Horwitz, *The Longest Raid of the War*, named the U.S. military units involved in a nice chronology in his appendix, p. 381; Hobson's aide, Lt. Weaver, later reported that Judah and Hobson were as ignorant of the naval officer's location as Fitch was of theirs. They "supposed he was jealously patrolling the river." Henry C. Weaver, "Morgan's Raid in Kentucky, Indiana, and Ohio, July 1863," in William H. Chamberlain, ed., *Sketches of War History, 1861–1865: Papers Prepared for the Ohio Commandary of the Military Order of the Loyal Legion of the United States*, Vol. 5 (Cincinnati: R Clarke, 1890–1908), 304.

28. Weaver, "Morgan's Raid in Kentucky, Indiana, and Ohio, July 1863," 304; ORN, 1, 25: 318; Duke, *A History of Morgan's Cavalry*, pp. 450–452; Weaver, "Morgan's Raid in Kentucky, Indiana, and Ohio, July 1863," 304; Logbook of the U.S.S. *Moose*, July 19, 1863; Horwitz, *The Longest Raid of the War*, pp. 215, 420; Cincinnati *Daily Gazette*, July 20, 1863, quoted in New York *Herald*, July 23, 1863; Schilling, "Morgan's Raid," *45th Ohio Volunteer Infantry Home Page*, http://www.homestead.com/ohi045/morgan~ns.4.html (accessed October 29, 2005). Captain Oakes of the *Imperial* later wrote of the battle to a colleague; his July 21 letter was reprinted in Vol. 4 of Frank Moore, ed., *The Rebellion Record: A Diary of American Events*. (New York: G. P. Putnam and D. Van Nostrand, 1861–1868), pp 391–392; A concise review of the entire episode is Mark F. Jenkins' "Operations of the Mississippi Squadron During Morgan's Raid," *Ironclads and Blockade Runners of the American Civil War Homepage*, www.wideopenwest.com/~jenkins/ironclads/buffingt.htm (accessed November 11, 2005) which has appeared at several URLs since it was first published in 1999.

29. OR, 1, 23, 1: 14, 640–645, 656–657, 660–662, 667–668, 774, 776–777, 781, 788; OR, 1, 30, 2: 547–552; OR, 1, 51, 1: 207; ORN, 1, 25: 256–257, 315; Cooling, *Fort Donelson's Legacy*, p. 282; Backs, *Ibid.*; Horwitz, *The Longest Raid of the War*, pp. 195–248; Keller, *Morgan's Raid*, pp. 162–178; Holland, *Morgan and His Raiders*, p. 242, 250; Smith, "Gunboats at Buffington": 108–110; Johnson, *Partisan Rangers of the Confederate Army*, pp. 149–150; Oakes letter, *The Rebellion Record*, p. 391–392; Cincinnati *Daily Gazette*, July 20, 1863, quoted in New York *Herald*, July 23, 1863; Indianapolis *Journal*, July 15, 1863; Louisville *Daily Journal*, July 21, 27, 1863; Nashville *Daily Union*, July 30, 1863; Logbook of the U.S.S. *Moose*, July 20–23, 1863; McCreary, "Journal of My Soldier Life," pp. 200–201; Rector, "Morgan Goes A-Raiding": 310–311; Williams, *Hayes of the 23rd*, p. 157; Weatherred, "Wartime Diary of John Weatherred;" Schilling, *Ibid*; Ramage, *Rebel Raider*, p. 178–179, 183; Mackey, *The Uncivil War*, pp. 190–191; Brown, *The Bold Cavaliers*, pp. 211–222, 228; Duke, *A History of Morgan's Cavalry*, pp. 453–454, 464; Stutler, *West Virginia in the Civil War*, pp. 233–241. Andrew R. L. Cayton, *Ohio: The History of a People* (Columbus: Ohio State University Press, 2002), p. 130; David Dixon Porter, *The Naval History of the Civil War* (New York: Sherman, 1886), p. 338; Bern Anderson, *By Sea and By River: The Naval History of the Civil War* (New York: Knopf, 1962), p. 155. Taken to prison in Columbus, Morgan and six of his officers effected the only successful 19th century escape from the Ohio Penitentiary on November 27. Later, he commanded in southwest Virginia and led another disastrous Kentucky raid. Cornered by Yankees again, in Greeneville, Tennessee, on September 4, 1864, he died trying to escape. In the 14 months between Buffington and Greeneville, Morgan and Fitch did not directly cross paths again.

30. Lenette S. Taylor, *"The Supply for Tomorrow Must Not Fail": The Civil War of Captain Simon Perkins, Jr., a Union Quartermaster* (Kent, OH: Kent State University Press, 2004), p. 121; ORN, 1, 23: 321; Cooling, *Fort Donelson's Legacy*, p. 291; Howard Papers, July 19, 1863; Nashville *Daily Union*, July 16, 1863. Acting Surgeon Howard late in July won a transfer to a shore facility; his letters home to Massachusetts, so important to any understanding of Sixth District naval activities, are no longer helpful.

Chapter Nine

1. Mark M. Boatner III, *The Civil War Dictionary* (New York: David McKay, 1959), pp. 149–150; Benjamin Franklin Cooling, *Fort Donelson's Legacy: War and Society in Kentucky and Tennessee, 1862–1863* (Knoxville: University of Tennessee Press, 1997), pp. 292–293; Charles Dana Gibson, with E. Kay Gibson, *Assault and Logistics, Vol. 2: Union Army Coastal and River Operations, 1861–1866* (Camden, ME: Ensign Press, 1995), pp. 369–371; William Glenn Robertson, et al., *Staff Ride Handbook for the Battle of Chickamauga, 18–20 September 1863* (Fort Leavenworth, KS: U.S. Army Command and General Staff College, Combat Studies Institute, 1992), pp. 27–28. Studies of the Chickamauga and Chattanooga campaigns are plentiful. For details, we have chosen to rely upon the work of fellow Tennessean John Bowers, *Chickamauga and Chattanooga: The Battles That Doomed the Confederacy* (New York: HarperPerennial, 1995) and the more recent work by Steven E. Woodward, *Six Armies in Tennessee: The Chickamauga and Chattanooga Campaigns* (Lincoln: University of Nebraska Press, 1999); the 15-page pamphlet by Harold S. Fink, *The Battle of Knoxville, (1863)*, published by the Knoxville-Knox County Civil War Centennial Committee in 1965, was a helpful introduction.

2. U.S. Navy Department, *Official Records of the Union and Confederate Navies in the War of the Rebellion* (Washington, DC: GPO, 1894–1922), Series 1, Vol. 25, 370, 372, 377–380 (cited hereafter as ORN, followed by a comma, the series number, a comma, the volume number, a colon, and the page number).

3. This brief review is based on the excellent campaign summary provided by Civil War historians Richard E. Beringer, Herman Hattaway, Archer Jones, and William N. Still, Jr., in their *Why the South Lost the Civil War* (Athens: University of Georgia Press, 1986), pp. 300–303. It should be noted that construction now finally began on a pre-war plan to build the Nashville and Northwestern Railroad from Kingston Springs, west of Nashville, to the Tennessee River. Upon its completion in 1864, under the direction since October 22, 1863, of Governor Andrew Johnson, it linked the capital with a huge military supply depot on the Tennessee River named for the Greeneville politician, thereby significantly increasing the Union army's western logistical apparatus. Cooling, *Fort Donelson's Legacy*, p. 295; Richard P. Gildrie, "Guerrilla Warfare in the Lower Cumberland River Valley, 1862–1865," *Tennessee Historical Quarterly* 49 (Fall 1990): 169; U.S. War Department, *The War of the Rebellion: A Compilation of the Official Records of the Union and Confederate Armies* (Washington, DC: GPO, 1880–1901), Series 1, Vol. 31, Pt. 3: 14–15 (cited hereafter as OR, followed by a comma, the series number, a comma, the volume number, a colon, and the page number); Clifton R. Hall, *Andrew Johnson: Military Governor of Tennessee* (Princeton, NJ: Princeton University Press, 1916), pp. 196–199.

4. ORN, 1, 25: 428, 438–439, 557. At the end of November, Fitch sent Rear Adm. Porter a report on the Ohio River, mentioning some of its communities. In general, all of the towns on the left bank were regarded as disloyal as were many of those on the right bank below Shawneetown. Evansville was a hotbed of contraband trading and needed watching. ORN, 1, 25: 610–611.

5. ORN, 1, 25: 438; 464–465; Lenette S. Taylor, *"The Supply for Tomorrow Must Not Fail": The Civil War of Captain Simon Perkins, Jr., a Union Quartermaster* (Kent, OH: Kent State University Press, 2004), pp. 150, 256–260; Perkins was the army's head quartermaster in Nashville at this time. It was he who now took charge of the army's three makeshift Cumberland River gunboats. The *Hagan* had grounded at Clarksville and was unable to move. The *Newsboy*, which was armed with a single 12-pounder gun, and *Silver Lake No. 2* were also out of action due to the water level, with the former assigned to "guard the wharves and bridges" at the capital city. Taylor, "The Supply for Tomorrow Must Not Fail," p. 151; OR, 1, 31, 3: 93; Stephen Starr, *The Union Cavalry in the Civil War: Vol. III, The War in the West, 1861–1865* (Baton Rouge: Louisiana State University Press, 1985), pp. 292–300.

6. David W. White, *Second Only to Grant: Quartermaster General Montgomery C. Meigs* (Shippensburg, PA: White Mane Books, 2000), pp. 214–220; Walter T. Durham, *Reluctant Partners: Nashville and the Union—July 1, 1863, to June 30, 1865* (Nashville: Tennessee Historical Society, 1987), p. 16; Wiley Sword, *Mountains Touched with Fire: Chattanooga Besieged, 1863* (New York: St. Martin's Press, 1995), pp. 116–118; OR, 1, 30, 1: 214–220; OR, 1, 30, 4: 475–476; OR, 1, 31, 1: 39, 678, 680, 712, 729, 774, 784, 788; OR, 1, 31, 3: 10, 16, 26, 34, 38; ORN, 1, 25: 466–472, 476, 482, 504, 509, 524–525, 592, 614; ORN, 1, 23: 322; Ulysses S. Grant, *The Papers of Ulysses S. Grant: Vol. 9, July 7–December 31, 1863*, edited by John Y. Simon (Edwardsville, IL: Southern Illinois University Press, 1967), p. 346; Cooling, *Fort Donelson's Legacy*, p. 325; Logbooks of the U.S.S. *Moose*, June 15, 1863–August 10, 1865, Records of the Bureau of Navigation, Record Group 19, U.S. National Archives, Washington, D.C., October 21–November 5, 1863 (cited hereafter as Logbook of the U.S.S. *Moose*, with date); *Nashville Daily Press*, November 3, 1863.

7. ORN, 1, 25: 534–535, 546–547, 592–594; OR, 1, 31, 3: 48–49, 60. Though only a lieutenant commander in rank like his colleagues Phelps, Shirk and others, Fitch, as a district commander, was entitled to yeoman services. It was these unnamed scribes who copied many of the communications and orders cited here. We know more about the *Newsboy* than any other U.S. Army gunboat employed on the Cumberland. The 53-ton stern-wheeler was built at Brownsville, Pennsylvania, in the spring of 1862 and originally homeported at Wheeling, Virginia. She was chartered by the U.S. Quartermaster Department from August 15 to 25, 1862, and again on November 16, just before her purchase by the government for $14,000. She was based at Nashville and when seen there in June 1865, her condition was rated as serviceable. Like the *Allegheny Belle* and other improvised army gunboats, she was undoubtedly protected with hay and cotton bales. William C. Lytle, comp., *Merchant Steam Vessels of the United States, 1807–1868 "The Lytle List"* (Mystic, CT: Steamship Historical Society of America, 1952), p. 138; Charles Dana Gibson, with E. Kay Gibson, *Assault and Logistics, Vol. 1: Dictionary of Transports and Combatant Vessels Steam and Sail Employed by the Union Army, 1861–1868* (Camden, ME: Ensign Press, 1995), p. 239; OR, 1, 31, 3: 93. James L. Donaldson was born in Maryland on March 17, 1814, and died there on November 4, 1885. Following his Seminole War and Mexican War service and postings in the west, he served as chief quartermaster with VIII Corps and later for the Department of the Cumberland, where he became an intimate of Maj. Gen. Thomas. He was chief quartermaster of the military divisions of the Tennessee and Missouri, 1865–1869, after which he retired. Donaldson is credited with the creation of military cemeteries for the scattered remains of soldiers and Decoration Day. "James Lowry Donaldson" in Vol. 2 of James Grant Wilson and John Fiske, eds., *Appleton's Cyclopaedia of American Biography* (New York: D. Appleton, 1888), p. 198.

8. ORN, 1, 25: 434–435, 541, 546–547, 549, 592–593; Durham, *Reluctant Partners*, p. 17; *Nashville Daily Press*, November 7, 1863; OR, 1, 31, 1: 74, 84–85; OR, 1, 31, 3: 64, 66, 75, 84–85, 94; Cooling, *Fort Donelson's Legacy*, p.

326; Logbook of the U.S.S. *Moose*, November 6–9, 1863. Rear Adm. Porter telegraphed his approval of Fitch's general orders 10 and 12 while the Hoosier was upstream: "Pursue the strictest measures and have the river banks cleared at all hazards; permit none but transports to go up."

9. OR, 1, 31, 3: 93, 115, 134–136; OR, 1, 31, 3: 107–108; Durham, *Reluctant Partners*, p. 17–18; Cooling, *Fort Donelson's Legacy*, p. 327; Logbook of the U.S.S. *Moose*, November 9–10, 1863. Cooling suggests Stockdale's mission was a self-initiated personal intervention by one Illinois captain. It was, in fact, a sanctioned commission from an anxious military superior who believed the naval district commander had failed in his duty when he did not put into Nashville. The Bowers-Stockdale incident would be followed by complaints from higher-ranking U.S. Army officers as old misunderstandings about Fitch's convoy methods resurfaced.

10. OR, 1, 31, 3: 115, 123, 134–136; ORN, 1, 25: 553–557; Logbook of the U.S.S. *Moose*, November 10–13, 1863. The copy of *Whistle Signal Code for Transport Fleets Under Convoy* written by Fitch was published in a one-page broadside in January 1864; a copy signed by the Indiana sailor, with ink stains obscuring parts of the text, later made it into the collections of the New York Historical Society. Stockdale did not make his report claiming that Fitch had Porter's orders on November 9 until sometime on November 13, by which time Bowers had already informed Grant that Fitch hadn't received instruction. Given that the Burnside mission did not subsequently, as Fitch probably anticipated, get off as immediately as Grant and Bowers desired could not but have strengthened Porter's faith in the Cumberland knowledge and expertise of his subordinate. John Y. Simon, editor of Grant's papers, does not pass judgment on the Fitch-Stockdale episode, but does call attention to their "rather different reports of the situation." Grant, *The Papers of Ulysses S. Grant*, p. 363.

11. John W. Donn, "War Record of J. W. Donn, Including Reminiscences of Frederick W. Dorr, July 1861 to June 1865," NOAA History Homepage, http://www.history.noaa.gov/stories_tales/donn.html (accessed April 4, 2005). In his recollections, Donn refers to the army gunboat employed on his trip as the *Pilot Boy*. As neither Lytle, in *Merchant Steam Vessels of the United States*, nor Gibson, in Vol. I of *Assault and Logistics*, show any steamer existing by that name in the West at this time and given that Lt. Col. Bowers wrote that he was sending the *Newsboy*, we must assume that Donn's memory was off concerning his boat's name.

12. ORN, 1, 25: 556–557, 564, 570, 579–582, 586, 592–595, 613; OR, 1, 31, 3: 156, 174, 177, 182; Cooling, *Fort Donelson's Legacy*, pp. 327, 332; Logbook of the U.S.S. *Moose*, November 13–30, 1863; Ralsa C. Rice, *Yankee Tigers: Through the Civil War with the One Hundred and Twenty-Fifth Ohio*, edited by Richard A. Baumgartner and Larry M. Strayer (Huntington, WV: Blue Acorn Press, 1992), pp. 75–77. In early December, Fitch was elated to write Rear Adm. Porter that "the captain, clerk and mate of the *Duke* are now under arrest in Nashville, and that the authorities have taken possession of the boat." The Eighth District chief promised his boss that he would query steamer captains with more caution and "take good care not to listen to any of their cock and bull stories in future." ORN, 1, 25: 631.

13. ORN, 1, 25: 557, 608, 612–614; Logbook of the U.S.S. *Moose*, November 29-December 2, 1863; Cooling, *Fort Donelson's Legacy*, p. 327.

14. ORN, 1, 25: 630, 681; OR, 3, 4: 880–881; William Tecumseh Sherman, *Memoirs* (New York: Penguin Books, 2000), pp. 350–353; Louis C. Hunter, *Steamboats on the Western Waters: An Economic and Technological History* (Cambridge, MA: Harvard University Press, 1949), p. 555; Nashville *Dispatch*, December 12, 14, 1863; Nashville *Daily Union*, December 16, 1863; Durham, *Reluctant Partners*, p. 18. The Navy announced in the public press in mid-December, before arrangements could be worked out between Fitch and his superior, that no private boats or steamers would be permitted to enter the Cumberland River from the Ohio unless they were transporting government freight or were under U.S. charter. On January 5, 1864, Parsons wrote Porter on his concerns; the admiral informed the river quartermaster on January 10 that the Cumberland was safe for private steamers and that Fitch had acknowledged orders lifting the embargo against them.

15. ORN, 1, 25: 630, 641–642, 644; OR, 1, 31, 3: 463; Nashville *Dispatch*, December 12, 14, 1863; Sherman, *Memoirs*, p. 357. Removal of the iron to Smithland would continue through February 1864. An effort by the Nashville District commander, Maj. Gen. Lovell H. Rousseau, to countermand the admiral's orders on behalf of "the heirs or interested parties" was ignored by Fitch, who went so far to protect the prize with the guard boat U.S.S. *Springfield*. Maj. Gen. Grant himself eventually checked with Porter to see if, in fact, he had ordered the seizure; once reassured, the claim was ignored. ORN, 1, 25: 743–745, 761.

16. ORN, 1, 25: 657–659.

17. ORN, 1, 25: 647–651; OR, 1, 31, 1: 644–645; Byrd Douglas, *Steamboatin' on the Cumberland* (Nashville: Tennessee Book, 1961), p. 149; Grant, *Papers of Ulysses S. Grant*, p. 549; Donn, "War Record of J. W. Donn." Rather than return downstream with the gunboats, Capt. Donn acquired a horse and rode overland through Kentucky to Camp Nelson, returning to Nashville from that point.

Chapter Ten

1. Ulysses S. Grant, *Personal Memoirs of U.S. Grant: A Modern Abridgment* (New York: Premier Books, 1962), pp. 264–265; U.S. War Department, *The War of the Rebellion: A Compilation of the Official Records of the Union and Confederate Armies* (Washington, DC: GPO, 1880–1901), Series 1, Vol. 32, Pt. 2: 99–101 (cited hereafter as OR, followed by a comma, the series number, a comma, the volume number, a colon, and the page number). On January 11, Brig. Gen. Eleazer Paine, headquartered at Gallatin and charged with guarding the Louisville and Nashville Railroad from Nashville to Kentucky, made an aggressive proposal to Governor Andrew Johnson. It was suggested that his infantry and Col. William B. Stokes' 5th Tennessee Cavalry (U.S.) be allowed to accompany the *Newsboy* and the next USN convoy to clear out the guerrillas all the way up the Cumberland to Burkesville. The sortie was sanctioned. Walter T. Durham, *Reluctant Partners: Nashville and the Union—July 1, 1863, to June 30, 1865* (Nashville: Tennessee Historical Society, 1987), p. 83.

2. U.S. Navy Department, *Official Records of the Union and Confederate Navies in the War of the Rebellion* (Washington, DC: GPO, 1894–1922), Series 1, Vol. 25, 714, 716–717, 720–721 (cited hereafter as ORN, followed by a comma, the series number, a comma, the volume number, a colon, and the page number); Logbooks of the U.S.S. *Moose*, June 15, 1863–August 10, 1865, Records of the Bureau of Navigation, Record Group 19, U.S. National Archives, Washington, D.C., January 1–January 31, 1864 (cited hereafter as Logbook of the U.S.S. *Moose*, with date).

3. ORN, 1, 25: 730; OR, 1, 32, 1: 162; OR, 1, 32, 2: 103, 365–366; Evansville *Daily Journal*, January 11–13, 1864;

Nashville *Daily Union*, February 10, 1864; Nashville *Dispatch*, February 24, 27, 1864. Ulysses S. Grant, *The Papers of Ulysses S. Grant: Vol. 10, January 1–May 31, 1864*, edited by John Y. Simon (Edwardsville, IL: Southern Illinois University Press, 1967), p. 104, 536. On February 20, Col. Parsons advised Grant that a fleet of canal boats and barges was being loaded at St. Louis for Nashville and would be started down "as soon as ice permits."

4. OR, 1, 20, 2: 332, 338–339; the Meigs-Rosecrans exchange on armed transports is reviewed in David W. Miller's *Second Only to Grant: Quartermaster General Montgomery C. Meigs* (Shippensburg, PA: White Mane Books, 2000), pp. 182–183; the story of "The Little Steamboat That Opened the Cracker Line" was well-told by eyewitness Brig. Gen. William G. Le Duc in *Battles and Leaders of the Civil War*, vol. 3, edited by Robert V. Johnson and Clarence C. Buel (New York: Century, 1884–1887; reprint, New York: Thomas Yoseloff, 1956), 676–678 (cited hereafter as B&L, followed by a comma, the volume number, a comma, and the page numbers); Donald Davidson, *The Tennessee, Vol. II: The New River, Civil War to TVA* (New York: Rinehart, 1948), pp. 64–67.

5. OR, 1, 31, 2: 56; OR, 1, 32, 2: 104–105; OR, 1, 52, 1: 713; ORN, 1, 25: 681, 698–700, 733, 741; Grant, *The Papers of Ulysses S. Grant: Vol. 10*, p. 104; Charles Dana Gibson, with E. Kay Gibson, *Assault and Logistics, Vol. 2: Union Army Coastal and River Operations, 1861–1866* (Camden, ME: Ensign Press, 1995), p. 411; Logbook of the U.S.S. *Moose*, January 24–February 5, 1864. Historian Davidson credits Dana with urging "the building of the gunboat squadron which Rosecrans had asked for the year before." Davidson, *The Tennessee*, p. 67. The *Alone* and *Convoy #2* would never steam over Muscle Shoals and the attempt, which all concerned hoped might occur in early March, was abandoned by April 4 when Maj. Gen. Sherman wrote to Fleet Captain Pennock: "I think we can build gunboats above the shoals and I agree with you that it is too late to pass the shoals now." OR, 1, 32, 3, 14–18, 30; ORN, 1, 26: 211; Grant, *The Papers of Ulysses S. Grant: Vol. 10*, p. 194.

6. OR, 3, 4: 881; ORN, 1, 25: 733, 741–746, 752–753, 756; Richard P. Gildrie, "Guerrilla Warfare in the Lower Cumberland River Valley, 1862–1865," *Tennessee Historical Quarterly* 49 (Fall 1990): 170. The case of the pig iron brought an inquiry from Maj. Gen. Grant on February 12 to Rear Adm. Porter concerning authorization for the removal in light of claims by the guardian of the minor heirs of the owner. Grant the next day received an extensive statement of facts in the matter by a Nashville attorney acting on behalf of the trustee of the estate, Mr. Daniel Hillman. Having checked out the attorney and Hillman, Grant endorsed the brief and sent the message and the trustee on to Porter, stating that Hillman would be asking the admiral for his advice on how best to obtain possession of the iron. Ulysses S. Grant, *The Papers of Ulysses S. Grant: Vol. 9, July 7–December 31, 1863*, edited by John Y. Simon (Edwardsville, IL: Southern Illinois University Press, 1967), pp. 571–572.

7. OR, 1, 52, 1: 706; Durham, *Reluctant Partners*, p. 118. It should be noted here that Fleet Captain Pennock, upon the departure of Admiral Porter to Louisiana for the joint operation up the Red River, had again assumed local responsibility for operations on the Cumberland, Ohio, and Tennessee rivers. It was he who, on March 11, ordered Lt. Cmdr. Fitch to send the damaged *Reindeer* to Cairo for her long-needed repairs. Porter reached the mouth of the Red River on April 2. ORN, 1, 26: 22.

8. OR, 1, 32, 1: 607; ORN, 1, 26: 183, 195–196, 203–204, 206–207; Logbook of the U.S.S. *Moose*, March 1–28, 1864; Nashville *Times*, March 9, 1864; William Tecumseh Sherman, *Memoirs* (New York: Penguin Books, 2000), pp. 365, 379, 382; John Allan Wyeth, *Life of General Nathan Bedford Forrest* (New York: Harper & Bros., 1904), pp. 315–319, 326–330; Byrd Douglas, *Steamboatin' on the Cumberland* (Nashville: Tennessee Book, 1961), p. 159.

9. OR, 1, 52, 1: 621.

10. ORN, 1, 26: 214–216; Logbook of the U.S.S. *Moose*, April 1–12, 1864; Davidson, *The Tennessee*, p. 67.

11. OR, 1, 32, 1: 556–614; ORN, 1, 215–218, 226–233; Logbook of the U.S.S. *Moose*, April 1–16, 1864; Wyeth, *Life of General Nathan Bedford Forrest*, pp. 333–361; Thomas Jordan and J. P. Pryor, *The Campaigns of Lieut. Gen. N. B. Forrest and of Forrest's Cavalry* (New Orleans and New York: Blelock, 1868; reprint, New York: DaCapo Press, 1996), pp. 424–454; Andrew Ward, *River Runs Red: The Fort Pillow Massacre in the American Civil War* (New York: Viking Press, 2005), pp. 280–282. It is not our purpose to tell the story of the Fort Pillow combat or review the charges of massacre, a matter which has been hashed and rehashed in the nearly 150 years since. We have noted several titles in our bibliography and call the reader's attention to Robert C. Mainfort, Jr., "Fort Pillow Massacre: A Statistical Note." *Journal of American History* 76 (December 1989): 836–837.

12. ORN, 1, 26: 245, 273; Edmund J. Huling, *Reminiscences of Gunboat Life in the Mississippi Squadron* (Saratoga Springs, NY: Sentinel Print, 1881), p. 15; Logbook of the U.S.S. *Moose*, April 16–20, 1864.

13. ORN, 1, 26: 265, 272, 274; OR, 1, 52, 1, 706; Logbook of the U.S.S. *Moose*, April 21–30, 1864.

14. ORN, 1, 26: 279, 286, 295, 366; OR, 1, 32, 1: 21. On April 15, the battered main body of the Mississippi Squadron returned to the mouth of the Red River from its unsuccessful sojourn into Louisiana. Four days later, Fitch and the other 13 lieutenant commanders serving in the unit were recommended for promotion; most, in light of Porter's failure, would wait years for advancement. On April 19, the squadron was reorganized; Fitch's Eighth District became the Tenth. Even as the squadron had become the largest in the Union Navy, Rear Adm. Porter still had but 14 regular naval officers in command, while, for example, Rear Adm. Farragut had 45. Fitch was now among the most senior in length of service. ORN, 1, 26: 311–312, 317–318, 445.

15. ORN, 1, 26: 326, 328; OR, 1, 52, 1:620, 706; Douglas, *Steamboatin' on the Cumberland*, p. 145; Logbook of the U.S.S. *Moose*, May 25–31, 1864. In May, Brig. Gen. George Crook undertook a campaign up the Kanawha and New rivers in West Virginia and destroyed the Confederate depot at Dublin. Fitch, who had wondered about the Kanawha back in February, had no boats or orders to participate in the undertaking. Edward O. Guerrant, "Operations in East Tennessee and South-West Virginia," in *Battles and Leaders of the Civil War*, vol. 4, edited by Robert V. Johnson and Clarence C. Buel (New York: Century, 1884–1887, reprint, Thomas Yoseloff, 1956), 477. Also in May, in a development which would impact Lt. Cmdr. Fitch in late fall, the Nashville and Northwest Railroad was completed between the state capital and the site of a growing supply depot and arsenal at Johnsonville on the Tennessee River.

16. ORN, 1, 26: 338–339, 358, 366–367, 375, 381, 401; Logbook of the U.S.S. *Moose*, June 1–10, 1864.

17. ORN, 1, 26: 382–383, 405; OR, 1, 38, 4: 460.

18. ORN, 1, 26: 384–385, 387, 408, 412, 439–441; Nashville *Dispatch*, June 22, 1864; Gildrie, "Guerrilla Warfare in the Lower Cumberland River Valley"; Logbook of the U.S.S. *Moose*, June 11–30, 1864.

19. ORN, 1, 26: 476, 488, 566, 573, 577; Bern Anderson, *By Sea and By River: The Naval History of the Civil War* (New York: Knopf, 1962), p. 264; ORN, 2, 92–93; "General

Burnside," "General Grant," "General Sherman," and "General Thomas," in Vol. 3 of *Dictionary of American Naval Fighting Ships* (Washington, DC: GPO, 1968), pp. 38, 43, 58, 61. Previously commander of the tinclad *Hastings*, Acting Volunteer Master Morehead was honorably discharged on September 12, 1865. Acting Volunteer Master Morton, who had begun as an acting gunner in 1862, rose to become the *pro tempore* captain of the timberclad *Conestoga*. He would remain in the navy until he retired in 1874. Lt. Forrest would be promoted to the rank of lieutenant commander on July 25, 1866, but died that Christmas Eve. Edward W. Callahan, *List of Officers of the Navy of the United States and of the Marine Corps, from 1775 to 1900, Comprising a Complete Register of All Present and Former Commissioned, Warranted, and Appointed Officers of the United States Navy, and of the Marine Corps, Regular and Volunteer. Compiled from the Official Records of the Navy Department* (New York: L.R. Hamersly, 1901; reprint, New York: Haskell House, 1969), pp. 390, 394, 200.

20. ORN, 1, 26, 485, 487–488, 491, 493–494, 498, 501–502, 514; Nashville *Daily Times and True Union*, July 21, 1864; Charles Dana Gibson and E. Kay Gibson, comps., *Dictionary of Transports and Combat Vessels, Steam and Sail, Employed by the Union Army, 1861-1868* (Camden, ME: Ensign Press, 1995), p. 282; *The New York Times*, July 21, 1864; Gildrie, "Guerrilla Warfare in the Lower Cumberland River Valley," 172; Logbook of the U.S.S. *Moose*, July 1–31, 1864.

21. ORN, 1, 26: 498–499, 509, 512–514; OR, 1, 39, 2: 254, 256, 259; OR, 3, 4: 891; Kentucky, Adjutant General, "Forty-Eighth Kentucky Mounted Infantry," *Union Regiments of Kentucky Homepage*, http://www.unionregimentsof kentucky.com/thomasspeed/infantry/48kyinf.html, December 25, 2005; Regimental Association, *History of the 46th Regiment, Indiana Volunteer Infantry, September 1861-September 1865* (Logansport, IN: Press of Wilson, Humphries, 1888), pp. 106–107. Steven E. Woodworth tells the story of the Atlanta campaign most recently in four chapters in his *Nothing but Victory: The Army of the Tennessee, 1861-1865* (New York: Alfred A. Knopf, 2005), pp. 506–587 while the Battle of Mobile Bay and subsequent events are recalled in Jack Friend's *West Tide, Flood Tide: The Battle of Mobile Bay* (Annapolis, MD: Naval Institute Press, 2004). The *Lou Eaves*, which Fitch had first encountered nearly two years earlier, was officially purchased by the U.S. Quartermaster Department on October 15, 1864, and would still be in service the following June 30. Known locally as "Gunboat No. 76" (USN tinclad numbers went only as high as 63), she was sold out of service during the summer. Gibson, *Dictionary*, p. 205; Milford M. Miller, "Evansville Steamboats During the Civil War," *Indiana Magazine of History* 37 (December 1941): 378. No printed operational history of those various gunboats, regular or auxiliary, employed by the U.S. Army on western waters during the Civil War has ever been written—not even a periodical article. Documentation of their activities undoubtedly lies buried deeply within the pages of river newspapers and Quartermaster General records. Still, the project would be a golden opportunity for any popular naval historian or aspiring Ph.D. candidate.

22. OR, 1, 52, 1, 619; Nashville *Daily Press*, August 26, October 11, 1864.

23. James R. Soley, "Closing Operations in the Gulf and Western Rivers," *B&L*, 4, 412.

Chapter Eleven

1. William Tecumseh Sherman, *Memoirs* (New York: Penguin Books, 2000), p. 519; U.S. War Department, *The War of the Rebellion: A Compilation of the Official Records of the Union and Confederate Armies* (Washington, DC: GPO, 1880–1901), Series 1, Vol. 39, Pt. 3: 162 (cited hereafter as OR, followed by a comma, the series number, a comma, the volume number, a colon, and the page number); Lloyd Lewis, *Sherman: Fighting Prophet* (New York: Harcourt, Brace and World, 1960), p. 430.

2. Bruce Catton, *Never Call Retreat* (New York: Pocket Books, 1973), p. 388; John Bell Hood, *Advance and Retreat: Personal Experiences in the United States and Confederate States Armies* (New Orleans: Published for the Hood Orphan Memorial Fund, 1880), pp. 263–269; Hood, "The Invasion of Tennessee," in *Battles and Leaders of the Civil War*, edited by Robert V. Johnson and Clarence C. Buel, vol. 4, (New York: Century, 1884–1887, reprinted Thomas Yoseloff, 1956), 425; OR, 1, 39, 2: 121; Benson J. Lossing, *Pictorial Field Book of the Civil War: Journeys Through the Battlefields in the Wake of Conflict*, vol. 3 (Hartford, CT: T. Belknap, 1874, reprinted Johns Hopkins University Press, 1997), 398–399.

3. OR, 1, 39,1, 539–541; OR, 1, 39, 3: 238–239, 815–817; U.S. Navy Department, *Official Records of the Union and Confederate Navies in the War of the Rebellion* (Washington, DC: GPO, 1894–1922), Series 1, Vol. 26, 582–583 (cited hereafter as ORN, followed by a comma, the series number, a comma, the volume number, a colon, and the page number); ORN, 2, 121, 229; David Dixon Porter, *Naval History of the Civil War* (New York: Sherman, 1886; reprinted, Mineola, NY: Dover, 1998), p. 563; William C. Lytle, comp. *Merchant Steam Vessels of the United States, 1807-1868 "The Lytle List"* (Mystic, CT: Steamship Historical Society of America, 1952), 18, 107; "Undine," in Vol. 7 of *Dictionary of American Naval Fighting Ships* (Washington, DC: GPO, 1981), p. 404; "Key West," in Vol. 3 of *Dictionary of American Naval Fighting Ships* (Washington, DC: GPO, 1968), 638; Donald H. Steenburn, "The United States Ship *Undine*," *Civil War Times Illustrated* 35 (August 1996): 27; W. Calvin Dickinson, "Temperance," in Carroll Van West, ed., *The Tennessee Encyclopedia of History and Culture* (Nashville: Rutledge Hill Press for the Tennessee Historical Society, 1998), p. 913; "'The Kelly Rangers/Kelly Troopers," Company F, Forrest's Battalion (3rd Tennessee Cavalry) and Company K, 4th Alabama Cavalry Regiment," Confederate Units of Madison County homepage, <http://www.rootsweb.com/~almadiso/confunit.htm> (accessed March 4, 2006); John E. Fisher, *They Rode with Forrest and Wheeler: A Chronicle of Five Tennessee Brothers' Service in the Confederate Western Cavalry* (Jefferson, NC: McFarland, 1995), pp.244–245, 250; "Reverend Dr. D. C. Kelley," *The Vanderbilt University Quarterly* 9 (October 1909): 236; Teresa Gray, public services archivist, Special Collections and University Archives, Jean and Alexander Heard Library, Vanderbilt University, "Re: David Campbell Kelley," March 13, 2006, personal e-mail. March 13, 2006; Jacob D. Cox, *March to the Sea: Franklin and Nashville*, Campaigns of the Civil War, no. 10 (New York: Scribner's, 1882), p. 12; Thomas Jordan and J. P. Pryor, *The Campaigns of Lieut. Gen. N. B. Forrest and of Forrest's Cavalry* (New Orleans and New York: Blelock, 1868; reprinted, New York: DaCapo Press, 1996), p. 575; John Allan Wyeth, *Life of General Nathan Bedford Forrest* (New York: Harper & Bros., 1904), pp. 47, 50; Robert Selph Henry, *"First with the Most" Forrest* (Indianapolis: Bobbs-Merrill, 1944), pp. 368–369; Ben Earl Kitchens, *Gunboats and Cavalry: A History of Eastport, Mississippi* (Florence, AL: Thornwood, 1985), pp. 119–124; Herschel K. Smith, Jr., *Some Encounters with General Forrest* (McKenzie, TN: Priv. Print., 1959?), p. 3; John Watson Morton, *The Artillery of Nathan Bedford Forrest's Cavalry* (Nashville: Publishing House of the Methodist Episcopal Church, South, 1909), p. 252; E. F.

Williams and H. K. Humphreys, eds., *Gunboats and Cavalry: The Story of Forrest's 1864 Johnsonville Campaign, as Told to J. P. Pryor and Thomas Jordan, by Nathan Bedford Forrest* (Memphis, TN: Nathan Bedford Forrest Trail Committee, 1965), p. 6; Edward F. Williams III, "The Johnsonville Raid and Nathan Bedford Forrest State Park," *Tennessee Historical Quarterly* 28 (Fall 1969): 227; Campbell H. Brown, "Forrest's Johnsonville Raid," *Civil War Times Illustrated* 4 (June 1965): 53; Norman R. Denny, "The Devil's Navy," *Civil War Times Illustrated* 35 (August 1996): 28; Mark Zimmerman, *Guide to Civil War Nashville* (Nashville: Battle of Nashville Preservation Society, 2004), p. 14. The literature on Forrest vs. the gunboats in October-November 1864 is huge, largely because the cavalry-naval aspect of the adventure is so unique. Donald H. Steenburn's recent work is very helpful, *Silent Echoes of Johnsonville: Rebel Cavalry and Yankee Gunboats* (Rogersville, AL: Elk River Press, 1994).

4. Wyeth, *Life of General Nathan Bedford Forrest*, p. 516; Jordan and Pryor, *The Campaigns*, pp. 589-590; Brown, "Forrest's Johnsonville Raid," 49; Henry, *"First with the Most" Forrest*, p. 371; ORN, 1, 26: 693, 699-700; Dudley Taylor Cornish and Virginia Jeans Laas, *Lincoln's Cornish: The Life of Samuel Phillips Lee, United States Navy, 1812-1897* (Lawrence, KS: University Press of Kansas, 1986), p. 140; Johnny H. Whisenant, "Samuel Phillips Lee, U.S.N.: Commander, Mississippi Squadron (October 19, 1864-August 14, 1865)")unpublished master's thesis, Pittsburg, KS: Kansas State College of Pittsburg, 1968), pp. 12-20; "Sameul Phillips Lee," in William B. Cogar, *Dictionary of Admirals of the U.S. Navy*, vol. 1 (Annapolis, MD: Naval Institute Press, 1989), 96-97; "Nashville," in *Major General George Thomas Blog Site*, http://home.earthline.net/~oneplez/majorgeneral georgehthomasblogsite/id20.html (accessed February 28, 2006), which is cited hereafter as Thomas Blog Site. On October 26, Gen. Thomas received a warning from Memphis: "It is reported that Forrest has sent to Mobile for a battery of heavy guns to plant on the Tennessee River." OR, 1, 39, 3: 459.

5. OR, 1, 39, 3: 524; Brown, "Forrest's Johnsonville Raid," 50-53; John W. Morton, "Raid of Forrest's Cavalry on the Tennessee River in 1864," *Southern Historical Society Papers* 10 (1882): 261-268; Lytle, *Merchant Steam Vessels of the United States*, pp. 9, 125. Morton later erroneously reported in this article that a white flag was raised over the *Undine* by the wife of Acting Master John L. Bryant, who was killed, but that it was quickly "snatched down" by the executive officer. Bryant was not killed and it is highly unlikely that his wife would have been aboard.

6. OR, 1, 39, 1: 863; ORN, 1, 26: 598-607; ORN, 2, 220; "Tawah," in Vol. 7 of *Dictionary of American Naval Fighting Ships* (Washington, DC: GPO, 1981), p. 66; Lytle, *Merchant Steam Vessels of the United States*, p. 53, 94, 194; Brown, "Forrest's Johnsonville Raid": 51-52; John W. Morton, "Raid of Forrest's Cavalry," 261-268; Wyeth, *Life of General Nathan Bedford Forrest*, pp. 522-526; Henry, *"First with the Most" Forrest*, p. 374; John A. Eisterhold, "Fort Heiman, Forgotten Fortress," *West Tennessee Historical Society Papers* 38 (1974): 53. James B. Williams was named an acting ensign on March 11, 1863, and was reinstated as an acting master on September 1, 1864; he would be honorably discharged on December 20, 1865. Edward W. Callahan, *List of Officers of the Navy of the United States and of the Marine Corps, from 1775 to 1900, Comprising a Complete Register of All Present and Former Commissioned, Warranted, and Appointed Officers of the United States Navy, and of the Marine Corps, Regular and Volunteer. Compiled from the Official Records of the Navy Department* (New York: L.R. Hamersly, 1901; reprinted, New York: Haskell House, 1969), p. 591; Steenburn, "The United States Ship *Undine*":

27. After the Civil War, Capt. Gracey became a distinguished Clarksburg citizen "very active in the affairs of the Cumberland." Byrd Douglas, *Steamboatin' on the Cumberland* (Nashville: Tennessee Book, 1961), p. 158. Certain aspects of the *Undine* and *Pueblo* captures are eerily similar as testimony at the respective inquiries demonstrates. I looked at the literature of the *Pueblo* incident in my *The United States Navy and Coast Guard, 1946-1983* (Jefferson, NC: McFarland, 1984), pp. 294-296.

7. ORN, 1, 26: 604; OR, 1, 39, 1: 864; OR, 1, 39, 3: 548, 602; Charles Dana Gibson and E. Kay Gibson, comps., *Dictionary of Transports and Combat Vessels, Steam and Sail, Employed by the Union Army, 1861-1868* (Camden, ME: Ensign Press, 1995), p. 81.

8. ORN, 1, 26: 706-707; ORN, 2, 1: 77; OR, 1, 52, 1: 120-122; "Elfin," in Vol. 2 of *Dictionary of American Naval Fighting Ships* (Washington, DC: GPO, 1963), p. 338; Porter, *Naval History of the Civil War*, p. 802. Lee was quite rank-conscious given his recent experience of demotion from and promotion to different squadron commands, even rebuking theater commander Gen. Thomas over a perceived breach of protocol in a message sent on December 2. Thomas, who would work closely with the Virginia-born naval commander, and who himself had known the heartbreak of being passed over, quickly made matters right. ORN, 1, 26: 638-639; Stanley F. Horn, *The Decisive Battle of Nashville* (Baton Rouge: Louisiana State University Press, 1956), p. 30; Whisenant, "Samuel Phillips Lee": pp. 43-44.

9. OR, 1, 39, 1: 869, 874; Williams, "The Johnsonville Raid": 237; James Dinkins, *1861 to 1865, by an Old Johnnie: Personal Recollections and Experiences in the Confederate Army* (Cincinnati: Robert Clarke, 1897), p. 205; Wyeth, *Life of General Nathan Bedford Forrest*, pp. 524-525; Brown, "Forrest's Johnsonville Raid": 53-54.

10. ORN, 1, 26: 603-605; OR, 1, 39, 3: 590. Built at Cincinnati in 1861, the 211-ton side-wheeler *Fairy* was 157 feet long, with a beam of 31.6 feet and a depth of hold of 5 feet. Purchased into the navy in early 1864, she was supposedly able to steam at six knots. Armed with eight 24-pounder howitzers, she began service under Acting Master Henry S. Wetmore on March 10. "Fairy" In Vol. 2 of *Dictionary of American Naval Fighting Ships* (Washington, DC: GPO, 1963), p. 385; a notoriously slow steamer according to "Gunboat" and others, the center-wheeler *St. Charles* was purchased from J. Van Vartwick of Chicago by the USN on April 9, 1863. She was converted into a tinclad at Cairo and renamed *Paw Paw*, prior to her commissioning on July 25. New acting master Augustus F. Thompson's 175-ton boat was 120 feet long, with a beam of 34 feet and a depth of hold of 3.10 feet and a six-foot draft. Rated at four mph, she was armed with two 30-pounder Parrott rifles (larger than those Forrest had placed on the *Venus*) and six 24-pounder howitzers. "Paw Paw" in Vol. 5 of *Dictionary of American Naval Fighting Ships* (Washington, DC: GPO, 1970), p. 238. Thompson, who was given command of the tinclad *Elfin* in May 1864, was honorably discharged on Oct. 20, 1865. Wetmore was trice rated a mate, being discharged the first time (1858), resigning the second (1862), and returning to that rank on October 1, 1862. He was promoted to acting master on December 14, 1863, became an Acting Volunteer Lieutenant on July 9, 1864, and was honorably discharged on Dec. 29, 1865. H. B. O'Neill would resign on March 2, 1865, while the *Paw Paw's* commander, Martin V. B. Haines, did not muster out until August 27, 1868. Callahan, *List of Officers of the Navy of the United States and of the Marine Corps*, pp. 237, 415, 541, 580.

11. ORN, 1, 26: 600-603, 611-612; OR, 1, 39, 3: 611 Logbooks of the U.S.S. *Moose*, June 15, 1863-August 10,

1865, Records of the Bureau of Navigation, Record Group 19, U.S. National Archives, Washington, D.C., November 1–2, 1864 (cited hereafter as Logbook of the U.S.S. *Moose*, with date). The *Undine's* captain was "severely chastised" by the investigating board for loss of the tinclad's signal book. Thereafter, all vessels were to be issued weighted bags for quick disposal in times of emergency. The Fitch-Shirk strategy has been criticized as an "overcautious approach." Williams, "The Johnsonville Raid": 238.

12. ORN, 1, 26: 615; OR, 1, 52, 1: 122; ORN, 1, 39, 1: 874; Wyeth, *Life of General Nathan Bedford Forrest*, p. 525; Jordan and Pryor, *The Campaigns*, p. 598; Jeffrey L. Patrick, "A Fighting Sailor on the Western Rivers: The Civil War Letters of 'Gunboat.'" *The Journal of Mississippi History* 58 (Fall 1996): 279; the *Paw Paw* could barely make four mph steaming upstream. Robert W. Kaeuper, "The Forgotten Triumph of the *Paw Paw*," *American Heritage* 46 (October 1995): 88; Stephen E. Ambrose, *Halleck: Lincoln's Chief of Staff* (Baton Rouge: Louisiana State University Press, 1962), pp. 190–191; Thomas Blog Site.

13. ORN, 1, 26: 611; Patrick, "A Fighting Sailor on the Western Rivers": 279; Logbook of the U.S.S. *Moose*, November 3, 1864. The last Confederate elements to leave Paris were Col. Hinchie P. Mabry's cavalry brigade and the 12-pounder howitzers from Capt. John C. Thrall's battery, nicknamed "The Arkansas Rats." These took position above Johnsonville later in the day. OR, 1, 39, 1: 874–875; Wyeth, *Life of General Nathan Bedford Forrest*, p. 527.

14. ORN, 1, 26: 630; Williams, "The Johnsonville Raid": 239; J. B. Irion and D. V. Beard, *Underwater Archaeological Assessment of Civil War Shipwrecks in Kentucky Lake, Benton and Humphreys Counties, Tennessee* (New Orleans: R. Christopher Goodwin & Associates, Inc., for the Tennessee Division of Archaeology, Department of Environment and Conservation, State of Tennessee, 1993), p. 3. The island, Johnsonville, Reynoldsburg, and the surrounding area were covered by the TVA's Kentucky Lake in 1944. "The Archaeological Investigations of the Battle of Johnsonville," *PanAm Consultants Homepage*, http://www.panamconsultants.com/PAGE (accessed June 8, 2004).

15. ORN, 1, 26: 612, 616; OR, 1, 39, 1: 122, 124, 869; Brown, "Forrest's Johnsonville Raid": 54.

16. ORN, 1, 26: 612; OR, 1, 39, 1: 869, 871, 875; Brown, "Forrest's Johnsonville Raid": 54; Morton, *The Artillery of Nathan Bedford Forrest's Cavalry*, pp. 252–255; Logbook of the U.S.S. *Moose*, November 3, 1864.

17. ORN, 1, 26: 612–613; OR, 1, 52, 1: 123; John M. Latham, *Raising the Civil War Gunboats and Building the Magic Valley History Tower* (Camden, TN: J. M. Latham, 1997), pp. 161–162; Logbook of the U.S.S. *Moose*, November 4, 1864; Brown, "Forrest's Johnsonville Raid": 55–56; Denny, "The Devil's Navy": 29; Patrick, "A Fighting Sailor on the Western Rivers": 280–281; Kaeuper, "The Forgotten Triumph of the *Paw Paw*:" 92. Morton, *The Artillery of Nathan Bedford Forrest's Cavalry*, p. 251; Williams, "The Johnsonville Raid": 239–240; Lonnie E. Maness, *An Untutored Genius: The Military Career of General Nathan Bedford Forrest* (Oxford, MS: Guild Bindery Press, 1990), p. 313; the loss of the *Undine* was reported in *The New York Times* on November 7. Callahan, *List of Officers of the Navy of the United States and of the Marine Corps*, p. 415. O'Neill was appointed to his rank in August 1863 and resigned from the service on March 2, 1865. The Alexandria losses are covered in ORN, 1, 26: 112–124.

18. OR, 1, 39, 1: 871; OR, 1, 52, 1: 123; ORN, 1, 26: 614; Jordan and Pryor, *The Campaigns*, p. 602; Logbook of the U.S.S. *Moose*, November 4, 1864. Fitch sent a written report of the day's activities by dispatch boat to Paducah for Lt. Cmdr. Shirk to forward on to Rear Admiral Lee. In his endorsement, Shirk was complementary of his colleagues, Fitch and King, pointing out that both "have done all that men could do to defeat the plans of the enemy and to uphold the honor of the flag." He went on to add: "If they were not successful, it was not because they were not brave, prudent, and faithful officers, but because they were met by an overwhelming force of the enemy." ORN, 1, 26: 615.

19. OR, 1, 39, 1: 871; OR, 1, 52, 1: 123–124; ORN, 1, 26: 610–611, 620; Morton, *The Artillery of Nathan Beford Forrest's Cavalry*, p. 255; Brown, "Forrest's Johnsonville Raid": 57; "The Archaeological Investigations of the Battle of Johnsonville," *PanAm Consultants Homepage*, http://www.panamconsultants.com/PAGE (accessed June 8, 2004).

20. OR, 1, 52, 1: 682–683; Denny, "The Devil's Navy": 30; Brown, "Forrest's Johnsonville Raid": 57; Williams, "The Johnsonville Raid": pp. 243–244; Alfred T. Mahan, *The Gulf and Inland Waters*, Vol. 3 of the *Navy in the Civil War* (New York: Scribner's, 1883), pp. 214–215; Cox, *March to the Sea*, p. 18; Williams and Humphreys, *Gunboats and Cavalry*, p. 24; Thomas Van Horne, ed., *History of the Army of the Cumberland: Its Organization, Campaigns, and Battles, Written at the Request of Major General George H. Thomas Chiefly from His Private Military Journal and Official and Other Documents Furnished by Him*, vol. 2 (Cincinnati: R. Clarke, 1875; reprinted, Wilmington, NC: Broadfoot, 1988), 484; Porter, *Naval History of the Civil War*, p. 802. Acting Volunteer Lieutenant King was court-martialed on May 8, 1865, for ordering the burning of the Johnsonville gunboats, but was found not guilty. Witness after witness pointed out that, had the naval craft been scuttled rather than destroyed, the water, only five feet deep, would not have covered their gun decks and had Forrest occupied the depot, as many feared possible, veterans of his Tennessee River Navy could have raised them in six hours' time. Latham, *Raising the Civil War Gunboats*, p. 166–167. The King court-martial proceedings are one of the great untapped sources on the entire campaign. U.S. Navy Department, Records of General Courts-Martial and Courts of Inquiry of the Navy Department, "Case of Acting Vol. Lieut E. M. King, Lately of the U.S.S. *Key West*," Microfilm Publications, M273, National Archives, Washington, D.C.

21. OR, 1, 39, 1: 871; OR, 1, 45, 1: 752;ORN, 1, 26: 614, 616, 629, 717–718; Logbook of the U.S.S. *Moose*, November 4–6, 1864; Wiley Sword, *Embrace an Angry Wind—The Confederacy's Last Hurrah: Spring Hill, Franklin & Nashville* (New York: HarperCollins, 1992), pp. 67–68; Patrick, "A Fighting Sailor on the Western Rivers": 280–281; Cornish and Laas, *Lincoln's Lee*, pp. 142–145; Nashville *Daily Press*, November 7–8, 1864; Nashville *Dispatch*, November 8–10, 1864; *The New York Times*, November 10, 1864.

Chapter Twelve

1. U.S. Navy Department, *Official Records of the Union and Confederate Navies in the War of the Rebellion* (Washington, DC: GPO, 1894–1922), Series 1, Vol. 26, 627, 717, 719 (cited hereafter as ORN, followed by a comma, the series number, a comma, the volume number, a colon, and the page number); ORN, 2, 1: 52, 58; OR, 1, 52, 1: 712; Logbooks of the U.S.S. *Moose*, June 15, 1863–August 10, 1865, Records of the Bureau of Navigation, Record Group 19, U.S. National Archives, Washington, D.C., November 7, 1864 (cited hereafter as Logbook of the U.S.S. *Moose*, with date). Lucius F. Hubbard, "Minnesota in the Battles of Nashville, December 15 and 16, 1864: Read Before the Minnesota Commandery of the Loyal Legion of the United States, March 14, 1905," Collections of the Minnesota Historical Society, Volume 12 http://memory.loc.gov/cgi-bin/

query/r?ammem/lhbum:@field%28DOCID+@lit%281hbum0 (accessed January 9, 2006); Paul H. Silverstone, *Warships of the Civil War Navies* (Annapolis, MD: Naval Institute Press, 1989), pp. 151–153; H. Allen Gosnell, *Guns on the Western Waters: The Story of the River Gunboats in the Civil War* (Baton Rouge: Louisiana State University Press, 1949), p. ii; Henry Walke, *Naval Scenes and Reminiscences of the Civil War in the United States on the Southern and Western Waters During the Years 1861, 1862 and 1863 with the History of That Period Compared and Corrected from Authentic Sources* (New York: F. R. Reed, 1877), p. 53; Myron J. Smith, Jr., "A Construction and Recruiting History of the U.S. Steam Gunboat *Carondelet*, 1861–1862" (unpublished master's thesis, Shippensburg State University, 1969), p. iv; Donald L. Canney, *The Old Steam Navy: Vol. 2, The Ironclads, 1842–1885* (Annapolis, MD: Naval Institute Press, 1993), pp. 47–55.

2. ORN, 2, 1: 157; Silverstone, *Warships*, p. 149; Canney, *The Old Steam Navy*, pp. 107–110. Acting Volunteer Lieutenant Howard, *Neosho's* captain, remained with the USN until honorably discharged on November 4, 1868. Edward W. Callahan, *List of Officers of the Navy of the United States and of the Marine Corps, from 1775 to 1900, Comprising a Complete Register of All Present and Former Commissioned, Warranted, and Appointed Officers of the United States Navy, and of the Marine Corps, Regular and Volunteer. Compiled from the Official Records of the Navy Department* (New York: L.R. Hamersly, 1901; reprinted, New York: Haskell House, 1969), p. 278.

3. U.S. War Department, *The War of the Rebellion: A Compilation of the Official Records of the Union and Confederate Armies* (Washington, DC: GPO, 1880–1901), Series I, Vol. 39, Pt. 1: 370 (cited hereafter as OR, followed by a comma, the series number, a comma, the volume number, a colon, and the page number); OR, 1, 39, 2: 250; OR, 1, 39, 3: 509, 537, 595, 692–693, 746; Wiley Sword, *Embrace an Angry Wind—The Confederacy's Last Hurrah: Spring Hill, Franklin & Nashville* (New York: HarperCollins, 1992), p. 85; ORN, 1, 26: 616, 627, 629–630, 720–721; Logbook of the U.S.S. *Moose*, November 8, 1864.

4. ORN, 1, 26: 628–629, 706–707, 724; Logbook of the U.S.S. *Moose*, November 9, 1864.

5. ORN, 1, 26: 631; Logbook of the U.S.S. *Moose*, November 10, 1864.

6. Logbook of the U.S.S. *Moose*, November 10, 1864.

7. Mark M. Boatner III, *The Civil War Dictionary* (New York: David McKay, 1959), pp. 308–309; OR, 1, 45, 1: 32–34; Sword, *Embrace an Angry Wind*, pp. 84–120; Logbook of the U.S.S. *Moose*, November 11–30, 1864.

8. Byrd Douglas, *Steamboatin' on the Cumberland* (Nashville: Tennessee Book, 1961), pp. 162–164. Luckily for the Union, Gen. Hood elected to keep Forrest with him, allowing only a few mounted units to be split off and sent against logistical targets along the Cumberland. "No longer would this ingenious leader be left," wrote Douglas, "to harass Thomas." On the other hand, Maj. Gen. Thomas would continue to overestimate Forrest's strength and threat, with his concern for "the devil" a major reason Nashville was placed into a defensive position; Sword, *Embrace an Angry Wind*, p. 278.

9. ORN, 1, 26: 632, 732–733. The *Carondelet* reached Illinois on November 15. Logbooks of the U.S.S. *Carondelet*, May 1862–June 1865, Records of the Bureau of Navigation, Record Group 19, U.S. National Archives, Washington, D.C., November 15, 1864 (cited hereafter as Logbook of the U.S.S. *Carondelet*, with date); John Hagerty, "Letter, November 15, 1864," in "'Dear Maggie...' The Letters of John Hagerty, 1st Class Fireman, U.S.S. *Carondelet* to Margaret 'Maggie' O'Neil, September 8, 1864–May 28, 1865," *Letters of John Hagerty* homepage, *http://www.webnation.com/~spectrum/usn-cw/diaries/HagertyJohnHome.htm* (accessed April 10, 2000).

10. OR, 1, 45, 1, 1032–1033; Nashville *Daily Union*, November 25, 1864; Walter T. Durham, *Reluctant Partners: Nashville and the Union—July 1, 1863, to June 30, 1865* (Nashville: Tennessee Historical Society, 1987), p. 206; Henry Stone, "Repelling Hood's Invasion of Tennessee," in *Battles and Leaders of the Civil War*, edited by Robert V. Johnson and Clarence C. Buel (New York: Century, 1884–1887; reprinted, New York: Thomas Yoseloff, 1956), p. 443.

11. OR, 1, 45, 1, 1055; Nashville *Dispatch*, November 26, 1864; Durham, *Reluctant Partners*, p. 205.

12. OR, 1, 45, 1, 1056–1057, 1075; ORN, 1, 26: 632–633, 647.

13. ORN, 1, 26: 632–633, 647, 746; Logbook of the *Carondelet*, November 27, 1864.

14. OR, 1, 45, I: 1104.

15. ORN, 1, 26: 633–634; Douglas, *Steamboatin' on the Cumberland*, p. 163; Logbook of the U.S.S. *Carondelet*, November 27, 1864; Logbook of the U.S.S. *Moose*, November 25–27, 1864.

16. ORN, 1, 26: 634–635; Logbook of the U.S.S. *Carondelet*, November 28, 1864.

17. ORN, 1, 26: 647; OR, 1, 45, 1: 1131–1132, 1135; Minnesota, Board of Commissioners on Publication of History of Minnesota in the Civil and Indian Wars, *Minnesota in the Civil and Indian Wars, 1861–1865*, vol. 1 (St. Paul, MN: Printed for the State of Minnesota by Pioneer Press, 1889), 274; Logbook of the U.S.S. *Moose*, November 29, 1864; Logbook of the U.S.S. *Carondelet*, November 29, 1864.

18. ORN, 1, 26: 636–637, 647–648; OR, 1, 45, 1: 34; OR, 1, 45, 2: 3, 17; Hubbard, "Minnesota in the Battles of Nashville"; Minnesota, *Minnesota in the Civil and Indian Wars*; Edwin G. Huddleston, *The Civil War in Middle Tennessee* (Nashville: Nashville Banner, 1965), pp. 118–119; Logbook of the U.S.S. *Moose*, November 30–December 1, 1864; Logbook of the U.S.S. *Carondelet*, November 30–December 1, 1864; Nashville *Daily Press*, November 30–December 2, 1864; Thomas Blog Site; John E. Fisher, *They Rode with Forrest and Wheeler: A Chronicle of Five Tennessee Brothers' Service in the Confederate Western Cavalry* (Jefferson, NC: McFarland, 1995), p. 161; Robert Selph Henry, *"First with the Most" Forrest* (Indianapolis: Bobbs-Merrill, 1944), pp. 399–400; Stanley F. Horn, *The Army of Tennessee: A Military History* (Indianapolis: Bobbs-Merrill, 1941, reprinted, Norman, OK: University of Oklahoma Press, 1968), p. 404; Stanley F. Horn, *The Decisive Battle of Nashville* (Baton Rouge: Louisiana State University Press, 1956), pp. 30–31; James F. Rusling, *Men and Things I Saw in Civil War Days*, new ed. (New York: Methodist Book Concern, 1914), pp. 87–88; Stanley F. Horn, comp., *Tennessee's War, 1861–1865: Described by Participants* (Nashville: Tennessee Civil War Centennial Commission, 1965), pp. 321–322; Robert Wayne "Bob" Henderson, Jr., *The Battlefield Beneath Us*, unpublished paper (Nashville, TN, May 2006), p. 3; Sword, *Embrace an Angry Wind*, pp. 272–274; Durham, *Reluctant Partners*, pp. 211–214. From the beginning of December until his advance from the city in mid-month, Maj. Gen. Thomas engaged in a verbal conflict with Lt. Gen. Grant and others in Washington over his perceived need to fully outfit his cavalry before moving. This requirement, seen as a case of the "slows" in Washington, nearly got Thomas replaced. The matter has been reviewed many times from different angles. Although outside the scope of this work, we saw the arguments many times in various memoirs, reports, and histories, including those cited here and some not, for example, Donald M. Lynne's, "Wilson's Cavalry at Nashville," *Civil War History*, 1, 1955: 141–159.

19. OR, 1, 45, 1: 79–83; OR, 1, 45, 2: 27; ORN, 1, 26: 636–639; Sword, *Embrace an Angry Wind*, p. 281; Henry, *"First with the Most" Forrest*, p. 401; Henderson, *The Battlefield Beneath Us*, p. 8; Logbook of the U.S.S. *Moose*, December 2, 1864; Logbook of the U.S.S. *Carondelet*, December 2, 1864; Mark Zimmerman, *Battle of Nashville Preservation Society Guide to Civil War Nashville* (Nashville: Lithographics, 2004), p. 49; Stanley F. Horn, "Nashville During the Civil War," *Tennessee Historical Quarterly* 4 (March 1945): 19.

20. Thomas L. Connelly, *Autumn of Glory: The Army of Tennessee, 1862-1865* (Baton Rouge: Louisiana State University Press, 1971), p. 508; James Lee McDonough, *Nashville: The Western Confederacy's Final Gamble* (Knoxville, TN: University of Tennessee Press, 2004), pp. 141–142; Steven E. Woodward, *Jefferson Davis and His Generals: The Failure of Confederate Command in the West* (Lawrence, KS: University Press of Kansas, 1990), p. 301; Douglas, *Steamboatin' on the Cumberland*, p. 165; Durham, *Reluctant Partners*, pp. 214–215; ORN, 1, 26: 646; OR, 1, 45, 1: 764; OR, 1, 45, 2: 18, 27, 191; Fisher, *They Rode with Forrest and Wheeler*, p. 162; John Allan Wyeth, *Life of General Nathan Bedford Forrest* (New York: Harper & Bros., 1904), p. 547; Thomas Jordan and J. P. Pryor, *The Campaigns of Lieut. Gen. N. B. Forrest and of Forrest's Cavalry* (New Orleans and New York: Blelock & Co., 1868; reprinted, New York: DaCapo Press, 1996), p. 636; Henderson, *The Battlefield Beneath Us*, pp. 1, 5, 7, 10.

21. Logbook of the U.S.S. *Carondelet*, December 3, 1864; Logbook of the U.S.S. *Moose*, December 3, 1864.

22. OR, 1, 45, 2: 30–31, 52; ORN, 1, 26: 639–640.

23. Logbook of the U.S.S. *Carondelet*, December 3–4, 1864; Logbook of the U.S.S. *Moose*, December 3–4, 1864; David Dixon Porter, *Naval History of the Civil War* (New York: Sherman, 1886; reprinted, Mineola, NY: Dover Publications, 1998), pp. 803–804; Alfred T. Mahan, *The Gulf and Inland Waters*, Vol. 3 of the *Navy in the Civil War*. (New York: Scribner's, 1883), pp. 215–216; Stephen Starr, *The Union Cavalry in the Civil War: Vol. 3, The War in the West, 1861-1865* (Baton Rouge: Louisiana State University Press, 1985), p. 284; ORN, 1, 26: 641–647; OR, 1, 45, 2: 37, 43, 48–49, 54; Rowland Stafford True, "Life Aboard a Gunboat," *Civil War Times Illustrated* 9 (February 1971): 39–40; Jordan and Pryor, *Campaigns of Lieut. Gen. N. B. Forrest*, p. 636; Wyeth, *Life of General Nathan Bedford Forrest*, pp. 547–548; OR, 1, 45, 2: 51–52; Walke, *Naval Scenes and Reminiscences of the Civil*, p. 124; Henderson, *The Battlefield Beneath Us*, pp. 10–11. Garrard was aboard the *Carondelet* to inform Miller that he had halted the Buena Vista-Hyde's Ferries by taking their boats under guard. OR, 1, 45, 2: 36–37.

24. Logbook of the U.S.S. *Carondelet*, December 5, 1864; Logbook of the U.S.S. *Moose*, December 5, 1864; Starr, *Union Cavalry in the Civil War*, pp. 283–284; Durham, *Reluctant Partners*, p. 226; *Nashville Dispatch*, December 6, 1864; *Nashville Daily Times and True Union*, December 8, 1864; McDonough, *Nashville: The Western Confederacy's Final Gamble*, p. 144; OR, 1, 45, 1: 631–632, 652, 654, 658, 660, 744, 754–755; OR, 1, 45, 2: 651, 657, 758; ORN, 1, 26: 648, 758; Jordan and Pryor, *Campaigns of Lieut. Gen. N. B. Forrest*, pp. 630–631; Henderson, *The Battlefield Beneath Us*, pp. 10–11; Mike Fitzpatrick, "Miasma Fogs and River Mists," *Military Images* 25 (January-February 2004): 29; Wyeth, *Life of General Nathan Bedford Forrest*, p. 548. Rice had been appointed an acting ensign on December 30, 1862, and an acting master on July 20, 1864; he would retain command of the *Brilliant* over the next six months and be honorably discharged on October 26, 1865. Callahan, *List of Officers of the Navy of the United States and of the Marine Corps*, p. 460.

25. ORN, 1, 26: 650–652; Logbook of the U.S.S. *Carondelet*, December 6, 1864; Logbook of the U.S.S. *Moose*, December 6, 1864; Bern Anderson, *By Sea and By River: The Naval History of the Civil War* (New York: Knopf, 1962), p. 266; Durham, *Reluctant Partners*, p. 218; True, "Life Aboard a Gunboat": 40; James McCague, *The Cumberland, Rivers of America* (New York: Holt, Rinehart and Winston, 1973), p. 180; Horn, *The Decisive Battle of Nashville*, p. 80; Henderson, *The Battlefield Beneath Us*, pp. 5, 7, 12–14; Zimmerman, *Battle of Nashville Preservation Society Guide*, p. 9; Terry Foenander, "Fact File No. 1," *Union Navy Medal of Honor Fact File* <http://home.ozconnect.net/tfoen/mohfactfile1.htm> (accessed March 12, 2006). Civilian pilot John H. Ferrell was born in Bedford County, Tennessee, on April 15, 1823, and entered naval service at Cairo. Upon his death, he was buried in Price Cemetery at Elizabethtown, Illinois. "Medal of Honor Recipients Buried in Illinois," *Home of Heroes Homepage*, < http://www.homeofheroes.com/moh/cemeteries/il.html (accessed March 12, 2006); John Ditzenback was born at New York City in 1828 and enlisted in Indiana, to which state his medal is credited. The quartermaster's fate after the war is unknown as is his burial site. "Find-a-Grave of Famous People: D-Di," in *Wikipedia: The Free Encyclopedia*, <http://en.wikipedia.org/wiki/Wikipedia:Find-A-Grave_famous_people/D/Di> (accessed March 12, 2006).

26. Dudley Taylor Cornish and Virginia Jeans Laas, *Lincoln's Lee: The Life of Samuel Phillips Lee, United States Navy, 1812-1897* (Lawrence, KS: University Press of Kansas, 1986), p. 146; OR, 1, 45, 2: 85–86; 101; Logbook of the U.S.S. *Carondelet*, December 7, 1864; Logbook of the U.S.S. *Moose*, December 7, 1864; *Nashville Daily Press*, December 8, 1864; Starr, *Union Cavalry in the Civil War*, p. 302; Durham, *Reluctant Partners*, p. 228.

27. Logbook of the U.S.S. *Carondelet*, December 8, 1864; Logbook of the U.S.S. *Moose*, December 8, 1864; OR, 1, 45, 2: 97–101, 105–106; ORN, 1, 26: 654–659, 662; Starr, *Union Cavalry in the Civil War*, pp. 284–285.

28. Logbook of the U.S.S. *Carondelet*, December 9, 1864; Logbook of the U.S.S. *Moose*, December 9–14, 1864; OR, 1, 45, 2:117; ORN, 1, 26: 184; McDonough, *Nashville: The Western Confederacy's Final Gamble*, pp. 149–151; Tamara Moser Melia, *"Damn the Torpedoes": A Short History of U.S. Naval Mine Countermeasures, 1777-1991*, Contributions in Naval History, no. 4 (Washington, DC: Naval Historical Center, Department of the Navy, 1991), p. 12. Fitch in his official report for the period from December 6 to 16 speaks of the "severity of the weather." ORN, 1, 26: 650.

29. OR, 1, 45, 2: 116–117, 125, 128; Logbook of the U.S.S. *Moose*, December 9, 1864; Starr, *Union Cavalry in the Civil War*, p. 303.

30. OR, 1, 45, 1: 803–804; OR, 1, 45: 2: 55, 70, 145, 152–154; ORN, 1, 26: 662, 688, 758; *The New York Times*, December 24, 1864; *The London Times*, December 24, 1864; Henderson, *The Battlefield Beneath Us*, p. 14; Starr, *Union Cavalry in the Civil War*, p. 303. An acting master after August 29, 1861, French was promoted an acting volunteer lieutenant on July 15, 1864, upon the recommendation of his commanding officer. He would be honorably discharged on December 22, 1865. An 1861 naval academy graduate, Pennsylvanian Naile served in the West Gulf Coast Blockading Squadron until early 1864. Promoted to ensign in 1863 and lieutenant in February 1864, he would achieve the rank of lieutenant commander in mid–1866. By January 1871, he would be on the retired list. Callahan, *List of Officers of the Navy of the United States and of the Marine Corps*, pp. 206, 400; Lewis B. Hamersly, *The Records of Living Officers of the U.S. Navy and Marine Corps* (Philadelphia: J. B. Lippincott, 1870), p. 225.

31. ORN, 1, 26: 650, 653; ORN, 1, 26: 661–662;

Durham, *Reluctant Partners*, p. 237; Nashville *Daily Press*, December 12, 14, 1864; Starr, *Union Cavalry in the Civil War*, p. 303.

32. ORN, 1, 26: 652, 662–664, 688, 803–806; OR, 1, 45, 2: 168–171; Rusling, *Men and Things I Saw*, p. 340; Starr, *Union Cavalry in the Civil War*, pp. 303, 317–319; Logbook of the U.S.S. *Moose*, December 12–13, 1864; Logbook of the U.S.S. *Carondelet*, December 12–13, 1864; John Hagerty, "Letter, December 13, 1864," in "'Dear Maggie'"; Douglas, *Steamboatin' on the Cumberland*, pp. 164–165.

33. OR, 1, 45, 2: 160, 180–184, 191–192; OR, 1, 45, 1:154; ORN, 1, 26: 653, 664; Henderson, *The Battlefield Beneath Us*, pp. 5, 16; James Dickins, *Personal Recollections & Experiences in the Confederate Army* (Cincinnati: Robert Clarke, 1897), p. 245; Starr, *Union Cavalry in the Civil War*, pp. 317–318; Logbook of the U.S.S. *Moose*, December 14–15, 1864; Logbook of the U.S.S. *Carondelet*, December 14–15, 1864.

34. Logbook of the U.S.S. *Moose*, December 15, 1864; Logbook of the U.S.S. *Carondelet*, December 15, 1864; Henderson, *The Battlefield Beneath Us*, pp. 14–15; Sarah Foster Kelly, *West Knoxville: Its People and Environs* (Nashville: S. F. Kelly, 1987), pp. 52, 59; Sword, *Embrace an Angry Wind*, pp. 319–322; OR, 1, 45, 1: 37–38, 128, 765; OR, 1, 45, 2: 185,197; ORN, 1, 26: 650–651; Durham, *Reluctant Partners*, p. 245.

35. OR, 1, 45, 1, 599–600, 606, 765; OR, 1, 45, 2: 205–206; ORN, 1, 26: 651; Logbook of the U.S.S. *Carondelet*, December 15, 1864; Sword, *Embrace an Angry Wind*, pp. 326–328; Henderson, *The Battlefield Beneath Us*, pp. 16–17; Dickins, *Personal Recollections*, p. 246; Durham, *Reluctant Partners.*, p. 250; Horn, *The Decisive Battle of Nashville*, p. 39; McDonough, *Nashville: The Western Confederacy's Final Gamble*, p.157, 175–176. Johnson's capture by Morgan near Gallatin on August 21, 1862, is told on pp. 116–117 of James A. Ramage, *Rebel Raider: The Life of General John Hunt Morgan* (Lexington: University Press of Kentucky, 1986).

36. OR, 1, 45, 1: 600; OR, 1, 45, 2: 197, 205; ORN, 1, 26: 651; John Johnston, "Cavalry of Hoods Left at Nashville," *Confederate Veteran* 13 (1905): 28–29; Horn, *The Decisive Battle of Nashville*, p. 84; Henderson, *The Battlefield Beneath Us*; McDonough, *Nashville: The Western Confederacy's Final Gamble*, p. 176–177; Sword, *Embrace an Angry Wind.*, pp. 327–328; McCague, *The Cumberland*, p. 180; Logbook of the U.S.S. *Moose*, December 15, 1864; Logbook of the U.S.S. *Carondelet*, December 15, 1864; Zimmerman, *Battle of Nashville Preservation Society Guide*, p. 69; Colleen Creamer, "Civil War Battle Site Gets Commemorative Marker: Reprinted from The City Paper, Nashville Tennessee, n.d.," American Civil War Round Table of the United Kingdom homepage, http://www.americancivilwar.org.uk/preservation/city_paper_nashville.htm (accessed April 1, 2006).

37. OR, 1, 45, 1: 38–39; OR, 1, 45, 2: 194, 196–197; *The New York Times*, December 19, 1864; James H. Wilson, *Under the Old Flag*, vol. 2 (New York: D. Appleton, 1912), pp. 109–112; Isaac R. Sherwood, *Memories of the War* (Toledo, OH: H. J. Crittenden, 1923), p. 149; Lynne, "Wilson's Cavalry at Nashville": p. 150; Sword, *Embrace an Angry Wind*, pp. 328–350. Fitch's belief that Kelley's batteries were captured formed the basis for the nautical history of the Battle of Nashville for a century. Among those giving this version credence early on were Admirals Porter and Mahan, both of whom knew Fitch and wrote their histories in the decade after his death. Porter, *Naval History of the Civil War*, p. 805; Mahan, *The Gulf and Inland Waters*, p. 216.

38. Sword, *Embrace an Angry Wind*, pp. 328, 350–351; Johnston, "Cavalry of Hoods Left at Nashville": 29; OR, 1, 45, 1: 601, 765–766 ; OR, 1, 45, 2: 213, 220; ORN, 1, 26: 651, 668; Henderson, *The Battlefield Beneath Us*, p. 6; ORN, 1, 27: 153; Wyeth, *Life of General Nathan Bedford Forrest*, pp. 555–556; Logbook of the U.S.S. *Moose*, December 16, 1864; Logbook of the U.S.S. *Carondelet*, December 16, 1864.

39. Horn, *The Decisive Battle of Nashville*, pp. 150–152; Horn, *Army of Tennessee*, p. 418; Horn, "Nashville During the Civil War," 22; Wyeth, *Life of General Nathan Bedford Forrest*, p. 556–559; Fisher, *They Rode with Forrest and Wheeler*, pp. 168–171; OR, 1, 45, 2: 210, 231, 245; Durham, *Reluctant Partners*, p. 261, 266; Nashville *Daily Union*, December 20, 22, 1864; Milwaukee *Daily Sentinel*, December 24, 1864.

40. ORN, 1, 26: 651; Logbook of the U.S.S. *Moose*, December 16, 1864; Logbook of the U.S.S. *Carondelet*, December 16, 1864.

41. OR, 1, 45, 2: 231; Nashville *Daily Union*, December 17, 1864.

42. ORN, 1, 26: 670–671; Cornish and Laas, *Lincoln's Lee*, p. 148.

43. ORN, 1, 26: 671–672; OR, 1, 45, 2: 251; Logbook of the U.S.S. *Moose*, December 18, 1864; Logbook of the U.S.S. *Carondelet*, December 18, 1864.

44. ORN, 1, 26: 670, 673; Logbook of the U.S.S. *Moose*, December 19, 1864; Logbook of the U.S.S. *Carondelet*, December 19, 1864; Cornish and Laas, *Lincoln's Lee*, p. 148. It is possible that Fitch, from his knowledge of the rivers gained in two years of war, might have suspected that, based on intelligence reports, Hood was heading for Alabama via Great Muscle Shoals. Low water on the obstruction would prevent any naval pursuit into the upper Tennessee.

45. OR, 1, 45, 1: 674; OR, 1, 45, 2: 357,371, 507; ORN, 1, 26: 672–679; ORN, 1, 27: 9–28; McDonough, *Nashville: The Western Confederacy's Final Gamble*, pp. 273–274; Starr, *Union Cavalry in the Civil War*, pp. 421, 423; Wyeth, *Life of General Nathan Bedford Forrest*, pp. 564–575; Cornish and Laas, *Lincoln's Lee*, pp. 149–150; Horn, "Nashville During the Civil War": 22.

Chapter Thirteen

1. Thomas Connelly, *Autumn of Glory: The Army of Tennessee, 1862-1865* (Baton Rouge: Louisiana State University Press, 1971), p. 513; Allen C. Guelzo, *The Crisis of the American Republic: A History of the Civil War and Reconstruction* (New York: St. Martin's Press, 1995), p. 368; Richard P. Gildrie, "Guerrilla Warfare in the Lower Cumberland River Valley, 1862–1865," *Tennessee Historical Quarterly* 49 (Fall 1990): 173. Maj. Gen. Sherman's staff judge advocate and provost marshal from October 1863 to September 1864, Henry Satterlee Fitch, had originally tendered his resignation in January 1863. It was finally accepted on January 11, 1865. John T. Fitch jtfitch@fitchfamily.com, "Re: Another Fitch," personal e-mail, May 23, 2000.

2. Dudley Taylor Cornish and Virginia Jeans Laas, *Lincoln's Lee: The Life of Samuel Phillips Lee, United States Navy, 1812-1897* (Lawrence, KS: University Press of Kansas, 1986), pp. 150–151; Johnny H. Whisenant, "Samuel Phillips Lee, U.S.N.: Commander, Mississippi Squadron (October 19, 1864–August 14, 1865)," (unpublished master's thesis; Pittsburg, KS: Kansas State College of Pittsburg, 1968), pp. 74–75; Samuel Phillips Lee, "Letter of Rear Admiral Samuel Phillips Lee to Senator James Rood Doolittle" (contributed by Duane Mowry), *Southern Historical Association* 19 (March 1905): 111–122.

3. Between mid–February and mid–March, Gen. Lee lost 8 percent of his army "either into the Union lines or

into North Carolina." Guelzo, *The Crisis of the American Republic*, p. 369; Gildrie, "Guerrilla Warfare in the Lower Cumberland River Valley": 173; Whisenant, "Samuel Phillips Lee, U.S.N.": 67.

4. Lewis B. Hamersly, *The Records of Living Officers of the U.S. Navy and Marine Corps* (Philadelphia: J. B. Lippincott, 1870), pp. 170, 250-251; U.S. Navy Department, *Official Records of the Union and Confederate Navies in the War of the Rebellion* (Washington, DC: GPO, 1894-1922), Series 1, Vol. 27, 14-15 (cited hereafter as ORN, followed by a comma, the series number, a comma, the volume number, a colon, and the page number); Cornish and Laas, *Lincoln's Lee*, p 149. Interestingly, Boyd would remain on duty with the Mississippi Squadron into late 1865 at which point he would be posted with Fitch to an instructor's billet at the U.S. Naval Academy. His most exciting and memorable service would be aboard the revolutionary test steamer U.S.S. *Wampanoag*, September 1867-June 1968. Boyd was promoted to the rank of commander in 1871 and captain in 1882. He died on July 30, 1890. Edward W. Callahan, *List of Officers of the Navy of the United States and of the Marine Corps, from 1775 to 1900, Comprising a Complete Register of All Present and Former Commissioned, Warranted, and Appointed Officers of the United States Navy, and of the Marine Corps, Regular and Volunteer. Compiled from the Official Records of the Navy Department* (New York: L.R. Hamersly, 1901; reprinted, New York: Haskell House, 1969), p. 70.

5. ORN, 1, 27: 14, 27, 36,56; Logbooks of the U.S.S. *Moose*, June 15, 1863-August 10, 1865, Records of the Bureau of Navigation, Record Group 19, U.S. National Archives, Washington, D.C., January 20-31, 1865 (cited hereafter as Logbook for the U.S.S. *Moose*, with date); David Dixon Porter, *Naval History of the Civil War* (New York: Sherman, 1886; reprinted, Mineola, NY: Dover, 1998), pp. 549, 807-808, 811.

6. Logbook of the U.S.S. *Moose*, February 1-March 1, 1865; Richmond *Daily Examiner*, March 1, 1865.

7. ORN, 1, 27: 78, 86-87, 92-93, 102, 104-105; Cornish and Laas, *Lincoln's Lee*, p. 151; Logbook of the U.S.S. *Moose*, March 8-18, 1864; *Louisville Journal*, March 9, 1864.

8. ORN, 1, 27: 125, 131.

9. ORN, 1, 27: 4, 40, 136-137.

10. ORN, 1, 27: 141.

11. ORN, 2, 1: 27; "Abeona" In: Vol. 1, Part A of *Dictionary of American Naval Fighting Ships*, (Washington, DC: GPO, 1991), p. 17.

12. ORN, 1, 27: 149, 711; Guelzo, *The Crisis of the American Republic*, pp. 377-379. The literature surrounding Lincoln's assassination is enormous. The details may be found in any recent biography of the 16th president.

13. ORN, 1, 27: 154, 160-184, 202-203.

14. ORN, 1, 27: 185-187, 200; Logbook of the U.S.S. *Moose*, April 28-May 3, 1865; Thomas Jordan and J. P. Pryor. *The Campaigns of Lieut. Gen. N. B. Forrest and of Forrest's Cavalry* (New Orleans and New York: Blelock, 1868; reprinted, New York: DaCapo Press, 1996), pp 685-703; Cornish and Laas, *Lincoln's Lee*, p. 153.

15. ORN, 1, 27: 199, 214, 218, 254, 283; "Fitch, Le Roy," Entry No. 415, Abstracts of Service Records of Naval Officers: Records of Officers, 1798-1893, U.S. Navy Department, Bureau of Navigation, U.S. National Archives and Records Service, Record Group 24, Reel 11, January 1864-December 1871 cited hereafter as Fitch, with reel number and date, kindly provided in photocopy by Alice C. Creighton, head, Special Collections and Archives, Nimitz Library, USNA, May 13, 1997; Porter, *Naval History of the Civil War*, pp. 803-804.

16. The population of Cass County was 16,843 in 1860. It swelled upwards 7,350 persons by 1870 to 24,193. Francis A. Walker, *A Compendium of the Ninth Census, June 1, 1870* (Washington, DC: GPO, 1872), p. 41.

17. William B. Cogar, *Dictionary of Admirals of the U.S. Navy*, vol. 1 (Annapolis, MD: Naval Institute Press, 1989), 132; James Russell Soley, *Historical Sketch of the United States Naval Academy, Prepared by Direction of Rear Admiral C. R. P. Rodgers, U.S.N.* (Washington, DC: GPO, 1876), p. 328; Jack Sweetman, *The U.S. Naval Academy: An Illustrated History* (Annapolis, MD: Naval Institute Press, 1979), pp. 63-74, 83-84; ORN, 1, 27: 344.

18. Sweetman, *The U.S. Naval Academy*, pp. 63-74, 83-84; Stanley Sandler, "A Navy in Decline: Some Strategic Technological Results of Disarmament, 1865-1869," *Military Affairs* 35 (December 1971): 138, 141. Naval establishment activities are traced during our period of conflict and postwar peace in the annual *Report of the Secretary of the Navy*. (Washington, DC: GPO, 1862-1876); among the comments on the naval "dark ages" reviewed for this biography are those offered by Charles O. Paullin, *Paullin's History of Naval Administration, 1775-1911: A Collection of Articles from the U.S. Naval Institute Proceedings* (Annapolis, MD: Naval Institute Press, 1968), pp. 337-346; Harold Sprout and Margaret Sprout, *The Rise of American Naval Power, 1776-1918* (Princeton, NJ: Princeton University Press, 1946), pp. 164-182; Walter R. Herrick, Jr., *The American Naval Revolution* (Baton Rouge: Louisiana State University Press, 1966), 13-23; Edward W. Sloan III, *Benjamin Franklin Isherwood, Naval Engineer: The Years as Engineer in Chief, 1861-1869* (Annapolis, MD: Naval Institute Press, 1965), pp. 65, 166-188; William M. McBride, *Technological Change and the United States Navy, 1865-1945* (Baltimore: Johns Hopkins University Press, 2000), 8-63; Lance C. Buhl, "The Smooth Water Navy: American Naval Policy and Politics, 1865-1876," (unpublished Ph.D. dissertation, Harvard University, 1968), 329-341; Buhl, "Mariners and Machines: Resistance to Technological Change in the American Navy, 1865-1869," *The Journal of American History* 61 (December 1974): 703-727; Robert W. Love, Jr., *History of the U.S. Navy*, vol. 1 (Harrisburg, PA: Stackpole Books, 1992), 322-344.

19. Fitch, Reel No. 415, July 3, 1865, May 29, 1866; *The Logansport Journal*, July 5, 1865; "Santee," in Vol. 6 of *Dictionary of American Naval Fighting Ships* (Washington, DC: GPO, 1976), p. 325; Soley, *Historical Sketch of the United States Naval Academy*, pp. 192, 331; Buhl, "Mariners and Machines," 720; Lewis B. Hamersly, *The Records of Living Officers of the U.S. Navy and Marine Corps* (Philadelphia: J. B. Lippincott, 1870), pp. 159, 165, 171, 187, 197; Cogar, *Dictionary of Admirals*, pp. 74, 108, 202; Chester G. Hearn, *Admiral David Dixon Porter: The Civil War Years* (Annapolis, MD: Naval Institute Press, 1996), pp. 316-317; Sweetman, *The U.S. Naval Academy*, pp. 84-89.

20. U.S. Navy Department. "Pay Table," in *Register of the Commissioned, Warrant, and Volunteer Officers of the Navy of the United States, Including Officers of the Marine Corps and Others to January 1, 1863* (Washington, DC: GPO, 1863), p. 3; U.S. Navy Department, *Regulations for the Government of the United States Navy, 1865* (Washington, DC: GPO, 1865), p. 204; Cogar, *Dictionary of Admirals*, pp. 97, 127, 201; McBride, *Technological Change*, p. 19.

21. Fitch, Reel 415, December 14, 1866, August 27, 1868; ORN, 2, I: 134; "Marblehead," in Vol. 4 of *Dictionary of American Naval Fighting Ships* (Washington, DC: GPO, 1969), p. 229; Donald L. Canney, *Lincoln's Navy: The Ships, Men and Organization, 1861-65* (London and New York: Conway Maritime Press, 1998), pp. 58-59; Paul H. Silverstone, *Warships of the Civil War Navies* (Annapolis, MD: Naval Institute Press, 1989), pp. 49-52; Love, *History of the U.S. Navy*, pp. 324-325; *Annual Report of the Secretary of the Navy*, 1868, p. 71; A. Hyatt Verrill, *Porto Rico Past and Pre-*

sent and San Domingo of To-Day (New York: Dodd, Mead, 1930), p. 263. Walter LaFeber encapsuled U.S.-Caribbean activities in 1867–1868 in his *The American Search for Opportunity, 1865-1913*, Vol. 2 of *The Cambridge History of American Foreign Relations* (New York: Cambridge University Press, 1993), pp. 9, 15–17. The U.S.S. *Marblehead* became the civilian bark *Marblehead*. The final *Unadilla*-class gunboat sold was the lead ship herself, at Hong Kong in November 1869. Silverstone, *Warships of the Civil War Navies*, pp. 49–52; Canney, *Lincoln's Navy*, pp. 58–59.

22. Charles Oscar Paullin, *Paullin's History of Naval Administration, 1775-1911* (Annapolis, MD: Naval Institute Press, 1968), p. 319; Charles H. Davis, *Charles H. Davis: Life of Charles Henry Davis, Rear Admiral, 1807-1877* (Boston and New York: Houghton, Mifflin, 1899), p. 74; Fitch, Reel No. 415, August 27, 1868, September 24, 1870; Dean Arthington, "Leroy Fitch," Arthington Collection Local Names Scrapbook, Logansport Public Library, n.d., p. 2668; Rebecca A. Livingston, Archives 1 Reference Branch, Textual Reference Division, National Archives, to Myron J. Smith, Jr., Greeneville, TN, May 21, 1997, Personal Files of Myron J. Smith, Jr., Greeneville, TN (cited hereafter as Livingston to Smith); The *Logansport Journal*, August 10, 1870; Will Ball, "This Changing World," *The Logansport Pharos-Tribune and Logansport Journal*, August 17, 1958.

23. Buhl, "Mariners and Machines": 722; Buhl, "The Smooth Water Navy": pp. 1–29; Sandler, "A Navy in Decline": 141.

24. George F. Pearce. *The U.S. Navy in Pensacola* (Pensacola, FL: University Press of Florida, 1980), p. 92; Jack Friend, *West Wind, Flood Tide: The Battle of Mobile Bay* (Annapolis, MD: Naval Institute Press, 2004), p. 99; Canney, *Lincoln's Navy*, p. 50; L. W. Parrish, *Pictorial History of the Naval Air Station at Pensacola, Florida* (N.p.: 1941), pp. 11–20; Charles Henry Bliss, *Pensacola, Florida* (Pensacola, FL: C. H. Bliss, 1894), p. 27; Charles Henry Bliss, *The Port of Pensacola—The Nicaragua Canal: Facts for Tourists, Pleasure Seekers, Sportsmen, Homeseekers and Investors* (Pensacola, FL: C. H. Bliss, 1898), pp. 33–35. Just before the Spanish-American War, tourists were permitted to visit the Pensacola Navy Yard. At that time, the U.S. steam launch *Undine* was in commission at the yard and was regarded as a "handsome little craft." We do not know if she was named in honor of the tinclad lost at Johnsonville, Tennessee, in 1864. Bliss, *The Port of Pensacola*, p. 32.

25. United States Senate, "Journal of the Executive Proceedings of the Senate of the United States of America, 1869–1871: Thursday, December 8, 1870," in *A Century of Lawmaking for a New Nation: U.S. Congressional Documents and Debates, 1774-1875*, American Memory homepage http://memory.loc.gov/cgi-bin/query/D?hlaw:97:./temp/~ammem_Wegv::@@@mdb=mcc.htm (accessed February 24, 2006); Fitch, Reel No. 306, October 26, 1870, December 3.

26. *Logansport Journal*, February 10, 1869; *Logansport Pharos*, May 25, 1871; John T. Fitch, jtfitch@fitchfamily.com "Re: Another Fitch," personal e-mail. May 23, 2000, May 9, 2005; Dean Arthington, " Major Henry S. Fitch," Arthington Collection Local Names Scrapbook, Logansport Public Library, n.d., p. 2669; Bliss, *The Port of Pensacola*, p. 41.

27. Fitch, Reel No. 306, February 9, May 2, 1872; Dean Arthington, "Henry Alford (Alvord?) Fitch," Arthington Collection Local Names Scrapbook, Logansport Public Library, n.d., p. 2668; *Logansport Journal*, January 25, 1873; Will Ball, "This Changing World," *Logansport Pharos-Tribune and Logansport Press*, August 14, October 2, 1960. Ball's August 14 column included an undated photo of a somewhat gaunt man in civilian clothes wearing a Lincolnesque beard. It was captioned "Cmdr. Fitch." It was not the U.S. Navy photograph reproduced elsewhere in this book.

29. Thomas B. Helm, *History of Cass County, Indiana* (Chicago: Brant & Fuller, 1886), pp. 421–422, 437–438; *Logansport Daily Star*, April 14–15, 1875; *Logansport Pharos*, April 14, 1875; *Logansport Weekly Journal*, April 17, 1875; Will Ball, "This Changing World," The *Logansport Pharos-Tribune and Logansport Press*, August 17, 1958, October 2, 1960; Paul Kroeger, info@kroegerfuneralhome.com "Cmdr.. Le Roy Fitch, Civil War Naval Hero from Logansport," personal e-mail, May 28, 2006; Fitch, Reel No. 306, April 13, 17, 1875.

30. John T. Fitch jtfitch@fitchfamily.com "Re: Another Fitch," personal e-mail, May 6, 2000; Stephen E. Towne, Indiana State Archives arc@icpr.state.in.us "Re: Cmdr. Leroy Fitch, USN," personal e-mail, June 6, 2000. Mary Fitch filed her "Declaration for Widow's Army Pension" at the Cass County Courthouse on October 17, 1878. Biography 4008, "Cmdr. Le Roy," in John T. Fitch, *Descendants of the Reverend James Fitch, 1622-1702: Vol. II, Generations Six and Seven* (Rockport, ME: Picton Press, 1999), p. 565; "Pensioners on the Roll," *Genealogy and Local History Services, Kokomo-Howard County Public Library homepage*, < http://www.kokomo.lib.in.us/glhs/pensioners/D-G.html> (accessed April 1, 2006).

31. The *Logansport Journal*, May 5, 1875; Thomas F. Beckner, beckner@usit.net "Fitch at Last," personal e-mail, July 2, 2006; "Pensioners on the Roll," *Genealogy and Local History Services, Kokomo-Howard County Public Library homepage*, <http://www.kokomo.lib.in.us/glhs/pensioners/D-G.html>, <http://www.kokomo.lib.in.us/glhs/pensioners/S.html> (accessed April 1, 2006); Fitch, "Le Roy Fitch."

32. Will Ball, "This Changing World," The *Logansport Pharos-Tribune and Logansport Press*, October 2, 16, 1960; David Kitchell, Cass County Historical Society, David.Kitchell@cnhiindiana.com "Re: "The Fitches," personal e-mail. April 5, 2006; "Kenneth-Cass County Towns," *Cass County Historical Society Homepage*, http://casscountyin.tripod.com/casstowns.htm (accessed May 3, 2006); Fitch, "Hon. Graham Newell," p. 589; Fitch, Le Roy Fitch profile, p. 591–592; Paul Kroeger, info@kroegerfuneralhome.com, "Cmdr.. Le Roy Fitch, Civil War Naval Hero from Logansport," personal e-mail, May 28, 2006.

33. *Logansport Daily Star*, April 14, 1875.

34. Paul H. Silverstone, *U.S. Warships of World War II* (Garden City, NY: Doubleday, 1972), pp. 100, 102, 126, 132; Will Ball, "This Changing World," *Logansport Pharos-Tribune and Logansport Press*, October 9, 1960; "Fitch," in Vol. II of *Dictionary of American Naval Fighting Ships* (Washington, DC: GPO, 1963), p. 409; *Logansport Weekly Journal*, April 17, 1875.

Bibliography

Primary Sources

"Acting Midshipman LeRoy Fitch Conduct Roll," 1854-1855 and 1855-1856, photocopies provided by Alice S. Creighton, Special Collections and Archives, Nimitz Library, U.S. Naval Academy.

Arthington, Dean. Arthington Collection Local Names Scrapbook. Logansport Public Library.

Barry, William Wesley, Papers. New York Historical Society, New York City.

Bock, William N., Papers. Illinois State Historical Society, Springfield.

Boyd, Joseph B., Papers. Cincinnati Historical Society, Cincinnati.

Browne, Symmes., Papers. Ohio Historical Society, Columbus.

Carondelet, U.S.S., Logbook: May 1862–June 1865. Record Group 24: U.S. Navy Department, Records of the Bureau of Naval Personnel. National Archives, Washington, D.C.

Civil War, Confederate and Federal. Collection. Tennessee State Library and Archives, Nashville.

Civil War Times Illustrated. Collection. U.S. Army Military History Institute, Carlisle Barracks, Pennsylvania.

"Fitch, Le Roy." Extracts from the United States Naval Academy Roll of the Midshipmen, 1851-1852, photocopies provided by Alice C. Creighton, Special Collections and Archives, Nimitz Library, U.S. Naval Academy.

"Fitch, Le Roy," Entry No. 2080, Abstracts of Service Records of Naval Officers: Records of Officers, 1798–1893, U.S. Navy Department, Bureau of Navigation, U.S. National Archives and Records Service, Record Group 24, Reel 8, January 1846–December 1858.

"Fitch, Le Roy," Entry No. 1574, Abstracts of Service Records of Naval Officers: Records of Officers, 1798–1893, U.S. Navy Department, Bureau of Navigation, U.S. National Archives and Records Service, Record Group 24, Reel 10, January 1859–December 1863.

Fitch, Le Roy. *Whistle Signal Code for Transport Fleets Under Convoy*. OCLC 60952393. N.p., 1864. New York Historical Society, New York City.

Howard, William H., Papers. University of Tennessee Library, Knoxville.

Indiana. Morgan Raid Commission. Report of the Morgan Raid Commission to the Governor, December 31, 1867. N.p., 1867.

Irion, Jack B., and David V. Beard. *Underwater Archaeological Assessment of Civil War Shipwrecks in Kentucky Lake, Benton and Humphreys Counties, Tennessee*. New Orleans: R. Christopher Goodwin & Associates, Inc., for the Tennessee Division of Archaeology, Department of Environment and Conservation, State of Tennessee, 1993.

James, Stephen R. Jr., Michael C. Tuttle, and Michael C. Krivor. *Remote Sensing Survey and Archaeological Assessment of Submerged Cultural Resources Associated with the Battle of Johnsonville*. Memphis: Submitted to the Tennessee Historical Commission by Panamerican Maritime, L.L.C., 1999.

Johnson, Robert V., and Clarence C. Buel, eds. *Battles and Leaders of the Civil War*. 4 vols. New York: Century, 1884–1887. Reprinted by Thomas Yoseloff, 1956.

Meigs, Montgomery C., Papers. Manuscript Division, Library of Congress, Washington, D.C.

Minnesota. Board of Commissioners on Publication of History of Minnesota in the Civil and Indian Wars. *Minnesota in the Civil and Indian Wars, 1861–1865*. 2 vols. St. Paul, MN: Printed for the State of Minnesota by the Pioneer Press Company, 1889.

Moose, U.S.S., Logbook: June 15, 1863–August 10, 1865. Record Group 24: U.S. Navy Department, Records of the Bureau of Naval Personnel. National Archives, Washington, D.C.

Ohio. "Commissioners to Examine Claims Growing Out of the Morgan Raid." *Report of the Commissioners of Morgan Raid Claims, to the Governor the State of Ohio, December 15th, 1864*. Columbus, OH: Nevins, 1865.

Pennock, Alexander Mosley, Papers. Illinois State Historical Society, Springfield.
Phelps, Seth Ledyard, Papers. Missouri Historical Society, St. Louis.
Porter, David Dixon, Papers. Manuscript Division, Library of Congress, Washington, D.C.
____, ____. Missouri Historical Society, St. Louis.
Soley, James Russell. *Historical Sketch of the United States Naval Academy, Prepared by Direction of Rear Admiral C. R. P. Rodgers, U.S.N.* Washington, D.C.: GPO, 1876.
United States. Congress. 38th Cong., 1st sess. Joint Committee on the Conduct of the War. *Fort Pillow Massacre.* House Reports, no. 65. Washington, D.C., 1864.
____. Navy Department. *List of Rear-Admirals, Commodores, Captains, and Commanders, Showing the Dates on Which They Retire, and the Promotions Consequent.* Washington, D.C.: GPO, 1870.
____. ____. Records of General Courts-Martial and Courts of Inquiry of the Navy Department. "Case of Acting Vol. Lieut E. M. King, Lately of the U.S.S. *Key West.*" Microfilm Publications, M273. National Archives, Washington, D.C.
____. ____. Records of the Bureau of Naval Personnel: Record Group 24. National Archives, Washington, D.C.
____. ____. Records of the Office of Naval Records and Library, Naval Records Collection: Record Group 45. National Archives, Washington, D.C.
____. ____. *Report of the Secretary of the Navy.* Washington, D.C.: GPO, 1862–1876.
____. ____. *Register of the Commissioned, Warrant, and Volunteer Officers of the Navy of the United States, Including Officers of the Marine Corps and Others.* Volumes 47–64. Washington, D.C.: GPO, 1862–1876.
____. ____. *Regulations for the Government of the United States Navy, 1865.* Washington, D.C.: GPO, 1865.
____. ____. Mississippi Squadron. *General Orders. Rear Adm. D. D. Porter, Commanding, From Oct. 16, 1862 to Oct. 26, 1864.* St. Louis: R. P. Studley, 1864.
____. ____. ____. *General Orders. Rear Adm. S. P. Lee, Commanding, From Nov. 1st 1864 to April 24, 1865.* St. Louis, MO: R. P. Studley, 1865.
____. ____. Office of Naval Records and Library. *List of U.S. Naval Vessels, 1861–1865, Including the Ellet Ram Fleet and the Mississippi Marine Brigade.* Office Memorandum. Washington, D.C., 1891.
____. ____. ____. *Official Records of the Union and Confederate Navies in the War of the Rebellion.* 31 vols. Washington, D.C.: GPO, 1894–1922.
____. War Department. *Atlas to Accompany the Official Records of the War of the Rebellion.* 3 vols. Compiled by Calvin D. Cowles. Washington, D.C.: GPO, 1891–1895.
____. *The War of the Rebellion: A Compilation of the Official Records of the Union and Confederate Armies.* 128 vols. Washington, D.C.: GPO, 1880–1901.
____. ____. Quartermaster Department. *Reports to the War Department by Brev. Maj. Gen. Lewis B. Parsons, Chief of Rail and River Transportation.* St. Louis: G. Knapp, 1867.
Walker, Francis A. *A Compendium of the Ninth Census, June 1, 1870.* Washington, D.C.: GPO, 1872.
Welles, Gideon. Papers. Manuscript Division, Library of Congress, Washington, D.C.

Newspapers

Chattanooga *Gazette*
Chicago *Tribune*
Cincinnati *Daily Commercial*
Cincinnati *Daily Enquirer*
Cincinnati *Daily Gazette*
Cincinnati *Times*
Cleveland *Daily Plain Dealer*
Evansville *Daily Journal*
Frank Leslie's Illustrated Newspaper
Harper's Weekly
Indiana Herald
Indianapolis *Journal*
Indianapolis *News*
Logansport *Daily Star*
The *Logansport Journal*
Logansport *Pharos*
Logansport *Pharos-Tribune* and *Logansport Press*
The *Logansport Press*
Logansport *Weekly Journal*
Louisville *Daily Journal*
Memphis *Argus*
Milwaukee *Daily Sentinel*
Nashville Banner
Nashville *Daily Press*
Nashville *Daily Times and True Union*
Nashville *Daily Union*
Nashville *Dispatch*
New Albany *Ledger*
The New York Times
New York Tribune
Richmond *Daily Examiner*
St. Louis *Daily Democrat*
St. Louis *Missouri Democrat*
St. Louis *Missouri Republican*
Times of London

Internet Sources

"The Archaeological Investigations of the Battle of Johnsonville." *PanAm Consultants Homepage,* http://www.panamconsultants.com/PAGE, (accessed June 8, 2004; page no longer available).
Aronson, Alan. "Strategic Supply of Civil War Armies." *General Histories of the American Civil War* http://members.cox.net/rb2307/content/STRATEGIC_SUPPLY_OF_CIVIL_WAR_ARMIES.htm.
Backs, Jean. "Morgan's Raid." *Explore Magazine* (Spring 2001), Ohio Department of Natural Resources Home Page. http://www.dnr.state.oh.us/parks/explore/magazine/spru2001/morgan.htm. (accessed November 14, 2005; page no longer available).
Brainy Media. "Master," *Brainy Dictionary 2005* http://www.brainydictionary.com/words/ma/master188291.html.
Branson, Ronald. *County History Preservation Society Homepage* http://www.countyhistory.com/doc.cass/004.htm (accessed July 4, 2005; page no longer available).

Cass County Historical Society, "Legends," *Cass County Historical Society Homepage,* http://casscountyin.tripod.com/legends.htm.

Conklin, Susan L. "Genesee County History." *Genesee County, New York, Home Page* http://www.co.genesee.ny.us/frameset.html?/dpt/countyhistory/index.html&1.

Craig, Joe. "A Primer on 18th Century Medicine." *The Northern Campaign: Learn About the Past.* http://www.thenortherncampaign.org/past8.htm. (accessed June 27, 2005; site no longer available).

Creamer, Colleen. "Civil War Battle Site Gets Commemorative Marker: Reprinted from The City Paper, Nashville Tennessee, n.d.," American Civil War Round Table of the United Kingdom homepage, http://www.americancivilwar.org.uk/news_Civil%20War%20Battle%20Site%20Gets%20Commemorative%20Marker_56.htm.

"Cumberland River." in *Wikipedia: The Free Encyclopedia,* http://en.wikipedia.org/wiki/Cumberland_River.

Donn, John W. "War Record of J. W. Donn, Including Reminiscences of Frederick W. Dorr, July 1861 to June 1865." *NOAA History Homepage,* http://www.history.noaa.gov/stories_tales/donn.html.

"Find-a-Grave of Famous People: D." in *Wikipedia: The Free Encyclopedia,* http://en.wikipedia.org/wiki/Wikipedia:Find-A-Grave_famous_people/D.

Foenander, Terry. "Fact File No. 1." *Union Navy Medal of Honor Fact File.* <http://home.ozconnect.net/tfoen/mohfactfile1.htm> (accessed March 12, 2006; site no longer available).

"General Information." *Wabash and Erie Canal Organization Homepage,* http://www.wabasherieccanal.org/subpage/interpretive/generalinfo.html.

Gray, George N. "Narrow Escapes: Just a Little Bit of History," *Ironton [Ohio] Register,* December 23, 1886, submitted by Donald E. Darby to *Sons of Union Veterans of the Civil War Patriotic Recollections,* http://suvcw.org/pr/art008.htm.

Hagerty, John. "Dear Maggie ... The Letters of John Hagerty, 1st Class Fireman, U.S.S. *Carondolet* to Margaret 'Maggie' O'Neil, September 8, 1864–May 28, 1865." Letters of John Hagerty homepage, http://www.webnation.com/~spectrum/usn-cw/diaries/HagertyJohnHome.htm (accessed April 10, 2000; site no longer available).

"History—Encyclopedia: Washington County, New York." *Nationmaster.com* http://www.nationmaster.com/encyclopedia/Washington-County,-New-York.

"The History of the City of Pekin, Illinois." http://www.ci.pekin.il.us/history.asp.

Hogan, Brian, Conrad Bush, and Mike Brown. "The 76th New York and the Navy." *76th New York Infantry Regiment Homepage* http://www.bpmlegal.com/76NY/76navy.html.

Hubbard, Lucius F. "Minnesota in the Battles of Nashville, December 15 and 16, 1864: Read Before the Minnesota Commandery of the Loyal Legion of the United States, March 14, 1905." Collections of the Minnesota Historical Society, Volume 12 http://memory.loc.gov/cgi-bin/query/r?ammem/lhbum:@field%28DOCID+@lit%281hbum0 (January 9, 2006).

"Indiana: Mrs. Graham Newell Fitch, 1859–1880" in Portraits/Biographies of Regents and Vice Regents to 1874, *Mount Vernon Ladies Association Home Page* http://www.mountvernon.org/learn/collections/index.cfm/pid/333.

"Indiana Militia in the Antebellum Era." *Conner Prairie Organization Homepage* http://www.connerprairie.org/HistoryOnline/militia.html.

Indiana University School of Medicine, Ruth Lilly Medical Library, Special Collections Department, "Record No. 19271, Graham Newell Fitch," 19th Century Indiana Physicians Database, http://www.biblioserver.com/19centurydocs/index.php?m=search&id=&ftype=data&q=fitch.

Jenkins, Mark F. "Tinclads." *Ironclads and Blockade Runners of the Civil War Homepage.* http://www.wideopenwest.com/~jenkins/ironclads/tinclads.htm.

_____. "Operations of the Mississippi Squadron During Morgan's Raid." *Ironclads and Blockade Runners of the American Civil War Homepage.* www.wideopenwest.com/~jenkins/ironclads/buffingt.htm.

Jones, Jim, ed. *Tennessee Civil War Sourcebook.* http://www.tennessee.civilwarsourcebook.com.

"'The Kelly Rangers/Kelly Troopers,' Company F, Forrest's Battalion (3d Tennessee Cavalry) and Company K, 4th Alabama Cavalry Regiment." Confederate Units of Madison County homepage, <http://www.rootsweb.com/~almadiso/confunit.htm> (accessed March 4, 2006; site no longer available).

Kentucky, Adjutant General. "Forty-Eighth Kentucky Mounted Infantry." *Union Regiments of Kentucky Homepage,* http://www.unionregimentsofkentucky.com/thomasspeed/infantry/48kyinf.html (accessed December 25, 2005; site no longer available).

Kestenbaum, Lawrence. "Index to Politicians: Fitch." *The Political Graveyard: A Database of Famous Cemeteries.* http://politicalgraveyard.com/bio/fitch.html#S2Q1DKTZ3.

"Letters from William Hix (Persons)." *76th New York Regiment Homepage* http://www.bpmlegal.com/76NY/76personswh.html.

Looker, Bryan. "Early Cass County." *Cass County Historical Society and Museum Home Page,* http://casscountyin.tripod.com/earlycass.htm.

Lucy, Gary R. "The Battle of Island No. 10, 1862." *Gary Lucy Homepage,* http://www.garylucy.com/island.html.

"Maynadier, Henry E., maj. gen. U. S. A." in *American Biographical Library* http://search.ancestry.com/db-abl/P1084.aspx>, (July 12, 2005).

McDonnell, Kathy Mandusic. "Medicine of Jacksonian America." *Conner Prairie Organization Homepage* http://www.connerprairie.org/HistoryOnline/jmed.html.

"Medal of Honor Recipients Buried in Illinois." *Home of Heroes Homepage,* http://www.homeofheroes.com/moh/cemeteries/il.html.

Morris, William R. "The Burning of Clifton." *Wayne County Historian,* II (June 1989) reprinted on the Civil War Page http://www.netease.net/wayne/burningclifton.htm.

"Nashville," in *Major General George Thomas Blog Site,* http://home.earthline.net/~oneplez/majorgeneralgeorgehthomasblogsite/id20.html (February 28, 2006).

"My Pollard Family: Chapter 2 & Chapter 3, Daniel, the War Years." *My American Family, or ???? Homepage* http://freepages.family.rootsweb.com/~ricksgenealogy/e_book.htm.

Noomen, Eric-Jan. "The Transfer of Napoleon's Corpse." *The Second Page of the Dead* http://www.xs4all.nl/~ejnoomen/story101.html.

Northern Indiana Historical Society. "Canals." *Northern Indiana Center for History Homepage* http://www.centerforhistory.org/indiana_main4.html, (accessed July 20, 2005; page no longer available).

"Ohio River." in *Wikipedia: The Free Encyclopedia*, http://en.wikipedia.org/wiki/Ohio_River.

"The Origin of the Ranks and Rank Insignia Now Used by the United States Armed Forces, Officers: Lieutenants." *Traditions of the Naval Service* http://www.history.navy.mil/trivia/triv4-5d.htm.

"Our History," *Kroeger Funeral Home Homepage* http://www.kroegerfuneralhome.com/index/cfm.

Paxson, Frederic L. "The Railroads of the 'Old Northwest" Before the Civil War." In *Transactions of the Wisconsin Academy of Sciences, Arts, and Letters* 18, Part 1 (October 1912), reprinted in Thomas Ehrenreich, *Railroad Extra*, 2001 http://www.catskillarchive.com/rrextra/abonw.html.

"Pensioners on the Roll." *Genealogy and Local History Services, Kokomo-Howard County Public Library homepage*, http://www.kokomo.lib.in.us/glhs/pensioners/D-G.html and http://www.kokomo.lib.in.us/glhs/pensioners/S.html.

Restore, Jane. "Jarvis Island." *Jane's Oceanic Home Page* 2003 http://www.janeresture.com/jarvis.

Sayers, Alethea D. "The Paper War Between Rosecrans & Halleck." *Civil War Web* http://civilwarweb.com/articles/12-99/paperwar.htm, (accessed June 6, 2005; page no longer available).

Schilling, Mark Rae. "Morgan's Raid." *45th Ohio Volunteer Infantry Home Page.* http://www.homestead.com/ohio45/morgan~ns.4.html (accessed October 29, 2005; page no longer available).

Scoggs, William Oscar. "William Walker, 1824–1860." In *1911 Encyclopedia.* http://69.1911encyclopedia.org/W/WA/WALKER_WILLIAM.htm.

Seyburn, Lieut. S. Y. "Excerpts from *The Tenth Regiment of Infantry*." *U.S. Regulars Civil War Archives Home Page*, http://www.usregulars.com/usarmy/10us.html.

Smith, Neal. "Villages/Areas." *Welcome to LeRoy, Genesee County, New York.* http://www.rootsweb.com/~nygenese/leroy.htm.

"Steamboats.Org Glossary." *Steamboats.Org Homepage.* http://www.steamboats.org/cgi-bin/glossary/guru_glossary_all.cgi.

"A Tale of Three Tinclads, All Named *Argosy*." *Mid Missouri Civil War Roundtable Homepage*, 2005, http://www.mmcwrt.org/2005/default0501.htm (accessed July 29, 2005; page no longer available).

"Tennessee River." in *Wikipedia: The Free Encyclopedia*, http://en.wikipedia.org/wiki/Tennessee_River .

Terra Realty, "History of Logansport." *Welcome to Logansport and Cass County* [1997] http://www.terrarealty.com/relo/churches.htm, (June 28, 2005).

"Towns of the Cumberland." *Save the Cumberland Homepage*, http://www.savethecumberland.org/towns.htm.

U. S. Navy Department, Naval Historical Center, Navy Department Library. "Chapter 6: Dispositions and Instructions." *War Instructions United States Navy 1944* http://www.history.navy.mil/library/online/warinst-6.htm.

"Walker's Expeditions." *Global Security Page.* http://www.globalsecurity.org/military/ops/walker.htm.

Weatherred, John. "Wartime Diary of John Weatherred, Bennett's Regiment or 9th Tennessee Cavalry, John Hunt Morgan's Command." Edited by Jack Masters. *The Wartime Diary of John Weatherred.* http://www.jackmasters.net/we1863.html.

Williams, Scott K. "St Louis' Ships of Iron: The Ironclads and Monitors of Carondelet (St. Louis), Missouri." *Missouri Civil War Museum Home Page*, http://missouricivilwarmuseum.org/1ironclads.htm.

Books

Abdill, George R. *Civil War Railroads: Pictorial Story of the Iron Horse, 1861–1865.* Seattle, WA: Superior, 1961.

Alden, Carroll Storrs, and Ralph Earle. *Makers of Naval Tradition.* Boston: Ginn, 1925.

Ambrose, Stephen E. *Halleck: Lincoln's Chief of Staff.* Baton Rouge: Louisiana State University Press, 1962.

Anders, Curt. *Henry Halleck's War: A Fresh Look at Lincoln's Controversial General-in-Chief.* Indianapolis: Guild Press of Indiana, 1999.

Anderson, Bern. *By Sea and By River: The Naval History of the Civil War.* New York: Knopf, 1962.

Angle, Paul M., ed. *Illinois Guide and Gazetter: Prepared Under the Supervision of the Illinois Sesquicentennial Commission.* Chicago: Rand McNally, 1969.

Ash, Stephen V. *Middle Tennessee Society Transformed, 1860–1870: War and Peace in the Upper South.* Baton Rouge: Louisiana State University Press, 1988.

_____. *When the Yankees Came: Conflict and Chaos in the Occupied South, 1861–1865.* Chapel Hill: University of North Carolina Press, 1995.

Asprey, Robert B. *The War in the Shadows: The Guerrilla in History, Two Thousand Years of the Guerrilla at War from Ancient Persia to the Present.* 2 vols. New York: William Morrow, 1975.

Bacon, Benjamin W. *Sinews of War: How Technology, Industry and Transportation Won the Civil War.* Novato, CA: Presidio Press, 1997.

Bailey, Anne J. *The Chessboard of War: Sherman and Hood in the Autumn Campaigns of 1864.* Great Campaigns of the Civil War. Lincoln: University of Nebraska Press, 2000.

Banta, Richard E. *The Ohio.* Rivers of America. New York: Rinehard, 1949.

Barrett, Edward. *Gunnery Instruction Simplified for the Volunteer Officers of the U.S. Navy, with Hints for Executive and Other Officers.* New York: D. Van Nostrand, 1863.

Barron, Samuel B. *The Lone Star Defenders: A Chronicle of the Third Texas Cavalry, Ross' Brigade.* New York and Washington, D.C.: The Neale Publishing Co., 1908.

Bartols, Barnabas H. *A Treatise on the Marine Boilers of the United States.* Philadelphia, PA: R. W. Barnard, 1851.

Beach, Ursula Smith. *Along the Warioto; or, a History of Montgomery County, Tennessee.* Clarksville, TN: Clarksville Kiwanis Club and Tennessee Historical Commission, 1964.

Beale, Howard K., ed. *Diary of Gideon Welles: Secretary of the Navy Under Lincoln and Johnson*. 2 vols. New York: W. W. Norton, 1960.

Beard, William E. *The Battle of Nashville, Including an Outline of the Stirring Events Occurring in One of the Most Notable Movements of the Civil War—Hood's Invasion of Tennessee*. Nashville, TN: Marshall & Bruce, 1913.

Bearss, Edwin C. *The Fall of Fort Henry*. Dover, TN: Eastern National Park and Monument Association, 1989.

_____. *Hardluck Ironclad: The Sinking and Salvage of the Cairo*. Baton Rouge: Louisiana State University, 1966.

_____. *Unconditional Surrender: The Fall of Fort Donelson*. Dover, TN: Eastern National Park and Monument Association, 1991.

Bennett, Michael J. *Union Jacks: Yankee Sailors in the Civil War*. Chapel Hill: University of North Carolina Press, 2004.

Beringer, Richard E., Herman Hattaway, Archer Jones, and William N. Still, Jr. *Why the South Lost the Civil War*. Athens: University of Georgia Press, 1986.

Berry, Thomas Franklin. *Four Years with Morgan and Forrest*. Oklahoma City: Harlow-Ratliff, 1914.

Bickman, William. *Rosecrans' Campaigns with the 14th Army Corps; or, the Army of the Cumberland: A Narrative of Personal Observations*. Cincinnati: Moore, Wilstach, Keys, 1863.

Biographical History of Cass, Miami, Howard, and Tipton Counties, Indiana. 2 vols. Chicago: Lewis, 1898.

Birtle, Andrew J. *U.S. Army Counterinsurgency and Contingency Operations Doctrine, 1860–1941*. Washington, D.C.: GPO, 1998.

Bliss, Charles Henry. *Pensacola, Florida*. Pensacola, FL: C. H. Bliss, 1894.

_____. *The Port of Pensacola—The Nicaragua Canal: Facts for Tourists, Pleasure Seekers, Sportsmen, Homeseekers and Investors*. Pensacola, FL: C. H. Bliss, 1898.

Boatner, Mark M., III. *The Civil War Dictionary*. New York: David McKay, 1959.

Bonner, Thomas Neville. *Becoming a Physician: Medical Education in Britain, France, Germany and the United States, 1750–1945*. Baltimore: Johns Hopkins University Press, 1995.

Bothura, Arthur L. *History of Miami County, Indiana: A Narrative Account of Its Historical Progress, Its People, and Its Principal Interests*. 2 vols. Chicago: Lewis Publications, 1914.

Bowers, John. *Chickamauga and Chattanooga: The Battles That Doomed the Confederacy*. New York: HarperPerennial, 1995.

Boynton, Charles B. *History of the Navy During the Rebellion*. 2 vols. New York: D. Appleton, 1869–1870.

Brandenburg Methodist Church Men's Club. *The Brandenburg Story: With Particular Reference to John Hunt Morgan's Crossing of the Ohio July 8, 1863*. Brandenburg, KY, 1963.

Brandt, Robert. *Touring the Middle Tennessee Backroads*. Winston-Salem, NC: John F. Blair, Publisher, 1995.

Browne, Henry R., and Symmes E. Browne. *From the Fresh Water Navy, 1861–1864: Letters of Acting Master's Mate Henry R. Browne and Acting Ensign Symmes E. Browne*. Edited by John D. Milligan. Naval Letters Series, Volume 3. Annapolis, MD: Naval Institute Press, 1970.

Brownlee, Richard S., 3rd. *Gray Ghosts of the Confederacy: Guerrilla Warfare in the West, 1861–1865*. Baton Rouge: Louisiana State University Press, 1958.

Bucy, Carole. *A Path Divided: Tennessee's Civil War Years*. Nashville: Tennessee 200, 1996.

Butler, Lorine. *John Morgan and His Men*. Philadelphia: Dorrance, 1960.

Callahan, Edward W. *List of Officers of the Navy of the United States and of the Marine Corps, from 1775 to 1900, Comprising a Complete Register of All Present and Former Commissioned, Warranted, and Appointed Officers of the United States Navy, and of the Marine Corps, Regular and Volunteer. Compiled from the Official Records of the Navy Department*. New York: L.R. Hamersly, 1901. Reprint. New York: Haskell House, 1969.

Canfield, Eugene B. *Civil War Naval Ordnance*. Washington, D.C.: Naval History Division, U.S. Navy Department, 1969.

Canney, Donald L. *Lincoln's Navy: The Ships, Men and Organization, 1861–65*. London and New York: Conway Maritime Press, 1998.

_____. *The Old Steam Navy: Vol. 2, The Ironclads, 1842–1885*. Annapolis, MD: Naval Institute Press, 1993.

Capers, Gerald M. *The Biography of a River Town: Memphis—Its Heroic Age*. Chapel Hill: University of North Carolina Press, 1939.

Catton, Bruce. *The Centennial History of the Civil War*. 3 vols. Garden City, NY: Doubleday, 1961–1965.

_____. *Never Call Retreat*. New York: Pocket Books, 1973.

Cayton, Andrew R. L. *Frontier Indiana*. Bloomington: Indiana University Press, 1996.

_____. *Ohio: The History of a People*. Columbus: Ohio State University Press, 2002.

Chamberlain, William H., ed. *Sketches of War History, 1861–1865: Papers Prepared for the Ohio Commandry of the Military Order of the Loyal Legion of the United States*. 6 vols. Cincinnati: R. Clarke, 1890–1908.

Chappelle, Howard I. *History of the American Sailing Navy*. New York: W. W. Norton, 1935.

Christ, Mark K., ed. *Rugged and Sublime: The Civil War in Arkansas*. Fayetteville: University of Arkansas Press, 1994.

Cist, Henry M. *Army of the Cumberland*. Campaigns of the Civil War. New York: Charles Scribner's Sons, 1892.

Cleaves, Freeman. *Rock of Chickamauga: The Life of General George H. Thomas*. Norman, OK: University of Oklahoma Press, 1948.

Coffin, Charles C. *My Days and Nights on the Battlefield: A Book for Boys*. Boston: Ticknor and Fields, 1864.

Cogar, William B. *Dictionary of Admirals of the U.S. Navy*. 2 vols. Annapolis, MD: Naval Institute Press, 1989.

Connelly, Thomas Lawrence. *Army of the Heartland: The Army of Tennessee, 1861–1862*. Baton Rouge: Louisiana State University Press, 1967.

_____. *Autumn of Glory: The Army of Tennessee, 1862–1865*. Baton Rouge: Louisiana State University Press, 1971.

———. *Civil War Tennessee: Battles and Leaders*. Knoxville, TN: University of Tennessee Press, 1979.

Conway, Fred W. *Corydon: The Forgotten Battle of the Civil War*. New Albany, IN: FBH Publishers, 1991.

Cooling, Benjamin F. *Fort Donelson's Legacy: War and Society in Kentucky and Tennessee, 1862–1863*. Knoxville, TN: University of Tennessee Press, 1997.

———. *Forts Henry and Donelson: The Key to the Confederate Heartland*. Knoxville, TN: University of Tennessee Press, 1987.

Coombe, Jack D. *Thunder Along the Mississippi: The River Battles That Split the Confederacy*. New York: Sarpedon, 1996.

Cornish, Dudley Taylor, and Virginia Jeans Laas. *Lincoln's Lee: The Life of Samuel Phillips Lee, United States Navy, 1812–1897*. Lawrence, KS: University Press of Kansas, 1986.

Cox, Jacob D. *March to the Sea: Franklin and Nashville*. Campaigns of the Civil War, no. 10. New York: Scribner's, 1882.

———. *Military Reminiscences of the Civil War*. 2 vols. New York: Scribner's, 1900.

Cozzens, Peter. *The Battle of Stones River*. Civil War Series. Washington, D.C.: Eastern National Park and Monument Association, 1995.

———. *No Better Place to Die: The Battle of Stones River*. Urbana: University of Illinois Press, 1990.

———. *The Shipwreck of Their Hopes: The Battle of Chattanooga*. Urbana: University of Illinois Press, 1994.

———. *The Terrible Sound: The Battle of Chickamauga*. Urbana: University of Illinois Press, 1992.

Crandall, Warren D., and Isaac D. Newell. *History of the Ram Fleet and Mississippi Marine Brigade*. St. Louis: Buschart Brothers, 1907.

Crocker, Helen B. *The Green River of Kentucky*. Lexington: University Press of Kentucky, 1976.

Crook, George. *General George Crook: His Autobiography*. Edited by Martin F. Schmitt. Norman: University of Oklahoma Press, 1946.

Daniel, Larry J. *Days of Glory: The Army of the Cumberland, 1861–1865*. Baton Rouge: Louisiana State University Press, 2004.

———, and Lynn N. Bock. *Island No. 10: Struggle in the Mississippi Valley*. Tuscaloosa: University of Alabama Press, 1996.

Davidson, Donald. *The Tennessee, Vol. II: The New River, Civil War to TVA*. Rivers of America. New York: Rinehart, 1948.

Davis, Charles H. *Charles H. Davis: Life of Charles Henry Davis, Rear Admiral, 1807–1877*. Boston and New York: Houghton, Mifflin, 1899.

Dewey, George. *Autobiography of George Dewey: Admiral of the Navy*. New York: Charles Scribner's Sons, 1913.

Dickins, James. *Personal Recollections & Experiences in the Confederate Army*. Cincinnati: Robert Clarke, 1897.

Dictionary of American Naval Fighting Ships. 8 vols. Washington, D.C.: GPO, 1916–1981.

Dinkins, James. *1861 to 1865, by an Old Johnnie: Personal Recollections and Experiences in the Confederate Army*. Cincinnati: Robert Clarke, 1897.

Dodge, Grenville M. *The Battle of Atlanta and Other Campaigns, Addresses, Etc*. Council Bluffs, IA: Monarch Printing, 1911. Reprint, Denver: Sage Books, 1965.

Dodson, W. C. *Campaigns of Wheeler and His Cavalry*. Atlanta: Hudgins, 1897.

Douglas, Byrd. *Steamboatin' on the Cumberland*. Nashville: Tennessee Book, 1961.

Du Bose, John W. *General Joseph Wheeler and the Army of Tennessee*. New York: Neale, 1912.

Duke, Basil W. *The Great Indiana-Ohio Raid by Brig. Gen. John Hunt Morgan and His Men, July 1863*. Louisville, KY: Book Nook Press, 1956.

———. *The History of Morgan's Cavalry*. New York: Neale, 1906. Reprint, Bloomington, IN: Indiana University Press, 1960.

———. *Reminiscences of General Basil W. Duke*. Garden City, NY: Doubleday Page, 1911.

Dunnavent, R. Blake. *Brown Water Warfare: The U.S. Navy in Riverine Warfare and the Emergence of a Tactical Doctrine, 1775–1970*. New Perspectives on Maritime History and Nautical Archaeology. Gainesville, FL: University of Florida Press, 2003.

Durham, Walter T. *Nashville: The Occupied City—the First Seventeen Months—February 16, 1862–June 30, 1863*. Nashville: Tennessee Historical Society, 1985.

———. *Reluctant Partners: Nashville and the Union—July 1, 1863 to June 30, 1865*. Nashville: Tennessee Historical Society, 1987.

Dyer, Frederick H. *A Compendium of the War of the Rebellion*. 3 vols. Des Moines: Dyer, 1908. Reprint, New York: Thomas Yoseloff, 1959.

Dyer, Joseph P. *"Fightin' Joe" Wheeler*. Southern Biography Series. Baton Rouge: Louisiana State University Press, 1941.

———. *From Shiloh to San Juan: The Life of "Fighting Joe" Wheeler*. Baton Rouge: Louisiana State University Press, 1961.

Engle, Stephen D. *Struggle for the Heartland: The Campaigns from Fort Henry to Corinth*. Lincoln: University of Nebraska Press, 2001.

Evans, Robley D. *A Sailor's Log: Recollections of a Naval Life*. New York: D. Appleton, 1901.

Ferguson, John L., ed. *Arkansas and the Civil War*. Little Rock: Arkansas Historical Commission, 1962.

Fink, Harold S. *The Battle of Knoxville (1863)*. Knoxville, TN: Knoxville-Knox County Civil War Centennial Committee, 1965.

Fisher, John E. *They Rode with Forrest and Wheeler: A Chronicle of Five Tennessee Brothers' Service in the Confederate Western Cavalry*. Jefferson, NC: McFarland, 1995.

Fitch, John. *Annals of the Army of the Cumberland*. Philadelphia: J. B. Lippincott, 1864.

Fitch, John T. *Descendants of the Reverend James Fitch, 1622–1702*. 2 vols. Rockport, ME: Picton Press, 1999.

Folmsbee, Stanley J., Robert E. Corlew, and Enoch L. Mitchell. *Tennessee: A Short History*. Knoxville, TN: University of Tennessee Press, 1969.

Foote, Shelby. *The Civil War: A Narrative*. 3 vols. New York: Random House, 1958–1974. Reprint, New York: Vintage Books, 1986.

Force, Manning F. *From Fort Henry to Corinth*. Campaigns of the Civil War, No. 2. New York: Scribner's, 1882. Reprint, Broadfoot Press, 1989.

Fowler, William H. *Under Two Flags: The American Navy in the Civil War*. New York: W. W. Norton, 1990.

Fox, Gustavus Vasa. *Confidential Correspondence of Gustavus Vasa Fox, Assistant Secretary of the Navy, 1861–1865.* Edited by Robert Means Thompson and Richard Wainwright. 2 vols. New York: De Vinne Press, 1918–1919.

Franklin, Samuel R. *Memories of a Rear Admiral: Who Has Served for More Than Half a Century in the Navy of the United States.* New York: Harper and Brothers, 1898.

Freemon, Frank R. *Gangrene and Glory: Medical Care During the American Civil War.* Urbana: University of Illinois Press, 2001.

Friend, Jack. *West Tide, Flood Tide: The Battle of Mobile Bay.* Annapolis, MD: Naval Institute Press, 2004.

Fuchs, Richard L. *An Unerring Fire: The Massacre at Fort Pillow.* Harrisburg, PA: Stackpole Books, 2002.

Funk, Arville L. *The Battle of Corydon.* Corydon, IL: ALFCO Publications, 1975.

_____. *The Morgan Raid in Indiana and Ohio (1863).* Corydon, IN: ALFCO Publications, 1971.

Gibbons, Tony. *Warships and Naval Battles of the Civil War.* New York: Gallery Books, 1989.

Gibson, Charles Dana, with E. Kay Gibson. *Assault and Logistics, Vol. 2: Union Army Coastal and River Operations, 1861–1866.* Camden, ME: Ensign Press, 1995.

Gildrie, Richard, Philip Kemmerly, and Thomas H. Winn. *Clarksville, Tennessee, in the Civil War: A Chronology.* Clarksville, TN: Montgomery County Historical Society, 1984.

Gosnell, H. Allen. *Guns on the Western Waters: The Story of the River Gunboats in the Civil War.* Baton Rouge: Louisiana State University Press, 1949.

Graf, LeRoy P., and Ralph W. Haskins, eds. *The Papers of Andrew Johnson.* Vol. V. Knoxville, TN: University of Tennessee Press, 1979.

Grant, Ulysses S. *The Papers of Ulysses S. Grant.* Edited by John Y. Simon. 24 vols. to date. Edwardsville, Southern Illinois University Press, 1967–.

_____. *Personal Memoirs of U.S. Grant.* 2 vols. New York: C. L. Webster, 1885-1886. Reprint (2 vols. in 1), New York: Penguin Books, 1999.

_____. *Personal Memoirs of U.S. Grant: A Modern Abridgment.* New York: Premier Books, 1962.

Green, Francis Vinton. *The Mississippi.* Campaigns of the Civil War, vol. 8. New York: Charles Scribner's Sons, 1885.

Griess, Thomas E., ed. *Atlas for the American Civil War.* West Point Military History Series. Wayne, NJ: Avery, 1986.

Grimsley, Mark. *The Hard Hand of War: Union Military Policy Toward Southern Civilians.* New York: Cambridge University Press, 1995.

Groom, Winston. *Shrouds of Glory: From Atlanta to Nashville—The Last Great Campaign of the Civil War.* New York: Atlantic Monthly Press, 1995.

Haites, Erik F., James Mak, and Gary M. Walton. *Western River Transportation: The Era of Early Internal Developments, 1810–1860.* Baltimore: Johns Hopkins University Press, 1975.

Hall, Clifton R. *Andrew Johnson: Military Governor of Tennessee.* Princeton: Princeton University Press, 1916.

Hallock, Judith Lee. *Braxton Bragg and Confederate Defeat.* Tuscaloosa, AL: University of Alabama Press, 1991.

Hamersly, Lewis B. *The Records of Living Officers of the U.S. Navy and Marine Corps.* Philadelphia: J. B. Lippincott, 1870.

Hannaford, Ebenezer. *The Story of a Regiment: A History of the Campaigns and Associations in the Field of the Sixth Regiment Ohio Volunteer Infantry.* Cincinnati: privately printed, 1868.

Harrison, Lowell H. *The Civil War in Kentucky.* Lexington, KY: University Press of Kentucky, 1975.

Hartigen, Richard S. *Lieber's Code and the Law of War.* South Holland, IL: Precedent, 1983.

Hartjie, Robert C. *Van Dorn: Life and Times of a Confederate General.* Nashville, TN: Vanderbilt University Press, 1967.

Hay, Thomas Robson. *Hood's Tennessee Campaign.* New York: Neale, 1929.

Hearn, Chester G. *Admiral David Glasgow Farragut: The Civil War Years.* Annapolis, MD: Naval Institute Press, 1998.

_____. *Admiral David Dixon Porter: The Civil War Years.* Annapolis, MD: Naval Institute Press, 1996.

_____. *The Capture of New Orleans, 1862.* Baton Rouge: Louisiana State University Press, 1995.

_____. *Ellet's Brigade: The Strangest Outfit of All.* Baton Rouge: Louisiana State University Press, 2000.

Helm, Thomas B. *History of Cass County, Indiana.* Chicago: Brant & Fuller, 1886.

Henderson, Mary Bess McCain, Evelyn Janet McCain Young, and Anna Irene McCain Naheloffer. *"Dear Eliza": The Letters of Michel Andrew Thompson.* Ames, IA: Carter Press, 1976.

Henry, Robert Selph. *"First with the Most" Forrest.* Indianapolis: Bobbs-Merrill, 1944.

_____, ed. *As They Saw Forrest: Some Recollections and Comments of Contemporaries.* Jackson, TN: McCowat-Mercer, 1956.

Herr, Kincaid. *The Louisville and Nashville Railroad, 1850–1963.* Louisville, KY: Public Relations Department, L & N, 1964. Reprint, University of Kentucky Press, 2000.

Herrick, Walter R., Jr. *The American Naval Revolution.* Baton Rouge: Louisiana State University Press, 1966.

Holbrook, Stewart H. *The Story of American Railroads.* New York: Crown, 1947.

Holland, Cecil F. *Morgan and His Raiders: A Biography of the Confederate General.* New York: Macmillan, 1942.

Hoobler, James A. *Cities Under the Gun: Images of Occupied Nashville and Chattanooga.* Nashville, TN: Rutledge Hill Press, 1986.

Hood, John Bell. *Advance and Retreat: Personal Experiences in the United States and Confederate States Armies.* New Orleans: Published for the Hood Orphan Memorial Fund, 1880.

Hoppin, James M. *The Life of Andrew Hull Foote, Rear Admiral, United States Navy.* New York: Harper and Brothers, 1874.

Horan, James D. *Confederate Agent: A Discovery in History.* New York: Crown, 1954.

Horn, Stanley F. *The Army of Tennessee: A Military History.* Indianapolis: Bobbs-Merrill, 1941. Reprint, Norman, OK: University of Oklahoma Press, 1968.

_____. *The Decisive Battle of Nashville.* Baton Rouge: Louisiana State University Press, 1956.

_____, comp. *Tennessee's War, 1861-1865: Described by Participants.* Nashville: Tennessee Civil War Centennial Commission, 1965.

Horwitz, Lester V. *The Longest Raid of the War: Little Known and Untold Stories of Morgan's Raid into Kentucky, Indiana, and Ohio.* Cincinnati: Farmcourt, 1999.

Hubbart, Henry Clyde. *The Older Middle West, 1840-1880: Its Social, Economic and Political Life and Sectional Tendencies Before, During and After the Civil War.* New York: Russell & Russell, 1963.

Hubbell, John T., and James W. Geary, eds. *Biographical Dictionary of the Union: Northern Leaders of the Civil War.* Westport, CT: Greenwood Press, 1995.

Huddleston, Edwin G. *The Civil War in Middle Tennessee.* Nashville, TN: Nashville Banner, 1965.

Hughes, Nathaniel Cheairs, Jr. *The Battle of Belmont: Grant Strikes South.* Chapel Hill: University of North Carolina Press, 1991.

_____, and Roy P. Stonesifer, Jr. *The Life and Wars of Gideon J. Pillow.* Chapel Hill: University of North Carolina Press, 1993.

Huling, Edmund J. *Reminiscences of Gunboat Life in the Mississippi Squadron.* Saratoga Springs, NY: Sentinel Print, 1881.

Hunter, Louis C. *Steamboats on the Western Waters: An Economic and Technological History.* Cambridge, MA: Harvard University Press, 1949. Reprint, New York: Dover, 1993.

Huston, James A. *The Sinews of War: Army Logistics, 1775-1953.* Army Historical Series. Washington, D.C.: Office of the Chief of Military History, United States Army, 1966.

Johnson, Adam R. "Stovepipe." *The Partisan Rangers of the Confederate Army,* edited by William J. Davis. Louisville, KY: George G. Fetter, 1904. Reprint, Austin, TX: State House Press, 1995.

Johnson, Robert E. *Rear Admiral John Rodgers, 1812-1882.* Annapolis, MD: Naval Institute Press, 1967.

_____. *Thence Round Cape Horn: The Story of United States Naval Forces on Pacific Station, 1812-1923.* Annapolis, MD: Naval Institute Press, 1963.

Jones, Archer. *Confederate Strategy: From Shiloh to Vicksburg.* Baton Rouge, LA: Louisiana State University Press, 1961.

Jones, Virgil C. *Gray Ghosts and Rebel Raiders.* New York: Holt, 1956.

Jordan, Thomas, and J. P. Pryor. *The Campaigns of Lieut. Gen. N. B. Forrest and of Forrest's Cavalry.* New Orleans and New York: Blelock & Co., 1868. Reprint, New York: DaCapo Press, 1996.

_____. *Gunboats and Cavalry: The Story of Forrest's 1864 Johnsonville Campaign,* as told by J. P. Pryor and Thomas Jordan. Edited by E. F. Williams and H. K. Humphreys. Memphis, TN: Nathan Bedford Forrest Trail Committee, 1965.

Kane, Adam. *The Western River Steamboat.* College Station: Texas A & M University Press, 2004.

Keller, Allan. *Morgan's Raid.* New York: Collier, 1962.

Kelly, Sarah Foster. *West Knoxville: Its People and Environs.* Nashville, TN: S. F. Kelly, 1987.

Kerby, Robert L. *Kirby Smith's Confederacy: The Trans-Mississippi South, 1863-1865.* New York: Columbia University Press, 1972.

Killebrew, J. B. *Introduction to the Resources of Tennessee.* 2 vols. Nashville, TN: Tavel, Eastman, and Howell, 1874.

King, Lester L. *Transformations in American Medicine From Benjamin Rush to William Osler.* Baltimore: Johns Hopkins University Press, 1991.

Kitchens, Ben Earl. *Gunboats and Cavalry: A History of Eastport, Mississippi, with Special Emphasis on Events of the War Between the States.* Florence, AL: Thornwood, 1985.

Klein, Benjamin F. *The Ohio River Atlas: A Collection of the Best Known Maps of the Ohio River, from 1713 to 1854.* Cincinnati: Picture Marine, 1954.

Klein, Maury. *History of the Louisville and Nashville Railroad.* New York: Macmillan, 1972.

Knapp, David. *The Confederate Horsemen.* New York: Vantage, 1966.

LaFeber, Walter. *The American Search for Opportunity, 1865-1913.* Vol. 2 of *The Cambridge History of American Foreign Relations.* New York: Cambridge University Press, 1993.

Lamers, William M. *The Edge of Glory: A Biography of General William S. Rosecrans, USA.* New York: Harcourt, Brace, 1961.

Lansden, John M. *History of the City of Cairo, Illinois.* Chicago: R. R. Donnelley, 1910.

Latham, John M. *Raising the Civil War Gunboats and Building the Magic Valley History Tower.* Camden, TN: Press Pro, 1997.

Lewis Charles Lee. *David Glasgow Farragut.* Annapolis, MD: Naval Institute Press, 1943.

Lewis, Lloyd. *Sherman: Fighting Prophet.* New York: Harcourt, Brace and World, 1960.

Lieber, Francis. *Guerrilla Parties Considered with Reference to the Laws and Usages of War.* New York: D. Van Nostrand, 1862.

Longacre, Edward G. *Mounted Raids of the Civil War.* New York: A. S. Barnes, 1975.

Lonn, Ella. *Foreigners in the Union Army and Navy.* Baton Rouge: Louisiana State University Press, 1951.

Lossing, Benson J. *Pictorial Field Book of the Civil War: Journeys Through the Battlefields in the Wake of Conflict.* 3 vols. Hartford, CT: T. Belknap, 1874. Reprint, Johns Hopkins University Press, 1997.

Love, Robert W. Jr. *History of the U.S. Navy.* 2 vols. Harrisburg, PA: Stackpole Books, 1992.

Lytle, Andrew Nelson. *Bedford Forrest and His Critter Company.* New York: Milton, Balch, 1931. Reprint, Nashville, TN: J. S. Sanders, 1992.

Lytle, William C., comp. *Merchant Steam Vessels of the United States, 1807-1868, "The Lytle List."* Publication No. 6. Mystic, CT: Steamship Historical Society of America, 1952.

Mackey, Robert M. *The Uncivil War: Irregular Warfare in the Upper South, 1861-1865.* Norman: University of Oklahoma Press, 2004.

McBride, William M. *Technological Change and the United States Navy, 1865-1945.* Baltimore: Johns Hopkins University Press, 2000.

McCague, James. *The Cumberland.* Rivers of America. New York: Holt, Rinehart and Winston, 1973.

McCutchan, Kenneth P., ed. *"Dearest Lizzie": The Civil War as Seen Through the Eyes of Lieutenant Colonel James Maynard Shanklin, of Southwest Indiana's Own*

42nd Regiment, Indiana Volunteer Infantry, and Recounted in Letters to His Wife. Evansville, IN: Friends of Willard Library Press, 1988.

McDonough, James Lee. Nashville: The Western Confederacy's Final Gamble. Knoxville, TN: University of Tennessee Press, 2004.

_____. Stones River: Bloody Winter in Tennessee. Knoxville, TN: University of Tennessee Press, 1980.

McDowell, Robert Emmett. City of Conflict: Louisville in the Civil War, 1861–1865. Louisville, KY: Civil War Roundtable, 1962.

McMurry, Richard M. John Bell Hood and the War for Southern Independence. Lexington, KY: University Press of Kentucky, 1982.

_____. Two Great Rebel Armies. Chapel Hill: University of North Carolina Press, 1989.

McPherson, James M. Battle Cry of Freedom: The Civil War Era. New York: Oxford University Press, 1988.

McWhitney, Grady. Braxton Bragg and Confederate Defeat. New York: Columbia University Press, 1969.

Mahan, Alfred T. The Gulf and Inland Waters. Vol. III of The Navy in the Civil War. New York: Scribner's, 1883.

Maness, Lonnie E. An Untutored Genius: The Military Career of General Nathan Bedford Forrest. Oxford, MS: Guild Bindery Press, 1990.

Marshall, Edward Chauncey. History of the Naval Academy. New York: D. Van Nostrand, 1862.

Marszalek, John F. Sherman: A Soldier's Passion for Order. New York: The Free Press, 1993.

Marvel, William. Burnside. Chapel Hill: University of North Carolina Press, 1991.

Maslowski, Peter. "Treason Must Be Made Odious": Military Occupation and Wartime Reconstruction in Nashville, Tennessee, 1862–1865. New York: K.T.O. Press, 1978.

Mathes, Harvey J. General Forrest. New York: D. Appleton, 1902.

Melia, Tamara Moser. "Damn the Torpedoes": A Short History of U.S. Naval Mine Countermeasures, 1777–1991. Contributions in Naval History, no. 4. Washington, D.C.: Naval Historical Center, Department of the Navy, 1991.

Merrill, James M. Battle Flags South: The Story of the Civil War Navies on Western Waters. Rutherford, NJ: Fairleigh Dickinson University Press, 1970.

Miller, David W. Second Only to Grant: Quartermaster General Montgomery C. Meigs. Shippensburg, PA: White Mane Books, 2000.

Miller, Frank. The Photographic History of the Civil War. 10 vols. New York: Review of Reviews, 1911.

Milligan, John D. Gunboats Down the Mississippi. Annapolis, MD: Naval Institute Press, 1965.

Mitchell, Joseph B., ed. The Badge of Gallantry: Recollections of Civil War Congressional Medal of Honor Winners. New York: Macmillan, 1968.

Moore, Frank, ed. The Rebellion Record: A Diary of American Events. 11 vols. New York: G. P. Putnam, 1861–1863; D. Van Nostrand, 1864–1868.hell,.

Morgan, James Morris. Recollections of a Rebel Reefer. Boston: Houghton, Mifflin, 1917.

Morison, Samuel Eliot. The Oxford History of the American People. New York: Oxford University Press, 1965.

Morton, John Watson. The Artillery of Nathan Bedford Forrest's Cavalry. Nashville, TN: Publishing House of the Methodist Episcopal Church South, 1909.

Mulesky, Raymond. Thunder from a Clear Sky: Stovepipe Johnson's Confederate Raid on Newburgh, Indiana. New York: iUniverse, 2005.

Musican, Ivan. Divided Waters: The Naval History of the Civil War. New York: HarperCollins, 1995.

Musgrove, George D. Kentucky Cavaliers in Dixie: Reminiscences of a Confederate Cavalryman. Edited by Bell I. Wiley. Jackson, TN: McCowat-Mercer Press, 1957. Reprint, Lincoln: University of Nebraska Press, 1999.

Neal, Diane, and Thomas W. Kremm, Lion of the South: General Thomas C. Hindman. Macon, GA: Mercer University Press, 1993.

Neuman, Frederick G. The Story of Paducah, Kentucky. Paducah: Young Printing, 1927.

Nevins, Allan. The War for the Union: War Becomes Revolution. New York: Charles Scribner's Sons, 1960.

Niven, John. Gideon Welles: Lincoln's Secretary of the Navy. New York: Oxford University Press, 1973.

Noe, Kenneth W., ed. A Southern Boy in Blue: The Memoir of Marcus Woodcock, 9th Kentucky Infantry (U.S.A.). Knoxville, TN: University of Tennessee Press, 1996.

Paludan, Philip Shaw. A People's Contest: The Union and Civil War, 1861–1865. New York: Harper & Row, 1988.

_____. Victims: A True Story of the Civil War. Knoxville, TN: University of Tennessee Press, 1981.

Parker, Foxhall A. The Naval Howitzer Afloat. New York: D. Van Nostrand, 1866.

_____. The Naval Howitzer Ashore. New York: D. Van Nostrand, 1865.

Parks, Joseph H. General Leonidas Polk, C.S.A.: The Fighting Bishop. Baton Rouge: Louisiana State University Press, 1962.

Parrish. L. W. Pictorial History of the Naval Air Station at Pensacola, Florida. N.p.: 1941.

Paullin, Charles Oscar. Paullin's History of Naval Administration, 1775–1911: A Collection of Articles from the U.S. Naval Institute Proceedings. Annapolis, MD: Naval Institute Press, 1968.

Pearce, George F. The U.S. Navy in Pensacola. Pensacola, FL: University Press of Florida, 1980.

Perry, James M. A Bohemian Brigade: The Civil War Correspondents, Mostly Rough, Sometimes Ready. New York: John Wiley, 2000.

Plum, William R. The Military Telegraph During the Civil War in the United States. 2 vols. Chicago: Jansen, McClurg, 1882.

Porter, David Dixon. Incidents and Anecdotes of the Civil War. New York: D. Appleton, 1885.

_____. Naval History of the Civil War. New York: Sherman, 1886. Reprint, Mineola, NY: Dover Publications, 1998.

Powell, Jehu. History of Cass County, Indiana. Chicago, New York: Lewis, 1913.

Powers, Ron. Mark Twain: A Life. New York: The Free Press, 2005.

Pratt, Fletcher. The Civil War on Western Waters. New York: Holt, 1958.

Puleston, William D. Annapolis: Gangway to the Quarterdeck. New York: D. Appleton-Century, 1942.

Putnam, A. W. *History of Middle Tennessee.* Knoxville, TN: University of Tennessee Press, 1971.

Ramage, James A. *Rebel Raider: The Life of General John Hunt Morgan.* Lexington, TN: University Press of Kentucky, 1986.

Ramold, Steven J. *Slaves, Sailors, Citizens: African Americans in the Union Navy.* DeKalb, IL: Northern Illinois University Press, 2002.

Reed, Rowena. *Combined Operations in the Civil War.* Annapolis, MD: Naval Institute Press, 1978.

Regimental Association. *History of the 46th Regiment, Indiana Volunteer Infantry, September 1861–September 1865.* Logansport, IN: Press of Wilson, Humphries & Co., 1888.

Rice, Ralsa C. *Yankee Tigers: Through the Civil War with the One Hundred and Twenty-Fifth Ohio.* Edited by Richard A. Baumgartner and Larry M. Strayer. Huntington, WV: Blue Acorn Press, 1992.

Ringle, Dennis J. *Life in Mr. Lincoln's Navy.* Annapolis, MD: Naval Institute Press, 1998.

Roberts, William H. *Civil War Ironclads: The U.S. Navy and Industrial Mobilization.* Baltimore: Johns Hopkins University Press, 2002.

Robertson, William Glenn, et al. *Staff Ride Handbook for the Battle of Chickamauga, 18–20 September 1863.* Fort Leavenworth, KS: U.S. Army Command and General Staff College, Combat Studies Institute, 1992.

Roe, Francis Asbury. *Naval Duties and Discipline, with the Policy and Principles of Naval Organization.* New York: D. Van Nostrand, 1865.

Roman, Alfred. *Military Operations of General Beauregard.* 2 vols. New York: Harper and Brothers, 1884.

Rusling, James F. *Men and Things I Saw in Civil War Days.* New ed. New York: Methodist Book Concern, 1914.

Safford, James M. *Geology of Tennessee.* Nashville, TN: S. C. Mercer, 1869.

Scheina, Robert L. *Latin America's Wars: The Age of the Caudillo, 1791–1898.* Washington, D.C.: Brassy's, 2003.

Seitz, Don C. *Braxton Bragg: General of the Confederacy.* Columbia, SC: State, 1924.

Sharf, J. Thomas. *History of the Confederate Navy from its Organization to the Surrender of its Last Vessel.* New York: Rodgers and Sherwood, 1887. Reprint, New York: Fairfax Press, 1977.

Shea, William L., and Earl J. Hess. *Pea Ridge: Campaign in the West.* Chapel Hill: University of North Carolina Press, 1997.

Shepard, Eric W. *Bedford Forrest: The Confederacy's Greatest Cavalryman.* New York: Dial Press, 1930.

Sherman, William Tecumseh. *Memoirs.* 2 vols. New York: Appleton, 1875. Reprint, New York: Penguin Books, 2000.

Sherwood, Isaac R. *Memories of the War.* Toledo, OH: H. J. Crittenden, 1923.

Silverstone, Paul H. *The Sailing Navy, 1775–1854.* Annapolis, MD: Naval Institute Press, 2001.

_____. *U.S. Warships of World War II.* Garden City, NY: Doubleday, 1972.

_____. *Warships of the Civil War Navies.* Annapolis, MD: Naval Institute Press, 1989.

Slagle, Jay. *Ironclad Captain: Seth Ledyard Phelps and the U.S. Navy.* Kent, OH: Kent State University Press, 1996.

Sloan, Edward W., III. *Benjamin Franklin Isherwood, Naval Engineer: The Years as Engineer in Chief, 1861–1869.* Annapolis, MD: Naval Institute Press, 1965.

Smith, Herschel K., Jr. *Some Encounters with General Forrest.* McKenzie, TN: Privately printed, 1959?.

Smith, Myron J., Jr. *An Indiana Sailor Scuttles Morgan's Raid.* Fort Wayne, IN: Fort Wayne Public Library, 1972.

_____. *U.S.S. Carondelet, 1861–1865.* Manhattan, KS: MA/AH Publishing, 1982.

Sprout, Harold, and Margaret Sprout. *The Rise of American Naval Power, 1776–1918.* Princeton: Princeton University Press, 1946.

Stamp, Kenneth M. *America in 1857.* New York: Oxford University Press, 1990.

_____. *And the War Came: The North and the Secession Crisis, 1860–1861.* Baton Rouge: Louisiana State University Press, 1970.

Starr, Stephen. *The Union Cavalry in the Civil War: Vol. III, The War in the West, 1861–1865.* Baton Rouge: Louisiana State University Press, 1985.

Steenburn, Donald H. *Silent Echoes of Johnsonville: Rebel Cavalry and Yankee Gunboats.* Rogersville, AL: Elk River Press, 1994.

Still, William N., Jr., ed. *The Confederate Navy: The Ships, Men, and Organization, 1861–1865.* Annapolis, MD: Naval Institute Press, 1997.

Stutler, Boyd B. *West Virginia in the Civil War.* Charleston, WV: Education Foundation, 1963.

Swedberg, Claire E., ed. *Three Years with the 92nd Illinois: The Civil War Diary of John M. King.* Mechanicsburg, PA: Stackpole Books, 1999.

Sweetman, Jack. *The U.S. Naval Academy: An Illustrated History.* Annapolis, MD: Naval Institute Press, 1979.

Swiggert, Howard. *The Rebel Raider: A Life of John Hunt Morgan.* Indianapolis: Bobbs-Merrill, 1934.

Sword, Wiley. *The Confederacy's Last Hurrah: Spring Hill, Franklin and Nashville.* Lawrence, KS: University Press of Kansas, 1993.

_____. *Embrace an Angry Wind—The Confederacy's Last Hurrah: Spring Hill, Franklin & Nashville.* New York: HarperCollins, 1992.

_____. *Mountains Touched with Fire: Chattanooga Besieged.* New York: St. Martin's Press, 1995.

Taylor, David L. *With Bowie Knives and Pistols: Morgan's Raid in Indiana.* Lexington, IN: TaylorMade Write, 1993.

Taylor, Lenette S. *"The Supply for Tomorrow Must Not Fail": The Civil War of Captain Simon Perkins, Jr., a Union Quartermaster.* Kent, OH: Kent State University Press, 2004.

Thomas, Dean S. *Cannons: Introduction to Civil War Artillery.* Arendtsville, PA: Thomas Publications, 1985.

Thomas, Edison H. *John Hunt Morgan and His Raiders.* Lexington, KY: University Press of Kentucky, 1975.

Todorich, Charles. *The Spirited Years: A History of the Antebellum Naval Academy.* Annapolis, MD: Naval Institute Press, 1984.

Troutman, Richard, ed. *The Heavens Are Weeping: The Diaries of George R. Browder, 1852–1886.* Grand Rapids, MI: Zondervan, 1987.

Tucker, Louis L. *Cincinnati During the Civil War.* Publications of the Ohio Civil War Centennial Commission, no. 9. Columbus: Ohio State University Press, 1962.

Tucker, Spencer C. *Andrew Foote: Civil War Admiral on Western Waters*. Annapolis, MD: Naval Institute Press, 2000.

Turner, George Edgar. *Victory Rode the Rails: The Strategic Place of Railroads in the Civil War*. Indianapolis: Bobbs-Merrill, 1953.

Twain, Mark. *Life on the Mississippi*. New York: Harper & Brothers, 1950.

United States. Navy Department. *Laws of the United States Relating to the Navy*. Washington, D.C.: GPO, 1866.

____. ____. *Regulations for the Government of the United States Navy*. Washington, D.C.: GPO, 1865.

____. ____. Mississippi Squadron. *General Orders, Rear Adm. D. D. Porter, Commanding, From Oct. 16th 1862 to Oct. 26th 1864*. St. Louis, MO: R. P. Studley, 1864.

____. ____. ____. *General Orders, Rear Adm. S. P. Lee Commanding, From Nov. 1st 1864 to April 24th, 1865*. St. Louis, MO: R. P. Studley, 1865.

____. ____. Naval History Division. *Civil War Naval Chronology, 1861-1865*. 6 vols. In 1. Rev. ed. Washington, D.C.: GPO, 1966.

____. ____. *Riverine Warfare: The United States Navy's Operations on Inland Waters*. Rev. ed. Washington, D.C.: GPO, 1968.

____. ____. Office of the Secretary of the Navy. *Report of the Secretary of the Navy*. 6 vols. Washington, D.C.: GPO, 1861-1866.

Van Doren Stern, Philip, ed. *Soldier Life in the Union and Confederate Armies*. New York: Premier Books, 1961.

Van Horne, Thomas B., ed. *History of the Army of the Cumberland: Its Organization, Campaigns, and Battles, Written at the Request of Major General George H. Thomas Chiefly from His Private Military Journal and Official and Other Documents Furnished by Him*. 2 vols. Cincinnati: R. Clarke, 1875. Reprint, Wilmington, NC: Broadfoot, 1988.

Verrill, A. Hyatt. *Porto Rico Past and Present and San Domingo of To-Day*. New York: Dodd, Mead, 1930.

Walke, Henry. *Naval Scenes and Reminiscences of the Civil War in the United States on the Southern and Western Waters During the Years 1861, 1862 and 1863 with the History of That Period Compared and Corrected from Authentic Sources*. New York: F. R. Reed, 1877.

Walker, Jeanie Mort. *Life of Capt. Joseph Fry, the Cuban Martyr*. Hartford, CT: J. B. Burr, 1875.

Walker, William. *The War in Nicaragua*. Mobile, AL: S.H. Goetzel, 1860. Reprint, Tucson: University of Arizona Press, 1985.

Wallace, Edward. *Destiny and Glory*. New York: Coward-McCann, 1957.

Ward, Andrew. *River Runs Red: The Fort Pillow Massacre in the American Civil War*. New York: Viking Press, 2005.

Warner, Ezra. *Generals in Blue: Lives of Union Commanders*. Baton Rouge: Louisiana State University Press, 1964.

____. *Generals in Gray: Lives of Confederate Commanders*. Baton Rouge: Louisiana State University Press, 1959.

Waters, Charles M. *Historic Clarksville: The Bicentennial Story, 1784-1984*. Clarksville, TN: Historic Clarksville Publishing Co., 1983.

Way, Frederick, Jr. *Way's Packet Directory, 1848-1994: Passenger Steamboats of the Mississippi River System Since the Advent of Photography in Mid-Continent America*. Athens, OH: Ohio University Press, 1983.

Weigley, Russell F. *Quartermaster General of the Union Army: A Biography of M. C. Meigs*. New York: Columbia University Press, 1959.

Welcher, Frank J. *The Union Army, 1861-1865: Organization and Operations—Vol. III, The Western Theater*. Bloomington: Indiana University Press, 1993.

Welles, Gideon. *The Diary of Gideon Welles, Secretary of the Navy Under Lincoln and Johnson*, edited by John T. Morse, Jr. 3 vols. Boston: Houghton, Mifflin, 1911.

West, Richard S., Jr. *Mr. Lincoln's Navy*. New York: Longman's, Green, 1957.

Wideman, John C. *The Sinking of the U.S.S. Cairo*. Jackson: University Press of Mississippi, 1993.

Wiley, Bell I. *The Life of Billy Yank, the Common Soldier of the Union*. New York: Bobbs-Merrill, 1952. Reprint. Baton Rouge: Louisiana State University Press, 1991.

____. *The Life of Johnny Reb, the Common Soldier of the Confederacy*. New York: Bobbs-Merrill, 1943. Reprint. Baton Rouge: Louisiana State University Press, 1990.

Wilkie, Franc B. *Pen and Powder*. Boston: Ticknor, 1888.

Willett, Robert R. Jr. *The Lightning Mule Brigade: Abel Streight's 1863 Raid into Alabama*. Carmel, IN: Guild Press of Indiana, 1999.

Williams, Edward F. III. *Fustest with the Mostest: The Military Career of Tennessee's Greatest Confederate, Lt. Gen. Nathan Bedford Forrest*. Memphis, TN: Southern Books, 1969. Reprint, Memphis, TN: Historical Hiking Trails, 1973.

____, and H. K. Humphreys, eds. *Gunboats and Cavalry: The Story of Forrest's 1864 Johnsonville Campaign, as Told to J. P. Pryor and Thomas Jordan, by Nathan Bedford Forrest*. Memphis, TN: Nathan Bedford Forrest Trail Committee, 1965.

Williams, T. Harry. *Hayes of the 23rd*. New York: Knopf, 1965. Reprint, Lincoln: University of Nebraska Press, 1994.

____. *Lincoln and His Generals*. New York: Knopf, 1952. Reprint, New York: Vintage Books, 1962.

Wills, Brian Steel. *A Battle from the Start: The Life of Nathan Bedford Forrest*. New York: HarperCollins, 1992.

____. *The Confederacy's Greatest Cavalryman: Forrest*. Lawrence, KS: University Press of Kansas, 1992.

Wilson, James Grant, and John Fiske, eds. *Appleton's Cyclopaedia of American Biography*. 5 vols. New York: D. Appleton, 1888.

Wilson, James H. *Under the Old Flag*. 2 vols. New York: D. Appleton, 1912.

Woodward, Steven E. *Jefferson Davis and His Generals: The Failure of Confederate Command in the West*. Lawrence, KS: University Press of Kansas, 1990.

____. *Nothing But Victory: The Army of the Tennessee, 1861-1865*. New York: Knopf, 2005.

____. *Six Armies in Tennessee: The Chickamauga and Chattanooga Campaigns*. Great Campaigns of the Civil War Series. Lincoln: University of Nebraska Press, 1999.

_____, ed. *Grant's Lieutenants: From Cairo to Vicksburg.* Lawrence, KS: University Press of Kansas, 2001.
Wyeth, John Allan. *Life of General Nathan Bedford Forrest.* New York: Harper & Bros., 1904 ((c)1899). Reprint, New York: Harper, 1959.
Young, Bennett H. *Confederate Wizards of the Saddle, Being Reminiscences and Observations of One Who Rode with Morgan.* Boston: Chappel, 1914.
Zimmerman, Mark. *Battle of Nashville Preservation Society Guide to Civil War Nashville.* Nashville, TN: Lithographics, 2004.

Articles and Essays in Books or Journals

Ambrose, Stephen E. "The Union Command System and the Donelson Campaign." *Military Affairs* 24 (Summer 1960): 78–86.
Anderson, Bern. "The Naval Strategy of the Civil War." *Military Affairs* 26 (Spring 1962): 11–21.
Andrews, Peter. "The Rock of Chickamauga." *American Heritage* 41 (February 1990): 81–91.
Aptheker, Herbert. "The Negro in the Union Navy." *Journal of Negro History* 32 (April 1947): 169–200.
Ash, Stephen V. "A Community at War: Montgomery County, 1861–65." *Tennessee Historical Quarterly* 36 (Spring 1977): 30–43.
_____. "Sharks in an Angry Sea: Civilian Resistance and Guerrilla Warfare in Occupied Middle Tennessee, 1862–1865." *Tennessee Historical Quarterly* 45 (Fall 1986): 217–320.
Atack, Jeremy, et al. "The Profitability of Steamboating on Western Rivers, 1850." *Business History Review* 49 (Autumn 1975): 346–354.
Atwater, Edward C. "Making Fewer Mistakes: A History of Students and Patients." *Bulletin of the History of Medicine* 57 (1983): 168–171.
Bailey, Anne J. "The Mississippi Marine Brigade: Fighting Rebel Guerrillas on Western Waters." *Military History of the Southwest* 22 (Spring 1992): 34–41.
Beard, Dan W. "With Forrest in West Tennessee." *Southern Historical Society Papers* 37, 1909: 304–308.
Bearss, Edwin C. "Civil War Operations In and Around Pensacola." *Florida Historical Quarterly* 36 (October 1957): 125–165.
_____. "The Fall of Fort Henry." *West Tennessee Historical Society Publications* 17, 1963: 85–107.
_____. "A Federal Raid Up the Tennessee River." *Alabama Review* 17 (October 1964): 261–270.
_____. "Unconditional Surrender: The Fall of Fort Donelson." *Tennessee Historical Quarterly* 21 (June 1962): 47–62.
_____. "The Union Raid Down the Mississippi and Up the Yazoo—August 16–27, 1862." In Editors of *Military Affairs, Military Analysis of the Civil War: An Anthology.* Millwood, NY: KTO, 1977. pp. 213–224.
_____. "The White River Expedition, June 10–July 15, 1862." *Arkansas Historical Quarterly* 21 (Winter 1962): 305–207.
Benedict, James B., Jr. "General John Hunt Morgan: The Great Indiana-Ohio Raid." *Filson Club Historical Quarterly* 31 (April 1957): 147–171.
Bennet, B. Kevin, and Dave Roth. "The General's Tour: The Battle of Buffington Island." *Blue & Gray Magazine* 15 (April 1998): 60–65.
Bergeron, Paul H. "Andrew Johnson." In Carroll Van West, ed., *The Tennessee Encyclopedia of History and Culture.* Nashville, TN: Rutledge Hill Press for the Tennessee Historical Society, 1998. P. 482.
Blair, John L. "Morgan's Ohio Raid." *Filson Club Historical Quarterly* 37 (July 1962): 242–271.
Blake, W. H. "Coal Barging in Wartime, 1861–1865." *Gulf States Historical Magazine* 1 (May 1903): 409–412.
Bogle, Robert V. "Defeat Through Default: Confederate Naval Strategy for the Upper Tennessee and Its Tributaries, 1861–1862." *Tennessee Historical Quarterly* 18 (Spring 1968): 62–71.
Brewer, Charles C. "African-American Sailors and the Unvexing of the Mississippi River." *Prologue* 30 (Winter 1996): 279–286.
Brown, Campbell H. "Forrest's Johnsonville Raid." *Civil War Times Illustrated* 4 (June 1965): 48–57.
Brown, Fred. "Sultana Burning." *Appalachian Life* 41 (March 2000): 3–4, 8.
Brown, Henry. "The Dark and the Light Side of the River War." Edited by John D. Milligan. *Civil War Times Illustrated* 9 (December 1970): 12–18.
Buhl, Lance C. "Mariners and Machines: Resistance to Technological Change in the American Navy, 1865–1869," *The Journal of American History* 61 (December 1974): 703–727.
"Burning of the *Alice Dean.*" *Confederate Veteran* 21 (January–December 1913): 111–112.
Burt, Jesse C. Jr. "Sherman's Logistics and Andrew Johnson." *Tennessee Historical Quarterly* 15 (1956): 195–215.
Campbell, James Edwin. "Recent Addresses of James Edwin Campbell: The Mississippi Squadron." *Ohio Archaeological and Historical Quarterly* 34 (January 1925): 29–64.
Castel, Albert. "The Fort Pillow Massacre: A Fresh Examination of the Evidence." *Civil War History* 4 (March 1958): 37–50.
_____. "The Guerrilla War." *Civil War Times Illustrated* 34 (October 1974): 1–50.
Catton, Bruce. "Glory Road Began in the West." *Civil War History* 6 (June 1960): 229–237.
Chalmers, James R. "Forrest and His Campaigns." *Southern Historical Society Papers* 8, 1879: 457–489.
Cimprich, John, and Robert C. Mainfort, Jr. "Fort Pillow Revisited: New Evidence About an Old Controversy." *Civil War History* 28 (December 1982): 293–306.
_____. "Fort Pillow Massacre: A Statistical Note." *Journal of American History* 76 (December 1989): 830–837.
Coggins, Jack. "Civil War Naval Ordnance: Weapons and Equipment." *Civil War Times Illustrate,* 4 (November 1964): 16–20.
Cooling, Benjamin Franklin. "The Attack on Dover, Tenn." *Civil War Times Illustrated* 2 (August 1963): 10–13.
_____. "The Battle of Dover, February 3, 1863, "*Tennessee Historical Quarterly* 22 (June 1963): 143–151.
Coulter, E. Merton. "Effects of Secession Upon the

Commerce of the Mississippi Valley." *Mississippi Valley Historical Review* 3 (December 1916): 275–300.

Cowen, E. G. "The Battle of Johnsonville." *Confederate Veteran* 22 (January–December 1914): 174–175.

Denny, Norman R. "The Devil's Navy." *Civil War Times Illustrated* 35 (August 1996): 25–30.

Dinkins, James. "With Forrest in Middle Tennessee." *Confederate Veteran* 34 (1926): 218–220.

Duke, Basil W. "Morgan's Indiana and Ohio Raid." In *The Annals of the War: Written by Leading Participants North and South*. Philadelphia: Times, 1879. pp. 241–256.

____. "The Raid." *The Century Magazine* 41 (January 1891): 403–412.

East, Sherrod E. "Montgomery C. Meigs and the Quartermaster Department." *Military Affairs* 25 (Winter 1961-1962): 183–196.

Eisterhold, John A. "Fort Heiman: Forgotten Fortress." *West Tennessee Historical Society Papers* 28, 1974: 43–54.

Fisher, Noel C. "'Prepare Them for My Coming': General William T. Sherman, Total War, and Pacification in West Tennessee." *Tennessee Historical Quarterly* 51 (Summer 1992): 75–86.

Fitzpatrick, Mike. "Miasma Fogs and River Mists," *Military Images* 25 (January-February 2004): 25–29.

Foster, Carol H. "The Requirement for Admission to the Naval Academy: An Historical Review." *U.S. Naval Institute Proceedings* 44 (February 1918): 348.

Fraser, John. "The Battle of Queenstown Heights October 13, 1812." *Magazine of American History* 24 (September 1890): 203–211.

Freidel, Frank. "General Orders 100 and Military Government." *Mississippi Valley Historical Review* 32 (March 1946): 541–546.

Gildrie, Richard P. "Guerrilla Warfare in the Lower Cumberland River Valley, 1862–1865." *Tennessee Historical Quarterly* 59 (Fall 1990): 161–176.

"Great Guns: Top Images at the 1999 Gettysburg Show." *Military Images* 19 (November-December 1999): 12–23.

Grimsley, Mark. "The Life of Nathan Bedford Forrest." *Civil War Times Illustrated* 32 (April-May 1993): 58–61, 63–70, 72–73, 32–39, 94–97.

Hagerman, Edward. "Field Transportation and Strategic Mobility in the Union Armies." *Civil War History* 34 (June 1988): 143–171.

Hirsch, Charles B. "Gunboat Personnel on the Western Waters." *Mid-America* 34 (April 1952): 73–86.

Holbrook, Francis X. "The Navy's Cross: William Walker." *Military Affairs* 39 (December 1975): 197–203.

Horn, Stanley F. "The Battle of Perryville." *Civil War Times Illustrated* 5 (February 1966): 4–11, 42–47.

____. "Nashville During the Civil War." *Tennessee Historical Quarterly* 4 (March 1945): 3–22.

____. "Nashville: The Most Decisive Battle of the War." *Civil War Times Illustrated* 3 (December 1964): 4–11, 31–36.

Huston, James A. "Logistical Support of Federal Armies in the Field." *Civil War History* 7 (March 1961): 36–47.

"John Morgan Raid in Ohio." *Magazine of History* 11, 1910: 209–219.

Johnston, John. "Cavalry of Hood's Left at Nashville." *Confederate Veteran* 13, 1905: 28–30.

Jones, Archer. "Tennessee and Mississippi: Joe Johnston's Strategic Problem." *Tennessee Historical Quarterly* 18 (June 1959): 134–147.

Kaeuper, Richard W. "The Forgotten Triumph of the Paw Paw." *American Heritage* 46 (October 1995): 86–94.

Kellar, Allan. "Morgan's Raid Across the Ohio." *Civil War Times Illustrated* 2 (June 1963): 6–10.

Lynne, Donald M. "Wilson's Cavalry at Nashville," *Civil War History* 1, 1955: 141–159.

Maness, Lonnie E. "Andrew Foote and the Gunboats at Forts Henry and Donelson." *Journal of the Jackson Purchase Historical Society* 12 (June 1984): 45–55.

____. "Andrew H. Foote: From Fort Donelson to Fort Pillow." *Journal of the Jackson Purchase Historical Society* 13 (June 1985): 1–17.

____. "Fort Pillow Under Confederate and Union Control." *West Tennessee Historical Society Papers* 38, 1984: 84–98.

Martin, Hiram H. "Service Afield and Afloat: A Reminiscence of the Civil War, Edited by Guy R. Everson." *Indiana Magazine of History* 89 (March 1993): 35–56.

McCreary, James Bennett. "Journal of My Soldier Life." *Register of the Kentucky State Historical Society* 33 (April–July 1935):, 97–117, 191–211.

Merrill, James M. "Cairo, Illinois: Strategic Civil War River Port." *Journal of the Illinois State Historical Society* 76 (Winter 1983): 242–257.

____. "Capt. Andrew Hull Foote and the Civil War on Tennessee Waters." *Tennessee Historical Quarterly* 30 (1971), 83–93.

____. "Union Shipbuilding on Western Waters During the Civil War." *Smithsonian Journal of History* 3 (Winter 1968-1969): 17–44.

Miller, Milford M. "Evansville Steamboats During the Civil War." *Indiana Magazine of History* 37 (December 1941): 359–381.

Milligan, John D. "Navy Life on the Mississippi River." *Civil War Times Illustrated* 33 (May-June 1994): 16, 66–73.

Mingus, Scott L. "Morgan's Raid." *CHARGE! Magazine* 4 (August 2004): 12–14.

"Moose Chase: Morgan's Raid." *All Hands*, no. 519 (April 1960): 59–63.

Morton, John Watson. "The Battle of Johnsonville." *Southern Historical Society Papers* 10, 1882: 471–488.

____. "Raid of Forrest's Cavalry on the Tennessee River in 1864." *Southern Historical Society Papers* 10, 1882: 261–268.

Mullen, Jay C. "Pope's New Madrid and Island No. 10 Campaign." *Missouri Historical Review* 49 (April 1965): 325–343.

Musgrove, George D. "Last Raid of Morgan Through Indiana and Ohio." *Southern Historical Society Papers* 35, 1907: 110–121.

Nash, Howard P. "Island No. 10." *Civil War Times Illustrated* 5 (December 1966): 42–50.

Newcomer, Lee N. "The Battle of Memphis, 1862." *West Tennessee Historical Society Papers* 12, 1958: 41–57.

Nichols, George Ward. "Down the Mississippi." *Harper's*

New Monthly Magazine 41 (November 1870): 836–845.

Paschall, Rod. "Tactical Exercises—Mission: Protection." *MHQ: The Quarterly Journal of Military History* 4 (Spring 1992): 56–58.

Patrick, Jeffrey L., ed. "A Fighting Sailor on the Western Waters: The Civil War Letters of [De Witt C. Morse] 'Gunboat.'" *Journal of Mississippi History* 58 (September 1996): 255–283.

Quisenberry, Anderson C. "Morgan's Men in Ohio." *Southern Historical Society Papers* 39, 1914: 91–99.

Rector, Charles R. "Morgan 'Goes A-Raiding' and Views West Virginia: A Bit of Civil War History." *West Virginia Review* 6 (May 1929): 310–311, 322.

"Reverend Dr. D. C. Kelley." *The Vanderbilt University Quarterly* 9 (October 1909): 236.

Robert, Sarah Corbin. "The Naval Academy as Housekeeper: Feeding and Clothing the Midshipmen." *U.S. Naval Institute Proceedings* 72 (April 1946): 119–129.

Roberts, Bobby L. "General T. C. Hindman and the Trans-Mississippi District." *Arkansas Historical Quarterly* 32 (Winter 1973): 297–311.

Roberts, John C. "Gunboats in the River War, 1861–1865." *U.S. Naval Institute Proceedings* 91 (March 1965): 83–99.

Robertson, Middleton. "Recollections of Morgan's Raid." *Indiana Magazine of History* 34 (June 1938): 188–194.

Rogge, Robert E. "Crossing the Line: Bragg vs. Morgan." *Civil War* 11 (March-April 1993): 16–22.

Sandler, Stanley. "A Navy in Decline: Some Strategic Technological Results of Disarmament, 1865–1869." *Military Affairs* 35 (December 1971): 138–142.

Saunders, Herbert. "The Civil War Letters of Herbert Saunders." Edited by Ronald K. Hutch. *Register of the Kentucky Historical Society* 69 (March 1971): 17–29.

Sawyer, William D. "The Western River Engine." *Steamboat Bill* 35, 1978: 71–80.

Scroggs, William Oscar. "William Walker and the Steamship Company in Nicaragua." *The American Historical Review* 10 (July 1905): 792–811.

Sheldon, Yvonne, ed. "Peril in West Union: Ohio Prepares for Morgan's Raiders." *Civil War Times Illustrated* 23 (November 1984): 32–37.

Smith, Lawrence M. "Rise and Fall of the Strategy of Exhaustion." *Army Logistician*, November-December 2004: 33–37.

Smith, Myron J., Jr. "Gunboats at Buffington: The U.S. Navy and Morgan's Raid, 1863." *West Virginia History* 44 (Winter 1983): 97–110.

———. "An Indiana Sailor Scuttles Morgan's Raid." *Indiana History Bulletin* 48 (June 1971): 87–98.

Steenburn, Donald H. "The United States Ship *Undine*." *Civil War Times Illustrated* 35 (August 1996): 27.

Still, John S. "Blitzkrieg, 1863, Morgan's Raid and Rout." *Civil War History* 3 (1957): 291–306.

Still, William N., Jr. "The Common Sailor—The Civil War's Uncommon Man: Part I, Yankee Blue Jackets." *Civil War Times Illustrated* 23 (February 1985): 25–39.

Suhr, Robert C. "Personality: Charles Henry Davis' Brilliant U.S. Navy Career was Interrupted, Not Enhanced, by the Civil War." *Military History* 21 (January-February 2005): 74–75.

Sutherland, Daniel E. "Guerrillas: The Real War in Arkansas." *Arkansas Historical Quarterly* 52 (Autumn 1993): 257–285.

———. "Sideshow No Longer: A Historiographical Review of the Guerrilla War." *Civil War History* 46 (March 2000): 5–23.

Swift, John. "Letters from a Sailor on a Tinclad." Edited by Lester L. Swift. *Civil War History* 10 (March 1961): 48–62.

Tomlin, Carolyn Ross. "Nathan Bedford Forrest and His 'Horse Marines.'" *Tennessee Conservationist* 61 (March 1995): 26–29.

Toplovich, Ann. "Cumberland River." In Carroll Van West, ed., *The Tennessee Encyclopedia of History and Culture*. Nashville, TN: Rutledge Hill Press for the Tennessee Historical Society, 1998. pp. 227–228.

———. "Tennessee River System." In Carroll Van West, ed., *The Tennessee Encyclopedia of History and Culture*. Nashville, TN: Rutledge Hill Press for the Tennessee Historical Society, 1998. pp. 943–945.

True, Rowland Stafford. "Life Aboard a Gunboat [U.S.S. *Silver Lake*, No. 23]: A First-Person Account." *Civil War Times Illustrated* 9 (February 1971): 36–43.

Tucker, Glenn. "Untutored Genius [Forrest] of the War." *Civil War Times Illustrated* 3 (June 1964): 7–9, 35–39, 49.

United States Naval Historical Foundation. "River Navies in the Civil War." *Military Affairs* 18 (Spring 1954): 29–32.

Vitz, Carl. "Cincinnati: Civil War Port." *Museum Echoes* 34 (July 1961): 51–54.

Walker, Peter F. "Command Failure: The Fall of Forts Henry and Donelson." *Tennessee Historical Quarterly*, 16 (December 1957), 335–360.

———. "Holding the Tennessee Line: Winter 1861-1862." *Tennessee Historical Quarterly* 16 (September 1957): 228–249.

Walton, Gary M. "River Transportation and the Old Northwest Territory" in David C. Klingaman and Richard K. Vedder, eds. *Essays on the Economy of the Old Northwest*. Athens: Ohio University Press, 1987. pp. 225–242.

Weaver, H. C. "Morgan's Raid in Kentucky, Indiana, and Ohio, July 1863." In W. H. Chamberlain, ed. *Sketches of War History, 1861–1865: Papers Prepared for Presentation to the Ohio Commandery of the Loyal Legion of the United States, 1890–1896*. Cincinnati: Robert G. Clarke, 1896. pp. iv, 278–314.

Webber, Richard, and John C. Roberts, "James B. Eads: Master Builder," *The Navy* 8 (March 1965): 23–25.

Weigley, Russel F. "Montgomery C. Meigs: A Personality Profile." *Civil War Times Illustrated* 3 (November 1964): 42–48.

Weld, Stanley B., ed., "A Connecticut Surgeon in the Civil War: The Reminiscences of Nathan Mayer." *Journal of the History of Medicine and Allied Sciences* 19, 1964: 272–286.

Weller, Cornelia, and Jac Weller. "The Logistics of Bedford Forrest, Part Two: A Leader of Men." *The Army Quarterly* 121 (October 1991): 423–429.

Weller, Jac. "Bedford Forest: Tactical Teamwork was

His Secret Weapon." *Ordnance* 38 (September-October 1953): 248–251.

———. "Nathan Bedford Forrest: An Analysis of Untutored Military Genius." *Tennessee Historical Quarterly* 18 (September 1959): 213–259.

West, Richard, Jr. "Lincoln's Hand in Naval Matters," *Civil War History* 4 (June 1958): 175–181.

White, Lonnie J. "Federal Operations at New Madrid and Island No. 10." *West Tennessee Historical Society Papers* 17 (1963): 47–67.

Whitesell, Robert D. "Military and Naval Activity Between Cairo and Columbus." *Register of the Kentucky Historical Society* 61, 1963: 107–121.

Williams, Edward F., III. "The Johnsonville Raid and Nathan Bedford Forrest State Park." *Tennessee Historical Quarterly* 28 (Fall 1969): 225–251.

Wilson, Terry. "'Against Such Powerful Odds': The 83rd Illinois Infantry at the Battle of Dover, Tennessee, February 1863," *Tennessee Historical Quarterly* 53 (December 1994): 260–271.

Wilson, William E. "Thunderbolt of the Confederacy; or, King of Horse Thieves." *Indiana Magazine of History* 54 (June 1958): 119–130.

Yeiser, A. R. "The Capture of the *Alice Dean*." *Confederate Veteran* 22 (July 1914): 364–365.

Unpublished sources

Barksdale, Ethelbert. "Semi-Regular and Irregular Warfare in the Civil War." Unpublished Ph.D. dissertation, University of Texas at Austin, 1941.

Bogle, Victor M. "A 19th Century River Town: A Social-Economic Study of New Albany, Indiana." Unpublished Ph.D. dissertation, Boston University, 1951.

Buhl, Lance C. "The Smooth Water Navy: American Naval Policy and Politics, 1865–1876." Unpublished Ph.D. dissertation, Harvard University, 1968.

Chapman, Jesse L. "The Ellet Family and Riverine Warfare in the West, 1861–1865." Unpublished master's thesis, Old Dominion University, 1985.

Chunney, James Robert. "Don Carlos Buell: Gentleman General." Unpublished Ph.D. dissertation, Rice University, 1964.

Daniel, John S., Jr. "Special Warfare in Middle Tennessee and Surrounding Areas, 1861–1862." Unpublished master's thesis, University of Tennessee, 1971.

Goodman, Michael Harris. "The Black Tar: Negro Seamen in the Union Navy." Unpublished Ph.D. dissertation, University of Nottingham, 1975.

Grimsley, Mark. "A Directed Severity: The Evolution of Federal Policy Toward Southern Civilians and Property, 1861–1865." Unpublished Ph.D. dissertation, Ohio State University, 1992.

Henderson, Robert Wayne ("Bob"), Jr. *The Battlefield Beneath Us*. Unpublished paper. Nashville, TN, May 2006.

Hughes, Michael Anderson. "The Struggle for Chattanooga, 1862–1863." Unpublished Ph.D. dissertation, University of Arkansas, 1991.

Lighthall, Laurence J. "John Hunt Morgan: A Confederate Asset or Liability?" Unpublished master's thesis, Georgia State University, 1996.

Parker, Theodore R. "The Federal Gunboat Flotilla on the Western Waters During Its Administration by the War Department to October 1, 1862." Unpublished Ph.D. dissertation, University of Pittsburgh, 1939.

Polser, Aubrey Henry. "The Administration of the United States Navy, 1861–1865." Unpublished Ph.D. dissertation, University of Nebraska, 1975.

Scarborough, Paul G. "The Impact of the John Morgan Raid in Indiana and Ohio." Unpublished master's thesis, Miami University, 1955.

Schottenhamel, George Carl. "Lewis Baldwin Parsons and the Civil War Transportation." Unpublished Ph.D. dissertation, University of Illinois, 1954.

Sharpe, Hal F. "A Door Left Open: The Failure of the Confederate Government to Adequately Defend the Inland Rivers of Tennessee." Unpublished master's thesis, Austin Peay State University, 1981.

Smith, Myron J., Jr. "A Construction and Recruiting History of the U.S. Steam Gunboat *Carondelet*, 1861–1862." Unpublished master's thesis, Shippensburg State University, 1969.

Stowe, John Joel, Jr. "The Military Career of Nathan Bedford Forrest." Unpublished master's thesis, George Peabody College, 1930.

Whisenant, Johnny H. "Samuel Phillips Lee, U.S.N.: Commander, Mississippi Squadron (October 19, 1864–August 14, 1865." Unpublished master's thesis, Kansas State College of Pittsburg, 1968.

Wills, Brian S. "Bedford Forrest." Unpublished Ph.D. dissertation, University of Georgia, 1991.

Wright, Aubrey Gardner. "Henry Walke, 1809–1896: Romantic Painter and Naval Hero." Unpublished master's thesis, George Washington University, 1971.

Wynne, Robert Bruce. "Topographical Influences Upon the 1863 Campaigns in East Tennessee and North Georgia." Unpublished master's thesis, University of Tennessee, 1962.

Personal e-mails

Beckner, Thomas F. "Fitch at Last," July 2, 2006. Personal e-mail, July 2, 2006.

Fitch, John T. "Re: Another Fitch," May 6, 2000, May 9, 2005, June 14, 2005. Personal e-mail, May 6, 2000, May 9, 2005, June 14, 2005.

Kitchell, David, Cass County Historical Society. "Re: "The Fitches," April 5, 2006. Personal e-mail. April 5, 2006.

Kroeger, Paul. "Cmdr. Le Roy Fitch, Civil War Naval Hero from Logansport," May 28, 2006. Personal e-mail, May 28, 2006.

Towne, Stephen E., Indiana State Archives. "Re: Cmdr. Leroy Fitch, USN," June 6, 2000. Personal e-mail, June 6, 2000.

Index

In regimental listings, all units are infantry unless otherwise noted. Numbers in **bold** *italics* indicate pages with photographs.

A. Baker (steamer) 258
A. O. Tyler see *Tyler* (U.S. timberclad)
Abeona (U.S. tinclad) 340, 342
Aberdeen, AK 69; see also White River expedition (June-July 1862)
Acacia (steamer) 61
Accessory Transit Company 26
Adams, Capt. Henry 32
Adams (U.S. ram) 164
Adamson, Capt. Frederick C. 141
Adelaide (steamer) 131
Alabama, economic importance of 37
Alabama regiments: 4th Cavalry 160; 7th Cavalry 281–282, 329
Albany Law School (NY) 24
Albert Pearce (steamer) 300
Alexander, Lt. Col. A. J. 325; see also Nashville, Battle of (1864)
Alexandria, LA, Battle of (1864) 286; see also *Covington* (U.S. tinclad); *Signal* (U.S. tinclad)
Alfred Robb (steamer/1st U.S. tinclad) 76, 78, 81, 95, 97, 106, 108, 113–115, 122, 126–129, 132, 134, 136, 138, 140, 142, 147–151, 155–157, 165, 338; see also Goudy, Acting Volunteer Lt. Jason
Algee, Capt. James B. 95
Alice (steamer) 273
Alice Dean (steamer) 181–185, 194; see also Morgan's Indiana-Ohio Raid (1863)
Allegheny Belle (ersatz U.S. military gunboat) 194, 196, 198, 200–203, 264; see also Morgan's Indiana-Ohio Raid (1863)

Allen, Brig. Gen. Robert 120, 212–213, 226–228, 230–231, 234, 241–242, 251, 258, 262–263, 295, 316; see also Logistics, river
Alone (steamer) 243; see also Muscle Shoals (Tennessee River)
Alpha (steamer) 258
Amberson, John 192; see also Buffinton Island (Ohio River)
Amberson's Island 192; see also Buffington Island (Ohio River)
America (steamer) 300
America (yacht) 345; see also U.S. Naval Academy
American Civil War Roundtable of the United Kingdom 329
American Ephemeris and Nautical Almanac 25, 29
American Guano Company 28
American Panama Railroad Company 26
Amsterdam, IN see New Amsterdam, IN
Anaconda Plan 35, 37
Anderson & Louisville Steamship Co. see *John T. McCombs* (steamer)
Anna (steamer) 258, 273–274
Antietam, Battle of (1862) 97
Anti-guerrilla warfare see Counterinsurgency operations
Appomattox Court House, VA (1865) 340
Argosy (U.S. tinclad) 154, 159–160, 165, 211
Arizona (steamer) 131, 300, 312, 332
Arkansas see Hindman, Maj. Gen. Thomas C.; Irregular warfare;

White River expedition (June-July 1862)
Arkansas (Confederate armorclad) 56, 276, 294; see also *Carondolet* (U.S. ironclad gunboat); *Tyler* (U.S. timberclad gunboat)
Arkansas Post, Battle of (1863) 124, 154
Arkansas regiments: Jackson Light Artillery (Thrall's Battery) 282–283; see also Johnsonville, TN, Battle of (1864)
Arkansas River 58, 64
Army of Kentucky (U.S.) 129
Army of Northern Virginia (Confederate) 116
Army of Tennessee (Confederate) 58, 93, 174–176, 210, 302–303; see also Atlanta, Battle of (1864); Chattanooga, Battle of (1863–1864); Franklin, Battle of (1864); Nashville, Battle of (1864)
Army of the Cumberland (U.S.) 110–114, 116–117, 119, 129, 135, 137, 139, 147, 209–210, 212–213, 230, 235, 244, 301; see also Chattanooga, TN, Battle of (1863); Franklin, TN, Battle of (1864); Nashville, Battle of (1864); Stone's River, Battle of (1862–1863)
Army of the Mississippi (U.S.) 43–44, 50, 57–58
Army of the Ohio (U.S.) 50, 57–58, 214, 239; see also Knoxville, TN
Army of the Southwest (U.S.) 44, 63–64

407

Index

Army of the Tennessee (U.S.) 50, 57–58, 159, 215, 267
Army of the Tennessee Detachment (U.S.) 302, 305; *see also* Nashville, Battle of (1864)
Artillery regiments (U.S.): 4th 328; *see also* Nashville, Battle of (1864)
Asboth, Brig. Gen. Alexander 146–148
Ashland, KY 86
Ashland, TN 117, 316, 318–320; *see also* Cumberland River
Ashland City, TN 88
Ashport, TN 254; *see also* Fort Pillow (Mississippi River)
Athens County, OH 197; *see also* Morgan's Indiana-Ohio Raid (1863)
Atlanta, Battle of (1864) 264, 266–267; *see also* Sherman, Maj. Gen. William T.
Atlanta, GA 270, 272
Aurora, IN 189–191; *see also* Morgan's Indiana-Ohio Raid (1863)
Aurora, KY 87
Aurora (steamer) 258, 269
Autocrat (U.S. ram) 164

Badger, Lt. Cmdr. Oscar C. 174
Bailey, Cmdr. Theodorus 25
Bainbridge, TN 139
Baldwin, Col. O. L. 250; *see also* Fort Donelson (Cumberland River)
Bancroft, George (Navy secretary) 18; *see also* U.S. Naval Academy
Banker (steamer) *see Victory* (U.S. tinclad)
Bardstown, KY 178
Baron de Kalb (U.S. ironclad gunboat) 347; *see also St. Louis* (U.S. ironclad gunboat); Walker, Cmdr. John G.
Barringer, Capt. A. V. 201; *see also* Morgan's Indiana-Ohio Raid (1863)
Bars and obstructions, river *see* Navigation seasons and conditions on Western rivers
Bates, Edward (Attorney General) 35
Batesville, AK 63
Battery Rock (Ohio River) 211; *see also* Shawneetown, IL
Battle of Nashville Preservation Society 303–304, 329; *see also* Henderson, Robert
Beaman, Correspondent George W. 47
Bean's Station, TN 320
Beauregard, Gen Pierre G. T. 41, 43, 50, 57
Beaver Creek 204; *see also* Morgan's Indiana-Ohio Raid (1863)
Beavertown, OH 196; *see also* Morgan's Indiana-Ohio Raid (1863)
Becker, Dr. Thomas F. (provides modern diagnosis of Le Roy's mysterious terminal illness) 354

Bell, Brig. Gen. Tyree 311; *see also* Nashville, Battle of (1864)
Bell, Acting Engineer William 114
Bellaire, OH 191; *see also* Morgan's Indiana-Ohio Raid (1863)
Belle Peoria (steamer) 109
Belleville Island (Ohio River) 201–202; *see also* Morgan's Indiana-Ohio Raid (1863)
Bellona, NY 11
Bell's Bend (Cumberland River) *see* Bell's Mills, TN, Battle of (1864)
Bell's Landing (Cumberland River) *see* Bell's Mills, TN, Battle of (1864)
Bell's Mills, TN, Battle of (1864) 65, 306–315, 317–318, 324, 326–328, 330, 335; *see also* Kelley, Lt. Col. David C.; Nashville, Battle of (1864)
Belmont, MO, Battle of (1861) 36
Belpre, OH 86
Ben Gaylord (steamer) *see Undine* (U.S. tinclad)
Ben Smith (steamer) 320, 322; *see also* Gracey's Battery
Benefit (steamer) 292, 321
Bennett's Ferry (Cumberland River) 237; *see also* Big South Fork reconnaissance (Donn/Glassford, 1863)
Benton (U.S. ironclad gunboat) 36, 49, 54, 72, 347; *see also* Greer, Lt. Cmdr. James A.
Benton County, TN 62
Berryman, Lt. O. H. 33
Betsy's Landing (Cumberland River) 121, 126, 156
Betsytown, TN 88
Bickerstaff, Chief Engineer Samuel 60, 173; *see also General Sterling Price* (Confederate/U.S. gunboat)
Biddle, Judge Horace P. 24
Biddle, Col. James 326–327; *see also* Nashville, Battle of (1864)
Biffle, Col. Jacob B. 311, 321, 327; *see also* Kelley, Lt. Col. David C.
Big Bend Landing (Tennessee River) 87
Big Bend Shoals (Tennessee River) 164
Big Sandy River 86, 171, 273
Big Shanty, GA 268
Big South Fork (Cumberland River) 214–215, 218–219, 221–222, 227–228, 233, 235–241, 247–248, 338; *see also* Knoxville, TN; Logistics, river
Big South Fork reconnaissance (Donn, 1863) 227
Big South Fork reconnaissance (Donn/Glassford, 1863) 235–239
Birmingham, KY 87
Bishop, Lt. Joshua 59
Bismarck (German battleship) 193
Bixby, Pilot Horace 84; *see also* Twain, Mark
Black Hawk (U.S. tinclad/flag steamer) 169, 225, 229, 247, 260, 277, 292, 298–299, 301, 303, 321–323, 331, 333, 340–341–342, 346; *see also* Lee, Adm. Samuel Phillips; Porter, Adm. David Dixon
Blake, Capt. George S. (U.S. Naval Academy superintendent) 345; *see also* U.S. Naval Academy
Blennerhassett Island (Ohio River) 168, 172, 185, 192, 195
Blockhouse No. 3 (Nashville) 311; *see also* Morton's Battery; Nashville, Battle of (1864)
Blockhouse No. 4 (Nashville) 311; *see also* Nashville, Battle of
Blodgett, Lt. George 64
Bolton, Acting Surgeon Samuel L. 98, 114
Boone, Col. William P. 153, 156–157
Bowers, Lt. Col. Theodore S. 217–218, 220–227, 232, 240
Bowling Green, KY 41, 109, 117, 321, 337
Boyd, Lt. Cmdr. Robert, Jr. 336
Boyd's Landing (Tennessee River) 149–150
Boyle, Brig. Gen. Jeremiah T. 112–113, 145–146, 188, 190–191
Bradley, Mary Ann Fitch 15
Bradley, Stephen 15
Bragg, Gen. Braxton 58, 61, 93, 97–98, 105–107, 116–117, 119, 126, 157–158, 162, 174–175, 177–178, 208, 212, 232
Brandenburg, KY 86, 168, 179, 181–185, 187, 211
Brayman, Brig. Gen. Mason 249–252, 255; *see also* Cairo, IL; Paducah, KY, Battles of (1864); Union City, TN
Breckenridge, Maj. Gen. John C. 318
Breese, Cmdr. K. Randolph 346–347; *see also Black Hawk* (U.S. tinclad/flagboat); U.S. Naval Academy
Brice's Cross Roads, MS, Battle of (1864) 268; *see also* Forrest, Maj. Gen. Nathan Bedford
Bridgeport, AL 209, 212–213, 217, 228, 242–**243**, 244–249, 257–260, 262–263, 344; *see also* Edwards, Capt. Arthur; Tennessee River gunboat construciton (1863–1864)
Briggs, Lt. H. H. *see* Rice's Battery
Bright, Jesse (U.S. senator) 24
Brilliant (U.S. tinclad) 82–83, 98–100, 102, 106–108, 113–115, 121, 125–126, 132, 134–135, 138, 140, 142–143, 146–148, 155–157, 165, 168, 171–172, 175, 178, 206, 210–211, 218, 222, 228–229, 232, 251–252, 260–261, 266, 278, 281, 299, 301, 306–307, 309, 312, 315, 317, 326, 336, 342
Bringhurst, Maj. Thomas 43, 67
Bristol, TN 338 Tennessee River Confederate raid (Wharton, 1865)

Index

Brock, Gen. Sir Isaac 12; see also Queenstown Heights, Battle of
Brookhaven, NY 12
Brooklyn Navy Yard see New York Navy Yard (Brooklyn)
Brookport, IN 86
Brott, Maj. Elijah C. 132
Browder, Rev. George R. 93
Brown, Lt. Cmdr. George 190
Brown, Lt. J. W. see Morton's Battery
Brown County (OH) militia 193; see also Morgan's Indiana-Ohio Raid (1863)
Brown's Ferry (Tennessee River) 162
Brownsport, TN 87
Bruce, Col. Sanders D. 127, 134
Bryant, Acting Volunteer Master John L. 269, 275–279; see also *Undine* (U.S. tinclad)
Buchanan, President James 24, 30–31, 42
Buchanan, Lt. Col. Robert 320; see also *Thomas E. Tutt* (steamer)
Buck Creek 185
Buckner, Col. Robert 183
Buckner, Maj. Gen. Simon B. 96, 183
Buell, Maj. Gen. Don Carlos 39, 50, 57–58, 62, 90–91, 97–98, 103
Buffalo Landing (Tennessee River) 87
Buffalo River 86
Buffington, Joel 192; see also Buffington Island (Ohio River)
Buffington Island (Ohio River) 168, 175, 185, 192, 194–201, 203–207, 326; see also Morgan's Indiana-Ohio Raid (1863)
Buford, Brig. Gen. Abraham 250, 252–253, 271, 273, 277, 310–311, 342; see also Johnsonville, TN, Battle of (1864); Paducah, KY, Battles of (1864)
Buford, Col. Napoleon 49
Bull Run, First Battle of (1861) 42
Bullus, Capt. Oscar 336; see also Cincinnati, OH
Burbridge, Maj. Gen. Stephen G. 320; see also Bean's Station, TN
Bureau of Construction and Repair (U.S.N.) 344
Bureau of Ordnance and Hydrography (U.S.N.) 18, 174
Burkesville, KY 176–177, 216, 222, 338–339; see also Cumberland River
Burnside, Maj. Gen. Ambrose 168, 170, 172–173, 178, 187–189, 191–196, 198, 203–204, 206, 210, 212, 214, 216, 218, 222, 225–228, 232, 235; see also Morgan's Indiana-Ohio Raid (1863)
Burnside, TN 87–88, 241, 247–248, 338; see also Cumberland River
Byrne, Capt. Edward P. 175; see also Kentucky Artillery Brigade

C. Miller (steamer) 152
Cache River, AK 69; see also White River expedition (June-July 1862)
Cairo, IL 34–36, 38, 40–44, **45–46**, 49, 76, 85–86, 90, 93–94, 98, 101, 107, 113, 117, 120, 122–123, 127–128, 135, 137–139, 143, 146, 148, 155, 160, 162–163, 167, 169–173, 184, 186, 203, 214, 218, 220, 223–225, 227, 229, 232–233, 236, 240–241, 244, 248–255, 257, 265, 290, 292, 297–298, 303
Cairo (U.S. ironclad gunboat) 36–37, 54, 347; see also Selfridge, Lt. Cmdr. Thomas O., Jr.
Caledonia, IL 252
Callowaytown, KY 87
Calvary Presbyterian Church (Logansport, IN) 30
Camelia (steamer) 300
Campbell, James Edwin (sailor/Ohio governor) 84; see also *Naiad* (U.S. tinclad)
Caney Creek/Fork (Cumberland River) 160, 217, 227
Cannelton, IN 187, 260–261, 266; see also Morgan's Indiana-Ohio Raid (1863)
Canton, IN 188; see also Morgan's Indiana-Ohio Raid (1863)
Canton, KY 88, 231
Capen, Mary "Polly" see Fitch, Mary "Polly"
Capitola (steamer) 131
Carondelet, MO 80, 82, 98
Carondelet (U.S. ironclad gunboat) 36–37, 40–41, 49, 54, 284, 292–**293**, 294–295, 297–303, 305–309, 311–312, 314–315, 317–319, 322, 326–328, 330–332, 336; see also Bell's Mills, Battle of (1864); Island No. 10 (Mississippi River); Miller, Acting Volunteer Master Charles W.; Nashville, Battle of (1864); Walke, Adm. Henry
Carr, Seaman Norman 285
Carrington, Brig. Gen. Henry B. 264; see also Caseyville, KY
Carroll County, IN 43
Carrollville, TN 87
Carthage, TN 87–88, 139, 144–145, 147, 167, 214, 216–218, 221, 235–238, 240, 246, 305, 311, 315, 317–318, 323, 339; see also Big South Fork (Cumberland River); Cumberland River
Caseyville, KY 86, 97, 99–103, 106–107, 113–114, 216, 262, 264
Caseyville ransom by Fitch (1862) 101
Casparis Stone Company 355; see also Fitch's Glen (Cass County, IN)
Cass County, IN 13–18, 23–25, 43, 344; see also Logansport, IN
Cass County, IN, Agricultural, Horticultural & Mechanical Association 352
Cavalry divisions (U.S.) 6th see Johnson, Brig. Gen. Richard

Cave-in-the-Rock, IL 107
Cedar Creek, TN 87
Cedar Knob (Nashville site of Tennessee state capitol) 302
Celina, TN 228, 237, 339; see also Obey's River
Center Furnace, KY 342
Centerville, TN 136
Cerro Gordo, TN 87, 141
Chalmers, Brig. Gen. James R. 271, 274, 276, 278, 281, 303–304, 311–312, 321, 325–329; see also Johnsonville, TN, Battle of (1864); Nashville, TN, Battle of (1864)
Champion (U.S. tinclad) 165
Champion No. 3 (steamer) 60
Chancellorsville, Battle of (1863) 168
Channels, crooked river see Navigation seasons and conditions on Western rivers
Charleston, WV 193; see also Morgan's Indiana-Ohio Raid (1863)
Charlotte, TN 98, 136, 156
Charlotte County, NY see Washington County, NY
Charter (steamer) 117
Chattahoochee River 268
Chattanooga (steamer) 242, 246
Chattanooga, TN 58, 86–87, 114, 157–158, 176, 208–233, 238–244, 248, 259, 267, 270, 272, 301
Chauvenet, Prof. William 21; see also U.S. Naval Academy
Cheatham, Brig. Gen. Benjamin F. 106, 303; see also Nashville, Battle of (1864)
Chenault, Col. David W. 177; see also Morgan's Indiana-Ohio Raid (1863)
Cherokee Station, AL 268
Cheshire, OH 203; see also Eight Mile Island (Ohio River)
Chester, OH 196–198; see also Morgan's Indiana-Ohio Raid (1863)
Chickamauga, Battle of (1863) 210
Chickasaw, AL 87, 142, 150, 160
"Christmas Raid" (1862) see Morgan's Kentucky Raids (1862–1863)
Cincinnati, OH 80, 86, 112, 129, 147, 167–168, 170, 172–173, 178, 180, 184, 187–191, 193–195, 200, 203, 211, 215, 222–223, 241–242, 248, 257–258, 260, 264–265, 273, 336, 340; see also Morgan's Indiana-Ohio Raid (1863)
Cincinnati (U.S. ironclad gunboat) 36–37, 40, 67, 292, 294–295, 301–303, 305, 310, 312, 316–317, 319, 332; see also Lee, Adm. Samuel Phillips; Nashville, Battle of (1864)
City of Pekin (steamer) 258, 269
Clara Dolson (U.S. receiving ship) 93, 163
Clarendon, AK 69, 71; see also White River expedition (June-July 1862)

Index

Clark, Acting Assistant Paymaster Jason W. 336; *see also Moose* (U.S. tinclad)
Clarksville, IN 86
Clarksville, TN 38, 41, 88, 93, 98, 126–127, 134, 136, 139, 151, 153, 156–157, 168, 171, 211, 219–223, 226, 228, 230–231–232, 263, 266, 277, 297–298, 301–303, 310, 312, 314, 316–324, 330–333, 337–338; Confederate occupation (1862) 95; *see also* Cumberland River
Clifton, TN 87, 107, 127, 160, 162, 333
Clifton, TN, Battle of (1863) 141
Clinton, TN 214, 269
Coal Creek 253–254; *see also* Fort Pillow (Mississippi River)
Coast Survey (U.S.) 227, 236–238; *see also* Donn, Capt. John W.
Cockrill, Mark Robertson 327; *see also* Cockrill's Bend (Cumberland River); Nashville, Battle of (1864)
Cockrill's Bend (Cumberland River) *see* Cumberland River; Nashville, Battle of (1864)
Coffee's Landing (Tennessee River) 87
Colbert Shoals (Tennessee River) 150–151
Coleman, Dr. Asa (Logansport medical partner of Dr. Graham Newell Fitch, attended at Le Roy's deathbed) 16, 24, 43, 352–354
Coleman, Emma Fitch 24, 352
College of Physicians and Surgeons, Fairfield, NY 12
Collier, Allen *see Naumkeag* (U.S. tinclad)
Collins, Acting Engineer G. S. 114
Colored troop regiments (U.S.): 8th Artillery (Heavy) 261; 11th 252–253 *see also* Fort Pillow (Mississippi River); 12th 271 *see also* Johnsonville, TN, Battle of (1864); 13th 271 *see also* Johnsonville, TN, Battle of (1864); 61st 268–269; 100th 271 *see also* Johnsonville, TN, Battle of (1864)
Colossus (U.S. tinclad) 342
Columbia, KY 177–178
Columbia, TN 130, 140, 156, 296–298
Columbiana County, OH 204; *see also* Morgan's Indiana-Ohio Raid (1863)
Columbus, KY 36, 38, 41, 146, 251–252, 255, 272
Columbus, KY, Battle of (1864) 249–250
Commodore Marina (River Road, Nashville) *see* Hillsboro Landing (Cumberland River)
Comstock, Capt. James B. 297
Conant, Acting Volunteer Ensign Thaddeus 114
Concordia, KY 86
Conditions and seasons of navigation on Western rivers 39–40
Conestoga (U.S. timberclad) 35, 38–41, 49, 64, 66–67, 72, 88
Confederate River Defense Force 51–52, 54–55; *see also* Memphis, TN, Battle of (1862); Plum Point Bend (Mississippi River)
Congressional Medal of Honor recipients: Ditzenback, John 314 *see also* Bell's Mills, TN, Battle of (1864) and *Neosho* (U.S. monitor); Ferrell, Pilot John H. 314 *see also* Bell's Mills, TN, Battle of (1864) and *Neosho* (U.S. monitor); Miller, Quartermaster James 348 *see also* John's Island, SC, Battle of (1863) and *Marblehead* (U.S. steam gunboat)
Constitution (U.S. frigate) 345; *see also* U.S. Naval Academy
Construction of Tennessee River gunboats *see* Bridgeport, AL; Edwards, Capt. Arthur; Tennessee River gunboat construction (1863–1864)
Convoy, principles and practice of 124–125, 138, 144–146, 152–154, 171–172, 219, 222–231, 236, 247, 259, 263, 332; *see also* General Orders (Fitch)
Convoy No. 2 (steamer) 243; *see also* Muscle Shoals (Tennessee River)
Convoys *see* Cumberland River; Logistics, river; Tennessee River
Cook's Landing (Tennessee River) 160
Cordelia Ann (ersatz U.S. military gunboat) 96
Corinth, MS 140–141
Corps (U.S. Army): IV 295, 301–302 *see also* Stanley, Maj. Gen. Frank and Wood, Brig. Gen. Thomas J.; VIII 193; IX 213; XVI 159, 291, 297 *see also* Smith, Maj. Gen. Andrew J. "A. J."; XXII 176; XXIII 213, 287, 295, 301–302 *see also* Schofield, Maj. Gen. John M.; XXVI 297
Corydon, IN 182, 185
Coulson, Acting Master's Mate Washington C. 114
Coulson, Acting Volunteer Master Washington C. 308, 336, 342–343; *see also Moose* (U.S. tinclad)
Counterinsurgency operations *see* Irregular warfare, causes, principles, and counterinsurgency
Courier (steamer) 117
Courtland, AL 162
Covington, KY 86
Covington No. 2 (steamer) *see Convington* (U.S. tinclad)
Covington (U.S. tinclad) 154, 159–160, 165–166, 286; *see also* Alexandria, LA, Battle of (1864)
Cox, Brig. Gen. Jacob D. 206, 212, 268
Cox, Col. Nathaniel N. 149
Coyle, Acting Volunteer Ensign J. C. 114, 210, 215, 261, 340; *see also Silver Lake* (U.S. tinclad)
Cracker Line 242, 246; *see also Chattanooga* (steamer); Chattanooga, TN
Craven, Lt. Thomas T. 19; *see also* U. S. Naval Academy
Creelsboro, KY 238; *see also* Big South Fork reconnaissance (Donn/Glassford, 1863)
Cricket (U.S. tinclad) 165
Crittenden, John J. (U.S. senator) 30
Crittenden Compromise (1860) 30
Crooked Point Cutoff (White River) 67
Cropsey, Lt. Col. A. J. 237–238; *see also* Big South Fork reconnaissance (Donn/Glassford, 1863)
Crossville, TN 216
Cuba (steamer) 278
Cuba Ford (Tennessee River) 107
Cumberland City, TN 88, 320, 322
Cumberland Furnace 136
Cumberland Gap 213, 227, 239; *see also* Knoxville, TN; Logistics, general
Cumberland Iron Works 131
Cumberland River 30, 38–40, 72, 85–86, 87–88, 91, 98, 104–110, 112–**118**, 119–139, 143–149, 151–156, 158, 165–166, 168–169, 171, 173, 176–178, 180, 206, 208, 210–211, 213–235, 239–242, 246–249, 251, 253, 257–258, 261, 263, 266, 270–271, 273, 277–278, 288, 291–292, 294–296, 299–303, 305–306, 309–310, 312, 315–320, 322–324, 327–329, 331–332, 336–340, 342–343; *see also* Big South Fork (Cumberland River); Clarksville, TN; Harpeth Shoals (Cumberland River); Logistics, river; Nashville, TN
Cumberland University *see* Kelley, Lt. Col. David C.
Cunningham, Lt. Col. Richard D. 261
Cunningham, S P. 205; *see also* Duke, Col. Basil W.
Curlew, KY 102
Curlew (U.S. tinclad) 165, 277–278, 280–281, 283–285, 289–290, 336; *see also* Johnsonville, TN, Battle of (1864)
Currie, Lt. George E. 64; *see also* Mississippi Marine Brigade
Curtis, Maj. Gen. Samuel R. 44, 63, 68–69

D. A. January (steamer/hospital boat) 301
D. B. Campbell (steamer) 99
Dahlgren, Adm. John A. 19; *see also* U.S. Naval Academy
Dalton, GA 157–158; *see also* Streight Raid (1863)

Dana, Charles (Asst. War Secretary) 146, 242–243; see also Chattanooga, TN; Tennessee River gunboat construction (1863–1864)
Danville, TN 278, 320
David Hughes (steamer) 277–278
Davidson, Samuel, house of (Nashville) see Bell's Mills, TN, Battle of (1864)
Davidson County, TN 303; see also Nashville, TN; Nashville, Battle of (1864)
Davidson Landing (Cumberland River) see Bell's Mills, TN, Battle of (1864)
Davis, Adm. Henry H. 25, **26**–29, 40, 51–**53**, 55, 57–61, 63–64, 66–68, 72, 76–79, 81–83, 94, 97–98, 167, 202; see also Tinclads," description and evolution
Davis, Jefferson (Confederate president) 39, 210, 268, 340–341–342
Davis, Maj. Gen. Jefferson C. 130
Davis, Capt. William J. 179, 188–189; see also Morgan's Indiana-Ohio Raid (1863)
Davis' Ripple (Cumberland River) 217, 317–318
Dawson, Col. William A. 276, 283; see also Johnsonville, TN, Battle of (1864); *Venus* (steamer)
Decatur, AL 273
Decatur, TN 87, 147–148
DeHart, Richard Patten (Indiana legislator) 42
Democratic Party 23, 26, 42; see also Fitch, Dr. Graham Newell (half brother)
Denby, Edwin (Navy secretary) 24
Denby, Martha Fitch 24
Department of the Cumberland (U.S.) see Army of the Cumberland
Department of the Missouri (U.S.) 39, 273, 291
Department of the Ohio (U.S.) 39, 112, 129, 170, 176, 189, 194; see also Army of the Ohio; Morgan's Indiana-Ohio Raid (1863)
Department of the Tennessee (U.S.) see Army of the Tennessee
Derby, IN 86
Derby Landing, IN see Derby, IN
Dewey, Adm. George 21
Diadem (steamer) 131
Diana (U.S. ram) 164
Dickson, Capt. J. Bates 320; see also Lexington, TN
Dickson County, TN 98
Dillihunty plantation, TN 150
Dinkins, Capt. James 327; see also Nashville, Battle of (1864)
Distillery raids, Cumberland River (1863) 234
District of the Etowah, Provisional Detachment of the 301; see also Nashville, Battle of (1864)
Ditzenback, Quartermaster John 314; see also Bell's Mills, TN, Battle of (1864); Congressional Medal of Honor; *Neosho* (U.S. monitor)
Dixon's Springs, TN 339
Dodge, Maj. Gen. Grenville M. 113, 140–142, 151, 159–**161**, 162, 164–165, 319
Donaldson, Col. James L. 218, 228, 234–235, 248, 251, 258, 260, 263, 274, 276–278, 288, 301, 310, 316–317, 320–321, 332; see also Cumberland River; Logistics, river; Nashville, TN
Donaldson, Acting Volunteer Ensign Oliver 315; see also *Carondolet* (U.S. ironclad)
Donaldsonville, LA 211
Donelson see Fort Donelson
Donelson, Daniel S. (Tennessee attorney general) 38; see also Fort Donelson
Donn, Capt. John W. 227, 236–238; see also Coast Survey (U.S.)
Dougherty, Col. H. 108
Doughty, William (warship designer) 29
Douglas, Stephen A. (U.S. senator) 24
Dove (steamer) 131, 218
Dover, TN 88, 124–125, 130–136, 138–139, 145, 151, 154–155, 166, 219–220; see also Fort Donelson (Cumberland River)
Dry Run Creek 192; see also Morgan's Indiana-Ohio Raid (1863)
Duble, Master Jonathan A. 67; see also *Mound City* (U.S. ironclad)
Duck River 86, 106, 108, 136, 148, 151, 160, 296, 332–333
Duck River Sucks (Tennessee River) 87, 108, 164
Dudley, Acting Volunteer Ensign D. B. 336; see also *Moose* (U.S. tinclad)
Duke, Col. Basil W. 168, 175, 179, 181–184, 197, 200–201, 204; see also Morgan's Indiana-Ohio Raid (1863)
Duke (steamer) 231–232, 258, 287
Duke of Argyle (steamer) 258
Dunbar (steamer) 142, 246
Dunn, Acting Volunteer Lieutenant Martin 149–150
Dunningham, Lt. John W. 65; see also St. Charles, AK; White River expediton (June-July 1862)
Dupont, IN 188, 190; see also Morgan's Indiana-Ohio Raid (1863)
Dycusburg, TN 220

Eads, James B. (contractor) 35, 37–38, 45, 47, 294; see also *Carondolet* (U.S. ironclad gunboat); *Neosho* (U.S. monitor)
Eagle Nest Island (Tennessee River) 141
Eaglesville, TN 130
East Liverpool, OH 204; see also Morgan's Indiana-Ohio Raid (1863)
East Perryville, TN 87
Easton, Lt. Col. Langdon C. 244, 246; see also Edwards, Capt. Arthur; Tennessee River gunboat constuction (1863–1864)
Eastport, MS 87, 138, 157, 159–161, 164, 212, 215, 230, 268–269, 297, 336; see also Hodge, Col. George B.
Eastport (U.S. ironclad gunboat) 41, 94, 128
Ebenezer (steamer) see *Tawah* (U.S. tinclad)
Echo No. 2 (steamer) 258, 320, 322; see also Gracey's Battery
Eckert, Thomas 287, 318–319, 324, 329; see also Johnsonville, TN, Battle of (1864); Nashville, Battle of (1864); Van Duzer, Capt. John C.
Eclipse (racehorse) 352
Eclipse (steamer) 152
Ector, Brig. Gen. Matthew D. 312; see also Nashville, Battle of (1864)
Edgefield, TN 104
Eddyville, KY 88, 171, 250, 342
Edwards, Capt. Arthur 242–244, 246, 249, 257–259; see also Bridgeport, AL; Chattanooga (steamer); Tennessee River gunboat construction (1863–1864)
Eel River 13, 16
Eight Mile Island (Ohio River) 196, 204; see also Morgan's Indiana-Ohio Raid (1863)
Eleventh of April (Costa Rican brig) 27; see also Nicaraguan National War (1856–1857)
Elfin (U.S. tinclad) 252, 271, 277, 281–283, 286–287; see also Johnsonville, TN, Battle of (1864)
Elizabethtown, IL 86, 109
Elk (steamer) 183–184
Elk River 86
Ella Faber (steamer) 131
Ellet, Brig. Gen. Alfred W. 158–162; see also Mississippi Marine Brigade
Ellet, Col. Charles, Jr. 52–56, 59–60, 64; see also Memphis, TN, Battle of (1862); Mississippi Marine Brigade
Ellet, Charles River 55; see also Memphis, TN, Battle of (1862); Mississippi Marine Brigade
Ellsworth, George A. "Lightning" 178, 180, 191, 202; see also Morgan's Indiana-Ohio Raid (178)
Emma (steamer) 51, 258
Emma Duncan (steamer) see *Hastings* (U.S. tinclad)
Empire City (steamer) 131
Engle, Capt. Frederick K. 25
Enterprise, IN 86
Erben, Lt. Henry 59
Essex (U.S. ironclad gunboat) 36, 40, 72
Eugene (steamer) 99
Eureka, KY 88
Evansville, IN 80, 86, 91, 97–100,

103, 106–107, 109, 113–114, 117, 121, 184, 186, 211, 215–216, 241–242, 260–266, 342
Ewing, Col. G. W. 15; *see also* Patawatomi Indian Uprising
Excelsior (ersatz U.S. military gunboat) 157–158

Fairplay (U.S. tinclad) 95–**96**, 97, 99–100, 106–106, 108, 113–114, 122, 125–126, 128, 132–134, 136, 138, 140–143, 146–148, 152, 155, 165–166, 168, 171–172, 174–175, 178, 184, 186–187, 207, 210–211, 215–216, 222, 224, 226–228, 232, 240, 247, 251–252, 254, 260–261, 265–266, 289, 299, 306–309, 311–312, 326, 330–332, 336; *see also* Fitch, Cmdr. Le Roy; Groves, Acting Volunteer Lieutenant George J.
Fairy (U.S. tinclad) 253, 278, 280–284; *see also* Johnsonville, TN, Battle of (1864)
Falls of the Ohio 40, 74, 86, 181, 185–186, 189, 215 *see* Louisville, KY; Louisville and Portland Canal; Navigation seasons and conditions on Western rivers
Farmer, Acting Volunteer Ensign J. M. 340; see also *New National* (steamer)
Farragut, Adm. David G. 28, 264, 345, 349
Ferguson, Champ 237; *see also* Big South Fork reconnaissance (Donn/Glassford, 1863)
Ferrell, Pilot John H. 308, 312, 314; *see also* Congressional Medal of Honor; *Moose* (U.S. tinclad); *Neosho* (U.S. monitor)
Ferris woodyard (Cumberland River) 237; *see also* Big South Fork reconnaissance (Donn/Glassford, 1863)
Filibusterers *see* Nicaraguan National War (1856–1857); Walker, William
Financier (steamer) 300, 312, 332
Fitch, Egbert Bensen (half brother-uncle) 12, 15, 30
Fitch, Emma (half sister) 15, 24, 30
Fitch, Dr. Frederick (father) 11–13, 15, 17–19
Fitch, Frederick (half brother-nephew) 15, 30, 43
Fitch, Dr. Graham Newell (half brother): birth of 11; as colonel, 46th Indiana 43–71 *see also* White River expedition (June-July 1862); death 71, 355; as delegate 1868 Democratic National Convention 71; as Episcopalian 17, 353; marriage 12; medical education of 12; medical practice, Chicago, IL 17–18; medical practice, Indianapolis, IN 71; medical practice, Le Roy, NY 12; medical practice, Logansport, IN 13–14, 42, 71; militia captain 15; possible last wartime meeting with Le Roy 71; relocation to Logansport, IN 13, 42; state legislator 15–16; as U.S. Congressman 18–23; as U.S. Senator 23–31, 42; as ward of Le Roy and Henry Alvord Fitch 18
Fitch, Harriet V. (stepmother) 12–13, 16–17, 30–31, 352–354
Fitch, Henrietta Bradley (half sister) 12
Fitch, Henry Alvord (brother) 17–18, 24, 30, 352
Fitch, Henry Satterlee (half brother) 12, 24, 30, 51, 61, 72, 351–353
Fitch, Leander (brother) 17
Fitch, Le Roy: birth 13; relocation to Logansport, IN 15; Logansport boyhood 16–17; and Logansport Weeping Willow legend 16–17 *see also* Fitch, Harriet V. (stepmother); as Episcopalian 17; as ward of Graham Newell Fitch 18; as student, U.S. Naval Academy 18–**20**, 21–22; Howitzer proficiency 20, 33, **46**, 52; as Midshipman 24–29; aboard frigate *Wasbash* 25; aboard sloop of war *St. Mary's* 25–29; as Passed Midshipman 29; aboard frigate *Savannah* 29–30; as Master 29–31; marriage to Mary "Mollie" Smith 30; as Lieutenant 31–89; aboard gunboat *Water Witch* 31–32; aboard screw steamer *Wyandotte* 32–33; aboard ship-of-the-line *North Carolina* 33–**34**; posted to Western Flotilla 34, 42; birth of daughter, Marie L. 42; command of ordnance boat *Judge Torrence* 45–62; command of prize gunboat *General Sterling Price* 61–71; possible last wartime meeting with Graham Newell 71; as Lt. Cmdr. 90–351; as executive officer, Upper Mississippi Flotilla 95–169; in defense of Fort Donelson (1863) 130–135; as commander, 6th District, Mississippi Squadron 169–210; orders destruction of Palymyra, TN (1863) 152–156; orchestrates naval defense against Morgan's Indiana-Ohio Raid (1863) 167–204; commendation from Navy Secretary Welles (1863) 205–206; as commander, 8th District, Mississippi Squadron 210–258; hunting incident (1863) 221–226; as U.S.N. advisor/superintendent, Tennessee River gunboat construction (1863–1864) 246–249, 257–260, 262–263; investigates Fort Pillow massacre (1864) 253–255; as commander, 10th District, Mississippi Squadron 258–344; attempt to rescue Johnsonville, TN (1864) 278–290; Naval defender of Nashville, TN (1864) 291–334; detached from Mississippi Squadron (1865) 344; instructor, U.S. Naval Academy (1865–1866) 346–347; command of steam gunboat *Marblehead* (1866–1868) **346**, 347–348; as vice-president, Northern Indiana Shooting Association 349; as executive officer, Pensacola Navy Yard (1870–1873) 349–353; promoted to the rank of Commander (1870) **351**; retired to Logansport (1873–1875) 352–353; as member, Cass County, IN, Agricultural, Horticultural & Mechanical Association 352; displays art at 1874 Cass County Fair 352; conversion to Catholicism 353; mysterious terminal illness, including 1875 diagnosis by Dr. Asa Coleman and 2007 diagnosis by Dr. Thomas F. Beckner 352–354; death 353; funeral 353–354; tombstone, Mount Hope Cemetery (Logansport, IN) **354**
Fitch, Marie L. (daughter) 42, 344, 349, 355
Fitch, Martha (half sister) 13, 24, 30
Fitch, Mary Ann (half sister) 11, 15
Fitch, Mary Ann (sister) 13, 15
Fitch, Mary "Mollie" Smith (wife) 25, 30, 98, 344, 349, 354–355
Fitch, Mary "Polly" (mother) 11
Fitch, Rachel Thomas (mother) 13, 17
Fitch (U.S. destroyer, DD-426/DMS-25) 355, **356**–357
"Fitch Doctrine" *see* Irregular warfare, causes, principles, and counterinsurgency
Fitch expedition to White River *see* White River Expedition (June-July 1862)
Fitch home (Logansport, IN) **14**–15, 352–353; *see also* Kroeger Funeral Home (Logansport, IN)
Fitch-Lowe Tennessee River expedition (December 1862) 108
Fitch medical practice building (Logansport, IN) 16
Fitch's Glen (Cass County, IN) 16, 355; *see also* Casparis Stone Company
Fitzpatrick, Acting Volunteer Master James 155
Flint River 86
Florence, AL 87, 138–140, 142, 150–151, 161–162, 164, 212, 291, 332–333
Flynn's Lick (Cumberland River) 237; *see also* Big South Fork reconnaissance (Donn/Glassford, 1863)
Foote, Adm. Andrew Hull 33–34, 36, 39–41, **44**, 48, 50–51, 77, 97, 120
Ford's Ferry (Ohio River) 103

Forest Rose (U.S. tinclad) 165
Forrest, Lt. Moreau 263, 344; see also *General Burnside* (U.S. tinclad)
Forrest, Maj. Gen. Nathan Bedford 62, 88, 90–91, 104, 107–109, 111–112, 117, 126, 130, 134, 136, 140, 156–157, 160, 162, 248–251, **252**, 267–273, 276–282, 286–289, 291, 296, 298, 303, 310–311, 320, 333, 342; see also Brice's Cross Roads, MS, Battle of (1864); Fort Pillow (Mississippi River); Johnsonville, TN, Battle of (1864); Kelley, Lt. Col. David C.; Okolona, MS, Battle of (1864); Paducah, KY, Battles of
Forrest's Kentucky Raid (1862) 91
Forrest's Middle Tennessee Raid (1864) 268–269
Forrest's Tennessee Raids (1862–1863) 108
Fort Anderson (Ohio River) 250; see also Paducah, KY, Battles of (1864)
Fort Donelson (Cumberland River) 38, 40–41, 88, 123–124, 129–139, 143–144, 146, 152–155, 157, 168, 218, 220–221, 226, 228, 230, 232–234, 250, 261, 277, 301, 320, 322, 338
Fort Heiman (Tennessee River) 108, 146–151, 270, 273–276, 280, 289–290, 292, 294, 320
Fort Henry (Tennessee River) 38, 40, 108, 113, 115, 122, 128, 131, 140, 142, 146, 148, 158–161, 163, 165, 273, 280
Fort Johnson *see* Johnsonville, TN, Battle of (1864)
Fort Pillow (Mississippi River) 50–53, 251–255, **256** ,
Fort Randolph (Mississippi River) 53
Fort Sumter (SC), Bombardment (1861) 31–32, 35
Fortress Rosecrans (Murfreesboro, TN) 311; see also Nashville, Battle of (1864)
Foster, Maj. Gen. John 235–236; see also Knoxville, TN
Foster, Col. John W. 96, 103
Fouty, Acting Volunteer Master George W. 152–153, 155
Fowler's Landing (Tennessee River) 87
Fox, Gustavus V. (Navy assistant secretary) 40, 107–108, 120, 123, 244
Frake's Mill, IN 185
Frankfort, KY 179
Franklin, TN, Battle of (1864) 296, 300
Fredonia, IN 86, 186
Freeman, Dr. Asa 12; see also Fitch, Dr. Graham Newell
Freestone (steamer) 131
Frémont, Maj. Gen. John C. 36
French, Acting Volunteer Lt. James S. 321; see also *St. Clair* (U.S. tinclad)

French Broad River 86
"Freshes" *see* Navigation seasons and conditions on Western rivers
Fry, Capt. Joseph 65; see also St. Charles, AK; White River expedition (June-July 1862)
Fyffe, Col. James P. 193; see also Morgan's Indiana-Ohio Raid (1863)

Gaddis, Chaplain Maxwell P. 118–119; see also *Hastings* (steamer)
Gadsden, AL 272–273
Gainsboro, TN 237–238; see also Big South Fork reconnaissance (Donn/Glassford, 1863)
Gallatin, TN 88, 109, 116, 132, 305; see also Cumberland River
Gallipolis, OH 86, 193–194, 196; see also Morgan's Indiana-Ohio Raid (1863)
Garfield, Brig. Gen. James A. 151, 157–158, 206
Garrard, Col. Israel 306, 320, 327; see also Nashville, Battle of (1864)
Garretsville, KY 179
General Beauregard (Confederate gunboat) 52, 54–55, 59; see also Memphis, TN, Battle of (1862)
General Bragg (Confederate/U.S. gunboat) 52, 54, 59, 79; see also Memphis, TN, Battle of (1862)
General Burnside (U.S. tinclad) 258, 262–263, 344; see also Tennessee River gunboat construction (1863–1864)
General Earl Van Dorn (Confederate gunboat) 52, 54, 59; see also Memphis, TN, Battle of (1862)
General Grant (U.S. tinclad) 258–**259,** 262, 344; **see also** Tennessee River gunboat construction (1863–1864)
General Lovell (Confederate gunboat) 52, 54, 59; see also Memphis, TN, Battle of (1862)
General M. Jeff Thompson (Confederate gunboat) 52, 54, 59; see also Memphis, TN, Battle of (1862)
General Order No. 2 (Porter) 101–102
General Order No. 4 (Porter) 101–102
General Order No. 5 (Lee) 292
General Order No. 10 (Fitch) 219
General Order No. 12 (Fitch) 219
General Order No. 13 (Fitch) 222
General Order No. 16 (Lee) 297
General Order No. 17 "Bands of Ten" (Hindman) 63, 68–69; see also White River expediton (June-July 1862)
General Order No. 20 (Porter) 169
General Order No. 48 (Lee) 338
General Order No. 57 (Lee) 340
General Order No. 59 (Welles) 314; see also Congressional Medal of Honor
General Order No. 60 (Grant) 60; see also Irregular warfare

General Order No. 60 (Lee) 340
General Order No. 65 (Porter) 175
General Order No. 80 (Porter) 210
General Order No. 84 (Porter) 169
General Order No. 184 (Porter) 319
General Pillow (U.S. tinclad) 95–97, 106, 108, 115, 122, 128, 269
General Sherman (U.S. tinclad) 258, 262, 344; see also Tennessee River gunboat construction (1863–1864)
General Siegel (steamer) 236
General Sterling Price (Confederate/U.S. gunboat) 52, 54, **58**–61, 63, 70, 79, 88, 94; see also Memphis, TN, Battle of (1862)
General Sumter (Confederate gunboat) 52, 54, 59; see also Memphis, TN, Battle of (1862)
General Thomas (U.S. tinclad) 258, 262, 344; see also Tennessee River gunboat construction (1863–1864)
Genesee County, NY 11
Geneva College (NY) 12
Gennie Hopkins (steamer) 258
Georgetown, OH 194; see also Morgan's Indiana-Ohio Raid (1863)
Georgia, Economic importance of 37
Glasgow, KY 177
Glasgow, KY, Confederate capture (1862) 109
Glassford, Acting Volunteer Lt. Henry A. 70, 123, 140, 166, 170, 173, 210, 223, 226, 235–239, 241, 247–248, 253, 256, 260–262, 271, 289, 294, 307–308, 312–314, 317–318, 331–333, 337–340, 344; see also Big South Fork reconnaissance (Donn/Glassford, 1863); Carthage, TN; *General Burnside* (U.S. tinclad); *Reindeer* (U.S. tinclad); Tennessee River gunboat construction (1863–1864)
Glide II (U.S. tinclad) 74
Goddard, Brig. Gen. Calvin 119–120, 137
Golconda, IL 86
Golden Era (steamer) 131, 203
Goldsborough, Cmdr. Louis M. (U.S. Naval Academy superintendent) 20, 22; see also U.S. Naval Academy
Goose Island (Ohio River) 196
Goudy, Acting Volunteer Lt. Jason 77–78, 115, 122, 127–129, 150, 154, 166, 275, 278, 280; see also *Alfred Robb* (U.S. tinclad); *Tawah* (U.S. tinclad)
Gower's Island (Cumberland River) 152, 168
Gracey, Capt. Frank P *see* Gracey's Battery
Gracey's Battery 276, 280, 283–284, 286, 320; see also Johnsonville, TN, Battle of (1864); *Undine* (U.S. tinclad)

Grafton, Capt. John J. 199; *see also* Morgan's Indiana-Ohio Raid (1863)
Graham (steamer) 51
Granada (Nicraguan rebel schooner) 27–28; *see also* Nicaraguan National War (1856–1857)
Grandview, IN 86
Granger, Maj. Gen. Gordon 122, 129, 131–133, 136, 151
Grant, Lt. Gen. Ulysses S. 36, 38, 40, 50, 57–58, 68–70, 72, 102, 107–108, 113–115, 143, 158–159, 170, **213**–218, 220–226, 228, 232–233, 235–236, 238–242, 244, 249, 257, 267–268, 272–273, 278, 280, 289, 291, 298, 320, 335, 337, 340–341
Gratton, TN 88
Gray, Lt. George 65; *see also* St. Charles, AK; White River expedition (June-July 1862)
Great Bear Creek 160–161
Great Western (U.S. ordnance boat) 45, 47, 49, 51, 53
Green, Cmdr. Joseph F. 22; *see also* U. S. Naval Academy
Green Bottom Bar (Tennessee River) 163–164, 279, 281; *see also* Johnsonville, TN
Green River 103, 106–107, 109, 117, 180, 191, 260
Greeneville, TN 104, 213; *see also* Johnson, Andrew (Tennessee military governor); Morgan, Maj. Gen. John Hunt
Greer, Lt. Cmdr. James A. 347; *see also Benton* (U.S. ironclad gunboat); U.S. Naval Academy
Gregory, Acting Volunteeer Lieutenant Thomas B. 210
Grey Eagle (steamer) 183–184
Grierson, Col. Benjamin H. 168
Griggs, Lt. Col. Chauncey 149–151
Griswold, Acting Volunteer Master William N. 154, 162–163
Groves, Acting Volunteer Lieutenant George J. 97, 100, 103, 114, 210, 216, 261, 265, 307–308; *see also Fairplay* (U.S. tinclad)
Guano Act (1856) 28
Guano expeditions (1850s) 25, 28
Guerrilla Parties Considered with Reference to the Laws and Usages of War 62
Guerrilla warfare *see* Irregular warfare
"Gunboat," pseudo. *see* Morse, Acting Master's Mate DeWitt C.
Guthrie Grays 194, 203; *see also* Morgan's Indiana-Ohio Raid (1863)
Gwin, Lt. William 76

H. R. W. Hill (steamer) 61
Hagan (ersatz U.S. military gunboat) 223, 231
Hagerty, Fireman John 322–323; *see also Carondolet* (U.S. ironclad gunboat); Nashville, Battle of (1864)
Haines, Col. Thomas J. 215, 217–218; *see also* Logistics, river
Hall, Acting Volunteer Master Samuel 340, 342; *see also Abeona* (U.S. tinclad)
Hall, Acting Assistant First Engineer Thomas N. 336; *see also Moose* (U.S. tinclad)
Halleck, Maj. Gen. Henry "Old Brains" 38–40, 50, 57–58, 62–64, 68, **76,** 78, 105, 107–108, 119–120, 122–123, 138, 143, 145, 159, 170, 172, 178, 210, 216, 218, 240, 278, 302, 305, 310, 316, 323, 329; *see also* Tinclads," description and evolution
Hamburg Landing (Tennessee River) 127, 140, 165
Hamilton, Maj. Oliver P. 173, 237; *see also* Big South Fork reconnaissance (Donn/Glassford, 1863); Kettle Creek, KY, Battle of (1863)
Hamilton County, OH *see* Cincinnati, OH; Morgan's Indiana-Ohio Raid (1863)
Hammond, Brig. Gen. J. H. 312, 315; *see also* Louisville and Nashville Railroad (L&N)
Hanson, Lt. Col. Charles S. 178; *see also* Morgan's Indiana-Ohio Raid (1863)
Harding, Col. Albert C. 130–136, 138; *see also* Fort Donelson
Harpeth Shoals (Cumberland River) 40, 88, 98, 105, 109, 114–115, 117–119, 121, 125–126, 128, 132, 136–137, 156–157, 168, 170, 211, 214, 221, 228, 230, 232, 242, 251, 258, 266, 310–311, 316–317, 337; *see also* Cumberland River; Navigation seasons and conditions on Western rivers
Harris, Isham G. (Tennessee governor) 38
Harrison, IN 190; *see also* Morgan's Indiana-Ohio Raid (1863)
Harrison, Col. Thomas J. 326–327; *see also* Nashville, Battle of (1864)
Harroldsburg, KY 179
Hartsville, TN 106, 306, 310
Hartt, Naval Constructor Edward 81; *see also* "Tinclads," general description and evolution
Hartupee (steamer) 236
Hastings, Acting Masters Mate L. W. 306; *see also Carondolet* (U.S. ironclad)
Hastings (steamer) 117–119, 125
Hastings (U.S. tinclad) 82, 162–165, 253–255, 321, 331
Hatchee River 254; *see also* Fort Pillow (Mississippi River)
Havana (steamer) 300
Hayes, Col. Rutherford B. 193, 196, 201; *see also* Morgan's Indiana-Ohio Raid (1863)
Hays farm, TN 150

Hazel Dell (steamer) 99, 131, 236
Head of Chain (Ohio River) 252
Hedges, Acting Third Engineer J. D. 336; *see also Moose* (U.S. tinclad)
Heintzelman, Maj. Gen. Samuel P. 265
Helena, AK 69
Helena, AK, Battle of (1863) 178
Henderson, KY 86, 100, 103, 211, 260–261
Henderson, KY, Confederate occupation (1862) 92
Henderson, Robert, "Bob" 303–304, 312, 329; *see also* Battle of Nashville Preservation Society
Henderson Island (Ohio River) 103
Henry, Gustavus A. (Confederate senator) 38; *see also* Fort Henry
Henry Logan (steamer) 203
Henry Von Puhl (steamer) 55
Hettie Gilmore (steamer) 117
Hickman, KY 250, 253, 255–257
Hicks, Col. Stephen D. 250–251; *see also* Paducah, KY, Battles of (1864)
Hillsboro Landing (Cumberland River) 307; *see also* Bell's Mills, TN, Battle of (1864)
Hindman, Maj. Gen. Thomas C. 63, 68–69; *see also* White River expedition (June-July 1862)
Hines, Capt. Thomas Henry 172, 176, 179, 181; *see also* Morgan's Indiana-Ohio Raid (1863)
Hinton, TN 156
Hobson, Brig. Gen. Edward 176–178, 183–187, 191, 193–198, 200; *see also* Morgan's Indiana-Ohio Raid (1863)
Hockinsport, OH 201–202; *see also* Morgan's Indiana-Ohio Raid (1863)
Hodge, Col. George B. 268–269
Holden, Acting Master's Mate W. S. 336; *see also Moose* (U.S. tinclad)
Holly Springs, MS 114
Holman, Capt. D. W. 121
Holston River 86, 338; *see also* Tennessee River Confederate raid (Wharton, 1865)
Honduras filibuster plot (1860) 29; *see also* Walker, William (filibusterer)
Hood, Maj. Gen. John Bell 264, 266–266, 272–273, 278, 282, 289–291, 296–302, 305, 311, 318, 320–321, 325–327, 330–336; *see also* Atlanta, Battle of (1864); Columbia, TN; Franklin, TN, Battle of (1864); Nashville, Battle of (1864)
Hopkinsville, KY 231, 233, 251, 322
Horizon (steamer) 131
Hough, Maj. John 318; *see also Moose* (U.S. tinclad)
Houston, Lt. Thomas T. 28; *see*

also Nicaraguan National War (1856–1857)
Hovey, Brig. Gen. Alvin P. 71, 265
Howard, Acting Volunteer Lieutenant Samuel 292, 312–315, 322, 326; *see also* Bell's Mills, Battle of (1864); Nashville, Battle of (1864); *Neosho* (U.S. monitor)
Howard, Acting Assistant Surgeon William 83, 114, 121, 125, 135, 138, 140–141, 143, 148, 155–156, 168, 173, 175; *see also Brilliant* (U.S. tinclad)
Howland, Capt. Henry 274, 276–278, 281, 283, 286; *see also* Johnsonville, TN, Battle of (1864)
Huber, Chief Engineer Joseph 69; *see also* White River expedition (June-July 1862)
Hudson's Battery 282–283, 285, 287; *see also* Johnsonville, TN, Battle of (1864); Mississippi regiments, Hudson's Light Artillery (Hudson's Battery)
Hughes, John M. 237; *see also* Big South Fork reconnaissance (Donn/Glassford, 1863)
Huling, Acting Assistant Paymaster Edmund J. 257; *see also Huntress* (U.S. tinclad)
Hull, Cdr. Joseph B. 81–82, 145; *see also* "Tinclads," general description and evolution
Humbolt, TN 108
Hunter, Lt. W. O. *see* Walton's Battery
Huntington, TN 108
Huntington, WV 86
Huntress (steamer) 131
Huntress (U.S. tinclad) 257
Hurd, Acting Volunteer Lt. Jacob S. 98, 102, 121–122, 125–126, 137, 147, 149, 151–155, 166
Hurlbut, Brig. Gen. Stephen A. 57, 139, 146–147, 159, 232, 249
Hyde's Ferry (Cumberland River) 305–306, 309, 312, 318; *see also* Bell's Mills, TN, Battle of (1864); Nashville, Battle of (1864)

Ibex (U.S. tinclad) 342
Icarus (British steam sloop) 29; *see also* Walker, William (filibusterer)
Ida May (steamer) 203
Illinois regiments: 2nd Artillery 131; 14th Cavalry 199; 17th Mounted 199; 18th 158; 63rd 93; 83rd 130–136, 297; 92nd 129, 131–132, 135–136; 103rd 221; 113th 268–269; 120th 268–269; 129th 236–238; Chicago Board of Trade Battery 310; Henshaw's Independent Light Artillery 199
Illinois River 13
Imperial (steamer) 195–196, 198–199, 201–203, 205; *see also* Morgan's Indiana-Ohio Raid (1863)
In Harm's Way (motion picture) 307

Independent Provisional Brigade (U.S.) *see* Streight Raid (1863)
Indian Bay, AK 67; *see also* White River expedition (June-July 1862)
Indiana Brigade *see* Indiana regiments
Indiana Home Guard *see* Indiana-Ohio Raid (1863)
Indiana Militia 15; *see also* Patawatomi Indian Uprising
Indiana-Ohio Raid (1863) 167–207
Indiana regiments: 5th Cavalry 199; 23rd Battery 183; 24th 69; 34th 68–69; 43rd 43, 57, 68, 265; 46th (Col. Fitch) 43, 49–53, 55–58, 61, 64–71, 264–266; 51st 157; 71st 183; 73rd 158
Indianaola (U.S. ironclad) 190
Indianapolis, IN 186–188, 264
Ingram's Shoals (Cumberland River) 170, 228–230, 232, 261, 263; *see also* Cumberland River
Iowa regiments: 5th Cavalry 131, 133–134
Irene (steamer) 109, 297
Iron ore recovery dispute, Cumberland River (1863–1864) 234, 247
Ironton, OH 86
Irregular warfare, causes, principles, and counterinsurgency 61–63, 65–72, 88, 90–91, 93–95, 97, 99–102, 105–106, 108–109, 113, 115–**118**, 124–131, 140–142, 146–156, 165, 212, 217, 219–220, 229, 231–232, 234, 235–238, 248, 256–257, 260–266, 277, 336–339, 342–343; *see also* Big South Fork reconnaissance (Donn/ Glasford, 1863); Johnsonville, TN, Battle of (1864); Morgan's Indiana-Ohio Raid (1863)
Irvin, Lt. Col. William J. 181–184; *see also* Morgan's Indiana-Ohio Raid (1863)
Island No. 8 (Mississippi River) 256
Island No. 10 (Mississippi River) 41, 43–44, 253, 284, 293, 307; *see also Carondolet* (U.S. ironclad gunboat); Walke, Adm. Henry
Island No. 26 (Mississippi River) 253
Island No. 30 (Mississippi River) 254
Island No. 44 (Mississippi River) 53
Islands, river *see* Navigation seasons and conditions on Western rivers; names of specific islands
Iuka, KY 88
Iuka, MS 215

J. F. McComb (steamer) 300, 312
J. H. Done (steamer) 203
J. K. Baldwin (steamer) 297
J. W. Cheeseman (steamer) 258, 274–276, 278
J. W. Kellogg (steamer) 152–153, 155
Jackman, G. W., Jr. (shipbuilder) 347; *see also Marblehead* (U.S. steam gunboat)

Jackson, OH 196; *see also* Morgan's Indiana-Ohio Raid (1863)
Jackson, TN 107
Jackson County, TN 237–238, 240; *see also* Big South Fork reconnaissance (Donn/Glassford, 1863)
Jackson County, WV *see* Buffington Island (Ohio River)
Jackson Light Artillery *see* Arkansas regiments, Jackson Light Artillery (Thrall's Battery)
Jacksonport, AK 64
Jackson's Woodyard (Cumberland River) 230
Jacob Musselman (steamer) 64
James Raymond (steamer) 300
James Thompson (steamer) 131
Jarvis Island (Pacific Ocean) 25, 28
Jasper, OH 191, 196; *see also* Morgan's Indiana-Ohio Raid (1863)
Jeffersonville, IN 86, 188
Jeffersonville and Indianapolis Railroad 86
Jell-O, invention of 11
Jenkins, Capt. W. 120, 123–124
Jennie Hopkins (steamer) 264
Jersey, KY 254; *see also* Paducah, KY, Battles of (1864)
John A. Fisher (steamer) 131, 220
John Adams (U.S. sloop of war) 345; *see also* U.S. Naval Academy
John T. McCombs (steamer) 181–185; *see also* Morgan's Indiana-Ohio Raid (1863)
John's Island, SC, Battle of (1863) 348; *see also Marblehead* (U.S. steam gunboat); Meade, Lt. Cmdr. Richard W.
Johnson, Brig. Gen. Adam Rankin "Stovepipe" 62, 92, 95, 99–101, 107, 112, 175, 197, 201–202, 264–265
Johnson, Andrew (Tennessee military governor/U.S. president) 90, 104, 206, 238, 271, 341, 351; *see also* Gainesboro, TN; Johnsonville, TN; Nashville, TN
Johnson, Pfc. John 327–328; *see also* Nashville, Battle of (1864)
Johnson, Brig. Gen. Richard W. 65, 309, 325–328, 330–331 ; *see also* Nashville, Battle of (1864)
Johnson, "Stovepipe" *see* Johnson, Brig. Gen. Adam Rankin "Stovepipe"
Johnson Island (Union POW camp) 204
Johnsonville, TN 82, 84, 266, 268, 270–271, 273–**274**, 277, 279–280, 282, 289, 292, 295, 298–299, 333
Johnsonville, TN, Battle of (1864) 154, 270–291
Johnston, Gen. Albert Sidney 37–39, 41, 50
Johnston, Lt. John V. 65; *see also* Fry, Capt. Joseph; St. Charles, AK; *St. Louis* (U.S. ironclad gunboat)

Index

Johnston, Gen. Joseph E. 116
Jones, Capt. George 21; *see also* U.S. Naval Academy
Jonesboro, TN 213
Judah, Brig. Gen. Henry M. 176, 191–**192**, 193–199, 201; *see also* Morgan's Indiana-Ohio Raid (1863)
Judge Torrence (U.S. ordnance boat) 45, 47, 49, 51–53, 60
Julia (steamer) 300
Juliet (U.S. tinclad) 165, 342

Kanawha River 30, 171, 193, 248
Kansas regiments: 1st Battery 271; *see also* Johnsonville, TN, Battle of (1864)
Kate (U.S. tinclad) 342
Kate Kearney (steamer) 300
Kautz, Col. August V. 196; *see also* Morgan's Indiana-Ohio Raid (1863)
Kelley, Lt. Col. David C. **269**–270, 275–276, 281, 304–319, 323, 325–330; *see also* Bell's Mills, TN, Battle of (1864); Eastport, MS; Johnsonville, TN, Battle of (1864); Nashville, Battle of (1864)
Kenapakomoko (Native American village) *see* Logansport, IN
Kendall, Acting Naval Constructor Charles F. 249; *see also* Tennessee River gunboat construction (1863–1864)
Kenesaw, GA 268
Kenton (steamer) 258, 269
Kentucky Artillery Brigade 175
Kentucky Raids (1862) *see* Forrest's Kentucky Raid (1862); Morgan's Kentucky Raid (1862)
Kentucky regiments: 1st Cavalry (USA) 199; 2nd Cavalry (CSA) 95, 136, 151, 157, 175, 182; 3rd Cavalry (CSA) 276; 3rd Cavalry (USA) 177, 199; 5th Cavalry (CSA) 175, 198–199; 5th Cavalry (USA) 250; 6th Cavalry (CSA) 175, 177; 8th Cavalry (CSA) 175; 8th Cavalry (USA) 177; 9th Cavalry (CSA) 172, 175; 9th Cavalry (USA) 177; 10th Cavalry (CSA) 92, 95, 175, 179–180, 182; 11th Cavalry (CSA) 173, 175; 11th Cavalry (USA) 199; 12th Cavalry (USA) 199; 14th Cavalry (CSA) 175; 16th (USA) 200; 20th (USA) 178
Kenwood (U.S. tinclad) 74
Kettle Creek, KY, Battle of (1863) 173
Key West (U.S. tinclad) 82, 212, 251, 254, 269–271, 277, 279–280, 282–283, 286–287, 340; *see also* Johnsonville, TN, Battle of (1864)
Key West No. 3 (steamer) *see Key West* (U.S. tinclad)
Kilburn, Lt. Col. Charles L. 215, 217–218; *see also* Logistics, river

Kilty, Cmdr. Augustus H. 64–66, 323; *see also Mound City* (U.S. ironclad gunboat); White River expedition (June-July 1862)
King, Acting Volunteer Lieutenant Edward M. 163, 212, 269, 271, 276–277, 279–281, 283–289, 294; *see also* Johnsonville, TN, Battle of (1864); *Key West* (U.S. tinclad)
King, John M. 129, 131–132, 135–136
Kingsport, TN 338; *see also* Tennessee River Confederate raid (Wharton, 1865)
Kingston, TN 216–217, 338; *see also* Tennessee River Confederate raid (Wharton, 1865)
Klinck, Master Leonard G. 95; *see also W. B. Terry* (steamer)
Knox, Frank (U.S. Navy secretary) 356; *see also Fitch* (U.S. destroyer, DD-426/DMS-25),
Knoxville, TN 86, 93, 109, 168, 173, 210, 212–218, 227–228, 233, 235–236, 239–240, 242, 248; *see also* Big South Fork (Cumberland River); Burnside, Maj. Gen. Ambrose; Foster, Maj. Gen. John; Longstreet, Lt. Gen. James; Tennessee River Confederate raid (Wharton, 1865)
Koenig, Rev. Henry (pastor, St. Joseph's Catholic Church, Logansport, IN) 352–353
Kossuth, Louis (Hungarian revolutionary) 22
Kroeger, Paul 352–353, 355; *see also* Kroeger Funeral Home (Logansport, IN)
Kroeger Funeral Home (Logansport, IN) 352–353, 355; *see also* Fitch home (Logansport, IN)
Kuttawa, KY 88

La Belle-Poule (French frigate) 17
Lady Foote see Alfred Robb (steamer/1st U.S. tinclad)
Lady Franklin (steamer) 131, 300, 312, 332
Lady Pike (steamer) 182
Lamb's Landing (Tennessee River) 139
Landing parties, Fitch proposals for gunboat 229, 236
Laurent Millaudon (steamer) *see General Sterling Price* (Confederate/U.S. gunboat)
La Vergne, TN *see* Blockhouse No. 4 (Nashville)
Lawrence, Col. William H. 252–253; *see also* Columbus, KY; Fort Pillow (Mississippi River)
Lawrence (steamer) 258
Lawrenceburg, IN 189–190; *see also* Morgan's Indiana-Ohio Raid (1863)
Leavenworth, IN 86, 182, 187
Lebanon, KY 178
Lebanon, TN 88, 310–311, 315

Lee, Adm. Samuel Phillips **272**, 277, 279, 284, 286–287, 289–290, 292, 294–303, 305, 309–312, 314, 316–321, 323–324, 329, 331–333, 335–344, 347; *see also* Mississippi Squadron; Nashville, Battle of (1864); Thomas, Maj. Gen. George "Old Pap."
Lee, Maj. Gen. Stephen D. 296, 303; *see also* Nashville, Battle of (1864)
Lee Creek, WV 202; *see also* Morgan's Indiana-Ohio Raid (1863)
Lenthall, John (warship designer) 25
Le Roy, NY 11
Letcher County, KY 87
Lewisburg, WV 2003; *see also* Morgan's Indiana-Ohio Raid (1863)
Lewisport, KY 86
Lexington, IN 188; *see also* Morgan's Indiana-Ohio Raid (1863)
Lexington, KY 239
Lexington, TN 108, 320
Lexington (U.S. timberclad) 35, 40–41, 64, 67, 69, 72, 76, 124, 126–**127**, 128–130, 132, 134, 138, 140, 142–144, 146–151, 154–156, 159–166, 168, 170–171
Liberty (steamer) 258
Liberty No. 2 (steamer) 297
Lieber, Francis 62; *see also* Irregular warfare
Lieber Code 62
Light-draught gunboats *see* "Tinclads," description and evolution; Names of specific "tinclads," e.g., *Moose* (U.S. tinclad)
Liholiho (U.S. schooner) 28
Lilly (steamer) 258, 300, 312, 332
Lilly Martin (steamer) 300
Lincoln, President Abraham 30–31, 35, 42, 137–138, 331, 340
Linden (U.S. tinclad) 165
Line Island (Cumberland River) 232
Little Miami River 191; *see also* Morgan's Indiana-Ohio Raid (1863)
Little Rebel (Confederate/U.S. tinclad) 52, 54, 59, 79, 81, 122–123; *see also* Memphis, TN, Battle of (1862)
Little Sandy Creek 192, 198; *see also* Morgan's Indiana-Ohio Raid (1863)
Livingston, Cdr. John W. 312, 321, 337–338; *see also* Mound City, IL
Lizzie Martin (steamer) 109, 152
Locust Grove, OH 194; *see also* Morgan's Indiana-Ohio Raid (1863)
Logansport, IN 13–18, 23–25, 30, 344, 349; *see also* Cass County, IN
Logansport Dragoons (Indiana militia unit) 15; *see also* Patawatomi Indian Uprising
Logistics, general 84–85, 117, 212–214, 218, 239, 246, 270–271, 289

Index

Logistics, river 79–80, 85–89, 98, 104–105, **109–110**, 112–115, 117–119, 123–128, 136–140, 143–147, 149, 152, 161, 165, 168, 212–218, 220–243, 246, 248, 251, 257–259, 270–291, 299–300, 303, 309, 312, 315, 320–323, 332; see also Big South Fork (Cumberland River); Chattanooga, TN; Cumberland River; Johnsonville, TN; Knoxville, TN; Nashville, TN; Tennessee River

Logwood, Col. T. C. 275, 282; see also Johnsonville, TN, Battle of (1864)

Longstreet, Lt. Gen. James 116, 119, 210, 228, 233; see also Chattanooga, TN; Knoxville, TN

Lookout (steamer) 244–**245**; see also Bridgeport, AL; Edwards, Capt. Arthur; Tennessee River gunboat construction (1863–1864)

Lookout Mountain, Battle of (1863) 230

Loop Creek 193, 196; see also Morgan's Indiana-Ohio Raid (1863)

Lou Eaves (ersatz U.S. military gunboat) 96, 103, 241, 264–265

Loudon, KY 213

Louisville, KY 74, 86, 97, 101, 106–107, 112, 114, 119, 123, 126, 129, 131, 144–145, 152, 166, 171, 177–181, 183–185, 187, 189, 191, 206, 211–215, 217, 220, 234, 241, 249, 258–259, 261, 263–266, 270–271, 277, 295, 297, 316, 321, 338–339; see also Logistics, river; Morgan's Indiana-Ohio Raid (1863); Palmer, Maj. Gen. John M.

Louisville and Nashville Railroad (L&N) 88–89, 104–106, 109, 116, 178, 211, 270, 288, 312, 315, 321, 324

Louisville and Portland Canal 74, 86, 181, 215; see also Falls of the Ohio

Louisville (U.S. ironclad gunboat) 36–37, 41, 54, 342, 347; see also Meade, Lt. Cmdr. Richard W.

Love, Maj. Gen. John 93

Lowe, Col. William W. 108, 113, 115, 131–136, 153; see also Fitch-Lowe Tennessee River expedition (December 1862); Fort Donelson

Lucas Landing (Tennessee River) see Johnsonville, TN

Luminary (steamer) 152–153

Lyon, Brig. Gen. Tyree H. 273, 320–324, 333; see also Johnsonville, TN, Battle of (1864); Nashville, Battle of (1864)

Mabry, Col. Hinchie P. 281; see also Johnsonvile, TN, Battle of (1864)

Macedonian (U.S. sloop of war) 345; see also U.S. Naval Academy

Madison, IN 80, 86, 113–114, 117, 186–191, 265–266; see also Morgan's Indiana-Ohio Raid (1863)

Madison and Indianapolis Railroad 86

Madisonville, KY, Battle of (1862) 92

Maggie Hayes (steamer) 300

Magnet (steamer) 300, 305–306, 309, 312, 332; see also Bell's Mills, TN, Battle of (1864)

Magnolia (ersatz U.S. military gunboat) 194; see also Morgan's Indiana-Ohio Raid (1863)

Mahan, Adm. Alfred Thayer 21, 134, 288; see also U. S. Naval Academy

Mahatha, Acting Engineer Robert 114

Major, Jason (Fitch family servant) 23

Manassas, First Battle of (1861) 42

Manchester, OH 193–194, 197; see also Morgan's Indiana-Ohio Raid (1863)

Manning, Acting Carpenter Thomas 114

Marblehead (U.S. steam gunboat) 345–**346**, 347–348; see also U.S. Naval Academy

Mare Island, CA 28

Marietta, OH 86, 193, 195, 197; see also Morgan's Indiana-Ohio Raid (1863)

Mariner (steamer) 236

Marion (U.S. sloop of war) 345; see also U.S. Naval Academy

Mark R. Cheek (steamer) 61

Marmora (U.S. tinclad) 165, 342

Marmora No. 2 (steamer) 103, 203, 300

Marrowbone, KY 176

Mars (steamer) 310

Marshall, Eugene 134

Marshall, Acting Volunteer Master James 143, 250–255; see also Fort Pillow (Mississippi River)

Martin, First Class Fireman Hiram H. 162–163

Marvin's Bluffs, TN 87

Mary Crane (steamer) 121

Mary Hein (steamer) see *Silver Lake* (U.S. tinclad) **188**

Maryville, TN 213

Matthews, Lt. R. B. 320; see also Gracey's Battery

Mattie Cook (steamer) 117

Mauckport, IN 86, 181

Maumee River 16

Maurepas (Confederate gunboat) 65; see also St. Charles, AK; White River expedition (June-July 1862)

Maury, Lt. John 28; see also Nicaraguan National War (1856–1857)

May Duke (steamer) 103, 131

Maynadier, Capt. Henry E. 48–50, 52, 55; see also Mortar boats

Maysville, KY 193–194, 203, 260; see also Morgan's Indiana-Ohio Raid (1863)

Mazeppa (steamer) 273, 277–279, 288

McCann, Capt. Dick 117

McClellan, Maj. Gen. George B. 35, 48

McClernand, Maj. Gen. John A. 57

McCorkle, Lt. David P. 28; see also Nicaraguan National War (1856–1857)

McCown, Brig. Gen. John P. 44

McCreary, Maj. James Bennett 173, 176, 185–186

McFarland, Acting Chief Engineer William D. 258, 260, 336; see also *Moose* (U.S. tinclad); Tennessee River gunboat construction (1863–1864)

McMillan, Acting 2nd Assistant Engineer Charles, 175, 336; see also *Moose* (U.S. tinclad)

McMinnville, TN 212

Meade, Lt. Cmdr. Richard W. 347–348; see also *Louisville* (U.S. ironclad gunboat); *Marblehead* (U.S. steam gunboat); U.S Naval Academy

Meade County, KY 179; see also Morgan's Indiana-Ohio Raid (1863)

Medal of Honor see Congressional Medal of Honor

Meigs, Maj. Gen. Montgomery C. 33, 79, 120, 123, 143, 145, **214**, 215, 226–228, 230–231, 233, 242, 244, 246, 248, 258, 264, 288, 332, 344

Meigs County, OH 195–197; see also Morgan's Indiana-Ohio Raid (1863)

Memphis, IN 189; see also Morgan's Indiana-Ohio Raid (1863)

Memphis, TN 37, 50, 55, 58, 69, 85, 107, 115, 120, 139, 146, 159, 212, 232, 248–249, 272, 297, 341

Memphis, TN, Battle of (1862) 51–53, **54**–55, 60

Memphis & Charleston Railroad 58

Memphis & Ohio Railroad 278

Memphis *Argus* 69

Memphis, Clarksville and Louisville Railroad 104, 281

Mercury (steamer) 109, 300

Meredith, Brig. Gen. Solomon 278, 297, 299, 301, 310, 320; see also Paducah, KY

Meridian, MS 248

Meridian-Corinth-Tuscumbia Railroad 291

Meriwether, Capt. H. Clay 179; see also Morgan's Indiana-Ohio Raid (1863)

Merrimac (U.S. frigate) 22, 25

Mervine, Cdr. William 27

Metamora (steamer) 312, 332

Metcalf, Capt. Lynn S. 291; see also Logistics, river

Metropolis, IL 86, 252, 255; see also Paducah, KY

Mexican War of the *Reforma* (1859–1860) 29

Michigan regiments: 3rd Cavalry 141; 7th Cavalry 199; 8th Cavalry 177, 199, 203; 9th Cavalry 199; 11th Battery 199–200; 23rd 199; 25th 177

Middlebury Academy *see* Wyoming Academy

Miles, Acting Master's Mate O. W. 336; *see also Moose* (U.S. tinclad)

Military Land Bounty Act (1850) 18

Miller, Acting Volunteer Master Charles W. 298, 305, 314–315; *see also* Bell's Mills, TN, Battle of (1864); *Carondelet* (U.S. ironclad gunboat); Nashville, Battle of (1864)

Miller, Quartermaster James 348; *see also* John's Island, SC, Battle of (1863); *Marblehead* (U.S. steam gunboat)

Minersville, OH 196; *see also* Morgan's Indiana-Ohio Raid (1863)

Mingo (U.S. ram) 64

Minnehaha (steamer) 297

Minnie Bay (steamer) **75**

Mint Julep Springs, home of Lt. Col./M Benjamin Smith (Logansport) 349, 352–353, 355–356; *see also* St. Joseph's Hospital (Logansport, IN)

Missionary (steamer) 246

Missionary Ridge, Battle of (1863) 230, 232

Mississippi Marine Brigade 52–56, 158–164, 166, 229, 236; *see also* Ellet, Brig. Gen. Alfred W.; Ellet, Col. Charles, Jr.; Memphis, TN, Battle of (1862)

Mississippi regiments: Hudson's Light Artillery (Hudson's Battery) 282; *see also* Johnsonville, TN, Battle of (1864)

Mississippi River 30, 35, 37, 39–40, 43–44, 56, 122, 137, 215, 233, 251, 265; *see also* Logistics, river

Mississippi Squadron (U.S. Navy) 97–344

Mississippi Squadron District organization: 1st *see* Townsend, Cmdr. Robert; 4th 211; 5th *see* Phelps, Lt. Cmdr. S. Ledyard; 6th *see* Fitch, Le Roy; 7th *see* Phelps, Lt. Cmdr. S. Ledyard; Shirk, Lt. Cmdr. James W.; 8th *see* Fitch, Le Roy; 9th *see* Fitch, Le Roy; Shirk, Lt. Cmdr. James W.; Boyd, Lt. Cmdr. Robert, Jr.; Ramsey, Lt. Cmdr. Francis M.; 10th *see* Fitch, Le Roy; 11th *see* Forrest, Lt. Moreau

Mississippi Squadron reduction/decommissioning 339–344

Missouri regiments: 7th 320 *see also* Buchanan, Lt. Col. Robert; 2nd Light Artillery 268–269

Mitchell, Brig. Gen. Robert B. 119, 121, 126–128, 139, 143, 156; *see also* Nashville, TN

Mobile Bay, Battle of (1864) 264, 266

Mollie Able (steamer) 258

Mollie McPike (steamer) 300

Molony, Acting Master's Mate Daniel 336; *see also Moose* (U.S. tinclad)

Monarch (U.S. ram) 54, 164

Monroe County, AK 67–68, 101; *see also* Caseyville, KY; White River expedition (June-July 1862)

Montgomery, Cdr. J. Ed 55; *see also* Confederate River Defense Force

Montgomery County, TN 98

Moore, Col. Absalom 106; *see also* Hartsville, TN, Confederate raid (1862)

Moore, Col. Jonathan B. 318; *see also Moose* (U.S. tinclad)

Moore, Col. Orland H. 177; *see also* Morgan's Indiana-Ohio Raid (1863)

Moose (U.S. tinclad) 78, 174–207, 210–211, 215–216, 218, 222–223, 227, 229–234, 236, 240, 246–248, 251–257, 260–263, 266, 269, 278, 280–285, 287, 299, 301–302, 305–309, 312, 315, 317–319, 325–326, 330–333, 336, 338, 340–343; *see also* Bell's Mills, TN, Battle of (1864); Fitch, Le Roy; Johnsonville, TN, Battle of (1864); Morgan's Indiana-Ohio Raid (1863); Nashville, Battle of (1864)

Mora, Gen. Jose I. 28; *see also* Nicaraguan National War (1856–1857)

Morehead, Acting Volunteer Master Joseph W. 262; *see also General Sherman* (U.S. tinclad)

Morgan, Charlton 201; *see also* Morgan's Indiana-Ohio Raid (1863)

Morgan, Acting Volunteer Master Edmund 306, 312, 322, 330–332, 336–337; *see also Springfield* (U.S. tinclad)

Morgan, Maj. Gen. John Hunt 62, 88, 90–91, 104–106, 108–112, 116, 157, 167–173, **174**–207, 212, 240, 260, 326

Morgan, Richard 201; *see also* Morgan's Indiana-Ohio Raid (1863)

Morganfield, KY 265; *see also* White Oak Springs (KY), Battle of (1864)

Morgan's Indiana-Ohio Raid (1863) 167–176, **177**–179, **180**–207, 234

Morgan's Kentucky Raids (1862–1863) 91–92, 108–109

Morristown, TN 213

Morse, Acting Master's Mate DeWitt C. "Gunboat" 280, 283–285, 290; *see also Curlew* (U.S. tinclad); Johnsonville, TN, Battle of (1864)

Mortar boats 47, **48**–50, 52

Morton, Acting Volunteer Master Gilbert 262; *see also General Thomas* (U.S. tinclad)

Morton, Capt. John W. 273, 275–276, 278, 281–283, 287; *see also* Johnsonville, TN, Battle of (1864); Morton's Battery

Morton, Oliver P. (Indiana governor) 43, 92, 186

Morton's Battery 273–275, 281–282, 310; *see also* Blockhouse No. 3 (Nashville); Johnsonville, TN, Battle of (1864)

Morton's Landing (Ohio River) 182

Mound City, IL 80, 86, 252, 254–255, 258, 260, 277–279, 292, 294–295, 297, 302–303, 318, 321, 323, 337, 339–342, 343–344

Mound City (U.S. ironclad gunboat) 36–37, 53, 64–65, **66**–70, 293; *see also* Kilty, Cmdr. Augustus H.; White River expedition (June-July 1862)

Mount Vernon, IN 86, 264–265

Mount Vernon Ladies Association 17; *see also* Fitch, Harriet V. (stepmother)

Moyer, Acting Volunteer Ensign Joseph 115

Muldraugh's Hill, KY, railroad bridge destruction (1862) 109

"Mule Brigade" (U.S.) *see* Streight Raid (1863)

Mullany, Lt. J. R. M. 33

Mundfordville, KY, Confederate capture (1862) 97, 109

Murfreesboro, TN 110, 112, 114, 116–117, 119, 137–138, 140, 151–153, 303, 311, 321; *see also* Nashville, Battle of (1864); Stone's River, Battle of (1862–1863)

Muscle Shoals (Tennessee River) 40–41, 58, 87, 140, 142, 159, 167, 209, 243, 246, 297; *see also* Navigation seasons and conditions on Western rivers

Mustapha Island (Ohio River) 203; *see also* Morgan's Indiana-Ohio Raid (1863)

N. J. Bigley (steamer) 306, 310

Naiad (U.S. tinclad) 83–84

Naile, Lt. Frederick J. 321–323, 331; *see also* Nashville, Battle of

Nannie (steamer) 297

Napier, Col. T. Alonzo 62, 95, 107–108

Napoleon Bonaparte 16–17, 62

Narrows (Tennessee River) 242; *see also Chattanooga* (steamer); Chattanooga, TN

Nashville and Chattanooga Railroad 58, 116, 268, 311

Nashville and Northwestern Railroad 266, 268, 270–271

Nashville, Battle of (1864) 40, 154, 291–334; *see also* Bell's Mills, TN, Battle of (1864)

Index

Nashville (steamer) 102
Nashville, TN 26, 37–39, 41, 85, 87–88, 90–91, 103–107, **109–110,** 112–117, 119, 121–123, 125–129, 132, 135–140, 143–145, 147, 152–153, 156, 165–166, 171, 178, 206–207, 210–213, 215–218, 220, 222–227, 229–230, 232–235, 238–242, 246–251, 257–260, 263, 266–268, 270, 274, 277–278, 283, 287–288, 290–292, 294–295, 297–298, 300–306, 309–310, 314–321, 323, 332, 337–339, 341; *see also* Cumberland River; Logistics, river
Naugatuck (steamer) 273
Naumkeag (U.S. tinclad) 172–174, 184, 189–190, 196, 203, 207, 336, 342
Naval Reserve Officers Training Program 18
Navigation seasons and conditions on Western rivers 39–40, 74, 106, 113, 144, 211, 215–216, 241
Navigator (steamer) 203
Negley, Brig. Gen. James S. 62
Neosho (U.S. monitor) 130, 292, 294–295, 297–303, 306, 309–310, 312–**313,** 314–315, 317–320, 322–323, 326–330, 332, 342; *see also* Bell's Mills, TN, Battle of (1864); Nashville, Battle of (1864)
Nettie (steamer) 258
New Albany, IN 80, 86, 183, 185, 187–188, 241, 260–261; *see also* Morgan's Indiana-Ohio Raid (1863)
New Amsterdam, IN 86
New Era (U.S. tinclad) 252–255; *see also* Fort Pillow (Mississippi River)
New Jersey regiments: 34th 252–253; *see also* Lawrence, Col. William H.
New Lisbon, OH 204; *see also* Morgan's Indiana-Ohio Raid (1863)
New Madrid, MO, Siege and capture (1862) 43–44, 48
New Martinsville, WV 86
New National (steamer) 64, 67, 69, 255, 340; *see also* Farmer, Acting Volunteer Ensign J. M.
New Philadelphia, IN 188; *see also* Morgan's Indiana-Ohio Raid (1863)
New Portland, TN 87, 148
New York (steamer) 300, 332
New York City, Draft riots (1863) 191
New York Navy Yard (Brooklyn) 25, 33
Newburg, IN, Raid by Adam R. Johnson (1862) 91
Newcastle and Richmond Rail Road 24
Newell, Capt. Cicero 141
Newport, KY 86
Newsboy (ersatz U.S. military gunboat) 219, 222–227, 231, 240, 263, 299, 301–302, 306, 310, 332; *see also* Cumberland River
Newsom, Col. John F. 141
Niagara Falls, NY 12
Nicaraguan National War (1856–1857) 26–28
Nightingale (steamer) 220
Nixon, Col. G. H. 311
Nolichuckey River 39
Norman (steamer) 258
North Atlantic Blockading Squadron 272
North Carolina (U.S. ship-of-the-line/receiving ship) 33–**34**
Northern Indiana Shooting Association 349

Oakes, Capt. T. J. *see Imperial* (steamer)
Obey's River 228, 237–238, 339; *see also* Big South Fork (Cumberland River); Cumberland River
Odd Fellow (steamer) 203
Ohio Raid (1863) 167–207
Ohio regiments: 2nd Cavalry 196; 3rd 158; 7th Cavalry 196, 306, 319–320, 327; 11th Cavalry 199, 12th 193; 18th 194–195; 23rd 193, 196, 201; 45th 203; 91st 193
Ohio River 30, 38–40, 43, 72, 79–81, 85–86, 91, 93–94, 96–97, **100,** 102–103, 106–108, 112–113, 125, 131, 136, 138, 147, 158, 163, 167–170, 172–207, 210–212, 215–217, 222, 225–226, 234, 241, 244, 248, 252, 259–264, 266–267, 295, 298, 342; *see also* Logistics, river; Morgan's Indiana-Ohio Raid (1863); Shipyards and repair facilities
Ohio River Expedition (1862) *see* Pennock's Ohio River Expedition (1862)
Ohio State Penitentiary, plot to release Morgan from (1863) 212
Okolona, MS, Battle of (1864) 249
"Oldsters" *see* U.S. Naval Academy
Olive (steamer) 300
Ollie Sullivan (steamer) 131, 258
Olympus, TN 237–238; *see also* Big South Fork reconnaissance (Donn/Glassford, 1863)
Omaha (steamer) 300
O'Neil, Acting Volunteer Ensign H. B. 278, 285, 290; *see also Curlew* (U.S. tinclad)
O'Neil, Margaret "Maggie" *see* Hagerty, Fireman John
Osage (U.S. monitor) 294
Overton County, TN 237; *see also* Big South Fork reconnaissance (Donn/Glassford, 1863)
Owensboro, KY 86, 106, 186, 261, 266
Ozark (U.S. monitor) 342

Paden City, WV 86
Paducah, KY 38, 86–87, 95–96, 100, 103, 106–108, 113, 115, 128–129, 139, 142, 146–148, 151, 163, 165, 167, 212, 218, 251–253, 261, 265, 271–273, 275, 277–278, 286, 289, 295, 297–299, 301, 303, 310, 320, 332–333; *see also* Tennessee River
Paducah, KY, Battles of (1864) 249–252, 254–255
Paine, Brig. Gen. Eleazer 240–241; *see also* Nashville, TN
Palestine (steamer) 109
Palmer, Maj. Gen. John M. 338–339; *see also* Louisville, KY
Palmyra, TN 88, 98–99, 130–131, 136, 145, 151–156, 158, 160, 166, 221, 234, 237, 286; *see also St. Clair* (U.S. tinclad)
Paoli, IN 176
Paper, Capt. James H. 181; *see also Alice Dean* (steamer)
Paris, IN 188; *see also* Morgan's Indiana-Ohio Raid (1863)
Paris Landing (Tennessee River) 86–87, 273–276, 280, 292
Park, John (Memphis mayor) 55–56
Parker's Crossroads, TN 108
Parkersburg, WV 86, 184, 190, 193, 195, 2001; *see also* Morgan's Indiana-Ohio Raid (1863)
Parsons, Col. Charles 85, 147, 233–234, **235,** 241–244, 259, 261, 263; *see also* Logistics, river
Parthenia (steamer) 117–119
Partisan Ranger Act (Confederate 1862) 61
Partisan warfare *see* Irregular warfare
Patawatomi Indian Uprising (1836) 15
Patrols, gunboat *see* Irregular warfare, causes, principles, and counterinsurgency
Paulding, Cdr. Hiram 25, 33
Paw Paw (U.S. tinclad) 250, 278, 280–283, 287, 292, 294–295, 297, 300; *see also* Johnsonville, TN, Battle of (1864); Paducah, KY, Battles of (1864)
Pea Ridge, AK, Battle of (1862) 44, 63
Pekin, IL 13; *see also* Tazwell County, IL
Pemberton, Maj. Gen. John 116
Pendergast, Cdr. Garrett J. 22, 29
Pennock, Fleet Captain Alexander M. 72, 76–78, 81–83, 91–95, 107–108, 112–116, 119–121, 123–130, 135–136, 138–140, 143–149, 154–156, 159–161, 165, 167, 169–172, 174, 179, 184–186, 189–190, 203, 228, 247, 249–253, 255, 257, 263–264, 265, 273, 277–278, 286, 347; *see also* Tinclads," description and evolution
Pennock's Ohio River Expedition (1862) 91–94
Pennsylvania regiments: 19th Cavalry 297
Pensacola navy yard (FL): defense

(1861) 32–33, **350**; Fitch as executive officer of (1870–1873) 349–353
Peosta (U.S. tinclad) **250**–252, 254, 279, 292, 298–300, 336; *see also* Paducah, KY, Battles of (1864)
Pepper, Master Nat 194; *see also Alice Dean* (steamer); *Allegheny Belle* (ersatz U.S. military gunboat); Morgan's Indiana-Ohio Raid (1863)
Perkins, Acting Volunteer Lieutenant Charles G. 98, 102, 121–122, 125–126, 168, 210, 261, 279, 312; *see also Brilliant* (U.S. tinclad)
Perry, Cdr. Matthew C. 22
Perryville, KY, Battle of (1862) 98
Perryville, TN 87, 148
Peru Blues (Indiana militia unit) 15; *see also* Patawatomi Indian Uprising
Peters, Capt. ___ 12
Phelps, Lt. Cmdr. S. Ledyard 38–39, 70, 72, 124, 126–128, 130, 165–167, 169, 190, 210, 215, 263
Phythian, Lt. Cmdr. Robert L. 346; *see also* U.S. Naval Academy
Pickneyville, KY 88
Pierce, President Franklin 22, 26
Piketown, OH 196; *see also* Morgan's Indiana-Ohio Raid (1863)
Pillow, Maj. Gen. Gideon J. 38
Pilot Knob (Tennessee River) 283; *see also* Johnsonville, TN, Battle of (1864)
Pilots 84
Pine Bluff, TN 87, 274–277
Pioneer (steamer) 300, 312
Pittsburg (U.S. ironclad gunboat) 36–37, 41, 50, 53
Pittsburgh, PA 80, 85, 185, 264–265
Pittsburgh Landing, TN 78, 113, 141
Pittsburgh Landing, TN, Battle of (1862) 50, 76
Plum Point Bend (Mississippi River) 50–52, 254; *see also* Fort Pillow (Mississippi River)
Point Isabella (Cumberland River) 236
Point Pleasant, TN 87, 240
Poland (steamer) 131
Polk, Maj. Gen. Leonidas 37–39
Pollard, Daniel (steamboat captain) 46
Pomeroy, OH 86, 168, 191, 193–197, 203, 261; *see also* Morgan's Indiana-Ohio Raid (1863)
Pontchartrain (Confederate gunboat) 65
Pook, Naval Constructor Samuel M. 35–36
Pope, Maj. Gen. John 43–44, 48, 50, 57, 64
Porter, Adm. David Dixon 67, 75, 90, 97, 99, 100–102, 105–108, 116, 119–120, 122–123, 125, 128, 130, 138–139, 143–149, 151, 157–

161, 163, 165, 167–175, 178, 183, 187, 189–190, 203, 206, 210–215, 218–228, 230, 232–236, 238, 240–241, 243–244, 246–247, 249, 255, 257–258, 260, 262–263, 269, 272, 288, 335, 344–345; *see also* Mississippi Squadron; U. S Naval Academy
Portland, KY 181; *see also* Louisville and Portland Canal
Portland, OH 168, 175, 192, 197, 203; *see also* Morgan's Indiana-Ohio Raid (1863)
Portsmouth, OH 195; *see also* Morgan's Indiana-Ohio Raid (1863)
Post, Rev. Martin M. 30
Prairie State (steamer) 258, 300, 306–307, 309, 332; *see also* Bell's Mills, TN, Battle of (1864); Nashville, Battle of (1864
Preble (U.S. sloop-of-war) 19–22; *see also* U. S. Naval Academy
Price, Maj. Gen. Sterling 268, 291
Prima Donna (steamer) 258, 306–307, 309, 312, 332; *see also* Nashville, Battle of (1864)
Prince of Orange (Dutch frigate) 22
Prohibition Party and 1890 Tennessee gubernatorial election *see* Kelley, Lt. Col. David C.
Pueblo (AGER-2) 275
Pulaski, TN, Battle of (1864) 295–295
Purier's Ferry (Cumberland River) 106
Putnam, Col. William R. 194–195; *see also* Morgan's Indiana-Ohio Raid (1863)

Queen City (U.S. tinclad) 154, 156, 159–160, 164–166, 185
Queen of the West (U.S. ram) 54
Queenstown Heights, Battle of (1812) 12
Quinby, Brig. Gen. Isaac F. 52
Quinn, Acting Volunteer Ensign Thomas A. 327; *see also Carondolet* (U.S. ironclad gunboat); Nashville, Battle of (1864)

R. Christopher Goodwin and Associates 82; *see also* Johnsonville, TN, Battle of (1864)
R. R. Hudson (steamer) **75**
Racine, OH 196; *see also* Morgan's Indiana-Ohio Raid (1863)
Railroads 16, 84–85, 91, 108–109, 112, 208–209, 211–212, 214, 222, 241, 248–249, 264, 267–268, 270–271, 282; *see also* Chattanooga, TN; Johnsonville, TN; Nashville, TN; Logistics, general
Ramsey, Lt. Cmdr. Francis M. 347; *see also* U.S. Naval Academy
Ramsey, Capt. Robert H. 323, 332; *see also* Nashville, Battle of (1864)
Randolph, TN 99, 277
Rankin's Ferry (Tennessee River) 242; *see also Chattanooga* (steamer); Chattanooga, TN

Rapids, river *see* Falls of the Ohio; Navigation seasons and conditions on Western rivers
Rasin, Capt. Hanson 218, 263; *see also* Fort Donelson (Cumberland River); Logistics, river; Smithland, KY
Ravell, Acting Volunteer Ensign John 175
Ravenswood, WV 175, 197; *see also* Morgan's Indiana-Ohio Raid (1863)
Rawlins, Brig. Gen. John A. 115, 213, 280
Raymond (steamer) 127
Ray's Ferry (Cumberland River) 237; *see also* Big South Fork reconnaissance (Donn/Glassford, 1863)
Read, Acting Volunteer Ensign Frederick 179, 184–185, 189, 210, 229–230, 232, 261, 279, 321, 336, 338, 340; *see also Victory* (U.S. tinclad)
Reber, Acting Assistant Surgeon W. M. 336; *see also Moose* (U.S. tinclad)
Red River 30
Red Rover (U.S. hospital boat) 332
Reed, Capt. Henry P. 278, 310, 320, 331; *see also* Smithland, KY
Reed's Landing, WV 195, 201, 203; *see also* Morgan's Indiana-Ohio Raid (1863)
Reedsville, WV *see* Reed's Landing, WV
Regiments *see* Names of states, then regiment numbers
Reindeer (U.S. tinclad) 179, 181, 184, 189–190, 196, 203, 210, 215–216, 218, 222–223, 226–227, 232, 235–241, 247, 252–253, 256–257, 261–262, 265, 289, 299, 306–309, 311, 315, 317, 319, 326, 330–332, 337, 339–340; *see also* Big South Fork reconnaissance (Donn/Glassford, 1863); Glassford, Acting Volunteer Lieutenant Henry A.
Repair facilities *see* Shipyards and repair facilities
Republican (steamboat) 16
Republican Party 23
Restless (U.S. tugboat) 93
Reveille (steamer) 109
Revell, Acting Volunteer Ensign John 114, 336; *see also Moose* (U.S. tinclad)
Rexville, IN 188; *see also* Morgan's Indiana-Ohio Raid (1863)
Reynolds, Maj. Gen. Joseph J. 109
Reynoldsburg, TN 87, 148, 270–271, 277, 279–285, 287, 289, 294; *see also* Johnsonville, TN
Reynoldsburg Island (Tennessee River) *see* Johnsonville, TN; Reynoldsburg, TN
Rice, Acting Volunteer Master John H. 175, 184, 200, 223, 312, 315,

336–337; *see also Brilliant* (U.S. tinclad); *Reindeer* (U.S. tinclad)
Rice, Capt. T. W. *see* Rice's Battery
Rice's Battery 282–283, 303; *see also* Bell's Mills, TN, Battle of (1864); Kelley, Lt. Col. David C.; Johnsonville, TN, Battle of (1864); Tennessee regiments, Rice's Battery
Richardson, Col. Robert V. 237; *see also* Big South Fork reconnaissance (Donn/Glassford, 1863)
Riley, Acting Volunteer Lieutenant Robert K. 123, 128
Ripley, OH 192–194; *see also* Morgan's Indiana-Ohio Raid (1863)
"Rises" *see* Navigation seasons and conditions on Western rivers
Rivas, Gen. Patricio 26; *see also* Nicaraguan National War (1856–1857)
Rivas, Nicaragua, Battle of 27; *see also* Nicaraguan National War (1856–1857)
River navigational seasons and conditions on Western rivers 39–40
River shipping *see* Logistics, river
Riverboats, description, power and configuration 72–76
Rob Roy (steamer) 93, 109
Robb see Alfred Robb (U.S. tinclad)
Robert B. Hamilton (steamer) 131
Roberts, Lt John S. 236–238; *see also* Big South Fork reconnaissance (Donn/Glassford, 1863); *Silver Lake No. 2* (ersatz U.S. military gunboat)
Robertson's Island (Cumberland River) 312, 314, 317, 323; *see also* Cumberland River
Robinson Island (Cumberland River) *see* Robertson's Island
Rockcastle, KY 88
Rockhaven, KY 180
Rockport, IN 86
Roddy, Col. Philip D. 160, 162
Rodgers, Cmdr. John 35–36, 97, 120
Rome, GA 272
Rome, IN 86
Rome, TN 88
Romeo (U.S. tinclad) 342
Rosecrans, Maj. Gen. William S. "Old Rosy" 98–**99**, 103–105, 107, 109–117, 119–123, 125–128, 130, 132, 134, 137–140, 142–149, 151, 157–159, 165, 167–168, 172, 176, 206, 208–209–213, 223, 242, 273, 278, 280, 291, 298; *see also* Army of the Cumberland (U.S.); Department of the Missouri (U.S.)
Rousseau, Maj. Gen. Lovell 247, 250–251; *see also* Iron ore recovery dispute (1863–1864); Nashville, TN
Rowley, Pilot George W. 308; *see also Moose* (U.S. tinclad)

Rowley, Maj. William R. 217
Rucker, Col. Edmund, W. 271, 281, 303, 312, 326–327; *see also* Bell's Mills, TN, Battle of (1864)
Rush Medical College (Chicago) 17–18
Rusling, Col. James F. 301, 322; *see also* Nashville, TN
Russellville, GA 162
Rutherford, TN 108
Rutland, OH 196–197; *see also* Morgan's Indiana-Ohio Raid (1863)

S. C. Baker (steamer) 236
Sabine River 265–266
Sailor's Creek 263
St. Bridget's Catholic Church (Logansport, IN) 353
St. Charles, AK 64–65, **66**, 69, 323; *see also Mound City* (U.S. ironclad gunboat); White River expedition (June-July 1862)
St. Clair (U.S. tinclad) 82, 98–100, 103, 106–108, 113–115, 121, 125–126, 129, 132, 134, 137–138, 140, 142, 147–148, 152–**153**, 155–156, 165–166, 168, 171–172, 175, 178, 206, 211, 286, 321, 323, 331, 336; *see also* French, Acting Volunteer Lt. James S.; Palmyra, TN
St. Cloud (steamer) 131
St. Joseph's Catholic Church (Logansport, IN) 352–353
St. Joseph's Hospital (Logansport, IN) 355–356; *see also* Mint Julep Springs, home of Lt. Col./M Benjamin Smith
St. Louis (steamer) 203, 263, 277
St. Louis (U.S. ironclad gunboat) 36–37, 40–41, 54, 64, 67; *see also Baron de Kalb* (U.S. ironclad gunboat)
St. Louis, MO 213, 222, 241, 243–244, 259, 277–278, 280, 291, 295, 297–298, 300, 319
St. Mary's (U.S. sloop of war) 25–29
St. Mary's College (Chicago) 24
St. Vincent de Paul's Catholic Church (Logansport, IN) 353
Salem, IN 186, 188; *see also* Morgan's Indiana-Ohio Raid (1863)
Salineville, OH 204; *see also* Morgan's Indiana-Ohio Raid (1863)
Salmon, Cmdr. Norvell 29; *see also* Walker, William (filibusterer)
Salt River 179
Salt Sulphur Springs, WV 203; *see also* Morgan's Indiana-Ohio Raid (1863)
Sanders, Col. William P. 173, 176, 204
Sander's East Tennessee Raid (1863) 173, 176, 204
Sandy Island (Tennessee River) 274
Santee (U.S. frigate) 345; *see also* U.S. Naval Academy
Sardinia, OH 194; *see also* Morgan's Indiana-Ohio Raid (1863)

Satterlee, Hannah Swenzey (step aunt) 12
Satterlee, Harriet Valerie *see* Fitch, Harriet V.
Satterlee, Luther (step uncle) 12
Savannah (steamer) 258
Savannah (U.S. frigate) 29
Savannah, GA 268, 288
Savannah, TN 87, 127, 140, 149, 151, 160
Scammon, Brig. Gen. E. Parker 193, 196, 201–202; *see also* Morgan's Indiana-Ohio Raid (1863)
Schofield, Maj. Gen. John M. 287–288, 296, 300–302; *see also* Franklin, TN, Battle of (1864); Pulaski, TN, Battle of (1864)
Science (steamer) 131
Scott, Lt. Col. Newton 43
Scott, Gen. Winfield 35; *see also* Anaconda Plan
Scott-Eads Plan *see* Anaconda Plan
Scott's Ferry (Cumberland River) 176
Scuffletown Bar (Ohio River) 171, 178, 211
Sears, Acting Volunteer Ensign Amasa C. 179, 184
Seasons and conditions of navigation on Western rivers 39–40
Sebastian, Pilot John 194, 198; *see also Allegheny Belle* (ersatz U.S. military gunboat); Morgan's Indiana-Ohio Raid (1863)
Selfridge, Lt. Cmdr. Thomas O., Jr. 347; *see also Cairo* (U.S. ironclad gunboat); U.S. Naval Academy
Sequatchie Valley raid (1863) 212
Seven Mile Island (Cumberland River) 234
Seven Mile Island (Tennessee River) 139
Seybold, George 17
Seybold Dry Goods Company (Logansport, IN) 17
Seymour, IN 172
Shackelford, Brig. Gen. James M. 176, 199, 204; *see also* Morgan's Indiana-Ohio Raid (1863)
Shawneetown, IL 86, 93, 97, 102, 211, 215, 257, 261, 264–266
Shawneetown Bar (Ohio River) 171, 178, 211, 215, 264
Sheely, Pilot Samuel G. 60; *see also General Sterling Price* (Confederate/U.S. gunboat)
Shelbyville, TN 110, 114
Shelbyville, TN, preacher's anti-gunboat prayer 106
Shenango (steamer) 131
Sheridan, Brig. Gen. Philip H. 117
Sherman, Maj. Gen. William T. 57–58, 70, 72, 85, 102, 143, 212–213, 215, 232, 235, 249, 251, 257–258, 260, 263, 267–268, 270, 272, 278, 281, 288–289, 295–296, 335, 351; *see also* Atlanta, Battle of (1864)
Sherman, WV 192; *see also* Morgan's Indiana-Ohio Raid (1863)

Index

Shiloh, Battle of (1862) 50, 76
Shipping, river *see* Logistics, river
Shipyards and repair facilities 80–81, 113, 120, 137, 242–249; *see also* names of specific towns, e.g., Bridgeport, AL; Pensacola, FL; Madison, IN, Mound City, IL
Shirk, Lt. Cmdr. James W. 147, 250–255, 257, 263, 265, 269, 273, 277–279, 281, 285–287, 289, 292, 295–299; *see also* Johnsonville, TN, Battle of (1864); Paducah, KY, Battles of (1864); *Tuscumbia* (U.S. ironclad)
Shoals, river *see* Navigation seasons and conditions on Western rivers; names of specific shoals
Shreveport (steamer) 258
Shunk, John N. *see Elfin* (U.S. tinclad)
Sidell *see W. H. Sidell* (ersatz U.S. military gunboat)
Signal (U.S. tinclad) 97, 286; *see also* Alexandria, LA, Battle of (1864)
Silver Cloud (steamer) 300
Silver Cloud (U.S. tinclad) 254; *see also* Fort Pillow (Mississippi River)
Silver Lake (U.S. tinclad) 122–123, 128, 130, 132, 134, 137–138, 140, 143–144, 146, 149–151, 154–156, 165–166, 168, 171–172, 175, 184, 186–187, **188**, 207, 210–211, 215–216, 218, 222–223, 226–227, 232, 240, 247, 250–252, 266, 299, 306–307, 309, 312, 315, 326, 331, 333, 336, 339–340, 342; *see also* Coyle, Acting Volunteer Ensign J. C.
Silver Lake No. 2 (ersatz U.S. military gunboat) 236–238, 240, 263, 299; *see also* Big South Fork reconnaissance (Donn/Glassford, 1863); Cumberland River
Sligo Ferry (Cumberland River) 217
Smith, Maj. Gen. Andrew J. "A. J." 268, 291, 295–302, 305; *see also* Nashville, Battle of (1864)
Smith, Col. Arthur A. 297, 303, 310, 312, 321, 333; *see also* Clarksville, TN
Smith, Lt. Col. Benjamin H. (father-in-law) 17, 25, 349, 354–355
Smith, Maj. Gen. Edmund Kirby 109
Smith, Elihu (newspaperman, father of "Polly" Smith) 25
Smith, Lt. Frank G. 328; *see also* Nashville, Battle of (1864)
Smith, Pilot Joseph N. 76
Smith, Mary "Mollie" *see* Fitch, Mary "Mollie" Smith
Smith, Mary "Polly" (mother-in-law) 25, 349
Smith, Brig. Gen. William Sooey 248–249; *see also* Okolona, MS, Battle of (1864)
Smithland, KY 38, 86, 88, 100, 103, 107, 113, 115, 125–126, 128–130, 132, 138–140, 142, 145–146, 151–154, 156, 165, 167, 169, 171, 178, 211–212, 215–216, 218, 220–230, 232, 234–235, 239–240, 247, 251, 255, 257–258, 260–261, 263, 266, 278–279, 294–295, 297–299, 301–302, 310, 312, 317, 319–321, 323, 331–333, 337, 339–341, 343; *see also* Cumberland River
Snags, river *see* Navigation seasons and conditions on Western rivers
South Atlantic Blockading Squadron 336
Sparta, TN 216–217, 227, 318, 324
Special Field Order No. 23 (Sherman) 260; *see also* Tennessee River gunboat construction (1863–1864)
Special Field Order No. 342 (Thomas) 324; *see also* Nashville, Battle of (1864)
Spiteful (U.S. tugboat) 64, 67
Spooner, Acting Masters Mate Charles W. 175
Spottsville, KY, Confederate attack upon (1862) 96
Spray (steamer) 300
Spring Hill, TN 162, 268
Springfield, KY 178
Springfield (U.S. tinclad) 123, 139–140, 143, 147, 155–157, 165–166, 168, 171–173, 175, 178, 181–185, 187–190, 196, 207, 210–211, 215, 227–228, 234, 240, 247, 251, 261–262, 266, 299, 305, 310, 312, 317, 322, 330–331, 336–338, 340; *see also* Morgan, Acting Volunteer Master Edmund; Watson, Acting Volunteer Master Joseph.
Stanfield, N. B. 181; *see also* Morgan's Indiana-Ohio Raid (1863)
Stanley, Brig. Gen. David S. 158
Stanton, Edwin M. (war secretary) 52–53, 60, 63, 79, 119–121, 138, 146, 213–214, 242–243
"Star of the Cumberland" *see* Nashville, TN
Starlight (steamer) 195, 197, 203; *see also* Morgan's Indiana-Ohio Raid (1863)
Steamboats, description, power and configuration 72–76, 307
Steedman, Maj. Gen. James B. 301; *see also* District of the Etowah, Provisional Detachment of the
Stephen Bayard (steamer) 332
Stephensport, KY 86
Steubenville, OH 86
Stevens, Lt. S. H. 310; *see also* Hartsville, TN
Stevenson, AL 209
Stewart, Lt. Gen. Alexander P. 303, 325; *see also* Nashville, Battle of (1864)
Stillman, U.S.MC Lt. C. H. 255
Stockdale, Capt. Sidney A. "Sid" 220–228, 232
Stone, Col. Henry 297; *see also* Nashville, Battle of (1864)
Stone's River, Battle of (1862–1863) 109–114
Strawberry Plains, TN 239; *see also* Knoxville, TN
Streight, Col. Abel D. 157–162, 168, 173, 187
Streight Raid (1863) 157–162, 168, 173, 187
Stribling, Cdr. Cornelius K. (U.S. Naval Academy superintendent). 19, 21; *see also* U.S. Naval Academy
Strong, Capt. William 220; see also *John A. Fisher* (steamer)
Submarine No. 7 (snagboat) *see Benton* (U.S. ironclad gunboat)
Sullivan, Brig. Gen. Jeremiah C. 107
Sultana (steamer) 74
Summersville, IN 188, 190; *see also* Morgan's Indiana-Ohio Raid (1863)
Summons, Acting Master's Mate Isaac 114
Supply (U.S. supply ship) 33
Sutton, WV 203; *see also* Morgan's Indiana-Ohio Raid (1863)
Swift's Iron & Steel Co. 258; *see also* Tennessee River gunboat construction (1863–1864)
Sword, Col. Thomas 264; *see also* Cincinnati, OH
Sybil (U.S. tinclad) 292
Syracuse, OH 196; *see also* Morgan's Indiana-Ohio Raid (1863)

Taber, Cyrus 25
Taber, Jesse 25
Taber, Susan "Tune" Smith (sister-in-law) 25
Taberville, IN 24
Tacony (steamer) 332
Tariscon (steamer) 203
Tawah (U.S. tinclad) 82, 271, 275–276, 279–280, 282–283, 286–287; *see also* Johnsonville, TN, Battle of (1864)
Taylor, Surgeon I. Winthrop 28; *see also* Nicaraguan National War (1856–1857)
Taylor, Lt. Gen. Richard "Dick" 270, 282
Taylor, Capt. Samuel B. 179, 181; *see also Alice Dean* (steamer); Morgan's Indiana-Ohio Raid (1863)
Tazewell County, IL 12–13
Tebb's Bend (Cumberland River) 177
Tell City, IN 86
Tempest (steamer) 131–132
Tempest (U.S. tinclad) 342
Temple, Cmdr. William G. 351
Tennessee: defense of 37–39, 72 *see also* Irregular warfare; economic importance of 37–38, 104
Tennessee Regiments: 1st Middle Tennessee (USA) Cavalry 158;

Index

2nd Mounted (USA) 199; 3rd Cavalry (CSA) 270; 4th (CSA) 162; 6th Cavalry (USA) 297; 8th (CSA) 162; 9th (CSA) 182, 321; 10th (CSA) 149, 162, 321; 11th (CSA) 162; 11th (USA) 271; 14th Cavalry (USA) 327–328; 14th Cavalry (USA) 252–253; 15th Cavalry (CSA) 276, 282; 26th Cavalry (CSA) 269, 282; *see also* Kelley, Lt. David C.; Morton's Battery (CSA); Rice's Battery (CSA)

Tennessee River 30, 38–40, 72, 76, 85–87, 91, 106–108, 113–116, 122–129, 137–143, 146–151, 154, 156, 158–165, 167, 169–170, 208–209, 212, 214–216, 230, 233, 242–243, 246, 251, 266, 268–291, 293–296, 298–299, 320, 333–336

Tennessee River Confederate raid (Wharton 1865) 338

Tennessee River gunboat construction (1863–1864) 242–244, 246–249, 257–260, 262–263; *see also* Bridgeport, AL; Edwards, Capt. Arthur; Wiard, Norman

Tennessee River gunboat raids (1862) 41, 76; *see also Lexington* (U.S. timberclad); *Tyler* (U.S. timberclad)

Tennessee River Navy *see* Johnsonville, TN, Battle of (1864); *Undine* (U.S. tinclad); *Venus* (steamer)

Tennessee Rolling Mills (Tennessee River) 342

Tensas (U.S. tinclad) 336

Texas regiments: 6th Cavalry 162–164; 8th Cavalry 133

Thomas, Maj. Gen. George H. "Old Pap" 109, 213, 216, 238, 267, 273, 276, 278–280, 288, 290–291, **292**, 295–303, 305–306, 309–311, 315–321, 323–325, 329, 331–333, 336–337–339, 341–342, 344; *see also* Chattanooga, TN; Nashville, Battle of (1864)

Thomas, Madeline Fitch 356; *see also Fitch* (U.S. destroyer, DD-426/DMS-25)

Thomas, Rachel *see* Fitch, Rachel Thomas

Thomas E. Tutt (steamer) 300, 320, 322; *see also* Gracey's Battery

Thompson, Acting Volunteer Master Augustus F. 277; *see also Elfin* (U.S. tinclad); *Paw Paw* (U.S. tinclad)

Thompson, Col. Charles R. 271, 276–278, 287–288, 294 ; *see also* Johnsonville, TN, Battle of (1864)

Thompson, Brig. Gen. M. Jeff 55

Thompson, Michel Andrew 135

Thorp, Acting Assistant Surgeon Abner 175, 254; *see also Moose* (U.S. tinclad)

Thrall's Battery *see* Arkansas regiments, Jackson Light Artillery (Thrall's Battery); Johnsonville, TN, Battle of (1864)

Three-Mile Island (Ohio River) 103

"Timberclads" *see Conestoga* (U.S. timberclad); *Lexington* (U.S. timberclad); *Tyler* (U.S. timberclad)

"Tinclads," general description and evolution 72–83, 94, 145; *see also* names of specific vessels, e.g., *Moose* (U.S. tinclad)

Tod, David (Ohio governor) 196, 264

Totten, Brig. Gen. Joseph G. 79

Townsend, Cmdr. Robert 211

Trace Creek, TN 271, 281

Tradewater coal mines (Caseyville, KY) 114

Transport requirements 84–85; *see also* Logistics, general

Treat, Lt. Samuel W. 281; *see also* Johnsonville, TN, Battle of (1864)

Trenton, TN 108

Trinity Episcopal Church (Logansport, IN) 353, 355

Trio (steamer) 117–119

Troy, IN 86

True, Landsman Rowland S. 309, 315; *see also Silver Lake* (U.S. tinclad)

Truesdale, Col. William 137

Tullahoma, TN 110, 114, 175–176, 206, 208

Tupelo, MS 116

Turkey Island (Tennessee River) *see* Green Bottom Bar (Tennessee River)

Turkey Neck Bend (Cumberland River) 176

Tuscumbia, AL 87, 140–142, 151, 156–157, 160–162, 164, 291

Tuscumbia (U.S. ironclad) 147–148

Tusker, Acting Masters Mate Johnson M. 175

Twain, Mark 73, 84

Twelve Mile Island (Ohio River) 189; *see also* Morgan's Indiana-Ohio Raid (1863)

Tyler, Capt. H. A. 253; *see also* Columbus, KY

Tyler (U.S. timberclad) 35, 40–41, 72, 76, 178, 342

Unconventional warfare *see* Irregular warfare

Undine (U.S. tinclad) 269–271, 274–284, 286, 289; *see also* Johnsonville, TN, Battle of (1864)

Union City, TN 108, 249–250

Union County, KY 91, 100, 107, 265; *see also* Caseyville, KY

Union County, TN 238; *see also* Big South Fork reconnaissance (Donn/Glassford, 1863)

Uniontown, KY 86, 93, 99, 102, 107, 172, 260–263

U.S. Naval Academy 18–23, 345–348; *see also Marblehead* (U.S. steam gunboat)

University of Nashville *see* Kelley, Lt. Col. David C.

Upper Tennessee River *see* Bridgeport, AL; *Chattanooga* (steamer); Chattanooga, TN; Cracker Line; Knoxville, TN; Tennessee River; Tennessee River gunboat construction (1863–1864)

V. F. Wilson (steamer) 46, 253–254

Van Dorn, Maj. Gen. Earl 44, 116, 137–140, 145

Van Dorn, Lt. William 119

Van Duzer, Capt. John C. 287, 318–319, 324, 329; *see also* Eckert, Thomas; Johnsonville, TN, Battle of (1864)

Vanderbilt University *see* Kelley, Lt. Col. David C.

Venus (steamer) 258, 274–280, 287; *see also* Johnsonville, TN, Battle of (1864)

Vernon, IN 189–190; *see also* Morgan's Indiana-Ohio Raid (1863)

Vicksburg, MS 115–116, 119–120, 161, 168, 170, 173, 178

Victoria (steamer) 61

Victory (steamer) 300

Victory (U.S. tinclad) 179, 184–185, 187–190, 196, 210, 215–216, 218, 227, 229–232, 240–241, 252, 254–255, 257, 264–266, 278, 292, 312, 321, 323, 331, 336, 338–340, 342; *see also* Read, Acting Volunteer Ensign Frederick

Vienna, IN 188; *see also* Morgan's Indiana-Ohio Raid (1863)

Vineton, OH 197; *see also* Morgan's Indiana-Ohio Raid (1863)

Virginia (ersatz U.S. military gunboat) 264–265

Volunteer (steamer) 253, 255, 298–299, 337

W. A. Healy *see Springfield* (U.S. tinclad)

W. B. Terry (steamer) 95

W C. Mann (steamer) *see Elfin* (U.S. tinclad)

W. H. Sidell (ersatz U.S. military gunboat) 119, 122, 157

W. L. Ewing (steamer) 300

Wabash (U.S. frigate) 25

Wabash and Erie Canal 15–16, 24, 30, 355

Wabash Island (Ohio River) 103

Wabash River 30

Wade, Col. William B. 117–119

Wagon transport 84

Walden's Ridge, TN 87

Walke, Adm. Henry 17, 33, 49, 284–285, 293, 299, 307, 336, 347; *see also Carondolet* (U.S. ironclad gunboat); Island No. 10 (Mississippi River)

Walker, Cmdr. John G. 347; *see also Baron de Kalb* (U.S. ironclad gunboat); U.S. Naval Academy

Walker, William (filibusterer) 26–27, 28–29
Wallace, Maj. Gen. Lew 57, 69, 186
Walton, Capt. E. S. *see* Walton's Battery
Walton's Battery 273–274, 276, 303; *see also* Bells Mills, TN, Battle of (1864); Johnsonville, TN, Battle of (1864); Kelley, Lt. Col. David C.
Wananita (steamer) 297, 300
War Eagle (steamer) 258
War of 1812 11–12
Washburn, Maj. Gen. Calwallader C. 297; *see also* Memphis, TN
Washington County, NY 11
Washington County, OH 197; *see also* Morgan's Indiana-Ohio Raid (1863)
Water Witch (U.S. gunboat) 31–32
Waterloo, AL 87, 149–150
Waterman, Surgeon Luther D. 119
Watkins, TN 88
Watson, Acting Volunteer Master Joseph 181–185, 189, 210–211, 262, 321; *see also General Grant* (U.S. tinclad); *Hastings* (U.S. tinclad); *Springfield* (U.S. tinclad)
Wayne, John 307
Weaver, Lt. Henry C. 200; *see also* Morgan's Indiana-Ohio Raid (1863)
Weaver, Lt. Col. T R. 274, 276–277; *see also* Johnsonville, TN, Battle of (1864); Pine Bluff, TN
Weaver, Pilot William 283; *see also* Johnsonville, TN, Battle of (1864); *Undine* (U.S. tinclad)
Webster County, KY 265
Weirton, WV 86
Welles, Gideon (Navy secretary) 59, 64, 78–79, 81, 94, 98, 107, 115–116, 119–121, 123, 130, 138, 140, 143, 145–146, 149, 158–159, 170, 190, 203, 205–206, 212, 233, 253, 255, 258, 272 277, 314, 330, 339, 341, 343, 346
Wells, Foster 2002; *see also* Morgan's Indiana-Ohio Raid (1863)
Wells Farm, WV *see* Wells, Foster
West Franklin, IN, Confederate raid (1862) 99
West Gulf Coast Blockading Squadron *see* Farragut, Admiral David G.; Mobile Bay, Battle of (1864)

West Union, OH 193; *see also* Morgan's Indiana-Ohio Raid (1863)
West Virginia regiments: 13th 193, 196
Western Flotilla (U.S. Army) 35–98
Wharton, Lt. Arthur D. 338; *see also* Tennessee River Confederate raid (Wharton, 1865)
Wharton, Brig. Gen. John 126, 134, 136
Wheeler, Maj. Gen. Joseph 106, 110, 112, 116–119, 126, 130, **131**–136, 151, 174–177, 209, 212
Wheeler, Seaman Robert 162
Wheeling, WV 80, 86, 191; *see also* Morgan's Indiana-Ohio Raid (1863)
White, Maj. Robert M. 162–164
White Cloud (steamer) 64, 67
White County, IN 43
White Oak Island (Tennessee River) 294
White Oak Springs (KY), Battle of (1864) 265
White River 30, 40, 58; *see also* Logistics, river
White River expedition (June-July 1862) 63–65, **66**–70, 78, 132, 187, 202, 293, 323; *see also Mound City* (U.S. ironclad gunboat); St. Charles, AK
White's Bend (Cumberland River) *see* Cumberland River; Nashville, Battle of (1864)
Wiard, Norman (warship designer) 244, 246; *see also* Tennessee River gunboat construction (1863–1864)
Widow Reynolds' Bar (Tennessee River) 273
Wiggins, Samuel 154; *see also Queen City* (U.S. tinclad); *Covington No. 2*
Wild Cat (steamer) 131–133; *see also* Fort Donelson
Wilkie, Correspondent Franc Bangs 45–46
Willcox, Brig. Gen. Orlando B. 188
Williams, Capt. A. M. 65; *see also* St. Charles, AK; White River expedition (June-July 1862)
Williams, Capt. Isaac P. 320–321; *see also* Clarksville, TN
Williams, Acting Volunteer Master James B. 275–276; *see also Tawah* (U.S. tinclad); Johnsonville, TN, Battle of (1864)
Williamsburg, OH 191; *see also* Morgan's Indiana-Ohio Raid (1863)
Williamson, Lt. J. C. 33
Wilson, Maj. Gen. James H. 302, 318, 325, 327–328, 330, 332; *see also* Nashville, Battle of (1864)
Wilson (steamer) *see V. F. Wilson* (steamer)
Wiltse, Acting Volunteer Ensign Isaac 336; *see also Moose* (U.S. tinclad)
Winchester, OH 194, 197; *see also* Morgan's Indiana-Ohio Raid (1863)
Winslow, Capt. F. S. 234, 248; *see also* Cumberland River; Nashville, TN
Winslow, Cmdr. John A. 67–68, 94
Wisconsin regiments: 33rd 318 *see also* Nashville, Battle of (1864); 43rd 271 *see also* Johnsonville, TN, Battle of (1864)
Wise, Capt. George D. 78, 81–82, 93
Wise, Capt. Henry 72
Wolf Creek Shoals (Cumberland River) 338; *see also* Big South Fork (Cumberland River)
Wood, Capt. C. L. 194–195, 197; *see also* Morgan's Indiana-Ohio Raid (1863)
Wood, Brig. Gen. Thomas J. 301–302; *see also* Nashville, Battle of (1864)
Woodville, KY 88
Woodward, Col. Thomas G. 95, 107, 136, 151, 156–157, 164
Wright, Maj. Gen. Horatio G. 112–114, 129, 147
Wyandotte (U.S. screw steamer) 32–33
Wyoming, NY 12
Wyoming Academy 12

Yazoo River 130
Yellow Creek 98, 263
Young's Point (Cumberland River) 306, 310

www.ingramcontent.com/pod-product-compliance
Lightning Source LLC
Chambersburg PA
CBHW081532300426
44116CB00015B/2607